CONTENTS

Author's Note 5

Researching the Charts 7

Explanation of Chart Abbreviations and Symbols 9

#1 HITS SECTION 11
A week-by-week listing of every record to hit #1 on *Billboard*'s Pop, R&B and Country singles and albums charts, and Adult Contemporary singles charts from 1950-1991.

SINGLES TITLE SECTION 277
An alphabetical listing, by title, of all singles listed in the #1 Hits Section.

ROYAL COURT OF #1s

Kings of the Singles 322
Royal Court of *Pop* Singles 323
Royal Court of *R&B* Singles 324
Royal Court of *Country* Singles 325
Royal Court of *Adult Contemporary* Singles 326

Kings of the Albums 327
Royal Court of *Pop* Albums 328
Royal Court of *R&B* Albums 329
Royal Court of *Country* Albums 330

Triple Crown Winners 331
Songs Reaching #1 On The Most Charts 332

JOEL WHITBURN PRESENTS
Billboard.

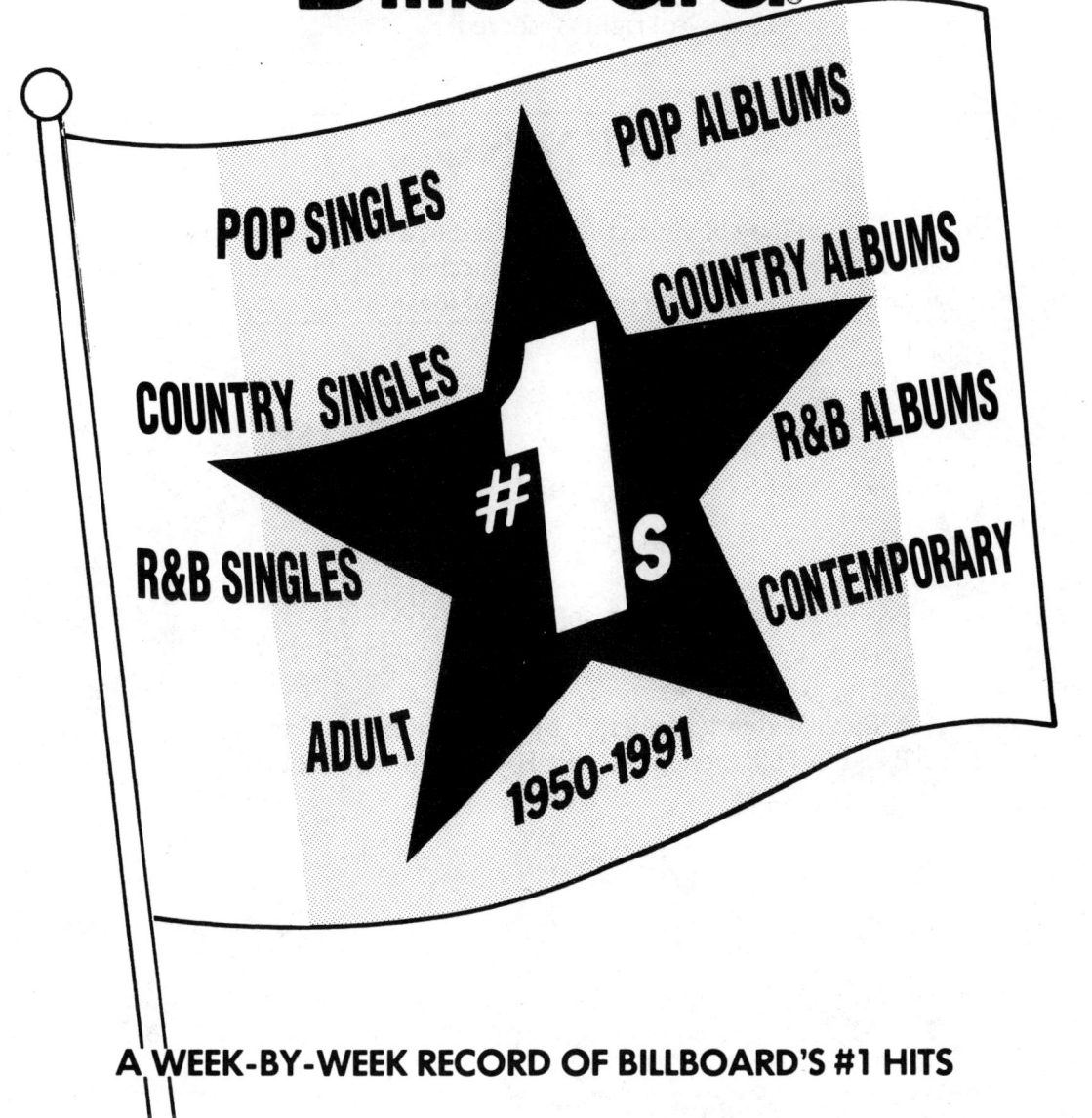

POP ALBUMS

POP SINGLES

COUNTRY ALBUMS

COUNTRY SINGLES

R&B ALBUMS

#1s

R&B SINGLES

CONTEMPORARY

ADULT

1950-1991

A WEEK-BY-WEEK RECORD OF BILLBOARD'S #1 HITS

Compiled from *Billboard's* Pop, R&B, Country and Adult Contemporary charts, 1950-1991.

Record Research Inc.
P.O. Box 200
Menomonee Falls, Wisconsin 53052-0200

Copyright © 1991 by Joel Whitburn

The Billboard chart data used in this work
is copyright © 1950-1991
by Billboard Publications, Inc.

All rights reserved.

WARNING

No part of this publication may be reproduced, stored in a retrieval system, or transmitted in any form by any means, electronic, mechanical, photocopying, recording or otherwise, without the prior written permission of the author.

ISBN 0-89820-080-6

Published independently by Record Research Inc.
P.O. Box 200, Menomonee Falls, Wisconsin 53052-0200

AUTHOR'S NOTE

The winner of baseball's Triple Crown is the player who leads his league in batting average, runs batted in and home runs over a single season. Fourteen players won the 16 Triple Crowns achieved in major league baseball's history. The two-time Triple Crown winners were Rogers Hornsby of the St. Louis Cardinals (1922 and 1925) and Ted Williams of the Boston Red Sox (1942 and 1947).

Apply the Triple Crown honor to the *Billboard* charts and you have the inspiration for this book: Which singles secured the most coveted spot on at least three of *Billboard's* main singles charts -- Pop, Country, R&B and Adult Contemporary? After compiling a master list of four decades worth of #1 hits of the premier music charts, we found that 40 singles had the good fortune of being three-time, chart-topping crossovers.

The frequency of crossover activity, greater in the early days of the rock era, has more to do with the nature of popular radio and the charts than with a song's crossover appeal. Nevertheless, the winners of *Billboard's* Triple Crown are no less deserving.

Not only does this master list of #1s reveal *Billboard's* Triple Crown winners, it gives a bird's-eye view of what was happening on the charts on any given week since 1950. For the years 1950-58, when *Billboard* published multiple charts in each of the Pop, R&B and Country formats, we listed all #1 titles from each of those charts. So, now for the first time, you can see exactly which weeks the multiple charting records or yo-yo chart-toppers claimed the chart summit.

Other research bonuses are a symbol showing a single's debut at #1 on any chart and a running total of each record's #1 weeks on each chart. For extra measure, we included the #1s of *Billboard's* Pop, R&B and Country albums charts.

Seeking out *Billboard's* Triple Crown winners led to new discoveries of what it means to be at the top of the charts. Check out this book's Royal Court of #1s and you'll find some unique achievements (and just which #1 hits were Triple Crown winners). In the pages ahead, I'm sure you'll dig up even more facts and feats.

Joel Whitburn

RESEARCHING THE CHARTS

<u>Billboard #1s 1950-1991</u> is a week-by-week listing of every #1 hit from *Billboard*'s Pop, R&B and Country singles and albums charts, and the Adult Contemporary singles charts. The research begins with the January 7, 1950 issue and ends on December 28, 1991.

From 1950 through March 17, 1956 only the Pop, R&B and Country <u>singles</u> charts are researched. The album chart research begins with *Billboard*'s first definitive weekly Pop album chart, published on March 24, 1956. Prior to this date, the Pop album chart was published sporadically--often 3 weeks between charts. From May 25, 1959 through August 10, 1963, *Billboard* published both monophonic and stereophonic Pop album charts. Both charts are researched for this book.

The Adult Contemporary singles research begins with *Billboard*'s first *Easy Listening* chart, published on July 17, 1961. That chart went through a number of name changes (*Middle-Road Singles, Pop-Standard Singles* and back to *Easy Listening Singles*) prior to becoming the *Adult Contemporary* chart on April 7, 1979. *Billboard* has never published an Adult Contemporary album chart.

The Country album and R&B album research begins with the first Country and R&B album charts, which were published by *Billboard* on January 11, 1964 and January 30, 1965, respectively.

In order to avoid any confusion, you should be aware that *Billboard* made the following name changes to their R&B and Country charts over the years. The R&B charts became the *Soul* charts in 1969 and then the *Black* charts in 1982, before reverting back to the R&B charts in late 1990. The Country singles chart was titled the *Folk (Country & Western)* chart from 1950 until late 1952, at which time *Folk* was dropped. The name *Country & Western* was abbreviated to *C&W* by mid-1956, and the *C&W* abbreviation was changed to simply *Country* by November of 1962.

During the years 1950 through 1958, Billboard published multiple singles charts for Pop, *R&B* and Country. The following is a breakdown, by chart category, of the multiple singles charts published.

POP SINGLES CHARTS 1950-1958

Chart Title	Dates Researched
Best Sellers In Stores	1/7/50 - 10/13/58 (chart ended)
Most Played By Jockeys	1/7/50 - 7/28/58 (chart ended)
Most Played In Juke Boxes	1/7/50 - 6/17/57 (chart ended)
Top 100	11/12/55 - 7/28/58 (chart ended)
Hot 100	8/4/58 - 12/28/91

R&B SINGLES CHARTS 1950-1958

Chart Title	Dates Researched
Best Sellers In Stores	1/7/50 - 10/13/58 (chart ended)
Most Played By Jockeys	1/22/55 - 10/13/58 (chart ended)
Most Played In Juke Boxes	1/7/50 - 6/17/57 (chart ended)

COUNTRY (C&W) SINGLES CHARTS 1950-1958

Chart Title	Dates Researched
Best Sellers In Stores	1/7/50 - 10/13/58 (chart ended)
Most Played By Jockeys	1/7/50 - 10/13/58 (chart ended)
Most Played In Juke Boxes	1/7/50 - 6/17/57 (chart ended)

As of 10/20/58, *Billboard* dropped all of the multiple singles charts and established one all-inclusive chart for Pop singles (the *Hot 100*), R&B singles (*Hot R&B Sides*) and Country singles (*Hot C&W Sides*). The *Hot 100* chart still exists today; however, the *Hot R&B Sides* chart is now titled *Hot R&B Singles*, and the *Hot C&W Sides* chart is now titled *Hot Country Singles & Tracks*.

R&B CHARTS DISCONTINUED

Billboard temporarily discontinued their *Hot R&B Singles* chart from November 30, 1963 through January 23, 1965. It was reinstated as the *Hot Rhythm & Blues Singles* chart on January 30, 1965. *Billboard* also discontinued their *Soul LP's* chart for a seven week period from August 26, 1972 through October 7, 1972.

FROZEN CHARTS

Beginning in 1976, *Billboard* ceased publishing an issue on the last week of the year. The year's last regular issue is considered frozen and the #1s are duplicated in this book for the unpublished week (the total weeks at the #1 position are increased by 1).

NON-SEQUENTIAL DATES

The date shown above each group of #1 hits is *Billboard's* issue date. In a few instances *Billboard's* issue dates did not adhere to a seven-day week, and those dates are as follows:

1. April 27, 1957 to April 29, 1957 (*Billboard* went from a Saturday to a Monday issue date)
2. December 25, 1961 to January 6, 1962 (*Billboard* went from a Monday to a permanent Saturday issue date)
3. December 31, 1960 (instead of January 2, 1961)
4. July 4, 1976 (instead of July 3, 1976)

EXPLANATION OF CHART ABBREVIATIONS AND SYMBOLS

The date shown above each group of #1 hits is *Billboard*'s issue date for that week. The titles for each date are listed in the following order, based on music category: Pop, R&B, Country and Adult Contemporary. Singles are always listed before the albums. During the period of multiple charts, the *Top 100* (or *Hot 100*) will always be shown first, followed by the *Best Sellers In Stores, Most Played By Jockeys* and *Most Played In Juke Boxes* charts. Also, from 1959 through 1963, when *Billboard* published both monophonic and stereophonic pop albums charts, the monophonic listing is always shown first.

CHART HEADINGS

- **POP** - Pop Singles and Albums
- **HOT** - *Hot 100* singles (shown for all Pop singles from August 4, 1958 to present)
- **R&B** - R&B/Soul/Black Singles and Albums
- **C&W** - Country/Country & Western Singles and Albums
- **A/C** - Adult Contemporary/Easy Listening Singles
- **LPS** - Pop Albums (shown until the Country albums chart began on January 11, 1964)

MULTIPLE CHART ABBREVIATIONS

SINGLES (1950-1958):
- BS - *Best Sellers In Stores*
- DJ - *Most Played By Disc Jockeys*
- JB - *Most Played In Juke Boxes*
- HT - *Hot 100*
- TP - *Top 100*

LPS (1959-1963):
- MO - *Best Selling Monophonic Pop Albums*
- ST - *Best Selling Stereophonic Pop Albums*

SYMBOLS

* Indicates the first time a single hit #1 on any chart; however, this symbol is not shown if the record hit #1 on only one chart. Also, symbol is not shown for albums.

Example: If a song hit #1 on the *Pop Best Sellers* chart on 5/20/57 and the *R&B Juke Box* chart on 5/27/57, an asterisk is shown next to the *Pop Best Sellers* entry only. The same is true of a song that hit #1 on the *Pop Best Sellers* chart on 5/20/57 and the *Pop Juke Box* chart on 5/27/57, an asterisk is shown next to the *Pop Best Sellers* entry only. If a song hit #1 for the first time on two charts on the same date, an asterisk is shown next to both titles.

/ Divides a two-sided single. If the A-side and B-side of a single were listed together at the #1 position on a chart, then both titles are shown herein and divided by a slash.

³ A superior number after each title indicates the cumulative number of weeks the record was at the #1 position on that chart.

In the 1950s *Billboard* occasionally listed ties at the #1 position. Those titles which tied are bracketed together for easy identification.

#1 HITS SECTION

A week-by-week listing of every record to hit #1 on *Billboard*'s Pop, R&B and Country singles and albums charts, and Adult Contemporary singles charts from 1950-1991.

January 7, 1950

POP
- BS *Rudolph, The Red-Nosed Reindeer [1]...Gene Autry
- DJ *I Can Dream, Can't I? [1]...Andrews Sisters
- JB Mule Train [5]...Frankie Laine and The Mule Skinners

R&B
- BS Saturday Night Fish Fry (Part I) [12]...Louis Jordan
- JB Saturday Night Fish Fry (Part I) [11]...Louis Jordan

C&W
- BS Slipping Around [14]...Margaret Whiting & Jimmy Wakely
- DJ *Rudolph, The Red-Nosed Reindeer [1]...Gene Autry
- JB Blue Christmas [1]...Ernest Tubb

January 14, 1950

POP
- BS I Can Dream, Can't I? [1]...Andrews Sisters
- DJ I Can Dream, Can't I? [2]...Andrews Sisters
- JB Mule Train [6]...Frankie Laine and The Mule Skinners

R&B
- BS For You, My Love [2]...Larry Darnell
- JB For You, My Love [3]...Larry Darnell

C&W
- BS Slipping Around [15]...Margaret Whiting & Jimmy Wakely
- DJ I Love You Because [1]...Leon Payne
- JB Blues Stay Away From Me [1]...Delmore Brothers

January 21, 1950

POP
- BS I Can Dream, Can't I? [2]...Andrews Sisters
- DJ I Can Dream, Can't I? [3]...Andrews Sisters
- JB I Can Dream, Can't I? [1]...Andrews Sisters

R&B
- BS For You, My Love [3]...Larry Darnell
- JB For You, My Love [4]...Larry Darnell

C&W
- BS Slipping Around [16]...Margaret Whiting & Jimmy Wakely
- DJ *Chattanoogie Shoe Shine Boy [1]...Red Foley
- JB Slipping Around [12]...Margaret Whiting & Jimmy Wakely

January 28, 1950

POP
- BS I Can Dream, Can't I? [3]...Andrews Sisters
- DJ I Can Dream, Can't I? [4]...Andrews Sisters
- JB I Can Dream, Can't I? [2]...Andrews Sisters

R&B
- BS For You, My Love [4]...Larry Darnell
- JB For You, My Love [5]...Larry Darnell

C&W
- BS Slipping Around [17]...Margaret Whiting & Jimmy Wakely
- DJ I Love You Because [2]...Leon Payne
- JB Take Me In Your Arms And Hold Me [1]...Eddy Arnold

February 4, 1950

POP
- BS I Can Dream, Can't I? [4]...Andrews Sisters
- DJ I Can Dream, Can't I? [5]...Andrews Sisters
- JB I Can Dream, Can't I? [3]...Andrews Sisters

R&B
- BS For You, My Love [5]...Larry Darnell
- JB For You, My Love [6]...Larry Darnell

C&W
- BS Chattanoogie Shoe Shine Boy [1]...Red Foley
- DJ Chattanoogie Shoe Shine Boy [2]...Red Foley
- JB Chattanoogie Shoe Shine Boy [1]...Red Foley

February 11, 1950

POP
- BS *Rag Mop [1]...Ames Brothers
- DJ *Rag Mop [1]...Ames Brothers
- JB Chattanoogie Shoe Shine Boy [1]...Red Foley

R&B
- BS For You, My Love [6]...Larry Darnell
- JB For You, My Love [7]...Larry Darnell

C&W
- BS Chattanoogie Shoe Shine Boy [2]...Red Foley
- DJ Chattanoogie Shoe Shine Boy [3]...Red Foley
- JB Chattanoogie Shoe Shine Boy [2]...Red Foley

February 18, 1950

POP
- BS Chattanoogie Shoe Shine Boy [1]...Red Foley
- DJ Rag Mop [2]...Ames Brothers
- JB Chattanoogie Shoe Shine Boy [2]...Red Foley

R&B
- BS *I Almost Lost My Mind [1]...Ivory Joe Hunter
- JB For You, My Love [8]...Larry Darnell

C&W
- BS Chattanoogie Shoe Shine Boy [3]...Red Foley
- DJ Chattanoogie Shoe Shine Boy [4]...Red Foley
- JB Chattanoogie Shoe Shine Boy [3]...Red Foley

February 25, 1950

POP
- BS Chattanoogie Shoe Shine Boy [2]...Red Foley
- DJ Chattanoogie Shoe Shine Boy [1]...Red Foley
- JB Chattanoogie Shoe Shine Boy [3]...Red Foley

R&B
- BS I Almost Lost My Mind [2]...Ivory Joe Hunter
- JB I Almost Lost My Mind [1]...Ivory Joe Hunter

C&W
- BS Chattanoogie Shoe Shine Boy [4]...Red Foley
- DJ Chattanoogie Shoe Shine Boy [5]...Red Foley
- JB Chattanoogie Shoe Shine Boy [4]...Red Foley

March 4, 1950

POP
- BS   Chattanoogie Shoe Shine Boy [3]...Red Foley
- DJ   Chattanoogie Shoe Shine Boy [2]...Red Foley
- JB   Chattanoogie Shoe Shine Boy [4]...Red Foley

R&B
- BS   *Double Crossing Blues [1]...
       Little Esther/Johnny Otis Orchestra
- JB   I Almost Lost My Mind [2]...Ivory Joe Hunter

C&W
- BS   Chattanoogie Shoe Shine Boy [5]...Red Foley
- DJ   Chattanoogie Shoe Shine Boy [6]...Red Foley
- JB   Chattanoogie Shoe Shine Boy [5]...Red Foley

March 11, 1950

POP
- BS   Chattanoogie Shoe Shine Boy [4]...Red Foley
- DJ   The Cry Of The Wild Goose [1]...Frankie Laine
- JB   Chattanoogie Shoe Shine Boy [5]...Red Foley

R&B
- BS   Double Crossing Blues [2]...
       Little Esther/Johnny Otis Orchestra
- JB   I Almost Lost My Mind [3]...Ivory Joe Hunter ⎫
- JB   Double Crossing Blues [1]...   ⎬ tie
       Little Esther/Johnny Otis Orchestra   ⎭

C&W
- BS   Chattanoogie Shoe Shine Boy [6]...Red Foley
- DJ   Chattanoogie Shoe Shine Boy [7]...Red Foley
- JB   Chattanoogie Shoe Shine Boy [6]...Red Foley

March 18, 1950

POP
- BS   *Music! Music! Music! [1]...
       Teresa Brewer with The Dixieland All Stars
- DJ   The Cry Of The Wild Goose [2]...Frankie Laine
- JB   Chattanoogie Shoe Shine Boy [6]...Red Foley

R&B
- BS   Double Crossing Blues [3]...
       Little Esther/Johnny Otis Orchestra
- JB   I Almost Lost My Mind [4]...Ivory Joe Hunter

C&W
- BS   Chattanoogie Shoe Shine Boy [7]...Red Foley
- DJ   Chattanoogie Shoe Shine Boy [8]...Red Foley
- JB   Chattanoogie Shoe Shine Boy [7]...Red Foley

March 25, 1950

POP
- BS   Music! Music! Music! [2]...
       Teresa Brewer with The Dixieland All Stars
- DJ   *If I Knew You Were Comin' I'd've Baked A Cake [1]...Eileen Barton
- JB   Chattanoogie Shoe Shine Boy [7]...Red Foley

R&B
- BS   Double Crossing Blues [4]...
       Little Esther/Johnny Otis Orchestra
- JB   Double Crossing Blues [2]...
       Little Esther/Johnny Otis Orchestra

C&W
- BS   Chattanoogie Shoe Shine Boy [8]...Red Foley
- DJ   Chattanoogie Shoe Shine Boy [9]...Red Foley
- JB   Chattanoogie Shoe Shine Boy [8]...Red Foley

April 1, 1950

POP
- BS   Music! Music! Music! [3]...
       Teresa Brewer with The Dixieland All Stars
- DJ   If I Knew You Were Comin' I'd've Baked A Cake [2]...Eileen Barton
- JB   Chattanoogie Shoe Shine Boy [8]...Red Foley

R&B
- BS   Double Crossing Blues [5]...
       Little Esther/Johnny Otis Orchestra
- JB   Double Crossing Blues [3]...
       Little Esther/Johnny Otis Orchestra

C&W
- BS   Chattanoogie Shoe Shine Boy [9]...Red Foley
- DJ   Chattanoogie Shoe Shine Boy [10]...Red Foley
- JB   Chattanoogie Shoe Shine Boy [9]...Red Foley

April 8, 1950

POP
- BS   Music! Music! Music! [4]...
       Teresa Brewer with The Dixieland All Stars
- DJ   If I Knew You Were Comin' I'd've Baked A Cake [3]...Eileen Barton
- JB   Music! Music! Music! [1]...
       Teresa Brewer with The Dixieland All Stars

R&B
- BS   Double Crossing Blues [6]...
       Little Esther/Johnny Otis Orchestra
- JB   Double Crossing Blues [4]...
       Little Esther/Johnny Otis Orchestra

C&W
- BS   Chattanoogie Shoe Shine Boy [10]...Red Foley
- DJ   Chattanoogie Shoe Shine Boy [11]...Red Foley
- JB   Chattanoogie Shoe Shine Boy [10]...Red Foley

April 15, 1950

POP
- BS If I Knew You Were Comin' I'd've Baked A Cake [1]...Eileen Barton
- DJ If I Knew You Were Comin' I'd've Baked A Cake [4]...Eileen Barton
- JB If I Knew You Were Comin' I'd've Baked A Cake [1]...Eileen Barton

R&B
- BS Double Crossing Blues [7]...
  Little Esther/Johnny Otis Orchestra
- JB *Mistrustin' Blues [1]...
  Little Esther with Mel Walker/The Johnny Otis Orch.

C&W
- BS Chattanoogie Shoe Shine Boy [11]...Red Foley
- DJ Chattanoogie Shoe Shine Boy [12]...Red Foley
- JB Chattanoogie Shoe Shine Boy [11]...Red Foley

April 22, 1950

POP
- BS If I Knew You Were Comin' I'd've Baked A Cake [2]...Eileen Barton
- DJ If I Knew You Were Comin' I'd've Baked A Cake [5]...Eileen Barton
- JB If I Knew You Were Comin' I'd've Baked A Cake [2]...Eileen Barton

R&B
- BS Double Crossing Blues [8]...
  Little Esther/Johnny Otis Orchestra
- JB Mistrustin' Blues [2]...
  Little Esther with Mel Walker/The Johnny Otis Orch.

C&W
- BS Chattanoogie Shoe Shine Boy [12]...Red Foley
- DJ *Long Gone Lonesome Blues [1]...Hank Williams
- JB Chattanoogie Shoe Shine Boy [12]...Red Foley

April 29, 1950

POP
- BS The Third Man Theme [1]...Anton Karas
- DJ If I Knew You Were Comin' I'd've Baked A Cake [6]...Eileen Barton
- JB If I Knew You Were Comin' I'd've Baked A Cake [3]...Eileen Barton

R&B
- BS Double Crossing Blues [9]...
  Little Esther/Johnny Otis Orchestra
- JB I Almost Lost My Mind [5]...Ivory Joe Hunter

C&W
- BS Long Gone Lonesome Blues [1]...Hank Williams
- DJ Chattanoogie Shoe Shine Boy [13]...Red Foley
- JB Chattanoogie Shoe Shine Boy [13]...Red Foley

May 6, 1950

POP
- BS The Third Man Theme [2]...Anton Karas
- DJ If I Knew You Were Comin' I'd've Baked A Cake [7]...Eileen Barton
- JB The 3rd Man Theme [1]...
  Guy Lombardo And His Royal Canadians

R&B
- BS Mistrustin' Blues [1]...
  Little Esther with Mel Walker/The Johnny Otis Orch.
- JB Mistrustin' Blues [3]...
  Little Esther with Mel Walker/The Johnny Otis Orch.

C&W
- BS Long Gone Lonesome Blues [2]...Hank Williams
- DJ Long Gone Lonesome Blues [2]...Hank Williams
- JB Long Gone Lonesome Blues [1]...Hank Williams

May 13, 1950

POP
- BS The Third Man Theme [3]...Anton Karas
- DJ If I Knew You Were Comin' I'd've Baked A Cake [8]...Eileen Barton
- JB The 3rd Man Theme [2]...
  Guy Lombardo And His Royal Canadians

R&B
- BS Mistrustin' Blues [2]...
  Little Esther with Mel Walker/The Johnny Otis Orch.
- JB I Need You So [1]...Ivory Joe Hunter ⎫ tie
- JB Mistrustin' Blues [4]...   ⎭
  Little Esther with Mel Walker/The Johnny Otis Orch.

C&W
- BS Long Gone Lonesome Blues [3]...Hank Williams
- DJ Long Gone Lonesome Blues [3]...Hank Williams
- JB Long Gone Lonesome Blues [2]...Hank Williams

May 20, 1950

POP
- BS The Third Man Theme [4]...Anton Karas
- DJ If I Knew You Were Comin' I'd've Baked A Cake [9]...Eileen Barton
- JB The 3rd Man Theme [3]...
  Guy Lombardo And His Royal Canadians

R&B
- BS Mistrustin' Blues [3]...
  Little Esther with Mel Walker/The Johnny Otis Orch.
- JB I Need You So [2]...Ivory Joe Hunter ⎫ tie
- JB Double Crossing Blues [5]...   ⎭
  Little Esther/Johnny Otis Orchestra

C&W
- BS Long Gone Lonesome Blues [4]...Hank Williams
- DJ Long Gone Lonesome Blues [4]...Hank Williams
- JB Long Gone Lonesome Blues [3]...Hank Williams

May 27, 1950

POP
- BS   The Third Man Theme [5]...Anton Karas
- DJ   If I Knew You Were Comin' I'd've Baked A Cake [10]...Eileen Barton
- JB   The 3rd Man Theme [4]...
       Guy Lombardo And His Royal Canadians

R&B
- BS   Mistrustin' Blues [4]...
       Little Esther with Mel Walker/The Johnny Otis Orch.
- JB   *Pink Champagne [1]...Joe Liggins & His "Honeydrippers"

C&W
- BS   *Birmingham Bounce [1]...Red Foley
- DJ   Long Gone Lonesome Blues [5]...Hank Williams
- JB   Long Gone Lonesome Blues [4]...Hank Williams

June 3, 1950

POP
- BS   The Third Man Theme [6]...Anton Karas
- DJ   Hoop-Dee-Doo [1]...Perry Como/The Fontane Sisters
- JB   The 3rd Man Theme [5]...
       Guy Lombardo And His Royal Canadians

R&B
- BS   Pink Champagne [1]...Joe Liggins & His "Honeydrippers"
- JB   Pink Champagne [2]...Joe Liggins & His "Honeydrippers"

C&W
- BS   Long Gone Lonesome Blues [5]...Hank Williams
- DJ   Long Gone Lonesome Blues [6]...Hank Williams
- JB   Birmingham Bounce [1]...Red Foley

June 10, 1950

POP
- BS   The Third Man Theme [7]...Anton Karas
- DJ   Sentimental Me [1]...Ames Brothers
- JB   The 3rd Man Theme [6]...
       Guy Lombardo And His Royal Canadians

R&B
- BS   Pink Champagne [2]...Joe Liggins & His "Honeydrippers"
- JB   Pink Champagne [3]...Joe Liggins & His "Honeydrippers"

C&W
- BS   Birmingham Bounce [2]...Red Foley
- DJ   Long Gone Lonesome Blues [7]...Hank Williams
- JB   Birmingham Bounce [2]...Red Foley

June 17, 1950

POP
- BS   The Third Man Theme [8]...Anton Karas
- DJ   Hoop-Dee-Doo [2]...Perry Como/The Fontane Sisters
- JB   The 3rd Man Theme [7]...
       Guy Lombardo And His Royal Canadians

R&B
- BS   Pink Champagne [3]...Joe Liggins & His "Honeydrippers"
- JB   Pink Champagne [4]...Joe Liggins & His "Honeydrippers"

C&W
- BS   *Why Don't You Love Me [1]...Hank Williams
- DJ   Long Gone Lonesome Blues [8]...Hank Williams
- JB   *I'll Sail My Ship Alone [1]...Moon Mullican

June 24, 1950

POP
- BS   The Third Man Theme [9]...Anton Karas
- DJ   I Wanna Be Loved [1]...Andrews Sisters
- JB   The 3rd Man Theme [8]...
       Guy Lombardo And His Royal Canadians

R&B
- BS   Pink Champagne [4]...Joe Liggins & His "Honeydrippers"
- JB   Pink Champagne [5]...Joe Liggins & His "Honeydrippers"

C&W
- BS   Birmingham Bounce [3]...Red Foley
- DJ   Why Don't You Love Me [1]...Hank Williams
- JB   Birmingham Bounce [3]...Red Foley ⎫
- JB   I'll Sail My Ship Alone [2]...Moon Mullican ⎬ tie

July 1, 1950

POP
- BS   The Third Man Theme [10]...Anton Karas
- DJ   I Wanna Be Loved [2]...Andrews Sisters
- JB   The 3rd Man Theme [9]...
       Guy Lombardo And His Royal Canadians

R&B
- BS   Pink Champagne [5]...Joe Liggins & His "Honeydrippers"
- JB   Pink Champagne [6]...Joe Liggins & His "Honeydrippers"

C&W
- BS   Birmingham Bounce [4]...Red Foley
- DJ   Why Don't You Love Me [2]...Hank Williams
- JB   I'll Sail My Ship Alone [3]...Moon Mullican

July 8, 1950

POP
- BS   The Third Man Theme [11]...Anton Karas
- DJ   *Mona Lisa [1]...Nat "King" Cole
- JB   The 3rd Man Theme [10]...
       Guy Lombardo And His Royal Canadians

R&B
- BS   Pink Champagne [6]...Joe Liggins & His "Honeydrippers"
- JB   Cupid's Boogie [1]...
       Little Esther/Johnny Otis Orchestra

C&W
- BS   Why Don't You Love Me [2]...Hank Williams
- DJ   Why Don't You Love Me [3]...Hank Williams
- JB   I'll Sail My Ship Alone [4]...Moon Mullican

July 15, 1950

POP
- BS   Mona Lisa [1]...Nat "King" Cole
- DJ   Mona Lisa [2]...Nat "King" Cole
- JB   The 3rd Man Theme [11]...
       Guy Lombardo And His Royal Canadians

R&B
- BS   Pink Champagne [7]...Joe Liggins & His "Honeydrippers"
- JB   Pink Champagne [7]...Joe Liggins & His "Honeydrippers"

C&W
- BS   Why Don't You Love Me [3]...Hank Williams
- DJ   Why Don't You Love Me [4]...Hank Williams
- JB   M-I-S-S-I-S-S-I-P-P-I [1]...Red Foley

July 22, 1950

POP
- BS   Mona Lisa [2]...Nat "King" Cole
- DJ   Mona Lisa [3]...Nat "King" Cole
- JB   Mona Lisa [1]...Nat "King" Cole

R&B
- BS   Pink Champagne [8]...Joe Liggins & His "Honeydrippers"
- JB   Pink Champagne [8]...Joe Liggins & His "Honeydrippers"

C&W
- BS   I'll Sail My Ship Alone [1]...Moon Mullican
- DJ   Why Don't You Love Me [5]...Hank Williams
- JB   Why Don't You Love Me [1]...Hank Williams

July 29, 1950

POP
- BS   Mona Lisa [3]...Nat "King" Cole
- DJ   Mona Lisa [4]...Nat "King" Cole
- JB   Mona Lisa [2]...Nat "King" Cole

R&B
- BS   Pink Champagne [9]...Joe Liggins & His "Honeydrippers"
- JB   Pink Champagne [9]...Joe Liggins & His "Honeydrippers"

C&W
- BS   Why Don't You Love Me [4]...Hank Williams
- DJ   Why Don't You Love Me [6]...Hank Williams
- JB   Why Don't You Love Me [2]...Hank Williams

August 5, 1950

POP
- BS   Mona Lisa [4]...Nat "King" Cole
- DJ   Mona Lisa [5]...Nat "King" Cole
- JB   Mona Lisa [3]...Nat "King" Cole

R&B
- BS   Pink Champagne [10]...Joe Liggins & His "Honeydrippers"
- JB   Pink Champagne [10]...Joe Liggins & His "Honeydrippers"

C&W
- BS   Why Don't You Love Me [5]...Hank Williams
- DJ   Why Don't You Love Me [7]...Hank Williams
- JB   Why Don't You Love Me [3]...Hank Williams

August 12, 1950

POP
- BS   Mona Lisa [5]...Nat "King" Cole
- DJ   Mona Lisa [6]...Nat "King" Cole
- JB   Mona Lisa [4]...Nat "King" Cole

R&B
- BS   Pink Champagne [11]...Joe Liggins & His "Honeydrippers"
- JB   Pink Champagne [11]...Joe Liggins & His "Honeydrippers"

C&W
- BS   Why Don't You Love Me [6]...Hank Williams
- DJ   Why Don't You Love Me [8]...Hank Williams
- JB   Why Don't You Love Me [4]...Hank Williams

August 19, 1950

POP
- BS   *Goodnight Irene [1]...
       Gordon Jenkins and The Weavers
- DJ   Mona Lisa [7]...Nat "King" Cole
- JB   Mona Lisa [5]...Nat "King" Cole

R&B
- BS   Hard Luck Blues [1]...Roy Brown
- JB   Pink Champagne [12]...Joe Liggins & His "Honeydrippers"

C&W
- BS   *I'm Moving On [1]...Hank Snow
- DJ   Why Don't You Love Me [9]...Hank Williams
- JB   Why Don't You Love Me [5]...Hank Williams

August 26, 1950

POP
- BS   Goodnight Irene [2]...
  Gordon Jenkins and The Weavers
- DJ   Mona Lisa [8]...Nat "King" Cole
- JB   Goodnight Irene [1]...
  Gordon Jenkins and The Weavers

R&B
- BS   Hard Luck Blues [2]...Roy Brown
- JB   Pink Champagne [13]...Joe Liggins & His "Honeydrippers"

C&W
- BS   *Goodnight, Irene [1]...Ernest Tubb & Red Foley
- DJ   Why Don't You Love Me [10]...Hank Williams
- JB   *Goodnight, Irene [1]...Ernest Tubb & Red Foley

September 2, 1950

POP
- BS   Goodnight Irene [3]...
  Gordon Jenkins and The Weavers
- DJ   Goodnight Irene [1]...
  Gordon Jenkins and The Weavers
- JB   Goodnight Irene [2]...
  Gordon Jenkins and The Weavers

R&B
- BS   Hard Luck Blues [3]...Roy Brown
- JB   Mona Lisa [1]...Nat "King" Cole

C&W
- BS   Goodnight, Irene [2]...Ernest Tubb & Red Foley
- DJ   I'm Moving On [1]...Hank Snow
- JB   Goodnight, Irene [2]...Ernest Tubb & Red Foley

September 9, 1950

POP
- BS   Goodnight Irene [4]...
  Gordon Jenkins and The Weavers
- DJ   Goodnight Irene [2]...
  Gordon Jenkins and The Weavers
- JB   Goodnight Irene [3]...
  Gordon Jenkins and The Weavers

R&B
- BS   *Blue Light Boogie - Parts 1 & 2 [1]...Louis Jordan
- JB   Mona Lisa [2]...Nat "King" Cole

C&W
- BS   I'm Moving On [2]...Hank Snow
- DJ   I'm Moving On [2]...Hank Snow
- JB   Goodnight, Irene [3]...Ernest Tubb & Red Foley

September 16, 1950

POP
- BS   Goodnight Irene [5]...
  Gordon Jenkins and The Weavers
- DJ   Goodnight Irene [3]...
  Gordon Jenkins and The Weavers
- JB   Goodnight Irene [4]...
  Gordon Jenkins and The Weavers

R&B
- BS   Blue Light Boogie - Parts 1 & 2 [2]...Louis Jordan
- JB   Mona Lisa [3]...Nat "King" Cole

C&W
- BS   I'm Moving On [3]...Hank Snow
- DJ   I'm Moving On [3]...Hank Snow
- JB   I'm Moving On [1]...Hank Snow

September 23, 1950

POP
- BS   Goodnight Irene [6]...
  Gordon Jenkins and The Weavers
- DJ   Goodnight Irene [4]...
  Gordon Jenkins and The Weavers
- JB   Goodnight Irene [5]...
  Gordon Jenkins and The Weavers

R&B
- BS   Blue Light Boogie - Parts 1 & 2 [3]...Louis Jordan
- JB   Mona Lisa [4]...Nat "King" Cole

C&W
- BS   I'm Moving On [4]...Hank Snow
- DJ   I'm Moving On [4]...Hank Snow
- JB   I'm Moving On [2]...Hank Snow

September 30, 1950

POP
- BS   Goodnight Irene [7]...
  Gordon Jenkins and The Weavers
- DJ   Goodnight Irene [5]...
  Gordon Jenkins and The Weavers
- JB   Goodnight Irene [6]...
  Gordon Jenkins and The Weavers

R&B
- BS   Blue Light Boogie - Parts 1 & 2 [4]...Louis Jordan
- JB   Blue Light Boogie - Parts 1 & 2 [1]...Louis Jordan

C&W
- BS   I'm Moving On [5]...Hank Snow
- DJ   I'm Moving On [5]...Hank Snow
- JB   I'm Moving On [3]...Hank Snow

October 7, 1950

POP
- BS Goodnight Irene [8]...
  Gordon Jenkins and The Weavers
- DJ Goodnight Irene [6]...
  Gordon Jenkins and The Weavers
- JB Goodnight Irene [7]...
  Gordon Jenkins and The Weavers

R&B
- BS Blue Light Boogie - Parts 1 & 2 [5]...Louis Jordan
- JB Blue Light Boogie - Parts 1 & 2 [2]...Louis Jordan

C&W
- BS I'm Moving On [6]...Hank Snow
- DJ I'm Moving On [6]...Hank Snow
- JB I'm Moving On [4]...Hank Snow

October 14, 1950

POP
- BS Goodnight Irene [9]...
  Gordon Jenkins and The Weavers
- DJ Goodnight Irene [7]...
  Gordon Jenkins and The Weavers
- JB Goodnight Irene [8]...
  Gordon Jenkins and The Weavers

R&B
- BS Blue Light Boogie - Parts 1 & 2 [6]...Louis Jordan
- JB Blue Light Boogie - Parts 1 & 2 [3]...Louis Jordan

C&W
- BS I'm Moving On [7]...Hank Snow
- DJ I'm Moving On [7]...Hank Snow
- JB I'm Moving On [5]...Hank Snow

October 21, 1950

POP
- BS Goodnight Irene [10]...
  Gordon Jenkins and The Weavers
- DJ Goodnight Irene [8]...
  Gordon Jenkins and The Weavers
- JB Goodnight Irene [9]...
  Gordon Jenkins and The Weavers

R&B
- BS Blue Light Boogie - Parts 1 & 2 [7]...Louis Jordan
- JB Blue Light Boogie - Parts 1 & 2 [4]...Louis Jordan

C&W
- BS I'm Moving On [8]...Hank Snow
- DJ I'm Moving On [8]...Hank Snow
- JB I'm Moving On [6]...Hank Snow

October 28, 1950

POP
- BS Goodnight Irene [11]...
  Gordon Jenkins and The Weavers
- DJ All My Love (Bolero) [1]...Patti Page
- JB Goodnight Irene [10]...
  Gordon Jenkins and The Weavers

R&B
- BS *Blue Shadows [1]...Lowell Fulsom
- JB *Blue Shadows [1]...Lowell Fulsom

C&W
- BS I'm Moving On [9]...Hank Snow
- DJ I'm Moving On [9]...Hank Snow
- JB I'm Moving On [7]...Hank Snow

November 4, 1950

POP
- BS Goodnight Irene [12]...
  Gordon Jenkins and The Weavers
- DJ All My Love (Bolero) [2]...Patti Page
- JB Goodnight Irene [11]...
  Gordon Jenkins and The Weavers

R&B
- BS *Anytime, Any Place, Anywhere [1]...Joe Morris
- JB Blue Shadows [2]...Lowell Fulsom

C&W
- BS I'm Moving On [10]...Hank Snow
- DJ I'm Moving On [10]...Hank Snow
- JB I'm Moving On [8]...Hank Snow

November 11, 1950

POP
- BS Goodnight Irene [13]...
  Gordon Jenkins and The Weavers
- DJ All My Love (Bolero) [3]...Patti Page
- JB Goodnight Irene [12]...
  Gordon Jenkins and The Weavers

R&B
- BS Anytime, Any Place, Anywhere [2]...Joe Morris
- JB Blue Shadows [3]...Lowell Fulsom

C&W
- BS I'm Moving On [11]...Hank Snow
- DJ I'm Moving On [11]...Hank Snow
- JB I'm Moving On [9]...Hank Snow

November 18, 1950

POP
- BS *Harbor Lights [1]...Sammy Kaye
- DJ All My Love (Bolero) [4]...Patti Page
- JB *Harbor Lights [1]...Sammy Kaye

R&B
- BS Anytime, Any Place, Anywhere [3]...Joe Morris
- JB Blue Shadows [4]...Lowell Fulsom

C&W
- BS I'm Moving On [12]...Hank Snow
- DJ I'm Moving On [12]...Hank Snow
- JB I'm Moving On [10]...Hank Snow

November 25, 1950

POP
- BS Harbor Lights [2]...Sammy Kaye
- DJ All My Love (Bolero) [5]...Patti Page
- JB Harbor Lights [2]...Sammy Kaye

R&B
- BS *Please Send Me Someone To Love [1]...Percy Mayfield
- JB Anytime, Any Place, Anywhere [1]...Joe Morris

C&W
- BS I'm Moving On [13]...Hank Snow
- DJ I'm Moving On [13]...Hank Snow
- JB I'm Moving On [11]...Hank Snow

December 2, 1950

POP
- BS *The Thing [1]...Phil Harris
- DJ *The Thing [1]...Phil Harris
- JB Harbor Lights [3]...Sammy Kaye

R&B
- BS Anytime, Any Place, Anywhere [4]...Joe Morris
- JB Anytime, Any Place, Anywhere [2]...Joe Morris

C&W
- BS I'm Moving On [14]...Hank Snow
- DJ I'm Moving On [14]...Hank Snow
- JB I'm Moving On [12]...Hank Snow

December 9, 1950

POP
- BS The Thing [2]...Phil Harris
- DJ The Thing [2]...Phil Harris
- JB Harbor Lights [4]...Sammy Kaye

R&B
- BS *Teardrops From My Eyes [1]...Ruth Brown
- JB Anytime, Any Place, Anywhere [3]...Joe Morris

C&W
- BS I'm Moving On [15]...Hank Snow
- DJ I'm Moving On [15]...Hank Snow
- JB I'm Moving On [13]...Hank Snow

December 16, 1950

POP
- BS The Thing [3]...Phil Harris
- DJ The Thing [3]...Phil Harris
- JB *The Tennessee Waltz [1]...Patti Page

R&B
- BS Please Send Me Someone To Love [2]...Percy Mayfield
- JB Please Send Me Someone To Love [1]...Percy Mayfield

C&W
- BS I'm Moving On [16]...Hank Snow
- DJ I'm Moving On [16]...Hank Snow
- JB I'm Moving On [14]...Hank Snow

December 23, 1950

POP
- BS The Thing [4]...Phil Harris
- DJ The Thing [4]...Phil Harris
- JB The Thing [1]...Phil Harris

R&B
- BS Teardrops From My Eyes [2]...Ruth Brown
- JB Teardrops From My Eyes [1]...Ruth Brown

C&W
- BS I'm Moving On [17]...Hank Snow
- DJ I'm Moving On [17]...Hank Snow
- JB If You've Got The Money I've Got The Time [1]...Lefty Frizzell

December 30, 1950

POP
- BS The Tennessee Waltz [1]...Patti Page
- DJ The Thing [5]...Phil Harris
- JB The Thing [2]...Phil Harris

R&B
- BS Teardrops From My Eyes [3]...Ruth Brown
- JB Teardrops From My Eyes [2]...Ruth Brown

C&W
- BS I'm Moving On [18]...Hank Snow
- DJ Moanin' The Blues [1]...Hank Williams
- JB If You've Got The Money I've Got The Time [2]...Lefty Frizzell

January 6, 1951

POP
- BS The Tennessee Waltz [2]...Patti Page
- DJ The Tennessee Waltz [1]...Patti Page
- JB The Tennessee Waltz [2]...Patti Page

R&B
- BS *Bad, Bad Whiskey [1]...Amos Milburn
- JB Teardrops From My Eyes [3]...Ruth Brown

C&W
- BS *The Golden Rocket [1]...Hank Snow
- DJ I Love You A Thousand Ways [1]...Lefty Frizzell
- JB If You've Got The Money I've Got The Time [3]...Lefty Frizzell

January 13, 1951

POP
- BS The Tennessee Waltz [3]...Patti Page
- DJ The Tennessee Waltz [2]...Patti Page
- JB The Tennessee Waltz [3]...Patti Page

R&B
- BS Teardrops From My Eyes [4]...Ruth Brown
- JB Bad, Bad Whiskey [1]...Amos Milburn

C&W
- BS The Golden Rocket [2]...Hank Snow
- DJ I'm Moving On [18]...Hank Snow
- JB *The Shot Gun Boogie [1]...Tennessee Ernie Ford

January 20, 1951

POP
- BS The Tennessee Waltz [4]...Patti Page
- DJ The Tennessee Waltz [3]...Patti Page
- JB The Tennessee Waltz [4]...Patti Page

R&B
- BS Teardrops From My Eyes [5]...Ruth Brown
- JB Bad, Bad Whiskey [2]...Amos Milburn

C&W
- BS I'm Moving On [19]...Hank Snow
- DJ I Love You A Thousand Ways [2]...Lefty Frizzell
- JB The Shot Gun Boogie [2]...Tennessee Ernie Ford

January 27, 1951

POP
- BS The Tennessee Waltz [5]...Patti Page
- DJ The Tennessee Waltz [4]...Patti Page
- JB The Tennessee Waltz [5]...Patti Page

R&B
- BS Teardrops From My Eyes [6]...Ruth Brown
- JB Teardrops From My Eyes [4]...Ruth Brown

C&W
- BS I'm Moving On [20]...Hank Snow
- DJ The Golden Rocket [1]...Hank Snow
- JB The Shot Gun Boogie [3]...Tennessee Ernie Ford

February 3, 1951

POP
- BS The Tennessee Waltz [6]...Patti Page
- DJ The Tennessee Waltz [5]...Patti Page
- JB The Tennessee Waltz [6]...Patti Page

R&B
- BS Teardrops From My Eyes [7]...Ruth Brown
- JB Teardrops From My Eyes [5]...Ruth Brown

C&W
- BS The Shot Gun Boogie [1]...Tennessee Ernie Ford
- DJ I Love You A Thousand Ways [3]...Lefty Frizzell
- JB The Shot Gun Boogie [4]...Tennessee Ernie Ford

February 10, 1951

POP
- BS The Tennessee Waltz [7]...Patti Page
- DJ The Tennessee Waltz [6]...Patti Page
- JB The Tennessee Waltz [7]...Patti Page

R&B
- BS Teardrops From My Eyes [8]...Ruth Brown
- JB Teardrops From My Eyes [6]...Ruth Brown

C&W
- BS I'm Moving On [21]...Hank Snow
- DJ *There's Been A Change In Me [1]...Eddy Arnold
- JB The Shot Gun Boogie [5]...Tennessee Ernie Ford

February 17, 1951

POP
- BS The Tennessee Waltz [8]...Patti Page
- DJ The Tennessee Waltz [7]...Patti Page
- JB The Tennessee Waltz [8]...Patti Page

R&B
- BS Teardrops From My Eyes [9]...Ruth Brown
- JB Teardrops From My Eyes [7]...Ruth Brown

C&W
- BS There's Been A Change In Me [1]...Eddy Arnold
- DJ There's Been A Change In Me [2]...Eddy Arnold
- JB The Shot Gun Boogie [6]...Tennessee Ernie Ford

February 24, 1951

POP
- BS The Tennessee Waltz [9]...Patti Page
- DJ The Tennessee Waltz [8]...Patti Page
- JB The Tennessee Waltz [9]...Patti Page

R&B
- BS Teardrops From My Eyes [10]...Ruth Brown
- JB Bad, Bad Whiskey [3]...Amos Milburn

C&W
- BS The Shot Gun Boogie [2]...Tennessee Ernie Ford
- DJ The Shot Gun Boogie [1]...Tennessee Ernie Ford
- JB The Shot Gun Boogie [7]...Tennessee Ernie Ford

March 3, 1951

POP
- BS *If [1]...Perry Como
- DJ *If [1]...Perry Como
- JB The Tennessee Waltz [10]...Patti Page

R&B
- BS Teardrops From My Eyes [11]...Ruth Brown
- JB *Black Night [1]...Charles Brown

C&W
- BS There's Been A Change In Me [2]...Eddy Arnold
- DJ There's Been A Change In Me [3]...Eddy Arnold
- JB The Shot Gun Boogie [8]...Tennessee Ernie Ford

March 10, 1951

POP
- BS Be My Love [1]...Mario Lanza
- DJ If [2]...Perry Como
- JB The Tennessee Waltz [11]...Patti Page

R&B
- BS Black Night [1]...Charles Brown
- JB Black Night [2]...Charles Brown

C&W
- BS There's Been A Change In Me [3]...Eddy Arnold
- DJ There's Been A Change In Me [4]...Eddy Arnold
- JB The Shot Gun Boogie [9]...Tennessee Ernie Ford

March 17, 1951

POP
- BS If [2]...Perry Como
- DJ If [3]...Perry Como
- JB The Tennessee Waltz [12]...Patti Page

R&B
- BS Black Night [2]...Charles Brown
- JB Black Night [3]...Charles Brown

C&W
- BS The Shot Gun Boogie [3]...Tennessee Ernie Ford
- DJ There's Been A Change In Me [5]...Eddy Arnold
- JB The Shot Gun Boogie [10]...Tennessee Ernie Ford

March 24, 1951

POP
- BS If [3]...Perry Como
- DJ If [4]...Perry Como
- JB The Tennessee Waltz [13]...Patti Page

R&B
- BS Black Night [3]...Charles Brown
- JB Black Night [4]...Charles Brown

C&W
- BS There's Been A Change In Me [4]...Eddy Arnold
- DJ There's Been A Change In Me [6]...Eddy Arnold
- JB The Shot Gun Boogie [11]...Tennessee Ernie Ford

March 31, 1951

POP
- BS If [4]...Perry Como
- DJ If [5]...Perry Como
- JB If [1]...Perry Como

R&B
- BS Black Night [4]...Charles Brown
- JB Black Night [5]...Charles Brown

C&W
- BS *Rhumba Boogie [1]...Hank Snow
- DJ There's Been A Change In Me [7]...Eddy Arnold
- JB The Shot Gun Boogie [12]...Tennessee Ernie Ford

April 7, 1951

POP
- BS If [5]...Perry Como
- DJ If [6]...Perry Como
- JB If [2]...Perry Como

R&B
- BS Black Night [5]...Charles Brown
- JB Black Night [6]...Charles Brown

C&W
- BS Rhumba Boogie [2]...Hank Snow
- DJ There's Been A Change In Me [8]...Eddy Arnold
- JB The Shot Gun Boogie [13]...Tennessee Ernie Ford

April 14, 1951

POP
- BS If [6]...Perry Como
- DJ If [7]...Perry Como
- JB If [3]...Perry Como

R&B
- BS Black Night [6]...Charles Brown
- JB Black Night [7]...Charles Brown

C&W
- BS Rhumba Boogie [3]...Hank Snow
- DJ There's Been A Change In Me [9]...Eddy Arnold
- JB The Shot Gun Boogie [14]...Tennessee Ernie Ford

April 21, 1951

POP
- BS *How High The Moon [1]...Les Paul and Mary Ford
- DJ If [8]...Perry Como
- JB If [4]...Perry Como

R&B
- BS Black Night [7]...Charles Brown
- JB Black Night [8]...Charles Brown

C&W
- BS Rhumba Boogie [4]...Hank Snow
- DJ There's Been A Change In Me [10]...Eddy Arnold
- JB Rhumba Boogie [1]...Hank Snow

April 28, 1951

POP
- BS How High The Moon [2]...Les Paul and Mary Ford
- DJ How High The Moon [1]...Les Paul and Mary Ford
- JB If [5]...Perry Como

R&B
- BS Black Night [8]...Charles Brown
- JB Black Night [9]...Charles Brown

C&W
- BS Rhumba Boogie [5]...Hank Snow
- DJ Rhumba Boogie [1]...Hank Snow
- JB Rhumba Boogie [2]...Hank Snow

May 5, 1951

POP
- BS How High The Moon [3]...Les Paul and Mary Ford
- DJ How High The Moon [2]...Les Paul and Mary Ford
- JB How High The Moon [1]...Les Paul and Mary Ford

R&B
- BS Black Night [9]...Charles Brown
- JB Black Night [10]...Charles Brown

C&W
- BS Rhumba Boogie [6]...Hank Snow
- DJ There's Been A Change In Me [11]...Eddy Arnold
- JB Rhumba Boogie [3]...Hank Snow

May 12, 1951

POP
- BS How High The Moon [4]...Les Paul and Mary Ford
- DJ How High The Moon [3]...Les Paul and Mary Ford
- JB How High The Moon [2]...Les Paul and Mary Ford

R&B
- BS Black Night [10]...Charles Brown
- JB Black Night [11]...Charles Brown

C&W
- BS Rhumba Boogie [7]...Hank Snow
- DJ Cold, Cold Heart [1]...Hank Williams
- JB Rhumba Boogie [4]...Hank Snow

May 19, 1951

POP
- BS How High The Moon [5]...Les Paul and Mary Ford
- DJ How High The Moon [4]...Les Paul and Mary Ford
- JB How High The Moon [3]...Les Paul and Mary Ford

R&B
- BS Black Night [11]...Charles Brown
- JB Black Night [12]...Charles Brown

C&W
- BS *Kentucky Waltz [1]...Eddy Arnold
- DJ Rhumba Boogie [2]...Hank Snow
- JB *Kentucky Waltz [1]...Eddy Arnold ⎫
- JB Rhumba Boogie [5]...Hank Snow ⎭ tie

May 26, 1951

POP
- BS How High The Moon [6]...Les Paul and Mary Ford
- DJ How High The Moon [5]...Les Paul and Mary Ford
- JB How High The Moon [4]...Les Paul and Mary Ford

R&B
- BS Black Night [12]...Charles Brown
- JB Black Night [13]...Charles Brown

C&W
- BS Rhumba Boogie [8]...Hank Snow
- DJ *I Want To Be With You Always [1]...Lefty Frizzell
- JB Kentucky Waltz [2]...Eddy Arnold

June 2, 1951

POP
- BS How High The Moon [7]...Les Paul and Mary Ford
- DJ How High The Moon [6]...Les Paul and Mary Ford
- JB How High The Moon [5]...Les Paul and Mary Ford

R&B
- BS Black Night [13]...Charles Brown
- JB Black Night [14]...Charles Brown

C&W
- BS Kentucky Waltz [2]...Eddy Arnold
- DJ I Want To Be With You Always [2]...Lefty Frizzell
- JB Kentucky Waltz [3]...Eddy Arnold

June 9, 1951

POP
- BS How High The Moon [8]...Les Paul and Mary Ford
- DJ How High The Moon [7]...Les Paul and Mary Ford
- JB How High The Moon [6]...Les Paul and Mary Ford

R&B
- BS *Rocket "88" [1]...Jackie Brenston
- JB Chica Boo [1]...Lloyd Glenn's Combo

C&W
- BS I Want To Be With You Always [1]...Lefty Frizzell
- DJ I Want To Be With You Always [3]...Lefty Frizzell
- JB I Want To Be With You Always [1]...Lefty Frizzell

June 16, 1951

POP
- BS How High The Moon [9]...Les Paul and Mary Ford
- DJ How High The Moon [8]...Les Paul and Mary Ford
- JB How High The Moon [7]...Les Paul and Mary Ford

R&B
- BS Rocket "88" [2]...Jackie Brenston
- JB Chica Boo [2]...Lloyd Glenn's Combo

C&W
- BS I Want To Be With You Always [2]...Lefty Frizzell
- DJ I Want To Be With You Always [4]...Lefty Frizzell
- JB I Want To Be With You Always [2]...Lefty Frizzell

June 23, 1951

POP
- BS *Too Young [1]...Nat "King" Cole
- DJ How High The Moon [9]...Les Paul and Mary Ford
- JB How High The Moon [8]...Les Paul and Mary Ford

R&B
- BS Rocket "88" [3]...Jackie Brenston
- JB Rocket "88" [1]...Jackie Brenston

C&W
- BS Kentucky Waltz [3]...Eddy Arnold
- DJ I Want To Be With You Always [5]...Lefty Frizzell
- JB I Want To Be With You Always [3]...Lefty Frizzell

June 30, 1951

POP
- BS Too Young [2]...Nat "King" Cole
- DJ Too Young [1]...Nat "King" Cole
- JB How High The Moon [9]...Les Paul and Mary Ford

R&B
- BS *Sixty Minute Man [1]...The Dominoes
- JB Rocket "88" [2]...Jackie Brenston

C&W
- BS I Want To Be With You Always [3]...Lefty Frizzell
- DJ I Want To Be With You Always [6]...Lefty Frizzell
- JB I Want To Be With You Always [4]...Lefty Frizzell

July 7, 1951

POP
- BS Too Young [3]...Nat "King" Cole
- DJ Too Young [2]...Nat "King" Cole
- JB Too Young [1]...Nat "King" Cole

R&B
- BS Sixty Minute Man [2]...The Dominoes
- JB Rocket "88" [3]...Jackie Brenston

C&W
- BS I Want To Be With You Always [4]...Lefty Frizzell
- DJ I Want To Be With You Always [7]...Lefty Frizzell
- JB I Want To Be With You Always [5]...Lefty Frizzell

July 14, 1951

POP
- BS Too Young [4]...Nat "King" Cole
- DJ Too Young [3]...Nat "King" Cole
- JB Too Young [2]...Nat "King" Cole

R&B
- BS Sixty Minute Man [3]...The Dominoes
- JB Rocket "88" [4]...Jackie Brenston

C&W
- BS I Want To Be With You Always [5]...Lefty Frizzell
- DJ I Want To Be With You Always [8]...Lefty Frizzell
- JB *I Wanna Play House With You [1]...Eddy Arnold

July 21, 1951

POP
- BS Too Young [5]...Nat "King" Cole
- DJ Too Young [4]...Nat "King" Cole
- JB Too Young [3]...Nat "King" Cole

R&B
- BS Sixty Minute Man [4]...The Dominoes
- JB Rocket "88" [5]...Jackie Brenston

C&W
- BS I Want To Be With You Always [6]...Lefty Frizzell
- DJ I Want To Be With You Always [9]...Lefty Frizzell
- JB I Wanna Play House With You [2]...Eddy Arnold

July 28, 1951

POP
- BS *Come On-a My House [1]...Rosemary Clooney
- DJ *Come On-a My House [1]...Rosemary Clooney
- JB Too Young [4]...Nat "King" Cole

R&B
- BS Sixty Minute Man [5]...The Dominoes
- JB Sixty Minute Man [1]...The Dominoes

C&W
- BS I Wanna Play House With You [1]...Eddy Arnold
- DJ I Want To Be With You Always [10]...Lefty Frizzell
- JB I Wanna Play House With You [3]...Eddy Arnold

August 4, 1951

POP
- BS Come On-a My House [2]...Rosemary Clooney
- DJ Come On-a My House [2]...Rosemary Clooney
- JB Come On-a My House [1]...Rosemary Clooney

R&B
- BS Sixty Minute Man [6]...The Dominoes
- JB Sixty Minute Man [2]...The Dominoes

C&W
- BS I Wanna Play House With You [2]...Eddy Arnold
- DJ I Want To Be With You Always [11]...Lefty Frizzell
- JB I Wanna Play House With You [4]...Eddy Arnold

August 11, 1951

POP
- BS Come On-a My House [3]...Rosemary Clooney
- DJ Come On-a My House [3]...Rosemary Clooney
- JB Come On-a My House [2]...Rosemary Clooney

R&B
- BS Sixty Minute Man [7]...The Dominoes
- JB Sixty Minute Man [3]...The Dominoes

C&W
- BS I Wanna Play House With You [3]...Eddy Arnold
- DJ Hey, Good Lookin' [1]...Hank Williams
- JB I Wanna Play House With You [5]...Eddy Arnold

August 18, 1951

POP
- *BS*   Come On-a My House [4]...Rosemary Clooney
- *DJ*   Come On-a My House [4]...Rosemary Clooney
- *JB*   Come On-a My House [3]...Rosemary Clooney

R&B
- *BS*   Sixty Minute Man [8]...The Dominoes
- *JB*   Sixty Minute Man [4]...The Dominoes

C&W
- *BS*   I Wanna Play House With You [4]...Eddy Arnold
- *DJ*   Hey, Good Lookin' [2]...Hank Williams
- *JB*   I Wanna Play House With You [6]...Eddy Arnold

August 25, 1951

POP
- *BS*   Come On-a My House [5]...Rosemary Clooney
- *DJ*   Come On-a My House [5]...Rosemary Clooney
- *JB*   Come On-a My House [4]...Rosemary Clooney

R&B
- *BS*   Sixty Minute Man [9]...The Dominoes
- *JB*   Sixty Minute Man [5]...The Dominoes

C&W
- *BS*   I Wanna Play House With You [5]...Eddy Arnold
- *DJ*   Hey, Good Lookin' [3]...Hank Williams
- *JB*   I Wanna Play House With You [7]...Eddy Arnold

September 1, 1951

POP
- *BS*   Come On-a My House [6]...Rosemary Clooney
- *DJ*   Come On-a My House [6]...Rosemary Clooney
- *JB*   Come On-a My House [5]...Rosemary Clooney

R&B
- *BS*   Don't You Know I Love You [1]...The Clovers
- *JB*   Sixty Minute Man [6]...The Dominoes

C&W
- *BS*   *Always Late (With Your Kisses) [1]...Lefty Frizzell
- *DJ*   Hey, Good Lookin' [4]...Hank Williams
- *JB*   I Wanna Play House With You [8]...Eddy Arnold

September 8, 1951

POP
- *BS*   *Because Of You [1]...Tony Bennett
- *DJ*   Come On-a My House [7]...Rosemary Clooney
- *JB*   Come On-a My House [6]...Rosemary Clooney

R&B
- *BS*   Don't You Know I Love You [2]...The Clovers
- *JB*   Sixty Minute Man [7]...The Dominoes

C&W
- *BS*   I Wanna Play House With You [6]...Eddy Arnold
- *DJ*   Hey, Good Lookin' [5]...Hank Williams
- *JB*   I Wanna Play House With You [9]...Eddy Arnold

September 15, 1951

POP
- *BS*   Because Of You [2]...Tony Bennett
- *DJ*   Come On-a My House [8]...Rosemary Clooney
- *JB*   Come On-a My House [7]...Rosemary Clooney

R&B
- *BS*   Sixty Minute Man [10]...The Dominoes
- *JB*   Sixty Minute Man [8]...The Dominoes

C&W
- *BS*   Always Late (With Your Kisses) [2]...Lefty Frizzell
- *DJ*   Always Late (With Your Kisses) [1]...Lefty Frizzell
- *JB*   I Wanna Play House With You [10]...Eddy Arnold

September 22, 1951

POP
- *BS*   Because Of You [3]...Tony Bennett
- *DJ*   Because Of You [1]...Tony Bennett
- *JB*   Come On-a My House [8]...Rosemary Clooney

R&B
- *BS*   Sixty Minute Man [11]...The Dominoes   ⎫
- *BS*   *The Glory Of Love [1]...The Five Keys   ⎬ tie
- *JB*   Sixty Minute Man [9]...The Dominoes

C&W
- *BS*   Always Late (With Your Kisses) [3]...Lefty Frizzell
- *DJ*   Always Late (With Your Kisses) [2]...Lefty Frizzell
- *JB*   I Wanna Play House With You [11]...Eddy Arnold

September 29, 1951

POP
- *BS*   Because Of You [4]...Tony Bennett
- *DJ*   Because Of You [2]...Tony Bennett
- *JB*   Because Of You [1]...Tony Bennett

R&B
- *BS*   Sixty Minute Man [12]...The Dominoes
- *JB*   Sixty Minute Man [10]...The Dominoes

C&W
- *BS*   Always Late (With Your Kisses) [4]...Lefty Frizzell
- *DJ*   Always Late (With Your Kisses) [3]...Lefty Frizzell
- *JB*   Always Late (With Your Kisses) [1]...Lefty Frizzell

October 6, 1951

POP
- *BS*   Because Of You [5]...Tony Bennett
- *DJ*   Because Of You [3]...Tony Bennett
- *JB*   Because Of You [2]...Tony Bennett

R&B
- *BS*   The Glory Of Love [2]...The Five Keys
- *JB*   Sixty Minute Man [11]...The Dominoes

C&W
- *BS*   Always Late (With Your Kisses) [5]...Lefty Frizzell
- *DJ*   Always Late (With Your Kisses) [4]...Lefty Frizzell
- *JB*   Always Late (With Your Kisses) [2]...Lefty Frizzell

October 13, 1951

POP
- BS Because Of You [6]...Tony Bennett
- DJ Because Of You [4]...Tony Bennett
- JB Because Of You [3]...Tony Bennett

R&B
- BS Sixty Minute Man [13]...The Dominoes
- JB Sixty Minute Man [12]...The Dominoes

C&W
- BS Always Late (With Your Kisses) [6]...Lefty Frizzell
- DJ Hey, Good Lookin' [6]...Hank Williams
- JB Always Late (With Your Kisses) [3]...Lefty Frizzell

October 20, 1951

POP
- BS Because Of You [7]...Tony Bennett
- DJ Because Of You [5]...Tony Bennett
- JB Because Of You [4]...Tony Bennett

R&B
- BS Sixty Minute Man [14]...The Dominoes
- JB The Glory Of Love [1]...The Five Keys

C&W
- BS Always Late (With Your Kisses) [7]...Lefty Frizzell
- DJ Always Late (With Your Kisses) [5]...Lefty Frizzell
- JB Always Late (With Your Kisses) [4]...Lefty Frizzell

October 27, 1951

POP
- BS Because Of You [8]...Tony Bennett
- DJ Because Of You [6]...Tony Bennett
- JB Because Of You [5]...Tony Bennett

R&B
- BS The Glory Of Love [3]...The Five Keys
- JB The Glory Of Love [2]...The Five Keys

C&W
- BS Always Late (With Your Kisses) [8]...Lefty Frizzell
- DJ Always Late (With Your Kisses) [6]...Lefty Frizzell
- JB Always Late (With Your Kisses) [5]...Lefty Frizzell

November 3, 1951

POP
- BS *Cold, Cold Heart [1]...Tony Bennett
- DJ Because Of You [7]...Tony Bennett
- JB Because Of You [6]...Tony Bennett

R&B
- BS The Glory Of Love [4]...The Five Keys
- JB "T" 99 Blues [1]...Jimmy Nelson

C&W
- BS Always Late (With Your Kisses) [9]...Lefty Frizzell
- DJ Hey, Good Lookin' [7]...Hank Williams
- JB Always Late (With Your Kisses) [6]...Lefty Frizzell } tie
- JB *Slow Poke [1]...Pee Wee King and his Golden West Cowboys

November 10, 1951

POP
- BS Cold, Cold Heart [2]...Tony Bennett
- DJ Because Of You [8]...Tony Bennett
- JB Because Of You [7]...Tony Bennett

R&B
- BS *Fool, Fool, Fool [1]...The Clovers
- JB *I Got Loaded [1]...Peppermint Harris

C&W
- BS Always Late (With Your Kisses) [10]...Lefty Frizzell
- DJ Slow Poke [1]...Pee Wee King and his Golden West Cowboys
- JB Slow Poke [2]...Pee Wee King and his Golden West Cowboys

November 17, 1951

POP
- BS Cold, Cold Heart [3]...Tony Bennett
- DJ *Sin [1]...Eddy Howard
- JB Because Of You [8]...Tony Bennett

R&B
- BS Fool, Fool, Fool [2]...The Clovers
- JB I'm In The Mood [1]...John Lee Hooker

C&W
- BS Always Late (With Your Kisses) [11]...Lefty Frizzell
- DJ Hey, Good Lookin' [8]...Hank Williams
- JB Slow Poke [3]...Pee Wee King and his Golden West Cowboys

November 24, 1951

POP
- BS Cold, Cold Heart [4]...Tony Bennett
- DJ Sin [2]...Eddy Howard
- JB Because Of You [9]...Tony Bennett

R&B
- BS Fool, Fool, Fool [3]...The Clovers
- JB I'm In The Mood [2]...John Lee Hooker

C&W
- BS Always Late (With Your Kisses) [12]...Lefty Frizzell
- DJ Slow Poke [2]...
  Pee Wee King and his Golden West Cowboys
- JB Slow Poke [4]...
  Pee Wee King and his Golden West Cowboys

December 1, 1951

POP
- BS Cold, Cold Heart [5]...Tony Bennett
- DJ Sin [3]...Eddy Howard
- JB Because Of You [10]...Tony Bennett

R&B
- BS Fool, Fool, Fool [4]...The Clovers
- JB I Got Loaded [2]...Peppermint Harris

C&W
- BS Slow Poke [1]...
  Pee Wee King and his Golden West Cowboys
- DJ Slow Poke [3]...
  Pee Wee King and his Golden West Cowboys
- JB Slow Poke [5]...
  Pee Wee King and his Golden West Cowboys

December 8, 1951

POP
- BS Cold, Cold Heart [6]...Tony Bennett
- DJ Sin [4]...Eddy Howard
- JB Cold, Cold Heart [1]...Tony Bennett

R&B
- BS Because Of You [1]...Tab Smith
- JB I'm In The Mood [3]...John Lee Hooker

C&W
- BS Slow Poke [2]...
  Pee Wee King and his Golden West Cowboys
- DJ Slow Poke [4]...
  Pee Wee King and his Golden West Cowboys
- JB Slow Poke [6]...
  Pee Wee King and his Golden West Cowboys

December 15, 1951

POP
- BS Sin [1]...Eddy Howard
- DJ Sin [5]...Eddy Howard
- JB Cold, Cold Heart [2]...Tony Bennett

R&B
- BS Because Of You [2]...Tab Smith
- JB I'm In The Mood [4]...John Lee Hooker

C&W
- BS Slow Poke [3]...
  Pee Wee King and his Golden West Cowboys
- DJ Slow Poke [5]...
  Pee Wee King and his Golden West Cowboys
- JB Slow Poke [7]...
  Pee Wee King and his Golden West Cowboys

December 22, 1951

POP
- BS Sin [2]...Eddy Howard
- DJ Sin [6]...Eddy Howard
- JB Cold, Cold Heart [3]...Tony Bennett

R&B
- BS Fool, Fool, Fool [5]...The Clovers ⎫ tie
- BS I Got Loaded [1]...Peppermint Harris ⎭
- JB Fool, Fool, Fool [1]...The Clovers

C&W
- BS Slow Poke [4]...
  Pee Wee King and his Golden West Cowboys
- DJ *Let Old Mother Nature Have Her Way [1]...Carl Smith
- JB Slow Poke [8]...
  Pee Wee King and his Golden West Cowboys

December 29, 1951

POP
- BS *Cry [1]...Johnnie Ray & The Four Lads
- DJ Sin [7]...Eddy Howard
- JB Sin [1]...Eddy Howard

R&B
- BS Flamingo [1]...Earl Bostic
- JB Fool, Fool, Fool [2]...The Clovers

C&W
- BS Slow Poke [5]...
  Pee Wee King and his Golden West Cowboys
- DJ Slow Poke [6]...
  Pee Wee King and his Golden West Cowboys
- JB Slow Poke [9]...
  Pee Wee King and his Golden West Cowboys

January 5, 1952

POP
- BS Cry [2]...Johnnie Ray & The Four Lads
- DJ Sin [8]...Eddy Howard
- DJ Cry [1]...Johnnie Ray & The Four Lads } tie
- JB Slow Poke [1]...
    Pee Wee King and his Golden West Cowboys

R&B
- BS Flamingo [2]...Earl Bostic
- JB Fool, Fool, Fool [3]...The Clovers

C&W
- BS Slow Poke [6]...
    Pee Wee King and his Golden West Cowboys
- DJ Let Old Mother Nature Have Her Way [2]...Carl Smith
- JB Slow Poke [10]...
    Pee Wee King and his Golden West Cowboys

January 12, 1952

POP
- BS Cry [3]...Johnnie Ray & The Four Lads
- DJ Cry [2]...Johnnie Ray & The Four Lads
- JB Slow Poke [2]...
    Pee Wee King and his Golden West Cowboys

R&B
- BS Cry [1]...Johnnie Ray & The Four Lads
- JB Weepin' And Cryin' [1]...Griffin Brothers

C&W
- BS Slow Poke [7]...
    Pee Wee King and his Golden West Cowboys
- DJ Let Old Mother Nature Have Her Way [3]...Carl Smith
- JB Slow Poke [11]...
    Pee Wee King and his Golden West Cowboys

January 19, 1952

POP
- BS Cry [4]...Johnnie Ray & The Four Lads
- DJ Cry [3]...Johnnie Ray & The Four Lads
- JB Slow Poke [3]...
    Pee Wee King and his Golden West Cowboys

R&B
- BS Fool, Fool, Fool [6]...The Clovers
- JB Weepin' And Cryin' [2]...Griffin Brothers

C&W
- BS Slow Poke [8]...
    Pee Wee King and his Golden West Cowboys
- DJ Slow Poke [7]...
    Pee Wee King and his Golden West Cowboys
- JB Slow Poke [12]...
    Pee Wee King and his Golden West Cowboys

January 26, 1952

POP
- BS Cry [5]...Johnnie Ray & The Four Lads
- DJ Cry [4]...Johnnie Ray & The Four Lads
- JB Cry [1]...Johnnie Ray & The Four Lads

R&B
- BS Flamingo [3]...Earl Bostic
- JB Weepin' And Cryin' [3]...Griffin Brothers

C&W
- BS Slow Poke [9]...
    Pee Wee King and his Golden West Cowboys
- DJ Slow Poke [8]...
    Pee Wee King and his Golden West Cowboys
- JB Slow Poke [13]...
    Pee Wee King and his Golden West Cowboys

February 2, 1952

POP
- BS Cry [6]...Johnnie Ray & The Four Lads
- DJ Cry [5]...Johnnie Ray & The Four Lads
- JB Cry [2]...Johnnie Ray & The Four Lads

R&B
- BS Flamingo [4]...Earl Bostic
- JB *Three O'Clock Blues [1]...B.B. King

C&W
- BS Slow Poke [10]...
    Pee Wee King and his Golden West Cowboys
- DJ *Give Me More, More, More (Of Your Kisses) [1]...
    Lefty Frizzell
- JB Slow Poke [14]...
    Pee Wee King and his Golden West Cowboys

February 9, 1952

POP
- BS Cry [7]...Johnnie Ray & The Four Lads
- DJ Cry [6]...Johnnie Ray & The Four Lads
- JB Cry [3]...Johnnie Ray & The Four Lads

R&B
- BS Three O'Clock Blues [1]...B.B. King
- JB Cry [1]...Johnnie Ray & The Four Lads

C&W
- BS Slow Poke [11]...
    Pee Wee King and his Golden West Cowboys
- DJ Slow Poke [9]...
    Pee Wee King and his Golden West Cowboys
- JB Give Me More, More, More (Of Your Kisses) [1]...
    Lefty Frizzell

February 16, 1952

POP
- BS   Cry [8]...Johnnie Ray & The Four Lads
- DJ   Cry [7]...Johnnie Ray & The Four Lads
- JB   Cry [4]...Johnnie Ray & The Four Lads

R&B
- BS   Three O'Clock Blues [2]...B.B. King
- JB   Three O'Clock Blues [2]...B.B. King

C&W
- BS   Slow Poke [12]...
        Pee Wee King and his Golden West Cowboys
- DJ   Give Me More, More, More (Of Your Kisses) [2]...
        Lefty Frizzell
- JB   Let Old Mother Nature Have Her Way [1]...Carl Smith

February 23, 1952

POP
- BS   Cry [9]...Johnnie Ray & The Four Lads
- DJ   Cry [8]...Johnnie Ray & The Four Lads
- JB   Cry [5]...Johnnie Ray & The Four Lads

R&B
- BS   Three O'Clock Blues [3]...B.B. King
- JB   Three O'Clock Blues [3]...B.B. King

C&W
- BS   Slow Poke [13]...
        Pee Wee King and his Golden West Cowboys
- DJ   Give Me More, More, More (Of Your Kisses) [3]...
        Lefty Frizzell
- JB   Slow Poke [15]...
        Pee Wee King and his Golden West Cowboys

March 1, 1952

POP
- BS   Cry [10]...Johnnie Ray & The Four Lads
- DJ   Cry [9]...Johnnie Ray & The Four Lads
- JB   Cry [6]...Johnnie Ray & The Four Lads

R&B
- BS   Three O'Clock Blues [4]...B.B. King
- JB   Three O'Clock Blues [4]...B.B. King

C&W
- BS   Slow Poke [14]...
        Pee Wee King and his Golden West Cowboys
- DJ   Wondering [1]...Webb Pierce
- JB   Let Old Mother Nature Have Her Way [2]...Carl Smith

March 8, 1952

POP
- BS   Cry [11]...Johnnie Ray & The Four Lads
- DJ   Cry [10]...Johnnie Ray & The Four Lads
- JB   Cry [7]...Johnnie Ray & The Four Lads

R&B
- BS   Three O'Clock Blues [5]...B.B. King
- JB   Three O'Clock Blues [5]...B.B. King

C&W
- BS   Let Old Mother Nature Have Her Way [1]...Carl Smith
- DJ   Wondering [2]...Webb Pierce
- JB   Let Old Mother Nature Have Her Way [3]...Carl Smith

March 15, 1952

POP
- BS   *Wheel Of Fortune [1]...Kay Starr
- DJ   *Wheel Of Fortune [1]...Kay Starr
- JB   Cry [8]...Johnnie Ray & The Four Lads

R&B
- BS   Booted [1]...Roscoe Gordon
- JB   *Night Train [1]...Jimmy Forrest

C&W
- BS   Let Old Mother Nature Have Her Way [2]...Carl Smith
- DJ   Wondering [3]...Webb Pierce
- JB   Give Me More, More, More (Of Your Kisses) [2]...
        Lefty Frizzell

March 22, 1952

POP
- BS   Wheel Of Fortune [2]...Kay Starr
- DJ   Wheel Of Fortune [2]...Kay Starr
- JB   Cry [9]...Johnnie Ray & The Four Lads

R&B
- BS   Night Train [1]...Jimmy Forrest
- JB   Night Train [2]...Jimmy Forrest

C&W
- BS   Let Old Mother Nature Have Her Way [3]...Carl Smith
- DJ   Wondering [4]...Webb Pierce
- JB   Give Me More, More, More (Of Your Kisses) [3]...
        Lefty Frizzell

March 29, 1952

POP
- BS Wheel Of Fortune [3]...Kay Starr
- DJ Wheel Of Fortune [3]...Kay Starr
- JB Wheel Of Fortune [1]...Kay Starr

R&B
- BS Night Train [2]...Jimmy Forrest
- JB Night Train [3]...Jimmy Forrest

C&W
- BS Let Old Mother Nature Have Her Way [4]...Carl Smith
- DJ *(When You Feel Like You're In Love) Don't Just Stand There [1]...Carl Smith
- JB Let Old Mother Nature Have Her Way [4]...Carl Smith

April 5, 1952

POP
- BS Wheel Of Fortune [4]...Kay Starr
- DJ Wheel Of Fortune [4]...Kay Starr
- JB Wheel Of Fortune [2]...Kay Starr

R&B
- BS Night Train [3]...Jimmy Forrest
- JB Night Train [4]...Jimmy Forrest

C&W
- BS Let Old Mother Nature Have Her Way [5]...Carl Smith
- DJ (When You Feel Like You're In Love) Don't Just Stand There [2]...Carl Smith
- JB Let Old Mother Nature Have Her Way [5]...Carl Smith

April 12, 1952

POP
- BS Wheel Of Fortune [5]...Kay Starr
- DJ Wheel Of Fortune [5]...Kay Starr
- JB Wheel Of Fortune [3]...Kay Starr

R&B
- BS Night Train [4]...Jimmy Forrest
- JB Night Train [5]...Jimmy Forrest

C&W
- BS (When You Feel Like You're In Love) Don't Just Stand There [1]...Carl Smith } tie
- BS Let Old Mother Nature Have Her Way [6]...Carl Smith
- DJ (When You Feel Like You're In Love) Don't Just Stand There [3]...Carl Smith
- JB (When You Feel Like You're In Love) Don't Just Stand There [1]...Carl Smith

April 19, 1952

POP
- BS Wheel Of Fortune [6]...Kay Starr
- DJ Wheel Of Fortune [6]...Kay Starr
- JB Wheel Of Fortune [4]...Kay Starr

R&B
- BS Night Train [5]...Jimmy Forrest
- JB Night Train [6]...Jimmy Forrest

C&W
- BS (When You Feel Like You're In Love) Don't Just Stand There [2]...Carl Smith
- DJ (When You Feel Like You're In Love) Don't Just Stand There [4]...Carl Smith
- JB Let Old Mother Nature Have Her Way [6]...Carl Smith

April 26, 1952

POP
- BS Wheel Of Fortune [7]...Kay Starr
- DJ Wheel Of Fortune [7]...Kay Starr
- JB Wheel Of Fortune [5]...Kay Starr

R&B
- BS Night Train [6]...Jimmy Forrest
- JB Night Train [7]...Jimmy Forrest

C&W
- BS (When You Feel Like You're In Love) Don't Just Stand There [3]...Carl Smith
- DJ (When You Feel Like You're In Love) Don't Just Stand There [5]...Carl Smith
- JB Let Old Mother Nature Have Her Way [7]...Carl Smith

May 3, 1952

POP
- BS Wheel Of Fortune [8]...Kay Starr
- DJ Wheel Of Fortune [8]...Kay Starr
- JB Wheel Of Fortune [6]...Kay Starr

R&B
- BS *5-10-15 Hours [1]...Ruth Brown
- JB *5-10-15 Hours [1]...Ruth Brown

C&W
- BS Easy On The Eyes [1]...Eddy Arnold
- DJ (When You Feel Like You're In Love) Don't Just Stand There [6]...Carl Smith
- JB Let Old Mother Nature Have Her Way [8]...Carl Smith

May 10, 1952

POP
- BS   Wheel Of Fortune [9]...Kay Starr
- DJ   Wheel Of Fortune [9]...Kay Starr
- JB   Wheel Of Fortune [7]...Kay Starr

R&B
- BS   5-10-15 Hours [2]...Ruth Brown
- JB   5-10-15 Hours [2]...Ruth Brown

C&W
- BS   (When You Feel Like You're In Love) Don't Just Stand There [4]...Carl Smith ⎫
- BS   *The Wild Side Of Life [1]...Hank Thompson ⎬ tie
- DJ   (When You Feel Like You're In Love) Don't Just Stand There [7]...Carl Smith
- JB   (When You Feel Like You're In Love) Don't Just Stand There [2]...Carl Smith

May 17, 1952

POP
- BS   Blue Tango [1]...Leroy Anderson
- DJ   *Kiss Of Fire [1]...Georgia Gibbs
- JB   Wheel Of Fortune [8]...Kay Starr

R&B
- BS   5-10-15 Hours [3]...Ruth Brown
- JB   5-10-15 Hours [3]...Ruth Brown

C&W
- BS   (When You Feel Like You're In Love) Don't Just Stand There [5]...Carl Smith ⎫
- BS   The Wild Side Of Life [2]...Hank Thompson ⎬ tie
- DJ   The Wild Side Of Life [1]...Hank Thompson
- JB   (When You Feel Like You're In Love) Don't Just Stand There [3]...Carl Smith

May 24, 1952

POP
- BS   Blue Tango [2]...Leroy Anderson
- DJ   Kiss Of Fire [2]...Georgia Gibbs
- JB   A Guy Is A Guy [1]...Doris Day

R&B
- BS   5-10-15 Hours [4]...Ruth Brown
- JB   5-10-15 Hours [4]...Ruth Brown

C&W
- BS   The Wild Side Of Life [3]...Hank Thompson
- DJ   (When You Feel Like You're In Love) Don't Just Stand There [8]...Carl Smith
- JB   The Wild Side Of Life [1]...Hank Thompson

May 31, 1952

POP
- BS   Blue Tango [3]...Leroy Anderson
- DJ   Kiss Of Fire [3]...Georgia Gibbs
- JB   Wheel Of Fortune [9]...Kay Starr

R&B
- BS   5-10-15 Hours [5]...Ruth Brown
- JB   5-10-15 Hours [5]...Ruth Brown

C&W
- BS   The Wild Side Of Life [4]...Hank Thompson
- DJ   The Wild Side Of Life [2]...Hank Thompson
- JB   The Wild Side Of Life [2]...Hank Thompson

June 7, 1952

POP
- BS   Blue Tango [4]...Leroy Anderson ⎫
- BS   *Here In My Heart [1]...Al Martino ⎬ tie
- DJ   Kiss Of Fire [4]...Georgia Gibbs
- JB   Wheel Of Fortune [10]...Kay Starr

R&B
- BS   5-10-15 Hours [6]...Ruth Brown
- JB   5-10-15 Hours [6]...Ruth Brown

C&W
- BS   The Wild Side Of Life [5]...Hank Thompson
- DJ   The Wild Side Of Life [3]...Hank Thompson
- JB   The Wild Side Of Life [3]...Hank Thompson

June 14, 1952

POP
- BS   Blue Tango [5]...Leroy Anderson
- DJ   Kiss Of Fire [5]...Georgia Gibbs
- JB   Kiss Of Fire [1]...Georgia Gibbs

R&B
- BS   5-10-15 Hours [7]...Ruth Brown
- JB   *Have Mercy Baby [1]...The Dominoes

C&W
- BS   The Wild Side Of Life [6]...Hank Thompson
- DJ   The Wild Side Of Life [4]...Hank Thompson
- JB   The Wild Side Of Life [4]...Hank Thompson

June 21, 1952

POP
- BS   Here In My Heart [2]...Al Martino
- DJ   Kiss Of Fire [6]...Georgia Gibbs
- JB   Kiss Of Fire [2]...Georgia Gibbs

R&B
- BS   Goin' Home [1]...Fats Domino
- JB   Have Mercy Baby [2]...The Dominoes

C&W
- BS   The Wild Side Of Life [7]...Hank Thompson
- DJ   The Wild Side Of Life [5]...Hank Thompson
- JB   The Wild Side Of Life [5]...Hank Thompson

June 28, 1952

POP
- BS Here In My Heart [3]...Al Martino
- DJ Here In My Heart [1]...Al Martino
- JB Kiss Of Fire [3]...Georgia Gibbs

R&B
- BS Have Mercy Baby [1]...The Dominoes
- JB Have Mercy Baby [3]...The Dominoes

C&W
- BS The Wild Side Of Life [8]...Hank Thompson
- DJ The Wild Side Of Life [6]...Hank Thompson
- JB The Wild Side Of Life [6]...Hank Thompson

July 5, 1952

POP
- BS Delicado [1]...Percy Faith & his Orch.
- DJ Kiss Of Fire [7]...Georgia Gibbs
- JB Kiss Of Fire [4]...Georgia Gibbs

R&B
- BS Have Mercy Baby [2]...The Dominoes
- JB Have Mercy Baby [4]...The Dominoes

C&W
- BS The Wild Side Of Life [9]...Hank Thompson
- DJ The Wild Side Of Life [7]...Hank Thompson
- JB The Wild Side Of Life [7]...Hank Thompson

July 12, 1952

POP
- BS *Auf Wiederseh'n Sweetheart [1]...Vera Lynn
- DJ Here In My Heart [2]...Al Martino
- JB Kiss Of Fire [5]...Georgia Gibbs

R&B
- BS Have Mercy Baby [3]...The Dominoes
- JB *Lawdy Miss Clawdy [1]...Lloyd Price

C&W
- BS The Wild Side Of Life [10]...Hank Thompson
- DJ That Heart Belongs To Me [1]...Webb Pierce
- JB The Wild Side Of Life [8]...Hank Thompson

July 19, 1952

POP
- BS Auf Wiederseh'n Sweetheart [2]...Vera Lynn
- DJ Here In My Heart [3]...Al Martino
- JB Kiss Of Fire [6]...Georgia Gibbs

R&B
- BS Have Mercy Baby [4]...The Dominoes
- JB Have Mercy Baby [5]...The Dominoes

C&W
- BS The Wild Side Of Life [11]...Hank Thompson
- DJ Are You Teasing Me [1]...Carl Smith
- JB The Wild Side Of Life [9]...Hank Thompson

July 26, 1952

POP
- BS Auf Wiederseh'n Sweetheart [3]...Vera Lynn
- DJ Auf Wiederseh'n Sweetheart [1]...Vera Lynn
- JB Half As Much [1]...Rosemary Clooney

R&B
- BS Have Mercy Baby [5]...The Dominoes
- JB Have Mercy Baby [6]...The Dominoes

C&W
- BS The Wild Side Of Life [12]...Hank Thompson
- DJ That Heart Belongs To Me [2]...Webb Pierce
- JB The Wild Side Of Life [10]...Hank Thompson

August 2, 1952

POP
- BS Auf Wiederseh'n Sweetheart [4]...Vera Lynn
- DJ Auf Wiederseh'n Sweetheart [2]...Vera Lynn
- JB Half As Much [2]...Rosemary Clooney

R&B
- BS Have Mercy Baby [6]...The Dominoes } tie
- BS Lawdy Miss Clawdy [1]...Lloyd Price } tie
- JB Have Mercy Baby [7]...The Dominoes

C&W
- BS The Wild Side Of Life [13]...Hank Thompson
- DJ The Wild Side Of Life [8]...Hank Thompson
- JB The Wild Side Of Life [11]...Hank Thompson

August 9, 1952

POP
- BS Auf Wiederseh'n Sweetheart [5]...Vera Lynn
- DJ Auf Wiederseh'n Sweetheart [3]...Vera Lynn
- JB Auf Wiederseh'n Sweetheart [1]...Vera Lynn

R&B
- BS Lawdy Miss Clawdy [2]...Lloyd Price
- JB Have Mercy Baby [8]...The Dominoes

C&W
- BS The Wild Side Of Life [14]...Hank Thompson
- DJ That Heart Belongs To Me [3]...Webb Pierce
- JB The Wild Side Of Life [12]...Hank Thompson

August 16, 1952

POP
- BS Auf Wiederseh'n Sweetheart [6]...Vera Lynn
- DJ Auf Wiederseh'n Sweetheart [4]...Vera Lynn
- JB Auf Wiederseh'n Sweetheart [2]...Vera Lynn

R&B
- BS Lawdy Miss Clawdy [3]...Lloyd Price
- JB Have Mercy Baby [9]...The Dominoes

C&W
- BS The Wild Side Of Life [15]...Hank Thompson
- DJ A Full Time Job [1]...Eddy Arnold
- JB The Wild Side Of Life [13]...Hank Thompson

August 23, 1952

POP
- BS Auf Wiederseh'n Sweetheart [7]...Vera Lynn
- DJ Auf Wiederseh'n Sweetheart [5]...Vera Lynn
- JB Auf Wiederseh'n Sweetheart [3]...Vera Lynn

R&B
- BS Lawdy Miss Clawdy [4]...Lloyd Price
- JB Mary Jo [1]...Four Blazes

C&W
- BS *It Wasn't God Who Made Honky Tonk Angels [1]...Kitty Wells
- DJ A Full Time Job [2]...Eddy Arnold
- JB The Wild Side Of Life [14]...Hank Thompson

August 30, 1952

POP
- BS Auf Wiederseh'n Sweetheart [8]...Vera Lynn
- DJ Auf Wiederseh'n Sweetheart [6]...Vera Lynn
- JB Auf Wiederseh'n Sweetheart [4]...Vera Lynn

R&B
- BS Lawdy Miss Clawdy [5]...Lloyd Price
- JB Mary Jo [2]...Four Blazes

C&W
- BS It Wasn't God Who Made Honky Tonk Angels [2]...Kitty Wells
- DJ A Full Time Job [3]...Eddy Arnold
- JB The Wild Side Of Life [15]...Hank Thompson

September 6, 1952

POP
- BS Auf Wiederseh'n Sweetheart [9]...Vera Lynn
- DJ Wish You Were Here [1]...Eddie Fisher
- JB Half As Much [3]...Rosemary Clooney

R&B
- BS *Ting-A-Ling [1]...The Clovers } tie
- BS Have Mercy Baby [7]...The Dominoes } tie
- JB Have Mercy Baby [10]...The Dominoes

C&W
- BS It Wasn't God Who Made Honky Tonk Angels [3]...Kitty Wells
- DJ *Jambalaya (On The Bayou) [1]...Hank Williams
- JB It Wasn't God Who Made Honky Tonk Angels [1]...Kitty Wells

September 13, 1952

POP
- BS *You Belong To Me [1]...Jo Stafford
- DJ *You Belong To Me [1]...Jo Stafford
- JB *You Belong To Me [1]...Jo Stafford

R&B
- BS Lawdy Miss Clawdy [6]...Lloyd Price
- JB Mary Jo [3]...Four Blazes

C&W
- BS It Wasn't God Who Made Honky Tonk Angels [4]...Kitty Wells
- DJ Jambalaya (On The Bayou) [2]...Hank Williams
- JB It Wasn't God Who Made Honky Tonk Angels [2]...Kitty Wells

September 20, 1952

POP
- BS You Belong To Me [2]...Jo Stafford
- DJ You Belong To Me [2]...Jo Stafford
- JB You Belong To Me [2]...Jo Stafford

R&B
- BS Lawdy Miss Clawdy [7]...Lloyd Price
- JB Ting-A-Ling [1]...The Clovers

C&W
- BS It Wasn't God Who Made Honky Tonk Angels [5]...Kitty Wells
- DJ A Full Time Job [4]...Eddy Arnold
- JB It Wasn't God Who Made Honky Tonk Angels [3]...Kitty Wells

September 27, 1952

POP
- BS You Belong To Me [3]...Jo Stafford
- DJ You Belong To Me [3]...Jo Stafford
- JB *I Went To Your Wedding [1]...Patti Page

R&B
- BS My Song [1]...Johnny Ace with The Beale Streeters
- JB *Juke [1]...Little Walter

C&W
- BS It Wasn't God Who Made Honky Tonk Angels [6]...Kitty Wells
- DJ Jambalaya (On The Bayou) [3]...Hank Williams
- JB It Wasn't God Who Made Honky Tonk Angels [4]...Kitty Wells

October 4, 1952

POP
- BS You Belong To Me [4]...Jo Stafford
- DJ You Belong To Me [4]...Jo Stafford
- JB I Went To Your Wedding [2]...Patti Page

R&B
- BS My Song [2]...Johnny Ace with The Beale Streeters
- JB Juke [2]...Little Walter

C&W
- BS Jambalaya (On The Bayou) [1]...Hank Williams
- DJ Jambalaya (On The Bayou) [4]...Hank Williams
- JB It Wasn't God Who Made Honky Tonk Angels [5]...Kitty Wells

October 11, 1952

POP
- BS You Belong To Me [5]...Jo Stafford
- DJ You Belong To Me [5]...Jo Stafford
- JB I Went To Your Wedding [3]...Patti Page

R&B
- BS My Song [3]...Johnny Ace with The Beale Streeters
- JB Juke [3]...Little Walter

C&W
- BS Jambalaya (On The Bayou) [2]...Hank Williams
- DJ Jambalaya (On The Bayou) [5]...Hank Williams
- JB Jambalaya (On The Bayou) [1]...Hank Williams

October 18, 1952

POP
- BS I Went To Your Wedding [1]...Patti Page
- DJ You Belong To Me [6]...Jo Stafford
- JB I Went To Your Wedding [4]...Patti Page

R&B
- BS My Song [4]...Johnny Ace with The Beale Streeters
- JB Juke [4]...Little Walter

C&W
- BS Jambalaya (On The Bayou) [3]...Hank Williams
- DJ Jambalaya (On The Bayou) [6]...Hank Williams
- JB Jambalaya (On The Bayou) [2]...Hank Williams

October 25, 1952

POP
- BS I Went To Your Wedding [2]...Patti Page
- DJ You Belong To Me [7]...Jo Stafford
- JB I Went To Your Wedding [5]...Patti Page

R&B
- BS My Song [5]...Johnny Ace with The Beale Streeters
- JB Juke [5]...Little Walter

C&W
- BS Jambalaya (On The Bayou) [4]...Hank Williams
- DJ Jambalaya (On The Bayou) [7]...Hank Williams
- JB Jambalaya (On The Bayou) [3]...Hank Williams

November 1, 1952

POP
- BS I Went To Your Wedding [3]...Patti Page
- DJ You Belong To Me [8]...Jo Stafford
- JB I Went To Your Wedding [6]...Patti Page

R&B
- BS My Song [6]...Johnny Ace with The Beale Streeters
- JB Juke [6]...Little Walter

C&W
- BS Jambalaya (On The Bayou) [5]...Hank Williams
- DJ Jambalaya (On The Bayou) [8]...Hank Williams
- JB Jambalaya (On The Bayou) [4]...Hank Williams

November 8, 1952

POP
- BS I Went To Your Wedding [4]...Patti Page
- DJ You Belong To Me [9]...Jo Stafford
- JB I Went To Your Wedding [7]...Patti Page

R&B
- BS My Song [7]...Johnny Ace with The Beale Streeters } tie
- BS You Know I Love You [1]...B.B. King
- JB *Five Long Years [1]...Eddie Boyd

C&W
- BS Jambalaya (On The Bayou) [6]...Hank Williams
- DJ Jambalaya (On The Bayou) [9]...Hank Williams
- JB Jambalaya (On The Bayou) [5]...Hank Williams

November 15, 1952

POP
- BS I Went To Your Wedding [5]...Patti Page
- DJ I Went To Your Wedding [1]...Patti Page
- JB I Went To Your Wedding [8]...Patti Page

R&B
- BS My Song [8]...Johnny Ace with The Beale Streeters
- JB Five Long Years [2]...Eddie Boyd

C&W
- BS Jambalaya (On The Bayou) [7]...Hank Williams
- DJ Jambalaya (On The Bayou) [10]...Hank Williams
- JB Jambalaya (On The Bayou) [6]...Hank Williams

November 22, 1952

POP
- BS It's In The Book [1]...Johnny Standley
- DJ You Belong To Me [10]...Jo Stafford
- JB I Went To Your Wedding [9]...Patti Page

R&B
- BS My Song [9]...Johnny Ace with The Beale Streeters
- JB Five Long Years [3]...Eddie Boyd

C&W
- BS Jambalaya (On The Bayou) [8]...Hank Williams
- DJ Jambalaya (On The Bayou) [11]...Hank Williams
- JB Jambalaya (On The Bayou) [7]...Hank Williams

November 29, 1952

POP
- BS *Why Don't You Believe Me [1]...Joni James } tie
- BS It's In The Book [2]...Johnny Standley
- DJ You Belong To Me [11]...Jo Stafford
- JB I Went To Your Wedding [10]...Patti Page

R&B
- BS You Know I Love You [2]...B.B. King
- JB Five Long Years [4]...Eddie Boyd

C&W
- BS Jambalaya (On The Bayou) [9]...Hank Williams
- DJ Jambalaya (On The Bayou) [12]...Hank Williams
- JB Jambalaya (On The Bayou) [8]...Hank Williams

December 6, 1952

POP
- BS Why Don't You Believe Me [2]...Joni James
- DJ You Belong To Me [12]...Jo Stafford
- JB The Glow-Worm [1]...Mills Brothers

R&B
- BS Juke [1]...Little Walter
- JB Five Long Years [5]...Eddie Boyd

C&W
- BS *Back Street Affair [1]...Webb Pierce
- DJ Don't Let The Stars Get In Your Eyes [1]...Slim Willet
- JB Jambalaya (On The Bayou) [9]...Hank Williams

December 13, 1952

POP
- BS Why Don't You Believe Me [3]...Joni James
- DJ Why Don't You Believe Me [1]...Joni James
- JB The Glow-Worm [2]...Mills Brothers

R&B
- BS Five Long Years [1]...Eddie Boyd
- JB Juke [7]...Little Walter

C&W
- BS Jambalaya (On The Bayou) [10]...Hank Williams
- DJ Back Street Affair [1]...Webb Pierce
- JB Jambalaya (On The Bayou) [10]...Hank Williams

December 20, 1952

POP
- BS Why Don't You Believe Me [4]...Joni James
- DJ Why Don't You Believe Me [2]...Joni James
- JB The Glow-Worm [3]...Mills Brothers

R&B
- BS Five Long Years [2]...Eddie Boyd
- JB Juke [8]...Little Walter

C&W
- BS Back Street Affair [2]...Webb Pierce } tie
- BS Jambalaya (On The Bayou) [11]...Hank Williams
- DJ Back Street Affair [2]...Webb Pierce
- JB Jambalaya (On The Bayou) [11]...Hank Williams

December 27, 1952

POP
- BS I Saw Mommy Kissing Santa Claus [1]...Jimmy Boyd
- DJ Why Don't You Believe Me [3]...Joni James
- JB Why Don't You Believe Me [1]...Joni James

R&B
- BS *I Don't Know [1]...Willie Mabon
- JB Five Long Years [6]...Eddie Boyd

C&W
- BS Jambalaya (On The Bayou) [12]...Hank Williams
- DJ Jambalaya (On The Bayou) [13]...Hank Williams
- JB Don't Let The Stars Get In Your Eyes [1]...
      Skeets McDonald

January 3, 1953

POP
- BS I Saw Mommy Kissing Santa Claus [2]...Jimmy Boyd
- DJ Why Don't You Believe Me [4]...Joni James
- JB Why Don't You Believe Me [2]...Joni James

R&B
- BS I Don't Know [2]...Willie Mabon
- JB Five Long Years [7]...Eddie Boyd

C&W
- BS Jambalaya (On The Bayou) [13]...Hank Williams
- DJ Jambalaya (On The Bayou) [14]...Hank Williams
- JB Don't Let The Stars Get In Your Eyes [2]... } tie
      Skeets McDonald
- JB Jambalaya (On The Bayou) [12]...Hank Williams

January 10, 1953

POP
- BS *Don't Let The Stars Get In Your Eyes [1]...
       Perry Como with The Ramblers
- DJ Why Don't You Believe Me [5]...Joni James
- JB Why Don't You Believe Me [3]...Joni James

R&B
- BS I Don't Know [3]...Willie Mabon
- JB I Don't Know [1]...Willie Mabon

C&W
- BS Midnight [1]...Red Foley
- DJ Back Street Affair [3]...Webb Pierce
- JB Don't Let The Stars Get In Your Eyes [3]...
       Skeets McDonald

January 17, 1953

POP
- BS Don't Let The Stars Get In Your Eyes [2]...
       Perry Como with The Ramblers
- DJ Why Don't You Believe Me [6]...Joni James
- JB Don't Let The Stars Get In Your Eyes [1]...
       Perry Como with The Ramblers

R&B
- BS I Don't Know [4]...Willie Mabon
- JB I Don't Know [2]...Willie Mabon

C&W
- BS Jambalaya (On The Bayou) [14]...Hank Williams
- DJ Back Street Affair [4]...Webb Pierce
- JB Back Street Affair [1]...Webb Pierce

January 24, 1953

POP
- BS Don't Let The Stars Get In Your Eyes [3]...
       Perry Como with The Ramblers
- DJ Don't Let The Stars Get In Your Eyes [1]...
       Perry Como with The Ramblers
- JB Don't Let The Stars Get In Your Eyes [2]...
       Perry Como with The Ramblers

R&B
- BS I Don't Know [5]...Willie Mabon
- JB I Don't Know [3]...Willie Mabon

C&W
- BS I'll Never Get Out Of This World Alive [1]...
       Hank Williams
- DJ I'll Go On Alone [1]...Marty Robbins
- JB Back Street Affair [2]...Webb Pierce

January 31, 1953

POP
- BS Don't Let The Stars Get In Your Eyes [4]...
       Perry Como with The Ramblers
- DJ Don't Let The Stars Get In Your Eyes [2]...
       Perry Como with The Ramblers
- JB Don't Let The Stars Get In Your Eyes [3]...
       Perry Como with The Ramblers

R&B
- BS I Don't Know [6]...Willie Mabon
- JB I Don't Know [4]...Willie Mabon

C&W
- BS Eddy's Song [1]...Eddy Arnold
- DJ *No Help Wanted [1]...The Carlisles
- JB Back Street Affair [3]...Webb Pierce

February 7, 1953

POP
- BS Don't Let The Stars Get In Your Eyes [5]...
       Perry Como with The Ramblers
- DJ Don't Let The Stars Get In Your Eyes [3]...
       Perry Como with The Ramblers
- JB Don't Let The Stars Get In Your Eyes [4]...
       Perry Como with The Ramblers

R&B
- BS I Don't Know [7]...Willie Mabon
- JB I Don't Know [5]...Willie Mabon

C&W
- BS Eddy's Song [2]...Eddy Arnold
- DJ I'll Go On Alone [2]...Marty Robbins
- JB I Let The Stars Get In My Eyes [1]...Goldie Hill

February 14, 1953

POP
- BS *Till I Waltz Again With You [1]...Teresa Brewer
- DJ *Till I Waltz Again With You [1]...Teresa Brewer
- JB *Till I Waltz Again With You [1]...Teresa Brewer

R&B
- BS I Don't Know [8]...Willie Mabon
- JB I Don't Know [6]...Willie Mabon

C&W
- BS Eddy's Song [3]...Eddy Arnold
- DJ No Help Wanted [2]...The Carlisles
- JB I Let The Stars Get In My Eyes [2]...Goldie Hill

February 21, 1953

POP
- BS Till I Waltz Again With You [2]...Teresa Brewer
- DJ Till I Waltz Again With You [2]...Teresa Brewer
- JB Till I Waltz Again With You [2]...Teresa Brewer

R&B
- BS *Baby, Don't Do It [1]...The "5" Royales
- JB I Don't Know [7]...Willie Mabon

C&W
- BS *Kaw-Liga [1]...Hank Williams
- DJ No Help Wanted [3]...The Carlisles
- JB I Let The Stars Get In My Eyes [3]...Goldie Hill

February 28, 1953

POP
- BS Till I Waltz Again With You [3]...Teresa Brewer
- DJ Till I Waltz Again With You [3]...Teresa Brewer
- JB Till I Waltz Again With You [3]...Teresa Brewer

R&B
- BS Baby, Don't Do It [2]...The "5" Royales
- JB Baby, Don't Do It [1]...The "5" Royales

C&W
- BS Kaw-Liga [2]...Hank Williams
- DJ No Help Wanted [4]...The Carlisles
- JB Kaw-Liga [1]...Hank Williams

March 7, 1953

POP
- BS Till I Waltz Again With You [4]...Teresa Brewer
- DJ Till I Waltz Again With You [4]...Teresa Brewer
- JB Till I Waltz Again With You [4]...Teresa Brewer

R&B
- BS *(Mama) He Treats Your Daughter Mean [1]...Ruth Brown
- JB Baby, Don't Do It [2]...The "5" Royales

C&W
- BS Kaw-Liga [3]...Hank Williams
- DJ Kaw-Liga [1]...Hank Williams
- JB Kaw-Liga [2]...Hank Williams

March 14, 1953

POP
- BS Till I Waltz Again With You [5]...Teresa Brewer
- DJ Till I Waltz Again With You [5]...Teresa Brewer
- JB Till I Waltz Again With You [5]...Teresa Brewer

R&B
- BS Baby, Don't Do It [3]...The "5" Royales
- JB Baby, Don't Do It [3]...The "5" Royales

C&W
- BS Kaw-Liga [4]...Hank Williams
- DJ Kaw-Liga [2]...Hank Williams
- JB Kaw-Liga [3]...Hank Williams

March 21, 1953

POP
- BS *The Doggie In The Window [1]...Patti Page
- DJ Till I Waltz Again With You [6]...Teresa Brewer
- JB Till I Waltz Again With You [6]...Teresa Brewer

R&B
- BS (Mama) He Treats Your Daughter Mean [2]...Ruth Brown
- JB (Mama) He Treats Your Daughter Mean [1]...Ruth Brown

C&W
- BS Kaw-Liga [5]...Hank Williams
- DJ Kaw-Liga [3]...Hank Williams
- JB Kaw-Liga [4]...Hank Williams

March 28, 1953

POP
- BS The Doggie In The Window [2]...Patti Page
- DJ The Doggie In The Window [1]...Patti Page
- JB The Doggie In The Window [1]...Patti Page

R&B
- BS (Mama) He Treats Your Daughter Mean [3]...Ruth Brown
- JB (Mama) He Treats Your Daughter Mean [2]...Ruth Brown

C&W
- BS Kaw-Liga [6]...Hank Williams
- DJ Kaw-Liga [4]...Hank Williams
- JB Kaw-Liga [5]...Hank Williams

April 4, 1953

POP
- BS The Doggie In The Window [3]...Patti Page
- DJ The Doggie In The Window [2]...Patti Page
- JB Till I Waltz Again With You [7]...Teresa Brewer

R&B
- BS (Mama) He Treats Your Daughter Mean [4]...Ruth Brown
- JB (Mama) He Treats Your Daughter Mean [3]...Ruth Brown

C&W
- BS Kaw-Liga [7]...Hank Williams
- DJ Kaw-Liga [5]...Hank Williams
- JB Kaw-Liga [6]...Hank Williams

April 11, 1953

POP
- BS   The Doggie In The Window [4]...Patti Page
- DJ   The Doggie In The Window [3]...Patti Page
- JB   The Doggie In The Window [2]...Patti Page

R&B
- BS   (Mama) He Treats Your Daughter Mean [5]...
       Ruth Brown
- JB   (Mama) He Treats Your Daughter Mean [4]...
       Ruth Brown

C&W
- BS   Kaw-Liga [8]...Hank Williams
- DJ   Kaw-Liga [6]...Hank Williams
- JB   *Your Cheatin' Heart [1]...Hank Williams

April 18, 1953

POP
- BS   The Doggie In The Window [5]...Patti Page
- DJ   The Doggie In The Window [4]...Patti Page
- JB   The Doggie In The Window [3]...Patti Page

R&B
- BS   *Hound Dog [1]...Willie Mae "Big Mama" Thornton
- JB   (Mama) He Treats Your Daughter Mean [5]...
       Ruth Brown

C&W
- BS   Kaw-Liga [9]...Hank Williams
- DJ   Kaw-Liga [7]...Hank Williams
- JB   Kaw-Liga [7]...Hank Williams

April 25, 1953

POP
- BS   The Doggie In The Window [6]...Patti Page
- DJ   The Doggie In The Window [5]...Patti Page
- JB   The Doggie In The Window [4]...Patti Page

R&B
- BS   Hound Dog [2]...Willie Mae "Big Mama" Thornton
- JB   Hound Dog [1]...Willie Mae "Big Mama" Thornton

C&W
- BS   Kaw-Liga [10]...Hank Williams
- DJ   Kaw-Liga [8]...Hank Williams
- JB   Kaw-Liga [8]...Hank Williams

May 2, 1953

POP
- BS   The Doggie In The Window [7]...Patti Page
- DJ   The Doggie In The Window [6]...Patti Page
- JB   The Doggie In The Window [5]...Patti Page

R&B
- BS   Hound Dog [3]...Willie Mae "Big Mama" Thornton
- JB   Hound Dog [2]...Willie Mae "Big Mama" Thornton

C&W
- BS   Kaw-Liga [11]...Hank Williams
- DJ   Your Cheatin' Heart [1]...Hank Williams
- JB   Your Cheatin' Heart [2]...Hank Williams

May 9, 1953

POP
- BS   The Doggie In The Window [8]...Patti Page
- DJ   The Doggie In The Window [7]...Patti Page
- JB   The Doggie In The Window [6]...Patti Page

R&B
- BS   Hound Dog [4]...Willie Mae "Big Mama" Thornton
- JB   Hound Dog [3]...Willie Mae "Big Mama" Thornton

C&W
- BS   *Mexican Joe [1]...Jim Reeves   } tie
- BS   Kaw-Liga [12]...Hank Williams
- DJ   Your Cheatin' Heart [2]...Hank Williams
- JB   No Help Wanted [1]...The Carlisles

May 16, 1953

POP
- BS   *The Song From Moulin Rouge (Where Is Your Heart) [1]...Percy Faith/Felicia Sanders
- DJ   *The Song From Moulin Rouge (Where Is Your Heart) [1]...Percy Faith/Felicia Sanders
- JB   The Doggie In The Window [7]...Patti Page

R&B
- BS   Hound Dog [5]...Willie Mae "Big Mama" Thornton
- JB   Hound Dog [4]...Willie Mae "Big Mama" Thornton

C&W
- BS   Kaw-Liga [13]...Hank Williams
- DJ   Your Cheatin' Heart [3]...Hank Williams
- JB   No Help Wanted [2]...The Carlisles

May 23, 1953

POP
- BS The Song From Moulin Rouge (Where Is Your Heart) [2]...Percy Faith/Felicia Sanders
- DJ The Song From Moulin Rouge (Where Is Your Heart) [2]...Percy Faith/Felicia Sanders
- JB The Song From Moulin Rouge (Where Is Your Heart) [1]...Percy Faith/Felicia Sanders

R&B
- BS Hound Dog [6]...Willie Mae "Big Mama" Thornton
- JB Hound Dog [5]...Willie Mae "Big Mama" Thornton

C&W
- BS Mexican Joe [2]...Jim Reeves
- DJ Your Cheatin' Heart [4]...Hank Williams
- JB No Help Wanted [3]...The Carlisles

May 30, 1953

POP
- BS The Song From Moulin Rouge (Where Is Your Heart) [3]...Percy Faith/Felicia Sanders
- DJ The Song From Moulin Rouge (Where Is Your Heart) [3]...Percy Faith/Felicia Sanders
- JB The Song From Moulin Rouge (Where Is Your Heart) [2]...Percy Faith/Felicia Sanders

R&B
- BS I'm Mad [1]...Willie Mabon & his Combo
- JB Hound Dog [6]...Willie Mae "Big Mama" Thornton

C&W
- BS Mexican Joe [3]...Jim Reeves
- DJ Your Cheatin' Heart [5]...Hank Williams
- JB No Help Wanted [4]...The Carlisles

June 6, 1953

POP
- BS The Song From Moulin Rouge (Where Is Your Heart) [4]...Percy Faith/Felicia Sanders
- DJ The Song From Moulin Rouge (Where Is Your Heart) [4]...Percy Faith/Felicia Sanders
- JB The Song From Moulin Rouge (Where Is Your Heart) [3]...Percy Faith/Felicia Sanders

R&B
- BS I'm Mad [2]...Willie Mabon & his Combo
- JB Hound Dog [7]...Willie Mae "Big Mama" Thornton

C&W
- BS Mexican Joe [4]...Jim Reeves ⎫
- BS Take These Chains From My Heart [1]...Hank Williams ⎬ tie
- DJ Mexican Joe [1]...Jim Reeves
- JB Mexican Joe [1]...Jim Reeves

June 13, 1953

POP
- BS The Song From Moulin Rouge (Where Is Your Heart) [5]...Percy Faith/Felicia Sanders
- DJ The Song From Moulin Rouge (Where Is Your Heart) [5]...Percy Faith/Felicia Sanders
- JB The Song From Moulin Rouge (Where Is Your Heart) [4]...Percy Faith/Felicia Sanders

R&B
- BS *Help Me Somebody [1]...The "5" Royales
- JB *Help Me Somebody [1]...The "5" Royales

C&W
- BS Mexican Joe [5]...Jim Reeves
- DJ Mexican Joe [2]...Jim Reeves
- JB Mexican Joe [2]...Jim Reeves

June 20, 1953

POP
- BS The Song From Moulin Rouge (Where Is Your Heart) [6]...Percy Faith/Felicia Sanders
- DJ The Song From Moulin Rouge (Where Is Your Heart) [6]...Percy Faith/Felicia Sanders
- JB The Song From Moulin Rouge (Where Is Your Heart) [5]...Percy Faith/Felicia Sanders

R&B
- BS Help Me Somebody [2]...The "5" Royales
- JB Help Me Somebody [2]...The "5" Royales

C&W
- BS Mexican Joe [6]...Jim Reeves
- DJ Mexican Joe [3]...Jim Reeves
- JB Mexican Joe [3]...Jim Reeves

June 27, 1953

POP
- BS The Song From Moulin Rouge (Where Is Your Heart) [7]...Percy Faith/Felicia Sanders
- DJ The Song From Moulin Rouge (Where Is Your Heart) [7]...Percy Faith/Felicia Sanders
- JB The Song From Moulin Rouge (Where Is Your Heart) [6]...Percy Faith/Felicia Sanders

R&B
- BS Help Me Somebody [3]...The "5" Royales
- JB Help Me Somebody [3]...The "5" Royales

C&W
- BS Take These Chains From My Heart [2]...Hank Williams
- DJ Mexican Joe [4]...Jim Reeves
- JB Mexican Joe [4]...Jim Reeves

July 4, 1953

POP
- BS The Song From Moulin Rouge (Where Is Your Heart) [8]...Percy Faith/Felicia Sanders
- DJ The Song From Moulin Rouge (Where Is Your Heart) [8]...Percy Faith/Felicia Sanders
- JB *I'm Walking Behind You [1]...Eddie Fisher

R&B
- BS Help Me Somebody [4]...The "5" Royales
- JB Please Love Me [1]...B.B. King

C&W
- BS Take These Chains From My Heart [3]...Hank Williams
- DJ Mexican Joe [5]...Jim Reeves
- JB Mexican Joe [5]...Jim Reeves

July 11, 1953

POP
- BS The Song From Moulin Rouge (Where Is Your Heart) [9]...Percy Faith/Felicia Sanders
- DJ The Song From Moulin Rouge (Where Is Your Heart) [9]...Percy Faith/Felicia Sanders
- JB I'm Walking Behind You [2]...Eddie Fisher

R&B
- BS Help Me Somebody [5]...The "5" Royales
- JB Help Me Somebody [4]...The "5" Royales

C&W
- BS *It's Been So Long [1]...Webb Pierce ⎫
- BS Take These Chains From My Heart [4]... Hank Williams ⎬ tie
- DJ Mexican Joe [6]...Jim Reeves
- JB Mexican Joe [6]...Jim Reeves

July 18, 1953

POP
- BS The Song From Moulin Rouge (Where Is Your Heart) [10]...Percy Faith/Felicia Sanders
- DJ I'm Walking Behind You [1]...Eddie Fisher
- JB I'm Walking Behind You [3]...Eddie Fisher

R&B
- BS *The Clock [1]...Johnny Ace
- JB Help Me Somebody [5]...The "5" Royales

C&W
- BS It's Been So Long [2]...Webb Pierce
- DJ Your Cheatin' Heart [6]...Hank Williams
- JB Mexican Joe [7]...Jim Reeves

July 25, 1953

POP
- BS I'm Walking Behind You [1]...Eddie Fisher
- DJ I'm Walking Behind You [2]...Eddie Fisher
- JB I'm Walking Behind You [4]...Eddie Fisher

R&B
- BS The Clock [2]...Johnny Ace
- JB Please Love Me [2]...B.B. King

C&W
- BS It's Been So Long [3]...Webb Pierce
- DJ It's Been So Long [1]...Webb Pierce ⎫
- DJ Mexican Joe [7]...Jim Reeves ⎬ tie
- JB Mexican Joe [8]...Jim Reeves

August 1, 1953

POP
- BS I'm Walking Behind You [2]...Eddie Fisher
- DJ I'm Walking Behind You [3]...Eddie Fisher
- JB I'm Walking Behind You [5]...Eddie Fisher

R&B
- BS The Clock [3]...Johnny Ace
- JB The Clock [1]...Johnny Ace

C&W
- BS It's Been So Long [4]...Webb Pierce
- DJ It's Been So Long [2]...Webb Pierce
- JB Rub-A-Dub-Dub [1]...Hank Thompson

August 8, 1953

POP
- BS *Vaya Con Dios [1]...Les Paul and Mary Ford
- DJ *Vaya Con Dios [1]...Les Paul and Mary Ford
- JB I'm Walking Behind You [6]...Eddie Fisher

R&B
- BS The Clock [4]...Johnny Ace
- JB The Clock [2]...Johnny Ace

C&W
- BS It's Been So Long [5]...Webb Pierce
- DJ It's Been So Long [3]...Webb Pierce
- JB Rub-A-Dub-Dub [2]...Hank Thompson

August 15, 1953

POP
- BS Vaya Con Dios [2]...Les Paul and Mary Ford
- DJ No Other Love [1]...Perry Como
- JB I'm Walking Behind You [7]...Eddie Fisher

R&B
- BS The Clock [5]...Johnny Ace
- JB The Clock [3]...Johnny Ace   ⎫ tie
- JB Please Love Me [3]...B.B. King ⎭

C&W
- BS It's Been So Long [6]...Webb Pierce
- DJ It's Been So Long [4]...Webb Pierce
- JB Mexican Joe [9]...Jim Reeves

August 22, 1953

POP
- BS Vaya Con Dios [3]...Les Paul and Mary Ford
- DJ No Other Love [2]...Perry Como
- JB Vaya Con Dios [1]...Les Paul and Mary Ford

R&B
- BS *Crying In The Chapel [1]...The Orioles
- JB The Clock [4]...Johnny Ace

C&W
- BS *Hey, Joe [1]...Carl Smith
- DJ It's Been So Long [5]...Webb Pierce
- JB It's Been So Long [1]...Webb Pierce

August 29, 1953

POP
- BS Vaya Con Dios [4]...Les Paul and Mary Ford
- DJ No Other Love [3]...Perry Como
- JB Vaya Con Dios [2]...Les Paul and Mary Ford

R&B
- BS Crying In The Chapel [2]...The Orioles
- JB Crying In The Chapel [1]...The Orioles

C&W
- BS *A Dear John Letter [1]...Jean Shepard & Ferlin Huskey
- DJ It's Been So Long [6]...Webb Pierce
- JB Rub-A-Dub-Dub [3]...Hank Thompson

September 5, 1953

POP
- BS Vaya Con Dios [5]...Les Paul and Mary Ford
- DJ No Other Love [4]...Perry Como
- JB Vaya Con Dios [3]...Les Paul and Mary Ford

R&B
- BS Crying In The Chapel [3]...The Orioles
- JB Crying In The Chapel [2]...The Orioles

C&W
- BS A Dear John Letter [2]...Jean Shepard & Ferlin Huskey
- DJ It's Been So Long [7]...Webb Pierce
- JB Hey, Joe [1]...Carl Smith

September 12, 1953

POP
- BS Vaya Con Dios [6]...Les Paul and Mary Ford
- DJ Vaya Con Dios [2]...Les Paul and Mary Ford
- JB Vaya Con Dios [4]...Les Paul and Mary Ford

R&B
- BS Crying In The Chapel [4]...The Orioles
- JB Crying In The Chapel [3]...The Orioles

C&W
- BS A Dear John Letter [3]...Jean Shepard & Ferlin Huskey
- DJ Hey, Joe [1]...Carl Smith
- JB Hey, Joe [2]...Carl Smith

September 19, 1953

POP
- BS Vaya Con Dios [7]...Les Paul and Mary Ford
- DJ Vaya Con Dios [3]...Les Paul and Mary Ford
- JB Vaya Con Dios [5]...Les Paul and Mary Ford

R&B
- BS *Shake A Hand [1]...Faye Adams
- JB *Shake A Hand [1]...Faye Adams

C&W
- BS Hey, Joe [2]...Carl Smith
- DJ It's Been So Long [8]...Webb Pierce
- JB Hey, Joe [3]...Carl Smith

September 26, 1953

POP
- BS Vaya Con Dios [8]...Les Paul and Mary Ford
- DJ *You You You [1]...The Ames Brothers
- JB Vaya Con Dios [6]...Les Paul and Mary Ford

R&B
- BS Shake A Hand [2]...Faye Adams
- JB Shake A Hand [2]...Faye Adams

C&W
- BS A Dear John Letter [4]...Jean Shepard & Ferlin Huskey
- DJ Hey, Joe [2]...Carl Smith
- JB Hey, Joe [4]...Carl Smith

October 3, 1953

POP
- BS Vaya Con Dios [9]...Les Paul and Mary Ford
- DJ You You You [2]...The Ames Brothers
- JB Vaya Con Dios [7]...Les Paul and Mary Ford

R&B
- BS Shake A Hand [3]...Faye Adams
- JB Shake A Hand [3]...Faye Adams

C&W
- BS A Dear John Letter [5]...Jean Shepard & Ferlin Huskey
- DJ Hey, Joe [3]...Carl Smith
- JB Hey, Joe [5]...Carl Smith

October 10, 1953

POP
- BS *St. George And The Dragonet [1]...Stan Freberg
- DJ You You You [3]...The Ames Brothers
- JB Vaya Con Dios [8]...Les Paul and Mary Ford

R&B
- BS Shake A Hand [4]...Faye Adams
- JB Crying In The Chapel [4]...The Orioles

C&W
- BS A Dear John Letter [6]...Jean Shepard & Ferlin Huskey
- DJ Hey, Joe [4]...Carl Smith
- JB A Dear John Letter [1]...Jean Shepard & Ferlin Huskey

October 17, 1953

POP
- BS St. George And The Dragonet [2]...Stan Freberg
- DJ You You You [4]...The Ames Brothers
- JB Vaya Con Dios [9]...Les Paul and Mary Ford

R&B
- BS Shake A Hand [5]...Faye Adams
- JB Shake A Hand [4]...Faye Adams } tie
- JB Crying In The Chapel [5]...The Orioles

C&W
- BS *I Forgot More Than You'll Ever Know [1]...The Davis Sisters
- DJ *I Forgot More Than You'll Ever Know [1]...The Davis Sisters
- JB Hey, Joe [6]...Carl Smith

October 24, 1953

POP
- BS St. George And The Dragonet [3]...Stan Freberg
- DJ St. George And The Dragonet [1]...Stan Freberg
- JB You You You [1]...The Ames Brothers

R&B
- BS Shake A Hand [6]...Faye Adams
- JB Shake A Hand [5]...Faye Adams

C&W
- BS I Forgot More Than You'll Ever Know [2]...The Davis Sisters
- DJ I Forgot More Than You'll Ever Know [2]...The Davis Sisters
- JB Hey, Joe [7]...Carl Smith

October 31, 1953

POP
- BS St. George And The Dragonet [4]...Stan Freberg
- DJ You You You [5]...The Ames Brothers
- JB You You You [2]...The Ames Brothers

R&B
- BS Shake A Hand [7]...Faye Adams
- JB Shake A Hand [6]...Faye Adams

C&W
- BS I Forgot More Than You'll Ever Know [3]...The Davis Sisters
- DJ I Forgot More Than You'll Ever Know [3]...The Davis Sisters
- JB A Dear John Letter [2]...Jean Shepard & Ferlin Huskey

November 7, 1953

POP
- BS Vaya Con Dios [10]...Les Paul and Mary Ford
- DJ You You You [6]...The Ames Brothers
- JB You You You [3]...The Ames Brothers

R&B
- BS Shake A Hand [8]...Faye Adams
- JB Shake A Hand [7]...Faye Adams

C&W
- BS I Forgot More Than You'll Ever Know [4]...The Davis Sisters
- DJ I Forgot More Than You'll Ever Know [4]...The Davis Sisters
- JB Hey, Joe [8]...Carl Smith

November 14, 1953

POP
- BS Vaya Con Dios [11]...Les Paul and Mary Ford
- DJ You You You [7]...The Ames Brothers
- JB You You You [4]...The Ames Brothers

R&B
- BS Shake A Hand [9]...Faye Adams
- JB Shake A Hand [8]...Faye Adams

C&W
- BS I Forgot More Than You'll Ever Know [5]...The Davis Sisters
- DJ I Forgot More Than You'll Ever Know [5]...The Davis Sisters
- JB I Forgot More Than You'll Ever Know [1]...The Davis Sisters

November 21, 1953

POP
- BS *Rags To Riches [1]...Tony Bennett
- DJ You You You [8]...The Ames Brothers
- JB You You You [5]...The Ames Brothers

R&B
- BS *Money Honey [1]...Clyde McPhatter & The Drifters
- JB *Money Honey [1]...Clyde McPhatter & The Drifters

C&W
- BS *There Stands The Glass [1]...Webb Pierce
- DJ I Forgot More Than You'll Ever Know [6]...
       The Davis Sisters
- JB A Dear John Letter [3]...Jean Shepard & Ferlin Huskey

November 28, 1953

POP
- BS Rags To Riches [2]...Tony Bennett
- DJ Rags To Riches [1]...Tony Bennett
- JB You You You [6]...The Ames Brothers

R&B
- BS Money Honey [2]...Clyde McPhatter & The Drifters
- JB Shake A Hand [9]...Faye Adams

C&W
- BS I Forgot More Than You'll Ever Know [6]...
       The Davis Sisters
- DJ I Forgot More Than You'll Ever Know [7]...
       The Davis Sisters
- JB A Dear John Letter [4]...Jean Shepard & Ferlin Huskey

December 5, 1953

POP
- BS Rags To Riches [3]...Tony Bennett
- DJ Rags To Riches [2]...Tony Bennett
- JB Rags To Riches [1]...Tony Bennett

R&B
- BS Money Honey [3]...Clyde McPhatter & The Drifters
- JB Shake A Hand [10]...Faye Adams } tie
- JB Honey Hush [1]...Joe Turner

C&W
- BS There Stands The Glass [2]...Webb Pierce
- DJ There Stands The Glass [1]...Webb Pierce
- JB There Stands The Glass [1]...Webb Pierce

December 12, 1953

POP
- BS Rags To Riches [4]...Tony Bennett
- DJ Rags To Riches [3]...Tony Bennett
- JB Rags To Riches [2]...Tony Bennett

R&B
- BS Money Honey [4]...Clyde McPhatter & The Drifters
- JB Honey Hush [2]...Joe Turner

C&W
- BS There Stands The Glass [3]...Webb Pierce
- DJ I Forgot More Than You'll Ever Know [8]...
       The Davis Sisters
- JB Caribbean [1]...Mitchell Torok

December 19, 1953

POP
- BS Rags To Riches [5]...Tony Bennett
- DJ Rags To Riches [4]...Tony Bennett
- JB Rags To Riches [3]...Tony Bennett

R&B
- BS Money Honey [5]...Clyde McPhatter & The Drifters
- JB Honey Hush [3]...Joe Turner

C&W
- BS There Stands The Glass [4]...Webb Pierce
- DJ *Let Me Be The One [1]...Hank Locklin
- JB Caribbean [2]...Mitchell Torok

December 26, 1953

POP
- BS Rags To Riches [6]...Tony Bennett
- DJ Rags To Riches [5]...Tony Bennett
- JB Rags To Riches [4]...Tony Bennett

R&B
- BS Money Honey [6]...Clyde McPhatter & The Drifters
- JB Honey Hush [4]...Joe Turner

C&W
- BS There Stands The Glass [5]...Webb Pierce
- DJ Let Me Be The One [2]...Hank Locklin
- JB I Forgot More Than You'll Ever Know [2]...
       The Davis Sisters

January 2, 1954

POP
- BS *Oh! My Pa-Pa [1]...Eddie Fisher
- DJ Rags To Riches [6]...Tony Bennett
- JB Rags To Riches [5]...Tony Bennett

R&B
- BS Money Honey [7]...Clyde McPhatter & The Drifters
- JB Honey Hush [5]...Joe Turner

C&W
- BS There Stands The Glass [6]...Webb Pierce
- DJ There Stands The Glass [2]...Webb Pierce
- JB Let Me Be The One [1]...Hank Locklin

January 9, 1954

POP
- BS Oh! My Pa-Pa [2]...Eddie Fisher
- DJ Rags To Riches [7]...Tony Bennett
- JB Rags To Riches [6]...Tony Bennett

R&B
- BS Money Honey [8]...Clyde McPhatter & The Drifters
- JB Honey Hush [6]...Joe Turner

C&W
- BS There Stands The Glass [7]...Webb Pierce
- DJ Let Me Be The One [3]...Hank Locklin } tie
- DJ Bimbo [1]...Jim Reeves
- JB There Stands The Glass [2]...Webb Pierce

January 16, 1954

POP
- BS Oh! My Pa-Pa [3]...Eddie Fisher
- DJ Oh! My Pa-Pa [1]...Eddie Fisher
- JB Rags To Riches [7]...Tony Bennett

R&B
- BS Money Honey [9]...Clyde McPhatter & The Drifters
- JB Honey Hush [7]...Joe Turner

C&W
- BS There Stands The Glass [8]...Webb Pierce
- DJ There Stands The Glass [3]...Webb Pierce
- JB There Stands The Glass [3]...Webb Pierce

January 23, 1954

POP
- BS Oh! My Pa-Pa [4]...Eddie Fisher
- DJ Oh! My Pa-Pa [2]...Eddie Fisher
- JB Rags To Riches [8]...Tony Bennett

R&B
- BS Money Honey [10]...Clyde McPhatter & The Drifters
- JB Honey Hush [8]...Joe Turner

C&W
- BS There Stands The Glass [9]...Webb Pierce
- DJ There Stands The Glass [4]...Webb Pierce
- JB There Stands The Glass [4]...Webb Pierce

January 30, 1954

POP
- BS Oh! My Pa-Pa [5]...Eddie Fisher
- DJ Oh! My Pa-Pa [3]...Eddie Fisher
- JB Oh! My Pa-Pa [1]...Eddie Fisher

R&B
- BS Money Honey [11]...Clyde McPhatter & The Drifters
- JB *Things That I Used To Do [1]...Guitar Slim

C&W
- BS There Stands The Glass [10]...Webb Pierce
- DJ Bimbo [2]...Jim Reeves
- JB There Stands The Glass [5]...Webb Pierce

February 6, 1954

POP
- BS Oh! My Pa-Pa [6]...Eddie Fisher
- DJ Oh! My Pa-Pa [4]...Eddie Fisher
- JB Oh! My Pa-Pa [2]...Eddie Fisher

R&B
- BS I'll Be True [1]...Faye Adams
- JB Things That I Used To Do [2]...Guitar Slim

C&W
- BS There Stands The Glass [11]...Webb Pierce
- DJ There Stands The Glass [5]...Webb Pierce
- JB There Stands The Glass [6]...Webb Pierce

February 13, 1954

POP
- BS Oh! My Pa-Pa [7]...Eddie Fisher
- DJ Oh! My Pa-Pa [5]...Eddie Fisher
- JB Oh! My Pa-Pa [3]...Eddie Fisher

R&B
- BS Things That I Used To Do [1]...Guitar Slim
- JB Things That I Used To Do [3]...Guitar Slim

C&W
- BS There Stands The Glass [12]...Webb Pierce
- DJ There Stands The Glass [6]...Webb Pierce
- JB Let Me Be The One [2]...Hank Locklin

February 20, 1954

POP
- BS Oh! My Pa-Pa [8]...Eddie Fisher
- DJ Oh! My Pa-Pa [6]...Eddie Fisher
- JB Oh! My Pa-Pa [4]...Eddie Fisher

R&B
- BS Things That I Used To Do [2]...Guitar Slim
- JB Things That I Used To Do [4]...Guitar Slim

C&W
- BS *Slowly [1]...Webb Pierce
- DJ Bimbo [3]...Jim Reeves
- JB There Stands The Glass [7]...Webb Pierce } tie
- JB Wake Up, Irene [1]...Hank Thompson

February 27, 1954

POP
- BS *Secret Love [1]...Doris Day
- DJ Oh! My Pa-Pa [7]...Eddie Fisher
- JB Oh! My Pa-Pa [5]...Eddie Fisher

R&B
- BS Things That I Used To Do [3]...Guitar Slim
- JB Things That I Used To Do [5]...Guitar Slim

C&W
- BS Slowly [2]...Webb Pierce
- DJ Slowly [1]...Webb Pierce
- JB There Stands The Glass [8]...Webb Pierce } tie
- JB Wake Up, Irene [2]...Hank Thompson

March 6, 1954

POP
- BS Secret Love [2]...Doris Day
- DJ Secret Love [1]...Doris Day
- JB Oh! My Pa-Pa [6]...Eddie Fisher

R&B
- BS Things That I Used To Do [4]...Guitar Slim
- JB Things That I Used To Do [6]...Guitar Slim

C&W
- BS Slowly [3]...Webb Pierce
- DJ Slowly [2]...Webb Pierce
- JB Slowly [1]...Webb Pierce
- JB There Stands The Glass [9]...Webb Pierce } tie

March 13, 1954

POP
- BS *Make Love To Me! [1]...Jo Stafford
- DJ Secret Love [2]...Doris Day
- JB *Make Love To Me! [1]...Jo Stafford

R&B
- BS Things That I Used To Do [5]...Guitar Slim
- JB Things That I Used To Do [7]...Guitar Slim

C&W
- BS Slowly [4]...Webb Pierce
- DJ Slowly [3]...Webb Pierce
- JB Slowly [2]...Webb Pierce

March 20, 1954

POP
- BS Secret Love [3]...Doris Day
- DJ Secret Love [3]...Doris Day
- JB Make Love To Me! [2]...Jo Stafford

R&B
- BS Things That I Used To Do [6]...Guitar Slim
- JB Things That I Used To Do [8]...Guitar Slim

C&W
- BS Slowly [5]...Webb Pierce
- DJ Slowly [4]...Webb Pierce
- JB Slowly [3]...Webb Pierce

March 27, 1954

POP
- BS Make Love To Me! [2]...Jo Stafford
- DJ Secret Love [4]...Doris Day
- JB Make Love To Me! [3]...Jo Stafford

R&B
- BS *You'll Never Walk Alone [1]...Roy Hamilton
- JB Things That I Used To Do [9]...Guitar Slim

C&W
- BS Slowly [6]...Webb Pierce
- DJ Slowly [5]...Webb Pierce
- JB Slowly [4]...Webb Pierce

April 3, 1954

POP
- BS Make Love To Me! [3]...Jo Stafford
- DJ Make Love To Me! [1]...Jo Stafford
- JB Make Love To Me! [4]...Jo Stafford

R&B
- BS You'll Never Walk Alone [2]...Roy Hamilton
- JB Things That I Used To Do [10]...Guitar Slim

C&W
- BS Slowly [7]...Webb Pierce
- DJ Slowly [6]...Webb Pierce
- JB Slowly [5]...Webb Pierce

April 10, 1954

POP
- BS *Wanted [1]...Perry Como
- DJ Make Love To Me! [2]...Jo Stafford
- JB Make Love To Me! [5]...Jo Stafford

R&B
- BS You'll Never Walk Alone [3]...Roy Hamilton
- JB Things That I Used To Do [11]...Guitar Slim

C&W
- BS Slowly [8]...Webb Pierce
- DJ Slowly [7]...Webb Pierce
- JB Slowly [6]...Webb Pierce

April 17, 1954

POP
- BS Wanted [2]...Perry Como
- DJ Make Love To Me! [3]...Jo Stafford
- JB Make Love To Me! [6]...Jo Stafford

R&B
- BS You'll Never Walk Alone [4]...Roy Hamilton
- JB Things That I Used To Do [12]...Guitar Slim

C&W
- BS Slowly [9]...Webb Pierce
- DJ Slowly [8]...Webb Pierce
- JB Slowly [7]...Webb Pierce

April 24, 1954

POP
- BS Wanted [3]...Perry Como
- DJ Wanted [1]...Perry Como
- JB Make Love To Me! [7]...Jo Stafford

R&B
- BS You'll Never Walk Alone [5]...Roy Hamilton
- JB Things That I Used To Do [13]...Guitar Slim

C&W
- BS Slowly [10]...Webb Pierce
- DJ Slowly [9]...Webb Pierce
- JB Slowly [8]...Webb Pierce

May 1, 1954

POP
- BS Wanted [4]...Perry Como
- DJ Wanted [2]...Perry Como
- JB Wanted [1]...Perry Como

R&B
- BS You'll Never Walk Alone [6]...Roy Hamilton
- JB Things That I Used To Do [14]...Guitar Slim

C&W
- BS Slowly [11]...Webb Pierce
- DJ Slowly [10]...Webb Pierce
- JB Slowly [9]...Webb Pierce

May 8, 1954

POP
- BS Wanted [5]...Perry Como
- DJ Wanted [3]...Perry Como
- JB Wanted [2]...Perry Como

R&B
- BS You'll Never Walk Alone [7]...Roy Hamilton
- JB You'll Never Walk Alone [1]...Roy Hamilton

C&W
- BS Slowly [12]...Webb Pierce
- DJ Slowly [11]...Webb Pierce
- JB Slowly [10]...Webb Pierce

May 15, 1954

POP
- BS Wanted [6]...Perry Como
- DJ Wanted [4]...Perry Como
- JB Wanted [3]...Perry Como

R&B
- BS You'll Never Walk Alone [8]...Roy Hamilton
- JB You'll Never Walk Alone [2]...Roy Hamilton

C&W
- BS Slowly [13]...Webb Pierce
- DJ Slowly [12]...Webb Pierce
- JB I Really Don't Want To Know [1]...Eddy Arnold

May 22, 1954

POP
- BS Wanted [7]...Perry Como
- DJ Wanted [5]...Perry Como
- JB Wanted [4]...Perry Como

R&B
- BS *Work With Me Annie [1]...Midnighters
- JB You'll Never Walk Alone [3]...Roy Hamilton

C&W
- BS Slowly [14]...Webb Pierce
- DJ Slowly [13]...Webb Pierce
- JB Slowly [11]...Webb Pierce

May 29, 1954

POP
- BS Wanted [8]...Perry Como
- DJ Wanted [6]...Perry Como
- JB Wanted [5]...Perry Como

R&B
- BS Work With Me Annie [2]...Midnighters
- JB You'll Never Walk Alone [4]...Roy Hamilton

C&W
- BS Slowly [15]...Webb Pierce
- DJ Slowly [14]...Webb Pierce
- JB Slowly [12]...Webb Pierce

June 5, 1954

POP
- BS *Little Things Mean A Lot [1]...Kitty Kallen
- DJ Wanted [7]...Perry Como
- JB Wanted [6]...Perry Como

R&B
- BS Work With Me Annie [3]...Midnighters
- JB You'll Never Walk Alone [5]...Roy Hamilton

C&W
- BS Slowly [16]...Webb Pierce
- DJ Slowly [15]...Webb Pierce
- JB Slowly [13]...Webb Pierce

June 12, 1954

POP
- BS Little Things Mean A Lot [2]...Kitty Kallen
- DJ Little Things Mean A Lot [1]...Kitty Kallen
- JB Wanted [7]...Perry Como

R&B
- BS Work With Me Annie [4]...Midnighters
- JB Shake, Rattle, And Roll [1]...Joe Turner

C&W
- BS Slowly [17]...Webb Pierce
- DJ Oh, Baby Mine (I Get So Lonely) [1]...Johnnie & Jack
- JB Slowly [14]...Webb Pierce

June 19, 1954

POP
- BS Little Things Mean A Lot [3]...Kitty Kallen
- DJ Little Things Mean A Lot [2]...Kitty Kallen
- JB Wanted [8]...Perry Como

R&B
- BS Work With Me Annie [5]...Midnighters
- JB Shake, Rattle, And Roll [2]...Joe Turner

C&W
- BS *I Don't Hurt Anymore [1]...Hank Snow
- DJ Oh, Baby Mine (I Get So Lonely) [2]...Johnnie & Jack
- JB Slowly [15]...Webb Pierce

June 26, 1954

POP
- BS Little Things Mean A Lot [4]...Kitty Kallen
- DJ Little Things Mean A Lot [3]...Kitty Kallen
- JB Little Things Mean A Lot [1]...Kitty Kallen

R&B
- BS Work With Me Annie [6]...Midnighters
- JB Shake, Rattle, And Roll [3]...Joe Turner

C&W
- BS I Don't Hurt Anymore [2]...Hank Snow
- DJ I Don't Hurt Anymore [1]...Hank Snow
- JB Slowly [16]...Webb Pierce

July 3, 1954

POP
- BS Little Things Mean A Lot [5]...Kitty Kallen
- DJ Little Things Mean A Lot [4]...Kitty Kallen
- JB Little Things Mean A Lot [2]...Kitty Kallen

R&B
- BS Work With Me Annie [7]...Midnighters
- JB Work With Me Annie [1]...Midnighters

C&W
- BS I Don't Hurt Anymore [3]...Hank Snow
- DJ Even Tho [1]...Webb Pierce
- JB Slowly [17]...Webb Pierce

July 10, 1954

POP
- BS Little Things Mean A Lot [6]...Kitty Kallen
- DJ Little Things Mean A Lot [5]...Kitty Kallen
- JB Little Things Mean A Lot [3]...Kitty Kallen

R&B
- BS *Honey Love [1]...Drifters featuring Clyde McPhatter
- JB Work With Me Annie [2]...Midnighters

C&W
- BS I Don't Hurt Anymore [4]...Hank Snow
- DJ Even Tho [2]...Webb Pierce
- JB I Don't Hurt Anymore [1]...Hank Snow

July 17, 1954

POP
- BS Little Things Mean A Lot [7]...Kitty Kallen
- DJ Little Things Mean A Lot [6]...Kitty Kallen
- JB Little Things Mean A Lot [4]...Kitty Kallen

R&B
- BS Honey Love [2]...Drifters featuring Clyde McPhatter
- JB Work With Me Annie [3]...Midnighters

C&W
- BS I Don't Hurt Anymore [5]...Hank Snow
- DJ I Don't Hurt Anymore [2]...Hank Snow
- JB I Don't Hurt Anymore [2]...Hank Snow

July 24, 1954

POP
- BS Little Things Mean A Lot [8]...Kitty Kallen
- DJ Little Things Mean A Lot [7]...Kitty Kallen
- JB Three Coins In The Fountain [1]... Four Aces Featuring Al Alberts

R&B
- BS Honey Love [3]...Drifters featuring Clyde McPhatter
- JB Work With Me Annie [4]...Midnighters

C&W
- BS I Don't Hurt Anymore [6]...Hank Snow
- DJ I Don't Hurt Anymore [3]...Hank Snow
- JB I Don't Hurt Anymore [3]...Hank Snow

July 31, 1954

POP
- BS Little Things Mean A Lot [9]...Kitty Kallen
- DJ Little Things Mean A Lot [8]...Kitty Kallen
- JB Little Things Mean A Lot [5]...Kitty Kallen

R&B
- BS Honey Love [4]...Drifters featuring Clyde McPhatter
- JB Honey Love [1]...Drifters featuring Clyde McPhatter

C&W
- BS I Don't Hurt Anymore [7]...Hank Snow
- DJ I Don't Hurt Anymore [4]...Hank Snow
- JB One By One [1]...Kitty Wells & Red Foley

August 7, 1954

POP
- BS *Sh-Boom [1]...The Crew-Cuts
- DJ *Sh-Boom [1]...The Crew-Cuts
- JB Little Things Mean A Lot [6]...Kitty Kallen

R&B
- BS Honey Love [5]...Drifters featuring Clyde McPhatter
- JB Honey Love [2]...Drifters featuring Clyde McPhatter

C&W
- BS I Don't Hurt Anymore [8]...Hank Snow
- DJ I Don't Hurt Anymore [5]...Hank Snow
- JB I Don't Hurt Anymore [4]...Hank Snow

August 14, 1954

POP
- BS Sh-Boom [2]...The Crew-Cuts
- DJ Sh-Boom [2]...The Crew-Cuts
- JB Little Things Mean A Lot [7]...Kitty Kallen

R&B
- BS Honey Love [6]...Drifters featuring Clyde McPhatter
- JB Honey Love [3]...Drifters featuring Clyde McPhatter

C&W
- BS I Don't Hurt Anymore [9]...Hank Snow
- DJ I Don't Hurt Anymore [6]...Hank Snow
- JB I Don't Hurt Anymore [5]...Hank Snow

August 21, 1954

POP
- BS Sh-Boom [3]...The Crew-Cuts
- DJ Sh-Boom [3]...The Crew-Cuts
- JB Sh-Boom [1]...The Crew-Cuts

R&B
- BS Honey Love [7]...Drifters featuring Clyde McPhatter
- JB Honey Love [4]...Drifters featuring Clyde McPhatter

C&W
- BS I Don't Hurt Anymore [10]...Hank Snow
- DJ I Don't Hurt Anymore [7]...Hank Snow
- JB I Don't Hurt Anymore [6]...Hank Snow

August 28, 1954

POP
- BS Sh-Boom [4]...The Crew-Cuts
- DJ Sh-Boom [4]...The Crew-Cuts
- JB Sh-Boom [2]...The Crew-Cuts

R&B
- BS Honey Love [8]...Drifters featuring Clyde McPhatter
- JB Honey Love [5]...Drifters featuring Clyde McPhatter

C&W
- BS I Don't Hurt Anymore [11]...Hank Snow
- DJ I Don't Hurt Anymore [8]...Hank Snow
- JB I Don't Hurt Anymore [7]...Hank Snow

September 4, 1954

POP
- BS Sh-Boom [5]...The Crew-Cuts
- DJ Sh-Boom [5]...The Crew-Cuts
- JB Sh-Boom [3]...The Crew-Cuts

R&B
- BS *Oh What A Dream [1]...Ruth Brown & Her Rhythmakers
- JB Honey Love [6]...Drifters featuring Clyde McPhatter

C&W
- BS I Don't Hurt Anymore [12]...Hank Snow
- DJ I Don't Hurt Anymore [9]...Hank Snow
- JB I Don't Hurt Anymore [8]...Hank Snow

September 11, 1954

POP
- BS Sh-Boom [6]...The Crew-Cuts
- DJ Sh-Boom [6]...The Crew-Cuts
- JB Sh-Boom [4]...The Crew-Cuts

R&B
- BS Oh What A Dream [2]...Ruth Brown & Her Rhythmakers
- JB Honey Love [7]...Drifters featuring Clyde McPhatter

C&W
- BS I Don't Hurt Anymore [13]...Hank Snow
- DJ I Don't Hurt Anymore [10]...Hank Snow
- JB I Don't Hurt Anymore [9]...Hank Snow

September 18, 1954

POP
- BS Sh-Boom [7]...The Crew-Cuts
- DJ Sh-Boom [7]...The Crew-Cuts
- JB Sh-Boom [5]...The Crew-Cuts

R&B
- BS Oh What A Dream [3]...Ruth Brown & Her Rhythmakers
- JB Honey Love [8]...Drifters featuring Clyde McPhatter

C&W
- BS I Don't Hurt Anymore [14]...Hank Snow
- DJ I Don't Hurt Anymore [11]...Hank Snow
- JB I Don't Hurt Anymore [10]...Hank Snow

September 25, 1954

POP
- BS *Hey There [1]...Rosemary Clooney
- DJ Sh-Boom [8]...The Crew-Cuts
- JB Sh-Boom [6]...The Crew-Cuts

R&B
- BS Annie Had A Baby [1]...Midnighters
- JB Oh What A Dream [1]...Ruth Brown & Her Rhythmakers

C&W
- BS I Don't Hurt Anymore [15]...Hank Snow
- DJ I Don't Hurt Anymore [12]...Hank Snow
- JB I Don't Hurt Anymore [11]...Hank Snow

October 2, 1954

POP
- BS Hey There [2]...Rosemary Clooney
- DJ Sh-Boom [9]...The Crew-Cuts
- JB Sh-Boom [7]...The Crew-Cuts

R&B
- BS Annie Had A Baby [2]...Midnighters
- JB Oh What A Dream [2]...Ruth Brown & Her Rhythmakers

C&W
- BS I Don't Hurt Anymore [16]...Hank Snow
- DJ I Don't Hurt Anymore [13]...Hank Snow
- JB I Don't Hurt Anymore [12]...Hank Snow

October 9, 1954

POP
- BS Hey There [3]...Rosemary Clooney
- DJ Hey There [1]...Rosemary Clooney
- JB Sh-Boom [8]...The Crew-Cuts

R&B
- BS Oh What A Dream [4]...Ruth Brown & Her Rhythmakers
- JB Oh What A Dream [3]...Ruth Brown & Her Rhythmakers

C&W
- BS I Don't Hurt Anymore [17]...Hank Snow
- DJ I Don't Hurt Anymore [14]...Hank Snow
- JB I Don't Hurt Anymore [13]...Hank Snow

October 16, 1954

POP
- BS Hey There [4]...Rosemary Clooney
- DJ Hey There [2]...Rosemary Clooney
- JB Hey There [1]...Rosemary Clooney

R&B
- BS *Hurts Me To My Heart [1]...Faye Adams
- JB Oh What A Dream [4]...Ruth Brown & Her Rhythmakers

C&W
- BS I Don't Hurt Anymore [18]...Hank Snow
- DJ I Don't Hurt Anymore [15]...Hank Snow
- JB I Don't Hurt Anymore [14]...Hank Snow

October 23, 1954

POP
- BS Hey There [5]...Rosemary Clooney
- DJ Hey There [3]...Rosemary Clooney
- JB Hey There [2]...Rosemary Clooney

R&B
- BS Hurts Me To My Heart [2]...Faye Adams
- JB Oh What A Dream [5]...Ruth Brown & Her Rhythmakers

C&W
- BS I Don't Hurt Anymore [19]...Hank Snow
- DJ I Don't Hurt Anymore [16]...Hank Snow
- JB I Don't Hurt Anymore [15]...Hank Snow

October 30, 1954

POP
- BS Hey There [6]...Rosemary Clooney
- DJ Hey There [4]...Rosemary Clooney
- JB Hey There [3]...Rosemary Clooney

R&B
- BS Hurts Me To My Heart [3]...Faye Adams
- JB Oh What A Dream [6]...Ruth Brown & Her Rhythmakers

C&W
- BS I Don't Hurt Anymore [20]...Hank Snow
- DJ I Don't Hurt Anymore [17]...Hank Snow
- JB I Don't Hurt Anymore [16]...Hank Snow

November 6, 1954

POP
- BS *This Ole House [1]...Rosemary Clooney
- DJ Hey There [5]...Rosemary Clooney
- JB Hey There [4]...Rosemary Clooney

R&B
- BS Hurts Me To My Heart [4]...Faye Adams
- JB Oh What A Dream [7]...Ruth Brown & Her Rhythmakers

C&W
- BS *More And More [1]...Webb Pierce
- DJ *More And More [1]...Webb Pierce
- JB I Don't Hurt Anymore [17]...Hank Snow

November 13, 1954

POP
- BS *I Need You Now [1]...Eddie Fisher
- DJ *I Need You Now [1]...Eddie Fisher
- JB This Ole House [1]...Rosemary Clooney

R&B
- BS Hurts Me To My Heart [5]...Faye Adams
- JB Oh What A Dream [8]...Ruth Brown & Her Rhythmakers

C&W
- BS More And More [2]...Webb Pierce
- DJ I Don't Hurt Anymore [18]...Hank Snow
- JB I Don't Hurt Anymore [18]...Hank Snow

November 20, 1954

POP
- BS I Need You Now [2]...Eddie Fisher
- DJ I Need You Now [2]...Eddie Fisher
- JB This Ole House [2]...Rosemary Clooney

R&B
- BS *Mambo Baby [1]...Ruth Brown & Her Rhythmakers
- JB Hurts Me To My Heart [1]...Faye Adams

C&W
- BS More And More [3]...Webb Pierce
- DJ More And More [2]...Webb Pierce
- JB I Don't Hurt Anymore [19]...Hank Snow

November 27, 1954

POP
- BS   I Need You Now [3]...Eddie Fisher
- DJ   *Mr. Sandman [1]...The Chordettes
- JB   This Ole House [3]...Rosemary Clooney

R&B
- BS   *Hearts Of Stone [1]...The Charms
- JB   Hurts Me To My Heart [2]...Faye Adams

C&W
- BS   More And More [4]...Webb Pierce
- DJ   More And More [3]...Webb Pierce
- JB   I Don't Hurt Anymore [20]...Hank Snow

December 4, 1954

POP
- BS   Mr. Sandman [1]...The Chordettes
- DJ   Mr. Sandman [2]...The Chordettes
- JB   I Need You Now [1]...Eddie Fisher

R&B
- BS   Hearts Of Stone [2]...The Charms
- JB   Hurts Me To My Heart [3]...Faye Adams

C&W
- BS   More And More [5]...Webb Pierce
- DJ   More And More [4]...Webb Pierce
- JB   More And More [1]...Webb Pierce

December 11, 1954

POP
- BS   Mr. Sandman [2]...The Chordettes
- DJ   Mr. Sandman [3]...The Chordettes
- JB   I Need You Now [2]...Eddie Fisher

R&B
- BS   Hearts Of Stone [3]...The Charms
- JB   Hurts Me To My Heart [4]...Faye Adams

C&W
- BS   More And More [6]...Webb Pierce
- DJ   More And More [5]...Webb Pierce
- JB   More And More [2]...Webb Pierce

December 18, 1954

POP
- BS   Mr. Sandman [3]...The Chordettes
- DJ   Mr. Sandman [4]...The Chordettes
- JB   Mr. Sandman [1]...The Chordettes

R&B
- BS   Hearts Of Stone [4]...The Charms
- JB   Hurts Me To My Heart [5]...Faye Adams

C&W
- BS   More And More [7]...Webb Pierce
- DJ   More And More [6]...Webb Pierce
- JB   More And More [3]...Webb Pierce

December 25, 1954

POP
- BS   Mr. Sandman [4]...The Chordettes
- DJ   Mr. Sandman [5]...The Chordettes
- JB   Mr. Sandman [2]...The Chordettes

R&B
- BS   Hearts Of Stone [5]...The Charms
- JB   You Upset Me Baby [1]...B.B. King

C&W
- BS   More And More [8]...Webb Pierce
- DJ   More And More [7]...Webb Pierce
- JB   More And More [4]...Webb Pierce

January 1, 1955

POP
- BS   Mr. Sandman [5]...The Chordettes
- DJ   *Let Me Go Lover [1]...Joan Weber
- JB   Mr. Sandman [3]...The Chordettes

R&B
- BS   Hearts Of Stone [6]...The Charms
- JB   You Upset Me Baby [2]...B.B. King

C&W
- BS   More And More [9]...Webb Pierce
- DJ   More And More [8]...Webb Pierce
- JB   More And More [5]...Webb Pierce

January 8, 1955

POP
- BS   Mr. Sandman [6]...The Chordettes
- DJ   Mr. Sandman [6]...The Chordettes
- JB   Mr. Sandman [4]...The Chordettes

R&B
- BS   Hearts Of Stone [7]...The Charms
- JB   Mambo Baby [1]...Ruth Brown & Her Rhythmakers

C&W
- BS   *Loose Talk [1]...Carl Smith
- DJ   *Loose Talk [1]...Carl Smith
- JB   More And More [6]...Webb Pierce

January 15, 1955

POP
- BS   Mr. Sandman [7]...The Chordettes
- DJ   Let Me Go Lover [2]...Joan Weber
- JB   Let Me Go Lover [1]...Joan Weber

R&B
- BS   Hearts Of Stone [8]...The Charms
- JB   *Earth Angel (Will You Be Mine) [1]...The Penguins

C&W
- BS   Loose Talk [2]...Carl Smith
- DJ   Loose Talk [2]...Carl Smith
- JB   More And More [7]...Webb Pierce

January 22, 1955
POP
- BS   Let Me Go Lover [1]...Joan Weber
- DJ   Mr. Sandman [7]...The Chordettes
- JB   Let Me Go Lover [2]...Joan Weber

R&B
- BS   Hearts Of Stone [9]...The Charms
- DJ   Hearts Of Stone [1]...The Charms
- JB   *Sincerely [1]...The Moonglows

C&W
- BS   Loose Talk [3]...Carl Smith
- DJ   Loose Talk [3]...Carl Smith
- JB   More And More [8]...Webb Pierce } tie
- JB   Loose Talk [1]...Carl Smith

January 29, 1955
POP
- BS   Let Me Go Lover [2]...Joan Weber
- DJ   Let Me Go Lover [3]...Joan Weber
- JB   Let Me Go Lover [3]...Joan Weber

R&B
- BS   Earth Angel (Will You Be Mine) [1]...The Penguins
- DJ   Hearts Of Stone [2]...The Charms
- JB   Hearts Of Stone [1]...The Charms

C&W
- BS   Loose Talk [4]...Carl Smith
- DJ   Let Me Go, Lover [1]...Hank Snow
- JB   Loose Talk [2]...Carl Smith

February 5, 1955
POP
- BS   *Hearts Of Stone [1]...The Fontane Sisters
- DJ   Let Me Go Lover [4]...Joan Weber
- JB   Let Me Go Lover [4]...Joan Weber

R&B
- BS   Earth Angel (Will You Be Mine) [2]...The Penguins
- DJ   Sincerely [1]...The Moonglows
- JB   Hearts Of Stone [2]...The Charms

C&W
- BS   Loose Talk [5]...Carl Smith
- DJ   Let Me Go, Lover [2]...Hank Snow
- JB   Loose Talk [3]...Carl Smith

February 12, 1955
POP
- BS   *Sincerely [1]...The McGuire Sisters
- DJ   *Sincerely [1]...The McGuire Sisters
- JB   Hearts Of Stone [1]...The Fontane Sisters

R&B
- BS   Earth Angel (Will You Be Mine) [3]...The Penguins
- DJ   *Pledging My Love [1]...Johnny Ace
- JB   Sincerely [2]...The Moonglows

C&W
- BS   Loose Talk [6]...Carl Smith
- DJ   Loose Talk [4]...Carl Smith
- JB   Loose Talk [4]...Carl Smith

February 19, 1955
POP
- BS   Sincerely [2]...The McGuire Sisters
- DJ   Sincerely [2]...The McGuire Sisters
- JB   Hearts Of Stone [2]...The Fontane Sisters

R&B
- BS   Pledging My Love [1]...Johnny Ace
- DJ   Earth Angel (Will You Be Mine) [1]...The Penguins
- JB   Earth Angel (Will You Be Mine) [2]...The Penguins

C&W
- BS   Loose Talk [7]...Carl Smith
- DJ   Loose Talk [5]...Carl Smith
- JB   More And More [9]...Webb Pierce

February 26, 1955
POP
- BS   Sincerely [3]...The McGuire Sisters
- DJ   Sincerely [3]...The McGuire Sisters
- JB   Hearts Of Stone [3]...The Fontane Sisters

R&B
- BS   Pledging My Love [2]...Johnny Ace
- DJ   Pledging My Love [2]...Johnny Ace
- JB   Earth Angel (Will You Be Mine) [3]...The Penguins

C&W
- BS   *In The Jailhouse Now [1]...Webb Pierce
- DJ   Loose Talk [6]...Carl Smith
- JB   More And More [10]...Webb Pierce

March 5, 1955
POP
- BS   Sincerely [4]...The McGuire Sisters
- DJ   Sincerely [4]...The McGuire Sisters
- JB   Sincerely [1]...The McGuire Sisters

R&B
- BS   Pledging My Love [3]...Johnny Ace
- DJ   Pledging My Love [3]...Johnny Ace
- JB   Pledging My Love [1]...Johnny Ace

C&W
- BS   In The Jailhouse Now [2]...Webb Pierce
- DJ   In The Jailhouse Now [1]...Webb Pierce
- JB   In The Jailhouse Now [1]...Webb Pierce

March 12, 1955
POP
- BS Sincerely [5]...The McGuire Sisters
- DJ Sincerely [5]...The McGuire Sisters
- JB Sincerely [2]...The McGuire Sisters

R&B
- BS Pledging My Love [4]...Johnny Ace
- DJ Pledging My Love [4]...Johnny Ace
- JB Pledging My Love [2]...Johnny Ace

C&W
- BS In The Jailhouse Now [3]...Webb Pierce
- DJ In The Jailhouse Now [2]...Webb Pierce
- JB In The Jailhouse Now [2]...Webb Pierce

March 19, 1955
POP
- BS Sincerely [6]...The McGuire Sisters
- DJ Sincerely [6]...The McGuire Sisters
- JB Sincerely [3]...The McGuire Sisters

R&B
- BS Pledging My Love [5]...Johnny Ace
- DJ Pledging My Love [5]...Johnny Ace
- JB Pledging My Love [3]...Johnny Ace

C&W
- BS In The Jailhouse Now [4]...Webb Pierce
- DJ In The Jailhouse Now [3]...Webb Pierce
- JB In The Jailhouse Now [3]...Webb Pierce

March 26, 1955
POP
- BS *The Ballad Of Davy Crockett [1]...Bill Hayes
- DJ Sincerely [7]...The McGuire Sisters
- JB Sincerely [4]...The McGuire Sisters

R&B
- BS Pledging My Love [6]...Johnny Ace
- DJ Pledging My Love [6]...Johnny Ace
- JB Pledging My Love [4]...Johnny Ace

C&W
- BS In The Jailhouse Now [5]...Webb Pierce
- DJ In The Jailhouse Now [4]...Webb Pierce
- JB In The Jailhouse Now [4]...Webb Pierce

April 2, 1955
POP
- BS The Ballad Of Davy Crockett [2]...Bill Hayes
- DJ Sincerely [8]...The McGuire Sisters
- JB Sincerely [5]...The McGuire Sisters

R&B
- BS Pledging My Love [7]...Johnny Ace
- DJ Pledging My Love [7]...Johnny Ace
- JB Pledging My Love [5]...Johnny Ace

C&W
- BS In The Jailhouse Now [6]...Webb Pierce
- DJ In The Jailhouse Now [5]...Webb Pierce
- JB In The Jailhouse Now [5]...Webb Pierce

April 9, 1955
POP
- BS The Ballad Of Davy Crockett [3]...Bill Hayes
- DJ Sincerely [9]...The McGuire Sisters
- JB Sincerely [6]...The McGuire Sisters

R&B
- BS Pledging My Love [8]...Johnny Ace
- DJ The Wallflower [1]...Etta James
- JB Pledging My Love [6]...Johnny Ace

C&W
- BS In The Jailhouse Now [7]...Webb Pierce
- DJ In The Jailhouse Now [6]...Webb Pierce
- JB In The Jailhouse Now/I'm Gonna Fall Out Of Love With You [6]...Webb Pierce

April 16, 1955
POP
- BS The Ballad Of Davy Crockett [4]...Bill Hayes
- DJ Sincerely [10]...The McGuire Sisters
- JB Sincerely [7]...The McGuire Sisters

R&B
- BS Pledging My Love [9]...Johnny Ace
- DJ Pledging My Love [8]...Johnny Ace
- JB Pledging My Love [7]...Johnny Ace

C&W
- BS In The Jailhouse Now [8]...Webb Pierce
- DJ In The Jailhouse Now [7]...Webb Pierce
- JB In The Jailhouse Now [7]...Webb Pierce

April 23, 1955
POP
- BS The Ballad Of Davy Crockett [5]...Bill Hayes
- DJ The Ballad Of Davy Crockett [1]...Bill Hayes
- JB The Ballad Of Davy Crockett [1]...Bill Hayes

R&B
- BS *My Babe [1]...Little Walter
- DJ Pledging My Love [9]...Johnny Ace
- JB Pledging My Love [8]...Johnny Ace

C&W
- BS In The Jailhouse Now [9]...Webb Pierce
- DJ In The Jailhouse Now [8]...Webb Pierce
- JB In The Jailhouse Now [8]...Webb Pierce

April 30, 1955

POP
- BS *Cherry Pink And Apple Blossom White [1]...
  Perez "Prez" Prado
- DJ The Ballad Of Davy Crockett [2]...Bill Hayes
- JB The Ballad Of Davy Crockett [2]...Bill Hayes

R&B
- BS My Babe [2]...Little Walter
- DJ Pledging My Love [10]...Johnny Ace
- JB My Babe [1]...Little Walter

C&W
- BS In The Jailhouse Now [10]...Webb Pierce
- DJ In The Jailhouse Now [9]...Webb Pierce
- JB In The Jailhouse Now [9]...Webb Pierce

May 7, 1955

POP
- BS Cherry Pink And Apple Blossom White [2]...
  Perez "Prez" Prado
- DJ The Ballad Of Davy Crockett [3]...Bill Hayes
- JB The Ballad Of Davy Crockett [3]...Bill Hayes

R&B
- BS My Babe [3]...Little Walter
- DJ The Wallflower [2]...Etta James
- JB I've Got A Woman [1]...Ray Charles

C&W
- BS In The Jailhouse Now [11]...Webb Pierce
- DJ In The Jailhouse Now [10]...Webb Pierce
- JB In The Jailhouse Now [10]...Webb Pierce

May 14, 1955

POP
- BS Cherry Pink And Apple Blossom White [3]...
  Perez "Prez" Prado
- DJ Unchained Melody [1]...Les Baxter
- JB Dance With Me Henry (Wallflower) [1]...
  Georgia Gibbs

R&B
- BS My Babe [4]...Little Walter
- DJ My Babe [1]...Little Walter
- JB Pledging My Love [9]...Johnny Ace

C&W
- BS In The Jailhouse Now [12]...Webb Pierce
- DJ In The Jailhouse Now [11]...Webb Pierce
- JB In The Jailhouse Now [11]...Webb Pierce

May 21, 1955

POP
- BS Cherry Pink And Apple Blossom White [4]...
  Perez "Prez" Prado
- DJ Cherry Pink And Apple Blossom White [1]...
  Perez "Prez" Prado
- JB Dance With Me Henry (Wallflower) [2]...
  Georgia Gibbs

R&B
- BS Unchained Melody [1]...Roy Hamilton
- DJ The Wallflower [3]...Etta James
- JB My Babe [2]...Little Walter

C&W
- BS In The Jailhouse Now [13]...Webb Pierce
- DJ In The Jailhouse Now [12]...Webb Pierce
- JB In The Jailhouse Now [12]...Webb Pierce

May 28, 1955

POP
- BS Cherry Pink And Apple Blossom White [5]...
  Perez "Prez" Prado
- DJ Cherry Pink And Apple Blossom White [2]...
  Perez "Prez" Prado
- JB Dance With Me Henry (Wallflower) [3]...
  Georgia Gibbs

R&B
- BS Unchained Melody [2]...Roy Hamilton
- DJ The Wallflower [4]...Etta James
- JB My Babe [3]...Little Walter

C&W
- BS In The Jailhouse Now [14]...Webb Pierce
- DJ In The Jailhouse Now [13]...Webb Pierce
- JB In The Jailhouse Now [13]...Webb Pierce

June 4, 1955

POP
- BS Cherry Pink And Apple Blossom White [6]...
  Perez "Prez" Prado
- DJ Unchained Melody [2]...Les Baxter
- JB Cherry Pink And Apple Blossom White [1]...
  Perez "Prez" Prado

R&B
- BS Unchained Melody [3]...Roy Hamilton
- DJ My Babe [2]...Little Walter
- JB My Babe [4]...Little Walter

C&W
- BS In The Jailhouse Now [15]...Webb Pierce
- DJ In The Jailhouse Now [14]...Webb Pierce
- JB In The Jailhouse Now [14]...Webb Pierce

June 11, 1955

POP
- BS Cherry Pink And Apple Blossom White [7]...
  Perez "Prez" Prado
- DJ Cherry Pink And Apple Blossom White [3]...
  Perez "Prez" Prado
- JB Cherry Pink And Apple Blossom White [2]...
  Perez "Prez" Prado

R&B
- BS *Ain't That A Shame [1]...Fats Domino
- DJ *Ain't That A Shame [1]...Fats Domino
- JB My Babe [5]...Little Walter

C&W
- BS In The Jailhouse Now [16]...Webb Pierce
- DJ In The Jailhouse Now [15]...Webb Pierce
- JB In The Jailhouse Now [15]...Webb Pierce

June 18, 1955

POP
- BS Cherry Pink And Apple Blossom White [8]...
  Perez "Prez" Prado
- DJ Cherry Pink And Apple Blossom White [4]...
  Perez "Prez" Prado
- JB Cherry Pink And Apple Blossom White [3]...
  Perez "Prez" Prado

R&B
- BS Ain't That A Shame [2]...Fats Domino
- DJ Ain't That A Shame [2]...Fats Domino
- JB Unchained Melody [1]...Al Hibbler

C&W
- BS In The Jailhouse Now [17]...Webb Pierce
- DJ Live Fast, Love Hard, Die Young [1]...Faron Young
- JB In The Jailhouse Now [16]...Webb Pierce

June 25, 1955

POP
- BS Cherry Pink And Apple Blossom White [9]...
  Perez "Prez" Prado
- DJ Cherry Pink And Apple Blossom White [5]...
  Perez "Prez" Prado
- JB Cherry Pink And Apple Blossom White [4]...
  Perez "Prez" Prado

R&B
- BS Ain't That A Shame [3]...Fats Domino
- DJ Ain't That A Shame [3]...Fats Domino
- JB Bo Diddley/I'm A Man [1]...Bo Diddley

C&W
- BS In The Jailhouse Now [18]...Webb Pierce
- DJ Live Fast, Love Hard, Die Young [2]...Faron Young
- JB In The Jailhouse Now [17]...Webb Pierce

July 2, 1955

POP
- BS Cherry Pink And Apple Blossom White [10]...
  Perez "Prez" Prado
- DJ Cherry Pink And Apple Blossom White [6]...
  Perez "Prez" Prado
- JB Cherry Pink And Apple Blossom White [5]...
  Perez "Prez" Prado

R&B
- BS Ain't That A Shame [4]...Fats Domino
- DJ Ain't That A Shame [4]...Fats Domino
- JB Ain't That A Shame [1]...Fats Domino

C&W
- BS In The Jailhouse Now [19]...Webb Pierce
- DJ Live Fast, Love Hard, Die Young [3]...Faron Young
- JB In The Jailhouse Now [18]...Webb Pierce

July 9, 1955

POP
- BS *(We're Gonna) Rock Around The Clock [1]...
  Bill Haley & His Comets
- DJ Learnin' The Blues [1]...Frank Sinatra
- JB Cherry Pink And Apple Blossom White [6]...
  Perez "Prez" Prado

R&B
- BS Ain't That A Shame [5]...Fats Domino
- DJ Ain't That A Shame [5]...Fats Domino
- JB Ain't That A Shame [2]...Fats Domino

C&W
- BS In The Jailhouse Now [20]...Webb Pierce
- DJ A Satisfied Mind [1]...Porter Wagoner
- JB In The Jailhouse Now [19]...Webb Pierce

July 16, 1955

POP
- BS (We're Gonna) Rock Around The Clock [2]...
  Bill Haley & His Comets
- DJ (We're Gonna) Rock Around The Clock [1]...
  Bill Haley & His Comets
- JB Cherry Pink And Apple Blossom White [7]...
  Perez "Prez" Prado

R&B
- BS Ain't That A Shame [6]...Fats Domino
- DJ Ain't That A Shame [6]...Fats Domino
- JB Ain't That A Shame [3]...Fats Domino

C&W
- BS *I Don't Care/Your Good For Nothing Heart [1]...
  Webb Pierce
- DJ A Satisfied Mind [2]...Porter Wagoner
- JB In The Jailhouse Now [20]...Webb Pierce

July 23, 1955

POP
- BS (We're Gonna) Rock Around The Clock [3]...
   Bill Haley & His Comets
- DJ (We're Gonna) Rock Around The Clock [2]...
   Bill Haley & His Comets
- JB Cherry Pink And Apple Blossom White [8]...
   Perez "Prez" Prado

R&B
- BS Ain't That A Shame [7]...Fats Domino
- DJ Ain't That A Shame [7]...Fats Domino
- JB Ain't That A Shame [4]...Fats Domino

C&W
- BS I Don't Care/Your Good For Nothing Heart [2]...
   Webb Pierce
- DJ A Satisfied Mind [3]...Porter Wagoner
- JB In The Jailhouse Now [21]...Webb Pierce

July 30, 1955

POP
- BS (We're Gonna) Rock Around The Clock [4]...
   Bill Haley & His Comets
- DJ Learnin' The Blues [2]...Frank Sinatra
- JB (We're Gonna) Rock Around The Clock [1]...
   Bill Haley & His Comets

R&B
- BS Ain't That A Shame [8]...Fats Domino
- DJ Ain't That A Shame [8]...Fats Domino
- JB Ain't That A Shame [5]...Fats Domino

C&W
- BS I Don't Care [3]...Webb Pierce
- DJ A Satisfied Mind [4]...Porter Wagoner
- JB I Don't Care [1]...Webb Pierce

August 6, 1955

POP
- BS (We're Gonna) Rock Around The Clock [5]...
   Bill Haley & His Comets
- DJ (We're Gonna) Rock Around The Clock [3]...
   Bill Haley & His Comets
- JB (We're Gonna) Rock Around The Clock [2]...
   Bill Haley & His Comets

R&B
- BS Ain't That A Shame [9]...Fats Domino
- DJ A Fool For You [1]...Ray Charles
- JB Bo Diddley [2]...Bo Diddley

C&W
- BS I Don't Care/Your Good For Nothing Heart [4]...
   Webb Pierce
- DJ I Don't Care [1]...Webb Pierce
- JB I Don't Care/Your Good For Nothing Heart [2]...
   Webb Pierce

August 13, 1955

POP
- BS (We're Gonna) Rock Around The Clock [6]...
   Bill Haley & His Comets
- DJ (We're Gonna) Rock Around The Clock [4]...
   Bill Haley & His Comets
- JB (We're Gonna) Rock Around The Clock [3]...
   Bill Haley & His Comets

R&B
- BS Ain't That A Shame [10]...Fats Domino
- DJ Ain't That A Shame [9]...Fats Domino
- JB Ain't That A Shame [6]...Fats Domino

C&W
- BS I Don't Care/Your Good For Nothing Heart [5]...
   Webb Pierce
- DJ I Don't Care [2]...Webb Pierce
- JB I Don't Care/Your Good For Nothing Heart [3]...
   Webb Pierce

August 20, 1955

POP
- BS (We're Gonna) Rock Around The Clock [7]...
   Bill Haley & His Comets
- DJ (We're Gonna) Rock Around The Clock [5]...
   Bill Haley & His Comets
- JB (We're Gonna) Rock Around The Clock [4]...
   Bill Haley & His Comets

R&B
- BS Ain't That A Shame [11]...Fats Domino
- DJ *Maybellene [1]...Chuck Berry } tie
- DJ Ain't That A Shame [10]...Fats Domino
- JB Ain't That A Shame [7]...Fats Domino

C&W
- BS I Don't Care [6]...Webb Pierce
- DJ I Don't Care [3]...Webb Pierce
- JB I Don't Care/Your Good For Nothing Heart [4]...
   Webb Pierce

August 27, 1955

POP
- BS (We're Gonna) Rock Around The Clock [8]...
   Bill Haley & His Comets
- DJ (We're Gonna) Rock Around The Clock [6]...
   Bill Haley & His Comets
- JB (We're Gonna) Rock Around The Clock [5]...
   Bill Haley & His Comets

R&B
- BS Maybellene [1]...Chuck Berry
- DJ Maybellene [2]...Chuck Berry
- JB Ain't That A Shame [8]...Fats Domino

C&W
- BS I Don't Care [7]...Webb Pierce
- DJ I Don't Care [4]...Webb Pierce
- JB I Don't Care [5]...Webb Pierce

September 3, 1955
POP
- BS *The Yellow Rose Of Texas [1]...Mitch Miller
- DJ *The Yellow Rose Of Texas [1]...Mitch Miller
- JB (We're Gonna) Rock Around The Clock [6]...
      Bill Haley & His Comets

R&B
- BS Maybellene [2]...Chuck Berry
- DJ Maybellene [3]...Chuck Berry
- JB Maybellene [1]...Chuck Berry

C&W
- BS I Don't Care [8]...Webb Pierce
- DJ I Don't Care [5]...Webb Pierce
- JB I Don't Care [6]...Webb Pierce

September 10, 1955
POP
- BS The Yellow Rose Of Texas [2]...Mitch Miller
- DJ The Yellow Rose Of Texas [2]...Mitch Miller
- JB (We're Gonna) Rock Around The Clock [7]...
      Bill Haley & His Comets

R&B
- BS Maybellene [3]...Chuck Berry
- DJ Maybellene [4]...Chuck Berry
- JB Maybellene [2]...Chuck Berry

C&W
- BS I Don't Care [9]...Webb Pierce
- DJ I Don't Care [6]...Webb Pierce
- JB I Don't Care [7]...Webb Pierce

September 17, 1955
POP
- BS The Yellow Rose Of Texas [3]...Mitch Miller
- DJ The Yellow Rose Of Texas [3]...Mitch Miller
- JB Ain't That A Shame [1]...Pat Boone

R&B
- BS Maybellene [4]...Chuck Berry
- DJ Maybellene [5]...Chuck Berry
- JB Maybellene [3]...Chuck Berry

C&W
- BS I Don't Care [10]...Webb Pierce
- DJ I Don't Care [7]...Webb Pierce
- JB I Don't Care/Your Good For Nothing Heart [8]...
      Webb Pierce

September 24, 1955
POP
- BS The Yellow Rose Of Texas [4]...Mitch Miller
- DJ The Yellow Rose Of Texas [4]...Mitch Miller
- JB Ain't That A Shame [2]...Pat Boone

R&B
- BS Maybellene [5]...Chuck Berry
- DJ Maybellene [6]...Chuck Berry
- JB Maybellene [4]...Chuck Berry

C&W
- BS I Don't Care [11]...Webb Pierce
- DJ I Don't Care [8]...Webb Pierce
- JB I Don't Care [9]...Webb Pierce

October 1, 1955
POP
- BS The Yellow Rose Of Texas [5]...Mitch Miller
- DJ The Yellow Rose Of Texas [5]...Mitch Miller
- JB The Yellow Rose Of Texas [1]...Mitch Miller

R&B
- BS Maybellene [6]...Chuck Berry
- DJ Maybellene [7]...Chuck Berry
- JB Maybellene [5]...Chuck Berry

C&W
- BS I Don't Care [12]...Webb Pierce
- DJ I Don't Care [9]...Webb Pierce
- JB I Don't Care [10]...Webb Pierce

October 8, 1955
POP
- BS *Love Is A Many-Splendored Thing [1]...Four Aces
- DJ The Yellow Rose Of Texas [6]...Mitch Miller
- JB The Yellow Rose Of Texas [2]...Mitch Miller

R&B
- BS Maybellene [7]...Chuck Berry
- DJ Maybellene [8]...Chuck Berry
- JB Maybellene [6]...Chuck Berry

C&W
- BS The Cattle Call/The Kentuckian Song [1]...
      Eddy Arnold
- DJ I Don't Care [10]...Webb Pierce
- JB I Don't Care [11]...Webb Pierce

October 15, 1955
POP
- BS The Yellow Rose Of Texas [6]...Mitch Miller
- DJ Love Is A Many-Splendored Thing [1]...Four Aces
- JB The Yellow Rose Of Texas [3]...Mitch Miller

R&B
- BS Maybellene [8]...Chuck Berry
- DJ Maybellene [9]...Chuck Berry
- JB Maybellene [7]...Chuck Berry

C&W
- BS The Cattle Call/The Kentuckian Song [2]...Eddy Arnold
- DJ I Don't Care [11]...Webb Pierce
- JB I Don't Care [12]...Webb Pierce

October 22, 1955
POP
- BS Love Is A Many-Splendored Thing [2]...Four Aces
- DJ Love Is A Many-Splendored Thing [2]...Four Aces
- JB The Yellow Rose Of Texas [4]...Mitch Miller

R&B
- BS Maybellene [9]...Chuck Berry
- DJ *Only You (And You Alone) [1]...The Platters
- JB Maybellene [8]...Chuck Berry

C&W
- BS *Love, Love, Love/If You Were Me [1]...Webb Pierce
- DJ I Don't Care [12]...Webb Pierce
- JB That Do Make It Nice/Just Call Me Lonesome [1]...Eddy Arnold

October 29, 1955
POP
- BS Autumn Leaves [1]...Roger Williams
- DJ Love Is A Many-Splendored Thing [3]...Four Aces
- JB The Yellow Rose Of Texas [5]...Mitch Miller

R&B
- BS Only You (And You Alone) [1]...The Platters
- DJ All By Myself [1]...Fats Domino
- JB Maybellene [9]...Chuck Berry

C&W
- BS Love, Love, Love/If You Were Me [2]...Webb Pierce
- DJ Love, Love, Love [1]...Webb Pierce
- JB That Do Make It Nice [2]...Eddy Arnold

November 5, 1955
POP
- BS Autumn Leaves [2]...Roger Williams
- DJ Love Is A Many-Splendored Thing [4]...Four Aces
- JB The Yellow Rose Of Texas [6]...Mitch Miller

R&B
- BS Only You (And You Alone) [2]...The Platters
- DJ All By Myself [2]...Fats Domino
- JB Maybellene [10]...Chuck Berry

C&W
- BS Love, Love, Love/If You Were Me [3]...Webb Pierce
- DJ Love, Love, Love [2]...Webb Pierce
- JB Love, Love, Love/If You Were Me [1]...Webb Pierce

November 12, 1955
POP
- TP Love Is A Many-Splendored Thing [1]...Four Aces
- BS Autumn Leaves [3]...Roger Williams
- DJ Love Is A Many-Splendored Thing [5]...Four Aces
- JB Love Is A Many-Splendored Thing [1]...Four Aces

R&B
- BS Only You (And You Alone) [3]...The Platters
- DJ All By Myself [3]...Fats Domino
- JB Maybellene [11]...Chuck Berry

C&W
- BS Love, Love, Love [4]...Webb Pierce
- DJ Love, Love, Love [3]...Webb Pierce
- JB Love, Love, Love/If You Were Me [2]...Webb Pierce

November 19, 1955
POP
- TP Love Is A Many-Splendored Thing [2]...Four Aces
- BS Autumn Leaves [4]...Roger Williams
- DJ Love Is A Many-Splendored Thing [6]...Four Aces
- JB Love Is A Many-Splendored Thing [2]...Four Aces

R&B
- BS Only You (And You Alone) [4]...The Platters
- DJ Only You (And You Alone) [2]...The Platters
- JB Only You (And You Alone) [1]...The Platters

C&W
- BS Love, Love, Love/If You Were Me [5]...Webb Pierce
- DJ Love, Love, Love [4]...Webb Pierce
- JB Love, Love, Love/If You Were Me [3]...Webb Pierce

November 26, 1955
POP
- TP   Love Is A Many-Splendored Thing [3]...Four Aces
- BS   *Sixteen Tons [1]...Tennessee Ernie Ford
- DJ   *Sixteen Tons [1]...Tennessee Ernie Ford
- JB   Love Is A Many-Splendored Thing [3]...Four Aces

R&B
- BS   Only You (And You Alone) [5]...The Platters
- DJ   Only You (And You Alone) [3]...The Platters
- JB   Only You (And You Alone) [2]...The Platters

C&W
- BS   Love, Love, Love/If You Were Me [6]...Webb Pierce
- DJ   Love, Love, Love [5]...Webb Pierce
- JB   Love, Love, Love/If You Were Me [4]...Webb Pierce

December 3, 1955
POP
- TP   Sixteen Tons [1]...Tennessee Ernie Ford
- BS   Sixteen Tons [2]...Tennessee Ernie Ford
- DJ   Sixteen Tons [2]...Tennessee Ernie Ford
- JB   Sixteen Tons [1]...Tennessee Ernie Ford

R&B
- BS   Only You (And You Alone) [6]...The Platters
- DJ   Only You (And You Alone) [4]...The Platters
- JB   Only You (And You Alone) [3]...The Platters

C&W
- BS   Love, Love, Love/If You Were Me [7]...Webb Pierce
- DJ   Love, Love, Love [6]...Webb Pierce
- JB   Love, Love, Love [5]...Webb Pierce

December 10, 1955
POP
- TP   Sixteen Tons [2]...Tennessee Ernie Ford
- BS   Sixteen Tons [3]...Tennessee Ernie Ford
- DJ   Sixteen Tons [3]...Tennessee Ernie Ford
- JB   Sixteen Tons [2]...Tennessee Ernie Ford

R&B
- BS   Only You (And You Alone) [7]...The Platters
- DJ   Only You (And You Alone) [5]...The Platters
- JB   Only You (And You Alone) [4]...The Platters

C&W
- BS   Love, Love, Love/If You Were Me [8]...Webb Pierce
- DJ   Love, Love, Love [7]...Webb Pierce
- JB   Love, Love, Love/If You Were Me [6]...Webb Pierce

December 17, 1955
POP
- TP   Sixteen Tons [3]...Tennessee Ernie Ford
- BS   Sixteen Tons [4]...Tennessee Ernie Ford
- DJ   Sixteen Tons [4]...Tennessee Ernie Ford
- JB   Sixteen Tons [3]...Tennessee Ernie Ford

R&B
- BS   *Hands Off [1]...Jay McShann
- DJ   *Hands Off [1]...Jay McShann
- JB   Only You (And You Alone) [5]...The Platters

C&W
- BS   Sixteen Tons [1]...Tennessee Ernie Ford
- DJ   Love, Love, Love [8]...Webb Pierce
- JB   Love, Love, Love/If You Were Me [7]...Webb Pierce

December 24, 1955
POP
- TP   Sixteen Tons [4]...Tennessee Ernie Ford
- BS   Sixteen Tons [5]...Tennessee Ernie Ford
- DJ   Sixteen Tons [5]...Tennessee Ernie Ford
- JB   Sixteen Tons [4]...Tennessee Ernie Ford

R&B
- BS   Hands Off [2]...Jay McShann
- DJ   Hands Off [2]...Jay McShann
- JB   Only You (And You Alone) [6]...The Platters

C&W
- BS   Sixteen Tons [2]...Tennessee Ernie Ford
- DJ   Love, Love, Love [9]...Webb Pierce
- JB   Love, Love, Love/If You Were Me [8]...Webb Pierce

December 31, 1955
POP
- TP   Sixteen Tons [5]...Tennessee Ernie Ford
- BS   Sixteen Tons [6]...Tennessee Ernie Ford
- DJ   Sixteen Tons [6]...Tennessee Ernie Ford
- JB   Sixteen Tons [5]...Tennessee Ernie Ford

R&B
- BS   Hands Off [3]...Jay McShann
- DJ   Poor Me [1]...Fats Domino
- JB   Adorable/Steamboat [1]...The Drifters

C&W
- BS   Sixteen Tons [3]...Tennessee Ernie Ford
- DJ   Love, Love, Love [10]...Webb Pierce
- JB   Sixteen Tons [1]...Tennessee Ernie Ford

January 7, 1956

POP
- TP Sixteen Tons [6]...Tennessee Ernie Ford
- BS Sixteen Tons [7]...Tennessee Ernie Ford
- DJ *Memories Are Made Of This [1]...Dean Martin
- JB Sixteen Tons [6]...Tennessee Ernie Ford

R&B
- BS *The Great Pretender [1]...The Platters
- DJ *The Great Pretender [1]...The Platters
- JB At My Front Door [1]...The El Dorados

C&W
- BS Sixteen Tons [4]...Tennessee Ernie Ford
- DJ Sixteen Tons [1]...Tennessee Ernie Ford
- JB Love, Love, Love [9]...Webb Pierce

January 14, 1956

POP
- TP Memories Are Made Of This [1]...Dean Martin
- BS Memories Are Made Of This [1]...Dean Martin
- DJ Memories Are Made Of This [2]...Dean Martin
- JB Sixteen Tons [7]...Tennessee Ernie Ford

R&B
- BS The Great Pretender [2]...The Platters
- DJ The Great Pretender [2]...The Platters
- JB Hands Off [1]...Jay McShann

C&W
- BS Sixteen Tons [5]...Tennessee Ernie Ford
- DJ Love, Love, Love [11]...Webb Pierce
- JB Sixteen Tons [2]...Tennessee Ernie Ford

January 21, 1956

POP
- TP Memories Are Made Of This [2]...Dean Martin
- BS Memories Are Made Of This [2]...Dean Martin
- DJ Memories Are Made Of This [3]...Dean Martin
- JB Sixteen Tons [8]...Tennessee Ernie Ford

R&B
- BS The Great Pretender [3]...The Platters
- DJ The Great Pretender [3]...The Platters
- JB Hands Off [2]...Jay McShann

C&W
- BS Sixteen Tons [6]...Tennessee Ernie Ford
- DJ Sixteen Tons [2]...Tennessee Ernie Ford
- JB Sixteen Tons [3]...Tennessee Ernie Ford

January 28, 1956

POP
- TP Memories Are Made Of This [3]...Dean Martin
- BS Memories Are Made Of This [3]...Dean Martin
- DJ Memories Are Made Of This [4]...Dean Martin
- JB Memories Are Made Of This [1]...Dean Martin

R&B
- BS The Great Pretender [4]...The Platters
- DJ The Great Pretender [4]...The Platters
- JB The Great Pretender [1]...The Platters

C&W
- BS Sixteen Tons [7]...Tennessee Ernie Ford
- DJ Sixteen Tons [3]...Tennessee Ernie Ford
- JB Sixteen Tons [4]...Tennessee Ernie Ford

February 4, 1956

POP
- TP Memories Are Made Of This [4]...Dean Martin
- BS Memories Are Made Of This [4]...Dean Martin
- DJ Memories Are Made Of This [5]...Dean Martin
- JB Memories Are Made Of This [2]...Dean Martin

R&B
- BS The Great Pretender [5]...The Platters
- DJ The Great Pretender [5]...The Platters
- JB The Great Pretender [2]...The Platters

C&W
- BS Sixteen Tons [8]...Tennessee Ernie Ford
- DJ Love, Love, Love [12]...Webb Pierce
- JB Sixteen Tons [5]...Tennessee Ernie Ford

February 11, 1956

POP
- TP Memories Are Made Of This [5]...Dean Martin
- BS Memories Are Made Of This [5]...Dean Martin
- DJ Memories Are Made Of This [6]...Dean Martin
- JB Memories Are Made Of This [3]...Dean Martin

R&B
- BS The Great Pretender [6]...The Platters
- DJ The Great Pretender [6]...The Platters
- JB The Great Pretender [3]...The Platters

C&W
- BS Sixteen Tons [9]...Tennessee Ernie Ford
- DJ *Why Baby Why [1]...Red Sovine & Webb Pierce
- JB Sixteen Tons [6]...Tennessee Ernie Ford

February 18, 1956
POP
- TP   The Great Pretender [1]...The Platters
- BS   *Rock And Roll Waltz [1]...Kay Starr
- DJ   The Great Pretender [1]...The Platters
- JB   Memories Are Made Of This [4]...Dean Martin

R&B
- BS   The Great Pretender [7]...The Platters
- DJ   The Great Pretender [7]...The Platters
- JB   The Great Pretender [4]...The Platters

C&W
- BS   Sixteen Tons [10]...Tennessee Ernie Ford
- DJ   Why Baby Why [2]...Red Sovine & Webb Pierce
- JB   Sixteen Tons [7]...Tennessee Ernie Ford

February 25, 1956
POP
- TP   The Great Pretender [2]...The Platters   ⎫
- TP   Rock And Roll Waltz [1]...Kay Starr   ⎬ tie
- BS   *Lisbon Antigua [1]...Nelson Riddle
- DJ   The Great Pretender [2]...The Platters
- JB   The Great Pretender [1]...The Platters

R&B
- BS   The Great Pretender [8]...The Platters
- DJ   The Great Pretender [8]...The Platters
- JB   The Great Pretender [5]...The Platters

C&W
- BS   *I Forgot To Remember To Forget [1]...Elvis Presley
- DJ   Love, Love, Love [13]...Webb Pierce
- JB   Why Baby Why [1]...Red Sovine & Webb Pierce

March 3, 1956
POP
- TP   Rock And Roll Waltz [2]...Kay Starr
- BS   Lisbon Antigua [2]...Nelson Riddle
- DJ   Lisbon Antigua [1]...Nelson Riddle
- JB   Rock And Roll Waltz [1]...Kay Starr

R&B
- BS   The Great Pretender [9]...The Platters
- DJ   The Great Pretender [9]...The Platters
- JB   The Great Pretender [6]...The Platters

C&W
- BS   I Forgot To Remember To Forget/Mystery Train [2]...Elvis Presley
- DJ   Why Baby Why [3]...Red Sovine & Webb Pierce
- JB   I Forgot To Remember To Forget [1]...Elvis Presley

March 10, 1956
POP
- TP   Rock And Roll Waltz [3]...Kay Starr
- BS   Lisbon Antigua [3]...Nelson Riddle
- DJ   Rock And Roll Waltz [1]...Kay Starr
- JB   Rock And Roll Waltz [2]...Kay Starr

R&B
- BS   The Great Pretender [10]...The Platters
- DJ   The Great Pretender [10]...The Platters
- JB   The Great Pretender [7]...The Platters

C&W
- BS   Why Baby Why [1]...Red Sovine & Webb Pierce
- DJ   Why Baby Why [4]...Red Sovine & Webb Pierce
- JB   I Forgot To Remember To Forget/Mystery Train [2]...Elvis Presley

March 17, 1956
POP
- TP   Rock And Roll Waltz [4]...Kay Starr
- BS   Lisbon Antigua [4]...Nelson Riddle
- DJ   *The Poor People Of Paris [1]...Les Baxter
- JB   Rock And Roll Waltz [3]...Kay Starr

R&B
- BS   *Why Do Fools Fall In Love [1]...Teenagers featuring Frankie Lymon
- DJ   The Great Pretender [11]...The Platters
- JB   The Great Pretender [8]...The Platters

C&W
- BS   *Heartbreak Hotel/I Was The One [1]...Elvis Presley
- DJ   I Don't Believe You've Met My Baby [1]...The Louvin Brothers
- JB   I Forgot To Remember To Forget/Mystery Train [3]...Elvis Presley

March 24, 1956
POP
- TP   The Poor People Of Paris [1]...Les Baxter
- BS   The Poor People Of Paris [1]...Les Baxter
- DJ   The Poor People Of Paris [2]...Les Baxter
- JB   Rock And Roll Waltz [4]...Kay Starr

R&B
- BS   Why Do Fools Fall In Love [2]...Teenagers featuring Frankie Lymon
- DJ   *Drown In My Own Tears [1]...Ray Charles
- JB   The Great Pretender [9]...The Platters

C&W
- BS   Heartbreak Hotel/I Was The One [2]...Elvis Presley
- DJ   I Don't Believe You've Met My Baby [2]...The Louvin Brothers
- JB   I Forgot To Remember To Forget/Mystery Train [4]...Elvis Presley

- LPS   Belafonte [1]...Harry Belafonte

March 31, 1956

POP
- TP The Poor People Of Paris [2]...Les Baxter
- BS The Poor People Of Paris [2]...Les Baxter
- DJ The Poor People Of Paris [3]...Les Baxter
- JB Rock And Roll Waltz [5]...Kay Starr

R&B
- BS Why Do Fools Fall In Love [3]...
     Teenagers featuring Frankie Lymon
- DJ Why Do Fools Fall In Love [1]...
     Teenagers featuring Frankie Lymon
- JB Drown In My Own Tears [1]...Ray Charles

C&W
- BS Heartbreak Hotel/I Was The One [3]...Elvis Presley
- DJ Heartbreak Hotel [1]...Elvis Presley
- JB I Forgot To Remember To Forget/Mystery Train [5]...Elvis Presley

- LPS Belafonte [2]...Harry Belafonte

April 7, 1956

POP
- TP The Poor People Of Paris [3]...Les Baxter
- BS The Poor People Of Paris [3]...Les Baxter
- DJ The Poor People Of Paris [4]...Les Baxter
- JB Rock And Roll Waltz [6]...Kay Starr

R&B
- BS Why Do Fools Fall In Love [4]...
     Teenagers featuring Frankie Lymon
- DJ Why Do Fools Fall In Love [2]...
     Teenagers featuring Frankie Lymon
- JB Drown In My Own Tears [2]...Ray Charles

C&W
- BS Heartbreak Hotel/I Was The One [4]...Elvis Presley
- DJ Heartbreak Hotel [2]...Elvis Presley
- JB Blue Suede Shoes [1]...Carl Perkins } tie
- JB Heartbreak Hotel [1]...Elvis Presley

- LPS Belafonte [3]...Harry Belafonte

April 14, 1956

POP
- TP The Poor People Of Paris [4]...Les Baxter
- BS The Poor People Of Paris [4]...Les Baxter
- DJ Lisbon Antigua [2]...Nelson Riddle
- JB The Poor People Of Paris [1]...Les Baxter

R&B
- BS Why Do Fools Fall In Love [5]...
     Teenagers featuring Frankie Lymon
- DJ *Long Tall Sally [1]...Little Richard
- JB *Long Tall Sally [1]...Little Richard

C&W
- BS Heartbreak Hotel/I Was The One [5]...Elvis Presley
- DJ Heartbreak Hotel [3]...Elvis Presley
- JB Blue Suede Shoes [2]...Carl Perkins

- LPS Belafonte [4]...Harry Belafonte

April 21, 1956

POP
- TP The Poor People Of Paris [5]...Les Baxter
- BS Heartbreak Hotel/I Was The One [1]...Elvis Presley
- DJ The Poor People Of Paris [5]...Les Baxter
- JB The Poor People Of Paris [2]...Les Baxter

R&B
- BS Long Tall Sally/Slippin' And Slidin' (Peepin' And Hidin') [1]...Little Richard
- DJ Long Tall Sally [2]...Little Richard
- JB Long Tall Sally/Slippin' And Slidin' (Peepin' And Hidin') [2]...Little Richard

C&W
- BS Heartbreak Hotel/I Was The One [6]...Elvis Presley
- DJ Heartbreak Hotel [4]...Elvis Presley
- JB Blue Suede Shoes [3]...Carl Perkins

- LPS Belafonte [5]...Harry Belafonte

April 28, 1956

POP
- TP The Poor People Of Paris [6]...Les Baxter
- BS Heartbreak Hotel/I Was The One [2]...Elvis Presley
- DJ The Poor People Of Paris [6]...Les Baxter
- JB The Poor People Of Paris [3]...Les Baxter

R&B
- BS Long Tall Sally/Slippin' And Slidin' (Peepin' And Hidin') [2]...Little Richard
- DJ Long Tall Sally [3]...Little Richard
- JB Long Tall Sally/Slippin' And Slidin' (Peepin' And Hidin') [3]...Little Richard

C&W
- BS Heartbreak Hotel/I Was The One [7]...Elvis Presley
- DJ Heartbreak Hotel [5]...Elvis Presley
- JB Heartbreak Hotel/I Was The One [2]...Elvis Presley

- LPS Belafonte [6]...Harry Belafonte

May 5, 1956

POP
- TP Heartbreak Hotel [1]...Elvis Presley
- BS Heartbreak Hotel [3]...Elvis Presley
- DJ Hot Diggity (Dog Ziggity Boom) [1]...Perry Como
- JB Heartbreak Hotel/I Was The One [1]...Elvis Presley

R&B
- BS Long Tall Sally/Slippin' And Slidin' (Peepin' And Hidin') [3]...Little Richard
- DJ Long Tall Sally [4]...Little Richard
- JB Long Tall Sally/Slippin' And Slidin' (Peepin' And Hidin') [4]...Little Richard

C&W
- BS Heartbreak Hotel/I Was The One [8]...Elvis Presley
- DJ Heartbreak Hotel [6]...Elvis Presley
- JB Heartbreak Hotel/I Was The One [3]...Elvis Presley

- LPS Elvis Presley [1]...Elvis Presley

May 12, 1956

POP
- TP Heartbreak Hotel [2]...Elvis Presley
- BS Heartbreak Hotel [4]...Elvis Presley
- DJ Heartbreak Hotel [1]...Elvis Presley
- JB Heartbreak Hotel [2]...Elvis Presley

R&B
- BS Long Tall Sally/Slippin' And Slidin' (Peepin' And Hidin') [4]...Little Richard
- DJ Long Tall Sally [5]...Little Richard
- JB Long Tall Sally/Slippin' And Slidin' (Peepin' And Hidin') [5]...Little Richard

C&W
- BS Heartbreak Hotel/I Was The One [9]...Elvis Presley
- DJ Heartbreak Hotel [7]...Elvis Presley
- JB Heartbreak Hotel/I Was The One [4]...Elvis Presley

- LPS Elvis Presley [2]...Elvis Presley

May 19, 1956

POP
- TP Heartbreak Hotel [3]...Elvis Presley
- BS Heartbreak Hotel [5]...Elvis Presley
- DJ Heartbreak Hotel [2]...Elvis Presley
- JB Heartbreak Hotel [3]...Elvis Presley

R&B
- BS Long Tall Sally/Slippin' And Slidin' (Peepin' And Hidin') [5]...Little Richard
- DJ *I'm In Love Again [1]...Fats Domino
- JB Long Tall Sally/Slippin' And Slidin' (Peepin' And Hidin') [6]...Little Richard

C&W
- BS Heartbreak Hotel [10]...Elvis Presley
- DJ Heartbreak Hotel [8]...Elvis Presley
- JB Heartbreak Hotel/I Was The One [5]...Elvis Presley

- LPS Elvis Presley [3]...Elvis Presley

May 26, 1956

POP
- TP Heartbreak Hotel [4]...Elvis Presley
- BS Heartbreak Hotel [6]...Elvis Presley
- DJ Heartbreak Hotel [3]...Elvis Presley
- JB Heartbreak Hotel/I Was The One [4]...Elvis Presley

R&B
- BS Long Tall Sally/Slippin' And Slidin' (Peepin' And Hidin') [6]...Little Richard
- DJ I'm In Love Again [2]...Fats Domino
- JB Long Tall Sally/Slippin' And Slidin' (Peepin' And Hidin') [7]...Little Richard

C&W
- BS Heartbreak Hotel/I Was The One [11]...Elvis Presley
- DJ Heartbreak Hotel [9]...Elvis Presley
- JB Heartbreak Hotel/I Was The One [6]...Elvis Presley

- LPS Elvis Presley [4]...Elvis Presley

June 2, 1956

POP
- TP Heartbreak Hotel [5]...Elvis Presley
- BS Heartbreak Hotel [7]...Elvis Presley
- DJ Moonglow and Theme From "Picnic" [1]...Morris Stoloff
- JB Heartbreak Hotel [5]...Elvis Presley

R&B
- BS I'm In Love Again/My Blue Heaven [1]...Fats Domino
- DJ I'm In Love Again [3]...Fats Domino
- JB Long Tall Sally/Slippin' And Slidin' (Peepin' And Hidin') [8]...Little Richard

C&W
- BS Heartbreak Hotel/I Was The One [12]...Elvis Presley
- DJ Heartbreak Hotel [10]...Elvis Presley
- JB Heartbreak Hotel/I Was The One [7]...Elvis Presley

- LPS Elvis Presley [5]...Elvis Presley

June 9, 1956

POP
- TP Heartbreak Hotel [6]...Elvis Presley
- BS Heartbreak Hotel [8]...Elvis Presley
- DJ Moonglow and Theme From "Picnic" [2]...Morris Stoloff
- JB Heartbreak Hotel [6]...Elvis Presley

R&B
- BS I'm In Love Again/My Blue Heaven [2]...Fats Domino
- DJ I'm In Love Again [4]...Fats Domino
- JB I'm In Love Again/My Blue Heaven [1]...Fats Domino

C&W
- BS Heartbreak Hotel/I Was The One [13]...Elvis Presley
- DJ Heartbreak Hotel [11]...Elvis Presley
- JB Heartbreak Hotel/I Was The One [8]...Elvis Presley

- LPS Elvis Presley [6]...Elvis Presley

June 16, 1956

POP
- TP *The Wayward Wind [1]...Gogi Grant ⎱ tie
- TP Heartbreak Hotel [7]...Elvis Presley ⎰
- BS *The Wayward Wind [1]...Gogi Grant
- DJ Moonglow and Theme From "Picnic" [3]...Morris Stoloff
- JB Heartbreak Hotel [7]...Elvis Presley

R&B
- BS I'm In Love Again/My Blue Heaven [3]...Fats Domino
- DJ I'm In Love Again [5]...Fats Domino
- JB I'm In Love Again [2]...Fats Domino

C&W
- BS Heartbreak Hotel [14]...Elvis Presley
- DJ Heartbreak Hotel [12]...Elvis Presley
- JB Heartbreak Hotel/I Was The One [9]...Elvis Presley

- LPS Elvis Presley [7]...Elvis Presley

June 23, 1956

POP
- TP The Wayward Wind [2]...Gogi Grant
- BS The Wayward Wind [2]...Gogi Grant
- DJ The Wayward Wind [1]...Gogi Grant
- JB Heartbreak Hotel [8]...Elvis Presley

R&B
- BS I'm In Love Again/My Blue Heaven [4]...Fats Domino
- DJ I'm In Love Again [6]...Fats Domino
- JB I'm In Love Again/My Blue Heaven [3]...Fats Domino

C&W
- BS Heartbreak Hotel/I Was The One [15]...Elvis Presley
- DJ *Crazy Arms [1]...Ray Price
- JB Heartbreak Hotel/I Was The One [10]...Elvis Presley

- LPS Elvis Presley [8]...Elvis Presley

June 30, 1956

POP
- TP The Wayward Wind [3]...Gogi Grant
- BS The Wayward Wind [3]...Gogi Grant
- DJ The Wayward Wind [2]...Gogi Grant
- JB The Wayward Wind [1]...Gogi Grant

R&B
- BS I'm In Love Again/My Blue Heaven [5]...Fats Domino
- DJ I'm In Love Again [7]...Fats Domino
- JB I'm In Love Again/My Blue Heaven [4]...Fats Domino

C&W
- BS Heartbreak Hotel/I Was The One [16]...Elvis Presley
- DJ Crazy Arms [2]...Ray Price
- JB Heartbreak Hotel/I Was The One [11]...Elvis Presley

- LPS Elvis Presley [9]...Elvis Presley

July 7, 1956

POP
- TP The Wayward Wind [4]...Gogi Grant
- BS The Wayward Wind [4]...Gogi Grant
- DJ The Wayward Wind [3]...Gogi Grant
- JB The Wayward Wind [2]...Gogi Grant

R&B
- BS I'm In Love Again [6]...Fats Domino
- DJ I'm In Love Again [8]...Fats Domino
- JB I'm In Love Again/My Blue Heaven [5]...Fats Domino

C&W
- BS Heartbreak Hotel [17]...Elvis Presley
- DJ Crazy Arms [3]...Ray Price
- JB Heartbreak Hotel/I Was The One [12]...Elvis Presley

- LPS Elvis Presley [10]...Elvis Presley

July 14, 1956

POP
- TP The Wayward Wind [5]...Gogi Grant
- BS The Wayward Wind [5]...Gogi Grant
- DJ The Wayward Wind [4]...Gogi Grant
- JB The Wayward Wind [3]...Gogi Grant

R&B
- BS I'm In Love Again/My Blue Heaven [7]...Fats Domino
- DJ I'm In Love Again [9]...Fats Domino
- JB I'm In Love Again/My Blue Heaven [6]...Fats Domino

C&W
- BS *I Want You, I Need You, I Love You/My Baby Left Me [1]...Elvis Presley
- DJ Crazy Arms [4]...Ray Price
- JB Heartbreak Hotel/I Was The One [13]...Elvis Presley

- LPS My Fair Lady [1]...Original Cast

July 21, 1956

POP
- TP The Wayward Wind [6]...Gogi Grant
- BS The Wayward Wind [6]...Gogi Grant
- DJ The Wayward Wind [5]...Gogi Grant
- JB The Wayward Wind [4]...Gogi Grant

R&B
- BS *Fever [1]...Little Willie John
- DJ *Fever [1]...Little Willie John
- JB I'm In Love Again/My Blue Heaven [7]...Fats Domino

C&W
- BS I Want You, I Need You, I Love You [2]...Elvis Presley
- DJ Crazy Arms [5]...Ray Price
- JB *I Walk The Line/Get Rhythm [1]...Johnny Cash

- LPS My Fair Lady [2]...Original Cast

July 28, 1956

POP
- TP The Wayward Wind [7]...Gogi Grant
- BS I Want You, I Need You, I Love You/My Baby Left Me [1]...Elvis Presley
- DJ The Wayward Wind [6]...Gogi Grant
- JB *I Almost Lost My Mind [1]...Pat Boone

R&B
- BS Fever [2]...Little Willie John
- DJ Fever [2]...Little Willie John
- JB Treasure Of Love [1]...Clyde McPhatter

C&W
- BS Crazy Arms/You Done Me Wrong [1]...Ray Price
- DJ Crazy Arms [6]...Ray Price
- JB Crazy Arms/You Done Me Wrong [1]...Ray Price

- LPS My Fair Lady [3]...Original Cast

August 4, 1956

POP
- TP I Almost Lost My Mind [1]...Pat Boone
- BS *My Prayer/Heaven On Earth [1]...The Platters
- DJ The Wayward Wind [7]...Gogi Grant
- JB I Almost Lost My Mind [2]...Pat Boone

R&B
- BS *Rip It Up [1]...Little Richard
- DJ Fever [3]...Little Willie John
- JB I'm In Love Again/My Blue Heaven [8]...Fats Domino } tie
- JB *Rip It Up/Ready Teddy [1]...Little Richard

C&W
- BS Crazy Arms [2]...Ray Price
- DJ Crazy Arms [7]...Ray Price
- JB I Walk The Line/Get Rhythm [2]...Johnny Cash

- LPS My Fair Lady [4]...Original Cast

August 11, 1956

POP
- TP I Almost Lost My Mind [2]...Pat Boone
- BS My Prayer/Heaven On Earth [2]...The Platters
- DJ The Wayward Wind [8]...Gogi Grant
- JB I Almost Lost My Mind [3]...Pat Boone

R&B
- BS Rip It Up/Ready Teddy [2]...Little Richard
- DJ Fever [4]...Little Willie John
- JB I'm In Love Again/My Blue Heaven [9]...Fats Domino

C&W
- BS Crazy Arms [3]...Ray Price
- DJ Crazy Arms [8]...Ray Price
- JB I Want You, I Need You, I Love You/My Baby Left Me [1]...Elvis Presley

- LPS My Fair Lady [5]...Original Cast

August 18, 1956

POP
- TP My Prayer [1]...The Platters
- BS *Hound Dog/Don't Be Cruel [1]...Elvis Presley
- DJ My Prayer [1]...The Platters
- JB I Almost Lost My Mind [4]...Pat Boone

R&B
- BS Fever [3]...Little Willie John
- DJ Fever [5]...Little Willie John
- JB My Prayer [1]...The Platters

C&W
- BS Crazy Arms [4]...Ray Price
- DJ Crazy Arms [9]...Ray Price
- JB I Walk The Line [3]...Johnny Cash

- LPS My Fair Lady [6]...Original Cast

August 25, 1956

POP
- TP My Prayer [2]...The Platters
- BS Hound Dog/Don't Be Cruel [2]...Elvis Presley
- DJ My Prayer [2]...The Platters
- JB My Prayer [1]...The Platters

R&B
- BS *Honky Tonk (Parts 1 & 2) [1]...Bill Doggett
- DJ My Prayer [1]...The Platters
- JB My Prayer [2]...The Platters

C&W
- BS Crazy Arms [5]...Ray Price
- DJ Crazy Arms [10]...Ray Price
- JB I Walk The Line/Get Rhythm [4]...Johnny Cash

- LPS My Fair Lady [7]...Original Cast

September 1, 1956

POP
- TP My Prayer [3]...The Platters
- BS Hound Dog/Don't Be Cruel [3]...Elvis Presley
- DJ My Prayer [3]...The Platters
- JB Hound Dog/Don't Be Cruel [1]...Elvis Presley

R&B
- BS Honky Tonk (Parts 1 & 2) [2]...Bill Doggett
- DJ *Let The Good Times Roll [1]...Shirley & Lee
- JB Fever [1]...Little Willie John

C&W
- BS Crazy Arms [6]...Ray Price
- DJ Crazy Arms [11]...Ray Price
- JB I Walk The Line/Get Rhythm [5]...Johnny Cash

- LPS My Fair Lady [8]...Original Cast

September 8, 1956

POP
- TP My Prayer [4]...The Platters
- BS Hound Dog/Don't Be Cruel [4]...Elvis Presley
- DJ Don't Be Cruel [1]...Elvis Presley
- JB Hound Dog/Don't Be Cruel [2]...Elvis Presley

R&B
- BS Honky Tonk (Parts 1 & 2) [3]...Bill Doggett
- DJ My Prayer [2]...The Platters
- JB Let The Good Times Roll [1]...Shirley & Lee

C&W
- BS Crazy Arms [7]...Ray Price
- DJ Crazy Arms [12]...Ray Price
- JB I Walk The Line/Get Rhythm [6]...Johnny Cash

- LPS Calypso [1]...Harry Belafonte

September 15, 1956

POP
- TP My Prayer [5]...The Platters ⎫
- TP Don't Be Cruel [1]...Elvis Presley ⎬ tie
- BS Hound Dog/Don't Be Cruel [5]...Elvis Presley
- DJ Don't Be Cruel [2]...Elvis Presley
- JB Hound Dog/Don't Be Cruel [3]...Elvis Presley

R&B
- BS Honky Tonk (Parts 1 & 2) [4]...Bill Doggett
- DJ Let The Good Times Roll [2]...Shirley & Lee
- JB Hound Dog/Don't Be Cruel [1]...Elvis Presley

C&W
- BS Crazy Arms [8]...Ray Price
- DJ Crazy Arms [13]...Ray Price
- JB Hound Dog/Don't Be Cruel [1]...Elvis Presley

- LPS Calypso [2]...Harry Belafonte

September 22, 1956

POP
- TP Don't Be Cruel [2]...Elvis Presley
- BS Don't Be Cruel [6]...Elvis Presley
- DJ Don't Be Cruel [3]...Elvis Presley
- JB Don't Be Cruel/Hound Dog [4]...Elvis Presley

R&B
- BS Honky Tonk (Parts 1 & 2) [5]...Bill Doggett
- DJ Let The Good Times Roll [3]...Shirley & Lee
- JB Hound Dog [2]...Elvis Presley

C&W
- BS Crazy Arms [9]...Ray Price
- DJ Crazy Arms [14]...Ray Price
- JB Hound Dog/Don't Be Cruel [2]...Elvis Presley

- LPS Calypso [3]...Harry Belafonte

September 29, 1956

POP
- TP Don't Be Cruel [3]...Elvis Presley
- BS Don't Be Cruel/Hound Dog [7]...Elvis Presley
- DJ Don't Be Cruel [4]...Elvis Presley
- JB Hound Dog/Don't Be Cruel [5]...Elvis Presley

R&B
- BS Honky Tonk (Parts 1 & 2) [6]...Bill Doggett
- DJ Honky Tonk (Parts 1 & 2) [1]...Bill Doggett
- JB Don't Be Cruel/Hound Dog [3]...Elvis Presley

C&W
- BS Don't Be Cruel/Hound Dog [1]...Elvis Presley
- DJ Crazy Arms [15]...Ray Price
- JB Don't Be Cruel/Hound Dog [3]...Elvis Presley

- LPS Calypso [4]...Harry Belafonte

October 6, 1956

POP
- TP Don't Be Cruel [4]...Elvis Presley
- BS Don't Be Cruel/Hound Dog [8]...Elvis Presley
- DJ Don't Be Cruel [5]...Elvis Presley
- JB Don't Be Cruel/Hound Dog [6]...Elvis Presley

R&B
- BS Honky Tonk (Parts 1 & 2) [7]...Bill Doggett
- DJ Honky Tonk (Parts 1 & 2) [2]...Bill Doggett
- JB Hound Dog/Don't Be Cruel [4]...Elvis Presley

C&W
- BS Don't Be Cruel/Hound Dog [2]...Elvis Presley
- DJ Crazy Arms [16]...Ray Price
- JB Hound Dog/Don't Be Cruel [4]...Elvis Presley

- LPS The King And I [1]...Soundtrack

October 13, 1956

POP
- TP Don't Be Cruel [5]...Elvis Presley
- BS Don't Be Cruel/Hound Dog [9]...Elvis Presley
- DJ Don't Be Cruel [6]...Elvis Presley
- JB Don't Be Cruel/Hound Dog [7]...Elvis Presley

R&B
- BS Honky Tonk (Parts 1 & 2) [8]...Bill Doggett
- DJ Honky Tonk (Parts 1 & 2) [3]...Bill Doggett
- JB Let The Good Times Roll [2]...Shirley & Lee

C&W
- BS Don't Be Cruel/Hound Dog [3]...Elvis Presley
- DJ Crazy Arms [17]...Ray Price
- JB Don't Be Cruel/Hound Dog [5]...Elvis Presley

- LPS The Eddy Duchin Story [1]...
        Carmen Cavallaro/Soundtrack

October 20, 1956

POP
- TP Don't Be Cruel [6]...Elvis Presley
- BS Don't Be Cruel/Hound Dog [10]...Elvis Presley
- DJ Don't Be Cruel [7]...Elvis Presley
- JB Don't Be Cruel/Hound Dog [8]...Elvis Presley

R&B
- BS Honky Tonk (Parts 1 & 2) [9]...Bill Doggett
- DJ Honky Tonk (Parts 1 & 2) [4]...Bill Doggett
- JB Honky Tonk (Parts 1 & 2) [1]...Bill Doggett

C&W
- BS Don't Be Cruel/Hound Dog [4]...Elvis Presley
- DJ Crazy Arms [18]...Ray Price
- JB Don't Be Cruel/Hound Dog [6]...Elvis Presley

- LPS Calypso [5]...Harry Belafonte

October 27, 1956

POP
- TP Don't Be Cruel [7]...Elvis Presley
- BS Don't Be Cruel/Hound Dog [11]...Elvis Presley
- DJ Don't Be Cruel [8]...Elvis Presley
- JB Don't Be Cruel/Hound Dog [9]...Elvis Presley

R&B
- BS Don't Be Cruel/Hound Dog [1]...Elvis Presley
- DJ Honky Tonk (Parts 1 & 2) [5]...Bill Doggett
- JB Hound Dog/Don't Be Cruel [5]...Elvis Presley

C&W
- BS Don't Be Cruel/Hound Dog [5]...Elvis Presley
- DJ I Walk The Line [1]...Johnny Cash
- JB Don't Be Cruel/Hound Dog [7]...Elvis Presley

- LPS Calypso [6]...Harry Belafonte

November 3, 1956

POP
- TP *The Green Door [1]...Jim Lowe
- BS *Love Me Tender [1]...Elvis Presley
- DJ *Love Me Tender [1]...Elvis Presley
- JB Don't Be Cruel/Hound Dog [10]...Elvis Presley

R&B
- BS Honky Tonk (Parts 1 & 2) [10]...Bill Doggett
- DJ *Blueberry Hill [1]...Fats Domino
- JB *Blueberry Hill [1]...Fats Domino
- JB Don't Be Cruel/Hound Dog [6]...Elvis Presley } tie

C&W
- BS Crazy Arms [10]...Ray Price
- DJ Crazy Arms [19]...Ray Price
- JB Don't Be Cruel/Hound Dog [8]...Elvis Presley

- LPS Calypso [7]...Harry Belafonte

November 10, 1956

POP
- TP The Green Door [2]...Jim Lowe
- BS Love Me Tender/Anyway You Want Me (That's How I Will Be) [2]...Elvis Presley
- DJ Love Me Tender [2]...Elvis Presley
- JB Don't Be Cruel/Hound Dog [11]...Elvis Presley

R&B
- BS Honky Tonk (Parts 1 & 2) [11]...Bill Doggett
- DJ Blueberry Hill [2]...Fats Domino
- JB Blueberry Hill [2]...Fats Domino

C&W
- BS Crazy Arms [11]...Ray Price
- DJ *Singing The Blues [1]...Marty Robbins
- JB Don't Be Cruel/Hound Dog [9]...Elvis Presley

- LPS Calypso [8]...Harry Belafonte

November 17, 1956

POP
- TP The Green Door [3]...Jim Lowe
- TP Love Me Tender [1]...Elvis Presley } tie
- BS Love Me Tender/Anyway You Want Me (That's How I Will Be) [3]...Elvis Presley
- DJ Love Me Tender [3]...Elvis Presley
- JB The Green Door [1]...Jim Lowe

R&B
- BS Honky Tonk (Parts 1 & 2) [12]...Bill Doggett
- DJ Blueberry Hill [3]...Fats Domino
- JB Let The Good Times Roll [3]...Shirley & Lee

C&W
- BS Singing The Blues [1]...Marty Robbins
- DJ Crazy Arms [20]...Ray Price
- JB Don't Be Cruel/Hound Dog [10]...Elvis Presley

- LPS Calypso [9]...Harry Belafonte

November 24, 1956

POP
- TP Love Me Tender [2]...Elvis Presley
- BS Love Me Tender [4]...Elvis Presley
- DJ Love Me Tender [4]...Elvis Presley
- JB The Green Door [2]...Jim Lowe

R&B
- BS Blueberry Hill [1]...Fats Domino
- DJ Blueberry Hill [4]...Fats Domino
- JB Blueberry Hill [3]...Fats Domino

C&W
- BS Singing The Blues [2]...Marty Robbins
- DJ Singing The Blues [2]...Marty Robbins
- JB Singing The Blues [1]...Marty Robbins

- LPS Calypso [10]...Harry Belafonte

December 1, 1956

POP
- TP Love Me Tender [3]...Elvis Presley
- BS Love Me Tender [5]...Elvis Presley
- DJ Love Me Tender [5]...Elvis Presley
- JB The Green Door [3]...Jim Lowe

R&B
- BS Honky Tonk (Parts 1 & 2) [13]...Bill Doggett
- DJ Blueberry Hill [5]...Fats Domino
- JB Blueberry Hill [4]...Fats Domino

C&W
- BS Singing The Blues [3]...Marty Robbins
- DJ Singing The Blues [3]...Marty Robbins
- JB Singing The Blues [2]...Marty Robbins

- LPS Calypso [11]...Harry Belafonte

December 8, 1956
POP
- TP *Singing The Blues [1]...Guy Mitchell
- BS *Singing The Blues [1]...Guy Mitchell
- DJ *Singing The Blues [1]...Guy Mitchell
- JB Love Me Tender/Anyway You Want Me (That's How I Will Be) [1]...Elvis Presley

R&B
- BS Blueberry Hill [2]...Fats Domino
- DJ Blueberry Hill [6]...Fats Domino
- JB Blueberry Hill [5]...Fats Domino

C&W
- BS Singing The Blues [4]...Marty Robbins
- DJ Singing The Blues [4]...Marty Robbins
- JB Singing The Blues [3]...Marty Robbins

LPS Elvis [1]...Elvis Presley

December 15, 1956
POP
- TP Singing The Blues [2]...Guy Mitchell
- BS Singing The Blues [2]...Guy Mitchell
- DJ Singing The Blues [2]...Guy Mitchell
- JB Singing The Blues [1]...Guy Mitchell

R&B
- BS Blueberry Hill [3]...Fats Domino
- DJ Blueberry Hill [7]...Fats Domino
- JB Blueberry Hill [6]...Fats Domino

C&W
- BS Singing The Blues [5]...Marty Robbins
- DJ Singing The Blues [5]...Marty Robbins
- JB Singing The Blues [4]...Marty Robbins

LPS Elvis [2]...Elvis Presley

December 22, 1956
POP
- TP Singing The Blues [3]...Guy Mitchell } tie
- TP Love Me Tender [4]...Elvis Presley
- BS Singing The Blues [3]...Guy Mitchell
- DJ Singing The Blues [3]...Guy Mitchell
- JB Singing The Blues [2]...Guy Mitchell

R&B
- BS Blueberry Hill [4]...Fats Domino
- DJ Blueberry Hill [8]...Fats Domino
- JB Blueberry Hill [7]...Fats Domino

C&W
- BS Singing The Blues [6]...Marty Robbins
- DJ Singing The Blues [6]...Marty Robbins
- JB Singing The Blues [5]...Marty Robbins

LPS Elvis [3]...Elvis Presley

December 29, 1956
POP
- TP Singing The Blues [4]...Guy Mitchell
- BS Singing The Blues [4]...Guy Mitchell
- DJ Singing The Blues [4]...Guy Mitchell
- JB Singing The Blues [3]...Guy Mitchell

R&B
- BS Blueberry Hill [5]...Fats Domino
- DJ Blueberry Hill [9]...Fats Domino
- JB Blueberry Hill [8]...Fats Domino

C&W
- BS Singing The Blues [7]...Marty Robbins
- DJ Singing The Blues [7]...Marty Robbins
- JB Singing The Blues [6]...Marty Robbins

LPS Elvis [4]...Elvis Presley

January 5, 1957
POP
- TP Singing The Blues [5]...Guy Mitchell
- BS Singing The Blues [5]...Guy Mitchell
- DJ Singing The Blues [5]...Guy Mitchell
- JB Singing The Blues [4]...Guy Mitchell

R&B
- BS Blueberry Hill [6]...Fats Domino
- DJ Blueberry Hill [10]...Fats Domino
- JB *Since I Met You Baby [1]...Ivory Joe Hunter

C&W
- BS Singing The Blues [8]...Marty Robbins
- DJ Singing The Blues [8]...Marty Robbins
- JB Singing The Blues [7]...Marty Robbins

LPS Elvis [5]...Elvis Presley

January 12, 1957
POP
- TP Singing The Blues [6]...Guy Mitchell
- BS Singing The Blues [6]...Guy Mitchell
- DJ Singing The Blues [6]...Guy Mitchell
- JB Singing The Blues [5]...Guy Mitchell

R&B
- BS Blueberry Hill [7]...Fats Domino
- DJ Since I Met You Baby [1]...Ivory Joe Hunter
- JB Since I Met You Baby [2]...Ivory Joe Hunter

C&W
- BS Singing The Blues [9]...Marty Robbins
- DJ Singing The Blues [9]...Marty Robbins
- JB Singing The Blues [8]...Marty Robbins

LPS Calypso [12]...Harry Belafonte

January 19, 1957

POP
- TP Singing The Blues [7]...Guy Mitchell
- BS Singing The Blues [7]...Guy Mitchell
- DJ Singing The Blues [7]...Guy Mitchell
- JB Singing The Blues [6]...Guy Mitchell

R&B
- BS Blueberry Hill [8]...Fats Domino
- DJ Blueberry Hill [11]...Fats Domino
- JB Since I Met You Baby [3]...Ivory Joe Hunter

C&W
- BS Singing The Blues [10]...Marty Robbins
- DJ Singing The Blues [10]...Marty Robbins
- JB Singing The Blues [9]...Marty Robbins

LPS Calypso [13]...Harry Belafonte

January 26, 1957

POP
- TP Singing The Blues [8]...Guy Mitchell
- BS Singing The Blues [8]...Guy Mitchell
- DJ Singing The Blues [8]...Guy Mitchell
- JB Singing The Blues [7]...Guy Mitchell

R&B
- BS *Blue Monday/What's The Reason I'm Not Pleasing You [1]...Fats Domino
- DJ *Blue Monday [1]...Fats Domino
- JB *Blue Monday/What's The Reason I'm Not Pleasing You [1]...Fats Domino

C&W
- BS Singing The Blues [11]...Marty Robbins
- DJ Singing The Blues [11]...Marty Robbins
- JB Singing The Blues [10]...Marty Robbins

LPS Calypso [14]...Harry Belafonte

February 2, 1957

POP
- TP Singing The Blues [9]...Guy Mitchell
- BS Singing The Blues [9]...Guy Mitchell
- DJ Singing The Blues [9]...Guy Mitchell
- JB Singing The Blues [8]...Guy Mitchell

R&B
- BS Blue Monday/What's The Reason I'm Not Pleasing You [2]...Fats Domino
- DJ Blue Monday [2]...Fats Domino
- JB Blue Monday/What's The Reason I'm Not Pleasing You [2]...Fats Domino

C&W
- BS Singing The Blues [12]...Marty Robbins
- DJ *Young Love [1]...Sonny James
- JB Singing The Blues [11]...Marty Robbins

LPS Calypso [15]...Harry Belafonte

February 9, 1957

POP
- TP *Don't Forbid Me [1]...Pat Boone
- BS *Too Much/Playing For Keeps [1]...Elvis Presley
- DJ Young Love [1]...Sonny James
- JB Singing The Blues [9]...Guy Mitchell

R&B
- BS Blue Monday [3]...Fats Domino
- DJ Blue Monday [3]...Fats Domino
- JB Blue Monday [3]...Fats Domino

C&W
- BS Singing The Blues [13]...Marty Robbins
- DJ Young Love [2]...Sonny James
- JB Singing The Blues [12]...Marty Robbins

LPS Calypso [16]...Harry Belafonte

February 16, 1957

POP
- TP *Young Love [1]...Tab Hunter
- BS Too Much [2]...Elvis Presley
- DJ *Young Love [1]...Tab Hunter
- JB Singing The Blues [10]...Guy Mitchell

R&B
- BS Blue Monday [4]...Fats Domino
- DJ Blue Monday [4]...Fats Domino
- JB Blue Monday [4]...Fats Domino

C&W
- BS Young Love [1]...Sonny James
- DJ Young Love [3]...Sonny James
- JB Singing The Blues [13]...Marty Robbins

LPS Calypso [17]...Harry Belafonte

February 23, 1957

POP
- TP Young Love [2]...Tab Hunter
- BS Too Much [3]...Elvis Presley
- DJ Young Love [2]...Tab Hunter
- JB Don't Forbid Me [1]...Pat Boone

R&B
- BS Blue Monday [5]...Fats Domino
- DJ Blue Monday [5]...Fats Domino
- JB Blue Monday [5]...Fats Domino

C&W
- BS Young Love [2]...Sonny James
- DJ Young Love [4]...Sonny James
- JB Young Love [1]...Sonny James

LPS Calypso [18]...Harry Belafonte

March 2, 1957

POP
- TP   Young Love [3]...Tab Hunter
- BS   Young Love [1]...Tab Hunter
- DJ   Young Love [3]...Tab Hunter
- JB   Young Love [1]...Tab Hunter

R&B
- BS   Blue Monday [6]...Fats Domino
- DJ   Blue Monday [6]...Fats Domino
- JB   Blue Monday [6]...Fats Domino

C&W
- BS   Young Love [3]...Sonny James
- DJ   Young Love [5]...Sonny James
- JB   There You Go/Train Of Love [1]...Johnny Cash

- LPS   Calypso [19]...Harry Belafonte

March 9, 1957

POP
- TP   Young Love [4]...Tab Hunter
- BS   Young Love [2]...Tab Hunter
- DJ   Young Love [4]...Tab Hunter
- JB   Too Much/Playing For Keeps [1]...Elvis Presley

R&B
- BS   Blue Monday [7]...Fats Domino
- DJ   Jim Dandy [1]...LaVern Baker & The Gliders } tie
- DJ   Blue Monday [7]...Fats Domino
- JB   Blue Monday/What's The Reason I'm Not Pleasing You [7]...Fats Domino

C&W
- BS   Young Love [4]...Sonny James
- DJ   Young Love [6]...Sonny James
- JB   There You Go/Train Of Love [2]...Johnny Cash

- LPS   Calypso [20]...Harry Belafonte

March 16, 1957

POP
- TP   Young Love [5]...Tab Hunter
- BS   Young Love [3]...Tab Hunter
- DJ   Young Love [5]...Tab Hunter
- JB   Young Love [2]...Tab Hunter

R&B
- BS   Blue Monday [8]...Fats Domino
- DJ   Love Is Strange [1]...Mickey & Sylvia
- JB   Blue Monday/What's The Reason I'm Not Pleasing You [8]...Fats Domino

C&W
- BS   Young Love/You're The Reason I'm In Love [5]...Sonny James
- DJ   Young Love [7]...Sonny James
- JB   Young Love [2]...Sonny James

- LPS   Calypso [21]...Harry Belafonte

March 23, 1957

POP
- TP   Young Love [6]...Tab Hunter
- BS   Young Love [4]...Tab Hunter
- DJ   Young Love [6]...Tab Hunter
- JB   Young Love [3]...Tab Hunter

R&B
- BS   *I'm Walkin' [1]...Fats Domino
- DJ   Love Is Strange [2]...Mickey & Sylvia
- JB   *I'm Walkin' [1]...Fats Domino

C&W
- BS   Young Love/You're The Reason I'm In Love [6]...Sonny James
- DJ   Young Love [8]...Sonny James
- JB   Young Love [3]...Sonny James

- LPS   Calypso [22]...Harry Belafonte

March 30, 1957

POP
- TP   *Butterfly [1]...Andy Williams
- BS   Party Doll [1]...Buddy Knox
- DJ   *Butterfly [1]...Andy Williams
- JB   Young Love [4]...Tab Hunter

R&B
- BS   I'm Walkin' [2]...Fats Domino
- DJ   I'm Walkin' [1]...Fats Domino
- JB   I'm Walkin' [2]...Fats Domino

C&W
- BS   Young Love/You're The Reason I'm In Love [7]...Sonny James
- DJ   Young Love [9]...Sonny James
- JB   There You Go [3]...Johnny Cash

- LPS   Calypso [23]...Harry Belafonte

April 6, 1957

POP
- TP   Butterfly [2]...Andy Williams
- BS   *Round And Round [1]...Perry Como
- DJ   Butterfly [2]...Andy Williams
- JB   Young Love [5]...Tab Hunter

R&B
- BS   I'm Walkin' [3]...Fats Domino
- DJ   I'm Walkin' [2]...Fats Domino
- JB   I'm Walkin' [3]...Fats Domino

C&W
- BS   *Gone [1]...Ferlin Husky
- DJ   *Gone [1]...Ferlin Husky
- JB   There You Go/Train Of Love [4]...Johnny Cash

- LPS   Calypso [24]...Harry Belafonte

April 13, 1957

POP
- TP Butterfly [3]...Andy Williams
- BS *All Shook Up [1]...Elvis Presley
- DJ Round And Round [1]...Perry Como
- JB Butterfly [1]...Charlie Gracie

R&B
- BS I'm Walkin' [4]...Fats Domino
- DJ I'm Walkin' [3]...Fats Domino
- JB I'm Walkin' [4]...Fats Domino

C&W
- BS Gone [2]...Ferlin Husky
- DJ Gone [2]...Ferlin Husky
- JB There You Go/Train Of Love [5]...Johnny Cash

- LPS Calypso [25]...Harry Belafonte

April 20, 1957

POP
- TP Round And Round [1]...Perry Como } tie
- TP All Shook Up [1]...Elvis Presley
- BS All Shook Up [2]...Elvis Presley
- DJ Round And Round [2]...Perry Como
- JB Butterfly [2]...Charlie Gracie

R&B
- BS I'm Walkin' [5]...Fats Domino
- DJ I'm Walkin' [4]...Fats Domino
- JB I'm Walkin' [5]...Fats Domino

C&W
- BS Gone [3]...Ferlin Husky
- DJ Gone [3]...Ferlin Husky
- JB Gone [1]...Ferlin Husky

- LPS Calypso [26]...Harry Belafonte

April 27, 1957

POP
- TP All Shook Up [2]...Elvis Presley
- BS All Shook Up [3]...Elvis Presley
- DJ All Shook Up [1]...Elvis Presley
- JB All Shook Up [1]...Elvis Presley

R&B
- BS I'm Walkin' [6]...Fats Domino
- DJ I'm Walkin' [5]...Fats Domino
- JB Lucille/Send Me Some Lovin' [1]...Little Richard

C&W
- BS Gone [4]...Ferlin Husky
- DJ Gone [4]...Ferlin Husky
- JB Gone [2]...Ferlin Husky

- LPS Calypso [27]...Harry Belafonte

April 29, 1957

POP
- TP All Shook Up [3]...Elvis Presley
- BS All Shook Up [4]...Elvis Presley
- DJ All Shook Up [2]...Elvis Presley
- JB All Shook Up [2]...Elvis Presley

R&B
- BS All Shook Up [1]...Elvis Presley
- DJ *School Day [1]...Chuck Berry
- JB Lucille/Send Me Some Lovin' [2]...Little Richard

C&W
- BS Gone [5]...Ferlin Husky
- DJ Gone [5]...Ferlin Husky
- JB Gone [3]...Ferlin Husky

- LPS Calypso [28]...Harry Belafonte

May 6, 1957

POP
- TP All Shook Up [4]...Elvis Presley
- BS All Shook Up [5]...Elvis Presley
- DJ All Shook Up [3]...Elvis Presley
- JB All Shook Up [3]...Elvis Presley

R&B
- BS All Shook Up [2]...Elvis Presley
- DJ All Shook Up [1]...Elvis Presley
- JB All Shook Up [1]...Elvis Presley

C&W
- BS Gone [6]...Ferlin Husky
- DJ Gone [6]...Ferlin Husky
- JB Gone [4]...Ferlin Husky

- LPS Calypso [29]...Harry Belafonte

May 13, 1957

POP
- TP All Shook Up [5]...Elvis Presley
- BS All Shook Up [6]...Elvis Presley
- DJ All Shook Up [4]...Elvis Presley
- JB All Shook Up [4]...Elvis Presley

R&B
- BS All Shook Up [3]...Elvis Presley
- DJ School Day [2]...Chuck Berry
- JB All Shook Up [2]...Elvis Presley

C&W
- BS Gone [7]...Ferlin Husky
- DJ Gone [7]...Ferlin Husky
- JB All Shook Up [1]...Elvis Presley

- LPS Calypso [30]...Harry Belafonte

May 20, 1957

POP
- TP   All Shook Up [6]...Elvis Presley
- BS   All Shook Up [7]...Elvis Presley
- DJ   All Shook Up [5]...Elvis Presley
- JB   All Shook Up [5]...Elvis Presley

R&B
- BS   All Shook Up [4]...Elvis Presley
- DJ   School Day [3]...Chuck Berry
- JB   School Day [1]...Chuck Berry

C&W
- BS   Gone [8]...Ferlin Husky
- DJ   Gone [8]...Ferlin Husky ⎫ tie
- DJ   Honky Tonk Song [1]...Webb Pierce ⎭
- JB   Gone [5]...Ferlin Husky ⎫ tie
- JB   *A White Sport Coat (And A Pink Carnation) [1]...Marty Robbins ⎭

- LPS Calypso [31]...Harry Belafonte

May 27, 1957

POP
- TP   All Shook Up [7]...Elvis Presley
- BS   All Shook Up [8]...Elvis Presley
- DJ   All Shook Up [6]...Elvis Presley
- JB   All Shook Up [6]...Elvis Presley

R&B
- BS   School Day [1]...Chuck Berry
- DJ   All Shook Up [2]...Elvis Presley
- JB   All Shook Up [3]...Elvis Presley

C&W
- BS   Gone [9]...Ferlin Husky
- DJ   Gone [9]...Ferlin Husky ⎫ tie
- DJ   Four Walls [1]...Jim Reeves ⎭
- JB   A White Sport Coat (And A Pink Carnation) [2]...Marty Robbins

- LPS Love Is The Thing [1]...Nat "King" Cole

June 3, 1957

POP
- TP   All Shook Up [8]...Elvis Presley
- BS   *Love Letters In The Sand/Bernardine [1]...Pat Boone
- DJ   All Shook Up [7]...Elvis Presley
- JB   All Shook Up [7]...Elvis Presley

R&B
- BS   *Young Blood/Searchin' [1]...The Coasters
- DJ   School Day [4]...Chuck Berry
- JB   All Shook Up [4]...Elvis Presley

C&W
- BS   Gone [10]...Ferlin Husky
- DJ   A White Sport Coat (And A Pink Carnation) [1]...Marty Robbins
- JB   A White Sport Coat (And A Pink Carnation) [3]...Marty Robbins

- LPS Love Is The Thing [2]...Nat "King" Cole

June 10, 1957

POP
- TP   Love Letters In The Sand [1]...Pat Boone
- BS   Love Letters In The Sand/Bernardine [2]...Pat Boone
- DJ   Love Letters In The Sand [1]...Pat Boone
- JB   All Shook Up [8]...Elvis Presley

R&B
- BS   Searchin'/Young Blood [2]...The Coasters
- DJ   School Day [5]...Chuck Berry
- JB   Searchin'/Young Blood [1]...The Coasters

C&W
- BS   A White Sport Coat (And A Pink Carnation) [1]...Marty Robbins
- DJ   Four Walls [2]...Jim Reeves
- JB   A White Sport Coat (And A Pink Carnation) [4]...Marty Robbins

- LPS Love Is The Thing [3]...Nat "King" Cole

June 17, 1957

POP
- TP   Love Letters In The Sand [2]...Pat Boone
- BS   Love Letters In The Sand [3]...Pat Boone
- DJ   Love Letters In The Sand [2]...Pat Boone
- JB   All Shook Up [9] **...Elvis Presley

R&B
- BS   Searchin'/Young Blood [3]...The Coasters
- DJ   C.C. Rider [1]...Chuck Willis
- JB   Searchin'/Young Blood [2] **...The Coasters

C&W
- BS   A White Sport Coat (And A Pink Carnation) [2]...Marty Robbins
- DJ   Four Walls [3]...Jim Reeves
- JB   A White Sport Coat (And A Pink Carnation) [5] **...Marty Robbins

- LPS Love Is The Thing [4]...Nat "King" Cole

  **final Billboard Juke Box charts*

June 24, 1957

POP
- TP   Love Letters In The Sand [3]...Pat Boone
- BS   Love Letters In The Sand/Bernardine [4]...Pat Boone
- DJ   Love Letters In The Sand [3]...Pat Boone

R&B
- BS   Searchin' [4]...The Coasters
- DJ   Searchin' [1]...The Coasters

C&W
- BS   A White Sport Coat (And A Pink Carnation) [3]...Marty Robbins
- DJ   Four Walls [4]...Jim Reeves

- LPS Love Is The Thing [5]...Nat "King" Cole

July 1, 1957
POP
- TP Love Letters In The Sand [4]...Pat Boone
- BS Love Letters In The Sand/Bernardine [5]...Pat Boone
- DJ Love Letters In The Sand [4]...Pat Boone

R&B
- BS Searchin'/Young Blood [5]...The Coasters
- DJ C.C. Rider [2]...Chuck Willis

C&W
- BS A White Sport Coat (And A Pink Carnation) [4]...Marty Robbins
- DJ Four Walls [5]...Jim Reeves

LPS Love Is The Thing [6]...Nat "King" Cole

July 8, 1957
POP
- TP Love Letters In The Sand [5]...Pat Boone
- BS *(Let Me Be Your) Teddy Bear/Loving You [1]...Elvis Presley
- DJ Love Letters In The Sand [5]...Pat Boone

R&B
- BS Searchin'/Young Blood [6]...The Coasters
- DJ Searchin' [2]...The Coasters

C&W
- BS A White Sport Coat (And A Pink Carnation) [5]...Marty Robbins
- DJ Four Walls [6]...Jim Reeves

LPS Love Is The Thing [7]...Nat "King" Cole

July 15, 1957
POP
- TP (Let Me Be Your) Teddy Bear [1]...Elvis Presley
- BS (Let Me Be Your) Teddy Bear/Loving You [2]...Elvis Presley
- DJ Love Letters In The Sand [6]...Pat Boone

R&B
- BS Searchin'/Young Blood [7]...The Coasters
- DJ Searchin' [3]...The Coasters

C&W
- BS *Bye Bye Love [1]...The Everly Brothers
- DJ Four Walls [7]...Jim Reeves

LPS Love Is The Thing [8]...Nat "King" Cole

July 22, 1957
POP
- TP (Let Me Be Your) Teddy Bear [2]...Elvis Presley
- BS (Let Me Be Your) Teddy Bear/Loving You [3]...Elvis Presley
- DJ Love Letters In The Sand [7]...Pat Boone

R&B
- BS Searchin'/Young Blood [8]...The Coasters
- DJ Searchin' [4]...The Coasters

C&W
- BS Bye Bye Love [2]...The Everly Brothers
- DJ Four Walls [8]...Jim Reeves

LPS Around The World In 80 Days [1]...Soundtrack

July 29, 1957
POP
- TP (Let Me Be Your) Teddy Bear [3]...Elvis Presley
- BS (Let Me Be Your) Teddy Bear/Loving You [4]...Elvis Presley
- DJ (Let Me Be Your) Teddy Bear [1]...Elvis Presley

R&B
- BS Searchin'/Young Blood [9]...The Coasters
- DJ Searchin' [5]...The Coasters } tie
- DJ Short Fat Fannie [1]...Larry Williams

C&W
- BS Bye Bye Love [3]...The Everly Brothers
- DJ Bye Bye Love [1]...The Everly Brothers

LPS Loving You [1]...Elvis Presley/Soundtrack

August 5, 1957
POP
- TP (Let Me Be Your) Teddy Bear [4]...Elvis Presley
- BS (Let Me Be Your) Teddy Bear/Loving You [5]...Elvis Presley
- DJ (Let Me Be Your) Teddy Bear [2]...Elvis Presley

R&B
- BS Searchin'/Young Blood [10]...The Coasters
- DJ Searchin' [6]...The Coasters

C&W
- BS (Let Me Be Your) Teddy Bear/Loving You [1]...Elvis Presley
- DJ Bye Bye Love [2]...The Everly Brothers

LPS Loving You [2]...Elvis Presley/Soundtrack

August 12, 1957

POP
- TP (Let Me Be Your) Teddy Bear [5]...Elvis Presley
- BS (Let Me Be Your) Teddy Bear/Loving You [6]...Elvis Presley
- DJ (Let Me Be Your) Teddy Bear [3]...Elvis Presley

R&B
- BS Searchin'/Young Blood [11]...The Coasters
- DJ Searchin' [7]...The Coasters

C&W
- BS Bye Bye Love [4]...The Everly Brothers
- DJ Bye Bye Love [3]...The Everly Brothers

- LPS Loving You [3]...Elvis Presley/Soundtrack

August 19, 1957

POP
- TP (Let Me Be Your) Teddy Bear [6]...Elvis Presley
- BS (Let Me Be Your) Teddy Bear/Loving You [7]...Elvis Presley
- DJ *Tammy [1]...Debbie Reynolds

R&B
- BS Searchin'/Young Blood [12]...The Coasters
- DJ Send For Me [1]...Nat "King" Cole

C&W
- BS Bye Bye Love [5]...The Everly Brothers
- DJ Bye Bye Love [4]...The Everly Brothers

- LPS Loving You [4]...Elvis Presley/Soundtrack

August 26, 1957

POP
- TP (Let Me Be Your) Teddy Bear [7]...Elvis Presley
- BS Tammy [1]...Debbie Reynolds
- DJ Tammy [2]...Debbie Reynolds

R&B
- BS Searchin'/Young Blood [13]...The Coasters
- DJ Send For Me [2]...Nat "King" Cole

C&W
- BS Bye Bye Love [6]...The Everly Brothers
- DJ Bye Bye Love [5]...The Everly Brothers

- LPS Loving You [5]...Elvis Presley/Soundtrack

September 2, 1957

POP
- TP Tammy [1]...Debbie Reynolds
- BS Tammy [2]...Debbie Reynolds
- DJ Tammy [3]...Debbie Reynolds

R&B
- BS (Let Me Be Your) Teddy Bear/Loving You [1]...Elvis Presley
- DJ Farther Up The Road [1]...Bobby "Blue" Bland

C&W
- BS Bye Bye Love [7]...The Everly Brothers
- DJ Bye Bye Love [6]...The Everly Brothers

- LPS Loving You [6]...Elvis Presley/Soundtrack

September 9, 1957

POP
- TP Tammy [2]...Debbie Reynolds
- BS *Diana [1]...Paul Anka
- DJ Tammy [4]...Debbie Reynolds

R&B
- BS *Whole Lot Of Shakin' Going On [1]...Jerry Lee Lewis
- DJ *Whole Lot Of Shakin' Going On [1]...Jerry Lee Lewis

C&W
- BS *Whole Lot Of Shakin' Going On [1]...Jerry Lee Lewis
- DJ Bye Bye Love [7]...The Everly Brothers

- LPS Loving You [7]...Elvis Presley/Soundtrack

September 16, 1957

POP
- TP Tammy [3]...Debbie Reynolds
- BS Tammy [3]...Debbie Reynolds
- DJ Tammy [5]...Debbie Reynolds

R&B
- BS Whole Lot Of Shakin' Going On [2]...Jerry Lee Lewis
- DJ Long Lonely Nights [1]...Clyde McPhatter

C&W
- BS Whole Lot Of Shakin' Going On [2]...Jerry Lee Lewis
- DJ *Fraulein [1]...Bobby Helms ⎱ tie
- DJ My Shoes Keep Walking Back To You [1]...Ray Price ⎰

- LPS Loving You [8]...Elvis Presley/Soundtrack

September 23, 1957

POP
- TP Tammy [4]...Debbie Reynolds
- BS That'll Be The Day [1]...The Crickets
- DJ *Honeycomb [1]...Jimmie Rodgers

R&B
- BS Diana [1]...Paul Anka
- DJ Farther Up The Road [2]...Bobby "Blue" Bland

C&W
- BS Fraulein [1]...Bobby Helms
- DJ Fraulein [2]...Bobby Helms

- LPS Loving You [9]...Elvis Presley/Soundtrack

September 30, 1957

POP
- TP Tammy [5]...Debbie Reynolds
- BS Honeycomb [1]...Jimmie Rodgers
- DJ Honeycomb [2]...Jimmie Rodgers

R&B
- BS Diana [2]...Paul Anka
- DJ Mr. Lee [1]...The Bobbettes

C&W
- BS Fraulein [2]...Bobby Helms
- DJ My Shoes Keep Walking Back To You [2]...Ray Price

- LPS Loving You [10]...Elvis Presley/Soundtrack

October 7, 1957

POP
- TP Honeycomb [1]...Jimmie Rodgers
- BS Honeycomb [2]...Jimmie Rodgers
- DJ Honeycomb [3]...Jimmie Rodgers

R&B
- BS Honeycomb [1]...Jimmie Rodgers
- DJ Mr. Lee [2]...The Bobbettes

C&W
- BS Fraulein [3]...Bobby Helms
- DJ Fraulein [3]...Bobby Helms

- LPS Around The World In 80 Days [2]...Soundtrack

October 14, 1957

POP
- TP Honeycomb [2]...Jimmie Rodgers
- BS *Wake Up Little Susie [1]...The Everly Brothers
- DJ Honeycomb [4]...Jimmie Rodgers

R&B
- BS Honeycomb [2]...Jimmie Rodgers
- DJ Honeycomb [1]...Jimmie Rodgers

C&W
- BS *Wake Up Little Susie [1]...The Everly Brothers
- DJ Fraulein [4]...Bobby Helms

- LPS Around The World In 80 Days [3]...Soundtrack

October 21, 1957

POP
- TP Wake Up Little Susie [1]...The Everly Brothers
- BS *Jailhouse Rock/Treat Me Nice [1]...Elvis Presley
- DJ Chances Are [1]...Johnny Mathis

R&B
- BS *Jailhouse Rock [1]...Elvis Presley
- DJ Mr. Lee [3]...The Bobbettes

C&W
- BS Wake Up Little Susie [2]...The Everly Brothers
- DJ My Shoes Keep Walking Back To You [3]...Ray Price

- LPS Around The World In 80 Days [4]...Soundtrack

October 28, 1957

POP
- TP Wake Up Little Susie [2]...The Everly Brothers
- BS Jailhouse Rock/Treat Me Nice [2]...Elvis Presley
- DJ Wake Up Little Susie [1]...The Everly Brothers

R&B
- BS Jailhouse Rock [2]...Elvis Presley
- DJ Mr. Lee [4]...The Bobbettes
- DJ Wake Up Little Susie [1]...The Everly Brothers } tie

C&W
- BS Wake Up Little Susie [3]...The Everly Brothers
- DJ Wake Up Little Susie [1]...The Everly Brothers

- LPS Around The World In 80 Days [5]...Soundtrack

November 4, 1957

POP
- TP Jailhouse Rock [1]...Elvis Presley
- BS Jailhouse Rock/Treat Me Nice [3]...Elvis Presley
- DJ Wake Up Little Susie [2]...The Everly Brothers

R&B
- BS Jailhouse Rock [3]...Elvis Presley
- DJ Jailhouse Rock [1]...Elvis Presley

C&W
- BS Wake Up Little Susie [4]...The Everly Brothers
- DJ Wake Up Little Susie [2]...The Everly Brothers

- LPS Around The World In 80 Days [6]...Soundtrack

November 11, 1957

POP
- TP Jailhouse Rock [2]...Elvis Presley
- BS Jailhouse Rock/Treat Me Nice [4]...Elvis Presley
- DJ Wake Up Little Susie [3]...The Everly Brothers

R&B
- BS Jailhouse Rock/Treat Me Nice [4]...Elvis Presley
- DJ Jailhouse Rock [2]...Elvis Presley

C&W
- BS Wake Up Little Susie [5]...The Everly Brothers
- DJ Wake Up Little Susie [3]...The Everly Brothers

- LPS Around The World In 80 Days [7]...Soundtrack

November 18, 1957
POP
- TP Jailhouse Rock [3]...Elvis Presley
- BS Jailhouse Rock/Treat Me Nice [5]...Elvis Presley
- DJ Wake Up Little Susie [4]...The Everly Brothers

R&B
- BS Jailhouse Rock/Treat Me Nice [5]...Elvis Presley
- DJ Jailhouse Rock [3]...Elvis Presley

C&W
- BS Wake Up Little Susie [6]...The Everly Brothers
- DJ Wake Up Little Susie [4]...The Everly Brothers

LPS My Fair Lady [9]...Original Cast

November 25, 1957
POP
- TP Jailhouse Rock [4]...Elvis Presley
- BS Jailhouse Rock/Treat Me Nice [6]...Elvis Presley
- DJ Jailhouse Rock [1]...Elvis Presley

R&B
- BS *You Send Me [1]...Sam Cooke
- DJ *You Send Me [1]...Sam Cooke

C&W
- BS Wake Up Little Susie [7]...The Everly Brothers
- DJ Wake Up Little Susie [5]...The Everly Brothers

LPS Around The World In 80 Days [8]...Soundtrack

December 2, 1957
POP
- TP Jailhouse Rock [5]...Elvis Presley
- BS You Send Me/Summertime [1]...Sam Cooke
- DJ Jailhouse Rock [2]...Elvis Presley

R&B
- BS You Send Me [2]...Sam Cooke
- DJ You Send Me [2]...Sam Cooke

C&W
- BS Jailhouse Rock/Treat Me Nice [1]...Elvis Presley
- DJ Wake Up Little Susie [6]...The Everly Brothers

LPS Around The World In 80 Days [9]...Soundtrack

December 9, 1957
POP
- TP You Send Me [1]...Sam Cooke } tie
- TP Jailhouse Rock [6]...Elvis Presley
- BS You Send Me/Summertime [2]...Sam Cooke
- DJ You Send Me [1]...Sam Cooke

R&B
- BS You Send Me [3]...Sam Cooke
- DJ You Send Me [3]...Sam Cooke

C&W
- BS *My Special Angel [1]...Bobby Helms
- DJ Wake Up Little Susie [7]...The Everly Brothers

LPS Around The World In 80 Days [10]...Soundtrack

December 16, 1957
POP
- TP You Send Me [2]...Sam Cooke
- BS Jailhouse Rock/Treat Me Nice [7]...Elvis Presley
- DJ *April Love [1]...Pat Boone

R&B
- BS You Send Me [4]...Sam Cooke
- DJ You Send Me [4]...Sam Cooke

C&W
- BS My Special Angel [2]...Bobby Helms
- DJ My Shoes Keep Walking Back To You [4]...Ray Price

LPS Elvis' Christmas Album [1]...Elvis Presley

December 23, 1957
POP
- TP You Send Me [3]...Sam Cooke
- BS April Love/When The Swallows Come Back To Capistrano [1]...Pat Boone
- DJ April Love [2]...Pat Boone

R&B
- BS You Send Me [5]...Sam Cooke
- DJ You Send Me [5]...Sam Cooke

C&W
- BS My Special Angel [3]...Bobby Helms
- DJ Wake Up Little Susie [8]...The Everly Brothers

LPS Elvis' Christmas Album [2]...Elvis Presley

December 30, 1957
POP
- TP April Love [1]...Pat Boone
- BS April Love [2]...Pat Boone
- DJ April Love [3]...Pat Boone

R&B
- BS You Send Me [6]...Sam Cooke
- DJ You Send Me [6]...Sam Cooke

C&W
- BS My Special Angel [4]...Bobby Helms
- DJ My Special Angel [1]...Bobby Helms

LPS Elvis' Christmas Album [3]...Elvis Presley

January 6, 1958
POP
- TP *At The Hop [1]...Danny & The Juniors
- BS *At The Hop [1]...Danny & The Juniors
- DJ April Love [4]...Pat Boone

R&B
- BS *At The Hop [1]...Danny & The Juniors
- DJ Raunchy [1]...Ernie Freeman

C&W
- BS Great Balls Of Fire [1]...Jerry Lee Lewis
- DJ *The Story Of My Life [1]...Marty Robbins

LPS Merry Christmas [1]...Bing Crosby

January 13, 1958

POP
- TP At The Hop [2]...Danny & The Juniors
- BS At The Hop [2]...Danny & The Juniors
- DJ April Love [5]...Pat Boone

R&B
- BS At The Hop [2]...Danny & The Juniors
- DJ Raunchy [2]...Ernie Freeman

C&W
- BS Great Balls Of Fire [2]...Jerry Lee Lewis
- DJ The Story Of My Life [2]...Marty Robbins
- LPS Elvis' Christmas Album [4]...Elvis Presley

January 20, 1958

POP
- TP At The Hop [3]...Danny & The Juniors
- BS At The Hop [3]...Danny & The Juniors
- DJ April Love [6]...Pat Boone

R&B
- BS At The Hop [3]...Danny & The Juniors
- DJ Raunchy [1]...Bill Justis

C&W
- BS The Story Of My Life [1]...Marty Robbins
- DJ The Story Of My Life [3]...Marty Robbins
- LPS Ricky [1]...Ricky Nelson

January 27, 1958

POP
- TP At The Hop [4]...Danny & The Juniors
- BS At The Hop [4]...Danny & The Juniors
- DJ At The Hop [1]...Danny & The Juniors

R&B
- BS At The Hop [4]...Danny & The Juniors
- DJ I'll Come Running Back To You [1]...Sam Cooke

C&W
- BS The Story Of My Life [2]...Marty Robbins
- DJ The Story Of My Life [4]...Marty Robbins
- LPS Ricky [2]...Ricky Nelson

February 3, 1958

POP
- TP At The Hop [5]...Danny & The Juniors
- BS At The Hop [5]...Danny & The Juniors
- DJ At The Hop [2]...Danny & The Juniors

R&B
- BS At The Hop [5]...Danny & The Juniors
- DJ *Get A Job [1]...The Silhouettes

C&W
- BS The Story Of My Life [3]...Marty Robbins
- DJ *Ballad Of A Teenage Queen [1]...Johnny Cash
- LPS My Fair Lady [10]...Original Cast

February 10, 1958

POP
- TP At The Hop [6]...Danny & The Juniors
- BS *Don't/I Beg Of You [1]...Elvis Presley
- DJ At The Hop [3]...Danny & The Juniors

R&B
- BS Get A Job [1]...The Silhouettes
- DJ Get A Job [2]...The Silhouettes

C&W
- BS The Story Of My Life [4]...Marty Robbins
- DJ Ballad Of A Teenage Queen [2]...Johnny Cash
- LPS Come fly with me [1]...Frank Sinatra

February 17, 1958

POP
- TP At The Hop [7]...Danny & The Juniors
- BS Don't/I Beg Of You [2]...Elvis Presley
- DJ Sugartime [1]...The McGuire Sisters

R&B
- BS Get A Job [2]...The Silhouettes
- DJ Get A Job [3]...The Silhouettes

C&W
- BS Ballad Of A Teenage Queen [1]...Johnny Cash
- DJ Ballad Of A Teenage Queen [3]...Johnny Cash
- LPS Come fly with me [2]...Frank Sinatra

February 24, 1958

POP
- TP Get A Job [1]...The Silhouettes
- BS Don't/I Beg Of You [3]...Elvis Presley
- DJ Sugartime [2]...The McGuire Sisters

R&B
- BS Get A Job [3]...The Silhouettes
- DJ Get A Job [4]...The Silhouettes

C&W
- BS Ballad Of A Teenage Queen [2]...Johnny Cash
- DJ Ballad Of A Teenage Queen [4]...Johnny Cash
- LPS Come fly with me [3]...Frank Sinatra

March 3, 1958

POP
- TP Get A Job [2]...The Silhouettes
- BS Don't/I Beg Of You [4]...Elvis Presley
- DJ Sugartime [3]...The McGuire Sisters

R&B
- BS Get A Job [4]...The Silhouettes
- DJ Get A Job [5]...The Silhouettes

C&W
- BS Ballad Of A Teenage Queen/Big River [3]...Johnny Cash
- DJ Ballad Of A Teenage Queen [5]...Johnny Cash
- LPS Come fly with me [4]...Frank Sinatra

March 10, 1958

POP
- TP Don't [1]...Elvis Presley
- BS Don't/I Beg Of You [5]...Elvis Presley
- DJ Sugartime [4]...The McGuire Sisters

R&B
- BS *Sweet Little Sixteen [1]...Chuck Berry
- DJ Get A Job [6]...The Silhouettes

C&W
- BS Ballad Of A Teenage Queen/Big River [4]...Johnny Cash
- DJ Ballad Of A Teenage Queen [6]...Johnny Cash

LPS Come fly with me [5]...Frank Sinatra

March 17, 1958

POP
- TP *Tequila [1]...The Champs
- BS *Tequila [1]...The Champs
- DJ Don't [1]...Elvis Presley

R&B
- BS Sweet Little Sixteen [2]...Chuck Berry
- DJ Sweet Little Sixteen [1]...Chuck Berry

C&W
- BS Ballad Of A Teenage Queen/Big River [5]...Johnny Cash
- DJ Ballad Of A Teenage Queen [7]...Johnny Cash

LPS The Music Man [1]...Original Cast

March 24, 1958

POP
- TP Tequila [2]...The Champs
- BS Tequila [2]...The Champs
- DJ Catch A Falling Star [1]...Perry Como

R&B
- BS Sweet Little Sixteen [3]...Chuck Berry
- DJ Sweet Little Sixteen [2]...Chuck Berry

C&W
- BS Ballad Of A Teenage Queen/Big River [6]...Johnny Cash
- DJ Ballad Of A Teenage Queen [8]...Johnny Cash

LPS The Music Man [2]...Original Cast

March 31, 1958

POP
- TP Tequila [3]...The Champs
- BS Tequila [3]...The Champs
- DJ Tequila [1]...The Champs

R&B
- BS Tequila [1]...The Champs
- DJ Sweet Little Sixteen [3]...Chuck Berry

C&W
- BS Ballad Of A Teenage Queen/Big River [7]...Johnny Cash
- DJ Ballad Of A Teenage Queen [9]...Johnny Cash

LPS The Music Man [3]...Original Cast

April 7, 1958

POP
- TP Tequila [4]...The Champs
- BS Tequila [4]...The Champs
- DJ Tequila [2]...The Champs

R&B
- BS Tequila [2]...The Champs
- DJ Tequila [1]...The Champs

C&W
- BS Ballad Of A Teenage Queen [8]...Johnny Cash
- DJ Ballad Of A Teenage Queen [10]...Johnny Cash

LPS My Fair Lady [11]...Original Cast

April 14, 1958

POP
- TP Tequila [5]...The Champs
- BS Tequila [5]...The Champs
- DJ He's Got The Whole World (In His Hands) [1]...Laurie London

R&B
- BS Tequila [3]...The Champs
- DJ Tequila [2]...The Champs

C&W
- BS *Oh Lonesome Me/I Can't Stop Lovin' You [1]...Don Gibson
- DJ *Oh Lonesome Me [1]...Don Gibson

LPS My Fair Lady [12]...Original Cast

April 21, 1958
POP
- TP *Twilight Time [1]...The Platters
- BS *Twilight Time [1]...The Platters
- DJ He's Got The Whole World (In His Hands) [2]...Laurie London

R&B
- BS Tequila [4]...The Champs
- DJ Tequila [3]...The Champs

C&W
- BS Oh Lonesome Me/I Can't Stop Lovin' You [2]...Don Gibson
- DJ Oh Lonesome Me [2]...Don Gibson

- LPS The Music Man [4]...Original Cast

April 28, 1958
POP
- TP *Witch Doctor [1]...David Seville
- BS *Witch Doctor [1]...David Seville
- DJ He's Got The Whole World (In His Hands) [3]...Laurie London

R&B
- BS Twilight Time [1]...The Platters
- DJ Tequila [4]...The Champs

C&W
- BS Oh Lonesome Me/I Can't Stop Lovin' You [3]...Don Gibson
- DJ Oh Lonesome Me [3]...Don Gibson

- LPS The Music Man [5]...Original Cast

May 5, 1958
POP
- TP Witch Doctor [2]...David Seville
- BS Witch Doctor [2]...David Seville
- DJ He's Got The Whole World (In His Hands) [4]...Laurie London

R&B
- BS Twilight Time [2]...The Platters
- DJ Wear My Ring Around Your Neck [1]...Elvis Presley

C&W
- BS Oh Lonesome Me/I Can't Stop Lovin' You [4]...Don Gibson
- DJ Oh Lonesome Me [4]...Don Gibson

- LPS The Music Man [6]...Original Cast

May 12, 1958
POP
- TP Witch Doctor [3]...David Seville
- BS *All I Have To Do Is Dream/Claudette [1]...The Everly Brothers
- DJ Twilight Time [1]...The Platters

R&B
- BS Twilight Time [3]...The Platters
- DJ Wear My Ring Around Your Neck [2]...Elvis Presley

C&W
- BS Oh Lonesome Me/I Can't Stop Lovin' You [5]...Don Gibson
- DJ Oh Lonesome Me [5]...Don Gibson

- LPS The Music Man [7]...Original Cast

May 19, 1958
POP
- TP All I Have To Do Is Dream [1]...The Everly Brothers
- BS All I Have To Do Is Dream/Claudette [2]...The Everly Brothers
- DJ All I Have To Do Is Dream [1]...The Everly Brothers

R&B
- BS All I Have To Do Is Dream [1]...The Everly Brothers
- DJ Wear My Ring Around Your Neck [3]...Elvis Presley

C&W
- BS Oh Lonesome Me/I Can't Stop Lovin' You [6]...Don Gibson
- DJ Oh Lonesome Me [6]...Don Gibson

- LPS South Pacific [1]...Soundtrack

May 26, 1958
POP
- TP All I Have To Do Is Dream [2]...The Everly Brothers
- BS All I Have To Do Is Dream/Claudette [3]...The Everly Brothers
- DJ All I Have To Do Is Dream [2]...The Everly Brothers

R&B
- BS All I Have To Do Is Dream [2]...The Everly Brothers
- DJ Witch Doctor [1]...David Seville

C&W
- BS Oh Lonesome Me/I Can't Stop Lovin' You [7]...Don Gibson
- DJ Just Married [1]...Marty Robbins

- LPS The Music Man [8]...Original Cast

June 2, 1958

POP
- TP   All I Have To Do Is Dream [3]...The Everly Brothers
- BS   All I Have To Do Is Dream/Claudette [4]...
       The Everly Brothers
- DJ   All I Have To Do Is Dream [3]...The Everly Brothers

R&B
- BS   All I Have To Do Is Dream [3]...The Everly Brothers
- DJ   All I Have To Do Is Dream [1]...The Everly Brothers

C&W
- BS   All I Have To Do Is Dream/Claudette [1]...
       The Everly Brothers
- DJ   All I Have To Do Is Dream [1]...The Everly Brothers

- LPS The Music Man [9]...Original Cast

June 9, 1958

POP
- TP   *The Purple People Eater [1]...Sheb Wooley
- BS   *The Purple People Eater [1]...Sheb Wooley
- DJ   All I Have To Do Is Dream [4]...The Everly Brothers

R&B
- BS   All I Have To Do Is Dream [4]...The Everly Brothers
- DJ   All I Have To Do Is Dream [2]...The Everly Brothers

C&W
- BS   All I Have To Do Is Dream/Claudette [2]...
       The Everly Brothers
- DJ   Just Married [2]...Marty Robbins

- LPS Johnny's Greatest Hits [1]...Johnny Mathis

June 16, 1958

POP
- TP   The Purple People Eater [2]...Sheb Wooley
- BS   The Purple People Eater [2]...Sheb Wooley
- DJ   All I Have To Do Is Dream [5]...The Everly Brothers

R&B
- BS   All I Have To Do Is Dream [5]...The Everly Brothers
- DJ   All I Have To Do Is Dream [3]...The Everly Brothers

C&W
- BS   All I Have To Do Is Dream/Claudette [3]...
       The Everly Brothers
- DJ   Oh Lonesome Me [7]...Don Gibson

- LPS Johnny's Greatest Hits [2]...Johnny Mathis

June 23, 1958

POP
- TP   The Purple People Eater [3]...Sheb Wooley
- BS   The Purple People Eater [3]...Sheb Wooley
- DJ   The Purple People Eater [1]...Sheb Wooley

R&B
- BS   *Yakety Yak [1]...The Coasters
- DJ   What Am I Living For [1]...Chuck Willis

C&W
- BS   Oh Lonesome Me/I Can't Stop Lovin' You [8]...
       Don Gibson
- DJ   *Guess Things Happen That Way [1]...Johnny Cash

- LPS The Music Man [10]...Original Cast

June 30, 1958

POP
- TP   The Purple People Eater [4]...Sheb Wooley
- BS   The Purple People Eater [4]...Sheb Wooley
- DJ   The Purple People Eater [2]...Sheb Wooley

R&B
- BS   Yakety Yak [2]...The Coasters
- DJ   Yakety Yak [1]...The Coasters

C&W
- BS   Guess Things Happen That Way/Come In
       Stranger [1]...Johnny Cash
- DJ   Oh Lonesome Me [8]...Don Gibson

- LPS The Music Man [11]...Original Cast

July 7, 1958

POP
- TP   The Purple People Eater [5]...Sheb Wooley
- BS   The Purple People Eater [5]...Sheb Wooley
- DJ   The Purple People Eater [3]...Sheb Wooley

R&B
- BS   Yakety Yak [3]...The Coasters
- DJ   Yakety Yak [2]...The Coasters

C&W
- BS   Guess Things Happen That Way/Come In
       Stranger [2]...Johnny Cash
- DJ   Guess Things Happen That Way [2]...Johnny Cash

- LPS Johnny's Greatest Hits [3]...Johnny Mathis

July 14, 1958

POP
- TP The Purple People Eater [6]...Sheb Wooley
- BS The Purple People Eater [6]...Sheb Wooley
- DJ The Purple People Eater [4]...Sheb Wooley

R&B
- BS Yakety Yak [4]...The Coasters
- DJ Yakety Yak [3]...The Coasters

C&W
- BS Guess Things Happen That Way/Come In Stranger [3]...Johnny Cash
- DJ Guess Things Happen That Way [3]...Johnny Cash
- LPS The Music Man [12]...Original Cast

July 21, 1958

POP
- TP Yakety Yak [1]...The Coasters
- BS *Hard Headed Woman/Don't Ask Me Why [1]...Elvis Presley
- DJ *Hard Headed Woman [1]...Elvis Presley

R&B
- BS Yakety Yak [5]...The Coasters
- DJ Yakety Yak [4]...The Coasters

C&W
- BS Guess Things Happen That Way/Come In Stranger [4]...Johnny Cash
- DJ Alone With You [1]...Faron Young
- LPS Gigi [1]...Soundtrack

July 28, 1958

POP
- TP *Patricia [1]...Perez Prado
- BS Hard Headed Woman/Don't Ask Me Why [2]...Elvis Presley
- DJ *Patricia [1]...Perez Prado
  final Billboard Pop Disc Jockey chart

R&B
- BS Yakety Yak [6]...The Coasters
- DJ Yakety Yak [5]...The Coasters

C&W
- BS Guess Things Happen That Way/Come In Stranger [5]...Johnny Cash
- DJ Alone With You [2]...Faron Young
- LPS Gigi [2]...Soundtrack

August 4, 1958

POP
- HT *Poor Little Fool [1]...Ricky Nelson
- BS *Poor Little Fool [1]...Ricky Nelson

R&B
- BS Yakety Yak [7]...The Coasters
- DJ Splish Splash [1]...Bobby Darin

C&W
- BS Guess Things Happen That Way/Come In Stranger [6]...Johnny Cash
- DJ Alone With You [3]...Faron Young
- LPS Gigi [3]...Soundtrack

August 11, 1958

POP
- HT Poor Little Fool [2]...Ricky Nelson
- BS Poor Little Fool [2]...Ricky Nelson

R&B
- BS Patricia [1]...Perez Prado
- DJ Splish Splash [2]...Bobby Darin

C&W
- BS Guess Things Happen That Way/Come In Stranger [7]...Johnny Cash
- DJ Alone With You [4]...Faron Young
- LPS Tchaikovsky: Piano Concerto No. 1 [1]...Van Cliburn

August 18, 1958

POP
- HT *Nel Blu Dipinto Di Blu (Volare) [1]...Domenico Modugno
- BS *Nel Blu Dipinto Di Blu (Volare) [1]...Domenico Modugno

R&B
- BS Patricia [2]...Perez Prado
- DJ Yakety Yak [6]...The Coasters

C&W
- BS Guess Things Happen That Way/Come In Stranger [8]...Johnny Cash
- DJ Alone With You [5]...Faron Young
- LPS Tchaikovsky: Piano Concerto No. 1 [2]...Van Cliburn

August 25, 1958

POP
- HT *Little Star [1]...The Elegants
- BS *Bird Dog/Devoted To You [1]...The Everly Brothers

R&B
- BS Just A Dream [1]...Jimmy Clanton
- DJ Patricia [1]...Perez Prado

C&W
- BS Blue Blue Day [1]...Don Gibson
- DJ Alone With You [6]...Faron Young
- LPS Tchaikovsky: Piano Concerto No. 1 [3]...Van Cliburn

September 1, 1958

POP
- HT Nel Blu Dipinto Di Blu (Volare) [2]...
  Domenico Modugno
- BS Nel Blu Dipinto Di Blu (Volare) [2]...
  Domenico Modugno

R&B
- BS Little Star [1]...The Elegants
- DJ When [1]...Kalin Twins

C&W
- BS Blue Blue Day [2]...Don Gibson
- DJ Alone With You [7]...Faron Young
- LPS Tchaikovsky: Piano Concerto No. 1 [4]...Van Cliburn

September 8, 1958

POP
- HT Nel Blu Dipinto Di Blu (Volare) [3]...
  Domenico Modugno
- BS Nel Blu Dipinto Di Blu (Volare) [3]...
  Domenico Modugno

R&B
- BS Little Star [2]...The Elegants
- DJ Little Star [1]...The Elegants

C&W
- BS Bird Dog/Devoted To You [1]...The Everly Brothers
- DJ Alone With You [8]...Faron Young
- LPS Tchaikovsky: Piano Concerto No. 1 [5]...Van Cliburn

September 15, 1958

POP
- HT Nel Blu Dipinto Di Blu (Volare) [4]...
  Domenico Modugno
- BS Nel Blu Dipinto Di Blu (Volare) [4]...
  Domenico Modugno

R&B
- BS Little Star [3]...The Elegants
- DJ Little Star [2]...The Elegants

C&W
- BS Bird Dog/Devoted To You [2]...The Everly Brothers
- DJ Alone With You [9]...Faron Young
- LPS South Pacific [2]...Soundtrack

September 22, 1958

POP
- HT Nel Blu Dipinto Di Blu (Volare) [5]...
  Domenico Modugno
- BS Nel Blu Dipinto Di Blu (Volare) [5]...
  Domenico Modugno

R&B
- BS Little Star [4]...The Elegants
- DJ Little Star [3]...The Elegants

C&W
- BS Bird Dog/Devoted To You [3]...The Everly Brothers
- DJ Alone With You [10]...Faron Young
- LPS Tchaikovsky: Piano Concerto No. 1 [6]...Van Cliburn

September 29, 1958

POP
- HT *It's All In The Game [1]...Tommy Edwards
- BS *It's All In The Game [1]...Tommy Edwards

R&B
- BS *It's All In The Game [1]...Tommy Edwards
- DJ Little Star [4]...The Elegants

C&W
- BS Bird Dog/Devoted To You [4]...The Everly Brothers
- DJ Alone With You [11]...Faron Young
- LPS Tchaikovsky: Piano Concerto No. 1 [7]...Van Cliburn

October 6, 1958

POP
- HT It's All In The Game [2]...Tommy Edwards
- BS It's All In The Game [2]...Tommy Edwards

R&B
- BS It's All In The Game [2]...Tommy Edwards
- DJ *Rock-in Robin [1]...Bobby Day

C&W
- BS Bird Dog/Devoted To You [5]...The Everly Brothers
- DJ Alone With You [12]...Faron Young
- LPS Sing Along With Mitch [1]...Mitch Miller & The Gang

October 13, 1958

POP
- HT It's All In The Game [3]...Tommy Edwards
- BS It's All In The Game [3]...Tommy Edwards
  final Billboard Pop Best Sellers chart

R&B
- BS It's All In The Game [3]...Tommy Edwards
- DJ Rock-in Robin [2]...Bobby Day
  final Billboard R&B Best Sellers and Disc Jockey charts

C&W
- BS Bird Dog/Devoted To You [6]...The Everly Brothers
- DJ Alone With You [13]...Faron Young
  final Billboard C&W Best Sellers and Disc Jockey charts
- LPS Frank Sinatra sings for Only The Lonely [1]...
  Frank Sinatra

October 20, 1958
- *HOT* It's All In The Game [4]...Tommy Edwards
- *R&B* Rock-in Robin [1]...Bobby Day
- *C&W* City Lights [1]...Ray Price
- *LPS* Frank Sinatra sings for Only The Lonely [2]...Frank Sinatra

October 27, 1958
- *HOT* It's All In The Game [5]...Tommy Edwards
- *R&B* Topsy II [1]...Cozy Cole
- *C&W* City Lights [2]...Ray Price
- *LPS* Frank Sinatra sings for Only The Lonely [3]...Frank Sinatra

November 3, 1958
- *HOT* It's All In The Game [6]...Tommy Edwards
- *R&B* Topsy II [2]...Cozy Cole
- *C&W* City Lights [3]...Ray Price
- *LPS* Frank Sinatra sings for Only The Lonely [4]...Frank Sinatra

November 10, 1958
- *HOT* It's Only Make Believe [1]...Conway Twitty
- *R&B* Topsy II [3]...Cozy Cole
- *C&W* City Lights [4]...Ray Price
- *LPS* Frank Sinatra sings for Only The Lonely [5]...Frank Sinatra

November 17, 1958
- *HOT* Tom Dooley [1]...The Kingston Trio
- *R&B* Topsy II [4]...Cozy Cole
- *C&W* City Lights [5]...Ray Price
- *LPS* South Pacific [3]...Soundtrack

November 24, 1958
- *HOT* It's Only Make Believe [2]...Conway Twitty
- *R&B* Topsy II [5]...Cozy Cole
- *C&W* City Lights [6]...Ray Price
- *LPS* The Kingston Trio [1]...The Kingston Trio

December 1, 1958
- *HOT* To Know Him, Is To Love Him [1]...The Teddy Bears
- *R&B* Topsy II [6]...Cozy Cole
- *C&W* City Lights [7]...Ray Price
- *LPS* Sing Along With Mitch [2]...Mitch Miller & The Gang

December 8, 1958
- *HOT* To Know Him, Is To Love Him [2]...The Teddy Bears
- *R&B* A Lover's Question [1]...Clyde McPhatter
- *C&W* City Lights [8]...Ray Price
- *LPS* Sing Along With Mitch [3]...Mitch Miller & The Gang

December 15, 1958
- *HOT* To Know Him, Is To Love Him [3]...The Teddy Bears
- *R&B* Lonely Teardrops [1]...Jackie Wilson
- *C&W* City Lights [9]...Ray Price
- *LPS* Sing Along With Mitch [4]...Mitch Miller & The Gang

December 22, 1958
- *HOT* The Chipmunk Song [1]...The Chipmunks
- *R&B* Lonely Teardrops [2]...Jackie Wilson
- *C&W* City Lights [10]...Ray Price
- *LPS* Sing Along With Mitch [5]...Mitch Miller & The Gang

December 29, 1958
- *HOT* The Chipmunk Song [2]...The Chipmunks
- *R&B* Lonely Teardrops [3]...Jackie Wilson
- *C&W* City Lights [11]...Ray Price
- *LPS* Christmas Sing-Along With Mitch [1]...Mitch Miller & The Gang

January 5, 1959
- *HOT* The Chipmunk Song [3]...The Chipmunks
- *R&B* Lonely Teardrops [4]...Jackie Wilson
- *C&W* City Lights [12]...Ray Price
- *LPS* Christmas Sing-Along With Mitch [2]...Mitch Miller & The Gang

January 12, 1959
- *HOT* The Chipmunk Song [4]...The Chipmunks
- *R&B* Lonely Teardrops [5]...Jackie Wilson
- *C&W* City Lights [13]...Ray Price
- *LPS* Sing Along With Mitch [6]...Mitch Miller & The Gang

January 19, 1959
- *HOT* Smoke Gets In Your Eyes [1]...The Platters
- *R&B* Lonely Teardrops [6]...Jackie Wilson
- *C&W* Billy Bayou [1]...Jim Reeves
- *LPS* Sing Along With Mitch [7]...Mitch Miller & The Gang

January 26, 1959
- *HOT*   Smoke Gets In Your Eyes [2]...The Platters
- *R&B*   Lonely Teardrops [7]...Jackie Wilson
- *C&W*   Billy Bayou [2]...Jim Reeves
- *LPS*   Sing Along With Mitch [8]...Mitch Miller & The Gang

February 2, 1959
- *HOT*   Smoke Gets In Your Eyes [3]...The Platters
- *R&B*   Try Me [1]...James Brown
- *C&W*   Billy Bayou [3]...Jim Reeves
- *LPS*   Flower Drum Song [1]...Original Cast

February 9, 1959
- *HOT*   *Stagger Lee [1]...Lloyd Price
- *R&B*   *Stagger Lee [1]...Lloyd Price
- *C&W*   Billy Bayou [4]...Jim Reeves
- *LPS*   Flower Drum Song [2]...Original Cast

February 16, 1959
- *HOT*   Stagger Lee [2]...Lloyd Price
- *R&B*   Stagger Lee [2]...Lloyd Price
- *C&W*   Billy Bayou [5]...Jim Reeves
- *LPS*   Flower Drum Song [3]...Original Cast

February 23, 1959
- *HOT*   Stagger Lee [3]...Lloyd Price
- *R&B*   Stagger Lee [3]...Lloyd Price
- *C&W*   Don't Take Your Guns To Town [1]...Johnny Cash
- *LPS*   The Music From Peter Gunn [1]...Henry Mancini

March 2, 1959
- *HOT*   Stagger Lee [4]...Lloyd Price
- *R&B*   Stagger Lee [4]...Lloyd Price
- *C&W*   Don't Take Your Guns To Town [2]...Johnny Cash
- *LPS*   The Music From Peter Gunn [2]...Henry Mancini

March 9, 1959
- *HOT*   *Venus [1]...Frankie Avalon
- *R&B*   It's Just A Matter Of Time [1]...Brook Benton
- *C&W*   Don't Take Your Guns To Town [3]...Johnny Cash
- *LPS*   The Music From Peter Gunn [3]...Henry Mancini

March 16, 1959
- *HOT*   Venus [2]...Frankie Avalon
- *R&B*   It's Just A Matter Of Time [2]...Brook Benton
- *C&W*   Don't Take Your Guns To Town [4]...Johnny Cash
- *LPS*   The Music From Peter Gunn [4]...Henry Mancini

March 23, 1959
- *HOT*   Venus [3]...Frankie Avalon
- *R&B*   It's Just A Matter Of Time [3]...Brook Benton
- *C&W*   Don't Take Your Guns To Town [5]...Johnny Cash
- *LPS*   The Music From Peter Gunn [5]...Henry Mancini

March 30, 1959
- *HOT*   Venus [4]...Frankie Avalon
- *R&B*   It's Just A Matter Of Time [4]...Brook Benton
- *C&W*   Don't Take Your Guns To Town [6]...Johnny Cash
- *LPS*   The Music From Peter Gunn [6]...Henry Mancini

April 6, 1959
- *HOT*   Venus [5]...Frankie Avalon
- *R&B*   It's Just A Matter Of Time [5]...Brook Benton
- *C&W*   When It's Springtime In Alaska (It's Forty Below) [1]...Johnny Horton
- *LPS*   The Music From Peter Gunn [7]...Henry Mancini

April 13, 1959
- *HOT*   Come Softly To Me [1]...Fleetwoods
- *R&B*   It's Just A Matter Of Time [6]...Brook Benton
- *C&W*   White Lightning [1]...George Jones
- *LPS*   The Music From Peter Gunn [8]...Henry Mancini

April 20, 1959
- *HOT*   Come Softly To Me [2]...Fleetwoods
- *R&B*   It's Just A Matter Of Time [7]...Brook Benton
- *C&W*   White Lightning [2]...George Jones
- *LPS*   The Music From Peter Gunn [9]...Henry Mancini

April 27, 1959
- *HOT*   Come Softly To Me [3]...Fleetwoods
- *R&B*   It's Just A Matter Of Time [8]...Brook Benton
- *C&W*   White Lightning [3]...George Jones
- *LPS*   The Music From Peter Gunn [10]...Henry Mancini

May 4, 1959
- *HOT*   Come Softly To Me [4]...Fleetwoods
- *R&B*   It's Just A Matter Of Time [9]...Brook Benton
- *C&W*   White Lightning [4]...George Jones
- *LPS*   Gigi [4]...Soundtrack

May 11, 1959

- HOT The Happy Organ [1]...Dave 'Baby' Cortez
- R&B *Kansas City [1]...Wilbert Harrison
- C&W White Lightning [5]...George Jones
- LPS Gigi [5]...Soundtrack

May 18, 1959

- HOT Kansas City [1]...Wilbert Harrison
- R&B Kansas City [2]...Wilbert Harrison
- C&W *The Battle Of New Orleans [1]...Johnny Horton
- LPS Gigi [6]...Soundtrack

May 25, 1959

- HOT Kansas City [2]...Wilbert Harrison
- R&B Kansas City [3]...Wilbert Harrison
- C&W The Battle Of New Orleans [2]...Johnny Horton
- LPS
  - MO Gigi [7]...Soundtrack
  - ST South Pacific [4]...Soundtrack
      first hit #1 on 5/19/58

June 1, 1959

- HOT The Battle Of New Orleans [1]...Johnny Horton
- R&B Kansas City [4]...Wilbert Harrison
- C&W The Battle Of New Orleans [3]...Johnny Horton
- LPS
  - MO Gigi [8]...Soundtrack
  - ST South Pacific [5]...Soundtrack

June 8, 1959

- HOT The Battle Of New Orleans [2]...Johnny Horton
- R&B Kansas City [5]...Wilbert Harrison
- C&W The Battle Of New Orleans [4]...Johnny Horton
- LPS
  - MO Gigi [9]...Soundtrack
  - ST South Pacific [6]...Soundtrack

June 15, 1959

- HOT The Battle Of New Orleans [3]...Johnny Horton
- R&B Kansas City [6]...Wilbert Harrison
- C&W The Battle Of New Orleans [5]...Johnny Horton
- LPS
  - MO Gigi [10]...Soundtrack
  - ST My Fair Lady [1]...Original Cast

June 22, 1959

- HOT The Battle Of New Orleans [4]...Johnny Horton
- R&B Kansas City [7]...Wilbert Harrison
- C&W The Battle Of New Orleans [6]...Johnny Horton
- LPS
  - MO Exotica [1]...Martin Denny
  - ST My Fair Lady [2]...Original Cast

June 29, 1959

- HOT The Battle Of New Orleans [5]...Johnny Horton
- R&B Personality [1]...Lloyd Price
- C&W The Battle Of New Orleans [7]...Johnny Horton
- LPS
  - MO Exotica [2]...Martin Denny
  - ST My Fair Lady [3]...Original Cast

July 6, 1959

- HOT The Battle Of New Orleans [6]...Johnny Horton
- R&B Personality [2]...Lloyd Price
- C&W The Battle Of New Orleans [8]...Johnny Horton
- LPS
  - MO Exotica [3]...Martin Denny
  - ST South Pacific [7]...Soundtrack

July 13, 1959

- HOT Lonely Boy [1]...Paul Anka
- R&B Personality [3]...Lloyd Price
- C&W The Battle Of New Orleans [9]...Johnny Horton
- LPS
  - MO Exotica [4]...Martin Denny
  - ST Film Encores [1]...Mantovani and his orchestra

July 20, 1959

- HOT Lonely Boy [2]...Paul Anka
- R&B Personality [4]...Lloyd Price
- C&W The Battle Of New Orleans [10]...Johnny Horton
- LPS
  - MO Exotica [5]...Martin Denny
  - ST South Pacific [8]...Soundtrack

July 27, 1959

- HOT Lonely Boy [3]...Paul Anka
- R&B There Goes My Baby [1]...The Drifters
- C&W Waterloo [1]...Stonewall Jackson
- LPS
  - MO The Kingston Trio At Large [1]...The Kingston Trio
  - ST South Pacific [9]...Soundtrack

August 3, 1959
- **HOT** Lonely Boy [4]...Paul Anka
- **R&B** What'd I Say (Part I) [1]...Ray Charles
- **C&W** Waterloo [2]...Stonewall Jackson
- **LPS**
  - *M0* The Kingston Trio At Large [2]...The Kingston Trio
  - *ST* South Pacific [10]...Soundtrack

August 10, 1959
- **HOT** A Big Hunk O' Love [1]...Elvis Presley
- **R&B** Thank You Pretty Baby [1]...Brook Benton
- **C&W** Waterloo [3]...Stonewall Jackson
- **LPS**
  - *M0* The Kingston Trio At Large [3]...The Kingston Trio
  - *ST* South Pacific [11]...Soundtrack

August 17, 1959
- **HOT** A Big Hunk O' Love [2]...Elvis Presley
- **R&B** Thank You Pretty Baby [2]...Brook Benton
- **C&W** Waterloo [4]...Stonewall Jackson
- **LPS**
  - *M0* The Kingston Trio At Large [4]...The Kingston Trio
  - *ST* South Pacific [12]...Soundtrack

August 24, 1959
- **HOT** *The Three Bells [1]...The Browns
- **R&B** Thank You Pretty Baby [3]...Brook Benton
- **C&W** Waterloo [5]...Stonewall Jackson
- **LPS**
  - *M0* The Kingston Trio At Large [5]...The Kingston Trio
  - *ST* South Pacific [13]...Soundtrack

August 31, 1959
- **HOT** The Three Bells [2]...The Browns
- **R&B** Thank You Pretty Baby [4]...Brook Benton
- **C&W** The Three Bells [1]...The Browns
- **LPS**
  - *M0* The Kingston Trio At Large [6]...The Kingston Trio
  - *ST* South Pacific [14]...Soundtrack

September 7, 1959
- **HOT** The Three Bells [3]...The Browns
- **R&B** I'm Gonna Get Married [1]...Lloyd Price
- **C&W** The Three Bells [2]...The Browns
- **LPS**
  - *M0* The Kingston Trio At Large [7]...The Kingston Trio
  - *ST* South Pacific [15]...Soundtrack

September 14, 1959
- **HOT** The Three Bells [4]...The Browns
- **R&B** I'm Gonna Get Married [2]...Lloyd Price
- **C&W** The Three Bells [3]...The Browns
- **LPS**
  - *M0* The Kingston Trio At Large [8]...The Kingston Trio
  - *ST* South Pacific [16]...Soundtrack

September 21, 1959
- **HOT** Sleep Walk [1]...Santo & Johnny
- **R&B** I Want To Walk You Home [1]...Fats Domino
- **C&W** The Three Bells [4]...The Browns
- **LPS**
  - *M0* The Kingston Trio At Large [9]...The Kingston Trio
  - *ST* South Pacific [17]...Soundtrack

September 28, 1959
- **HOT** Sleep Walk [2]...Santo & Johnny
- **R&B** I'm Gonna Get Married [3]...Lloyd Price
- **C&W** The Three Bells [5]...The Browns
- **LPS**
  - *M0* The Kingston Trio At Large [10]...The Kingston Trio
  - *ST* South Pacific [18]...Soundtrack

October 5, 1959
- **HOT** Mack The Knife [1]...Bobby Darin
- **R&B** Poison Ivy [1]...The Coasters
- **C&W** The Three Bells [6]...The Browns
- **LPS**
  - *M0* The Kingston Trio At Large [11]...The Kingston Trio
  - *ST* South Pacific [19]...Soundtrack

October 12, 1959
- **HOT** Mack The Knife [2]...Bobby Darin
- **R&B** Sea Of Love [1]...Phil Phillips
- **C&W** The Three Bells [7]...The Browns
- **LPS**
  - *M0* The Kingston Trio At Large [12]...The Kingston Trio
  - *ST* South Pacific [20]...Soundtrack

October 19, 1959
- **HOT** Mack The Knife [3]...Bobby Darin
- **R&B** You Better Know It [1]...Jackie Wilson
- **C&W** The Three Bells [8]...The Browns
- **LPS**
  - *M0* The Kingston Trio At Large [13]...The Kingston Trio
  - *ST* South Pacific [21]...Soundtrack

October 26, 1959

- *HOT* Mack The Knife [4]...Bobby Darin
- *R&B* Poison Ivy [2]...The Coasters
- *C&W* The Three Bells [9]...The Browns
- *LPS*
  - *M0* The Kingston Trio At Large [14]...The Kingston Trio
  - *ST* South Pacific [22]...Soundtrack

November 2, 1959

- *HOT* Mack The Knife [5]...Bobby Darin
- *R&B* Poison Ivy [3]...The Coasters
- *C&W* The Three Bells [10]...The Browns
- *LPS*
  - *M0* The Kingston Trio At Large [15]...The Kingston Trio
  - *ST* South Pacific [23]...Soundtrack

November 9, 1959

- *HOT* Mack The Knife [6]...Bobby Darin
- *R&B* Poison Ivy [4]...The Coasters
- *C&W* Country Girl [1]...Faron Young
- *LPS*
  - *M0* Heavenly [1]...Johnny Mathis
  - *ST* South Pacific [24]...Soundtrack

November 16, 1959

- *HOT* Mr. Blue [1]...The Fleetwoods
- *R&B* So Many Ways [1]...Brook Benton
- *C&W* Country Girl [2]...Faron Young
- *LPS*
  - *M0* Heavenly [2]...Johnny Mathis
  - *ST* South Pacific [25]...Soundtrack

November 23, 1959

- *HOT* Mack The Knife [7]...Bobby Darin
- *R&B* Don't You Know [1]...Della Reese
- *C&W* Country Girl [3]...Faron Young
- *LPS*
  - *M0* Heavenly [3]...Johnny Mathis
  - *ST* South Pacific [26]...Soundtrack

November 30, 1959

- *HOT* Mack The Knife [8]...Bobby Darin
- *R&B* Don't You Know [2]...Della Reese
- *C&W* Country Girl [4]...Faron Young
- *LPS*
  - *M0* Heavenly [4]...Johnny Mathis
  - *ST* South Pacific [27]...Soundtrack

December 7, 1959

- *HOT* Mack The Knife [9]...Bobby Darin
- *R&B* The Clouds [1]...The Spacemen
- *C&W* The Same Old Me [1]...Ray Price
- *LPS*
  - *M0* Heavenly [5]...Johnny Mathis
  - *ST* South Pacific [28]...Soundtrack

December 14, 1959

- *HOT* Heartaches By The Number [1]...Guy Mitchell
- *R&B* So Many Ways [2]...Brook Benton
- *C&W* The Same Old Me [2]...Ray Price
- *LPS*
  - *M0* Here We Go Again! [1]...The Kingston Trio
  - *ST* South Pacific [29]...Soundtrack

December 21, 1959

- *HOT* Heartaches By The Number [2]...Guy Mitchell
- *R&B* So Many Ways [3]...Brook Benton
- *C&W* *El Paso [1]...Marty Robbins
- *LPS*
  - *M0* Here We Go Again! [2]...The Kingston Trio
  - *ST* South Pacific [30]...Soundtrack

December 28, 1959

- *HOT* Why [1]...Frankie Avalon
- *R&B* The Clouds [2]...The Spacemen
- *C&W* El Paso [2]...Marty Robbins
- *LPS*
  - *M0* Here We Go Again! [3]...The Kingston Trio
  - *ST* South Pacific [31]...Soundtrack

January 4, 1960

- *HOT* El Paso [1]...Marty Robbins
- *R&B* The Clouds [3]...The Spacemen
- *C&W* El Paso [3]...Marty Robbins
- *LPS*
  - *M0* Here We Go Again! [4]...The Kingston Trio
  - *ST* Here We Go Again! [1]...The Kingston Trio

January 11, 1960

- *HOT* El Paso [2]...Marty Robbins
- *R&B* Smokie - Part 2 [1]...Bill Black's Combo
- *C&W* El Paso [4]...Marty Robbins
- *LPS*
  - *M0* Here We Go Again! [5]...The Kingston Trio
  - *ST* The Lord's Prayer [1]...Mormon Tabernacle Choir

January 18, 1960
- HOT Running Bear [1]...Johnny Preston
- R&B Smokie - Part 2 [2]...Bill Black's Combo
- C&W El Paso [5]...Marty Robbins
- **LPS**
  - MO Here We Go Again! [6]...The Kingston Trio
  - ST Here We Go Again! [2]...The Kingston Trio

January 25, 1960
- HOT Running Bear [2]...Johnny Preston
- R&B Smokie - Part 2 [3]...Bill Black's Combo
- C&W El Paso [6]...Marty Robbins
- **LPS**
  - MO Here We Go Again! [7]...The Kingston Trio
  - ST The Sound Of Music [1]...Original Cast

February 1, 1960
- HOT Running Bear [3]...Johnny Preston
- R&B Smokie - Part 2 [4]...Bill Black's Combo
- C&W El Paso [7]...Marty Robbins
- **LPS**
  - MO Here We Go Again! [8]...The Kingston Trio
  - ST The Sound Of Music [2]...Original Cast

February 8, 1960
- HOT Teen Angel [1]...Mark Dinning
- R&B Baby (You've Got What It Takes) [1]...
  Dinah Washington & Brook Benton
- C&W He'll Have To Go [1]...Jim Reeves
- **LPS**
  - MO The Sound Of Music [1]...Original Cast
  - ST The Sound Of Music [3]...Original Cast

February 15, 1960
- HOT Teen Angel [2]...Mark Dinning
- R&B Baby (You've Got What It Takes) [2]...
  Dinah Washington & Brook Benton
- C&W He'll Have To Go [2]...Jim Reeves
- **LPS**
  - MO The Sound Of Music [2]...Original Cast
  - ST The Sound Of Music [4]...Original Cast

February 22, 1960
- HOT The Theme From "A Summer Place" [1]...Percy Faith
- R&B Baby (You've Got What It Takes) [3]...
  Dinah Washington & Brook Benton
- C&W He'll Have To Go [3]...Jim Reeves
- **LPS**
  - MO The Sound Of Music [3]...Original Cast
  - ST The Sound Of Music [5]...Original Cast

February 29, 1960
- HOT The Theme From "A Summer Place" [2]...Percy Faith
- R&B Baby (You've Got What It Takes) [4]...
  Dinah Washington & Brook Benton
- C&W He'll Have To Go [4]...Jim Reeves
- **LPS**
  - MO The Sound Of Music [4]...Original Cast
  - ST The Sound Of Music [6]...Original Cast

March 7, 1960
- HOT The Theme From "A Summer Place" [3]...Percy Faith
- R&B Baby (You've Got What It Takes) [5]...
  Dinah Washington & Brook Benton
- C&W He'll Have To Go [5]...Jim Reeves
- **LPS**
  - MO The Sound Of Music [5]...Original Cast
  - ST The Sound Of Music [7]...Original Cast

March 14, 1960
- HOT The Theme From "A Summer Place" [4]...Percy Faith
- R&B Baby (You've Got What It Takes) [6]...
  Dinah Washington & Brook Benton
- C&W He'll Have To Go [6]...Jim Reeves
- **LPS**
  - MO The Sound Of Music [6]...Original Cast
  - ST The Sound Of Music [8]...Original Cast

March 21, 1960
- HOT The Theme From "A Summer Place" [5]...Percy Faith
- R&B Baby (You've Got What It Takes) [7]...
  Dinah Washington & Brook Benton
- C&W He'll Have To Go [7]...Jim Reeves
- **LPS**
  - MO The Sound Of Music [7]...Original Cast
  - ST The Sound Of Music [9]...Original Cast

March 28, 1960
- HOT The Theme From "A Summer Place" [6]...Percy Faith
- R&B Baby (You've Got What It Takes) [8]...
  Dinah Washington & Brook Benton
- C&W He'll Have To Go [8]...Jim Reeves
- **LPS**
  - MO The Sound Of Music [8]...Original Cast
  - ST The Sound Of Music [10]...Original Cast

April 4, 1960
- HOT The Theme From "A Summer Place" [7]...Percy Faith
- R&B Baby (You've Got What It Takes) [9]...
  Dinah Washington & Brook Benton
- C&W He'll Have To Go [9]...Jim Reeves
- **LPS**
  - MO The Sound Of Music [9]...Original Cast
  - ST The Sound Of Music [11]...Original Cast

April 11, 1960

- **HOT** The Theme From "A Summer Place" [8]...Percy Faith
- **R&B** Baby (You've Got What It Takes) [10]...
  Dinah Washington & Brook Benton
- **C&W** He'll Have To Go [10]...Jim Reeves
- **LPS**
  - **MO** The Sound Of Music [10]...Original Cast
  - **ST** The Sound Of Music [12]...Original Cast

April 18, 1960

- **HOT** The Theme From "A Summer Place" [9]...Percy Faith
- **R&B** Fannie Mae [1]...Buster Brown
- **C&W** He'll Have To Go [11]...Jim Reeves
- **LPS**
  - **MO** The Sound Of Music [11]...Original Cast
  - **ST** The Sound Of Music [13]...Original Cast

April 25, 1960

- **HOT** Stuck On You [1]...Elvis Presley
- **R&B** White Silver Sands [1]...Bill Black's Combo
- **C&W** He'll Have To Go [12]...Jim Reeves
- **LPS**
  - **MO** The Sound Of Music [12]...Original Cast
  - **ST** Persuasive Percussion [1]...
    Enoch Light/Terry Snyder and The All-Stars

May 2, 1960

- **HOT** Stuck On You [2]...Elvis Presley
- **R&B** White Silver Sands [2]...Bill Black's Combo
- **C&W** He'll Have To Go [13]...Jim Reeves
- **LPS**
  - **MO** Theme from A Summer Place [1]...
    Billy Vaughn and his orchestra
  - **ST** The Sound Of Music [14]...Original Cast

May 9, 1960

- **HOT** Stuck On You [3]...Elvis Presley
- **R&B** White Silver Sands [3]...Bill Black's Combo
- **C&W** He'll Have To Go [14]...Jim Reeves
- **LPS**
  - **MO** Sold Out [1]...The Kingston Trio
  - **ST** The Sound Of Music [15]...Original Cast

May 16, 1960

- **HOT** Stuck On You [4]...Elvis Presley
- **R&B** White Silver Sands [4]...Bill Black's Combo
- **C&W** Please Help Me, I'm Falling [1]...Hank Locklin
- **LPS**
  - **MO** Theme from A Summer Place [2]...
    Billy Vaughn and his orchestra
  - **ST** Persuasive Percussion [2]...
    Enoch Light/Terry Snyder and The All-Stars

May 23, 1960

- **HOT** *Cathy's Clown [1]...The Everly Brothers
- **R&B** Doggin' Around [1]...Jackie Wilson
- **C&W** Please Help Me, I'm Falling [2]...Hank Locklin
- **LPS**
  - **MO** Sold Out [2]...The Kingston Trio
  - **ST** Sold Out [1]...The Kingston Trio

May 30, 1960

- **HOT** Cathy's Clown [2]...The Everly Brothers
- **R&B** Doggin' Around [2]...Jackie Wilson
- **C&W** Please Help Me, I'm Falling [3]...Hank Locklin
- **LPS**
  - **MO** Sold Out [3]...The Kingston Trio
  - **ST** Persuasive Percussion [3]...
    Enoch Light/Terry Snyder and The All-Stars

June 6, 1960

- **HOT** Cathy's Clown [3]...The Everly Brothers
- **R&B** Doggin' Around [3]...Jackie Wilson
- **C&W** Please Help Me, I'm Falling [4]...Hank Locklin
- **LPS**
  - **MO** Sold Out [4]...The Kingston Trio
  - **ST** Persuasive Percussion [4]...
    Enoch Light/Terry Snyder and The All-Stars

June 13, 1960

- **HOT** Cathy's Clown [4]...The Everly Brothers
- **R&B** Cathy's Clown [1]...The Everly Brothers
- **C&W** Please Help Me, I'm Falling [5]...Hank Locklin
- **LPS**
  - **MO** Sold Out [5]...The Kingston Trio
  - **ST** Persuasive Percussion [5]...
    Enoch Light/Terry Snyder and The All-Stars

June 20, 1960

- **HOT** Cathy's Clown [5]...The Everly Brothers
- **R&B** A Rockin' Good Way (To Mess Around And
  Fall In Love) [1]...Dinah Washington & Brook Benton
- **C&W** Please Help Me, I'm Falling [6]...Hank Locklin
- **LPS**
  - **MO** Sold Out [6]...The Kingston Trio
  - **ST** Persuasive Percussion [6]...
    Enoch Light/Terry Snyder and The All-Stars

June 27, 1960

- **HOT** Everybody's Somebody's Fool [1]...Connie Francis
- **R&B** A Rockin' Good Way (To Mess Around And Fall In Love) [2]...Dinah Washington & Brook Benton
- **C&W** Please Help Me, I'm Falling [7]...Hank Locklin
- **LPS**
  - **MO** Sold Out [7]...The Kingston Trio
  - **ST** Persuasive Percussion [7]...
    Enoch Light/Terry Snyder and The All-Stars

July 4, 1960

- **HOT** Everybody's Somebody's Fool [2]...Connie Francis
- **R&B** A Rockin' Good Way (To Mess Around And Fall In Love) [3]...Dinah Washington & Brook Benton
- **C&W** Please Help Me, I'm Falling [8]...Hank Locklin
- **LPS**
  - **MO** Sold Out [8]...The Kingston Trio
  - **ST** Persuasive Percussion [8]...
    Enoch Light/Terry Snyder and The All-Stars

July 11, 1960

- **HOT** Alley-Oop [1]...Hollywood Argyles
- **R&B** There's Something On Your Mind, Part 2 [1]...Bobby Marchan
- **C&W** Please Help Me, I'm Falling [9]...Hank Locklin
- **LPS**
  - **MO** Sold Out [9]...The Kingston Trio
  - **ST** Persuasive Percussion [9]...
    Enoch Light/Terry Snyder and The All-Stars

July 18, 1960

- **HOT** I'm Sorry [1]...Brenda Lee
- **R&B** A Rockin' Good Way (To Mess Around And Fall In Love) [4]...Dinah Washington & Brook Benton
- **C&W** Please Help Me, I'm Falling [10]...Hank Locklin
- **LPS**
  - **MO** Sold Out [10]...The Kingston Trio
  - **ST** Persuasive Percussion [10]...
    Enoch Light/Terry Snyder and The All-Stars

July 25, 1960

- **HOT** I'm Sorry [2]...Brenda Lee
- **R&B** This Bitter Earth [1]...Dinah Washington
- **C&W** Please Help Me, I'm Falling [11]...Hank Locklin
- **LPS**
  - **MO** The Button-Down Mind Of Bob Newhart [1]...Bob Newhart
  - **ST** Persuasive Percussion [11]...
    Enoch Light/Terry Snyder and The All-Stars

August 1, 1960

- **HOT** I'm Sorry [3]...Brenda Lee
- **R&B** A Woman, A Lover, A Friend [1]...Jackie Wilson
- **C&W** Please Help Me, I'm Falling [12]...Hank Locklin
- **LPS**
  - **MO** The Button-Down Mind Of Bob Newhart [2]...Bob Newhart
  - **ST** Persuasive Percussion [12]...
    Enoch Light/Terry Snyder and The All-Stars

August 8, 1960

- **HOT** Itsy Bitsy Teenie Weenie Yellow Polkadot Bikini [1]...Brian Hyland
- **R&B** A Woman, A Lover, A Friend [2]...Jackie Wilson
- **C&W** Please Help Me, I'm Falling [13]...Hank Locklin
- **LPS**
  - **MO** The Button-Down Mind Of Bob Newhart [3]...Bob Newhart
  - **ST** Persuasive Percussion [13]...
    Enoch Light/Terry Snyder and The All-Stars

August 15, 1960

- **HOT** It's Now Or Never [1]...Elvis Presley
- **R&B** A Woman, A Lover, A Friend [3]...Jackie Wilson
- **C&W** Please Help Me, I'm Falling [14]...Hank Locklin
- **LPS**
  - **MO** The Button-Down Mind Of Bob Newhart [4]...Bob Newhart
  - **ST** Sold Out [2]...The Kingston Trio

August 22, 1960

- **HOT** It's Now Or Never [2]...Elvis Presley
- **R&B** A Woman, A Lover, A Friend [4]...Jackie Wilson
- **C&W** Alabam [1]...Cowboy Copas
- **LPS**
  - **MO** The Button-Down Mind Of Bob Newhart [5]...Bob Newhart
  - **ST** Sold Out [3]...The Kingston Trio

August 29, 1960

- **HOT** It's Now Or Never [3]...Elvis Presley
- **R&B** Kiddio [1]...Brook Benton
- **C&W** Alabam [2]...Cowboy Copas
- **LPS**
  - **MO** The Button-Down Mind Of Bob Newhart [6]...Bob Newhart
  - **ST** String Along [1]...The Kingston Trio

September 5, 1960

- **HOT** It's Now Or Never [4]...Elvis Presley
- **R&B** Kiddio [2]...Brook Benton
- **C&W** Alabam [3]...Cowboy Copas
- **LPS**
  - **MO** The Button-Down Mind Of Bob Newhart [7]...Bob Newhart
  - **ST** String Along [2]...The Kingston Trio

September 12, 1960

- **HOT** It's Now Or Never [5]...Elvis Presley
- **R&B** Kiddio [3]...Brook Benton
- **C&W** Alabam [4]...Cowboy Copas
- **LPS**
  - **MO** The Button-Down Mind Of Bob Newhart [8]...Bob Newhart
  - **ST** String Along [3]...The Kingston Trio

September 19, 1960

- **HOT** *The Twist [1]...Chubby Checker
- **R&B** Kiddio [4]...Brook Benton
- **C&W** Alabam [5]...Cowboy Copas
- **LPS**
  - **MO** String Along [1]...The Kingston Trio
  - **ST** String Along [4]...The Kingston Trio

September 26, 1960

- **HOT** My Heart Has A Mind Of Its Own [1]...Connie Francis
- **R&B** Kiddio [5]...Brook Benton
- **C&W** Alabam [6]...Cowboy Copas
- **LPS**
  - **MO** String Along [2]...The Kingston Trio
  - **ST** String Along [5]...The Kingston Trio

October 3, 1960

- **HOT** My Heart Has A Mind Of Its Own [2]...Connie Francis
- **R&B** Kiddio [6]...Brook Benton
- **C&W** Alabam [7]...Cowboy Copas
- **LPS**
  - **MO** String Along [3]...The Kingston Trio
  - **ST** String Along [6]...The Kingston Trio

October 10, 1960

- **HOT** Mr. Custer [1]...Larry Verne
- **R&B** Kiddio [7]...Brook Benton
- **C&W** Alabam [8]...Cowboy Copas
- **LPS**
  - **MO** String Along [4]...The Kingston Trio
  - **ST** String Along [7]...The Kingston Trio

October 17, 1960

- **HOT** *Save The Last Dance For Me [1]...The Drifters
- **R&B** Kiddio [8]...Brook Benton
- **C&W** Alabam [9]...Cowboy Copas
- **LPS**
  - **MO** String Along [5]...The Kingston Trio
  - **ST** String Along [8]...The Kingston Trio

October 24, 1960

- **HOT** I Want To Be Wanted [1]...Brenda Lee
- **R&B** Kiddio [9]...Brook Benton
- **C&W** Alabam [10]...Cowboy Copas
- **LPS**
  - **MO** Nice 'n' Easy [1]...Frank Sinatra
  - **ST** Nice 'n' Easy [1]...Frank Sinatra

October 31, 1960

- **HOT** Save The Last Dance For Me [2]...The Drifters
- **R&B** Save The Last Dance For Me [1]...The Drifters
- **C&W** Alabam [11]...Cowboy Copas
- **LPS**
  - **MO** The Button-Down Mind Of Bob Newhart [9]...Bob Newhart
  - **ST** Nice 'n' Easy [2]...Frank Sinatra

November 7, 1960

- **HOT** Save The Last Dance For Me [3]...The Drifters
- **R&B** Let's Go, Let's Go, Let's Go [1]...Hank Ballard & The Midnighters
- **C&W** Alabam [12]...Cowboy Copas
- **LPS**
  - **MO** The Button-Down Mind Of Bob Newhart [10]...Bob Newhart
  - **ST** Nice 'n' Easy [3]...Frank Sinatra

November 14, 1960

- **HOT** Georgia On My Mind [1]...Ray Charles
- **R&B** He Will Break Your Heart [1]...Jerry Butler
- **C&W** Wings Of A Dove [1]...Ferlin Husky
- **LPS**
  - **MO** The Button-Down Mind Of Bob Newhart [11]...Bob Newhart
  - **ST** String Along [9]...The Kingston Trio

November 21, 1960

- **HOT** Stay [1]...Maurice Williams
- **R&B** Let's Go, Let's Go, Let's Go [2]...Hank Ballard & The Midnighters
- **C&W** Wings Of A Dove [2]...Ferlin Husky
- **LPS**
  - **MO** The Button-Down Mind Of Bob Newhart [12]...Bob Newhart
  - **ST** Nice 'n' Easy [4]...Frank Sinatra

November 28, 1960

- **HOT** Are You Lonesome To-night? [1]...Elvis Presley
- **R&B** He Will Break Your Heart [2]...Jerry Butler
- **C&W** Wings Of A Dove [3]...Ferlin Husky
- **LPS**
  - **MO** The Button-Down Mind Of Bob Newhart [13]...
    Bob Newhart
  - **ST** Nice 'n' Easy [5]...Frank Sinatra

December 5, 1960

- **HOT** Are You Lonesome To-night? [2]...Elvis Presley
- **R&B** Let's Go, Let's Go, Let's Go [3]...
    Hank Ballard & The Midnighters
- **C&W** Wings Of A Dove [4]...Ferlin Husky
- **LPS**
  - **MO** G.I. Blues [1]...Elvis Presley/Soundtrack
  - **ST** Nice 'n' Easy [6]...Frank Sinatra

December 12, 1960

- **HOT** Are You Lonesome To-night? [3]...Elvis Presley
- **R&B** He Will Break Your Heart [3]...Jerry Butler
- **C&W** Wings Of A Dove [5]...Ferlin Husky
- **LPS**
  - **MO** The Button-Down Mind Of Bob Newhart [14]...
    Bob Newhart
  - **ST** Nice 'n' Easy [7]...Frank Sinatra

December 19, 1960

- **HOT** Are You Lonesome To-night? [4]...Elvis Presley
- **R&B** He Will Break Your Heart [4]...Jerry Butler
- **C&W** Wings Of A Dove [6]...Ferlin Husky
- **LPS**
  - **MO** G.I. Blues [2]...Elvis Presley/Soundtrack
  - **ST** Nice 'n' Easy [8]...Frank Sinatra

December 26, 1960

- **HOT** Are You Lonesome To-night? [5]...Elvis Presley
- **R&B** He Will Break Your Heart [5]...Jerry Butler
- **C&W** Wings Of A Dove [7]...Ferlin Husky
- **LPS**
  - **MO** G.I. Blues [3]...Elvis Presley/Soundtrack
  - **ST** String Along [10]...The Kingston Trio

December 31, 1960

- **HOT** Are You Lonesome To-night? [6]...Elvis Presley
- **R&B** He Will Break Your Heart [6]...Jerry Butler
- **C&W** Wings Of A Dove [8]...Ferlin Husky
- **LPS**
  - **MO** G.I. Blues [4]...Elvis Presley/Soundtrack
  - **ST** Nice 'n' Easy [9]...Frank Sinatra

January 9, 1961

- **HOT** Wonderland By Night [1]...Bert Kaempfert
- **R&B** He Will Break Your Heart [7]...Jerry Butler
- **C&W** North To Alaska [1]...Johnny Horton
- **LPS**
  - **MO** The Button-Down Mind Strikes Back! [1]...
    Bob Newhart
  - **ST** G.I. Blues [1]...Elvis Presley/Soundtrack

January 16, 1961

- **HOT** Wonderland By Night [2]...Bert Kaempfert
- **R&B** Shop Around [1]...The Miracles
- **C&W** North To Alaska [2]...Johnny Horton
- **LPS**
  - **MO** Wonderland By Night [1]...
    Bert Kaempfert and his orchestra
  - **ST** G.I. Blues [2]...Elvis Presley/Soundtrack

January 23, 1961

- **HOT** Wonderland By Night [3]...Bert Kaempfert
- **R&B** Shop Around [2]...The Miracles
- **C&W** North To Alaska [3]...Johnny Horton
- **LPS**
  - **MO** Wonderland By Night [2]...
    Bert Kaempfert and his orchestra
  - **ST** Exodus [1]...Soundtrack

January 30, 1961

- **HOT** Will You Love Me Tomorrow [1]...The Shirelles
- **R&B** Shop Around [3]...The Miracles
- **C&W** North To Alaska [4]...Johnny Horton
- **LPS**
  - **MO** Wonderland By Night [3]...
    Bert Kaempfert and his orchestra
  - **ST** Exodus [2]...Soundtrack

February 6, 1961

- **HOT** Will You Love Me Tomorrow [2]...The Shirelles
- **R&B** Shop Around [4]...The Miracles
- **C&W** North To Alaska [5]...Johnny Horton
- **LPS**
  - **MO** Exodus [1]...Soundtrack
  - **ST** Exodus [3]...Soundtrack

February 13, 1961

- **HOT** Calcutta [1]...Lawrence Welk
- **R&B** Shop Around [5]...The Miracles
- **C&W** Wings Of A Dove [9]...Ferlin Husky
- **LPS**
  - **MO** Wonderland By Night [4]...
    Bert Kaempfert and his orchestra
  - **ST** Exodus [4]...Soundtrack

February 20, 1961

- HOT   Calcutta [2]...Lawrence Welk
- R&B   Shop Around [6]...The Miracles
- C&W   Wings Of A Dove [10]...Ferlin Husky
- **LPS**
  - M0   Wonderland By Night [5]...
    Bert Kaempfert and his orchestra
  - ST   Exodus [5]...Soundtrack

February 27, 1961

- HOT   *Pony Time [1]...Chubby Checker
- R&B   Shop Around [7]...The Miracles
- C&W   Don't Worry [1]...Marty Robbins
- **LPS**
  - M0   Exodus [2]...Soundtrack
  - ST   Exodus [6]...Soundtrack

March 6, 1961

- HOT   Pony Time [2]...Chubby Checker
- R&B   Shop Around [8]...The Miracles
- C&W   Don't Worry [2]...Marty Robbins
- **LPS**
  - M0   Exodus [3]...Soundtrack
  - ST   Exodus [7]...Soundtrack

March 13, 1961

- HOT   Pony Time [3]...Chubby Checker
- R&B   Pony Time [1]...Chubby Checker
- C&W   Don't Worry [3]...Marty Robbins
- **LPS**
  - M0   Calcutta! [1]...Lawrence Welk
  - ST   Calcutta! [1]...Lawrence Welk

March 20, 1961

- HOT   Surrender [1]...Elvis Presley
- R&B   Pony Time [2]...Chubby Checker
- C&W   Don't Worry [4]...Marty Robbins
- **LPS**
  - M0   Calcutta! [2]...Lawrence Welk
  - ST   Calcutta! [2]...Lawrence Welk

March 27, 1961

- HOT   Surrender [2]...Elvis Presley
- R&B   I Pity The Fool [1]...Bobby Bland
- C&W   Don't Worry [5]...Marty Robbins
- **LPS**
  - M0   Calcutta! [3]...Lawrence Welk
  - ST   Calcutta! [3]...Lawrence Welk

April 3, 1961

- HOT   *Blue Moon [1]...The Marcels
- R&B   *Blue Moon [1]...The Marcels
- C&W   Don't Worry [6]...Marty Robbins
- **LPS**
  - M0   G.I. Blues [5]...Elvis Presley/Soundtrack
  - ST   Calcutta! [4]...Lawrence Welk

April 10, 1961

- HOT   Blue Moon [2]...The Marcels
- R&B   Blue Moon [2]...The Marcels
- C&W   Don't Worry [7]...Marty Robbins
- **LPS**
  - M0   Calcutta! [4]...Lawrence Welk
  - ST   Calcutta! [5]...Lawrence Welk

April 17, 1961

- HOT   Blue Moon [3]...The Marcels
- R&B   One Mint Julep [1]...Ray Charles
- C&W   Don't Worry [8]...Marty Robbins
- **LPS**
  - M0   Calcutta! [5]...Lawrence Welk
  - ST   Calcutta! [6]...Lawrence Welk

April 24, 1961

- HOT   Runaway [1]...Del Shannon
- R&B   *Mother-In-Law [1]...Ernie K-Doe
- C&W   Don't Worry [9]...Marty Robbins
- **LPS**
  - M0   Calcutta! [6]...Lawrence Welk
  - ST   Calcutta! [7]...Lawrence Welk

May 1, 1961

- HOT   Runaway [2]...Del Shannon
- R&B   Mother-In-Law [2]...Ernie K-Doe
- C&W   Don't Worry [10]...Marty Robbins
- **LPS**
  - M0   Calcutta! [7]...Lawrence Welk
  - ST   Calcutta! [8]...Lawrence Welk

May 8, 1961

- HOT   Runaway [3]...Del Shannon
- R&B   Mother-In-Law [3]...Ernie K-Doe
- C&W   Hello Walls [1]...Faron Young
- **LPS**
  - M0   Calcutta! [8]...Lawrence Welk
  - ST   Calcutta! [9]...Lawrence Welk

May 15, 1961

- **HOT** Runaway [4]...Del Shannon
- **R&B** Mother-In-Law [4]...Ernie K-Doe
- **C&W** Hello Walls [2]...Faron Young
- **LPS**
  - **MO** G.I. Blues [6]...Elvis Presley/Soundtrack
  - **ST** Calcutta! [10]...Lawrence Welk

May 22, 1961

- **HOT** Mother-In-Law [1]...Ernie K-Doe
- **R&B** Mother-In-Law [5]...Ernie K-Doe
- **C&W** Hello Walls [3]...Faron Young
- **LPS**
  - **MO** G.I. Blues [7]...Elvis Presley/Soundtrack
  - **ST** Exodus [8]...Soundtrack

May 29, 1961

- **HOT** Travelin' Man [1]...Ricky Nelson
- **R&B** Stand By Me [1]...Ben E. King
- **C&W** Hello Walls [4]...Faron Young
- **LPS**
  - **MO** G.I. Blues [8]...Elvis Presley/Soundtrack
  - **ST** Calcutta! [11]...Lawrence Welk

June 5, 1961

- **HOT** Running Scared [1]...Roy Orbison
- **R&B** Stand By Me [2]...Ben E. King
- **C&W** Hello Walls [5]...Faron Young
- **LPS**
  - **MO** Camelot [1]...Original Cast
  - **ST** Exodus [9]...Soundtrack

June 12, 1961

- **HOT** Travelin' Man [2]...Ricky Nelson
- **R&B** Stand By Me [3]...Ben E. King
- **C&W** Hello Walls [6]...Faron Young
- **LPS**
  - **MO** Camelot [2]...Original Cast
  - **ST** Exodus [10]...Soundtrack

June 19, 1961

- **HOT** Moody River [1]...Pat Boone
- **R&B** Stand By Me [4]...Ben E. King
- **C&W** Hello Walls [7]...Faron Young
- **LPS**
  - **MO** Camelot [3]...Original Cast
  - **ST** Exodus [11]...Soundtrack

June 26, 1961

- **HOT** Quarter To Three [1]...U.S. Bonds
- **R&B** Every Beat Of My Heart [1]...Pips
- **C&W** Hello Walls [8]...Faron Young
- **LPS**
  - **MO** Camelot [4]...Original Cast
  - **ST** Exodus [12]...Soundtrack

July 3, 1961

- **HOT** Quarter To Three [2]...U.S. Bonds
- **R&B** *Tossin' And Turnin' [1]...Bobby Lewis
- **C&W** Hello Walls [9]...Faron Young
- **LPS**
  - **MO** Camelot [5]...Original Cast
  - **ST** Exodus [13]...Soundtrack

July 10, 1961

- **HOT** Tossin' And Turnin' [1]...Bobby Lewis
- **R&B** Tossin' And Turnin' [2]...Bobby Lewis
- **C&W** Heartbreak U.S.A. [1]...Kitty Wells
- **LPS**
  - **MO** Camelot [6]...Original Cast
  - **ST** Exodus [14]...Soundtrack

July 17, 1961

- **HOT** Tossin' And Turnin' [2]...Bobby Lewis
- **R&B** Tossin' And Turnin' [3]...Bobby Lewis
- **C&W** Heartbreak U.S.A. [2]...Kitty Wells
- **A/C** The Boll Weevil Song [1]...Brook Benton
- **LPS**
  - **MO** Carnival [1]...Original Cast
  - **ST** Stars For A Summer Night [1]...Various Artists

July 24, 1961

- **HOT** Tossin' And Turnin' [3]...Bobby Lewis
- **R&B** Tossin' And Turnin' [4]...Bobby Lewis
- **C&W** Heartbreak U.S.A. [3]...Kitty Wells
- **A/C** The Boll Weevil Song [2]...Brook Benton
- **LPS**
  - **MO** Stars For A Summer Night [1]...Various Artists
  - **ST** Stars For A Summer Night [2]...Various Artists

July 31, 1961

- **HOT** Tossin' And Turnin' [4]...Bobby Lewis
- **R&B** Tossin' And Turnin' [5]...Bobby Lewis
- **C&W** Heartbreak U.S.A. [4]...Kitty Wells
- **A/C** The Boll Weevil Song [3]...Brook Benton
- **LPS**
  - **MO** Stars For A Summer Night [2]...Various Artists
  - **ST** Stars For A Summer Night [3]...Various Artists

August 7, 1961

- HOT   Tossin' And Turnin' [5]...Bobby Lewis
- R&B   Tossin' And Turnin' [6]...Bobby Lewis
- C&W   I Fall To Pieces [1]...Patsy Cline
- A/C   Together [1]...Connie Francis
- LPS
  - MO   Stars For A Summer Night [3]...Various Artists
  - ST   Stars For A Summer Night [4]...Various Artists

August 14, 1961

- HOT   Tossin' And Turnin' [6]...Bobby Lewis
- R&B   Tossin' And Turnin' [7]...Bobby Lewis
- C&W   I Fall To Pieces [2]...Patsy Cline
- A/C   *Wooden Heart [1]...Joe Dowell
- LPS
  - MO   Stars For A Summer Night [4]...Various Artists
  - ST   Stars For A Summer Night [5]...Various Artists

August 21, 1961

- HOT   Tossin' And Turnin' [7]...Bobby Lewis
- R&B   Tossin' And Turnin' [8]...Bobby Lewis
- C&W   Tender Years [1]...George Jones
- A/C   Wooden Heart [2]...Joe Dowell
- LPS
  - MO   Something for Everybody [1]...Elvis Presley
  - ST   Stars For A Summer Night [6]...Various Artists

August 28, 1961

- HOT   Wooden Heart [1]...Joe Dowell
- R&B   Tossin' And Turnin' [9]...Bobby Lewis
- C&W   Tender Years [2]...George Jones
- A/C   Wooden Heart [3]...Joe Dowell
- LPS
  - MO   Something for Everybody [2]...Elvis Presley
  - ST   Stars For A Summer Night [7]...Various Artists

September 4, 1961

- HOT   *Michael [1]...The Highwaymen
- R&B   Tossin' And Turnin' [10]...Bobby Lewis
- C&W   Tender Years [3]...George Jones
- A/C   *Michael [1]...The Highwaymen
- LPS
  - MO   Something for Everybody [3]...Elvis Presley
  - ST   Stars For A Summer Night [8]...Various Artists

September 11, 1961

- HOT   Michael [2]...The Highwaymen
- R&B   My True Story [1]...The Jive Five
- C&W   Tender Years [4]...George Jones
- A/C   Michael [2]...The Highwaymen
- LPS
  - MO   Judy At Carnegie Hall [1]...Judy Garland
  - ST   Stars For A Summer Night [9]...Various Artists

September 18, 1961

- HOT   Take Good Care Of My Baby [1]...Bobby Vee
- R&B   My True Story [2]...The Jive Five
- C&W   Tender Years [5]...George Jones
- A/C   Michael [3]...The Highwaymen
- LPS
  - MO   Judy At Carnegie Hall [2]...Judy Garland
  - ST   Judy At Carnegie Hall [1]...Judy Garland

September 25, 1961

- HOT   Take Good Care Of My Baby [2]...Bobby Vee
- R&B   My True Story [3]...The Jive Five
- C&W   Walk On By [1]...Leroy Van Dyke
- A/C   Michael [4]...The Highwaymen
- LPS
  - MO   Judy At Carnegie Hall [3]...Judy Garland
  - ST   Judy At Carnegie Hall [2]...Judy Garland

October 2, 1961

- HOT   Take Good Care Of My Baby [3]...Bobby Vee
- R&B   *Hit The Road Jack [1]...Ray Charles
- C&W   Tender Years [6]...George Jones
- A/C   Michael [5]...The Highwaymen
- LPS
  - MO   Judy At Carnegie Hall [4]...Judy Garland
  - ST   Judy At Carnegie Hall [3]...Judy Garland

October 9, 1961

- HOT   Hit The Road Jack [1]...Ray Charles
- R&B   Hit The Road Jack [2]...Ray Charles
- C&W   Tender Years [7]...George Jones
- A/C   Mexico [1]...Bob Moore
- LPS
  - MO   Judy At Carnegie Hall [5]...Judy Garland
  - ST   Judy At Carnegie Hall [4]...Judy Garland

October 16, 1961

- **HOT** Hit The Road Jack [2]...Ray Charles
- **R&B** Hit The Road Jack [3]...Ray Charles
- **C&W** Walk On By [2]...Leroy Van Dyke
- **A/C** Sad Movies (Make Me Cry) [1]...Sue Thompson
- **LPS**
  - **MO** Judy At Carnegie Hall [6]...Judy Garland
  - **ST** Judy At Carnegie Hall [5]...Judy Garland

October 23, 1961

- **HOT** Runaround Sue [1]...Dion
- **R&B** Hit The Road Jack [4]...Ray Charles
- **C&W** Walk On By [3]...Leroy Van Dyke
- **A/C** *Big Bad John [1]...Jimmy Dean
- **LPS**
  - **MO** Judy At Carnegie Hall [7]...Judy Garland
  - **ST** Judy At Carnegie Hall [6]...Judy Garland

October 30, 1961

- **HOT** Runaround Sue [2]...Dion
- **R&B** Hit The Road Jack [5]...Ray Charles
- **C&W** Walk On By [4]...Leroy Van Dyke
- **A/C** Big Bad John [2]...Jimmy Dean
- **LPS**
  - **MO** Judy At Carnegie Hall [8]...Judy Garland
  - **ST** Judy At Carnegie Hall [7]...Judy Garland

November 6, 1961

- **HOT** Big Bad John [1]...Jimmy Dean
- **R&B** Ya Ya [1]...Lee Dorsey
- **C&W** Walk On By [5]...Leroy Van Dyke
- **A/C** Big Bad John [3]...Jimmy Dean
- **LPS**
  - **MO** Judy At Carnegie Hall [9]...Judy Garland
  - **ST** Judy At Carnegie Hall [8]...Judy Garland

November 13, 1961

- **HOT** Big Bad John [2]...Jimmy Dean
- **R&B** *Please Mr. Postman [1]...The Marvelettes
- **C&W** Walk On By [6]...Leroy Van Dyke
- **A/C** Big Bad John [4]...Jimmy Dean
- **LPS**
  - **MO** Judy At Carnegie Hall [10]...Judy Garland
  - **ST** Judy At Carnegie Hall [9]...Judy Garland

November 20, 1961

- **HOT** Big Bad John [3]...Jimmy Dean
- **R&B** Please Mr. Postman [2]...The Marvelettes
- **C&W** Big Bad John [1]...Jimmy Dean
- **A/C** Big Bad John [5]...Jimmy Dean
- **LPS**
  - **MO** Judy At Carnegie Hall [11]...Judy Garland
  - **ST** Stereo 35/MM [1]...Enoch Light & The Light Brigade

November 27, 1961

- **HOT** Big Bad John [4]...Jimmy Dean
- **R&B** Please Mr. Postman [3]...The Marvelettes
- **C&W** Big Bad John [2]...Jimmy Dean
- **A/C** Big Bad John [6]...Jimmy Dean
- **LPS**
  - **MO** Judy At Carnegie Hall [12]...Judy Garland
  - **ST** Stereo 35/MM [2]...Enoch Light & The Light Brigade

December 4, 1961

- **HOT** Big Bad John [5]...Jimmy Dean
- **R&B** Please Mr. Postman [4]...The Marvelettes
- **C&W** Walk On By [7]...Leroy Van Dyke
- **A/C** Big Bad John [7]...Jimmy Dean
- **LPS**
  - **MO** Judy At Carnegie Hall [13]...Judy Garland
  - **ST** Stereo 35/MM [3]...Enoch Light & The Light Brigade

December 11, 1961

- **HOT** Please Mr. Postman [1]...The Marvelettes
- **R&B** Please Mr. Postman [5]...The Marvelettes
- **C&W** Walk On By [8]...Leroy Van Dyke
- **A/C** Big Bad John [8]...Jimmy Dean
- **LPS**
  - **MO** Blue Hawaii [1]...Elvis Presley/Soundtrack
  - **ST** Stereo 35/MM [4]...Enoch Light & The Light Brigade

December 18, 1961

- **HOT** The Lion Sleeps Tonight [1]...The Tokens
- **R&B** Please Mr. Postman [6]...The Marvelettes
- **C&W** Walk On By [9]...Leroy Van Dyke
- **A/C** Big Bad John [9]...Jimmy Dean
- **LPS**
  - **MO** Blue Hawaii [2]...Elvis Presley/Soundtrack
  - **ST** Stereo 35/MM [5]...Enoch Light & The Light Brigade

December 25, 1961

- **HOT** The Lion Sleeps Tonight [2]...The Tokens
- **R&B** Please Mr. Postman [7]...The Marvelettes
- **C&W** Walk On By [10]...Leroy Van Dyke
- **A/C** Big Bad John [10]...Jimmy Dean
- **LPS**
  - **MO** Blue Hawaii [3]...Elvis Presley/Soundtrack
  - **ST** Stereo 35/MM [6]...Enoch Light & The Light Brigade

January 6, 1962

- **HOT** The Lion Sleeps Tonight [3]...The Tokens
- **R&B** Unchain My Heart [1]...Ray Charles
- **C&W** Walk On By [11]...Leroy Van Dyke
- **A/C** When I Fall In Love [1]...The Lettermen
- **LPS**
  - **MO** Blue Hawaii [4]...Elvis Presley/Soundtrack
  - **ST** Stereo 35/MM [7]...Enoch Light & The Light Brigade

January 13, 1962

- **HOT** The Twist [2]...Chubby Checker
  first hit #1 on 9/19/60
- **R&B** Unchain My Heart [2]...Ray Charles
- **C&W** Walk On By [12]...Leroy Van Dyke
- **A/C** Can't Help Falling In Love [1]...Elvis Presley
- **LPS**
  - **MO** Blue Hawaii [5]...Elvis Presley/Soundtrack
  - **ST** Holiday Sing Along With Mitch [1]...
    Mitch Miller And The Gang

January 20, 1962

- **HOT** The Twist [3]...Chubby Checker
- **R&B** I Know (You Don't Love Me No More) [1]...
  Barbara George
- **C&W** Walk On By [13]...Leroy Van Dyke
- **A/C** Can't Help Falling In Love [2]...Elvis Presley
- **LPS**
  - **MO** Blue Hawaii [6]...Elvis Presley/Soundtrack
  - **ST** Blue Hawaii [1]...Elvis Presley/Soundtrack

January 27, 1962

- **HOT** Peppermint Twist - Part I [1]...
  Joey Dee & the Starliters
- **R&B** I Know (You Don't Love Me No More) [2]...
  Barbara George
- **C&W** Walk On By [14]...Leroy Van Dyke
- **A/C** Can't Help Falling In Love [3]...Elvis Presley
- **LPS**
  - **MO** Blue Hawaii [7]...Elvis Presley/Soundtrack
  - **ST** Blue Hawaii [2]...Elvis Presley/Soundtrack

February 3, 1962

- **HOT** Peppermint Twist - Part I [2]...
  Joey Dee & the Starliters
- **R&B** I Know (You Don't Love Me No More) [3]...
  Barbara George
- **C&W** Walk On By [15]...Leroy Van Dyke
- **A/C** Can't Help Falling In Love [4]...Elvis Presley
- **LPS**
  - **MO** Blue Hawaii [8]...Elvis Presley/Soundtrack
  - **ST** Blue Hawaii [3]...Elvis Presley/Soundtrack

February 10, 1962

- **HOT** Peppermint Twist - Part I [3]...
  Joey Dee & the Starliters
- **R&B** I Know (You Don't Love Me No More) [4]...
  Barbara George
- **C&W** Walk On By [16]...Leroy Van Dyke
- **A/C** Can't Help Falling In Love [5]...Elvis Presley
- **LPS**
  - **MO** Blue Hawaii [9]...Elvis Presley/Soundtrack
  - **ST** Breakfast At Tiffany's [1]...
    Henry Mancini/Soundtrack

February 17, 1962

- **HOT** *Duke Of Earl [1]...Gene Chandler
- **R&B** *Duke Of Earl [1]...Gene Chandler
- **C&W** Walk On By [17]...Leroy Van Dyke
- **A/C** Can't Help Falling In Love [6]...Elvis Presley
- **LPS**
  - **MO** Blue Hawaii [10]...Elvis Presley/Soundtrack
  - **ST** Breakfast At Tiffany's [2]...
    Henry Mancini/Soundtrack

February 24, 1962

- **HOT** Duke Of Earl [2]...Gene Chandler
- **R&B** Duke Of Earl [2]...Gene Chandler
- **C&W** Walk On By [18]...Leroy Van Dyke
- **A/C** A Little Bitty Tear [1]...Burl Ives
- **LPS**
  - **MO** Blue Hawaii [11]...Elvis Presley/Soundtrack
  - **ST** Breakfast At Tiffany's [3]...
    Henry Mancini/Soundtrack

March 3, 1962

- **HOT** Duke Of Earl [3]...Gene Chandler
- **R&B** Duke Of Earl [3]...Gene Chandler
- **C&W** Walk On By [19]...Leroy Van Dyke
- **A/C** Midnight In Moscow [1]...Kenny Ball
- **LPS**
  - **MO** Blue Hawaii [12]...Elvis Presley/Soundtrack
  - **ST** Breakfast At Tiffany's [4]...
    Henry Mancini/Soundtrack

March 10, 1962

- HOT Hey! Baby [1]...Bruce Channel
- R&B Duke Of Earl [4]...Gene Chandler
- C&W Misery Loves Company [1]...Porter Wagoner
- A/C Midnight In Moscow [2]...Kenny Ball
- LPS
  - MO Blue Hawaii [13]...Elvis Presley/Soundtrack
  - ST Breakfast At Tiffany's [5]...
    Henry Mancini/Soundtrack

March 17, 1962

- HOT Hey! Baby [2]...Bruce Channel
- R&B Duke Of Earl [5]...Gene Chandler
- C&W That's My Pa [1]...Sheb Wooley
- A/C Midnight In Moscow [3]...Kenny Ball
- LPS
  - MO Blue Hawaii [14]...Elvis Presley/Soundtrack
  - ST Breakfast At Tiffany's [6]...
    Henry Mancini/Soundtrack

March 24, 1962

- HOT Hey! Baby [3]...Bruce Channel
- R&B Twistin' The Nite Away [1]...Sam Cooke
- C&W Misery Loves Company [2]...Porter Wagoner
- A/C *Don't Break The Heart That Loves You [1]...
  Connie Francis
- LPS
  - MO Blue Hawaii [15]...Elvis Presley/Soundtrack
  - ST Breakfast At Tiffany's [7]...
    Henry Mancini/Soundtrack

March 31, 1962

- HOT Don't Break The Heart That Loves You [1]...
  Connie Francis
- R&B Twistin' The Nite Away [2]...Sam Cooke
- C&W She's Got You [1]...Patsy Cline
- A/C Don't Break The Heart That Loves You [2]...
  Connie Francis
- LPS
  - MO Blue Hawaii [16]...Elvis Presley/Soundtrack
  - ST Breakfast At Tiffany's [8]...
    Henry Mancini/Soundtrack

April 7, 1962

- HOT Johnny Angel [1]...Shelley Fabares
- R&B Twistin' The Nite Away [3]...Sam Cooke
- C&W She's Got You [2]...Patsy Cline
- A/C Don't Break The Heart That Loves You [3]...
  Connie Francis
- LPS
  - MO Blue Hawaii [17]...Elvis Presley/Soundtrack
  - ST Blue Hawaii [4]...Elvis Presley/Soundtrack

April 14, 1962

- HOT Johnny Angel [2]...Shelley Fabares
- R&B Soul Twist [1]...King Curtis
- C&W She's Got You [3]...Patsy Cline
- A/C Don't Break The Heart That Loves You [4]...
  Connie Francis
- LPS
  - MO Blue Hawaii [18]...Elvis Presley/Soundtrack
  - ST Breakfast At Tiffany's [9]...
    Henry Mancini/Soundtrack

April 21, 1962

- HOT Good Luck Charm [1]...Elvis Presley
- R&B Soul Twist [2]...King Curtis
- C&W She's Got You [4]...Patsy Cline
- A/C *Stranger On The Shore [1]...Mr. Acker Bilk
- LPS
  - MO Blue Hawaii [19]...Elvis Presley/Soundtrack
  - ST Breakfast At Tiffany's [10]...
    Henry Mancini/Soundtrack

April 28, 1962

- HOT Good Luck Charm [2]...Elvis Presley
- R&B Mashed Potato Time [1]...Dee Dee Sharp
- C&W Charlie's Shoes [1]...Billy Walker
- A/C Stranger On The Shore [2]...Mr. Acker Bilk
- LPS
  - MO Blue Hawaii [20]...Elvis Presley/Soundtrack
  - ST Breakfast At Tiffany's [11]...
    Henry Mancini/Soundtrack

May 5, 1962

- HOT Soldier Boy [1]...The Shirelles
- R&B Mashed Potato Time [2]...Dee Dee Sharp
- C&W She's Got You [5]...Patsy Cline
- A/C Stranger On The Shore [3]...Mr. Acker Bilk
- LPS
  - MO West Side Story [1]...Soundtrack
  - ST Breakfast At Tiffany's [12]...
    Henry Mancini/Soundtrack

May 12, 1962

- HOT Soldier Boy [2]...The Shirelles
- R&B Mashed Potato Time [3]...Dee Dee Sharp
- C&W Charlie's Shoes [2]...Billy Walker
- A/C Stranger On The Shore [4]...Mr. Acker Bilk
- LPS
  - MO West Side Story [2]...Soundtrack
  - ST West Side Story [1]...Soundtrack

May 19, 1962

- HOT Soldier Boy [3]...The Shirelles
- R&B Mashed Potato Time [4]...Dee Dee Sharp
- C&W She Thinks I Still Care [1]...George Jones
- A/C Stranger On The Shore [5]...Mr. Acker Bilk
- LPS
  - M0 West Side Story [3]...Soundtrack
  - ST West Side Story [2]...Soundtrack

May 26, 1962

- HOT Stranger On The Shore [1]...Mr. Acker Bilk
- R&B *I Can't Stop Loving You [1]...Ray Charles
- C&W She Thinks I Still Care [2]...George Jones
- A/C Stranger On The Shore [6]...Mr. Acker Bilk
- LPS
  - M0 West Side Story [4]...Soundtrack
  - ST West Side Story [3]...Soundtrack

June 2, 1962

- HOT I Can't Stop Loving You [1]...Ray Charles
- R&B I Can't Stop Loving You [2]...Ray Charles
- C&W She Thinks I Still Care [3]...George Jones
- A/C Stranger On The Shore [7]...Mr. Acker Bilk
- LPS
  - M0 West Side Story [5]...Soundtrack
  - ST West Side Story [4]...Soundtrack

June 9, 1962

- HOT I Can't Stop Loving You [2]...Ray Charles
- R&B I Can't Stop Loving You [3]...Ray Charles
- C&W She Thinks I Still Care [4]...George Jones
- A/C I Can't Stop Loving You [1]...Ray Charles
- LPS
  - M0 West Side Story [6]...Soundtrack
  - ST West Side Story [5]...Soundtrack

June 16, 1962

- HOT I Can't Stop Loving You [3]...Ray Charles
- R&B I Can't Stop Loving You [4]...Ray Charles
- C&W She Thinks I Still Care [5]...George Jones
- A/C I Can't Stop Loving You [2]...Ray Charles
- LPS
  - M0 West Side Story [7]...Soundtrack
  - ST West Side Story [6]...Soundtrack

June 23, 1962

- HOT I Can't Stop Loving You [4]...Ray Charles
- R&B I Can't Stop Loving You [5]...Ray Charles
- C&W She Thinks I Still Care [6]...George Jones
- A/C I Can't Stop Loving You [3]...Ray Charles
- LPS
  - M0 Modern Sounds In Country And Western Music [1]...Ray Charles
  - ST West Side Story [7]...Soundtrack

June 30, 1962

- HOT I Can't Stop Loving You [5]...Ray Charles
- R&B I Can't Stop Loving You [6]...Ray Charles
- C&W Wolverton Mountain [1]...Claude King
- A/C I Can't Stop Loving You [4]...Ray Charles
- LPS
  - M0 Modern Sounds In Country And Western Music [2]...Ray Charles
  - ST West Side Story [8]...Soundtrack

July 7, 1962

- HOT *The Stripper [1]...David Rose
- R&B I Can't Stop Loving You [7]...Ray Charles
- C&W Wolverton Mountain [2]...Claude King
- A/C *The Stripper [1]...David Rose
- LPS
  - M0 Modern Sounds In Country And Western Music [3]...Ray Charles
  - ST West Side Story [9]...Soundtrack

July 14, 1962

- HOT *Roses Are Red (My Love) [1]...Bobby Vinton
- R&B I Can't Stop Loving You [8]...Ray Charles
- C&W Wolverton Mountain [3]...Claude King
- A/C The Stripper [2]...David Rose
- LPS
  - M0 Modern Sounds In Country And Western Music [4]...Ray Charles
  - ST West Side Story [10]...Soundtrack

July 21, 1962

- HOT Roses Are Red (My Love) [2]...Bobby Vinton
- R&B I Can't Stop Loving You [9]...Ray Charles
- C&W Wolverton Mountain [4]...Claude King
- A/C I Can't Stop Loving You [5]...Ray Charles
- LPS
  - M0 Modern Sounds In Country And Western Music [5]...Ray Charles
  - ST West Side Story [11]...Soundtrack

July 28, 1962

- HOT   Roses Are Red (My Love) [3]...Bobby Vinton
- R&B   I Can't Stop Loving You [10]...Ray Charles
- C&W   Wolverton Mountain [5]...Claude King
- A/C   Roses Are Red (My Love) [1]...Bobby Vinton
- LPS
  - M0   Modern Sounds In Country And Western Music [6]...Ray Charles
  - ST   West Side Story [12]...Soundtrack

August 4, 1962

- HOT   Roses Are Red (My Love) [4]...Bobby Vinton
- R&B   You'll Lose A Good Thing [1]...Barbara Lynn
- C&W   Wolverton Mountain [6]...Claude King
- A/C   Roses Are Red (My Love) [2]...Bobby Vinton
- LPS
  - M0   Modern Sounds In Country And Western Music [7]...Ray Charles
  - ST   West Side Story [13]...Soundtrack

August 11, 1962

- HOT   Breaking Up Is Hard To Do [1]...Neil Sedaka
- R&B   You'll Lose A Good Thing [2]...Barbara Lynn
- C&W   Wolverton Mountain [7]...Claude King
- A/C   Roses Are Red (My Love) [3]...Bobby Vinton
- LPS
  - M0   Modern Sounds In Country And Western Music [8]...Ray Charles
  - ST   Modern Sounds In Country And Western Music [1]...Ray Charles

August 18, 1962

- HOT   Breaking Up Is Hard To Do [2]...Neil Sedaka
- R&B   You'll Lose A Good Thing [3]...Barbara Lynn
- C&W   Wolverton Mountain [8]...Claude King
- A/C   Roses Are Red (My Love) [4]...Bobby Vinton
- LPS
  - M0   Modern Sounds In Country And Western Music [9]...Ray Charles
  - ST   West Side Story [14]...Soundtrack

August 25, 1962

- HOT   *The Loco-Motion [1]...Little Eva
- R&B   *The Loco-Motion [1]...Little Eva
- C&W   Wolverton Mountain [9]...Claude King
- A/C   You Don't Know Me [1]...Ray Charles
- LPS
  - M0   Modern Sounds In Country And Western Music [10]...Ray Charles
  - ST   West Side Story [15]...Soundtrack

September 1, 1962

- HOT   Sheila [1]...Tommy Roe
- R&B   The Loco-Motion [2]...Little Eva
- C&W   Devil Woman [1]...Marty Robbins
- A/C   You Don't Know Me [2]...Ray Charles
- LPS
  - M0   Modern Sounds In Country And Western Music [11]...Ray Charles
  - ST   West Side Story [16]...Soundtrack

September 8, 1962

- HOT   Sheila [2]...Tommy Roe
- R&B   The Loco-Motion [3]...Little Eva
- C&W   Devil Woman [2]...Marty Robbins
- A/C   You Don't Know Me [3]...Ray Charles
- LPS
  - M0   Modern Sounds In Country And Western Music [12]...Ray Charles
  - ST   West Side Story [17]...Soundtrack

September 15, 1962

- HOT   *Sherry [1]...The 4 Seasons
- R&B   Green Onions [1]...Booker T. & The MG's
- C&W   Devil Woman [3]...Marty Robbins
- A/C   Ramblin' Rose [1]...Nat "King" Cole
- LPS
  - M0   Modern Sounds In Country And Western Music [13]...Ray Charles
  - ST   West Side Story [18]...Soundtrack

September 22, 1962

- HOT   Sherry [2]...The 4 Seasons
- R&B   You Beat Me To The Punch [1]...Mary Wells
- C&W   Devil Woman [4]...Marty Robbins
- A/C   Ramblin' Rose [2]...Nat "King" Cole
- LPS
  - M0   Modern Sounds In Country And Western Music [14]...Ray Charles
  - ST   West Side Story [19]...Soundtrack

September 29, 1962

- HOT   Sherry [3]...The 4 Seasons
- R&B   Green Onions [2]...Booker T. & The MG's
- C&W   Devil Woman [5]...Marty Robbins
- A/C   Ramblin' Rose [3]...Nat "King" Cole
- LPS
  - M0   West Side Story [8]...Soundtrack
  - ST   West Side Story [20]...Soundtrack

October 6, 1962

- HOT Sherry [4]...The 4 Seasons
- R&B Sherry [1]...The 4 Seasons
- C&W Devil Woman [6]...Marty Robbins
- A/C Ramblin' Rose [4]...Nat "King" Cole
- LPS
  - M0 West Side Story [9]...Soundtrack
  - ST West Side Story [21]...Soundtrack

October 13, 1962

- HOT Sherry [5]...The 4 Seasons
- R&B Green Onions [3]...Booker T. & The MG's
- C&W Devil Woman [7]...Marty Robbins
- A/C Ramblin' Rose [5]...Nat "King" Cole
- LPS
  - M0 West Side Story [10]...Soundtrack
  - ST West Side Story [22]...Soundtrack

October 20, 1962

- HOT Monster Mash [1]...Bobby "Boris" Pickett
- R&B Do You Love Me [1]...The Contours
- C&W Devil Woman [8]...Marty Robbins
- A/C I Remember You [1]...Frank Ifield
- LPS
  - M0 Peter, Paul and Mary [1]...Peter, Paul and Mary
  - ST West Side Story [23]...Soundtrack

October 27, 1962

- HOT Monster Mash [2]...Bobby "Boris" Pickett
- R&B Green Onions [4]...Booker T. & The MG's
- C&W Mama Sang A Song [1]...Bill Anderson
- A/C Only Love Can Break A Heart [1]...Gene Pitney
- LPS
  - M0 Peter, Paul and Mary [2]...Peter, Paul and Mary
  - ST West Side Story [24]...Soundtrack

November 3, 1962

- HOT He's A Rebel [1]...The Crystals
- R&B Do You Love Me [2]...The Contours
- C&W Mama Sang A Song [2]...Bill Anderson
- A/C Only Love Can Break A Heart [2]...Gene Pitney
- LPS
  - M0 Peter, Paul and Mary [3]...Peter, Paul and Mary
  - ST West Side Story [25]...Soundtrack

November 10, 1962

- HOT He's A Rebel [2]...The Crystals
- R&B Do You Love Me [3]...The Contours
- C&W I've Been Everywhere [1]...Hank Snow
- A/C All Alone Am I [1]...Brenda Lee
- LPS
  - M0 Peter, Paul and Mary [4]...Peter, Paul and Mary
  - ST West Side Story [26]...Soundtrack

November 17, 1962

- HOT *Big Girls Don't Cry [1]...The 4 Seasons
- R&B *Big Girls Don't Cry [1]...The 4 Seasons
- C&W Mama Sang A Song [3]...Bill Anderson
- A/C All Alone Am I [2]...Brenda Lee
- LPS
  - M0 Peter, Paul and Mary [5]...Peter, Paul and Mary
  - ST West Side Story [27]...Soundtrack

November 24, 1962

- HOT Big Girls Don't Cry [2]...The 4 Seasons
- R&B Big Girls Don't Cry [2]...The 4 Seasons
- C&W Mama Sang A Song [4]...Bill Anderson
- A/C All Alone Am I [3]...Brenda Lee
- LPS
  - M0 Peter, Paul and Mary [6]...Peter, Paul and Mary
  - ST West Side Story [28]...Soundtrack

December 1, 1962

- HOT Big Girls Don't Cry [3]...The 4 Seasons
- R&B Big Girls Don't Cry [3]...The 4 Seasons
- C&W Mama Sang A Song [5]...Bill Anderson
- A/C All Alone Am I [4]...Brenda Lee
- LPS
  - M0 My Son, The Folk Singer [1]...Allan Sherman
  - ST West Side Story [29]...Soundtrack

December 8, 1962

- HOT Big Girls Don't Cry [4]...The 4 Seasons
- R&B Release Me [1]...Esther Phillips
- C&W Mama Sang A Song [6]...Bill Anderson
- A/C All Alone Am I [5]...Brenda Lee
- LPS
  - M0 My Son, The Folk Singer [2]...Allan Sherman
  - ST West Side Story [30]...Soundtrack

December 15, 1962
- HOT Big Girls Don't Cry [5]...The 4 Seasons
- R&B You Are My Sunshine [1]...Ray Charles
- C&W I've Been Everywhere [2]...Hank Snow
- A/C *Go Away Little Girl [1]...Steve Lawrence
- LPS
  - M0 The First Family [1]...Vaughn Meader
  - ST West Side Story [31]...Soundtrack

December 22, 1962
- HOT Telstar [1]...The Tornadoes
- R&B Release Me [2]...Esther Phillips
- C&W Mama Sang A Song [7]...Bill Anderson
- A/C Go Away Little Girl [2]...Steve Lawrence
- LPS
  - M0 The First Family [2]...Vaughn Meader
  - ST West Side Story [32]...Soundtrack

December 29, 1962
- HOT Telstar [2]...The Tornadoes
- R&B You Are My Sunshine [2]...Ray Charles
- C&W Don't Let Me Cross Over [1]...Carl Butler & Pearl
- A/C Go Away Little Girl [3]...Steve Lawrence
- LPS
  - M0 The First Family [3]...Vaughn Meader
  - ST West Side Story [33]...Soundtrack

January 5, 1963
- HOT Telstar [3]...The Tornadoes
- R&B Release Me [3]...Esther Phillips
- C&W Ruby Ann [1]...Marty Robbins
- A/C Go Away Little Girl [4]...Steve Lawrence
- LPS
  - M0 The First Family [4]...Vaughn Meader
  - ST West Side Story [34]...Soundtrack

January 12, 1963
- HOT Go Away Little Girl [1]...Steve Lawrence
- R&B You Are My Sunshine [3]...Ray Charles
- C&W Don't Let Me Cross Over [2]...Carl Butler & Pearl
- A/C Go Away Little Girl [5]...Steve Lawrence
- LPS
  - M0 The First Family [5]...Vaughn Meader
  - ST West Side Story [35]...Soundtrack

January 19, 1963
- HOT Go Away Little Girl [2]...Steve Lawrence
- R&B Two Lovers [1]...Mary Wells
- C&W The Ballad Of Jed Clampett [1]...Flatt & Scruggs
- A/C Go Away Little Girl [6]...Steve Lawrence
- LPS
  - M0 The First Family [6]...Vaughn Meader
  - ST West Side Story [36]...Soundtrack

January 26, 1963
- HOT *Walk Right In [1]...The Rooftop Singers
- R&B Two Lovers [2]...Mary Wells
- C&W Don't Let Me Cross Over [3]...Carl Butler & Pearl
- A/C *Walk Right In [1]...The Rooftop Singers
- LPS
  - M0 The First Family [7]...Vaughn Meader
  - ST West Side Story [37]...Soundtrack

February 2, 1963
- HOT Walk Right In [2]...The Rooftop Singers
- R&B Two Lovers [3]...Mary Wells
- C&W The Ballad Of Jed Clampett [2]...Flatt & Scruggs
- A/C Walk Right In [2]...The Rooftop Singers
- LPS
  - M0 The First Family [8]...Vaughn Meader
  - ST West Side Story [38]...Soundtrack

February 9, 1963
- HOT *Hey Paula [1]...Paul & Paula
- R&B Two Lovers [4]...Mary Wells
- C&W The Ballad Of Jed Clampett [3]...Flatt & Scruggs
- A/C Walk Right In [3]...The Rooftop Singers
- LPS
  - M0 The First Family [9]...Vaughn Meader
  - ST West Side Story [39]...Soundtrack

February 16, 1963
- HOT Hey Paula [2]...Paul & Paula
- R&B You've Really Got A Hold On Me [1]...The Miracles
- C&W Don't Let Me Cross Over [4]...Carl Butler & Pearl
- A/C Walk Right In [4]...The Rooftop Singers
- LPS
  - M0 The First Family [10]...Vaughn Meader
  - ST West Side Story [40]...Soundtrack

February 23, 1963

- HOT   Hey Paula [3]...Paul & Paula
- R&B   Hey Paula [1]...Paul & Paula
- C&W   Don't Let Me Cross Over [5]...Carl Butler & Pearl
- A/C   Walk Right In [5]...The Rooftop Singers
- LPS
  - M0   The First Family [11]...Vaughn Meader
  - ST   West Side Story [41]...Soundtrack

March 2, 1963

- HOT   Walk Like A Man [1]...The 4 Seasons
- R&B   Hey Paula [2]...Paul & Paula
- C&W   Don't Let Me Cross Over [6]...Carl Butler & Pearl
- A/C   Rhythm Of The Rain [1]...The Cascades
- LPS
  - M0   The First Family [12]...Vaughn Meader
  - ST   West Side Story [42]...Soundtrack

March 9, 1963

- HOT   Walk Like A Man [2]...The 4 Seasons
- R&B   That's The Way Love Is [1]...Bobby Bland
- C&W   Don't Let Me Cross Over [7]...Carl Butler & Pearl
- A/C   Rhythm Of The Rain [2]...The Cascades
- LPS
  - M0   My Son, The Celebrity [1]...Allan Sherman
  - ST   Jazz Samba [1]...Stan Getz/Charlie Byrd

March 16, 1963

- HOT   Walk Like A Man [3]...The 4 Seasons
- R&B   That's The Way Love Is [2]...Bobby Bland
- C&W   Don't Let Me Cross Over [8]...Carl Butler & Pearl
- A/C   The End Of The World [1]...Skeeter Davis
- LPS
  - M0   Songs I Sing On The Jackie Gleason Show [1]...Frank Fontaine
  - ST   West Side Story [43]...Soundtrack

March 23, 1963

- HOT   *Our Day Will Come [1]...Ruby & The Romantics
- R&B   *Our Day Will Come [1]...Ruby & The Romantics
- C&W   Don't Let Me Cross Over [9]...Carl Butler & Pearl
- A/C   The End Of The World [2]...Skeeter Davis
- LPS
  - M0   Songs I Sing On The Jackie Gleason Show [2]...Frank Fontaine
  - ST   West Side Story [44]...Soundtrack

March 30, 1963

- HOT   *He's So Fine [1]...The Chiffons
- R&B   Our Day Will Come [2]...Ruby & The Romantics
- C&W   Don't Let Me Cross Over [10]...Carl Butler & Pearl
- A/C   The End Of The World [3]...Skeeter Davis
- LPS
  - M0   Songs I Sing On The Jackie Gleason Show [3]...Frank Fontaine
  - ST   West Side Story [45]...Soundtrack

April 6, 1963

- HOT   He's So Fine [2]...The Chiffons
- R&B   He's So Fine [1]...The Chiffons
- C&W   Don't Let Me Cross Over [11]...Carl Butler & Pearl
- A/C   The End Of The World [4]...Skeeter Davis
- LPS
  - M0   Songs I Sing On The Jackie Gleason Show [4]...Frank Fontaine
  - ST   West Side Story [46]...Soundtrack

April 13, 1963

- HOT   He's So Fine [3]...The Chiffons
- R&B   He's So Fine [2]...The Chiffons
- C&W   Still [1]...Bill Anderson
- A/C   Can't Get Used To Losing You [1]...Andy Williams
- LPS
  - M0   Songs I Sing On The Jackie Gleason Show [5]...Frank Fontaine
  - ST   West Side Story [47]...Soundtrack

April 20, 1963

- HOT   He's So Fine [4]...The Chiffons
- R&B   He's So Fine [3]...The Chiffons
- C&W   Still [2]...Bill Anderson
- A/C   Can't Get Used To Losing You [2]...Andy Williams
- LPS
  - M0   West Side Story [11]...Soundtrack
  - ST   West Side Story [48]...Soundtrack

April 27, 1963

- HOT   *I Will Follow Him [1]...Little Peggy March
- R&B   He's So Fine [4]...The Chiffons
- C&W   Still [3]...Bill Anderson
- A/C   Can't Get Used To Losing You [3]...Andy Williams
- LPS
  - M0   West Side Story [12]...Soundtrack
  - ST   West Side Story [49]...Soundtrack

May 4, 1963

- *HOT* I Will Follow Him [2]...Little Peggy March
- *R&B* Baby Workout [1]...Jackie Wilson
- *C&W* Lonesome 7-7203 [1]...Hawkshaw Hawkins
- *A/C* Can't Get Used To Losing You [4]...Andy Williams
- *LPS*
  - *MO* Days of Wine and Roses [1]...Andy Williams
  - *ST* West Side Story [50]...Soundtrack

May 11, 1963

- *HOT* I Will Follow Him [3]...Little Peggy March
- *R&B* Baby Workout [2]...Jackie Wilson
- *C&W* Still [4]...Bill Anderson
- *A/C* Puff The Magic Dragon [1]...Peter, Paul & Mary
- *LPS*
  - *MO* Days of Wine and Roses [2]...Andy Williams
  - *ST* West Side Story [51]...Soundtrack

May 18, 1963

- *HOT* *If You Wanna Be Happy [1]...Jimmy Soul
- *R&B* Baby Workout [3]...Jackie Wilson
- *C&W* Still [5]...Bill Anderson
- *A/C* Puff The Magic Dragon [2]...Peter, Paul & Mary
- *LPS*
  - *MO* Days of Wine and Roses [3]...Andy Williams
  - *ST* West Side Story [52]...Soundtrack

May 25, 1963

- *HOT* If You Wanna Be Happy [2]...Jimmy Soul
- *R&B* I Will Follow Him [1]...Little Peggy March
- *C&W* Still [6]...Bill Anderson
- *A/C* I Love You Because [1]...Al Martino
- *LPS*
  - *MO* Days of Wine and Roses [4]...Andy Williams
  - *ST* West Side Story [53]...Soundtrack

June 1, 1963

- *HOT* *It's My Party [1]...Lesley Gore
- *R&B* If You Wanna Be Happy [1]...Jimmy Soul
- *C&W* Lonesome 7-7203 [2]...Hawkshaw Hawkins
- *A/C* I Love You Because [2]...Al Martino
- *LPS*
  - *MO* Days of Wine and Roses [5]...Andy Williams
  - *ST* Days of Wine and Roses [1]...Andy Williams

June 8, 1963

- *HOT* It's My Party [2]...Lesley Gore
- *R&B* Another Saturday Night [1]...Sam Cooke
- *C&W* Lonesome 7-7203 [3]...Hawkshaw Hawkins
- *A/C* *Sukiyaki [1]...Kyu Sakamoto
- *LPS*
  - *MO* Days of Wine and Roses [6]...Andy Williams
  - *ST* Days of Wine and Roses [2]...Andy Williams

June 15, 1963

- *HOT* Sukiyaki [1]...Kyu Sakamoto
- *R&B* It's My Party [1]...Lesley Gore
- *C&W* Act Naturally [1]...Buck Owens
- *A/C* Sukiyaki [2]...Kyu Sakamoto
- *LPS*
  - *MO* Days of Wine and Roses [7]...Andy Williams
  - *ST* Days of Wine and Roses [3]...Andy Williams

June 22, 1963

- *HOT* Sukiyaki [2]...Kyu Sakamoto
- *R&B* It's My Party [2]...Lesley Gore
- *C&W* Lonesome 7-7203 [4]...Hawkshaw Hawkins
- *A/C* Sukiyaki [3]...Kyu Sakamoto
- *LPS*
  - *MO* Days of Wine and Roses [8]...Andy Williams
  - *ST* Days of Wine and Roses [4]...Andy Williams

June 29, 1963

- *HOT* Sukiyaki [3]...Kyu Sakamoto
- *R&B* It's My Party [3]...Lesley Gore
- *C&W* Act Naturally [2]...Buck Owens
- *A/C* Sukiyaki [4]...Kyu Sakamoto
- *LPS*
  - *MO* Days of Wine and Roses [9]...Andy Williams
  - *ST* Days of Wine and Roses [5]...Andy Williams

July 6, 1963

- *HOT* *Easier Said Than Done [1]...The Essex
- *R&B* Hello Stranger [1]...Barbara Lewis
- *C&W* Still [7]...Bill Anderson
- *A/C* Sukiyaki [5]...Kyu Sakamoto
- *LPS*
  - *MO* Days of Wine and Roses [10]...Andy Williams
  - *ST* Days of Wine and Roses [6]...Andy Williams

July 13, 1963
- HOT Easier Said Than Done [2]...The Essex
- R&B Hello Stranger [2]...Barbara Lewis
- C&W Act Naturally [3]...Buck Owens
- A/C Tie Me Kangaroo Down, Sport [1]...Rolf Harris
- LPS
  - M0 Days of Wine and Roses [11]...Andy Williams
  - ST Days of Wine and Roses [7]...Andy Williams

July 20, 1963
- HOT Surf City [1]...Jan & Dean
- R&B Easier Said Than Done [1]...The Essex
- C&W Act Naturally [4]...Buck Owens
- A/C Tie Me Kangaroo Down, Sport [2]...Rolf Harris
- LPS
  - M0 Days of Wine and Roses [12]...Andy Williams
  - ST Days of Wine and Roses [8]...Andy Williams

July 27, 1963
- HOT Surf City [2]...Jan & Dean
- R&B Easier Said Than Done [2]...The Essex
- C&W Ring Of Fire [1]...Johnny Cash
- A/C Tie Me Kangaroo Down, Sport [3]...Rolf Harris
- LPS
  - M0 Days of Wine and Roses [13]...Andy Williams
  - ST Days of Wine and Roses [9]...Andy Williams

August 3, 1963
- HOT So Much In Love [1]...The Tymes
- R&B *Fingertips - Pt 2 [1]...Little Stevie Wonder
- C&W Ring Of Fire [2]...Johnny Cash
- A/C Blowin' In The Wind [1]...Peter, Paul & Mary
- LPS
  - M0 Days of Wine and Roses [14]...Andy Williams
  - ST Days of Wine and Roses [10]...Andy Williams

August 10, 1963
- HOT Fingertips - Pt 2 [1]...Little Stevie Wonder
- R&B Fingertips - Pt 2 [2]...Little Stevie Wonder
- C&W Ring Of Fire [3]...Johnny Cash
- A/C Blowin' In The Wind [2]...Peter, Paul & Mary
- LPS
  - M0 Days of Wine and Roses [15]...Andy Williams
  - ST Days of Wine and Roses [11]...Andy Williams
  - *final week of separate mono and stereo album charts*

August 17, 1963
- HOT Fingertips - Pt 2 [2]...Little Stevie Wonder
- R&B Fingertips - Pt 2 [3]...Little Stevie Wonder
- C&W Ring Of Fire [4]...Johnny Cash
- A/C Blowin' In The Wind [3]...Peter, Paul & Mary
- LPS Days of Wine and Roses [16]...Andy Williams

August 24, 1963
- HOT Fingertips - Pt 2 [3]...Little Stevie Wonder
- R&B Fingertips - Pt 2 [4]...Little Stevie Wonder
- C&W Ring Of Fire [5]...Johnny Cash
- A/C Blowin' In The Wind [4]...Peter, Paul & Mary
- LPS Little Stevie Wonder/The 12 Year Old Genius [1]...Stevie Wonder

August 31, 1963
- HOT My Boyfriend's Back [1]...The Angels
- R&B Fingertips - Pt 2 [5]...Little Stevie Wonder
- C&W Ring Of Fire [6]...Johnny Cash
- A/C Blowin' In The Wind [5]...Peter, Paul & Mary
- LPS My Son, The Nut [1]...Allan Sherman

September 7, 1963
- HOT My Boyfriend's Back [2]...The Angels
- R&B Fingertips - Pt 2 [6]...Little Stevie Wonder
- C&W Ring Of Fire [7]...Johnny Cash
- A/C *Blue Velvet [1]...Bobby Vinton
- LPS My Son, The Nut [2]...Allan Sherman

September 14, 1963
- HOT My Boyfriend's Back [3]...The Angels
- R&B Heat Wave [1]...Martha & The Vandellas
- C&W Abilene [1]...George Hamilton IV
- A/C Blue Velvet [2]...Bobby Vinton
- LPS My Son, The Nut [3]...Allan Sherman

September 21, 1963
- HOT Blue Velvet [1]...Bobby Vinton
- R&B Heat Wave [2]...Martha & The Vandellas
- C&W Abilene [2]...George Hamilton IV
- A/C Blue Velvet [3]...Bobby Vinton
- LPS My Son, The Nut [4]...Allan Sherman

September 28, 1963
- HOT Blue Velvet [2]...Bobby Vinton
- R&B Heat Wave [3]...Martha & The Vandellas
- C&W Abilene [3]...George Hamilton IV
- A/C Blue Velvet [4]...Bobby Vinton
- LPS My Son, The Nut [5]...Allan Sherman

October 5, 1963
- HOT Blue Velvet [3]...Bobby Vinton
- R&B Heat Wave [4]...Martha & The Vandellas
- C&W Abilene [4]...George Hamilton IV
- A/C Blue Velvet [5]...Bobby Vinton
- LPS My Son, The Nut [6]...Allan Sherman

October 12, 1963
- HOT *Sugar Shack [1]...Jimmy Gilmer and The Fireballs
- R&B Cry Baby [1]...Garnet Mimms & The Enchanters
- C&W Talk Back Trembling Lips [1]...Ernest Ashworth
- A/C Blue Velvet [6]...Bobby Vinton
- LPS My Son, The Nut [7]...Allan Sherman

October 19, 1963
- HOT Sugar Shack [2]...Jimmy Gilmer and The Fireballs
- R&B Part Time Love [1]...Little Johnny Taylor
- C&W Love's Gonna Live Here [1]...Buck Owens
- A/C Blue Velvet [7]...Bobby Vinton
- LPS My Son, The Nut [8]...Allan Sherman

October 26, 1963
- HOT Sugar Shack [3]...Jimmy Gilmer and The Fireballs
- R&B Cry Baby [2]...Garnet Mimms & The Enchanters
- C&W Love's Gonna Live Here [2]...Buck Owens
- A/C Blue Velvet [8]...Bobby Vinton
- LPS Peter, Paul and Mary [7]...Peter, Paul and Mary
    first hit #1 on 10/20/62

November 2, 1963
- HOT Sugar Shack [4]...Jimmy Gilmer and The Fireballs
- R&B Cry Baby [3]...Garnet Mimms & The Enchanters
- C&W Love's Gonna Live Here [3]...Buck Owens
- A/C Washington Square [1]...The Village Stompers
- LPS In The Wind [1]...Peter, Paul and Mary

November 9, 1963
- HOT Sugar Shack [5]...Jimmy Gilmer and The Fireballs
- R&B It's All Right [1]...The Impressions
- C&W Love's Gonna Live Here [4]...Buck Owens
- A/C Washington Square [2]...The Village Stompers
- LPS In The Wind [2]...Peter, Paul and Mary

November 16, 1963
- HOT Deep Purple [1]...Nino Tempo & April Stevens
- R&B It's All Right [2]...The Impressions
- C&W Love's Gonna Live Here [5]...Buck Owens
- A/C Washington Square [3]...The Village Stompers
- LPS In The Wind [3]...Peter, Paul and Mary

November 23, 1963
- HOT *I'm Leaving It Up To You [1]...Dale & Grace
- R&B Sugar Shack [1]...Jimmy Gilmer and The Fireballs
- C&W Love's Gonna Live Here [6]...Buck Owens
- A/C *I'm Leaving It Up To You [1]...Dale & Grace
- LPS In The Wind [4]...Peter, Paul and Mary

November 30, 1963
- HOT I'm Leaving It Up To You [2]...Dale & Grace
- R&B [CHART DISCONTINUED UNTIL 1/30/65]
- C&W Love's Gonna Live Here [7]...Buck Owens
- A/C I'm Leaving It Up To You [2]...Dale & Grace
- LPS In The Wind [5]...Peter, Paul and Mary

December 7, 1963
- HOT *Dominique [1]...The Singing Nun
- R&B [CHART DISCONTINUED UNTIL 1/30/65]
- C&W Love's Gonna Live Here [8]...Buck Owens
- A/C *Dominique [1]...The Singing Nun
- LPS The Singing Nun [1]...The Singing Nun

December 14, 1963
- HOT Dominique [2]...The Singing Nun
- R&B [CHART DISCONTINUED UNTIL 1/30/65]
- C&W Love's Gonna Live Here [9]...Buck Owens
- A/C Dominique [2]...The Singing Nun
- LPS The Singing Nun [2]...The Singing Nun

December 21, 1963
- HOT Dominique [3]...The Singing Nun
- R&B [CHART DISCONTINUED UNTIL 1/30/65]
- C&W Love's Gonna Live Here [10]...Buck Owens
- A/C Dominique [3]...The Singing Nun
- LPS The Singing Nun [3]...The Singing Nun

December 28, 1963
- HOT Dominique [4]...The Singing Nun
- R&B [CHART DISCONTINUED UNTIL 1/30/65]
- C&W Love's Gonna Live Here [11]...Buck Owens
- A/C Dominique [4]...The Singing Nun
- LPS The Singing Nun [4]...The Singing Nun

January 4, 1964
- HOT *There! I've Said It Again [1]...Bobby Vinton
- R&B [CHART DISCONTINUED UNTIL 1/30/65]
- C&W Love's Gonna Live Here [12]...Buck Owens
- A/C *There! I've Said It Again [1]...Bobby Vinton
- LPS The Singing Nun [5]...The Singing Nun

January 11, 1964
SINGLES
- HOT   There! I've Said It Again [2]...Bobby Vinton
- R&B   [CHART DISCONTINUED UNTIL 1/30/65]
- C&W   Love's Gonna Live Here [13]...Buck Owens
- A/C   There! I've Said It Again [2]...Bobby Vinton

ALBUMS
- POP   The Singing Nun [6]...The Singing Nun
- C&W   Ring Of Fire (The Best Of Johnny Cash) [1]...Johnny Cash

January 18, 1964
SINGLES
- HOT   There! I've Said It Again [3]...Bobby Vinton
- R&B   [CHART DISCONTINUED UNTIL 1/30/65]
- C&W   Love's Gonna Live Here [14]...Buck Owens
- A/C   There! I've Said It Again [3]...Bobby Vinton

ALBUMS
- POP   The Singing Nun [7]...The Singing Nun
- C&W   Night Life [1]...Ray Price

January 25, 1964
SINGLES
- HOT   There! I've Said It Again [4]...Bobby Vinton
- R&B   [CHART DISCONTINUED UNTIL 1/30/65]
- C&W   Love's Gonna Live Here [15]...Buck Owens
- A/C   There! I've Said It Again [4]...Bobby Vinton

ALBUMS
- POP   The Singing Nun [8]...The Singing Nun
- C&W   B.O. Sings Tommy Collins [1]...Buck Owens

February 1, 1964
SINGLES
- HOT   I Want To Hold Your Hand [1]...The Beatles
- R&B   [CHART DISCONTINUED UNTIL 1/30/65]
- C&W   Love's Gonna Live Here [16]...Buck Owens
- A/C   There! I've Said It Again [5]...Bobby Vinton

ALBUMS
- POP   The Singing Nun [9]...The Singing Nun
- C&W   B.O. Sings Tommy Collins [2]...Buck Owens

February 8, 1964
SINGLES
- HOT   I Want To Hold Your Hand [2]...The Beatles
- R&B   [CHART DISCONTINUED UNTIL 1/30/65]
- C&W   Begging To You [1]...Marty Robbins
- A/C   For You [1]...Ricky Nelson

ALBUMS
- POP   The Singing Nun [10]...The Singing Nun
- C&W   Ring Of Fire (The Best Of Johnny Cash) [2]...Johnny Cash

February 15, 1964
SINGLES
- HOT   I Want To Hold Your Hand [3]...The Beatles
- R&B   [CHART DISCONTINUED UNTIL 1/30/65]
- C&W   B.J. The D.J. [1]...Stonewall Jackson
- A/C   For You [2]...Ricky Nelson

ALBUMS
- POP   Meet The Beatles! [1]...The Beatles
- C&W   Ring Of Fire (The Best Of Johnny Cash) [3]...Johnny Cash

February 22, 1964
SINGLES
- HOT   I Want To Hold Your Hand [4]...The Beatles
- R&B   [CHART DISCONTINUED UNTIL 1/30/65]
- C&W   Begging To You [2]...Marty Robbins
- A/C   Java [1]...Al Hirt

ALBUMS
- POP   Meet The Beatles! [2]...The Beatles
- C&W   Ring Of Fire (The Best Of Johnny Cash) [4]...Johnny Cash

February 29, 1964
SINGLES
- HOT   I Want To Hold Your Hand [5]...The Beatles
- R&B   [CHART DISCONTINUED UNTIL 1/30/65]
- C&W   Begging To You [3]...Marty Robbins
- A/C   Java [2]...Al Hirt

ALBUMS
- POP   Meet The Beatles! [3]...The Beatles
- C&W   Ring Of Fire (The Best Of Johnny Cash) [5]...Johnny Cash

March 7, 1964
SINGLES
- HOT   I Want To Hold Your Hand [6]...The Beatles
- R&B   [CHART DISCONTINUED UNTIL 1/30/65]
- C&W   Saginaw, Michigan [1]...Lefty Frizzell
- A/C   Java [3]...Al Hirt

ALBUMS
- POP   Meet The Beatles! [4]...The Beatles
- C&W   Ring Of Fire (The Best Of Johnny Cash) [6]...Johnny Cash

March 14, 1964
SINGLES
- HOT   I Want To Hold Your Hand [7]...The Beatles
- R&B   [CHART DISCONTINUED UNTIL 1/30/65]
- C&W   Saginaw, Michigan [2]...Lefty Frizzell
- A/C   Java [4]...Al Hirt

ALBUMS
- POP   Meet The Beatles! [5]...The Beatles
- C&W   Ring Of Fire (The Best Of Johnny Cash) [7]...Johnny Cash

March 21, 1964
SINGLES
- HOT   She Loves You [1]...The Beatles
- R&B   [CHART DISCONTINUED UNTIL 1/30/65]
- C&W   Saginaw, Michigan [3]...Lefty Frizzell
- A/C   Navy Blue [1]...Diane Renay

ALBUMS
- POP   Meet The Beatles! [6]...The Beatles
- C&W   Ring Of Fire (The Best Of Johnny Cash) [8]...Johnny Cash

March 28, 1964
SINGLES
- HOT   She Loves You [2]...The Beatles
- R&B   [CHART DISCONTINUED UNTIL 1/30/65]
- C&W   Saginaw, Michigan [4]...Lefty Frizzell
- A/C   *Hello, Dolly! [1]...Louis Armstrong

ALBUMS
- POP   Meet The Beatles! [7]...The Beatles
- C&W   Ring Of Fire (The Best Of Johnny Cash) [9]...Johnny Cash

April 4, 1964
SINGLES
- HOT   Can't Buy Me Love [1]...The Beatles
- R&B   [CHART DISCONTINUED UNTIL 1/30/65]
- C&W   Understand Your Man [1]...Johnny Cash
- A/C   Hello, Dolly! [2]...Louis Armstrong

ALBUMS
- POP   Meet The Beatles! [8]...The Beatles
- C&W   Ring Of Fire (The Best Of Johnny Cash) [10]...Johnny Cash

April 11, 1964
SINGLES
- HOT   Can't Buy Me Love [2]...The Beatles
- R&B   [CHART DISCONTINUED UNTIL 1/30/65]
- C&W   Understand Your Man [2]...Johnny Cash
- A/C   Hello, Dolly! [3]...Louis Armstrong

ALBUMS
- POP   Meet The Beatles! [9]...The Beatles
- C&W   Ring Of Fire (The Best Of Johnny Cash) [11]...Johnny Cash

April 18, 1964
SINGLES
- HOT   Can't Buy Me Love [3]...The Beatles
- R&B   [CHART DISCONTINUED UNTIL 1/30/65]
- C&W   Understand Your Man [3]...Johnny Cash
- A/C   Hello, Dolly! [4]...Louis Armstrong

ALBUMS
- POP   Meet The Beatles! [10]...The Beatles
- C&W   Ring Of Fire (The Best Of Johnny Cash) [12]...Johnny Cash

April 25, 1964
SINGLES
- HOT   Can't Buy Me Love [4]...The Beatles
- R&B   [CHART DISCONTINUED UNTIL 1/30/65]
- C&W   Understand Your Man [4]...Johnny Cash
- A/C   Hello, Dolly! [5]...Louis Armstrong

ALBUMS
- POP   Meet The Beatles! [11]...The Beatles
- C&W   Ring Of Fire (The Best Of Johnny Cash) [13]...Johnny Cash

May 2, 1964
SINGLES
- HOT   Can't Buy Me Love [5]...The Beatles
- R&B   [CHART DISCONTINUED UNTIL 1/30/65]
- C&W   Understand Your Man [5]...Johnny Cash
- A/C   Hello, Dolly! [6]...Louis Armstrong

ALBUMS
- POP   The Beatles' Second Album [1]...The Beatles
- C&W   Ring Of Fire (The Best Of Johnny Cash) [14]...Johnny Cash

May 9, 1964
SINGLES
- HOT   Hello, Dolly! [1]...Louis Armstrong
- R&B   [CHART DISCONTINUED UNTIL 1/30/65]
- C&W   Understand Your Man [6]...Johnny Cash
- A/C   Hello, Dolly! [7]...Louis Armstrong

ALBUMS
- POP   The Beatles' Second Album [2]...The Beatles
- C&W   Guitar Country [1]...Chet Atkins

May 16, 1964
SINGLES
- HOT   My Guy [1]...Mary Wells
- R&B   [CHART DISCONTINUED UNTIL 1/30/65]
- C&W   My Heart Skips A Beat [1]...Buck Owens
- A/C   Hello, Dolly! [8]...Louis Armstrong

ALBUMS
- POP   The Beatles' Second Album [3]...The Beatles
- C&W   Guitar Country [2]...Chet Atkins

May 23, 1964
SINGLES
- HOT   My Guy [2]...Mary Wells
- R&B   [CHART DISCONTINUED UNTIL 1/30/65]
- C&W   My Heart Skips A Beat [2]...Buck Owens
- A/C   Hello, Dolly! [9]...Louis Armstrong

ALBUMS
- POP   The Beatles' Second Album [4]...The Beatles
- C&W   Guitar Country [3]...Chet Atkins

May 30, 1964
SINGLES
- *HOT*   Love Me Do [1]...The Beatles
- *R&B*   [CHART DISCONTINUED UNTIL 1/30/65]
- *C&W*   My Heart Skips A Beat [3]...Buck Owens
- *A/C*   Love Me With All Your Heart (Cuando Calienta El Sol) [1]...The Ray Charles Singers

ALBUMS
- *POP*   The Beatles' Second Album [5]...The Beatles
- *C&W*   Guitar Country [4]...Chet Atkins

June 6, 1964
SINGLES
- *HOT*   Chapel Of Love [1]...The Dixie Cups
- *R&B*   [CHART DISCONTINUED UNTIL 1/30/65]
- *C&W*   Together Again [1]...Buck Owens
- *A/C*   Love Me With All Your Heart (Cuando Calienta El Sol) [2]...The Ray Charles Singers

ALBUMS
- *POP*   Hello, Dolly! [1]...Original Cast
- *C&W*   Guitar Country [5]...Chet Atkins

June 13, 1964
SINGLES
- *HOT*   Chapel Of Love [2]...The Dixie Cups
- *R&B*   [CHART DISCONTINUED UNTIL 1/30/65]
- *C&W*   Together Again [2]...Buck Owens
- *A/C*   Love Me With All Your Heart (Cuando Calienta El Sol) [3]...The Ray Charles Singers

ALBUMS
- *POP*   Hello, Dolly! [1]...Louis Armstrong
- *C&W*   Guitar Country [6]...Chet Atkins

June 20, 1964
SINGLES
- *HOT*   Chapel Of Love [3]...The Dixie Cups
- *R&B*   [CHART DISCONTINUED UNTIL 1/30/65]
- *C&W*   My Heart Skips A Beat [4]...Buck Owens
- *A/C*   Love Me With All Your Heart (Cuando Calienta El Sol) [4]...The Ray Charles Singers

ALBUMS
- *POP*   Hello, Dolly! [2]...Louis Armstrong
- *C&W*   More Hank Snow Souvenirs [1]...Hank Snow

June 27, 1964
SINGLES
- *HOT*   A World Without Love [1]...Peter & Gordon
- *R&B*   [CHART DISCONTINUED UNTIL 1/30/65]
- *C&W*   My Heart Skips A Beat [5]...Buck Owens
- *A/C*   People [1]...Barbra Streisand

ALBUMS
- *POP*   Hello, Dolly! [3]...Louis Armstrong
- *C&W*   More Hank Snow Souvenirs [2]...Hank Snow

July 4, 1964
SINGLES
- *HOT*   I Get Around [1]...The Beach Boys
- *R&B*   [CHART DISCONTINUED UNTIL 1/30/65]
- *C&W*   My Heart Skips A Beat [6]...Buck Owens
- *A/C*   People [2]...Barbra Streisand

ALBUMS
- *POP*   Hello, Dolly! [4]...Louis Armstrong
- *C&W*   Moonlight and Roses [1]...Jim Reeves

July 11, 1964
SINGLES
- *HOT*   I Get Around [2]...The Beach Boys
- *R&B*   [CHART DISCONTINUED UNTIL 1/30/65]
- *C&W*   My Heart Skips A Beat [7]...Buck Owens
- *A/C*   People [3]...Barbra Streisand

ALBUMS
- *POP*   Hello, Dolly! [5]...Louis Armstrong
- *C&W*   Moonlight and Roses [2]...Jim Reeves

July 18, 1964
SINGLES
- *HOT*   Rag Doll [1]...The 4 Seasons
- *R&B*   [CHART DISCONTINUED UNTIL 1/30/65]
- *C&W*   Dang Me [1]...Roger Miller
- *A/C*   The Girl From Ipanema [1]...Stan Getz/Astrud Gilberto

ALBUMS
- *POP*   Hello, Dolly! [6]...Louis Armstrong
- *C&W*   Moonlight and Roses [3]...Jim Reeves

July 25, 1964
SINGLES
- *HOT*   Rag Doll [2]...The 4 Seasons
- *R&B*   [CHART DISCONTINUED UNTIL 1/30/65]
- *C&W*   Dang Me [2]...Roger Miller
- *A/C*   The Girl From Ipanema [2]...Stan Getz/Astrud Gilberto

ALBUMS
- *POP*   A Hard Day's Night [1]...The Beatles/Soundtrack
- *C&W*   Moonlight and Roses [4]...Jim Reeves

August 1, 1964
SINGLES
- *HOT*   A Hard Day's Night [1]...The Beatles
- *R&B*   [CHART DISCONTINUED UNTIL 1/30/65]
- *C&W*   Dang Me [3]...Roger Miller
- *A/C*   *Everybody Loves Somebody [1]...Dean Martin

ALBUMS
- *POP*   A Hard Day's Night [2]...The Beatles/Soundtrack
- *C&W*   Moonlight and Roses [5]...Jim Reeves

August 8, 1964
SINGLES
- HOT A Hard Day's Night [2]...The Beatles
- R&B [CHART DISCONTINUED UNTIL 1/30/65]
- C&W Dang Me [4]...Roger Miller
- A/C Everybody Loves Somebody [2]...Dean Martin

ALBUMS
- POP A Hard Day's Night [3]...The Beatles/Soundtrack
- C&W Moonlight and Roses [6]...Jim Reeves

August 15, 1964
SINGLES
- HOT Everybody Loves Somebody [1]...Dean Martin
- R&B [CHART DISCONTINUED UNTIL 1/30/65]
- C&W Dang Me [5]...Roger Miller
- A/C Everybody Loves Somebody [3]...Dean Martin

ALBUMS
- POP A Hard Day's Night [4]...The Beatles/Soundtrack
- C&W Moonlight and Roses [7]...Jim Reeves

August 22, 1964
SINGLES
- HOT Where Did Our Love Go [1]...The Supremes
- R&B [CHART DISCONTINUED UNTIL 1/30/65]
- C&W Dang Me [6]...Roger Miller
- A/C Everybody Loves Somebody [4]...Dean Martin

ALBUMS
- POP A Hard Day's Night [5]...The Beatles/Soundtrack
- C&W Moonlight and Roses [8]...Jim Reeves

August 29, 1964
SINGLES
- HOT Where Did Our Love Go [2]...The Supremes
- R&B [CHART DISCONTINUED UNTIL 1/30/65]
- C&W I Guess I'm Crazy [1]...Jim Reeves
- A/C Everybody Loves Somebody [5]...Dean Martin

ALBUMS
- POP A Hard Day's Night [6]...The Beatles/Soundtrack
- C&W I Walk The Line [1]...Johnny Cash

September 5, 1964
SINGLES
- HOT The House Of The Rising Sun [1]...The Animals
- R&B [CHART DISCONTINUED UNTIL 1/30/65]
- C&W I Guess I'm Crazy [2]...Jim Reeves
- A/C Everybody Loves Somebody [6]...Dean Martin

ALBUMS
- POP A Hard Day's Night [7]...The Beatles/Soundtrack
- C&W I Walk The Line [2]...Johnny Cash

September 12, 1964
SINGLES
- HOT The House Of The Rising Sun [2]...The Animals
- R&B [CHART DISCONTINUED UNTIL 1/30/65]
- C&W I Guess I'm Crazy [3]...Jim Reeves
- A/C Everybody Loves Somebody [7]...Dean Martin

ALBUMS
- POP A Hard Day's Night [8]...The Beatles/Soundtrack
- C&W I Walk The Line [3]...Johnny Cash

September 19, 1964
SINGLES
- HOT The House Of The Rising Sun [3]...The Animals
- R&B [CHART DISCONTINUED UNTIL 1/30/65]
- C&W I Guess I'm Crazy [4]...Jim Reeves
- A/C Everybody Loves Somebody [8]...Dean Martin

ALBUMS
- POP A Hard Day's Night [9]...The Beatles/Soundtrack
- C&W I Walk The Line [4]...Johnny Cash

September 26, 1964
SINGLES
- HOT Oh, Pretty Woman [1]...Roy Orbison
- R&B [CHART DISCONTINUED UNTIL 1/30/65]
- C&W I Guess I'm Crazy [5]...Jim Reeves
- A/C We'll Sing In The Sunshine [1]...Gale Garnett

ALBUMS
- POP A Hard Day's Night [10]...The Beatles/Soundtrack
- C&W The Best Of Jim Reeves [1]...Jim Reeves

October 3, 1964
SINGLES
- HOT Oh, Pretty Woman [2]...Roy Orbison
- R&B [CHART DISCONTINUED UNTIL 1/30/65]
- C&W I Guess I'm Crazy [6]...Jim Reeves
- A/C We'll Sing In The Sunshine [2]...Gale Garnett

ALBUMS
- POP A Hard Day's Night [11]...The Beatles/Soundtrack
- C&W The Best Of Jim Reeves [2]...Jim Reeves

October 10, 1964
SINGLES
- HOT Oh, Pretty Woman [3]...Roy Orbison
- R&B [CHART DISCONTINUED UNTIL 1/30/65]
- C&W I Guess I'm Crazy [7]...Jim Reeves
- A/C We'll Sing In The Sunshine [3]...Gale Garnett

ALBUMS
- POP A Hard Day's Night [12]...The Beatles/Soundtrack
- C&W The Best Of Jim Reeves [3]...Jim Reeves

October 17, 1964

SINGLES
- HOT Do Wah Diddy Diddy [1]...Manfred Mann
- R&B [CHART DISCONTINUED UNTIL 1/30/65]
- C&W I Don't Care (Just as Long as You Love Me) [1]...Buck Owens
- A/C We'll Sing In The Sunshine [4]...Gale Garnett

ALBUMS
- POP A Hard Day's Night [13]...The Beatles/Soundtrack
- C&W The Best Of Jim Reeves [4]...Jim Reeves

October 24, 1964

SINGLES
- HOT Do Wah Diddy Diddy [2]...Manfred Mann
- R&B [CHART DISCONTINUED UNTIL 1/30/65]
- C&W I Don't Care (Just as Long as You Love Me) [2]...Buck Owens
- A/C We'll Sing In The Sunshine [5]...Gale Garnett

ALBUMS
- POP A Hard Day's Night [14]...The Beatles/Soundtrack
- C&W The Best Of Jim Reeves [5]...Jim Reeves

October 31, 1964

SINGLES
- HOT Baby Love [1]...The Supremes
- R&B [CHART DISCONTINUED UNTIL 1/30/65]
- C&W I Don't Care (Just as Long as You Love Me) [3]...Buck Owens
- A/C We'll Sing In The Sunshine [6]...Gale Garnett

ALBUMS
- POP People [1]...Barbra Streisand
- C&W The Best Of Jim Reeves [6]...Jim Reeves

November 7, 1964

SINGLES
- HOT Baby Love [2]...The Supremes
- R&B [CHART DISCONTINUED UNTIL 1/30/65]
- C&W I Don't Care (Just as Long as You Love Me) [4]...Buck Owens
- A/C We'll Sing In The Sunshine [7]...Gale Garnett

ALBUMS
- POP People [2]...Barbra Streisand
- C&W The Best Of Jim Reeves [7]...Jim Reeves

November 14, 1964

SINGLES
- HOT Baby Love [3]...The Supremes
- R&B [CHART DISCONTINUED UNTIL 1/30/65]
- C&W I Don't Care (Just as Long as You Love Me) [5]...Buck Owens
- A/C The Door Is Still Open To My Heart [1]...Dean Martin

ALBUMS
- POP People [3]...Barbra Streisand
- C&W The Best Of Jim Reeves [8]...Jim Reeves

November 21, 1964

SINGLES
- HOT Baby Love [4]...The Supremes
- R&B [CHART DISCONTINUED UNTIL 1/30/65]
- C&W I Don't Care (Just as Long as You Love Me) [6]...Buck Owens
- A/C *Ringo [1]...Lorne Greene

ALBUMS
- POP People [4]...Barbra Streisand
- C&W Together Again/My Heart Skips A Beat [1]...Buck Owens

November 28, 1964

SINGLES
- HOT Leader Of The Pack [1]...The Shangri-Las
- R&B [CHART DISCONTINUED UNTIL 1/30/65]
- C&W Once A Day [1]...Connie Smith
- A/C Ringo [2]...Lorne Greene

ALBUMS
- POP People [5]...Barbra Streisand
- C&W Together Again/My Heart Skips A Beat [2]...Buck Owens

December 5, 1964

SINGLES
- HOT Ringo [1]...Lorne Greene
- R&B [CHART DISCONTINUED UNTIL 1/30/65]
- C&W Once A Day [2]...Connie Smith
- A/C Ringo [3]...Lorne Greene

ALBUMS
- POP Beach Boys Concert [1]...The Beach Boys
- C&W Together Again/My Heart Skips A Beat [3]...Buck Owens

December 12, 1964

SINGLES
- HOT Mr. Lonely [1]...Bobby Vinton
- R&B [CHART DISCONTINUED UNTIL 1/30/65]
- C&W Once A Day [3]...Connie Smith
- A/C Ringo [4]...Lorne Greene

ALBUMS
- POP Beach Boys Concert [2]...The Beach Boys
- C&W Together Again/My Heart Skips A Beat [4]...Buck Owens

December 19, 1964

SINGLES
- HOT Come See About Me [1]...The Supremes
- R&B [CHART DISCONTINUED UNTIL 1/30/65]
- C&W Once A Day [4]...Connie Smith
- A/C Ringo [5]...Lorne Greene

ALBUMS
- POP Beach Boys Concert [3]...The Beach Boys
- C&W Together Again/My Heart Skips A Beat [5]...Buck Owens

December 26, 1964
SINGLES
- HOT   I Feel Fine [1]...The Beatles
- R&B   [CHART DISCONTINUED UNTIL 1/30/65]
- C&W   Once A Day [5]...Connie Smith
- A/C   Ringo [6]...Lorne Greene

ALBUMS
- POP   Beach Boys Concert [4]...The Beach Boys
- C&W   Together Again/My Heart Skips A Beat [6]...Buck Owens

January 2, 1965
SINGLES
- HOT   I Feel Fine [2]...The Beatles
- R&B   [CHART DISCONTINUED UNTIL 1/30/65]
- C&W   Once A Day [6]...Connie Smith
- A/C   The Wedding [1]...Julie Rogers

ALBUMS
- POP   Roustabout [1]...Elvis Presley/Soundtrack
- C&W   Together Again/My Heart Skips A Beat [7]...Buck Owens

January 9, 1965
SINGLES
- HOT   I Feel Fine [3]...The Beatles
- R&B   [CHART DISCONTINUED UNTIL 1/30/65]
- C&W   Once A Day [7]...Connie Smith
- A/C   The Wedding [2]...Julie Rogers

ALBUMS
- POP   Beatles '65 [1]...The Beatles
- C&W   I Don't Care [1]...Buck Owens

January 16, 1965
SINGLES
- HOT   Come See About Me [2]...The Supremes
- R&B   [CHART DISCONTINUED UNTIL 1/30/65]
- C&W   Once A Day [8]...Connie Smith
- A/C   The Wedding [3]...Julie Rogers

ALBUMS
- POP   Beatles '65 [2]...The Beatles
- C&W   I Don't Care [2]...Buck Owens

January 23, 1965
SINGLES
- HOT   Downtown [1]...Petula Clark
- R&B   [CHART DISCONTINUED UNTIL 1/30/65]
- C&W   You're The Only World I Know [1]...Sonny James
- A/C   Willow Weep For Me [1]...Chad & Jeremy

ALBUMS
- POP   Beatles '65 [3]...The Beatles
- C&W   I Don't Care [3]...Buck Owens

January 30, 1965
SINGLES
- HOT   Downtown [2]...Petula Clark
- R&B   *My Girl [1]...The Temptations
- C&W   You're The Only World I Know [2]...Sonny James
- A/C   You're Nobody Till Somebody Loves You [1]...Dean Martin

ALBUMS
- POP   Beatles '65 [4]...The Beatles
- R&B   Where Did Our Love Go [1]...The Supremes
- C&W   I Don't Care [4]...Buck Owens

February 6, 1965
SINGLES
- HOT   You've Lost That Lovin' Feelin' [1]...The Righteous Brothers
- R&B   My Girl [2]...The Temptations
- C&W   You're The Only World I Know [3]...Sonny James
- A/C   Have You Looked Into Your Heart [1]...Jerry Vale

ALBUMS
- POP   Beatles '65 [5]...The Beatles
- R&B   Sam Cooke At The Copa [1]...Sam Cooke
- C&W   I Don't Care [5]...Buck Owens

February 13, 1965
SINGLES
- HOT   You've Lost That Lovin' Feelin' [2]...The Righteous Brothers
- R&B   My Girl [3]...The Temptations
- C&W   You're The Only World I Know [4]...Sonny James
- A/C   *King Of The Road [1]...Roger Miller

ALBUMS
- POP   Beatles '65 [6]...The Beatles
- R&B   Sam Cooke At The Copa [2]...Sam Cooke
- C&W   I Don't Care [6]...Buck Owens

February 20, 1965
SINGLES
- HOT   This Diamond Ring [1]...Gary Lewis & The Playboys
- R&B   My Girl [4]...The Temptations
- C&W   I've Got A Tiger By The Tail [1]...Buck Owens
- A/C   King Of The Road [2]...Roger Miller

ALBUMS
- POP   Beatles '65 [7]...The Beatles
- R&B   Sam Cooke At The Copa [3]...Sam Cooke
- C&W   I Don't Care [7]...Buck Owens

February 27, 1965
SINGLES
- HOT This Diamond Ring [2]...Gary Lewis & The Playboys
- R&B My Girl [5]...The Temptations
- C&W I've Got A Tiger By The Tail [2]...Buck Owens
- A/C King Of The Road [3]...Roger Miller

ALBUMS
- POP Beatles '65 [8]...The Beatles
- R&B Shake [1]...Sam Cooke
- C&W I Don't Care [8]...Buck Owens

March 6, 1965
SINGLES
- HOT My Girl [1]...The Temptations
- R&B My Girl [6]...The Temptations
- C&W I've Got A Tiger By The Tail [3]...Buck Owens
- A/C King Of The Road [4]...Roger Miller

ALBUMS
- POP Beatles '65 [9]...The Beatles
- R&B Shake [2]...Sam Cooke
- C&W I Don't Care [9]...Buck Owens

March 13, 1965
SINGLES
- HOT Eight Days A Week [1]...The Beatles
- R&B Shotgun [1]...Jr. Walker & The All Stars
- C&W I've Got A Tiger By The Tail [4]...Buck Owens
- A/C King Of The Road [5]...Roger Miller

ALBUMS
- POP Mary Poppins [1]...Soundtrack
- R&B Shake [3]...Sam Cooke
- C&W I Don't Care [10]...Buck Owens

March 20, 1965
SINGLES
- HOT Eight Days A Week [2]...The Beatles
- R&B Shotgun [2]...Jr. Walker & The All Stars
- C&W I've Got A Tiger By The Tail [5]...Buck Owens
- A/C King Of The Road [6]...Roger Miller

ALBUMS
- POP Goldfinger [1]...Soundtrack
- R&B Shake [4]...Sam Cooke
- C&W I Don't Care [11]...Buck Owens

March 27, 1965
SINGLES
- HOT Stop! In The Name Of Love [1]...The Supremes
- R&B Shotgun [3]...Jr. Walker & The All Stars
- C&W King Of The Road [1]...Roger Miller
- A/C King Of The Road [7]...Roger Miller

ALBUMS
- POP Goldfinger [2]...Soundtrack
- R&B People Get Ready [1]...The Impressions
- C&W I Don't Care [12]...Buck Owens

April 3, 1965
SINGLES
- HOT Stop! In The Name Of Love [2]...The Supremes
- R&B Got To Get You Off My Mind [1]...Solomon Burke
- C&W King Of The Road [2]...Roger Miller
- A/C King Of The Road [8]...Roger Miller

ALBUMS
- POP Goldfinger [3]...Soundtrack
- R&B People Get Ready [2]...The Impressions
- C&W I Don't Care [13]...Buck Owens

April 10, 1965
SINGLES
- HOT I'm Telling You Now [1]...Freddie & The Dreamers
- R&B Got To Get You Off My Mind [2]...Solomon Burke
- C&W King Of The Road [3]...Roger Miller
- A/C King Of The Road [9]...Roger Miller

ALBUMS
- POP Mary Poppins [2]...Soundtrack
- R&B The Temptations Sing Smokey [1]...The Temptations
- C&W I've Got A Tiger By The Tail [1]...Buck Owens

April 17, 1965
SINGLES
- HOT I'm Telling You Now [2]...Freddie & The Dreamers
- R&B Got To Get You Off My Mind [3]...Solomon Burke
- C&W King Of The Road [4]...Roger Miller
- A/C King Of The Road [10]...Roger Miller

ALBUMS
- POP Mary Poppins [3]...Soundtrack
- R&B The Temptations Sing Smokey [2]...The Temptations
- C&W I've Got A Tiger By The Tail [2]...Buck Owens

April 24, 1965
SINGLES
- HOT Game Of Love [1]...Wayne Fontana & The Mindbenders
- R&B Shotgun [4]...Jr. Walker & The All Stars
- C&W King Of The Road [5]...Roger Miller
- A/C The Race Is On [1]...Jack Jones

ALBUMS
- POP Mary Poppins [4]...Soundtrack
- R&B The Temptations Sing Smokey [3]...The Temptations
- C&W I've Got A Tiger By The Tail [3]...Buck Owens

May 1, 1965
SINGLES
- HOT Mrs. Brown You've Got A Lovely Daughter [1]...Herman's Hermits
- R&B We're Gonna Make It [1]...Little Milton
- C&W This Is It [1]...Jim Reeves
- A/C Cast Your Fate To The Wind [1]...Sounds Orchestral

ALBUMS
- POP Mary Poppins [5]...Soundtrack
- R&B The Temptations Sing Smokey [4]...The Temptations
- C&W I've Got A Tiger By The Tail [4]...Buck Owens

May 8, 1965
SINGLES
- *HOT* Mrs. Brown You've Got A Lovely Daughter [2]...Herman's Hermits
- *R&B* We're Gonna Make It [2]...Little Milton
- *C&W* This Is It [2]...Jim Reeves
- *A/C* Cast Your Fate To The Wind [2]...Sounds Orchestral

ALBUMS
- *POP* Mary Poppins [6]...Soundtrack
- *R&B* The Temptations Sing Smokey [5]...The Temptations
- *C&W* I've Got A Tiger By The Tail [5]...Buck Owens

May 15, 1965
SINGLES
- *HOT* Mrs. Brown You've Got A Lovely Daughter [3]...Herman's Hermits
- *R&B* We're Gonna Make It [3]...Little Milton
- *C&W* Girl On The Billboard [1]...Del Reeves
- *A/C* Cast Your Fate To The Wind [3]...Sounds Orchestral

ALBUMS
- *POP* Mary Poppins [7]...Soundtrack
- *R&B* The Temptations Sing Smokey [6]...The Temptations
- *C&W* I've Got A Tiger By The Tail [6]...Buck Owens

May 22, 1965
SINGLES
- *HOT* Ticket To Ride [1]...The Beatles
- *R&B* I'll Be Doggone [1]...Marvin Gaye
- *C&W* Girl On The Billboard [2]...Del Reeves
- *A/C* Crying In The Chapel [1]...Elvis Presley

ALBUMS
- *POP* Mary Poppins [8]...Soundtrack
- *R&B* The Temptations Sing Smokey [7]...The Temptations
- *C&W* I've Got A Tiger By The Tail [7]...Buck Owens

May 29, 1965
SINGLES
- *HOT* Help Me, Rhonda [1]...The Beach Boys
- *R&B* *Back In My Arms Again [1]...The Supremes
- *C&W* This Is It [3]...Jim Reeves
- *A/C* Crying In The Chapel [2]...Elvis Presley

ALBUMS
- *POP* Mary Poppins [9]...Soundtrack
- *R&B* The Temptations Sing Smokey [8]...The Temptations
- *C&W* I've Got A Tiger By The Tail [8]...Buck Owens

June 5, 1965
SINGLES
- *HOT* Help Me, Rhonda [2]...The Beach Boys
- *R&B* *I Can't Help Myself [1]...Four Tops
- *C&W* What's He Doing In My World [1]...Eddy Arnold
- *A/C* Crying In The Chapel [3]...Elvis Presley

ALBUMS
- *POP* Mary Poppins [10]...Soundtrack
- *R&B* The Temptations Sing Smokey [9]...The Temptations
- *C&W* I've Got A Tiger By The Tail [9]...Buck Owens

June 12, 1965
SINGLES
- *HOT* Back In My Arms Again [1]...The Supremes
- *R&B* I Can't Help Myself [2]...Four Tops
- *C&W* What's He Doing In My World [2]...Eddy Arnold
- *A/C* Crying In The Chapel [4]...Elvis Presley

ALBUMS
- *POP* Mary Poppins [11]...Soundtrack
- *R&B* The Temptations Sing Smokey [10]...The Temptations
- *C&W* I've Got A Tiger By The Tail [10]...Buck Owens

June 19, 1965
SINGLES
- *HOT* I Can't Help Myself [1]...Four Tops
- *R&B* I Can't Help Myself [3]...Four Tops
- *C&W* Ribbon Of Darkness [1]...Marty Robbins
- *A/C* Crying In The Chapel [5]...Elvis Presley

ALBUMS
- *POP* Mary Poppins [12]...Soundtrack
- *R&B* The Temptations Sing Smokey [11]...The Temptations
- *C&W* I've Got A Tiger By The Tail [11]...Buck Owens

June 26, 1965
SINGLES
- *HOT* Mr. Tambourine Man [1]...The Byrds
- *R&B* I Can't Help Myself [4]...Four Tops
- *C&W* Before You Go [1]...Buck Owens
- *A/C* Crying In The Chapel [6]...Elvis Presley

ALBUMS
- *POP* Mary Poppins [13]...Soundtrack
- *R&B* The Temptations Sing Smokey [12]...The Temptations
- *C&W* I've Got A Tiger By The Tail [12]...Buck Owens

July 3, 1965
SINGLES
- *HOT* I Can't Help Myself [2]...Four Tops
- *R&B* I Can't Help Myself [5]...Four Tops
- *C&W* Before You Go [2]...Buck Owens
- *A/C* Crying In The Chapel [7]...Elvis Presley

ALBUMS
- *POP* Mary Poppins [14]...Soundtrack
- *R&B* Four Tops [1]...Four Tops
- *C&W* I've Got A Tiger By The Tail [13]...Buck Owens

July 10, 1965

SINGLES
- HOT (I Can't Get No) Satisfaction [1]...The Rolling Stones
- R&B I Can't Help Myself [6]...Four Tops
- C&W Before You Go [3]...Buck Owens
- A/C A Walk In The Black Forest [1]...Horst Jankowski

ALBUMS
- POP Beatles VI [1]...The Beatles
- R&B Four Tops [2]...Four Tops
- C&W Connie Smith [1]...Connie Smith

July 17, 1965

SINGLES
- HOT (I Can't Get No) Satisfaction [2]...The Rolling Stones
- R&B I Can't Help Myself [7]...Four Tops
- C&W Before You Go [4]...Buck Owens
- A/C A Walk In The Black Forest [2]...Horst Jankowski

ALBUMS
- POP Beatles VI [2]...The Beatles
- R&B Four Tops [3]...Four Tops
- C&W Connie Smith [2]...Connie Smith

July 24, 1965

SINGLES
- HOT (I Can't Get No) Satisfaction [3]...The Rolling Stones
- R&B I Can't Help Myself [8]...Four Tops
- C&W Before You Go [5]...Buck Owens
- A/C (Such An) Easy Question [1]...Elvis Presley

ALBUMS
- POP Beatles VI [3]...The Beatles
- R&B Shotgun [1]...Jr. Walker & The All Stars
- C&W Connie Smith [3]...Connie Smith

July 31, 1965

SINGLES
- HOT (I Can't Get No) Satisfaction [4]...The Rolling Stones
- R&B I Can't Help Myself [9]...Four Tops
- C&W Before You Go [6]...Buck Owens
- A/C (Such An) Easy Question [2]...Elvis Presley

ALBUMS
- POP Beatles VI [4]...The Beatles
- R&B The Temptations Sing Smokey [13]...The Temptations
- C&W Connie Smith [4]...Connie Smith

August 7, 1965

SINGLES
- HOT I'm Henry VIII, I Am [1]...Herman's Hermits
- R&B In The Midnight Hour [1]...Wilson Pickett
- C&W The First Thing Ev'ry Morning (And The Last Thing Ev'ry Night) [1]...Jimmy Dean
- A/C Save Your Heart For Me [1]...Gary Lewis & The Playboys

ALBUMS
- POP Beatles VI [5]...The Beatles
- R&B The Temptations Sing Smokey [14]...The Temptations
- C&W Connie Smith [5]...Connie Smith

August 14, 1965

SINGLES
- HOT I Got You Babe [1]...Sonny & Cher
- R&B Papa's Got A Brand New Bag (Part I) [1]...James Brown
- C&W The First Thing Ev'ry Morning (And The Last Thing Ev'ry Night) [2]...Jimmy Dean
- A/C Save Your Heart For Me [2]...Gary Lewis & The Playboys

ALBUMS
- POP Beatles VI [6]...The Beatles
- R&B The Temptations Sing Smokey [15]...The Temptations
- C&W The Easy Way [1]...Eddy Arnold

August 21, 1965

SINGLES
- HOT I Got You Babe [2]...Sonny & Cher
- R&B Papa's Got A Brand New Bag (Part I) [2]...James Brown
- C&W Yes, Mr. Peters [1]...Roy Drusky & Priscilla Mitchell
- A/C Save Your Heart For Me [3]...Gary Lewis & The Playboys

ALBUMS
- POP Out Of Our Heads [1]...The Rolling Stones
- R&B The Temptations Sing Smokey [16]...The Temptations
- C&W The Easy Way [2]...Eddy Arnold

August 28, 1965

SINGLES
- HOT I Got You Babe [3]...Sonny & Cher
- R&B Papa's Got A Brand New Bag (Part I) [3]...James Brown
- C&W Yes, Mr. Peters [2]...Roy Drusky & Priscilla Mitchell
- A/C Hold Me, Thrill Me, Kiss Me [1]...Mel Carter

ALBUMS
- POP Out Of Our Heads [2]...The Rolling Stones
- R&B The Temptations Sing Smokey [17]...The Temptations
- C&W Connie Smith [6]...Connie Smith

September 4, 1965
SINGLES
- HOT   Help! [1]...The Beatles
- R&B   Papa's Got A Brand New Bag (Part I) [4]...James Brown
- C&W   The Bridge Washed Out [1]...Warner Mack
- A/C   You Were On My Mind [1]...We Five

ALBUMS
- POP   Out Of Our Heads [3]...The Rolling Stones
- R&B   The Temptations Sing Smokey [18]...The Temptations
- C&W   Connie Smith [7]...Connie Smith

September 11, 1965
SINGLES
- HOT   Help! [2]...The Beatles
- R&B   Papa's Got A Brand New Bag (Part I) [5]...James Brown
- C&W   Is It Really Over? [1]...Jim Reeves
- A/C   You Were On My Mind [2]...We Five

ALBUMS
- POP   Help! [1]...The Beatles/Soundtrack
- R&B   The In Crowd [1]...Ramsey Lewis Trio
- C&W   I've Got A Tiger By The Tail [14]...Buck Owens

September 18, 1965
SINGLES
- HOT   Help! [3]...The Beatles
- R&B   Papa's Got A Brand New Bag (Part I) [6]...James Brown
- C&W   Is It Really Over? [2]...Jim Reeves
- A/C   You Were On My Mind [3]...We Five

ALBUMS
- POP   Help! [2]...The Beatles/Soundtrack
- R&B   The In Crowd [2]...Ramsey Lewis Trio
- C&W   I've Got A Tiger By The Tail [15]...Buck Owens

September 25, 1965
SINGLES
- HOT   Eve Of Destruction [1]...Barry McGuire
- R&B   Papa's Got A Brand New Bag (Part I) [7]...James Brown
- C&W   Is It Really Over? [3]...Jim Reeves
- A/C   You Were On My Mind [4]...We Five

ALBUMS
- POP   Help! [3]...The Beatles/Soundtrack
- R&B   The In Crowd [3]...Ramsey Lewis Trio
- C&W   The 3rd Time Around [1]...Roger Miller

October 2, 1965
SINGLES
- HOT   Hang On Sloopy [1]...The McCoys
- R&B   Papa's Got A Brand New Bag (Part I) [8]...James Brown
- C&W   Only You (Can Break My Heart) [1]...Buck Owens
- A/C   You Were On My Mind [5]...We Five

ALBUMS
- POP   Help! [4]...The Beatles/Soundtrack
- R&B   The In Crowd [4]...Ramsey Lewis Trio
- C&W   The 3rd Time Around [2]...Roger Miller

October 9, 1965
SINGLES
- HOT   Yesterday [1]...The Beatles
- R&B   I Want To (Do Everything For You) [1]...Joe Tex
- C&W   Behind The Tear [1]...Sonny James
- A/C   I'm Yours [1]...Elvis Presley

ALBUMS
- POP   Help! [5]...The Beatles/Soundtrack
- R&B   The In Crowd [5]...Ramsey Lewis Trio
- C&W   Before You Go/No One But You [1]...Buck Owens

October 16, 1965
SINGLES
- HOT   Yesterday [2]...The Beatles
- R&B   I Want To (Do Everything For You) [2]...Joe Tex
- C&W   Behind The Tear [2]...Sonny James
- A/C   I'm Yours [2]...Elvis Presley

ALBUMS
- POP   Help! [6]...The Beatles/Soundtrack
- R&B   The In Crowd [6]...Ramsey Lewis Trio
- C&W   Up Through The Years [1]...Jim Reeves

October 23, 1965
SINGLES
- HOT   Yesterday [3]...The Beatles
- R&B   I Want To (Do Everything For You) [3]...Joe Tex
- C&W   Hello Vietnam [1]...Johnny Wright
- A/C   I'm Yours [3]...Elvis Presley

ALBUMS
- POP   Help! [7]...The Beatles/Soundtrack
- R&B   The In Crowd [7]...Ramsey Lewis Trio
- C&W   Up Through The Years [2]...Jim Reeves

October 30, 1965
SINGLES
- HOT   Yesterday [4]...The Beatles
- R&B   Rescue Me [1]...Fontella Bass
- C&W   Hello Vietnam [2]...Johnny Wright
- A/C   Taste Of Honey [1]...Herb Alpert

ALBUMS
- POP   Help! [8]...The Beatles/Soundtrack
- R&B   Otis Blue/Otis Redding Sings Soul [1]...Otis Redding
- C&W   My World [1]...Eddy Arnold

November 6, 1965
SINGLES
- HOT   Get Off Of My Cloud [1]...The Rolling Stones
- R&B   Rescue Me [2]...Fontella Bass
- C&W   Hello Vietnam [3]...Johnny Wright
- A/C   Taste Of Honey [2]...Herb Alpert

ALBUMS
- POP   Help! [9]...The Beatles/Soundtrack
- R&B   The In Crowd [8]...Ramsey Lewis Trio
- C&W   My World [2]...Eddy Arnold

November 13, 1965
SINGLES
- HOT   Get Off Of My Cloud [2]...The Rolling Stones
- R&B   Rescue Me [3]...Fontella Bass
- C&W   Behind The Tear [3]...Sonny James
- A/C   Taste Of Honey [3]...Herb Alpert

ALBUMS
- POP   The Sound Of Music [1]...Soundtrack
- R&B   The In Crowd [9]...Ramsey Lewis Trio
- C&W   The First Thing Ev'ry Morning [1]...Jimmy Dean

November 20, 1965
SINGLES
- HOT   I Hear A Symphony [1]...The Supremes
- R&B   Rescue Me [4]...Fontella Bass
- C&W   May The Bird Of Paradise Fly Up Your Nose [1]..."Little" Jimmy Dickens
- A/C   Taste Of Honey [4]...Herb Alpert

ALBUMS
- POP   The Sound Of Music [2]...Soundtrack
- R&B   The In Crowd [10]...Ramsey Lewis Trio
- C&W   The First Thing Ev'ry Morning [2]...Jimmy Dean

November 27, 1965
SINGLES
- HOT   I Hear A Symphony [2]...The Supremes
- R&B   Ain't That Peculiar [1]...Marvin Gaye
- C&W   May The Bird Of Paradise Fly Up Your Nose [2]..."Little" Jimmy Dickens
- A/C   Taste Of Honey [5]...Herb Alpert

ALBUMS
- POP   Whipped Cream & Other Delights [1]...Herb Alpert's Tijuana Brass
- R&B   The In Crowd [11]...Ramsey Lewis Trio
- C&W   My World [3]...Eddy Arnold

December 4, 1965
SINGLES
- HOT   Turn! Turn! Turn! (To Everything There Is A Season) [1]...The Byrds
- R&B   I Got You (I Feel Good) [1]...James Brown
- C&W   *Make The World Go Away [1]...Eddy Arnold
- A/C   *Make The World Go Away [1]...Eddy Arnold

ALBUMS
- POP   Whipped Cream & Other Delights [2]...Herb Alpert's Tijuana Brass
- R&B   The In Crowd [12]...Ramsey Lewis Trio
- C&W   My World [4]...Eddy Arnold

December 11, 1965
SINGLES
- HOT   Turn! Turn! Turn! (To Everything There Is A Season) [2]...The Byrds
- R&B   I Got You (I Feel Good) [2]...James Brown
- C&W   Make The World Go Away [2]...Eddy Arnold
- A/C   Make The World Go Away [2]...Eddy Arnold

ALBUMS
- POP   Whipped Cream & Other Delights [3]...Herb Alpert's Tijuana Brass
- R&B   Temptin' Temptation's [1]...The Temptations
- C&W   My World [5]...Eddy Arnold

December 18, 1965
SINGLES
- HOT   Turn! Turn! Turn! (To Everything There Is A Season) [3]...The Byrds
- R&B   I Got You (I Feel Good) [3]...James Brown
- C&W   Make The World Go Away [3]...Eddy Arnold
- A/C   Make The World Go Away [3]...Eddy Arnold

ALBUMS
- POP   Whipped Cream & Other Delights [4]...Herb Alpert's Tijuana Brass
- R&B   Temptin' Temptation's [2]...The Temptations
- C&W   My World [6]...Eddy Arnold

December 25, 1965
SINGLES
- HOT   Over And Over [1]...The Dave Clark Five
- R&B   I Got You (I Feel Good) [4]...James Brown
- C&W   Buckaroo [1]...Buck Owens
- A/C   Make The World Go Away [4]...Eddy Arnold

ALBUMS
- POP   Whipped Cream & Other Delights [5]...Herb Alpert's Tijuana Brass
- R&B   Temptin' Temptation's [3]...The Temptations
- C&W   Cute 'N' Country [1]...Connie Smith

January 1, 1966
SINGLES
- HOT The Sounds Of Silence [1]...Simon & Garfunkel
- R&B I Got You (I Feel Good) [5]...James Brown
- C&W Buckaroo [2]...Buck Owens
- A/C England Swings [1]...Roger Miller

ALBUMS
- POP Whipped Cream & Other Delights [6]...
       Herb Alpert's Tijuana Brass
- R&B Temptin' Temptation's [4]...The Temptations
- C&W Cute 'N' Country [2]...Connie Smith

January 8, 1966
SINGLES
- HOT We Can Work It Out [1]...The Beatles
- R&B A Sweet Woman Like You [1]...Joe Tex
- C&W Giddyup Go [1]...Red Sovine
- A/C Spanish Eyes [1]...Al Martino

ALBUMS
- POP Rubber Soul [1]...The Beatles
- R&B Temptin' Temptation's [5]...The Temptations
- C&W My World [7]...Eddy Arnold

January 15, 1966
SINGLES
- HOT We Can Work It Out [2]...The Beatles
- R&B I Got You (I Feel Good) [6]...James Brown
- C&W Giddyup Go [2]...Red Sovine
- A/C Spanish Eyes [2]...Al Martino

ALBUMS
- POP Rubber Soul [2]...The Beatles
- R&B Going To A Go-Go [1]...
       Smokey Robinson & The Miracles
- C&W My World [8]...Eddy Arnold

January 22, 1966
SINGLES
- HOT The Sounds Of Silence [2]...Simon & Garfunkel
- R&B Uptight (Everything's Alright) [1]...Stevie Wonder
- C&W Giddyup Go [3]...Red Sovine
- A/C Spanish Eyes [3]...Al Martino

ALBUMS
- POP Rubber Soul [3]...The Beatles
- R&B Temptin' Temptation's [6]...The Temptations
- C&W My World [9]...Eddy Arnold

January 29, 1966
SINGLES
- HOT We Can Work It Out [3]...The Beatles
- R&B Uptight (Everything's Alright) [2]...Stevie Wonder
- C&W Giddyup Go [4]...Red Sovine
- A/C Spanish Eyes [4]...Al Martino

ALBUMS
- POP Rubber Soul [4]...The Beatles
- R&B Temptin' Temptation's [7]...The Temptations
- C&W My World [10]...Eddy Arnold

February 5, 1966
SINGLES
- HOT My Love [1]...Petula Clark
- R&B Uptight (Everything's Alright) [3]...Stevie Wonder
- C&W Giddyup Go [5]...Red Sovine
- A/C It Was A Very Good Year [1]...Frank Sinatra

ALBUMS
- POP Rubber Soul [5]...The Beatles
- R&B Temptin' Temptation's [8]...The Temptations
- C&W My World [11]...Eddy Arnold

February 12, 1966
SINGLES
- HOT My Love [2]...Petula Clark
- R&B Uptight (Everything's Alright) [4]...Stevie Wonder
- C&W Giddyup Go [6]...Red Sovine
- A/C Crying Time [1]...Ray Charles

ALBUMS
- POP Rubber Soul [6]...The Beatles
- R&B Going To A Go-Go [2]...
       Smokey Robinson & The Miracles
- C&W My World [12]...Eddy Arnold

February 19, 1966
SINGLES
- HOT Lightnin' Strikes [1]...Lou Christie
- R&B Uptight (Everything's Alright) [5]...Stevie Wonder
- C&W Waitin' In Your Welfare Line [1]...Buck Owens
- A/C Crying Time [2]...Ray Charles

ALBUMS
- POP Whipped Cream & Other Delights [7]...
       Herb Alpert's Tijuana Brass
- R&B Temptin' Temptation's [9]...The Temptations
- C&W My World [13]...Eddy Arnold

February 26, 1966

SINGLES
- HOT These Boots Are Made For Walkin' [1]...Nancy Sinatra
- R&B Baby Scratch My Back [1]...Slim Harpo
- C&W Waitin' In Your Welfare Line [2]...Buck Owens
- A/C Crying Time [3]...Ray Charles

ALBUMS
- POP Whipped Cream & Other Delights [8]...Herb Alpert's Tijuana Brass
- R&B Temptin' Temptation's [10]...The Temptations
- C&W My World [14]...Eddy Arnold

March 5, 1966

SINGLES
- HOT *The Ballad Of The Green Berets [1]...SSgt Barry Sadler
- R&B Baby Scratch My Back [2]...Slim Harpo
- C&W Waitin' In Your Welfare Line [3]...Buck Owens
- A/C *The Ballad Of The Green Berets [1]...SSgt Barry Sadler

ALBUMS
- POP Going Places [1]...Herb Alpert And The Tijuana Brass
- R&B Going To A Go-Go [3]...Smokey Robinson & The Miracles
- C&W My World [15]...Eddy Arnold

March 12, 1966

SINGLES
- HOT The Ballad Of The Green Berets [2]...SSgt Barry Sadler
- R&B 634-5789 (Soulsville, U.S.A.) [1]...Wilson Pickett
- C&W Waitin' In Your Welfare Line [4]...Buck Owens
- A/C The Ballad Of The Green Berets [2]...SSgt Barry Sadler

ALBUMS
- POP Ballads of the Green Berets [1]...SSgt Barry Sadler
- R&B Going To A Go-Go [4]...Smokey Robinson & The Miracles
- C&W My World [16]...Eddy Arnold

March 19, 1966

SINGLES
- HOT The Ballad Of The Green Berets [3]...SSgt Barry Sadler
- R&B 634-5789 (Soulsville, U.S.A.) [2]...Wilson Pickett
- C&W Waitin' In Your Welfare Line [5]...Buck Owens
- A/C The Ballad Of The Green Berets [3]...SSgt Barry Sadler

ALBUMS
- POP Ballads of the Green Berets [2]...SSgt Barry Sadler
- R&B Going To A Go-Go [5]...Smokey Robinson & The Miracles
- C&W My World [17]...Eddy Arnold

March 26, 1966

SINGLES
- HOT The Ballad Of The Green Berets [4]...SSgt Barry Sadler
- R&B 634-5789 (Soulsville, U.S.A.) [3]...Wilson Pickett
- C&W Waitin' In Your Welfare Line [6]...Buck Owens
- A/C The Ballad Of The Green Berets [4]...SSgt Barry Sadler

ALBUMS
- POP Ballads of the Green Berets [3]...SSgt Barry Sadler
- R&B Temptin' Temptation's [11]...The Temptations
- C&W Ballads of the Green Berets [1]...SSgt Barry Sadler

April 2, 1966

SINGLES
- HOT The Ballad Of The Green Berets [5]...SSgt Barry Sadler
- R&B 634-5789 (Soulsville, U.S.A.) [4]...Wilson Pickett
- C&W Waitin' In Your Welfare Line [7]...Buck Owens
- A/C The Ballad Of The Green Berets [5]...SSgt Barry Sadler

ALBUMS
- POP Ballads of the Green Berets [4]...SSgt Barry Sadler
- R&B Temptin' Temptation's [12]...The Temptations
- C&W Ballads of the Green Berets [2]...SSgt Barry Sadler

April 9, 1966

SINGLES
- HOT (You're My) Soul And Inspiration [1]...The Righteous Brothers
- R&B 634-5789 (Soulsville, U.S.A.) [5]...Wilson Pickett
- C&W *I Want To Go With You [1]...Eddy Arnold
- A/C *I Want To Go With You [1]...Eddy Arnold

ALBUMS
- POP Ballads of the Green Berets [5]...SSgt Barry Sadler
- R&B Temptin' Temptation's [13]...The Temptations
- C&W Roll out the red carpet for Buck Owens and his Buckaroos [1]...Buck Owens

April 16, 1966

SINGLES
- HOT (You're My) Soul And Inspiration [2]...The Righteous Brothers
- R&B 634-5789 (Soulsville, U.S.A.) [6]...Wilson Pickett
- C&W I Want To Go With You [2]...Eddy Arnold
- A/C I Want To Go With You [2]...Eddy Arnold

ALBUMS
- POP Going Places [2]...Herb Alpert And The Tijuana Brass
- R&B Temptin' Temptation's [14]...The Temptations
- C&W Roll out the red carpet for Buck Owens and his Buckaroos [2]...Buck Owens

April 23, 1966
SINGLES
- HOT (You're My) Soul And Inspiration [3]...The Righteous Brothers
- R&B 634-5789 (Soulsville, U.S.A.) [7]...Wilson Pickett
- C&W I Want To Go With You [3]...Eddy Arnold
- A/C I Want To Go With You [3]...Eddy Arnold

ALBUMS
- POP Going Places [3]...Herb Alpert And The Tijuana Brass
- R&B I Hear A Symphony [1]...The Supremes
- C&W I Want To Go With You [1]...Eddy Arnold

April 30, 1966
SINGLES
- HOT Good Lovin' [1]...Young Rascals
- R&B Get Ready [1]...The Temptations
- C&W I Want To Go With You [4]...Eddy Arnold
- A/C Together Again [1]...Ray Charles

ALBUMS
- POP Going Places [4]...Herb Alpert And The Tijuana Brass
- R&B Get My Mojo Workin' [1]...Jimmy Smith
- C&W I Want To Go With You [2]...Eddy Arnold

May 7, 1966
SINGLES
- HOT Monday, Monday [1]...Mama's & The Papa's
- R&B *When A Man Loves A Woman [1]...Percy Sledge
- C&W I Want To Go With You [5]...Eddy Arnold
- A/C Together Again [2]...Ray Charles

ALBUMS
- POP Going Places [5]...Herb Alpert And The Tijuana Brass
- R&B Get My Mojo Workin' [2]...Jimmy Smith
- C&W Roll out the red carpet for Buck Owens and his Buckaroos [3]...Buck Owens

May 14, 1966
SINGLES
- HOT Monday, Monday [2]...Mama's & The Papa's
- R&B When A Man Loves A Woman [2]...Percy Sledge
- C&W I Want To Go With You [6]...Eddy Arnold
- A/C Together Again [3]...Ray Charles

ALBUMS
- POP Going Places [6]...Herb Alpert And The Tijuana Brass
- R&B Crying Time [1]...Ray Charles
- C&W Roll out the red carpet for Buck Owens and his Buckaroos [4]...Buck Owens

May 21, 1966
SINGLES
- HOT Monday, Monday [3]...Mama's & The Papa's
- R&B When A Man Loves A Woman [3]...Percy Sledge
- C&W Distant Drums [1]...Jim Reeves
- A/C Band Of Gold [1]...Mel Carter

ALBUMS
- POP If You Can Believe Your Eyes And Ears [1]...The Mamas And The Papas
- R&B Lou Rawls Live! [1]...Lou Rawls
- C&W Roll out the red carpet for Buck Owens and his Buckaroos [5]...Buck Owens

May 28, 1966
SINGLES
- HOT When A Man Loves A Woman [1]...Percy Sledge
- R&B When A Man Loves A Woman [4]...Percy Sledge
- C&W Distant Drums [2]...Jim Reeves
- A/C Band Of Gold [2]...Mel Carter

ALBUMS
- POP What Now My Love [1]...Herb Alpert & The Tijuana Brass
- R&B Lou Rawls Live! [2]...Lou Rawls
- C&W Roll out the red carpet for Buck Owens and his Buckaroos [6]...Buck Owens

June 4, 1966
SINGLES
- HOT When A Man Loves A Woman [2]...Percy Sledge
- R&B It's A Man's Man's Man's World [1]...James Brown
- C&W Distant Drums [3]...Jim Reeves
- A/C *Strangers In The Night [1]...Frank Sinatra

ALBUMS
- POP What Now My Love [2]...Herb Alpert & The Tijuana Brass
- R&B Lou Rawls Live! [3]...Lou Rawls
- C&W Roll out the red carpet for Buck Owens and his Buckaroos [7]...Buck Owens

June 11, 1966
SINGLES
- HOT Paint It, Black [1]...The Rolling Stones
- R&B It's A Man's Man's Man's World [2]...James Brown
- C&W Distant Drums [4]...Jim Reeves
- A/C Strangers In The Night [2]...Frank Sinatra

ALBUMS
- POP What Now My Love [3]...Herb Alpert & The Tijuana Brass
- R&B Lou Rawls Live! [4]...Lou Rawls
- C&W Roll out the red carpet for Buck Owens and his Buckaroos [8]...Buck Owens

June 18, 1966
SINGLES
- HOT Paint It, Black [2]...The Rolling Stones
- R&B Hold On! I'm A Comin' [1]...Sam & Dave
- C&W Take Good Care Of Her [1]...Sonny James
- A/C Strangers In The Night [3]...Frank Sinatra

ALBUMS
- POP What Now My Love [4]...
  Herb Alpert & The Tijuana Brass
- R&B Lou Rawls Live! [5]...Lou Rawls
- C&W Distant Drums [1]...Jim Reeves

June 25, 1966
SINGLES
- HOT Paperback Writer [1]...The Beatles
- R&B Ain't Too Proud To Beg [1]...The Temptations
- C&W Take Good Care Of Her [2]...Sonny James
- A/C Strangers In The Night [4]...Frank Sinatra

ALBUMS
- POP What Now My Love [5]...
  Herb Alpert & The Tijuana Brass
- R&B Lou Rawls Live! [6]...Lou Rawls
- C&W Distant Drums [2]...Jim Reeves

July 2, 1966
SINGLES
- HOT Strangers In The Night [1]...Frank Sinatra
- R&B Ain't Too Proud To Beg [2]...The Temptations
- C&W Think Of Me [1]...Buck Owens
- A/C Strangers In The Night [5]...Frank Sinatra

ALBUMS
- POP What Now My Love [6]...
  Herb Alpert & The Tijuana Brass
- R&B Lou Rawls Live! [7]...Lou Rawls
- C&W Distant Drums [3]...Jim Reeves

July 9, 1966
SINGLES
- HOT Paperback Writer [2]...The Beatles
- R&B Ain't Too Proud To Beg [3]...The Temptations
- C&W Think Of Me [2]...Buck Owens
- A/C Strangers In The Night [6]...Frank Sinatra

ALBUMS
- POP What Now My Love [7]...
  Herb Alpert & The Tijuana Brass
- R&B Lou Rawls Live! [8]...Lou Rawls
- C&W Distant Drums [4]...Jim Reeves

July 16, 1966
SINGLES
- HOT Hanky Panky [1]...Tommy James & The Shondells
- R&B Ain't Too Proud To Beg [4]...The Temptations
- C&W Think Of Me [3]...Buck Owens
- A/C Strangers In The Night [7]...Frank Sinatra

ALBUMS
- POP What Now My Love [8]...
  Herb Alpert & The Tijuana Brass
- R&B Lou Rawls Live! [9]...Lou Rawls
- C&W Distant Drums [5]...Jim Reeves

July 23, 1966
SINGLES
- HOT Hanky Panky [2]...Tommy James & The Shondells
- R&B Let's Go Get Stoned [1]...Ray Charles
- C&W Think Of Me [4]...Buck Owens
- A/C The Impossible Dream [1]...Jack Jones

ALBUMS
- POP Strangers In The Night [1]...Frank Sinatra
- R&B Lou Rawls Live! [10]...Lou Rawls
- C&W Distant Drums [6]...Jim Reeves

July 30, 1966
SINGLES
- HOT Wild Thing [1]...The Troggs
- R&B Ain't Too Proud To Beg [5]...The Temptations
- C&W Think Of Me [5]...Buck Owens
- A/C Somewhere My Love [1]...Ray Conniff & The Singers

ALBUMS
- POP "Yesterday"...And Today [1]...The Beatles
- R&B Gettin' Ready [1]...The Temptations
- C&W Distant Drums [7]...Jim Reeves

August 6, 1966
SINGLES
- HOT Wild Thing [2]...The Troggs
- R&B Ain't Too Proud To Beg [6]...The Temptations
- C&W Think Of Me [6]...Buck Owens
- A/C Somewhere My Love [2]...Ray Conniff & The Singers

ALBUMS
- POP "Yesterday"...And Today [2]...The Beatles
- R&B Gettin' Ready [2]...The Temptations
- C&W I'm A People [1]...George Jones

August 13, 1966
SINGLES
- HOT Summer In The City [1]...The Lovin' Spoonful
- R&B Ain't Too Proud To Beg [7]...The Temptations
- C&W Almost Persuaded [1]...David Houston
- A/C Somewhere My Love [3]...Ray Conniff & The Singers

ALBUMS
- POP "Yesterday"...And Today [3]...The Beatles
- R&B Gettin' Ready [3]...The Temptations
- C&W I'm A People [2]...George Jones

August 20, 1966
SINGLES
- HOT   Summer In The City [2]...The Lovin' Spoonful
- R&B   Ain't Too Proud To Beg [8]...The Temptations
- C&W   Almost Persuaded [2]...David Houston
- A/C   Somewhere My Love [4]...Ray Conniff & The Singers

ALBUMS
- POP   "Yesterday"...And Today [4]...The Beatles
- R&B   Hold On, I'm Comin' [1]...Sam & Dave
- C&W   Dust On Mother's Bible [1]...Buck Owens

August 27, 1966
SINGLES
- HOT   Summer In The City [3]...The Lovin' Spoonful
- R&B   Blowin' In The Wind [1]...Stevie Wonder
- C&W   Almost Persuaded [3]...David Houston
- A/C   I Couldn't Live Without Your Love [1]...Petula Clark

ALBUMS
- POP   "Yesterday"...And Today [5]...The Beatles
- R&B   Gettin' Ready [4]...The Temptations
- C&W   Dust On Mother's Bible [2]...Buck Owens

September 3, 1966
SINGLES
- HOT   Sunshine Superman [1]...Donovan
- R&B   *You Can't Hurry Love [1]...The Supremes
- C&W   Almost Persuaded [4]...David Houston
- A/C   Born Free [1]...Roger Williams

ALBUMS
- POP   What Now My Love [9]...Herb Alpert & The Tijuana Brass
- R&B   Gettin' Ready [5]...The Temptations
- C&W   The Last Word Is Lonesome [1]...Eddy Arnold

September 10, 1966
SINGLES
- HOT   You Can't Hurry Love [1]...The Supremes
- R&B   You Can't Hurry Love [2]...The Supremes
- C&W   Almost Persuaded [5]...David Houston
- A/C   Born Free [2]...Roger Williams

ALBUMS
- POP   Revolver [1]...The Beatles
- R&B   Gettin' Ready [6]...The Temptations
- C&W   Carnegie Hall Concert [1]...Buck Owens

September 17, 1966
SINGLES
- HOT   You Can't Hurry Love [2]...The Supremes
- R&B   Land Of 1,000 Dances [1]...Wilson Pickett
- C&W   Almost Persuaded [6]...David Houston
- A/C   Born Free [3]...Roger Williams

ALBUMS
- POP   Revolver [2]...The Beatles
- R&B   Lou Rawls Live! [11]...Lou Rawls
- C&W   Carnegie Hall Concert [2]...Buck Owens

September 24, 1966
SINGLES
- HOT   Cherish [1]...The Association
- R&B   Beauty Is Only Skin Deep [1]...The Temptations
- C&W   Almost Persuaded [7]...David Houston
- A/C   Born Free [4]...Roger Williams

ALBUMS
- POP   Revolver [3]...The Beatles
- R&B   Lou Rawls Live! [12]...Lou Rawls
- C&W   Carnegie Hall Concert [3]...Buck Owens

October 1, 1966
SINGLES
- HOT   Cherish [2]...The Association
- R&B   Beauty Is Only Skin Deep [2]...The Temptations
- C&W   Almost Persuaded [8]...David Houston
- A/C   In The Arms Of Love [1]...Andy Williams

ALBUMS
- POP   Revolver [4]...The Beatles
- R&B   Lou Rawls Soulin' [1]...Lou Rawls
- C&W   Carnegie Hall Concert [4]...Buck Owens

October 8, 1966
SINGLES
- HOT   Cherish [3]...The Association
- R&B   Beauty Is Only Skin Deep [3]...The Temptations
- C&W   Almost Persuaded [9]...David Houston
- A/C   In The Arms Of Love [2]...Andy Williams

ALBUMS
- POP   Revolver [5]...The Beatles
- R&B   Lou Rawls Soulin' [2]...Lou Rawls
- C&W   Almost Persuaded [1]...David Houston

October 15, 1966
SINGLES
- HOT   *Reach Out I'll Be There [1]...Four Tops
- R&B   Beauty Is Only Skin Deep [4]...The Temptations
- C&W   Blue Side Of Lonesome [1]...Jim Reeves
- A/C   Summer Wind [1]...Frank Sinatra

ALBUMS
- POP   Revolver [6]...The Beatles
- R&B   Lou Rawls Soulin' [3]...Lou Rawls
- C&W   I Love You Drops [1]...Bill Anderson

October 22, 1966
SINGLES
- HOT   Reach Out I'll Be There [2]...Four Tops
- R&B   Beauty Is Only Skin Deep [5]...The Temptations
- C&W   Open Up Your Heart [1]...Buck Owens
- A/C   Born Free [5]...Roger Williams

ALBUMS
- POP   The Supremes A' Go-Go [1]...The Supremes
- R&B   The Supremes A' Go-Go [1]...The Supremes
- C&W   I Love You Drops [2]...Bill Anderson

October 29, 1966
SINGLES
- HOT 96 Tears [1]...? (Question Mark) & The Mysterians
- R&B Reach Out I'll Be There [1]...Four Tops
- C&W Open Up Your Heart [2]...Buck Owens
- A/C Born Free [6]...Roger Williams

ALBUMS
- POP The Supremes A' Go-Go [2]...The Supremes
- R&B The Supremes A' Go-Go [2]...The Supremes
- C&W Carnegie Hall Concert [5]...Buck Owens

November 5, 1966
SINGLES
- HOT Last Train To Clarksville [1]...The Monkees
- R&B Reach Out I'll Be There [2]...Four Tops
- C&W Open Up Your Heart [3]...Buck Owens
- A/C The Wheel Of Hurt [1]...Margaret Whiting

ALBUMS
- POP Doctor Zhivago [1]...Soundtrack
- R&B The Supremes A' Go-Go [3]...The Supremes
- C&W Another Bridge To Burn [1]...Ray Price

November 12, 1966
SINGLES
- HOT Poor Side Of Town [1]...Johnny Rivers
- R&B Love Is A Hurtin' Thing [1]...Lou Rawls
- C&W Open Up Your Heart [4]...Buck Owens
- A/C The Wheel Of Hurt [2]...Margaret Whiting

ALBUMS
- POP The Monkees [1]...The Monkees
- R&B The Supremes A' Go-Go [4]...The Supremes
- C&W You Ain't Woman Enough [1]...Loretta Lynn

November 19, 1966
SINGLES
- HOT *You Keep Me Hangin' On [1]...The Supremes
- R&B Knock On Wood [1]...Eddie Floyd
- C&W I Get The Fever [1]...Bill Anderson
- A/C The Wheel Of Hurt [3]...Margaret Whiting

ALBUMS
- POP The Monkees [2]...The Monkees
- R&B Lou Rawls Soulin' [4]...Lou Rawls
- C&W You Ain't Woman Enough [2]...Loretta Lynn

November 26, 1966
SINGLES
- HOT You Keep Me Hangin' On [2]...The Supremes
- R&B You Keep Me Hangin' On [1]...The Supremes
- C&W Somebody Like Me [1]...Eddy Arnold
- A/C The Wheel Of Hurt [4]...Margaret Whiting

ALBUMS
- POP The Monkees [3]...The Monkees
- R&B Lou Rawls Soulin' [5]...Lou Rawls
- C&W Another Bridge To Burn [2]...Ray Price

December 3, 1966
SINGLES
- HOT *Winchester Cathedral [1]...The New Vaudeville Band
- R&B You Keep Me Hangin' On [2]...The Supremes
- C&W Somebody Like Me [2]...Eddy Arnold
- A/C *Winchester Cathedral [1]...The New Vaudeville Band

ALBUMS
- POP The Monkees [4]...The Monkees
- R&B Lou Rawls Soulin' [6]...Lou Rawls
- C&W Born To Sing [1]...Connie Smith

December 10, 1966
SINGLES
- HOT Good Vibrations [1]...The Beach Boys
- R&B You Keep Me Hangin' On [3]...The Supremes
- C&W Somebody Like Me [3]...Eddy Arnold
- A/C Winchester Cathedral [2]...The New Vaudeville Band

ALBUMS
- POP The Monkees [5]...The Monkees
- R&B Lou Rawls Soulin' [7]...Lou Rawls
- C&W Swinging Doors [1]...Merle Haggard

December 17, 1966
SINGLES
- HOT Winchester Cathedral [2]...The New Vaudeville Band
- R&B You Keep Me Hangin' On [4]...The Supremes
- C&W Somebody Like Me [4]...Eddy Arnold
- A/C Winchester Cathedral [3]...The New Vaudeville Band

ALBUMS
- POP The Monkees [6]...The Monkees
- R&B Lou Rawls Soulin' [8]...Lou Rawls
- C&W Swinging Doors [2]...Merle Haggard

December 24, 1966
SINGLES
- HOT Winchester Cathedral [3]...The New Vaudeville Band
- R&B (I Know) I'm Losing You [1]...The Temptations
- C&W There Goes My Everything [1]...Jack Greene
- A/C Winchester Cathedral [4]...The New Vaudeville Band

ALBUMS
- POP The Monkees [7]...The Monkees
- R&B Lou Rawls Soulin' [9]...Lou Rawls
- C&W The Best Of Sonny James [1]...Sonny James

December 31, 1966
SINGLES
- HOT I'm A Believer [1]...The Monkees
- R&B (I Know) I'm Losing You [2]...The Temptations
- C&W There Goes My Everything [2]...Jack Greene
- A/C That's Life [1]...Frank Sinatra

ALBUMS
- POP The Monkees [8]...The Monkees
- R&B The Temptations Greatest Hits [1]...The Temptations
- C&W The Best Of Sonny James [2]...Sonny James

January 7, 1967

SINGLES
- HOT   I'm A Believer [2]...The Monkees
- R&B   Tell It Like It Is [1]...Aaron Neville
- C&W   There Goes My Everything [3]...Jack Greene
- A/C   That's Life [2]...Frank Sinatra

ALBUMS
- POP   The Monkees [9]...The Monkees
- R&B   The Temptations Greatest Hits [2]...The Temptations
- C&W   The Best Of Sonny James [3]...Sonny James

January 14, 1967

SINGLES
- HOT   I'm A Believer [3]...The Monkees
- R&B   Tell It Like It Is [2]...Aaron Neville
- C&W   There Goes My Everything [4]...Jack Greene
- A/C   That's Life [3]...Frank Sinatra

ALBUMS
- POP   The Monkees [10]...The Monkees
- R&B   The Temptations Greatest Hits [3]...The Temptations
- C&W   The Best Of Sonny James [4]...Sonny James

January 21, 1967

SINGLES
- HOT   I'm A Believer [4]...The Monkees
- R&B   Tell It Like It Is [3]...Aaron Neville
- C&W   There Goes My Everything [5]...Jack Greene
- A/C   Sugar Town [1]...Nancy Sinatra

ALBUMS
- POP   The Monkees [11]...The Monkees
- R&B   The Temptations Greatest Hits [4]...The Temptations
- C&W   Somebody Like Me [1]...Eddy Arnold

January 28, 1967

SINGLES
- HOT   I'm A Believer [5]...The Monkees
- R&B   Tell It Like It Is [4]...Aaron Neville
- C&W   There Goes My Everything [6]...Jack Greene
- A/C   Sugar Town [2]...Nancy Sinatra

ALBUMS
- POP   The Monkees [12]...The Monkees
- R&B   The Temptations Greatest Hits [5]...The Temptations
- C&W   Somebody Like Me [2]...Eddy Arnold

February 4, 1967

SINGLES
- HOT   I'm A Believer [6]...The Monkees
- R&B   Tell It Like It Is [5]...Aaron Neville
- C&W   There Goes My Everything [7]...Jack Greene
- A/C   My Cup Runneth Over [1]...Ed Ames

ALBUMS
- POP   The Monkees [13]...The Monkees
- R&B   Four Tops Live! [1]...Four Tops
- C&W   The Best Of Sonny James [5]...Sonny James

February 11, 1967

SINGLES
- HOT   I'm A Believer [7]...The Monkees
- R&B   Are You Lonely For Me [1]...Freddie Scott
- C&W   Don't Come Home A'Drinkin' (With Lovin' On Your Mind) [1]...Loretta Lynn
- A/C   My Cup Runneth Over [2]...Ed Ames

ALBUMS
- POP   More Of The Monkees [1]...The Monkees
- R&B   The Temptations Greatest Hits [6]...The Temptations
- C&W   There Goes My Everything [1]...Jack Greene

February 18, 1967

SINGLES
- HOT   Kind Of A Drag [1]...The Buckinghams
- R&B   Are You Lonely For Me [2]...Freddie Scott
- C&W   Where Does The Good Times Go [1]...Buck Owens
- A/C   My Cup Runneth Over [3]...Ed Ames

ALBUMS
- POP   More Of The Monkees [2]...The Monkees
- R&B   The Temptations Greatest Hits [7]...The Temptations
- C&W   There Goes My Everything [2]...Jack Greene

February 25, 1967

SINGLES
- HOT   Kind Of A Drag [2]...The Buckinghams
- R&B   Are You Lonely For Me [3]...Freddie Scott
- C&W   Where Does The Good Times Go [2]...Buck Owens
- A/C   My Cup Runneth Over [4]...Ed Ames

ALBUMS
- POP   More Of The Monkees [3]...The Monkees
- R&B   The Temptations Greatest Hits [8]...The Temptations
- C&W   There Goes My Everything [3]...Jack Greene

March 4, 1967

SINGLES
- HOT   Ruby Tuesday [1]...The Rolling Stones
- R&B   Are You Lonely For Me [4]...Freddie Scott
- C&W   The Fugitive [1]...Merle Haggard
- A/C   Lady [1]...Jack Jones

ALBUMS
- POP   More Of The Monkees [4]...The Monkees
- R&B   The Temptations Greatest Hits [9]...The Temptations
- C&W   There Goes My Everything [4]...Jack Greene

March 11, 1967
SINGLES
- HOT *Love Is Here And Now You're Gone [1]...The Supremes
- R&B *Love Is Here And Now You're Gone [1]...The Supremes
- C&W Where Does The Good Times Go [3]...Buck Owens
- A/C Lady [2]...Jack Jones

ALBUMS
- POP More Of The Monkees [5]...The Monkees
- R&B The Supremes sing Holland-Dozier-Holland [1]...The Supremes
- C&W There Goes My Everything [5]...Jack Greene

March 18, 1967
SINGLES
- HOT Penny Lane [1]...The Beatles
- R&B Love Is Here And Now You're Gone [2]...The Supremes
- C&W Where Does The Good Times Go [4]...Buck Owens
- A/C Lady [3]...Jack Jones

ALBUMS
- POP More Of The Monkees [6]...The Monkees
- R&B The Supremes sing Holland-Dozier-Holland [2]...The Supremes
- C&W Open Up Your Heart [1]...Buck Owens

March 25, 1967
SINGLES
- HOT Happy Together [1]...The Turtles
- R&B I Never Loved A Man (The Way I Loved You) [1]...Aretha Franklin
- C&W I Won't Come In While He's There [1]...Jim Reeves
- A/C Lady [4]...Jack Jones

ALBUMS
- POP More Of The Monkees [7]...The Monkees
- R&B The Supremes sing Holland-Dozier-Holland [3]...The Supremes
- C&W There Goes My Everything [6]...Jack Greene

April 1, 1967
SINGLES
- HOT Happy Together [2]...The Turtles
- R&B I Never Loved A Man (The Way I Loved You) [2]...Aretha Franklin
- C&W Walk Through This World With Me [1]...George Jones
- A/C *Somethin' Stupid [1]...Nancy Sinatra & Frank Sinatra

ALBUMS
- POP More Of The Monkees [8]...The Monkees
- R&B Mercy, Mercy, Mercy! [1]..."Cannonball" Adderley
- C&W There Goes My Everything [7]...Jack Greene

April 8, 1967
SINGLES
- HOT Happy Together [3]...The Turtles
- R&B I Never Loved A Man (The Way I Loved You) [3]...Aretha Franklin
- C&W Walk Through This World With Me [2]...George Jones
- A/C Somethin' Stupid [2]...Nancy Sinatra & Frank Sinatra

ALBUMS
- POP More Of The Monkees [9]...The Monkees
- R&B Temptations Live! [1]...The Temptations
- C&W There Goes My Everything [8]...Jack Greene

April 15, 1967
SINGLES
- HOT Somethin' Stupid [1]...Nancy Sinatra & Frank Sinatra
- R&B I Never Loved A Man (The Way I Loved You) [4]...Aretha Franklin
- C&W Lonely Again [1]...Eddy Arnold
- A/C Somethin' Stupid [3]...Nancy Sinatra & Frank Sinatra

ALBUMS
- POP More Of The Monkees [10]...The Monkees
- R&B Temptations Live! [2]...The Temptations
- C&W Lonely Again [1]...Eddy Arnold

April 22, 1967
SINGLES
- HOT Somethin' Stupid [2]...Nancy Sinatra & Frank Sinatra
- R&B I Never Loved A Man (The Way I Loved You) [5]...Aretha Franklin
- C&W Lonely Again [2]...Eddy Arnold
- A/C Somethin' Stupid [4]...Nancy Sinatra & Frank Sinatra

ALBUMS
- POP More Of The Monkees [11]...The Monkees
- R&B Temptations Live! [3]...The Temptations
- C&W Lonely Again [2]...Eddy Arnold

April 29, 1967
SINGLES
- HOT Somethin' Stupid [3]...Nancy Sinatra & Frank Sinatra
- R&B I Never Loved A Man (The Way I Loved You) [6]...Aretha Franklin
- C&W Need You [1]...Sonny James
- A/C Somethin' Stupid [5]...Nancy Sinatra & Frank Sinatra

ALBUMS
- POP More Of The Monkees [12]...The Monkees
- R&B I Never Loved A Man The Way I Love You [1]...Aretha Franklin
- C&W Touch My Heart [1]...Ray Price

May 6, 1967

SINGLES
- *HOT* **Somethin' Stupid** [4]...Nancy Sinatra & Frank Sinatra
- *R&B* **I Never Loved A Man (The Way I Loved You)** [7]...Aretha Franklin
- *C&W* **Need You** [2]...Sonny James
- *A/C* **Somethin' Stupid** [6]...Nancy Sinatra & Frank Sinatra

ALBUMS
- *POP* **More Of The Monkees** [13]...The Monkees
- *R&B* **I Never Loved A Man The Way I Love You** [2]...Aretha Franklin
- *C&W* **Lonely Again** [3]...Eddy Arnold

May 13, 1967

SINGLES
- *HOT* **The Happening** [1]...The Supremes
- *R&B* **Jimmy Mack** [1]...Martha & The Vandellas
- *C&W* **Sam's Place** [1]...Buck Owens
- *A/C* **Somethin' Stupid** [7]...Nancy Sinatra & Frank Sinatra

ALBUMS
- *POP* **More Of The Monkees** [14]...The Monkees
- *R&B* **I Never Loved A Man The Way I Love You** [3]...Aretha Franklin
- *C&W* **There Goes My Everything** [9]...Jack Greene

May 20, 1967

SINGLES
- *HOT* **Groovin'** [1]...Young Rascals
- *R&B* ***Respect** [1]...Aretha Franklin
- *C&W* **Sam's Place** [2]...Buck Owens
- *A/C* **Somethin' Stupid** [8]...Nancy Sinatra & Frank Sinatra

ALBUMS
- *POP* **More Of The Monkees** [15]...The Monkees
- *R&B* **I Never Loved A Man The Way I Love You** [4]...Aretha Franklin
- *C&W* **Don't Come Home A Drinkin'** [1]...Loretta Lynn

May 27, 1967

SINGLES
- *HOT* **Groovin'** [2]...Young Rascals
- *R&B* **Respect** [2]...Aretha Franklin
- *C&W* **Sam's Place** [3]...Buck Owens
- *A/C* **Somethin' Stupid** [9]...Nancy Sinatra & Frank Sinatra

ALBUMS
- *POP* **More Of The Monkees** [16]...The Monkees
- *R&B* **I Never Loved A Man The Way I Love You** [5]...Aretha Franklin
- *C&W* **The Best Of Eddy Arnold** [1]...Eddy Arnold

June 3, 1967

SINGLES
- *HOT* **Respect** [1]...Aretha Franklin
- *R&B* **Respect** [3]...Aretha Franklin
- *C&W* **It's Such A Pretty World Today** [1]...Wynn Stewart
- *A/C* **Casino Royale** [1]...Herb Alpert

ALBUMS
- *POP* **More Of The Monkees** [17]...The Monkees
- *R&B* **I Never Loved A Man The Way I Love You** [6]...Aretha Franklin
- *C&W* **The Best Of Eddy Arnold** [2]...Eddy Arnold

June 10, 1967

SINGLES
- *HOT* **Respect** [2]...Aretha Franklin
- *R&B* **Respect** [4]...Aretha Franklin
- *C&W* **It's Such A Pretty World Today** [2]...Wynn Stewart
- *A/C* **Casino Royale** [2]...Herb Alpert

ALBUMS
- *POP* **More Of The Monkees** [18]...The Monkees
- *R&B* **I Never Loved A Man The Way I Love You** [7]...Aretha Franklin
- *C&W* **The Best Of Eddy Arnold** [3]...Eddy Arnold

June 17, 1967

SINGLES
- *HOT* **Groovin'** [3]...Young Rascals
- *R&B* **Respect** [5]...Aretha Franklin
- *C&W* **All The Time** [1]...Jack Greene
- *A/C* **Time, Time** [1]...Ed Ames

ALBUMS
- *POP* **Sounds Like** [1]...Herb Alpert & The Tijuana Brass
- *R&B* **I Never Loved A Man The Way I Love You** [8]...Aretha Franklin
- *C&W* **The Best Of Eddy Arnold** [4]...Eddy Arnold

June 24, 1967

SINGLES
- *HOT* **Groovin'** [4]...Young Rascals
- *R&B* **Respect** [6]...Aretha Franklin
- *C&W* **All The Time** [2]...Jack Greene
- *A/C* **Stop! And Think It Over** [1]...Perry Como

ALBUMS
- *POP* **Headquarters** [1]...The Monkees
- *R&B* **I Never Loved A Man The Way I Love You** [9]...Aretha Franklin
- *C&W* **The Best Of Eddy Arnold** [5]...Eddy Arnold

July 1, 1967

SINGLES
- HOT   Windy [1]...The Association
- R&B   Respect [7]...Aretha Franklin
- C&W   All The Time [3]...Jack Greene
- A/C   Mary In The Morning [1]...Al Martino

ALBUMS
- POP   Sgt. Pepper's Lonely Hearts Club Band [1]...
        The Beatles
- R&B   I Never Loved A Man The Way I Love You [10]...
        Aretha Franklin
- C&W   The Best Of Eddy Arnold [6]...Eddy Arnold

July 8, 1967

SINGLES
- HOT   Windy [2]...The Association
- R&B   Respect [8]...Aretha Franklin
- C&W   All The Time [4]...Jack Greene
- A/C   Mary In The Morning [2]...Al Martino

ALBUMS
- POP   Sgt. Pepper's Lonely Hearts Club Band [2]...
        The Beatles
- R&B   I Never Loved A Man The Way I Love You [11]...
        Aretha Franklin
- C&W   The Best Of Eddy Arnold [7]...Eddy Arnold

July 15, 1967

SINGLES
- HOT   Windy [3]...The Association
- R&B   I Was Made To Love Her [1]...Stevie Wonder
- C&W   All The Time [5]...Jack Greene
- A/C   Don't Sleep In The Subway [1]...Petula Clark

ALBUMS
- POP   Sgt. Pepper's Lonely Hearts Club Band [3]...
        The Beatles
- R&B   Revenge [1]...Bill Cosby
- C&W   Need You [1]...Sonny James

July 22, 1967

SINGLES
- HOT   Windy [4]...The Association
- R&B   Make Me Yours [1]...Bettye Swann
- C&W   With One Exception [1]...David Houston
- A/C   Don't Sleep In The Subway [2]...Petula Clark

ALBUMS
- POP   Sgt. Pepper's Lonely Hearts Club Band [4]...
        The Beatles
- R&B   Revenge [2]...Bill Cosby
- C&W   Buck Owens & His Buckaroos In Japan [1]...
        Buck Owens

July 29, 1967

SINGLES
- HOT   Light My Fire [1]...The Doors
- R&B   Make Me Yours [2]...Bettye Swann
- C&W   Tonight Carmen [1]...Marty Robbins
- A/C   Don't Sleep In The Subway [3]...Petula Clark

ALBUMS
- POP   Sgt. Pepper's Lonely Hearts Club Band [5]...
        The Beatles
- R&B   Here Where There Is Love [1]...Dionne Warwick
- C&W   All The Time [1]...Jack Greene

August 5, 1967

SINGLES
- HOT   Light My Fire [2]...The Doors
- R&B   I Was Made To Love Her [2]...Stevie Wonder
- C&W   I'll Never Find Another You [1]...Sonny James
- A/C   It's Such A Pretty World Today [1]...Andy Russell

ALBUMS
- POP   Sgt. Pepper's Lonely Hearts Club Band [6]...
        The Beatles
- R&B   Here Where There Is Love [2]...Dionne Warwick
- C&W   All The Time [2]...Jack Greene

August 12, 1967

SINGLES
- HOT   Light My Fire [3]...The Doors
- R&B   I Was Made To Love Her [3]...Stevie Wonder
- C&W   I'll Never Find Another You [2]...Sonny James
- A/C   In The Chapel in The Moonlight [1]...Dean Martin

ALBUMS
- POP   Sgt. Pepper's Lonely Hearts Club Band [7]...
        The Beatles
- R&B   I Never Loved A Man The Way I Love You [12]...
        Aretha Franklin
- C&W   All The Time [3]...Jack Greene

August 19, 1967

SINGLES
- HOT   All You Need Is Love [1]...The Beatles
- R&B   I Was Made To Love Her [4]...Stevie Wonder
- C&W   I'll Never Find Another You [3]...Sonny James
- A/C   In The Chapel in The Moonlight [2]...Dean Martin

ALBUMS
- POP   Sgt. Pepper's Lonely Hearts Club Band [8]...
        The Beatles
- R&B   I Never Loved A Man The Way I Love You [13]...
        Aretha Franklin
- C&W   All The Time [4]...Jack Greene

August 26, 1967

SINGLES
- HOT Ode To Billie Joe [1]...Bobbie Gentry
- R&B Baby I Love You [1]...Aretha Franklin
- C&W I'll Never Find Another You [4]...Sonny James
- A/C In The Chapel in The Moonlight [3]...Dean Martin

ALBUMS
- POP Sgt. Pepper's Lonely Hearts Club Band [9]...
  The Beatles
- R&B I Never Loved A Man The Way I Love You [14]...
  Aretha Franklin
- C&W It's Such A Pretty World Today [1]...Wynn Stewart

September 2, 1967

SINGLES
- HOT Ode To Billie Joe [2]...Bobbie Gentry
- R&B Baby I Love You [2]...Aretha Franklin
- C&W Branded Man [1]...Merle Haggard
- A/C The World We Knew (Over And Over) [1]...
  Frank Sinatra

ALBUMS
- POP Sgt. Pepper's Lonely Hearts Club Band [10]...
  The Beatles
- R&B With A Lot O' Soul [1]...The Temptations
- C&W It's Such A Pretty World Today [2]...Wynn Stewart

September 9, 1967

SINGLES
- HOT Ode To Billie Joe [3]...Bobbie Gentry
- R&B Cold Sweat (Part 1) [1]...James Brown
- C&W Your Tender Loving Care [1]...Buck Owens
- A/C The World We Knew (Over And Over) [2]...
  Frank Sinatra

ALBUMS
- POP Sgt. Pepper's Lonely Hearts Club Band [11]...
  The Beatles
- R&B Aretha Arrives [1]...Aretha Franklin
- C&W All The Time [5]...Jack Greene

September 16, 1967

SINGLES
- HOT Ode To Billie Joe [4]...Bobbie Gentry
- R&B Cold Sweat (Part 1) [2]...James Brown
- C&W My Elusive Dreams [1]...
  David Houston & Tammy Wynette
- A/C The World We Knew (Over And Over) [3]...
  Frank Sinatra

ALBUMS
- POP Sgt. Pepper's Lonely Hearts Club Band [12]...
  The Beatles
- R&B Aretha Arrives [2]...Aretha Franklin
- C&W Johnny Cash's Greatest Hits, Volume 1 [1]...
  Johnny Cash

September 23, 1967

SINGLES
- HOT The Letter [1]...The Box Tops
- R&B Cold Sweat (Part 1) [3]...James Brown
- C&W My Elusive Dreams [2]...
  David Houston & Tammy Wynette
- A/C The World We Knew (Over And Over) [4]...
  Frank Sinatra

ALBUMS
- POP Sgt. Pepper's Lonely Hearts Club Band [13]...
  The Beatles
- R&B Aretha Arrives [3]...Aretha Franklin
- C&W Johnny Cash's Greatest Hits, Volume 1 [2]...
  Johnny Cash

September 30, 1967

SINGLES
- HOT The Letter [2]...The Box Tops
- R&B Funky Broadway [1]...Wilson Pickett
- C&W Laura (What's He Got That I Ain't Got) [1]...
  Leon Ashley
- A/C The World We Knew (Over And Over) [5]...
  Frank Sinatra

ALBUMS
- POP Sgt. Pepper's Lonely Hearts Club Band [14]...
  The Beatles
- R&B Aretha Arrives [4]...Aretha Franklin
- C&W Johnny Cash's Greatest Hits, Volume 1 [3]...
  Johnny Cash

October 7, 1967

SINGLES
- HOT The Letter [3]...The Box Tops
- R&B (Your Love Keeps Lifting Me) Higher And Higher [1]...Jackie Wilson
- C&W Turn The World Around [1]...Eddy Arnold
- A/C A Banda [1]...Herb Alpert

ALBUMS
- POP Sgt. Pepper's Lonely Hearts Club Band [15]...
  The Beatles
- R&B Aretha Arrives [5]...Aretha Franklin
- C&W Ode To Billie Joe [1]...Bobbie Gentry

October 14, 1967

SINGLES
- HOT The Letter [4]...The Box Tops
- R&B Soul Man [1]...Sam & Dave
- C&W I Don't Wanna Play House [1]...Tammy Wynette
- A/C A Banda [2]...Herb Alpert

ALBUMS
- POP Ode To Billie Joe [1]...Bobbie Gentry
- R&B Diana Ross and the Supremes Greatest Hits [1]...
  Diana Ross & The Supremes
- C&W Ode To Billie Joe [2]...Bobbie Gentry

October 21, 1967
SINGLES
- *HOT* To Sir With Love [1]...Lulu
- *R&B* Soul Man [2]...Sam & Dave
- *C&W* I Don't Wanna Play House [2]...Tammy Wynette
- *A/C* It Must Be Him [1]...Vikki Carr

ALBUMS
- *POP* Ode To Billie Joe [2]...Bobbie Gentry
- *R&B* Diana Ross and the Supremes Greatest Hits [2]...
  Diana Ross & The Supremes
- *C&W* Ode To Billie Joe [3]...Bobbie Gentry

October 28, 1967
SINGLES
- *HOT* To Sir With Love [2]...Lulu
- *R&B* Soul Man [3]...Sam & Dave
- *C&W* I Don't Wanna Play House [3]...Tammy Wynette
- *A/C* It Must Be Him [2]...Vikki Carr

ALBUMS
- *POP* Diana Ross and the Supremes Greatest Hits [1]...
  Diana Ross & The Supremes
- *R&B* Diana Ross and the Supremes Greatest Hits [3]...
  Diana Ross & The Supremes
- *C&W* Your Tender Loving Care [1]...Buck Owens

November 4, 1967
SINGLES
- *HOT* To Sir With Love [3]...Lulu
- *R&B* Soul Man [4]...Sam & Dave
- *C&W* You Mean The World To Me [1]...David Houston
- *A/C* It Must Be Him [3]...Vikki Carr

ALBUMS
- *POP* Diana Ross and the Supremes Greatest Hits [2]...
  Diana Ross & The Supremes
- *R&B* Diana Ross and the Supremes Greatest Hits [4]...
  Diana Ross & The Supremes
- *C&W* Turn The World Around [1]...Eddy Arnold

November 11, 1967
SINGLES
- *HOT* To Sir With Love [4]...Lulu
- *R&B* Soul Man [5]...Sam & Dave
- *C&W* You Mean The World To Me [2]...David Houston
- *A/C* More Than The Eye Can See [1]...Al Martino

ALBUMS
- *POP* Diana Ross and the Supremes Greatest Hits [3]...
  Diana Ross & The Supremes
- *R&B* Diana Ross and the Supremes Greatest Hits [5]...
  Diana Ross & The Supremes
- *C&W* Turn The World Around [2]...Eddy Arnold

November 18, 1967
SINGLES
- *HOT* To Sir With Love [5]...Lulu
- *R&B* Soul Man [6]...Sam & Dave
- *C&W* It's The Little Things [1]...Sonny James
- *A/C* More Than The Eye Can See [2]...Al Martino

ALBUMS
- *POP* Diana Ross and the Supremes Greatest Hits [4]...
  Diana Ross & The Supremes
- *R&B* Diana Ross and the Supremes Greatest Hits [6]...
  Diana Ross & The Supremes
- *C&W* Turn The World Around [3]...Eddy Arnold

November 25, 1967
SINGLES
- *HOT* Incense And Peppermints [1]...Strawberry Alarm Clock
- *R&B* Soul Man [7]...Sam & Dave
- *C&W* It's The Little Things [2]...Sonny James
- *A/C* When The Snow Is On The Roses [1]...Ed Ames

ALBUMS
- *POP* Diana Ross and the Supremes Greatest Hits [5]...
  Diana Ross & The Supremes
- *R&B* Diana Ross and the Supremes Greatest Hits [7]...
  Diana Ross & The Supremes
- *C&W* Turn The World Around [4]...Eddy Arnold

December 2, 1967
SINGLES
- *HOT* Daydream Believer [1]...The Monkees
- *R&B* I Heard It Through The Grapevine [1]...
  Gladys Knight & The Pips
- *C&W* It's The Little Things [3]...Sonny James
- *A/C* When The Snow Is On The Roses [2]...Ed Ames

ALBUMS
- *POP* Pisces, Aquarius, Capricorn & Jones Ltd. [1]...
  The Monkees
- *R&B* Diana Ross and the Supremes Greatest Hits [8]...
  Diana Ross & The Supremes
- *C&W* Turn The World Around [5]...Eddy Arnold

December 9, 1967
SINGLES
- *HOT* Daydream Believer [2]...The Monkees
- *R&B* I Heard It Through The Grapevine [2]...
  Gladys Knight & The Pips
- *C&W* It's The Little Things [4]...Sonny James
- *A/C* When The Snow Is On The Roses [3]...Ed Ames

ALBUMS
- *POP* Pisces, Aquarius, Capricorn & Jones Ltd. [2]...
  The Monkees
- *R&B* Diana Ross and the Supremes Greatest Hits [9]...
  Diana Ross & The Supremes
- *C&W* Turn The World Around [6]...Eddy Arnold

December 16, 1967

SINGLES
- *HOT* Daydream Believer [3]...The Monkees
- *R&B* I Heard It Through The Grapevine [3]...
  Gladys Knight & The Pips
- *C&W* It's The Little Things [5]...Sonny James
- *A/C* When The Snow Is On The Roses [4]...Ed Ames

ALBUMS
- *POP* Pisces, Aquarius, Capricorn & Jones Ltd. [3]...
  The Monkees
- *R&B* Diana Ross and the Supremes Greatest Hits [10]...
  Diana Ross & The Supremes
- *C&W* Branded Man [1]...Merle Haggard

December 23, 1967

SINGLES
- *HOT* Daydream Believer [4]...The Monkees
- *R&B* I Heard It Through The Grapevine [4]...
  Gladys Knight & The Pips
- *C&W* For Loving You [1]...Bill Anderson & Jan Howard
- *A/C* Cold [1]...John Gary

ALBUMS
- *POP* Pisces, Aquarius, Capricorn & Jones Ltd. [4]...
  The Monkees
- *R&B* Diana Ross and the Supremes Greatest Hits [11]...
  Diana Ross & The Supremes
- *C&W* Turn The World Around [7]...Eddy Arnold

December 30, 1967

SINGLES
- *HOT* Hello Goodbye [1]...The Beatles
- *R&B* I Heard It Through The Grapevine [5]...
  Gladys Knight & The Pips
- *C&W* For Loving You [2]...Bill Anderson & Jan Howard
- *A/C* Cold [2]...John Gary

ALBUMS
- *POP* Pisces, Aquarius, Capricorn & Jones Ltd. [5]...
  The Monkees
- *R&B* Diana Ross and the Supremes Greatest Hits [12]...
  Diana Ross & The Supremes
- *C&W* Turn The World Around [8]...Eddy Arnold

January 6, 1968

SINGLES
- *HOT* Hello Goodbye [2]...The Beatles
- *R&B* I Heard It Through The Grapevine [6]...
  Gladys Knight & The Pips
- *C&W* For Loving You [3]...Bill Anderson & Jan Howard
- *A/C* Chattanooga Choo Choo [1]...Harpers Bizarre

ALBUMS
- *POP* Magical Mystery Tour [1]...The Beatles
- *R&B* The Temptations in a Mellow Mood [1]...
  The Temptations
- *C&W* Turn The World Around [9]...Eddy Arnold

January 13, 1968

SINGLES
- *HOT* Hello Goodbye [3]...The Beatles
- *R&B* I Second That Emotion [1]...
  Smokey Robinson & The Miracles
- *C&W* For Loving You [4]...Bill Anderson & Jan Howard
- *A/C* Chattanooga Choo Choo [2]...Harpers Bizarre

ALBUMS
- *POP* Magical Mystery Tour [2]...The Beatles
- *R&B* The Temptations in a Mellow Mood [2]...
  The Temptations
- *C&W* Turn The World Around [10]...Eddy Arnold

January 20, 1968

SINGLES
- *HOT* Judy In Disguise (With Glasses) [1]...
  John Fred & His Playboy Band
- *R&B* Chain Of Fools [1]...Aretha Franklin
- *C&W* Sing Me Back Home [1]...Merle Haggard
- *A/C* In The Misty Moonlight [1]...Dean Martin

ALBUMS
- *POP* Magical Mystery Tour [3]...The Beatles
- *R&B* The Temptations in a Mellow Mood [3]...
  The Temptations
- *C&W* Turn The World Around [11]...Eddy Arnold

January 27, 1968

SINGLES
- *HOT* Judy In Disguise (With Glasses) [2]...
  John Fred & His Playboy Band
- *R&B* Chain Of Fools [2]...Aretha Franklin
- *C&W* Sing Me Back Home [2]...Merle Haggard
- *A/C* In The Misty Moonlight [2]...Dean Martin

ALBUMS
- *POP* Magical Mystery Tour [4]...The Beatles
- *R&B* The Temptations in a Mellow Mood [4]...
  The Temptations
- *C&W* Turn The World Around [12]...Eddy Arnold

February 3, 1968

SINGLES
- *HOT* Green Tambourine [1]...The Lemon Pipers
- *R&B* Chain Of Fools [3]...Aretha Franklin
- *C&W* Skip A Rope [1]...Henson Cargill
- *A/C* Am I That Easy To Forget [1]...Engelbert Humperdinck

ALBUMS
- *POP* Magical Mystery Tour [5]...The Beatles
- *R&B* The Temptations in a Mellow Mood [5]...
  The Temptations
- *C&W* Turn The World Around [13]...Eddy Arnold

February 10, 1968
SINGLES
- HOT   *Love Is Blue [1]...Paul Mauriat
- R&B   Chain Of Fools [4]...Aretha Franklin
- C&W   Skip A Rope [2]...Henson Cargill
- A/C   The Lesson [1]...Vikki Carr

ALBUMS
- POP   Magical Mystery Tour [6]...The Beatles
- R&B   The Temptations in a Mellow Mood [6]...The Temptations
- C&W   By The Time I Get To Phoenix [1]...Glen Campbell

February 17, 1968
SINGLES
- HOT   Love Is Blue [2]...Paul Mauriat
- R&B   I Wish It Would Rain [1]...The Temptations
- C&W   Skip A Rope [3]...Henson Cargill
- A/C   Love Is Blue [1]...Paul Mauriat

ALBUMS
- POP   Magical Mystery Tour [7]...The Beatles
- R&B   The Temptations in a Mellow Mood [7]...The Temptations
- C&W   By The Time I Get To Phoenix [2]...Glen Campbell

February 24, 1968
SINGLES
- HOT   Love Is Blue [3]...Paul Mauriat
- R&B   I Wish It Would Rain [2]...The Temptations
- C&W   Skip A Rope [4]...Henson Cargill
- A/C   Love Is Blue [2]...Paul Mauriat

ALBUMS
- POP   Magical Mystery Tour [8]...The Beatles
- R&B   History Of Otis Redding [1]...Otis Redding
- C&W   By The Time I Get To Phoenix [3]...Glen Campbell

March 2, 1968
SINGLES
- HOT   Love Is Blue [4]...Paul Mauriat
- R&B   I Wish It Would Rain [3]...The Temptations
- C&W   Skip A Rope [5]...Henson Cargill
- A/C   Love Is Blue [3]...Paul Mauriat

ALBUMS
- POP   Blooming Hits [1]...Paul Mauriat and his orchestra
- R&B   Aretha: Lady Soul [1]...Aretha Franklin
- C&W   By The Time I Get To Phoenix [4]...Glen Campbell

March 9, 1968
SINGLES
- HOT   Love Is Blue [5]...Paul Mauriat
- R&B   We're A Winner [1]...The Impressions
- C&W   Take Me To Your World [1]...Tammy Wynette
- A/C   Love Is Blue [4]...Paul Mauriat

ALBUMS
- POP   Blooming Hits [2]...Paul Mauriat and his orchestra
- R&B   Aretha: Lady Soul [2]...Aretha Franklin
- C&W   Sing Me Back Home [1]...Merle Haggard

March 16, 1968
SINGLES
- HOT   *(Sittin' On) The Dock Of The Bay [1]...Otis Redding
- R&B   *(Sittin' On) The Dock Of The Bay [1]...Otis Redding
- C&W   A World Of Our Own [1]...Sonny James
- A/C   Love Is Blue [5]...Paul Mauriat

ALBUMS
- POP   Blooming Hits [3]...Paul Mauriat and his orchestra
- R&B   Aretha: Lady Soul [3]...Aretha Franklin
- C&W   It Takes People Like You To Make People Like Me [1]...Buck Owens

March 23, 1968
SINGLES
- HOT   (Sittin' On) The Dock Of The Bay [2]...Otis Redding
- R&B   (Sittin' On) The Dock Of The Bay [2]...Otis Redding
- C&W   A World Of Our Own [2]...Sonny James
- A/C   Love Is Blue [6]...Paul Mauriat

ALBUMS
- POP   Blooming Hits [4]...Paul Mauriat and his orchestra
- R&B   Aretha: Lady Soul [4]...Aretha Franklin
- C&W   It Takes People Like You To Make People Like Me [2]...Buck Owens

March 30, 1968
SINGLES
- HOT   (Sittin' On) The Dock Of The Bay [3]...Otis Redding
- R&B   (Sittin' On) The Dock Of The Bay [3]...Otis Redding
- C&W   A World Of Our Own [3]...Sonny James
- A/C   Love Is Blue [7]...Paul Mauriat

ALBUMS
- POP   Blooming Hits [5]...Paul Mauriat and his orchestra
- R&B   Aretha: Lady Soul [5]...Aretha Franklin
- C&W   It Takes People Like You To Make People Like Me [3]...Buck Owens

April 6, 1968

SINGLES
- HOT (Sittin' On) The Dock Of The Bay [4]...Otis Redding
- R&B (Sweet Sweet Baby) Since You've Been Gone [1]...Aretha Franklin
- C&W How Long Will My Baby Be Gone [1]...Buck Owens & The Buckaroos
- A/C Love Is Blue [8]...Paul Mauriat

ALBUMS
- POP The Graduate [1]...Simon & Garfunkel/Soundtrack
- R&B Aretha: Lady Soul [6]...Aretha Franklin
- C&W The Everlovin' World Of Eddy Arnold [1]...Eddy Arnold

April 13, 1968

SINGLES
- HOT *Honey [1]...Bobby Goldsboro
- R&B (Sweet Sweet Baby) Since You've Been Gone [2]...Aretha Franklin
- C&W You Are My Treasure [1]...Jack Greene
- A/C Love Is Blue [9]...Paul Mauriat

ALBUMS
- POP The Graduate [2]...Simon & Garfunkel/Soundtrack
- R&B Aretha: Lady Soul [7]...Aretha Franklin
- C&W The Everlovin' World Of Eddy Arnold [2]...Eddy Arnold

April 20, 1968

SINGLES
- HOT Honey [2]...Bobby Goldsboro
- R&B (Sweet Sweet Baby) Since You've Been Gone [3]...Aretha Franklin
- C&W Fist City [1]...Loretta Lynn
- A/C Love Is Blue [10]...Paul Mauriat

ALBUMS
- POP The Graduate [3]...Simon & Garfunkel/Soundtrack
- R&B The Dock Of The Bay [1]...Otis Redding
- C&W It Takes People Like You To Make People Like Me [4]...Buck Owens

April 27, 1968

SINGLES
- HOT Honey [3]...Bobby Goldsboro
- R&B I Got The Feelin' [1]...James Brown
- C&W The Legend Of Bonnie And Clyde [1]...Merle Haggard
- A/C Love Is Blue [11]...Paul Mauriat

ALBUMS
- POP The Graduate [4]...Simon & Garfunkel/Soundtrack
- R&B Aretha: Lady Soul [8]...Aretha Franklin
- C&W The Everlovin' World Of Eddy Arnold [3]...Eddy Arnold

May 4, 1968

SINGLES
- HOT Honey [4]...Bobby Goldsboro
- R&B I Got The Feelin' [2]...James Brown
- C&W The Legend Of Bonnie And Clyde [2]...Merle Haggard
- A/C Honey [1]...Bobby Goldsboro

ALBUMS
- POP The Graduate [5]...Simon & Garfunkel/Soundtrack
- R&B Aretha: Lady Soul [9]...Aretha Franklin
- C&W The Everlovin' World Of Eddy Arnold [4]...Eddy Arnold

May 11, 1968

SINGLES
- HOT Honey [5]...Bobby Goldsboro
- R&B Cowboys To Girls [1]...The Intruders
- C&W Have A Little Faith [1]...David Houston
- A/C Honey [2]...Bobby Goldsboro

ALBUMS
- POP The Graduate [6]...Simon & Garfunkel/Soundtrack
- R&B The Dock Of The Bay [2]...Otis Redding
- C&W Promises Promises [1]...Lynn Anderson

May 18, 1968

SINGLES
- HOT *Tighten Up [1]...Archie Bell & The Drells
- R&B *Tighten Up [1]...Archie Bell & The Drells
- C&W I Wanna Live [1]...Glen Campbell
- A/C The Good, The Bad And The Ugly [1]...Hugo Montenegro

ALBUMS
- POP The Graduate [7]...Simon & Garfunkel/Soundtrack
- R&B Aretha: Lady Soul [10]...Aretha Franklin
- C&W The Country Way [1]...Charley Pride

May 25, 1968

SINGLES
- HOT Tighten Up [2]...Archie Bell & The Drells
- R&B Tighten Up [2]...Archie Bell & The Drells
- C&W Honey [1]...Bobby Goldsboro
- A/C The Good, The Bad And The Ugly [2]...Hugo Montenegro

ALBUMS
- POP Bookends [1]...Simon & Garfunkel
- R&B Aretha: Lady Soul [11]...Aretha Franklin
- C&W Honey [1]...Bobby Goldsboro

June 1, 1968
SINGLES
- HOT Mrs. Robinson [1]...Simon & Garfunkel
- R&B Shoo-Be-Doo-Be-Doo-Da-Day [1]...Stevie Wonder
- C&W Honey [2]...Bobby Goldsboro
- A/C The Good, The Bad And The Ugly [3]...Hugo Montenegro

ALBUMS
- POP Bookends [2]...Simon & Garfunkel
- R&B Aretha: Lady Soul [12]...Aretha Franklin
- C&W Honey [2]...Bobby Goldsboro

June 8, 1968
SINGLES
- HOT Mrs. Robinson [2]...Simon & Garfunkel
- R&B Ain't Nothing Like The Real Thing [1]...Marvin Gaye & Tammi Terrell
- C&W Honey [3]...Bobby Goldsboro
- A/C *This Guy's In Love With You [1]...Herb Alpert

ALBUMS
- POP Bookends [3]...Simon & Garfunkel
- R&B Aretha: Lady Soul [13]...Aretha Franklin
- C&W Hey, Little One [1]...Glen Campbell

June 15, 1968
SINGLES
- HOT Mrs. Robinson [3]...Simon & Garfunkel
- R&B Think [1]...Aretha Franklin
- C&W I Wanna Live [2]...Glen Campbell
- A/C This Guy's In Love With You [2]...Herb Alpert

ALBUMS
- POP The Graduate [8]...Simon & Garfunkel/Soundtrack
- R&B Aretha: Lady Soul [14]...Aretha Franklin
- C&W Fist City [1]...Loretta Lynn

June 22, 1968
SINGLES
- HOT This Guy's In Love With You [1]...Herb Alpert
- R&B Think [2]...Aretha Franklin
- C&W I Wanna Live [3]...Glen Campbell
- A/C This Guy's In Love With You [3]...Herb Alpert

ALBUMS
- POP The Graduate [9]...Simon & Garfunkel/Soundtrack
- R&B Wish It Would Rain [1]...The Temptations
- C&W Fist City [2]...Loretta Lynn

June 29, 1968
SINGLES
- HOT This Guy's In Love With You [2]...Herb Alpert
- R&B Think [3]...Aretha Franklin
- C&W D-I-V-O-R-C-E [1]...Tammy Wynette
- A/C This Guy's In Love With You [4]...Herb Alpert

ALBUMS
- POP Bookends [4]...Simon & Garfunkel
- R&B Wish It Would Rain [2]...The Temptations
- C&W Honey [3]...Bobby Goldsboro

July 6, 1968
SINGLES
- HOT This Guy's In Love With You [3]...Herb Alpert
- R&B I Could Never Love Another (After Loving You) [1]...The Temptations
- C&W D-I-V-O-R-C-E [2]...Tammy Wynette
- A/C This Guy's In Love With You [5]...Herb Alpert

ALBUMS
- POP Bookends [5]...Simon & Garfunkel
- R&B The Dock Of The Bay [3]...Otis Redding
- C&W Honey [4]...Bobby Goldsboro

July 13, 1968
SINGLES
- HOT This Guy's In Love With You [4]...Herb Alpert
- R&B *Grazing In The Grass [1]...Hugh Masekela
- C&W D-I-V-O-R-C-E [3]...Tammy Wynette
- A/C This Guy's In Love With You [6]...Herb Alpert

ALBUMS
- POP Bookends [6]...Simon & Garfunkel
- R&B Aretha: Lady Soul [15]...Aretha Franklin
- C&W Honey [5]...Bobby Goldsboro

July 20, 1968
SINGLES
- HOT Grazing In The Grass [1]...Hugh Masekela
- R&B Grazing In The Grass [2]...Hugh Masekela
- C&W Folsom Prison Blues [1]...Johnny Cash
- A/C This Guy's In Love With You [7]...Herb Alpert

ALBUMS
- POP Bookends [7]...Simon & Garfunkel
- R&B Aretha: Lady Soul [16]...Aretha Franklin
- C&W Johnny Cash At Folsom Prison [1]...Johnny Cash

July 27, 1968
SINGLES
- HOT Grazing In The Grass [2]...Hugh Masekela
- R&B Grazing In The Grass [3]...Hugh Masekela
- C&W Folsom Prison Blues [2]...Johnny Cash
- A/C This Guy's In Love With You [8]...Herb Alpert

ALBUMS
- POP The Beat Of The Brass [1]...
  Herb Alpert & The Tijuana Brass
- R&B Aretha Now [1]...Aretha Franklin
- C&W Johnny Cash At Folsom Prison [2]...Johnny Cash

August 3, 1968
SINGLES
- HOT Hello, I Love You [1]...The Doors
- R&B Grazing In The Grass [4]...Hugh Masekela
- C&W Folsom Prison Blues [3]...Johnny Cash
- A/C This Guy's In Love With You [9]...Herb Alpert

ALBUMS
- POP The Beat Of The Brass [2]...
  Herb Alpert & The Tijuana Brass
- R&B Aretha Now [2]...Aretha Franklin
- C&W Johnny Cash At Folsom Prison [3]...Johnny Cash

August 10, 1968
SINGLES
- HOT Hello, I Love You [2]...The Doors
- R&B Stay In My Corner [1]...The Dells
- C&W Folsom Prison Blues [4]...Johnny Cash
- A/C This Guy's In Love With You [10]...Herb Alpert

ALBUMS
- POP Wheels Of Fire [1]...Cream
- R&B Aretha Now [3]...Aretha Franklin
- C&W A New Place In The Sun [1]...Glen Campbell

August 17, 1968
SINGLES
- HOT People Got To Be Free [1]...The Rascals
- R&B Stay In My Corner [2]...The Dells
- C&W Heaven Says Hello [1]...Sonny James
- A/C Classical Gas [1]...Mason Williams

ALBUMS
- POP Wheels Of Fire [2]...Cream
- R&B Aretha Now [4]...Aretha Franklin
- C&W A New Place In The Sun [2]...Glen Campbell

August 24, 1968
SINGLES
- HOT People Got To Be Free [2]...The Rascals
- R&B Stay In My Corner [3]...The Dells
- C&W Already It's Heaven [1]...David Houston
- A/C Classical Gas [2]...Mason Williams

ALBUMS
- POP Wheels Of Fire [3]...Cream
- R&B Aretha Now [5]...Aretha Franklin
- C&W A New Place In The Sun [3]...Glen Campbell

August 31, 1968
SINGLES
- HOT People Got To Be Free [3]...The Rascals
- R&B You're All I Need To Get By [1]...
  Marvin Gaye & Tammi Terrell
- C&W Mama Tried [1]...Merle Haggard
- A/C Classical Gas [3]...Mason Williams

ALBUMS
- POP Wheels Of Fire [4]...Cream
- R&B Aretha Now [6]...Aretha Franklin
- C&W A New Place In The Sun [4]...Glen Campbell

September 7, 1968
SINGLES
- HOT People Got To Be Free [4]...The Rascals
- R&B You're All I Need To Get By [2]...
  Marvin Gaye & Tammi Terrell
- C&W Mama Tried [2]...Merle Haggard
- A/C The Fool On The Hill [1]...Sergio Mendes & Brasil '66

ALBUMS
- POP Waiting For The Sun [1]...The Doors
- R&B Aretha Now [7]...Aretha Franklin
- C&W A New Place In The Sun [5]...Glen Campbell

September 14, 1968
SINGLES
- HOT People Got To Be Free [5]...The Rascals
- R&B You're All I Need To Get By [3]...
  Marvin Gaye & Tammi Terrell
- C&W Mama Tried [3]...Merle Haggard
- A/C The Fool On The Hill [2]...Sergio Mendes & Brasil '66

ALBUMS
- POP Waiting For The Sun [2]...The Doors
- R&B Wish It Would Rain [3]...The Temptations
- C&W A New Place In The Sun [6]...Glen Campbell

September 21, 1968
SINGLES
- HOT *Harper Valley P.T.A. [1]...Jeannie C. Riley
- R&B You're All I Need To Get By [4]...Marvin Gaye & Tammi Terrell
- C&W Mama Tried [4]...Merle Haggard
- A/C The Fool On The Hill [3]...Sergio Mendes & Brasil '66

ALBUMS
- POP Waiting For The Sun [3]...The Doors
- R&B Aretha Now [8]...Aretha Franklin
- C&W D-I-V-O-R-C-E [1]...Tammy Wynette

September 28, 1968
SINGLES
- HOT Hey Jude [1]...The Beatles
- R&B You're All I Need To Get By [5]...Marvin Gaye & Tammi Terrell
- C&W Harper Valley P.T.A. [1]...Jeannie C. Riley
- A/C The Fool On The Hill [4]...Sergio Mendes & Brasil '66

ALBUMS
- POP Time Peace/The Rascals' Greatest Hits [1]...The Rascals
- R&B Aretha Now [9]...Aretha Franklin
- C&W D-I-V-O-R-C-E [2]...Tammy Wynette

October 5, 1968
SINGLES
- HOT Hey Jude [2]...The Beatles
- R&B Say It Loud - I'm Black And I'm Proud (Part 1) [1]...James Brown
- C&W Harper Valley P.T.A. [2]...Jeannie C. Riley
- A/C The Fool On The Hill [5]...Sergio Mendes & Brasil '66

ALBUMS
- POP Waiting For The Sun [4]...The Doors
- R&B Aretha Now [10]...Aretha Franklin
- C&W Johnny Cash At Folsom Prison [4]...Johnny Cash

October 12, 1968
SINGLES
- HOT Hey Jude [3]...The Beatles
- R&B Say It Loud - I'm Black And I'm Proud (Part 1) [2]...James Brown
- C&W Harper Valley P.T.A. [3]...Jeannie C. Riley
- A/C The Fool On The Hill [6]...Sergio Mendes & Brasil '66

ALBUMS
- POP Cheap Thrills [1]...Big Brother And The Holding Company
- R&B Aretha Now [11]...Aretha Franklin
- C&W Gentle On My Mind [1]...Glen Campbell

October 19, 1968
SINGLES
- HOT Hey Jude [4]...The Beatles
- R&B Say It Loud - I'm Black And I'm Proud (Part 1) [3]...James Brown
- C&W Then You Can Tell Me Goodbye [1]...Eddy Arnold
- A/C My Special Angel [1]...The Vogues

ALBUMS
- POP Cheap Thrills [2]...Big Brother And The Holding Company
- R&B Aretha Now [12]...Aretha Franklin
- C&W Gentle On My Mind [2]...Glen Campbell

October 26, 1968
SINGLES
- HOT Hey Jude [5]...The Beatles
- R&B Say It Loud - I'm Black And I'm Proud (Part 1) [4]...James Brown
- C&W Then You Can Tell Me Goodbye [2]...Eddy Arnold
- A/C My Special Angel [2]...The Vogues

ALBUMS
- POP Cheap Thrills [3]...Big Brother And The Holding Company
- R&B Aretha Now [13]...Aretha Franklin
- C&W Bobbie Gentry & Glen Campbell [1]...Bobbie Gentry & Glen Campbell

November 2, 1968
SINGLES
- HOT Hey Jude [6]...The Beatles
- R&B Say It Loud - I'm Black And I'm Proud (Part 1) [5]...James Brown
- C&W Next In Line [1]...Conway Twitty
- A/C Those Were The Days [1]...Mary Hopkin

ALBUMS
- POP Cheap Thrills [4]...Big Brother And The Holding Company
- R&B Aretha Now [14]...Aretha Franklin
- C&W Harper Valley P.T.A. [1]...Jeannie C. Riley

November 9, 1968
SINGLES
- HOT Hey Jude [7]...The Beatles
- R&B Say It Loud - I'm Black And I'm Proud (Part 1) [6]...James Brown
- C&W I Walk Alone [1]...Marty Robbins
- A/C Those Were The Days [2]...Mary Hopkin

ALBUMS
- POP Cheap Thrills [5]...Big Brother And The Holding Company
- R&B Aretha Now [15]...Aretha Franklin
- C&W Harper Valley P.T.A. [2]...Jeannie C. Riley

November 16, 1968

SINGLES
- HOT   Hey Jude [8]...The Beatles
- R&B   Hey, Western Union Man [1]...Jerry Butler
- C&W   I Walk Alone [2]...Marty Robbins
- A/C   Those Were The Days [3]...Mary Hopkin

ALBUMS
- POP   Electric Ladyland [1]...Jimi Hendrix Experience
- R&B   Aretha Now [16]...Aretha Franklin
- C&W   Harper Valley P.T.A. [3]...Jeannie C. Riley

November 23, 1968

SINGLES
- HOT   Hey Jude [9]...The Beatles
- R&B   Who's Making Love [1]...Johnnie Taylor
- C&W   Stand By Your Man [1]...Tammy Wynette
- A/C   Those Were The Days [4]...Mary Hopkin

ALBUMS
- POP   Electric Ladyland [2]...Jimi Hendrix Experience
- R&B   Hickory Holler Revisited [1]...O.C. Smith
- C&W   Harper Valley P.T.A. [4]...Jeannie C. Riley

November 30, 1968

SINGLES
- HOT   Love Child [1]...Diana Ross & The Supremes
- R&B   Who's Making Love [2]...Johnnie Taylor
- C&W   Stand By Your Man [2]...Tammy Wynette
- A/C   Those Were The Days [5]...Mary Hopkin

ALBUMS
- POP   Cheap Thrills [6]...Big Brother And The Holding Company
- R&B   Aretha Now [17]...Aretha Franklin
- C&W   Wichita Lineman [1]...Glen Campbell

December 7, 1968

SINGLES
- HOT   Love Child [2]...Diana Ross & The Supremes
- R&B   Who's Making Love [3]...Johnnie Taylor
- C&W   Stand By Your Man [3]...Tammy Wynette
- A/C   Those Were The Days [6]...Mary Hopkin

ALBUMS
- POP   Cheap Thrills [7]...Big Brother And The Holding Company
- R&B   Special Occasion [1]...Smokey Robinson & The Miracles
- C&W   Wichita Lineman [2]...Glen Campbell

December 14, 1968

SINGLES
- HOT   *I Heard It Through The Grapevine [1]...Marvin Gaye
- R&B   *I Heard It Through The Grapevine [1]...Marvin Gaye
- C&W   Born To Be With You [1]...Sonny James
- A/C   *Wichita Lineman [1]...Glen Campbell

ALBUMS
- POP   Cheap Thrills [8]...Big Brother And The Holding Company
- R&B   Special Occasion [2]...Smokey Robinson & The Miracles
- C&W   Wichita Lineman [3]...Glen Campbell

December 21, 1968

SINGLES
- HOT   I Heard It Through The Grapevine [2]...Marvin Gaye
- R&B   I Heard It Through The Grapevine [2]...Marvin Gaye
- C&W   Wichita Lineman [1]...Glen Campbell
- A/C   Wichita Lineman [2]...Glen Campbell

ALBUMS
- POP   Wichita Lineman [1]...Glen Campbell
- R&B   Diana Ross & the Supremes Join the Temptations [1]...Diana Ross & The Supremes and The Temptations
- C&W   Wichita Lineman [4]...Glen Campbell

December 28, 1968

SINGLES
- HOT   I Heard It Through The Grapevine [3]...Marvin Gaye
- R&B   I Heard It Through The Grapevine [3]...Marvin Gaye
- C&W   Wichita Lineman [2]...Glen Campbell
- A/C   Wichita Lineman [3]...Glen Campbell

ALBUMS
- POP   The Beatles [White Album] [1]...The Beatles
- R&B   Diana Ross & the Supremes Join the Temptations [2]...Diana Ross & The Supremes and The Temptations
- C&W   Wichita Lineman [5]...Glen Campbell

January 4, 1969

SINGLES
- HOT   I Heard It Through The Grapevine [4]...Marvin Gaye
- R&B   I Heard It Through The Grapevine [4]...Marvin Gaye
- C&W   Daddy Sang Bass [1]...Johnny Cash
- A/C   Wichita Lineman [4]...Glen Campbell

ALBUMS
- POP   The Beatles [White Album] [2]...The Beatles
- R&B   Diana Ross & the Supremes Join the Temptations [3]...Diana Ross & The Supremes and The Temptations
- C&W   Wichita Lineman [6]...Glen Campbell

January 11, 1969
SINGLES
- HOT   I Heard It Through The Grapevine [5]...Marvin Gaye
- R&B   I Heard It Through The Grapevine [5]...Marvin Gaye
- C&W   Daddy Sang Bass [2]...Johnny Cash
- A/C   Wichita Lineman [5]...Glen Campbell

ALBUMS
- POP   The Beatles [White Album] [3]...The Beatles
- R&B   Diana Ross & the Supremes Join the Temptations [4]...Diana Ross & The Supremes and The Temptations
- C&W   Wichita Lineman [7]...Glen Campbell

January 18, 1969
SINGLES
- HOT   I Heard It Through The Grapevine [6]...Marvin Gaye
- R&B   I Heard It Through The Grapevine [6]...Marvin Gaye
- C&W   Daddy Sang Bass [3]...Johnny Cash
- A/C   Wichita Lineman [6]...Glen Campbell

ALBUMS
- POP   The Beatles [White Album] [4]...The Beatles
- R&B   TCB [1]...Diana Ross & The Supremes with The Temptations
- C&W   Wichita Lineman [8]...Glen Campbell

January 25, 1969
SINGLES
- HOT   I Heard It Through The Grapevine [7]...Marvin Gaye
- R&B   I Heard It Through The Grapevine [7]...Marvin Gaye
- C&W   Daddy Sang Bass [4]...Johnny Cash
- A/C   I've Gotta Be Me [1]...Sammy Davis, Jr.

ALBUMS
- POP   The Beatles [White Album] [5]...The Beatles
- R&B   TCB [2]...Diana Ross & The Supremes with The Temptations
- C&W   Wichita Lineman [9]...Glen Campbell

February 1, 1969
SINGLES
- HOT   Crimson And Clover [1]...Tommy James & The Shondells
- R&B   Can I Change My Mind [1]...Tyrone Davis
- C&W   Daddy Sang Bass [5]...Johnny Cash
- A/C   I've Gotta Be Me [2]...Sammy Davis, Jr.

ALBUMS
- POP   The Beatles [White Album] [6]...The Beatles
- R&B   TCB [3]...Diana Ross & The Supremes with The Temptations
- C&W   Wichita Lineman [10]...Glen Campbell

February 8, 1969
SINGLES
- HOT   Crimson And Clover [2]...Tommy James & The Shondells
- R&B   Can I Change My Mind [2]...Tyrone Davis
- C&W   Daddy Sang Bass [6]...Johnny Cash
- A/C   I've Gotta Be Me [3]...Sammy Davis, Jr.

ALBUMS
- POP   TCB [1]...Diana Ross & The Supremes with The Temptations
- R&B   TCB [4]...Diana Ross & The Supremes with The Temptations
- C&W   Wichita Lineman [11]...Glen Campbell

February 15, 1969
SINGLES
- HOT   *Everyday People [1]...Sly & The Family Stone
- R&B   Can I Change My Mind [3]...Tyrone Davis
- C&W   Until My Dreams Come True [1]...Jack Greene
- A/C   I've Gotta Be Me [4]...Sammy Davis, Jr.

ALBUMS
- POP   The Beatles [White Album] [7]...The Beatles
- R&B   TCB [5]...Diana Ross & The Supremes with The Temptations
- C&W   Wichita Lineman [12]...Glen Campbell

February 22, 1969
SINGLES
- HOT   Everyday People [2]...Sly & The Family Stone
- R&B   Everyday People [1]...Sly & The Family Stone
- C&W   Until My Dreams Come True [2]...Jack Greene
- A/C   I've Gotta Be Me [5]...Sammy Davis, Jr.

ALBUMS
- POP   The Beatles [White Album] [8]...The Beatles
- R&B   TCB [6]...Diana Ross & The Supremes with The Temptations
- C&W   Wichita Lineman [13]...Glen Campbell

March 1, 1969
SINGLES
- HOT   Everyday People [3]...Sly & The Family Stone
- R&B   Everyday People [2]...Sly & The Family Stone
- C&W   To Make Love Sweeter For You [1]...Jerry Lee Lewis
- A/C   I've Gotta Be Me [6]...Sammy Davis, Jr.

ALBUMS
- POP   The Beatles [White Album] [9]...The Beatles
- R&B   Aretha Franklin: Soul '69 [1]...Aretha Franklin
- C&W   Wichita Lineman [14]...Glen Campbell

March 8, 1969
SINGLES
- HOT Everyday People [4]...Sly & The Family Stone
- R&B Give It Up Or Turnit A Loose [1]...James Brown
- C&W Only The Lonely [1]...Sonny James
- A/C I've Gotta Be Me [7]...Sammy Davis, Jr.

ALBUMS
- POP Wichita Lineman [2]...Glen Campbell
- R&B Aretha Franklin: Soul '69 [2]...Aretha Franklin
- C&W Wichita Lineman [15]...Glen Campbell

March 15, 1969
SINGLES
- HOT Dizzy [1]...Tommy Roe
- R&B Give It Up Or Turnit A Loose [2]...James Brown
- C&W Only The Lonely [2]...Sonny James
- A/C You Gave Me A Mountain [1]...Frankie Laine

ALBUMS
- POP Wichita Lineman [3]...Glen Campbell
- R&B Aretha Franklin: Soul '69 [3]...Aretha Franklin
- C&W Wichita Lineman [16]...Glen Campbell

March 22, 1969
SINGLES
- HOT Dizzy [2]...Tommy Roe
- R&B Run Away Child, Running Wild [1]...The Temptations
- C&W Only The Lonely [3]...Sonny James
- A/C You Gave Me A Mountain [2]...Frankie Laine

ALBUMS
- POP Wichita Lineman [4]...Glen Campbell
- R&B Aretha Franklin: Soul '69 [4]...Aretha Franklin
- C&W Wichita Lineman [17]...Glen Campbell

March 29, 1969
SINGLES
- HOT Dizzy [3]...Tommy Roe
- R&B Run Away Child, Running Wild [2]...The Temptations
- C&W Who's Gonna Mow Your Grass [1]...Buck Owens
- A/C *Galveston [1]...Glen Campbell

ALBUMS
- POP Blood, Sweat & Tears [1]...Blood, Sweat & Tears
- R&B Cloud Nine [1]...The Temptations
- C&W Wichita Lineman [18]...Glen Campbell

April 5, 1969
SINGLES
- HOT Dizzy [4]...Tommy Roe
- R&B Only The Strong Survive [1]...Jerry Butler
- C&W Who's Gonna Mow Your Grass [2]...Buck Owens
- A/C Galveston [2]...Glen Campbell

ALBUMS
- POP Wichita Lineman [5]...Glen Campbell
- R&B Cloud Nine [2]...The Temptations
- C&W Wichita Lineman [19]...Glen Campbell

April 12, 1969
SINGLES
- HOT *Aquarius/Let The Sunshine In [1]...The 5th Dimension
- R&B Only The Strong Survive [2]...Jerry Butler
- C&W Woman Of The World (Leave My World Alone) [1]...Loretta Lynn
- A/C Galveston [3]...Glen Campbell

ALBUMS
- POP Blood, Sweat & Tears [2]...Blood, Sweat & Tears
- R&B Cloud Nine [3]...The Temptations
- C&W Wichita Lineman [20]...Glen Campbell

April 19, 1969
SINGLES
- HOT Aquarius/Let The Sunshine In [2]...The 5th Dimension
- R&B It's Your Thing [1]...The Isley Brothers
- C&W Galveston [1]...Glen Campbell
- A/C Galveston [4]...Glen Campbell

ALBUMS
- POP Blood, Sweat & Tears [3]...Blood, Sweat & Tears
- R&B Cloud Nine [4]...The Temptations
- C&W Galveston [1]...Glen Campbell

April 26, 1969
SINGLES
- HOT Aquarius/Let The Sunshine In [3]...The 5th Dimension
- R&B It's Your Thing [2]...The Isley Brothers
- C&W Galveston [2]...Glen Campbell
- A/C Galveston [5]...Glen Campbell

ALBUMS
- POP Hair [1]...Original Cast
- R&B Cloud Nine [5]...The Temptations
- C&W Galveston [2]...Glen Campbell

May 3, 1969
SINGLES
- HOT Aquarius/Let The Sunshine In [4]...The 5th Dimension
- R&B It's Your Thing [3]...The Isley Brothers
- C&W Galveston [3]...Glen Campbell
- A/C Galveston [6]...Glen Campbell

ALBUMS
- POP Hair [2]...Original Cast
- R&B Cloud Nine [6]...The Temptations
- C&W Galveston [3]...Glen Campbell

May 10, 1969
SINGLES
- HOT Aquarius/Let The Sunshine In [5]...The 5th Dimension
- R&B It's Your Thing [4]...The Isley Brothers
- C&W Hungry Eyes [1]...Merle Haggard
- A/C Aquarius/Let The Sunshine In [1]...The 5th Dimension

ALBUMS
- POP Hair [3]...Original Cast
- R&B Cloud Nine [7]...The Temptations
- C&W Galveston [4]...Glen Campbell

May 17, 1969
SINGLES
- HOT Aquarius/Let The Sunshine In [6]...The 5th Dimension
- R&B The Chokin' Kind [1]...Joe Simon
- C&W My Life (Throw It Away If I Want To) [1]...Bill Anderson
- A/C Aquarius/Let The Sunshine In [2]...The 5th Dimension

ALBUMS
- POP Hair [4]...Original Cast
- R&B Cloud Nine [8]...The Temptations
- C&W Galveston [5]...Glen Campbell

May 24, 1969
SINGLES
- HOT Get Back [1]...Beatles with Billy Preston
- R&B The Chokin' Kind [2]...Joe Simon
- C&W My Life (Throw It Away If I Want To) [2]...Bill Anderson
- A/C Happy Heart [1]...Andy Williams

ALBUMS
- POP Hair [5]...Original Cast
- R&B Cloud Nine [9]...The Temptations
- C&W Galveston [6]...Glen Campbell

May 31, 1969
SINGLES
- HOT Get Back [2]...Beatles with Billy Preston
- R&B The Chokin' Kind [3]...Joe Simon
- C&W Singing My Song [1]...Tammy Wynette
- A/C Happy Heart [2]...Andy Williams

ALBUMS
- POP Hair [6]...Original Cast
- R&B Cloud Nine [10]...The Temptations
- C&W Galveston [7]...Glen Campbell

June 7, 1969
SINGLES
- HOT Get Back [3]...Beatles with Billy Preston
- R&B Too Busy Thinking About My Baby [1]...Marvin Gaye
- C&W Singing My Song [2]...Tammy Wynette
- A/C *Love Theme From Romeo & Juliet [1]...Henry Mancini

ALBUMS
- POP Hair [7]...Original Cast
- R&B Cloud Nine [11]...The Temptations
- C&W Galveston [8]...Glen Campbell

June 14, 1969
SINGLES
- HOT Get Back [4]...Beatles with Billy Preston
- R&B Too Busy Thinking About My Baby [2]...Marvin Gaye
- C&W Running Bear [1]...Sonny James
- A/C Love Theme From Romeo & Juliet [2]...Henry Mancini

ALBUMS
- POP Hair [8]...Original Cast
- R&B Cloud Nine [12]...The Temptations
- C&W Galveston [9]...Glen Campbell

June 21, 1969
SINGLES
- HOT Get Back [5]...Beatles with Billy Preston
- R&B Too Busy Thinking About My Baby [3]...Marvin Gaye
- C&W Running Bear [2]...Sonny James
- A/C Love Theme From Romeo & Juliet [3]...Henry Mancini

ALBUMS
- POP Hair [9]...Original Cast
- R&B M.P.G. [1]...Marvin Gaye
- C&W Galveston [10]...Glen Campbell

June 28, 1969
SINGLES
- HOT Love Theme From Romeo & Juliet [1]...Henry Mancini
- R&B Too Busy Thinking About My Baby [4]...Marvin Gaye
- C&W Running Bear [3]...Sonny James
- A/C Love Theme From Romeo & Juliet [4]...Henry Mancini

ALBUMS
- POP Hair [10]...Original Cast
- R&B M.P.G. [2]...Marvin Gaye
- C&W Galveston [11]...Glen Campbell

July 5, 1969
SINGLES
- HOT Love Theme From Romeo & Juliet [2]...Henry Mancini
- R&B Too Busy Thinking About My Baby [5]...Marvin Gaye
- C&W Statue Of A Fool [1]...Jack Greene
- A/C Love Theme From Romeo & Juliet [5]...Henry Mancini

ALBUMS
- POP Hair [11]...Original Cast
- R&B Cloud Nine [13]...The Temptations
- C&W Songs My Father Left Me [1]...Hank Williams, Jr.

July 12, 1969
SINGLES
- HOT *In The Year 2525 (Exordium & Terminus) [1]...Zager & Evans
- R&B Too Busy Thinking About My Baby [6]...Marvin Gaye
- C&W Statue Of A Fool [2]...Jack Greene
- A/C Love Theme From Romeo & Juliet [6]...Henry Mancini

ALBUMS
- POP Hair [12]...Original Cast
- R&B My Whole World Ended [1]...David Ruffin
- C&W Songs My Father Left Me [2]...Hank Williams, Jr.

July 19, 1969
SINGLES
- HOT In The Year 2525 (Exordium & Terminus) [2]...Zager & Evans
- R&B What Does It Take (To Win Your Love) [1]...Jr. Walker & The All Stars
- C&W I Love You More Today [1]...Conway Twitty
- A/C Love Theme From Romeo & Juliet [7]...Henry Mancini

ALBUMS
- POP Hair [13]...Original Cast
- R&B My Whole World Ended [2]...David Ruffin
- C&W Same Train, A Different Time [1]...Merle Haggard

July 26, 1969
SINGLES
- HOT In The Year 2525 (Exordium & Terminus) [3]...Zager & Evans
- R&B What Does It Take (To Win Your Love) [2]...Jr. Walker & The All Stars
- C&W Johnny B. Goode [1]...Buck Owens & The Buckaroos
- A/C Love Theme From Romeo & Juliet [8]...Henry Mancini

ALBUMS
- POP Blood, Sweat & Tears [4]...Blood, Sweat & Tears
- R&B Aretha's Gold [1]...Aretha Franklin
- C&W Same Train, A Different Time [2]...Merle Haggard

August 2, 1969
SINGLES
- HOT In The Year 2525 (Exordium & Terminus) [4]...Zager & Evans
- R&B Mother Popcorn (You Got To Have A Mother For Me) (Part 1) [1]...James Brown
- C&W Johnny B. Goode [2]...Buck Owens & The Buckaroos
- A/C Spinning Wheel [1]...Blood, Sweat & Tears

ALBUMS
- POP Blood, Sweat & Tears [5]...Blood, Sweat & Tears
- R&B Aretha's Gold [2]...Aretha Franklin
- C&W Johnny Cash At San Quentin [1]...Johnny Cash

August 9, 1969
SINGLES
- HOT In The Year 2525 (Exordium & Terminus) [5]...Zager & Evans
- R&B Mother Popcorn (You Got To Have A Mother For Me) (Part 1) [2]...James Brown
- C&W All I Have To Offer You (Is Me) [1]...Charley Pride
- A/C Spinning Wheel [2]...Blood, Sweat & Tears

ALBUMS
- POP Blood, Sweat & Tears [6]...Blood, Sweat & Tears
- R&B Aretha's Gold [3]...Aretha Franklin
- C&W Johnny Cash At San Quentin [2]...Johnny Cash

August 16, 1969
SINGLES
- HOT In The Year 2525 (Exordium & Terminus) [6]...Zager & Evans
- R&B Choice Of Colors [1]...The Impressions
- C&W Workin' Man Blues [1]...Merle Haggard
- A/C In The Year 2525 (Exordium & Terminus) [1]...Zager & Evans

ALBUMS
- POP Blood, Sweat & Tears [7]...Blood, Sweat & Tears
- R&B Aretha's Gold [4]...Aretha Franklin
- C&W Johnny Cash At San Quentin [3]...Johnny Cash

August 23, 1969
SINGLES
- HOT Honky Tonk Women [1]...The Rolling Stones
- R&B Share Your Love With Me [1]...Aretha Franklin
- C&W *A Boy Named Sue [1]...Johnny Cash
- A/C In The Year 2525 (Exordium & Terminus) [2]...Zager & Evans

ALBUMS
- POP Johnny Cash At San Quentin [1]...Johnny Cash
- R&B Hot Buttered Soul [1]...Isaac Hayes
- C&W Johnny Cash At San Quentin [4]...Johnny Cash

August 30, 1969
SINGLES
- HOT   Honky Tonk Women [2]...The Rolling Stones
- R&B   Share Your Love With Me [2]...Aretha Franklin
- C&W   A Boy Named Sue [2]...Johnny Cash
- A/C   A Boy Named Sue [1]...Johnny Cash

ALBUMS
- POP   Johnny Cash At San Quentin [2]...Johnny Cash
- R&B   Hot Buttered Soul [2]...Isaac Hayes
- C&W   Johnny Cash At San Quentin [5]...Johnny Cash

September 6, 1969
SINGLES
- HOT   Honky Tonk Women [3]...The Rolling Stones
- R&B   Share Your Love With Me [3]...Aretha Franklin
- C&W   A Boy Named Sue [3]...Johnny Cash
- A/C   A Boy Named Sue [2]...Johnny Cash

ALBUMS
- POP   Johnny Cash At San Quentin [3]...Johnny Cash
- R&B   Hot Buttered Soul [3]...Isaac Hayes
- C&W   Johnny Cash At San Quentin [6]...Johnny Cash

September 13, 1969
SINGLES
- HOT   Honky Tonk Women [4]...The Rolling Stones
- R&B   Share Your Love With Me [4]...Aretha Franklin
- C&W   A Boy Named Sue [4]...Johnny Cash
- A/C   I'll Never Fall In Love Again [1]...Tom Jones

ALBUMS
- POP   Johnny Cash At San Quentin [4]...Johnny Cash
- R&B   Hot Buttered Soul [4]...Isaac Hayes
- C&W   Johnny Cash At San Quentin [7]...Johnny Cash

September 20, 1969
SINGLES
- HOT   Sugar, Sugar [1]...The Archies
- R&B   Share Your Love With Me [5]...Aretha Franklin
- C&W   A Boy Named Sue [5]...Johnny Cash
- A/C   Jean [1]...Oliver

ALBUMS
- POP   Blind Faith [1]...Blind Faith
- R&B   Hot Buttered Soul [5]...Isaac Hayes
- C&W   Johnny Cash At San Quentin [8]...Johnny Cash

September 27, 1969
SINGLES
- HOT   Sugar, Sugar [2]...The Archies
- R&B   Oh, What A Night [1]...The Dells
- C&W   Tall Dark Stranger [1]...Buck Owens
- A/C   Jean [2]...Oliver

ALBUMS
- POP   Blind Faith [2]...Blind Faith
- R&B   Hot Buttered Soul [6]...Isaac Hayes
- C&W   Johnny Cash At San Quentin [9]...Johnny Cash

October 4, 1969
SINGLES
- HOT   Sugar, Sugar [3]...The Archies
- R&B   *I Can't Get Next To You [1]...The Temptations
- C&W   Since I Met You, Baby [1]...Sonny James
- A/C   Jean [3]...Oliver

ALBUMS
- POP   Green River [1]...Creedence Clearwater Revival
- R&B   Hot Buttered Soul [7]...Isaac Hayes
- C&W   Johnny Cash At San Quentin [10]...Johnny Cash

October 11, 1969
SINGLES
- HOT   Sugar, Sugar [4]...The Archies
- R&B   I Can't Get Next To You [2]...The Temptations
- C&W   Since I Met You, Baby [2]...Sonny James
- A/C   Jean [4]...Oliver

ALBUMS
- POP   Green River [2]...Creedence Clearwater Revival
- R&B   Hot Buttered Soul [8]...Isaac Hayes
- C&W   Johnny Cash At San Quentin [11]...Johnny Cash

October 18, 1969
SINGLES
- HOT   I Can't Get Next To You [1]...The Temptations
- R&B   I Can't Get Next To You [3]...The Temptations
- C&W   Since I Met You, Baby [3]...Sonny James
- A/C   Is That All There Is [1]...Peggy Lee

ALBUMS
- POP   Green River [3]...Creedence Clearwater Revival
- R&B   Hot Buttered Soul [9]...Isaac Hayes
- C&W   Johnny Cash At San Quentin [12]...Johnny Cash

October 25, 1969
SINGLES
- HOT   I Can't Get Next To You [2]...The Temptations
- R&B   I Can't Get Next To You [4]...The Temptations
- C&W   The Ways To Love A Man [1]...Tammy Wynette
- A/C   Is That All There Is [2]...Peggy Lee

ALBUMS
- POP   Green River [4]...Creedence Clearwater Revival
- R&B   Hot Buttered Soul [10]...Isaac Hayes
- C&W   Johnny Cash At San Quentin [13]...Johnny Cash

November 1, 1969
SINGLES
- HOT   Suspicious Minds [1]...Elvis Presley
- R&B   I Can't Get Next To You [5]...The Temptations
- C&W   The Ways To Love A Man [2]...Tammy Wynette
- A/C   *Wedding Bell Blues [1]...The 5th Dimension

ALBUMS
- POP   Abbey Road [1]...The Beatles
- R&B   Puzzle People [1]...The Temptations
- C&W   Johnny Cash At San Quentin [14]...Johnny Cash

November 8, 1969

SINGLES
- HOT   Wedding Bell Blues [1]...The 5th Dimension
- R&B   Baby I'm For Real [1]...The Originals
- C&W   To See My Angel Cry [1]...Conway Twitty
- A/C   Wedding Bell Blues [2]...The 5th Dimension

ALBUMS
- POP   Abbey Road [2]...The Beatles
- R&B   Puzzle People [2]...The Temptations
- C&W   Johnny Cash At San Quentin [15]...Johnny Cash

November 15, 1969

SINGLES
- HOT   Wedding Bell Blues [2]...The 5th Dimension
- R&B   Baby I'm For Real [2]...The Originals
- C&W   Okie From Muskogee [1]...Merle Haggard
- A/C   Try A Little Kindness [1]...Glen Campbell

ALBUMS
- POP   Abbey Road [3]...The Beatles
- R&B   Puzzle People [3]...The Temptations
- C&W   Johnny Cash At San Quentin [16]...Johnny Cash

November 22, 1969

SINGLES
- HOT   Wedding Bell Blues [3]...The 5th Dimension
- R&B   Baby I'm For Real [3]...The Originals
- C&W   Okie From Muskogee [2]...Merle Haggard
- A/C   *Leaving On A Jet Plane [1]...Peter, Paul & Mary

ALBUMS
- POP   Abbey Road [4]...The Beatles
- R&B   Puzzle People [4]...The Temptations
- C&W   Johnny Cash At San Quentin [17]...Johnny Cash

November 29, 1969

SINGLES
- HOT   Come Together/Something [1]...The Beatles
- R&B   Baby I'm For Real [4]...The Originals
- C&W   Okie From Muskogee [3]...Merle Haggard
- A/C   Leaving On A Jet Plane [2]...Peter, Paul & Mary

ALBUMS
- POP   Abbey Road [5]...The Beatles
- R&B   Puzzle People [5]...The Temptations
- C&W   Johnny Cash At San Quentin [18]...Johnny Cash

December 6, 1969

SINGLES
- HOT   Na Na Hey Hey Kiss Him Goodbye [1]...Steam
- R&B   Baby I'm For Real [5]...The Originals
- C&W   Okie From Muskogee [4]...Merle Haggard
- A/C   Leaving On A Jet Plane [3]...Peter, Paul & Mary

ALBUMS
- POP   Abbey Road [6]...The Beatles
- R&B   Puzzle People [6]...The Temptations
- C&W   Johnny Cash At San Quentin [19]...Johnny Cash

December 13, 1969

SINGLES
- HOT   Na Na Hey Hey Kiss Him Goodbye [2]...Steam
- R&B   *Someday We'll Be Together [1]...
        Diana Ross and The Supremes
- C&W   (I'm So) Afraid Of Losing You Again [1]...
        Charley Pride
- A/C   *Raindrops Keep Fallin' On My Head [1]...B.J. Thomas

ALBUMS
- POP   Abbey Road [7]...The Beatles
- R&B   Puzzle People [7]...The Temptations
- C&W   Johnny Cash At San Quentin [20]...Johnny Cash

December 20, 1969

SINGLES
- HOT   Leaving On A Jet Plane [1]...Peter, Paul & Mary
- R&B   Someday We'll Be Together [2]...
        Diana Ross and The Supremes
- C&W   (I'm So) Afraid Of Losing You Again [2]...
        Charley Pride
- A/C   Raindrops Keep Fallin' On My Head [2]...B.J. Thomas

ALBUMS
- POP   Abbey Road [8]...The Beatles
- R&B   Puzzle People [8]...The Temptations
- C&W   The Best Of Charley Pride [1]...Charley Pride

December 27, 1969

SINGLES
- HOT   Someday We'll Be Together [1]...
        Diana Ross and The Supremes
- R&B   Someday We'll Be Together [3]...
        Diana Ross and The Supremes
- C&W   (I'm So) Afraid Of Losing You Again [3]...
        Charley Pride
- A/C   Raindrops Keep Fallin' On My Head [3]...B.J. Thomas

ALBUMS
- POP   Led Zeppelin II [1]...Led Zeppelin
- R&B   Puzzle People [9]...The Temptations
- C&W   The Best Of Charley Pride [2]...Charley Pride

January 3, 1970

SINGLES
- HOT   Raindrops Keep Fallin' On My Head [1]...B.J. Thomas
- R&B   Someday We'll Be Together [4]...
        Diana Ross and The Supremes
- C&W   Baby, Baby (I Know You're A Lady) [1]...
        David Houston
- A/C   Raindrops Keep Fallin' On My Head [4]...B.J. Thomas

ALBUMS
- POP   Abbey Road [9]...The Beatles
- R&B   Puzzle People [10]...The Temptations
- C&W   The Best Of Charley Pride [3]...Charley Pride

January 10, 1970
SINGLES
- *HOT* Raindrops Keep Fallin' On My Head [2]...B.J. Thomas
- *R&B* *I Want You Back [1]...Jackson 5
- *C&W* Baby, Baby (I Know You're A Lady) [2]...David Houston
- *A/C* Raindrops Keep Fallin' On My Head [5]...B.J. Thomas

ALBUMS
- *POP* Abbey Road [10]...The Beatles
- *R&B* Puzzle People [11]...The Temptations
- *C&W* The Best Of Charley Pride [4]...Charley Pride

January 17, 1970
SINGLES
- *HOT* Raindrops Keep Fallin' On My Head [3]...B.J. Thomas
- *R&B* I Want You Back [2]...Jackson 5
- *C&W* Baby, Baby (I Know You're A Lady) [3]...David Houston
- *A/C* Raindrops Keep Fallin' On My Head [6]...B.J. Thomas

ALBUMS
- *POP* Led Zeppelin II [2]...Led Zeppelin
- *R&B* Puzzle People [12]...The Temptations
- *C&W* The Best Of Charley Pride [5]...Charley Pride

January 24, 1970
SINGLES
- *HOT* Raindrops Keep Fallin' On My Head [4]...B.J. Thomas
- *R&B* I Want You Back [3]...Jackson 5
- *C&W* Baby, Baby (I Know You're A Lady) [4]...David Houston
- *A/C* Raindrops Keep Fallin' On My Head [7]...B.J. Thomas

ALBUMS
- *POP* Abbey Road [11]...The Beatles
- *R&B* Puzzle People [13]...The Temptations
- *C&W* The Best Of Charley Pride [6]...Charley Pride

January 31, 1970
SINGLES
- *HOT* I Want You Back [1]...Jackson 5
- *R&B* I Want You Back [4]...Jackson 5
- *C&W* A Week In A Country Jail [1]...Tom T. Hall
- *A/C* Without Love (There Is Nothing) [1]...Tom Jones

ALBUMS
- *POP* Led Zeppelin II [3]...Led Zeppelin
- *R&B* Puzzle People [14]...The Temptations
- *C&W* The Best Of Charley Pride [7]...Charley Pride

February 7, 1970
SINGLES
- *HOT* Venus [1]...The Shocking Blue
- *R&B* *Thank You (Falettinme Be Mice Elf Agin) [1]...Sly & The Family Stone
- *C&W* A Week In A Country Jail [2]...Tom T. Hall
- *A/C* I'll Never Fall In Love Again [1]...Dionne Warwick

ALBUMS
- *POP* Led Zeppelin II [4]...Led Zeppelin
- *R&B* Puzzle People [15]...The Temptations
- *C&W* The Best Of Charley Pride [8]...Charley Pride

February 14, 1970
SINGLES
- *HOT* Thank You (Falettinme Be Mice Elf Agin)/Everybody Is A Star [1]...Sly & The Family Stone
- *R&B* Thank You (Falettinme Be Mice Elf Agin) [2]...Sly & The Family Stone
- *C&W* It's Just A Matter Of Time [1]...Sonny James
- *A/C* I'll Never Fall In Love Again [2]...Dionne Warwick

ALBUMS
- *POP* Led Zeppelin II [5]...Led Zeppelin
- *R&B* Diana Ross Presents The Jackson 5 [1]...Jackson 5
- *C&W* The Best Of Charley Pride [9]...Charley Pride

February 21, 1970
SINGLES
- *HOT* Thank You (Falettinme Be Mice Elf Agin)/Everybody Is A Star [2]...Sly & The Family Stone
- *R&B* Thank You (Falettinme Be Mice Elf Agin) [3]...Sly & The Family Stone
- *C&W* It's Just A Matter Of Time [2]...Sonny James
- *A/C* I'll Never Fall In Love Again [3]...Dionne Warwick

ALBUMS
- *POP* Led Zeppelin II [6]...Led Zeppelin
- *R&B* Diana Ross Presents The Jackson 5 [2]...Jackson 5
- *C&W* The Best Of Charley Pride [10]...Charley Pride

February 28, 1970
SINGLES
- *HOT* *Bridge Over Troubled Water [1]...Simon & Garfunkel
- *R&B* Thank You (Falettinme Be Mice Elf Agin) [4]...Sly & The Family Stone
- *C&W* It's Just A Matter Of Time [3]...Sonny James
- *A/C* *Bridge Over Troubled Water [1]...Simon & Garfunkel

ALBUMS
- *POP* Led Zeppelin II [7]...Led Zeppelin
- *R&B* Diana Ross Presents The Jackson 5 [3]...Jackson 5
- *C&W* The Best Of Charley Pride [11]...Charley Pride

March 7, 1970
SINGLES
- HOT Bridge Over Troubled Water [2]...Simon & Garfunkel
- R&B Thank You (Falettinme Be Mice Elf Agin) [5]...Sly & The Family Stone
- C&W It's Just A Matter Of Time [4]...Sonny James
- A/C Bridge Over Troubled Water [2]...Simon & Garfunkel

ALBUMS
- POP Bridge Over Troubled Water [1]...Simon & Garfunkel
- R&B Diana Ross Presents The Jackson 5 [4]...Jackson 5
- C&W The Best Of Charley Pride [12]...Charley Pride

March 14, 1970
SINGLES
- HOT Bridge Over Troubled Water [3]...Simon & Garfunkel
- R&B Rainy Night In Georgia [1]...Brook Benton
- C&W The Fightin' Side Of Me [1]...Merle Haggard
- A/C Bridge Over Troubled Water [3]...Simon & Garfunkel

ALBUMS
- POP Bridge Over Troubled Water [2]...Simon & Garfunkel
- R&B Diana Ross Presents The Jackson 5 [5]...Jackson 5
- C&W The Best Of Charley Pride [13]...Charley Pride

March 21, 1970
SINGLES
- HOT Bridge Over Troubled Water [4]...Simon & Garfunkel
- R&B Call Me [1]...Aretha Franklin
- C&W The Fightin' Side Of Me [2]...Merle Haggard
- A/C Bridge Over Troubled Water [4]...Simon & Garfunkel

ALBUMS
- POP Bridge Over Troubled Water [3]...Simon & Garfunkel
- R&B Diana Ross Presents The Jackson 5 [6]...Jackson 5
- C&W Okie From Muskogee [1]...Merle Haggard

March 28, 1970
SINGLES
- HOT Bridge Over Troubled Water [5]...Simon & Garfunkel
- R&B Call Me [2]...Aretha Franklin
- C&W The Fightin' Side Of Me [3]...Merle Haggard
- A/C Bridge Over Troubled Water [5]...Simon & Garfunkel

ALBUMS
- POP Bridge Over Troubled Water [4]...Simon & Garfunkel
- R&B Diana Ross Presents The Jackson 5 [7]...Jackson 5
- C&W Hello, I'm Johnny Cash [1]...Johnny Cash

April 4, 1970
SINGLES
- HOT Bridge Over Troubled Water [6]...Simon & Garfunkel
- R&B *ABC [1]...Jackson 5
- C&W Tennessee Bird Walk [1]...Jack Blanchard & Misty Morgan
- A/C Bridge Over Troubled Water [6]...Simon & Garfunkel

ALBUMS
- POP Bridge Over Troubled Water [5]...Simon & Garfunkel
- R&B Diana Ross Presents The Jackson 5 [8]...Jackson 5
- C&W Hello, I'm Johnny Cash [2]...Johnny Cash

April 11, 1970
SINGLES
- HOT *Let It Be [1]...The Beatles
- R&B ABC [2]...Jackson 5
- C&W Tennessee Bird Walk [2]...Jack Blanchard & Misty Morgan
- A/C *Let It Be [1]...The Beatles

ALBUMS
- POP Bridge Over Troubled Water [6]...Simon & Garfunkel
- R&B Diana Ross Presents The Jackson 5 [9]...Jackson 5
- C&W Hello, I'm Johnny Cash [3]...Johnny Cash

April 18, 1970
SINGLES
- HOT Let It Be [2]...The Beatles
- R&B ABC [3]...Jackson 5
- C&W Is Anybody Goin' To San Antone [1]...Charley Pride
- A/C Let It Be [2]...The Beatles

ALBUMS
- POP Bridge Over Troubled Water [7]...Simon & Garfunkel
- R&B Psychedelic Shack [1]...The Temptations
- C&W Hello, I'm Johnny Cash [4]...Johnny Cash

April 25, 1970
SINGLES
- HOT ABC [1]...Jackson 5
- R&B ABC [4]...Jackson 5
- C&W Is Anybody Goin' To San Antone [2]...Charley Pride
- A/C Let It Be [3]...The Beatles

ALBUMS
- POP Bridge Over Troubled Water [8]...Simon & Garfunkel
- R&B Psychedelic Shack [2]...The Temptations
- C&W Just Plain Charley [1]...Charley Pride

May 2, 1970

SINGLES
- HOT ABC [2]...Jackson 5
- R&B Turn Back The Hands Of Time [1]...Tyrone Davis
- C&W My Woman My Woman, My Wife [1]...Marty Robbins
- A/C Let It Be [4]...The Beatles

ALBUMS
- POP Bridge Over Troubled Water [9]...Simon & Garfunkel
- R&B Psychedelic Shack [3]...The Temptations
- C&W Just Plain Charley [2]...Charley Pride

May 9, 1970

SINGLES
- HOT American Woman/No Sugar Tonight [1]...The Guess Who
- R&B Turn Back The Hands Of Time [2]...Tyrone Davis
- C&W The Pool Shark [1]...Dave Dudley
- A/C For The Love Of Him [1]...Bobbi Martin

ALBUMS
- POP Bridge Over Troubled Water [10]...Simon & Garfunkel
- R&B Psychedelic Shack [4]...The Temptations
- C&W Okie From Muskogee [2]...Merle Haggard

May 16, 1970

SINGLES
- HOT American Woman/No Sugar Tonight [2]...The Guess Who
- R&B Love On A Two-Way Street [1]...The Moments
- C&W My Love [1]...Sonny James
- A/C For The Love Of Him [2]...Bobbi Martin

ALBUMS
- POP Deja Vu [1]...Crosby, Stills, Nash & Young
- R&B The Isaac Hayes Movement [1]...Isaac Hayes
- C&W Okie From Muskogee [3]...Merle Haggard

May 23, 1970

SINGLES
- HOT American Woman/No Sugar Tonight [3]...The Guess Who
- R&B Love On A Two-Way Street [2]...The Moments
- C&W My Love [2]...Sonny James
- A/C *Everything Is Beautiful [1]...Ray Stevens

ALBUMS
- POP McCartney [1]...Paul McCartney
- R&B The Isaac Hayes Movement [2]...Isaac Hayes
- C&W Okie From Muskogee [4]...Merle Haggard

May 30, 1970

SINGLES
- HOT Everything Is Beautiful [1]...Ray Stevens
- R&B Love On A Two-Way Street [3]...The Moments
- C&W My Love [3]...Sonny James
- A/C Everything Is Beautiful [2]...Ray Stevens

ALBUMS
- POP McCartney [2]...Paul McCartney
- R&B The Isaac Hayes Movement [3]...Isaac Hayes
- C&W Okie From Muskogee [5]...Merle Haggard

June 6, 1970

SINGLES
- HOT Everything Is Beautiful [2]...Ray Stevens
- R&B Love On A Two-Way Street [4]...The Moments
- C&W Hello Darlin' [1]...Conway Twitty
- A/C Everything Is Beautiful [3]...Ray Stevens

ALBUMS
- POP McCartney [3]...Paul McCartney
- R&B The Isaac Hayes Movement [4]...Isaac Hayes
- C&W Just Plain Charley [3]...Charley Pride

June 13, 1970

SINGLES
- HOT The Long And Winding Road/For You Blue [1]...The Beatles
- R&B Love On A Two-Way Street [5]...The Moments
- C&W Hello Darlin' [2]...Conway Twitty
- A/C Daughter Of Darkness [1]...Tom Jones

ALBUMS
- POP Let It Be [1]...The Beatles/Soundtrack
- R&B The Isaac Hayes Movement [5]...Isaac Hayes
- C&W Just Plain Charley [4]...Charley Pride

June 20, 1970

SINGLES
- HOT The Long And Winding Road/For You Blue [2]...The Beatles
- R&B *The Love You Save [1]...Jackson 5
- C&W Hello Darlin' [3]...Conway Twitty
- A/C The Wonder Of You [1]...Elvis Presley

ALBUMS
- POP Let It Be [2]...The Beatles/Soundtrack
- R&B ABC [1]...Jackson 5
- C&W Just Plain Charley [5]...Charley Pride

June 27, 1970
SINGLES
- HOT   The Love You Save [1]...Jackson 5
- R&B   The Love You Save [2]...Jackson 5
- C&W   Hello Darlin' [4]...Conway Twitty
- A/C   A Song Of Joy [1]...Miguel Rios

ALBUMS
- POP   Let It Be [3]...The Beatles/Soundtrack
- R&B   ABC [2]...Jackson 5
- C&W   Just Plain Charley [6]...Charley Pride

July 4, 1970
SINGLES
- HOT   The Love You Save [2]...Jackson 5
- R&B   The Love You Save [3]...Jackson 5
- C&W   He Loves Me All The Way [1]...Tammy Wynette
- A/C   A Song Of Joy [2]...Miguel Rios

ALBUMS
- POP   Let It Be [4]...The Beatles/Soundtrack
- R&B   ABC [3]...Jackson 5
- C&W   Just Plain Charley [7]...Charley Pride

July 11, 1970
SINGLES
- HOT   Mama Told Me (Not To Come) [1]...Three Dog Night
- R&B   The Love You Save [4]...Jackson 5
- C&W   He Loves Me All The Way [2]...Tammy Wynette
- A/C   *(They Long To Be) Close To You [1]...Carpenters

ALBUMS
- POP   Woodstock [1]...Soundtrack
- R&B   ABC [4]...Jackson 5
- C&W   Just Plain Charley [8]...Charley Pride

July 18, 1970
SINGLES
- HOT   Mama Told Me (Not To Come) [2]...Three Dog Night
- R&B   The Love You Save [5]...Jackson 5
- C&W   He Loves Me All The Way [3]...Tammy Wynette
- A/C   (They Long To Be) Close To You [2]...Carpenters

ALBUMS
- POP   Woodstock [2]...Soundtrack
- R&B   ABC [5]...Jackson 5
- C&W   Just Plain Charley [9]...Charley Pride

July 25, 1970
SINGLES
- HOT   (They Long To Be) Close To You [1]...Carpenters
- R&B   The Love You Save [6]...Jackson 5
- C&W   Wonder Could I Live There Anymore [1]...Charley Pride
- A/C   (They Long To Be) Close To You [3]...Carpenters

ALBUMS
- POP   Woodstock [3]...Soundtrack
- R&B   ABC [6]...Jackson 5
- C&W   Tammy's Touch [1]...Tammy Wynette

August 1, 1970
SINGLES
- HOT   (They Long To Be) Close To You [2]...Carpenters
- R&B   Signed, Sealed, Delivered I'm Yours [1]...Stevie Wonder
- C&W   Wonder Could I Live There Anymore [2]...Charley Pride
- A/C   (They Long To Be) Close To You [4]...Carpenters

ALBUMS
- POP   Woodstock [4]...Soundtrack
- R&B   ABC [7]...Jackson 5
- C&W   Tammy's Touch [2]...Tammy Wynette

August 8, 1970
SINGLES
- HOT   (They Long To Be) Close To You [3]...Carpenters
- R&B   Signed, Sealed, Delivered I'm Yours [2]...Stevie Wonder
- C&W   Don't Keep Me Hangin' On [1]...Sonny James
- A/C   (They Long To Be) Close To You [5]...Carpenters

ALBUMS
- POP   Blood, Sweat & Tears 3 [1]...Blood, Sweat & Tears
- R&B   The Isaac Hayes Movement [6]...Isaac Hayes
- C&W   Charley Pride's 10th Album [1]...Charley Pride

August 15, 1970
SINGLES
- HOT   (They Long To Be) Close To You [4]...Carpenters
- R&B   Signed, Sealed, Delivered I'm Yours [3]...Stevie Wonder
- C&W   Don't Keep Me Hangin' On [2]...Sonny James
- A/C   (They Long To Be) Close To You [6]...Carpenters

ALBUMS
- POP   Blood, Sweat & Tears 3 [2]...Blood, Sweat & Tears
- R&B   The Isaac Hayes Movement [7]...Isaac Hayes
- C&W   Charley Pride's 10th Album [2]...Charley Pride

August 22, 1970
SINGLES
- HOT   Make It With You [1]...Bread
- R&B   Signed, Sealed, Delivered I'm Yours [4]...Stevie Wonder
- C&W   Don't Keep Me Hangin' On [3]...Sonny James
- A/C   I Just Can't Help Believing [1]...B.J. Thomas

ALBUMS
- POP   Cosmo's Factory [1]...Creedence Clearwater Revival
- R&B   ABC [8]...Jackson 5
- C&W   Charley Pride's 10th Album [3]...Charley Pride

August 29, 1970

SINGLES
- HOT War [1]...Edwin Starr
- R&B Signed, Sealed, Delivered I'm Yours [5]...Stevie Wonder
- C&W Don't Keep Me Hangin' On [4]...Sonny James
- A/C Snowbird [1]...Anne Murray

ALBUMS
- POP Cosmo's Factory [2]...Creedence Clearwater Revival
- R&B ABC [9]...Jackson 5
- C&W Charley Pride's 10th Album [4]...Charley Pride

September 5, 1970

SINGLES
- HOT War [2]...Edwin Starr
- R&B Signed, Sealed, Delivered I'm Yours [6]...Stevie Wonder
- C&W All For The Love Of Sunshine [1]...Hank Williams, Jr.
- A/C Snowbird [2]...Anne Murray

ALBUMS
- POP Cosmo's Factory [3]...Creedence Clearwater Revival
- R&B ABC [10]...Jackson 5
- C&W Charley Pride's 10th Album [5]...Charley Pride

September 12, 1970

SINGLES
- HOT War [3]...Edwin Starr
- R&B Don't Play That Song [1]...Aretha Franklin
- C&W All For The Love Of Sunshine [2]...Hank Williams, Jr.
- A/C Snowbird [3]...Anne Murray

ALBUMS
- POP Cosmo's Factory [4]...Creedence Clearwater Revival
- R&B ABC [11]...Jackson 5
- C&W Charley Pride's 10th Album [6]...Charley Pride

September 19, 1970

SINGLES
- HOT *Ain't No Mountain High Enough [1]...Diana Ross
- R&B Don't Play That Song [2]...Aretha Franklin
- C&W For The Good Times/Grazin' In Greener Pastures [1]...Ray Price
- A/C Snowbird [4]...Anne Murray

ALBUMS
- POP Cosmo's Factory [5]...Creedence Clearwater Revival
- R&B ABC [12]...Jackson 5
- C&W Charley Pride's 10th Album [7]...Charley Pride

September 26, 1970

SINGLES
- HOT Ain't No Mountain High Enough [2]...Diana Ross
- R&B Don't Play That Song [3]...Aretha Franklin
- C&W There Must Be More To Love Than This [1]...Jerry Lee Lewis
- A/C Snowbird [5]...Anne Murray

ALBUMS
- POP Cosmo's Factory [6]...Creedence Clearwater Revival
- R&B Diana Ross [1]...Diana Ross
- C&W Charley Pride's 10th Album [8]...Charley Pride

October 3, 1970

SINGLES
- HOT Ain't No Mountain High Enough [3]...Diana Ross
- R&B Ain't No Mountain High Enough [1]...Diana Ross
- C&W There Must Be More To Love Than This [2]...Jerry Lee Lewis
- A/C Snowbird [6]...Anne Murray

ALBUMS
- POP Cosmo's Factory [7]...Creedence Clearwater Revival
- R&B Diana Ross [2]...Diana Ross
- C&W Hello Darlin' [1]...Conway Twitty

October 10, 1970

SINGLES
- HOT Cracklin' Rosie [1]...Neil Diamond
- R&B *I'll Be There [1]...Jackson 5
- C&W Sunday Morning Coming Down [1]...Johnny Cash
- A/C We've Only Just Begun [1]...Carpenters

ALBUMS
- POP Cosmo's Factory [8]...Creedence Clearwater Revival
- R&B Third Album [1]...Jackson 5
- C&W The Fightin' Side Of Me [1]...Merle Haggard

October 17, 1970

SINGLES
- HOT I'll Be There [1]...Jackson 5
- R&B I'll Be There [2]...Jackson 5
- C&W Sunday Morning Coming Down [2]...Johnny Cash
- A/C We've Only Just Begun [2]...Carpenters

ALBUMS
- POP Cosmo's Factory [9]...Creedence Clearwater Revival
- R&B Third Album [2]...Jackson 5
- C&W The Fightin' Side Of Me [2]...Merle Haggard

October 24, 1970

SINGLES
- *HOT*   I'll Be There [2]...Jackson 5
- *R&B*   I'll Be There [3]...Jackson 5
- *C&W*   Run, Woman, Run [1]...Tammy Wynette
- *A/C*   We've Only Just Begun [3]...Carpenters

ALBUMS
- *POP*   Abraxas [1]...Santana
- *R&B*   Third Album [3]...Jackson 5
- *C&W*   The Fightin' Side Of Me [3]...Merle Haggard

October 31, 1970

SINGLES
- *HOT*   I'll Be There [3]...Jackson 5
- *R&B*   I'll Be There [4]...Jackson 5
- *C&W*   Run, Woman, Run [2]...Tammy Wynette
- *A/C*   We've Only Just Begun [4]...Carpenters

ALBUMS
- *POP*   Led Zeppelin III [1]...Led Zeppelin
- *R&B*   Third Album [4]...Jackson 5
- *C&W*   The Fightin' Side Of Me [4]...Merle Haggard

November 7, 1970

SINGLES
- *HOT*   I'll Be There [4]...Jackson 5
- *R&B*   I'll Be There [5]...Jackson 5
- *C&W*   I Can't Believe That You've Stopped Loving Me [1]...Charley Pride
- *A/C*   We've Only Just Begun [5]...Carpenters

ALBUMS
- *POP*   Led Zeppelin III [2]...Led Zeppelin
- *R&B*   Third Album [5]...Jackson 5
- *C&W*   The Fightin' Side Of Me [5]...Merle Haggard

November 14, 1970

SINGLES
- *HOT*   I'll Be There [5]...Jackson 5
- *R&B*   I'll Be There [6]...Jackson 5
- *C&W*   I Can't Believe That You've Stopped Loving Me [2]...Charley Pride
- *A/C*   We've Only Just Begun [6]...Carpenters

ALBUMS
- *POP*   Led Zeppelin III [3]...Led Zeppelin
- *R&B*   Third Album [6]...Jackson 5
- *C&W*   The Fightin' Side Of Me [6]...Merle Haggard

November 21, 1970

SINGLES
- *HOT*   I Think I Love You [1]...The Partridge Family
- *R&B*   Super Bad (Part 1 & Part 2) [1]...James Brown
- *C&W*   Fifteen Years Ago [1]...Conway Twitty
- *A/C*   We've Only Just Begun [7]...Carpenters

ALBUMS
- *POP*   Led Zeppelin III [4]...Led Zeppelin
- *R&B*   Third Album [7]...Jackson 5
- *C&W*   The Fightin' Side Of Me [7]...Merle Haggard

November 28, 1970

SINGLES
- *HOT*   I Think I Love You [2]...The Partridge Family
- *R&B*   Super Bad (Part 1 & Part 2) [2]...James Brown
- *C&W*   Endlessly [1]...Sonny James
- *A/C*   You Don't Have To Say You Love Me [1]...Elvis Presley

ALBUMS
- *POP*   Abraxas [2]...Santana
- *R&B*   Third Album [8]...Jackson 5
- *C&W*   For The Good Times [1]...Ray Price

December 5, 1970

SINGLES
- *HOT*   I Think I Love You [3]...The Partridge Family
- *R&B*   *The Tears Of A Clown [1]...Smokey Robinson & The Miracles
- *C&W*   Endlessly [2]...Sonny James
- *A/C*   It's Impossible [1]...Perry Como

ALBUMS
- *POP*   Abraxas [3]...Santana
- *R&B*   Third Album [9]...Jackson 5
- *C&W*   For The Good Times [2]...Ray Price

December 12, 1970

SINGLES
- *HOT*   The Tears Of A Clown [1]...Smokey Robinson & The Miracles
- *R&B*   The Tears Of A Clown [2]...Smokey Robinson & The Miracles
- *C&W*   Endlessly [3]...Sonny James
- *A/C*   It's Impossible [2]...Perry Como

ALBUMS
- *POP*   Abraxas [4]...Santana
- *R&B*   Third Album [10]...Jackson 5
- *C&W*   For The Good Times [3]...Ray Price

December 19, 1970

SINGLES
- HOT The Tears Of A Clown [2]...Smokey Robinson & The Miracles
- R&B The Tears Of A Clown [3]...Smokey Robinson & The Miracles
- C&W Coal Miner's Daughter [1]...Loretta Lynn
- A/C It's Impossible [3]...Perry Como

ALBUMS
- POP Abraxas [5]...Santana
- R&B Greatest Hits [1]...Sly & The Family Stone
- C&W The Johnny Cash Show [1]...Johnny Cash

December 26, 1970

SINGLES
- HOT My Sweet Lord/Isn't It A Pity [1]...George Harrison
- R&B Stoned Love [1]...The Supremes
- C&W Rose Garden [1]...Lynn Anderson
- A/C It's Impossible [4]...Perry Como

ALBUMS
- POP Abraxas [6]...Santana
- R&B To Be Continued [1]...Isaac Hayes
- C&W The Johnny Cash Show [2]...Johnny Cash

January 2, 1971

SINGLES
- HOT My Sweet Lord/Isn't It A Pity [2]...George Harrison
- R&B Groove Me [1]...King Floyd
- C&W Rose Garden [2]...Lynn Anderson
- A/C One Less Bell To Answer [1]...The 5th Dimension

ALBUMS
- POP All Things Must Pass [1]...George Harrison
- R&B To Be Continued [2]...Isaac Hayes
- C&W For The Good Times [4]...Ray Price

January 9, 1971

SINGLES
- HOT My Sweet Lord/Isn't It A Pity [3]...George Harrison
- R&B Groove Me [2]...King Floyd
- C&W Rose Garden [3]...Lynn Anderson
- A/C Watching Scotty Grow [1]...Bobby Goldsboro

ALBUMS
- POP All Things Must Pass [2]...George Harrison
- R&B To Be Continued [3]...Isaac Hayes
- C&W For The Good Times [5]...Ray Price

January 16, 1971

SINGLES
- HOT My Sweet Lord/Isn't It A Pity [4]...George Harrison
- R&B Groove Me [3]...King Floyd
- C&W Rose Garden [4]...Lynn Anderson
- A/C Watching Scotty Grow [2]...Bobby Goldsboro

ALBUMS
- POP All Things Must Pass [3]...George Harrison
- R&B To Be Continued [4]...Isaac Hayes
- C&W For The Good Times [6]...Ray Price

January 23, 1971

SINGLES
- HOT Knock Three Times [1]...Dawn
- R&B If I Were Your Woman [1]...Gladys Knight & The Pips
- C&W Rose Garden [5]...Lynn Anderson
- A/C Watching Scotty Grow [3]...Bobby Goldsboro

ALBUMS
- POP All Things Must Pass [4]...George Harrison
- R&B To Be Continued [5]...Isaac Hayes
- C&W For The Good Times [7]...Ray Price

January 30, 1971

SINGLES
- HOT Knock Three Times [2]...Dawn
- R&B Groove Me [4]...King Floyd
- C&W Flesh And Blood [1]...Johnny Cash
- A/C Watching Scotty Grow [4]...Bobby Goldsboro

ALBUMS
- POP All Things Must Pass [5]...George Harrison
- R&B To Be Continued [6]...Isaac Hayes
- C&W For The Good Times [8]...Ray Price

February 6, 1971

SINGLES
- HOT Knock Three Times [3]...Dawn
- R&B (Do The) Push And Pull, Part I [1]...Rufus Thomas
- C&W Joshua [1]...Dolly Parton
- A/C Watching Scotty Grow [5]...Bobby Goldsboro

ALBUMS
- POP All Things Must Pass [6]...George Harrison
- R&B Curtis [1]...Curtis Mayfield
- C&W For The Good Times [9]...Ray Price

February 13, 1971

SINGLES
- HOT One Bad Apple [1]...The Osmonds
- R&B (Do The) Push And Pull, Part I [2]...Rufus Thomas
- C&W Help Me Make It Through The Night [1]...Sammi Smith
- A/C Watching Scotty Grow [6]...Bobby Goldsboro

ALBUMS
- POP All Things Must Pass [7]...George Harrison
- R&B Curtis [2]...Curtis Mayfield
- C&W Rose Garden [1]...Lynn Anderson

February 20, 1971
SINGLES
- HOT One Bad Apple [2]...The Osmonds
- R&B Jody's Got Your Girl And Gone [1]...Johnnie Taylor
- C&W Help Me Make It Through The Night [2]...Sammi Smith
- A/C If You Could Read My Mind [1]...Gordon Lightfoot

ALBUMS
- POP Jesus Christ Superstar [1]...Various Artists
- R&B To Be Continued [7]...Isaac Hayes
- C&W Rose Garden [2]...Lynn Anderson

February 27, 1971
SINGLES
- HOT One Bad Apple [3]...The Osmonds
- R&B Jody's Got Your Girl And Gone [2]...Johnnie Taylor
- C&W Help Me Make It Through The Night [3]...Sammi Smith
- A/C For All We Know [1]...Carpenters

ALBUMS
- POP Pearl [1]...Janis Joplin
- R&B To Be Continued [8]...Isaac Hayes
- C&W Rose Garden [3]...Lynn Anderson

March 6, 1971
SINGLES
- HOT One Bad Apple [4]...The Osmonds
- R&B *Just My Imagination (Running Away With Me) [1]...The Temptations
- C&W I'd Rather Love You [1]...Charley Pride
- A/C For All We Know [2]...Carpenters

ALBUMS
- POP Pearl [2]...Janis Joplin
- R&B To Be Continued [9]...Isaac Hayes
- C&W Rose Garden [4]...Lynn Anderson

March 13, 1971
SINGLES
- HOT One Bad Apple [5]...The Osmonds
- R&B Just My Imagination (Running Away With Me) [2]...The Temptations
- C&W I'd Rather Love You [2]...Charley Pride
- A/C For All We Know [3]...Carpenters

ALBUMS
- POP Pearl [3]...Janis Joplin
- R&B Curtis [3]...Curtis Mayfield
- C&W Rose Garden [5]...Lynn Anderson

March 20, 1971
SINGLES
- HOT Me And Bobby McGee [1]...Janis Joplin
- R&B Just My Imagination (Running Away With Me) [3]...The Temptations
- C&W I'd Rather Love You [3]...Charley Pride
- A/C (Where Do I Begin) Love Story [1]...Andy Williams

ALBUMS
- POP Pearl [4]...Janis Joplin
- R&B Curtis [4]...Curtis Mayfield
- C&W Rose Garden [6]...Lynn Anderson

March 27, 1971
SINGLES
- HOT Me And Bobby McGee [2]...Janis Joplin
- R&B What's Going On [1]...Marvin Gaye
- C&W After The Fire Is Gone [1]...Conway Twitty & Loretta Lynn
- A/C (Where Do I Begin) Love Story [2]...Andy Williams

ALBUMS
- POP Pearl [5]...Janis Joplin
- R&B To Be Continued [10]...Isaac Hayes
- C&W Rose Garden [7]...Lynn Anderson

April 3, 1971
SINGLES
- HOT Just My Imagination (Running Away With Me) [1]...The Temptations
- R&B What's Going On [2]...Marvin Gaye
- C&W After The Fire Is Gone [2]...Conway Twitty & Loretta Lynn
- A/C When There's No You [1]...Engelbert Humperdinck

ALBUMS
- POP Pearl [6]...Janis Joplin
- R&B To Be Continued [11]...Isaac Hayes
- C&W Rose Garden [8]...Lynn Anderson

April 10, 1971
SINGLES
- HOT Just My Imagination (Running Away With Me) [2]...The Temptations
- R&B What's Going On [3]...Marvin Gaye
- C&W Empty Arms [1]...Sonny James
- A/C (Where Do I Begin) Love Story [3]...Andy Williams

ALBUMS
- POP Pearl [7]...Janis Joplin
- R&B Live In Cook County Jail [1]...B.B. King
- C&W Rose Garden [9]...Lynn Anderson

April 17, 1971
SINGLES
- HOT Joy To The World [1]...Three Dog Night
- R&B What's Going On [4]...Marvin Gaye
- C&W Empty Arms [2]...Sonny James
- A/C (Where Do I Begin) Love Story [4]...Andy Williams

ALBUMS
- POP Pearl [8]...Janis Joplin
- R&B Live In Cook County Jail [2]...B.B. King
- C&W Rose Garden [10]...Lynn Anderson

April 24, 1971
SINGLES
- HOT Joy To The World [2]...Three Dog Night
- R&B What's Going On [5]...Marvin Gaye
- C&W Empty Arms [3]...Sonny James
- A/C If [1]...Bread

ALBUMS
- POP Pearl [9]...Janis Joplin
- R&B Live In Cook County Jail [3]...B.B. King
- C&W Rose Garden [11]...Lynn Anderson

May 1, 1971
SINGLES
- HOT Joy To The World [3]...Three Dog Night
- R&B Never Can Say Goodbye [1]...Jackson 5
- C&W Empty Arms [4]...Sonny James
- A/C If [2]...Bread

ALBUMS
- POP Jesus Christ Superstar [2]...Various Artists
- R&B Curtis [5]...Curtis Mayfield
- C&W Rose Garden [12]...Lynn Anderson

May 8, 1971
SINGLES
- HOT Joy To The World [4]...Three Dog Night
- R&B Never Can Say Goodbye [2]...Jackson 5
- C&W How Much More Can She Stand [1]...Conway Twitty
- A/C If [3]...Bread

ALBUMS
- POP Jesus Christ Superstar [3]...Various Artists
- R&B Maybe Tomorrow [1]...Jackson 5
- C&W Help Me Make It Through The Night [1]...Sammi Smith

May 15, 1971
SINGLES
- HOT Joy To The World [5]...Three Dog Night
- R&B Never Can Say Goodbye [3]...Jackson 5
- C&W I Won't Mention It Again [1]...Ray Price
- A/C Me And You And A Dog Named Boo [1]...Lobo

ALBUMS
- POP 4 Way Street [1]...Crosby, Stills, Nash & Young
- R&B Maybe Tomorrow [2]...Jackson 5
- C&W Rose Garden [13]...Lynn Anderson

May 22, 1971
SINGLES
- HOT Joy To The World [6]...Three Dog Night
- R&B Bridge Over Troubled Water [1]...Aretha Franklin
- C&W I Won't Mention It Again [2]...Ray Price
- A/C Me And You And A Dog Named Boo [2]...Lobo

ALBUMS
- POP Sticky Fingers [1]...The Rolling Stones
- R&B Maybe Tomorrow [3]...Jackson 5
- C&W Hag [1]...Merle Haggard

May 29, 1971
SINGLES
- HOT Brown Sugar [1]...The Rolling Stones
- R&B *Want Ads [1]...The Honey Cone
- C&W I Won't Mention It Again [3]...Ray Price
- A/C Rainy Days And Mondays [1]...Carpenters

ALBUMS
- POP Sticky Fingers [2]...The Rolling Stones
- R&B Maybe Tomorrow [4]...Jackson 5
- C&W Hag [2]...Merle Haggard

June 5, 1971
SINGLES
- HOT Brown Sugar [2]...The Rolling Stones
- R&B Want Ads [2]...The Honey Cone
- C&W You're My Man [1]...Lynn Anderson
- A/C Rainy Days And Mondays [2]...Carpenters

ALBUMS
- POP Sticky Fingers [3]...The Rolling Stones
- R&B Maybe Tomorrow [5]...Jackson 5
- C&W Rose Garden [14]...Lynn Anderson

June 12, 1971
SINGLES
- HOT Want Ads [1]...The Honey Cone
- R&B Want Ads [3]...The Honey Cone
- C&W You're My Man [2]...Lynn Anderson
- A/C Rainy Days And Mondays [3]...Carpenters

ALBUMS
- POP Sticky Fingers [4]...The Rolling Stones
- R&B Maybe Tomorrow [6]...Jackson 5
- C&W Hag [3]...Merle Haggard

June 19, 1971
SINGLES
- HOT *It's Too Late/I Feel The Earth Move [1]...Carole King
- R&B Bridge Over Troubled Water/Brand New Me [2]...Aretha Franklin
- C&W When You're Hot, You're Hot [1]...Jerry Reed
- A/C Rainy Days And Mondays [4]...Carpenters

ALBUMS
- POP Tapestry [1]...Carole King
- R&B Aretha Live At Fillmore West [1]...Aretha Franklin
- C&W Hag [4]...Merle Haggard

June 26, 1971
SINGLES
- HOT   It's Too Late/I Feel The Earth Move [2]...Carole King
- R&B   Don't Knock My Love - Pt. 1 [1]...Wilson Pickett
- C&W   When You're Hot, You're Hot [2]...Jerry Reed
- A/C   It's Too Late [1]...Carole King

ALBUMS
- POP   Tapestry [2]...Carole King
- R&B   Aretha Live At Fillmore West [2]...Aretha Franklin
- C&W   Did You Think To Pray [1]...Charley Pride

July 3, 1971
SINGLES
- HOT   It's Too Late/I Feel The Earth Move [3]...Carole King
- R&B   Mr. Big Stuff [1]...Jean Knight
- C&W   When You're Hot, You're Hot [3]...Jerry Reed
- A/C   It's Too Late [2]...Carole King

ALBUMS
- POP   Tapestry [3]...Carole King
- R&B   Aretha Live At Fillmore West [3]...Aretha Franklin
- C&W   I Won't Mention It Again [1]...Ray Price

July 10, 1971
SINGLES
- HOT   It's Too Late/I Feel The Earth Move [4]...Carole King
- R&B   Mr. Big Stuff [2]...Jean Knight
- C&W   When You're Hot, You're Hot [4]...Jerry Reed
- A/C   It's Too Late [3]...Carole King

ALBUMS
- POP   Tapestry [4]...Carole King
- R&B   Aretha Live At Fillmore West [4]...Aretha Franklin
- C&W   I Won't Mention It Again [2]...Ray Price

July 17, 1971
SINGLES
- HOT   It's Too Late/I Feel The Earth Move [5]...Carole King
- R&B   Mr. Big Stuff [3]...Jean Knight
- C&W   When You're Hot, You're Hot [5]...Jerry Reed
- A/C   It's Too Late [4]...Carole King

ALBUMS
- POP   Tapestry [5]...Carole King
- R&B   Aretha Live At Fillmore West [5]...Aretha Franklin
- C&W   I Won't Mention It Again [3]...Ray Price

July 24, 1971
SINGLES
- HOT   Indian Reservation (The Lament Of The Cherokee Reservation Indian) [1]...Raiders
- R&B   Mr. Big Stuff [4]...Jean Knight
- C&W   Bright Lights, Big City [1]...Sonny James
- A/C   It's Too Late [5]...Carole King

ALBUMS
- POP   Tapestry [6]...Carole King
- R&B   What's Going On [1]...Marvin Gaye
- C&W   Man In Black [1]...Johnny Cash

July 31, 1971
SINGLES
- HOT   *You've Got A Friend [1]...James Taylor
- R&B   Mr. Big Stuff [5]...Jean Knight
- C&W   I'm Just Me [1]...Charley Pride
- A/C   *You've Got A Friend [1]...James Taylor

ALBUMS
- POP   Tapestry [7]...Carole King
- R&B   What's Going On [2]...Marvin Gaye
- C&W   Man In Black [2]...Johnny Cash

August 7, 1971
SINGLES
- HOT   How Can You Mend A Broken Heart [1]...Bee Gees
- R&B   Hot Pants (She Got To Use What She Got, To Get What She Wants) (Part 1) [1]...James Brown
- C&W   I'm Just Me [2]...Charley Pride
- A/C   If Not For You [1]...Olivia Newton-John

ALBUMS
- POP   Tapestry [8]...Carole King
- R&B   What's Going On [3]...Marvin Gaye
- C&W   I Won't Mention It Again [4]...Ray Price

August 14, 1971
SINGLES
- HOT   How Can You Mend A Broken Heart [2]...Bee Gees
- R&B   Mercy Mercy Me (The Ecology) [1]...Marvin Gaye
- C&W   I'm Just Me [3]...Charley Pride
- A/C   If Not For You [2]...Olivia Newton-John

ALBUMS
- POP   Tapestry [9]...Carole King
- R&B   What's Going On [4]...Marvin Gaye
- C&W   I'm Just Me [1]...Charley Pride

August 21, 1971
SINGLES
- HOT   How Can You Mend A Broken Heart [3]...Bee Gees
- R&B   Mercy Mercy Me (The Ecology) [2]...Marvin Gaye
- C&W   I'm Just Me [4]...Charley Pride
- A/C   If Not For You [3]...Olivia Newton-John

ALBUMS
- POP   Tapestry [10]...Carole King
- R&B   What's Going On [5]...Marvin Gaye
- C&W   I'm Just Me [2]...Charley Pride

August 28, 1971
SINGLES
- HOT   How Can You Mend A Broken Heart [4]...Bee Gees
- R&B   Spanish Harlem [1]...Aretha Franklin
- C&W   Good Lovin' (Makes It Right) [1]...Tammy Wynette
- A/C   Beginnings [1]...Chicago

ALBUMS
- POP   Tapestry [11]...Carole King
- R&B   What's Going On [6]...Marvin Gaye
- C&W   You're My Man [1]...Lynn Anderson

September 4, 1971
SINGLES
- HOT Uncle Albert/Admiral Halsey [1]...Paul & Linda McCartney
- R&B Spanish Harlem [2]...Aretha Franklin
- C&W Good Lovin' (Makes It Right) [2]...Tammy Wynette
- A/C The Night They Drove Old Dixie Down [1]...Joan Baez

ALBUMS
- POP Tapestry [12]...Carole King
- R&B What's Going On [7]...Marvin Gaye
- C&W You're My Man [2]...Lynn Anderson

September 11, 1971
SINGLES
- HOT Go Away Little Girl [1]...Donny Osmond
- R&B Spanish Harlem [3]...Aretha Franklin
- C&W Easy Loving [1]...Freddie Hart
- A/C The Night They Drove Old Dixie Down [2]...Joan Baez

ALBUMS
- POP Tapestry [13]...Carole King
- R&B What's Going On [8]...Marvin Gaye
- C&W You're My Man [3]...Lynn Anderson

September 18, 1971
SINGLES
- HOT Go Away Little Girl [2]...Donny Osmond
- R&B Stick-Up [1]...The Honey Cone
- C&W The Year That Clayton Delaney Died [1]...Tom T. Hall
- A/C The Night They Drove Old Dixie Down [3]...Joan Baez

ALBUMS
- POP Tapestry [14]...Carole King
- R&B What's Going On [9]...Marvin Gaye
- C&W You're My Man [4]...Lynn Anderson

September 25, 1971
SINGLES
- HOT Go Away Little Girl [3]...Donny Osmond
- R&B Stick-Up [2]...The Honey Cone
- C&W The Year That Clayton Delaney Died [2]...Tom T. Hall
- A/C The Night They Drove Old Dixie Down [4]...Joan Baez

ALBUMS
- POP Tapestry [15]...Carole King
- R&B Shaft [1]...Isaac Hayes/Soundtrack
- C&W You're My Man [5]...Lynn Anderson

October 2, 1971
SINGLES
- HOT Maggie May/Reason To Believe [1]...Rod Stewart
- R&B Make It Funky (Part 1) [1]...James Brown
- C&W Easy Loving [2]...Freddie Hart
- A/C The Night They Drove Old Dixie Down [5]...Joan Baez

ALBUMS
- POP Every Picture Tells A Story [1]...Rod Stewart
- R&B Shaft [2]...Isaac Hayes/Soundtrack
- C&W You're My Man [6]...Lynn Anderson

October 9, 1971
SINGLES
- HOT Maggie May/Reason To Believe [2]...Rod Stewart
- R&B Make It Funky (Part 1) [2]...James Brown
- C&W Easy Loving [3]...Freddie Hart
- A/C Superstar [1]...Carpenters

ALBUMS
- POP Every Picture Tells A Story [2]...Rod Stewart
- R&B Shaft [3]...Isaac Hayes/Soundtrack
- C&W You're My Man [7]...Lynn Anderson

October 16, 1971
SINGLES
- HOT Maggie May/Reason To Believe [3]...Rod Stewart
- R&B Thin Line Between Love & Hate [1]...The Persuaders
- C&W How Can I Unlove You [1]...Lynn Anderson
- A/C Superstar [2]...Carpenters

ALBUMS
- POP Every Picture Tells A Story [3]...Rod Stewart
- R&B Shaft [4]...Isaac Hayes/Soundtrack
- C&W I'm Just Me [3]...Charley Pride

October 23, 1971
SINGLES
- HOT Maggie May/Reason To Believe [4]...Rod Stewart
- R&B Thin Line Between Love & Hate [2]...The Persuaders
- C&W How Can I Unlove You [2]...Lynn Anderson
- A/C Never My Love [1]...The 5th Dimension

ALBUMS
- POP Every Picture Tells A Story [4]...Rod Stewart
- R&B Shaft [5]...Isaac Hayes/Soundtrack
- C&W I Won't Mention It Again [5]...Ray Price

October 30, 1971
SINGLES
- HOT Maggie May/Reason To Believe [5]...Rod Stewart
- R&B Trapped By A Thing Called Love [1]...Denise LaSalle
- C&W How Can I Unlove You [3]...Lynn Anderson
- A/C Peace Train [1]...Cat Stevens

ALBUMS
- POP Imagine [1]...John Lennon
- R&B Shaft [6]...Isaac Hayes/Soundtrack
- C&W Easy Loving [1]...Freddie Hart

November 6, 1971
SINGLES
- *HOT* Gypsys, Tramps & Thieves [1]...Cher
- *R&B* Inner City Blues (Make Me Wanna Holler) [1]...Marvin Gaye
- *C&W* Here Comes Honey Again [1]...Sonny James
- *A/C* Peace Train [2]...Cat Stevens

ALBUMS
- *POP* Shaft [1]...Isaac Hayes/Soundtrack
- *R&B* Shaft [7]...Isaac Hayes/Soundtrack
- *C&W* Easy Loving [2]...Freddie Hart

November 13, 1971
SINGLES
- *HOT* Gypsys, Tramps & Thieves [2]...Cher
- *R&B* Inner City Blues (Make Me Wanna Holler) [2]...Marvin Gaye
- *C&W* Lead Me On [1]...Conway Twitty & Loretta Lynn
- *A/C* Peace Train [3]...Cat Stevens

ALBUMS
- *POP* Santana III [1]...Santana
- *R&B* Shaft [8]...Isaac Hayes/Soundtrack
- *C&W* Easy Loving [3]...Freddie Hart

November 20, 1971
SINGLES
- *HOT* Theme From Shaft [1]...Isaac Hayes
- *R&B* Have You Seen Her [1]...The Chi-Lites
- *C&W* Daddy Frank (The Guitar Man) [1]...Merle Haggard
- *A/C* Baby I'm-A Want You [1]...Bread

ALBUMS
- *POP* Santana III [2]...Santana
- *R&B* Shaft [9]...Isaac Hayes/Soundtrack
- *C&W* Easy Loving [4]...Freddie Hart

November 27, 1971
SINGLES
- *HOT* Theme From Shaft [2]...Isaac Hayes
- *R&B* Have You Seen Her [2]...The Chi-Lites
- *C&W* Daddy Frank (The Guitar Man) [2]...Merle Haggard
- *A/C* All I Ever Need Is You [1]...Sonny & Cher

ALBUMS
- *POP* Santana III [3]...Santana
- *R&B* Shaft [10]...Isaac Hayes/Soundtrack
- *C&W* Easy Loving [5]...Freddie Hart

December 4, 1971
SINGLES
- *HOT* *Family Affair [1]...Sly & The Family Stone
- *R&B* *Family Affair [1]...Sly & The Family Stone
- *C&W* Kiss An Angel Good Mornin' [1]...Charley Pride
- *A/C* All I Ever Need Is You [2]...Sonny & Cher

ALBUMS
- *POP* Santana III [4]...Santana
- *R&B* Shaft [11]...Isaac Hayes/Soundtrack
- *C&W* Easy Loving [6]...Freddie Hart

December 11, 1971
SINGLES
- *HOT* Family Affair [2]...Sly & The Family Stone
- *R&B* Family Affair [2]...Sly & The Family Stone
- *C&W* Kiss An Angel Good Mornin' [2]...Charley Pride
- *A/C* All I Ever Need Is You [3]...Sonny & Cher

ALBUMS
- *POP* Santana III [5]...Santana
- *R&B* Shaft [12]...Isaac Hayes/Soundtrack
- *C&W* Easy Loving [7]...Freddie Hart

December 18, 1971
SINGLES
- *HOT* Family Affair [3]...Sly & The Family Stone
- *R&B* Family Affair [3]...Sly & The Family Stone
- *C&W* Kiss An Angel Good Mornin' [3]...Charley Pride
- *A/C* All I Ever Need Is You [4]...Sonny & Cher

ALBUMS
- *POP* There's A Riot Goin' On [1]...Sly & The Family Stone
- *R&B* Shaft [13]...Isaac Hayes/Soundtrack
- *C&W* Easy Loving [8]...Freddie Hart

December 25, 1971
SINGLES
- *HOT* Brand New Key [1]...Melanie
- *R&B* Family Affair [4]...Sly & The Family Stone
- *C&W* Kiss An Angel Good Mornin' [4]...Charley Pride
- *A/C* All I Ever Need Is You [5]...Sonny & Cher

ALBUMS
- *POP* There's A Riot Goin' On [2]...Sly & The Family Stone
- *R&B* Shaft [14]...Isaac Hayes/Soundtrack
- *C&W* Easy Loving [9]...Freddie Hart

January 1, 1972
SINGLES
- *HOT* Brand New Key [2]...Melanie
- *R&B* Family Affair [5]...Sly & The Family Stone
- *C&W* Kiss An Angel Good Mornin' [5]...Charley Pride
- *A/C* An Old Fashioned Love Song [1]...Three Dog Night

ALBUMS
- *POP* Music [1]...Carole King
- *R&B* There's A Riot Goin' On [1]...Sly & The Family Stone
- *C&W* Charley Pride Sings Heart Songs [1]...Charley Pride

January 8, 1972
SINGLES
- HOT   Brand New Key [3]...Melanie
- R&B   *Let's Stay Together [1]...Al Green
- C&W   Would You Take Another Chance On Me/ Me And Bobby McGee [1]...Jerry Lee Lewis
- A/C   Cherish [1]...David Cassidy

ALBUMS
- POP   Music [2]...Carole King
- R&B   There's A Riot Goin' On [2]...Sly & The Family Stone
- C&W   Charley Pride Sings Heart Songs [2]...Charley Pride

January 15, 1972
SINGLES
- HOT   *American Pie - Parts I & II [1]...Don McLean
- R&B   Let's Stay Together [2]...Al Green
- C&W   Carolyn [1]...Merle Haggard
- A/C   *American Pie - Parts I & II [1]...Don McLean

ALBUMS
- POP   Music [3]...Carole King
- R&B   Black Moses [1]...Isaac Hayes
- C&W   Charley Pride Sings Heart Songs [3]...Charley Pride

January 22, 1972
SINGLES
- HOT   American Pie - Parts I & II [2]...Don McLean
- R&B   Let's Stay Together [3]...Al Green
- C&W   Carolyn [2]...Merle Haggard
- A/C   American Pie - Parts I & II [2]...Don McLean

ALBUMS
- POP   American Pie [1]...Don McLean
- R&B   Black Moses [2]...Isaac Hayes
- C&W   Charley Pride Sings Heart Songs [4]...Charley Pride

January 29, 1972
SINGLES
- HOT   American Pie - Parts I & II [3]...Don McLean
- R&B   Let's Stay Together [4]...Al Green
- C&W   Carolyn [3]...Merle Haggard
- A/C   American Pie - Parts I & II [3]...Don McLean

ALBUMS
- POP   American Pie [2]...Don McLean
- R&B   Black Moses [3]...Isaac Hayes
- C&W   Charley Pride Sings Heart Songs [5]...Charley Pride

February 5, 1972
SINGLES
- HOT   American Pie - Parts I & II [4]...Don McLean
- R&B   Let's Stay Together [5]...Al Green
- C&W   One's On The Way [1]...Loretta Lynn
- A/C   Hurting Each Other [1]...Carpenters

ALBUMS
- POP   American Pie [3]...Don McLean
- R&B   Black Moses [4]...Isaac Hayes
- C&W   Charley Pride Sings Heart Songs [6]...Charley Pride

February 12, 1972
SINGLES
- HOT   Let's Stay Together [1]...Al Green
- R&B   Let's Stay Together [6]...Al Green
- C&W   One's On The Way [2]...Loretta Lynn
- A/C   Hurting Each Other [2]...Carpenters

ALBUMS
- POP   American Pie [4]...Don McLean
- R&B   Black Moses [5]...Isaac Hayes
- C&W   Charley Pride Sings Heart Songs [7]...Charley Pride

February 19, 1972
SINGLES
- HOT   *Without You [1]...Nilsson
- R&B   Let's Stay Together [7]...Al Green
- C&W   It's Four In The Morning [1]...Faron Young
- A/C   *Without You [1]...Nilsson

ALBUMS
- POP   American Pie [5]...Don McLean
- R&B   Black Moses [6]...Isaac Hayes
- C&W   Charley Pride Sings Heart Songs [8]...Charley Pride

February 26, 1972
SINGLES
- HOT   Without You [2]...Nilsson
- R&B   Let's Stay Together [8]...Al Green
- C&W   It's Four In The Morning [2]...Faron Young
- A/C   Without You [2]...Nilsson

ALBUMS
- POP   American Pie [6]...Don McLean
- R&B   Black Moses [7]...Isaac Hayes
- C&W   Charley Pride Sings Heart Songs [9]...Charley Pride

March 4, 1972
SINGLES
- HOT   Without You [3]...Nilsson
- R&B   Let's Stay Together [9]...Al Green
- C&W   Bedtime Story [1]...Tammy Wynette
- A/C   Without You [3]...Nilsson

ALBUMS
- POP   American Pie [7]...Don McLean
- R&B   Solid Rock [1]...The Temptations
- C&W   Charley Pride Sings Heart Songs [10]...Charley Pride

March 11, 1972
SINGLES
- HOT   Without You [4]...Nilsson
- R&B   Talking Loud And Saying Nothing (Part I) [1]...James Brown
- C&W   My Hang-Up Is You [1]...Freddie Hart
- A/C   Without You [4]...Nilsson

ALBUMS
- POP   Harvest [1]...Neil Young
- R&B   Solid Rock [2]...The Temptations
- C&W   Charley Pride Sings Heart Songs [11]...Charley Pride

March 18, 1972

SINGLES
- HOT Heart Of Gold [1]...Neil Young
- R&B I Gotcha [1]...Joe Tex
- C&W My Hang-Up Is You [2]...Freddie Hart
- A/C Without You [5]...Nilsson

ALBUMS
- POP Harvest [2]...Neil Young
- R&B Let's Stay Together [1]...Al Green
- C&W Charley Pride Sings Heart Songs [12]...Charley Pride

March 25, 1972

SINGLES
- HOT A Horse With No Name [1]...America
- R&B In The Rain [1]...The Dramatics
- C&W My Hang-Up Is You [3]...Freddie Hart
- A/C Rock And Roll Lullaby [1]...B.J. Thomas

ALBUMS
- POP America [1]...America
- R&B Let's Stay Together [2]...Al Green
- C&W Charley Pride Sings Heart Songs [13]...Charley Pride

April 1, 1972

SINGLES
- HOT A Horse With No Name [2]...America
- R&B In The Rain [2]...The Dramatics
- C&W My Hang-Up Is You [4]...Freddie Hart
- A/C *The First Time Ever I Saw Your Face [1]...
  Roberta Flack

ALBUMS
- POP America [2]...America
- R&B Let's Stay Together [3]...Al Green
- C&W Charley Pride Sings Heart Songs [14]...Charley Pride

April 8, 1972

SINGLES
- HOT A Horse With No Name [3]...America
- R&B In The Rain [3]...The Dramatics
- C&W My Hang-Up Is You [5]...Freddie Hart
- A/C The First Time Ever I Saw Your Face [2]...
  Roberta Flack

ALBUMS
- POP America [3]...America
- R&B Let's Stay Together [4]...Al Green
- C&W Charley Pride Sings Heart Songs [15]...Charley Pride

April 15, 1972

SINGLES
- HOT The First Time Ever I Saw Your Face [1]...
  Roberta Flack
- R&B In The Rain [4]...The Dramatics
- C&W My Hang-Up Is You [6]...Freddie Hart
- A/C The First Time Ever I Saw Your Face [3]...
  Roberta Flack

ALBUMS
- POP America [4]...America
- R&B Let's Stay Together [5]...Al Green
- C&W Charley Pride Sings Heart Songs [16]...Charley Pride

April 22, 1972

SINGLES
- HOT The First Time Ever I Saw Your Face [2]...
  Roberta Flack
- R&B Day Dreaming [1]...Aretha Franklin
- C&W Chantilly Lace/Think About It Darlin' [1]...
  Jerry Lee Lewis
- A/C The First Time Ever I Saw Your Face [4]...
  Roberta Flack

ALBUMS
- POP America [5]...America
- R&B Let's Stay Together [6]...Al Green
- C&W The Best Of Charley Pride, Volume 2 [1]...
  Charley Pride

April 29, 1972

SINGLES
- HOT The First Time Ever I Saw Your Face [3]...
  Roberta Flack
- R&B Day Dreaming [2]...Aretha Franklin
- C&W Chantilly Lace/Think About It Darlin' [2]...
  Jerry Lee Lewis
- A/C The First Time Ever I Saw Your Face [5]...
  Roberta Flack

ALBUMS
- POP First Take [1]...Roberta Flack
- R&B Let's Stay Together [7]...Al Green
- C&W The Best Of Charley Pride, Volume 2 [2]...
  Charley Pride

May 6, 1972

SINGLES
- HOT The First Time Ever I Saw Your Face [4]...
  Roberta Flack
- R&B *I'll Take You There [1]...The Staple Singers
- C&W Chantilly Lace/Think About It Darlin' [3]...
  Jerry Lee Lewis
- A/C The First Time Ever I Saw Your Face [6]...
  Roberta Flack

ALBUMS
- POP First Take [2]...Roberta Flack
- R&B Let's Stay Together [8]...Al Green
- C&W The Best Of Charley Pride, Volume 2 [3]...
  Charley Pride

May 13, 1972

SINGLES
- HOT   The First Time Ever I Saw Your Face [5]...Roberta Flack
- R&B   I'll Take You There [2]...The Staple Singers
- C&W   Grandma Harp/Turnin' Off A Memory [1]...Merle Haggard
- A/C   Morning Has Broken [1]...Cat Stevens

ALBUMS
- POP   First Take [3]...Roberta Flack
- R&B   Let's Stay Together [9]...Al Green
- C&W   The Best Of Charley Pride, Volume 2 [4]...Charley Pride

May 20, 1972

SINGLES
- HOT   The First Time Ever I Saw Your Face [6]...Roberta Flack
- R&B   I'll Take You There [3]...The Staple Singers
- C&W   Grandma Harp/Turnin' Off A Memory [2]...Merle Haggard
- A/C   *The Candy Man [1]...Sammy Davis, Jr.

ALBUMS
- POP   First Take [4]...Roberta Flack
- R&B   Let's Stay Together [10]...Al Green
- C&W   The Best Of Charley Pride, Volume 2 [5]...Charley Pride

May 27, 1972

SINGLES
- HOT   *Oh Girl [1]...Chi-Lites
- R&B   I'll Take You There [4]...The Staple Singers
- C&W   (Lost Her Love) On Our Last Date [1]...Conway Twitty
- A/C   The Candy Man [2]...Sammy Davis, Jr.

ALBUMS
- POP   First Take [5]...Roberta Flack
- R&B   First Take [1]...Roberta Flack
- C&W   The Best Of Charley Pride, Volume 2 [6]...Charley Pride

June 3, 1972

SINGLES
- HOT   I'll Take You There [1]...The Staple Singers
- R&B   Oh Girl [1]...Chi-Lites
- C&W   The Happiest Girl In The Whole U.S.A. [1]...Donna Fargo
- A/C   *Song Sung Blue [1]...Neil Diamond

ALBUMS
- POP   Thick As A Brick [1]...Jethro Tull
- R&B   First Take [2]...Roberta Flack
- C&W   The Best Of Charley Pride, Volume 2 [7]...Charley Pride

June 10, 1972

SINGLES
- HOT   The Candy Man [1]...Sammy Davis, Jr.
- R&B   Oh Girl [2]...The Chi-Lites
- C&W   The Happiest Girl In The Whole U.S.A. [2]...Donna Fargo
- A/C   Song Sung Blue [2]...Neil Diamond

ALBUMS
- POP   Thick As A Brick [2]...Jethro Tull
- R&B   A Lonely Man [1]...The Chi-Lites
- C&W   The Best Of Charley Pride, Volume 2 [8]...Charley Pride

June 17, 1972

SINGLES
- HOT   The Candy Man [2]...Sammy Davis, Jr.
- R&B   Woman's Gotta Have It [1]...Bobby Womack
- C&W   The Happiest Girl In The Whole U.S.A. [3]...Donna Fargo
- A/C   Song Sung Blue [3]...Neil Diamond

ALBUMS
- POP   Exile On Main St. [1]...The Rolling Stones
- R&B   A Lonely Man [2]...The Chi-Lites
- C&W   The Best Of Charley Pride, Volume 2 [9]...Charley Pride

June 24, 1972

SINGLES
- HOT   The Candy Man [3]...Sammy Davis, Jr.
- R&B   *Lean On Me [1]...Bill Withers
- C&W   That's Why I Love You Like I Do [1]...Sonny James
- A/C   Song Sung Blue [4]...Neil Diamond

ALBUMS
- POP   Exile On Main St. [2]...The Rolling Stones
- R&B   A Lonely Man [3]...The Chi-Lites
- C&W   The Best Of Charley Pride, Volume 2 [10]...Charley Pride

July 1, 1972

SINGLES
- HOT   Song Sung Blue [1]...Neil Diamond
- R&B   Outa-Space [1]...Billy Preston
- C&W   Eleven Roses [1]...Hank Williams, Jr.
- A/C   Song Sung Blue [5]...Neil Diamond

ALBUMS
- POP   Exile On Main St. [3]...The Rolling Stones
- R&B   A Lonely Man [4]...The Chi-Lites
- C&W   The Best Of Charley Pride, Volume 2 [11]...Charley Pride

July 8, 1972

SINGLES
- HOT Lean On Me [1]...Bill Withers
- R&B (If Loving You Is Wrong) I Don't Want To Be Right [1]...Luther Ingram
- C&W Eleven Roses [2]...Hank Williams, Jr.
- A/C Song Sung Blue [6]...Neil Diamond

ALBUMS
- POP Exile On Main St. [4]...The Rolling Stones
- R&B A Lonely Man [5]...The Chi-Lites
- C&W The Best Of Charley Pride, Volume 2 [12]...Charley Pride

July 15, 1972

SINGLES
- HOT Lean On Me [2]...Bill Withers
- R&B (If Loving You Is Wrong) I Don't Want To Be Right [2]...Luther Ingram
- C&W Made In Japan [1]...Buck Owens
- A/C Song Sung Blue [7]...Neil Diamond

ALBUMS
- POP Honky Chateau [1]...Elton John
- R&B Still Bill [1]...Bill Withers
- C&W The Best Of Charley Pride, Volume 2 [13]...Charley Pride

July 22, 1972

SINGLES
- HOT Lean On Me [3]...Bill Withers
- R&B (If Loving You Is Wrong) I Don't Want To Be Right [3]...Luther Ingram
- C&W It's Gonna Take A Little Bit Longer [1]...Charley Pride
- A/C *Where Is The Love [1]...Roberta Flack & Donny Hathaway

ALBUMS
- POP Honky Chateau [2]...Elton John
- R&B Still Bill [2]...Bill Withers
- C&W The Best Of Charley Pride, Volume 2 [14]...Charley Pride

July 29, 1972

SINGLES
- HOT *Alone Again (Naturally) [1]...Gilbert O'Sullivan
- R&B (If Loving You Is Wrong) I Don't Want To Be Right [4]...Luther Ingram
- C&W It's Gonna Take A Little Bit Longer [2]...Charley Pride
- A/C *Alone Again (Naturally) [1]...Gilbert O'Sullivan

ALBUMS
- POP Honky Chateau [3]...Elton John
- R&B Still Bill [3]...Bill Withers
- C&W The Best Of Charley Pride, Volume 2 [15]...Charley Pride

August 5, 1972

SINGLES
- HOT Alone Again (Naturally) [2]...Gilbert O'Sullivan
- R&B Where Is The Love [1]...Roberta Flack & Donny Hathaway
- C&W It's Gonna Take A Little Bit Longer [3]...Charley Pride
- A/C Alone Again (Naturally) [2]...Gilbert O'Sullivan

ALBUMS
- POP Honky Chateau [4]...Elton John
- R&B Still Bill [4]...Bill Withers
- C&W The Best Of Charley Pride, Volume 2 [16]...Charley Pride

August 12, 1972

SINGLES
- HOT Alone Again (Naturally) [3]...Gilbert O'Sullivan
- R&B I'm Still In Love With You [1]...Al Green
- C&W Bless Your Heart [1]...Freddie Hart
- A/C Alone Again (Naturally) [3]...Gilbert O'Sullivan

ALBUMS
- POP Honky Chateau [5]...Elton John
- R&B Still Bill [5]...Bill Withers
- C&W The Happiest Girl In The Whole U.S.A. [1]...Donna Fargo

August 19, 1972

SINGLES
- HOT Alone Again (Naturally) [4]...Gilbert O'Sullivan
- R&B I'm Still In Love With You [2]...Al Green
- C&W Bless Your Heart [2]...Freddie Hart
- A/C Alone Again (Naturally) [4]...Gilbert O'Sullivan

ALBUMS
- POP Chicago V [1]...Chicago
- R&B Still Bill [6]...Bill Withers
- C&W The Happiest Girl In The Whole U.S.A. [2]...Donna Fargo

August 26, 1972

SINGLES
- HOT Brandy (You're A Fine Girl) [1]...Looking Glass
- R&B Power Of Love [1]...Joe Simon
- C&W If You Leave Me Tonight I'll Cry [1]...Jerry Wallace
- A/C Alone Again (Naturally) [5]...Gilbert O'Sullivan

ALBUMS
- POP Chicago V [2]...Chicago
- R&B [CHART DISCONTINUED UNTIL 10/14/72]
- C&W The Happiest Girl In The Whole U.S.A. [3]...Donna Fargo

September 2, 1972
SINGLES
- HOT Alone Again (Naturally) [5]...Gilbert O'Sullivan
- R&B Power Of Love [2]...Joe Simon
- C&W Woman (Sensuous Woman) [1]...Don Gibson
- A/C Alone Again (Naturally) [6]...Gilbert O'Sullivan

ALBUMS
- POP Chicago V [3]...Chicago
- R&B [CHART DISCONTINUED UNTIL 10/14/72]
- C&W The Happiest Girl In The Whole U.S.A. [4]...Donna Fargo

September 9, 1972
SINGLES
- HOT Alone Again (Naturally) [6]...Gilbert O'Sullivan
- R&B Back Stabbers [1]...The O'Jays
- C&W If You Leave Me Tonight I'll Cry [2]...Jerry Wallace
- A/C The Guitar Man [1]...Bread

ALBUMS
- POP Chicago V [4]...Chicago
- R&B [CHART DISCONTINUED UNTIL 10/14/72]
- C&W To Get To You [1]...Jerry Wallace

September 16, 1972
SINGLES
- HOT *Black & White [1]...Three Dog Night
- R&B Get On The Good Foot (Part 1) [1]...James Brown
- C&W When The Snow Is On The Roses [1]...Sonny James
- A/C *Baby Don't Get Hooked On Me [1]...Mac Davis

ALBUMS
- POP Chicago V [5]...Chicago
- R&B [CHART DISCONTINUED UNTIL 10/14/72]
- C&W A Sunshine Day with Charley Pride [1]...Charley Pride

September 23, 1972
SINGLES
- HOT Baby Don't Get Hooked On Me [1]...Mac Davis
- R&B Get On The Good Foot (Part 1) [2]...James Brown
- C&W I Can't Stop Loving You [1]...Conway Twitty
- A/C Baby Don't Get Hooked On Me [2]...Mac Davis

ALBUMS
- POP Chicago V [6]...Chicago
- R&B [CHART DISCONTINUED UNTIL 10/14/72]
- C&W A Sunshine Day with Charley Pride [2]...Charley Pride

September 30, 1972
SINGLES
- HOT Baby Don't Get Hooked On Me [2]...Mac Davis
- R&B Get On The Good Foot (Part 1) [3]...James Brown
- C&W I Ain't Never [1]...Mel Tillis
- A/C Baby Don't Get Hooked On Me [3]...Mac Davis

ALBUMS
- POP Chicago V [7]...Chicago
- R&B [CHART DISCONTINUED UNTIL 10/14/72]
- C&W A Sunshine Day with Charley Pride [3]...Charley Pride

October 7, 1972
SINGLES
- HOT Baby Don't Get Hooked On Me [3]...Mac Davis
- R&B Get On The Good Foot (Part 1) [4]...James Brown
- C&W I Ain't Never [2]...Mel Tillis
- A/C Black & White [1]...Three Dog Night

ALBUMS
- POP Chicago V [8]...Chicago
- R&B [CHART DISCONTINUED UNTIL 10/14/72]
- C&W A Sunshine Day with Charley Pride [4]...Charley Pride

October 14, 1972
SINGLES
- HOT Ben [1]...Michael Jackson
- R&B I'll Be Around/How Could I Let You Get Away [1]...Spinners
- C&W Funny Face [1]...Donna Fargo
- A/C Garden Party [1]...Rick Nelson & The Stone Canyon Band

ALBUMS
- POP Chicago V [9]...Chicago
- R&B Superfly [1]...Curtis Mayfield/Soundtrack
- C&W A Sunshine Day with Charley Pride [5]...Charley Pride

October 21, 1972
SINGLES
- HOT My Ding-A-Ling [1]...Chuck Berry
- R&B I'll Be Around/How Could I Let You Get Away [2]...Spinners
- C&W Funny Face [2]...Donna Fargo
- A/C Garden Party [2]...Rick Nelson & The Stone Canyon Band

ALBUMS
- POP Superfly [1]...Curtis Mayfield/Soundtrack
- R&B Superfly [2]...Curtis Mayfield/Soundtrack
- C&W A Sunshine Day with Charley Pride [6]...Charley Pride

October 28, 1972
SINGLES
- HOT   My Ding-A-Ling [2]...Chuck Berry
- R&B   I'll Be Around [3]...Spinners
- C&W   Funny Face [3]...Donna Fargo
- A/C   If I Could Reach You [1]...The 5th Dimension

ALBUMS
- POP   Superfly [2]...Curtis Mayfield/Soundtrack
- R&B   Superfly [3]...Curtis Mayfield/Soundtrack
- C&W   A Sunshine Day with Charley Pride [7]...Charley Pride

November 4, 1972
SINGLES
- HOT   *I Can See Clearly Now [1]...Johnny Nash
- R&B   I'll Be Around [4]...Spinners
- C&W   It's Not Love (But It's Not Bad) [1]...Merle Haggard
- A/C   *I Can See Clearly Now [1]...Johnny Nash

ALBUMS
- POP   Superfly [3]...Curtis Mayfield/Soundtrack
- R&B   Superfly [4]...Curtis Mayfield/Soundtrack
- C&W   A Sunshine Day with Charley Pride [8]...Charley Pride

November 11, 1972
SINGLES
- HOT   I Can See Clearly Now [2]...Johnny Nash
- R&B   I'll Be Around [5]...Spinners
- C&W   My Man [1]...Tammy Wynette
- A/C   I Can See Clearly Now [2]...Johnny Nash

ALBUMS
- POP   Superfly [4]...Curtis Mayfield/Soundtrack
- R&B   Superfly [5]...Curtis Mayfield/Soundtrack
- C&W   A Sunshine Day with Charley Pride [9]...Charley Pride

November 18, 1972
SINGLES
- HOT   I Can See Clearly Now [3]...Johnny Nash
- R&B   If You Don't Know Me By Now [1]...Harold Melvin & The Blue Notes
- C&W   She's Too Good To Be True [1]...Charley Pride
- A/C   I Can See Clearly Now [3]...Johnny Nash

ALBUMS
- POP   Catch Bull At Four [1]...Cat Stevens
- R&B   Superfly [6]...Curtis Mayfield/Soundtrack
- C&W   A Sunshine Day with Charley Pride [10]...Charley Pride

November 25, 1972
SINGLES
- HOT   I Can See Clearly Now [4]...Johnny Nash
- R&B   If You Don't Know Me By Now [2]...Harold Melvin & The Blue Notes
- C&W   She's Too Good To Be True [2]...Charley Pride
- A/C   I Can See Clearly Now [4]...Johnny Nash

ALBUMS
- POP   Catch Bull At Four [2]...Cat Stevens
- R&B   All Directions [1]...The Temptations
- C&W   The Best Of The Best Of Merle Haggard [1]...Merle Haggard

December 2, 1972
SINGLES
- HOT   Papa Was A Rollin' Stone [1]...The Temptations
- R&B   You Ought To Be With Me [1]...Al Green
- C&W   She's Too Good To Be True [3]...Charley Pride
- A/C   I'd Love You To Want Me [1]...Lobo

ALBUMS
- POP   Catch Bull At Four [3]...Cat Stevens
- R&B   I'm Still In Love With You [1]...Al Green
- C&W   The Best Of The Best Of Merle Haggard [2]...Merle Haggard

December 9, 1972
SINGLES
- HOT   I Am Woman [1]...Helen Reddy
- R&B   *Me And Mrs. Jones [1]...Billy Paul
- C&W   Got The All Overs For You (All Over Me) [1]...Freddie Hart
- A/C   Clair [1]...Gilbert O'Sullivan

ALBUMS
- POP   Seventh Sojourn [1]...The Moody Blues
- R&B   I'm Still In Love With You [2]...Al Green
- C&W   The Best Of The Best Of Merle Haggard [3]...Merle Haggard

December 16, 1972
SINGLES
- HOT   Me And Mrs. Jones [1]...Billy Paul
- R&B   Me And Mrs. Jones [2]...Billy Paul
- C&W   Got The All Overs For You (All Over Me) [2]...Freddie Hart
- A/C   Clair [2]...Gilbert O'Sullivan

ALBUMS
- POP   Seventh Sojourn [2]...The Moody Blues
- R&B   I'm Still In Love With You [3]...Al Green
- C&W   The Best Of The Best Of Merle Haggard [4]...Merle Haggard

December 23, 1972
SINGLES
- HOT Me And Mrs. Jones [2]...Billy Paul
- R&B Me And Mrs. Jones [3]...Billy Paul
- C&W Got The All Overs For You (All Over Me) [3]...Freddie Hart
- A/C Clair [3]...Gilbert O'Sullivan

ALBUMS
- POP Seventh Sojourn [3]...The Moody Blues
- R&B I'm Still In Love With You [4]...Al Green
- C&W The Best Of The Best Of Merle Haggard [5]...Merle Haggard

December 30, 1972
SINGLES
- HOT Me And Mrs. Jones [3]...Billy Paul
- R&B Me And Mrs. Jones [4]...Billy Paul
- C&W She's Got To Be A Saint [1]...Ray Price
- A/C Sweet Surrender [1]...Bread

ALBUMS
- POP Seventh Sojourn [4]...The Moody Blues
- R&B I'm Still In Love With You [5]...Al Green
- C&W The Best Of The Best Of Merle Haggard [6]...Merle Haggard

January 6, 1973
SINGLES
- HOT *You're So Vain [1]...Carly Simon
- R&B *Superstition [1]...Stevie Wonder
- C&W She's Got To Be A Saint [2]...Ray Price
- A/C Sweet Surrender [2]...Bread

ALBUMS
- POP Seventh Sojourn [5]...The Moody Blues
- R&B 360 Degrees Of Billy Paul [1]...Billy Paul
- C&W The Best Of The Best Of Merle Haggard [7]...Merle Haggard

January 13, 1973
SINGLES
- HOT You're So Vain [2]...Carly Simon
- R&B Superstition [2]...Stevie Wonder
- C&W She's Got To Be A Saint [3]...Ray Price
- A/C Been To Canaan [1]...Carole King

ALBUMS
- POP No Secrets [1]...Carly Simon
- R&B 360 Degrees Of Billy Paul [2]...Billy Paul
- C&W Got The All Overs For You [1]...Freddie Hart

January 20, 1973
SINGLES
- HOT You're So Vain [3]...Carly Simon
- R&B Superstition [3]...Stevie Wonder
- C&W Soul Song [1]...Joe Stampley
- A/C You're So Vain [1]...Carly Simon

ALBUMS
- POP No Secrets [2]...Carly Simon
- R&B Talking Book [1]...Stevie Wonder
- C&W Got The All Overs For You [2]...Freddie Hart

January 27, 1973
SINGLES
- HOT Superstition [1]...Stevie Wonder
- R&B Why Can't We Live Together [1]...Timmy Thomas
- C&W (Old Dogs-Children And) Watermelon Wine [1]...Tom T. Hall
- A/C You're So Vain [2]...Carly Simon

ALBUMS
- POP No Secrets [3]...Carly Simon
- R&B Talking Book [2]...Stevie Wonder
- C&W It's Not Love (But It's Not Bad) [1]...Merle Haggard

February 3, 1973
SINGLES
- HOT Crocodile Rock [1]...Elton John
- R&B Why Can't We Live Together [2]...Timmy Thomas
- C&W She Needs Someone To Hold Her (When She Cries) [1]...Conway Twitty
- A/C Don't Expect Me To Be Your Friend [1]...Lobo

ALBUMS
- POP No Secrets [4]...Carly Simon
- R&B Talking Book [3]...Stevie Wonder
- C&W It's Not Love (But It's Not Bad) [2]...Merle Haggard

February 10, 1973
SINGLES
- HOT Crocodile Rock [2]...Elton John
- R&B Could It Be I'm Falling In Love [1]...Spinners
- C&W She Needs Someone To Hold Her (When She Cries) [2]...Conway Twitty
- A/C Don't Expect Me To Be Your Friend [2]...Lobo

ALBUMS
- POP No Secrets [5]...Carly Simon
- R&B The World Is A Ghetto [1]...War
- C&W It's Not Love (But It's Not Bad) [3]...Merle Haggard

February 17, 1973
SINGLES
- HOT Crocodile Rock [3]...Elton John
- R&B *Love Train [1]...O'Jays
- C&W I Wonder If They Ever Think Of Me [1]...Merle Haggard
- A/C Dueling Banjos [1]...Eric Weissberg & Steve Mandell

ALBUMS
- POP The World Is A Ghetto [1]...War
- R&B The World Is A Ghetto [2]...War
- C&W Songs of Love by Charley Pride [1]...Charley Pride

February 24, 1973
SINGLES
- HOT Killing Me Softly With His Song [1]...Roberta Flack
- R&B Love Train [2]...O'Jays
- C&W Rated "X" [1]...Loretta Lynn
- A/C Dueling Banjos [2]...Eric Weissberg & Steve Mandell

ALBUMS
- POP The World Is A Ghetto [2]...War
- R&B The World Is A Ghetto [3]...War
- C&W Songs of Love by Charley Pride [2]...Charley Pride

March 3, 1973
SINGLES
- HOT Killing Me Softly With His Song [2]...Roberta Flack
- R&B Love Train [3]...O'Jays
- C&W The Lord Knows I'm Drinking [1]...Cal Smith
- A/C Last Song [1]...Edward Bear

ALBUMS
- POP Don't Shoot Me I'm Only The Piano Player [1]...Elton John
- R&B The World Is A Ghetto [4]...War
- C&W Songs of Love by Charley Pride [3]...Charley Pride

March 10, 1973
SINGLES
- HOT Killing Me Softly With His Song [3]...Roberta Flack
- R&B Love Train [4]...O'Jays
- C&W 'Til I Get It Right [1]...Tammy Wynette
- A/C Last Song [2]...Edward Bear

ALBUMS
- POP Don't Shoot Me I'm Only The Piano Player [2]...Elton John
- R&B The World Is A Ghetto [5]...War
- C&W Songs of Love by Charley Pride [4]...Charley Pride

March 17, 1973
SINGLES
- HOT Killing Me Softly With His Song [4]...Roberta Flack
- R&B Neither One Of Us (Wants To Be The First To Say Goodbye) [1]...Gladys Knight & The Pips
- C&W Teddy Bear Song [1]...Barbara Fairchild
- A/C Danny's Song [1]...Anne Murray

ALBUMS
- POP Dueling Banjos [1]...Eric Weissberg
- R&B The World Is A Ghetto [6]...War
- C&W Dueling Banjos [1]...Eric Weissberg

March 24, 1973
SINGLES
- HOT Love Train [1]...O'Jays
- R&B Neither One Of Us (Wants To Be The First To Say Goodbye) [2]...Gladys Knight & The Pips
- C&W Teddy Bear Song [2]...Barbara Fairchild
- A/C Danny's Song [2]...Anne Murray

ALBUMS
- POP Dueling Banjos [2]...Eric Weissberg
- R&B The World Is A Ghetto [7]...War
- C&W Dueling Banjos [2]...Eric Weissberg

March 31, 1973
SINGLES
- HOT Killing Me Softly With His Song [5]...Roberta Flack
- R&B Neither One Of Us (Wants To Be The First To Say Goodbye) [3]...Gladys Knight & The Pips
- C&W Keep Me In Mind [1]...Lynn Anderson
- A/C Sing [1]...Carpenters

ALBUMS
- POP Dueling Banjos [3]...Eric Weissberg
- R&B Wattstax: The Living Word [1]...Soundtrack
- C&W Dueling Banjos [3]...Eric Weissberg

April 7, 1973
SINGLES
- HOT The Night The Lights Went Out In Georgia [1]...Vicki Lawrence
- R&B Neither One Of Us (Wants To Be The First To Say Goodbye) [4]...Gladys Knight & The Pips
- C&W Super Kind Of Woman [1]...Freddie Hart
- A/C *Tie A Yellow Ribbon Round The Ole Oak Tree [1]...Dawn featuring Tony Orlando

ALBUMS
- POP Lady Sings The Blues [1]...Diana Ross/Soundtrack
- R&B Wattstax: The Living Word [2]...Soundtrack
- C&W Dueling Banjos [4]...Eric Weissberg

April 14, 1973

SINGLES
- HOT The Night The Lights Went Out In Georgia [2]...Vicki Lawrence
- R&B Masterpiece [1]...The Temptations
- C&W A Shoulder To Cry On [1]...Charley Pride
- A/C Sing [2]...Carpenters

ALBUMS
- POP Lady Sings The Blues [2]...Diana Ross/Soundtrack
- R&B Neither One Of Us [1]...Gladys Knight & The Pips
- C&W Aloha from Hawaii via Satellite [1]...Elvis Presley

April 21, 1973

SINGLES
- HOT Tie A Yellow Ribbon Round The Ole Oak Tree [1]...Dawn featuring Tony Orlando
- R&B Masterpiece [2]...The Temptations
- C&W Superman [1]...Donna Fargo
- A/C Tie A Yellow Ribbon Round The Ole Oak Tree [2]...Dawn featuring Tony Orlando

ALBUMS
- POP Billion Dollar Babies [1]...Alice Cooper
- R&B Neither One Of Us [2]...Gladys Knight & The Pips
- C&W Aloha from Hawaii via Satellite [2]...Elvis Presley

April 28, 1973

SINGLES
- HOT Tie A Yellow Ribbon Round The Ole Oak Tree [2]...Dawn featuring Tony Orlando
- R&B Pillow Talk [1]...Sylvia
- C&W Behind Closed Doors [1]...Charlie Rich
- A/C *You Are The Sunshine Of My Life [1]...Stevie Wonder

ALBUMS
- POP The Dark Side Of The Moon [1]...Pink Floyd
- R&B Masterpiece [1]...The Temptations
- C&W Aloha from Hawaii via Satellite [3]...Elvis Presley

May 5, 1973

SINGLES
- HOT Tie A Yellow Ribbon Round The Ole Oak Tree [3]...Dawn featuring Tony Orlando
- R&B Pillow Talk [2]...Sylvia
- C&W Behind Closed Doors [2]...Charlie Rich
- A/C You Are The Sunshine Of My Life [2]...Stevie Wonder

ALBUMS
- POP Aloha from Hawaii via Satellite [1]...Elvis Presley
- R&B Masterpiece [2]...The Temptations
- C&W Aloha from Hawaii via Satellite [4]...Elvis Presley

May 12, 1973

SINGLES
- HOT Tie A Yellow Ribbon Round The Ole Oak Tree [4]...Dawn featuring Tony Orlando
- R&B Funky Worm [1]...Ohio Players
- C&W Come Live With Me [1]...Roy Clark
- A/C Daniel [1]...Elton John

ALBUMS
- POP Houses Of The Holy [1]...Led Zeppelin
- R&B Spinners [1]...Spinners
- C&W My Second Album [1]...Donna Fargo

May 19, 1973

SINGLES
- HOT You Are The Sunshine Of My Life [1]...Stevie Wonder
- R&B Leaving Me [1]...The Independents
- C&W What's Your Mama's Name [1]...Tanya Tucker
- A/C Daniel [2]...Elton John

ALBUMS
- POP Houses Of The Holy [2]...Led Zeppelin
- R&B Spinners [2]...Spinners
- C&W Super Kind Of Woman [1]...Freddie Hart

May 26, 1973

SINGLES
- HOT Frankenstein [1]...Edgar Winter Group
- R&B I'm Gonna Love You Just A Little More Baby [1]...Barry White
- C&W Satin Sheets [1]...Jeanne Pruett
- A/C And I Love You So [1]...Perry Como

ALBUMS
- POP The Beatles/1967-1970 [1]...The Beatles
- R&B Spinners [3]...Spinners
- C&W introducing Johnny Rodriguez [1]...Johnny Rodriguez

June 2, 1973

SINGLES
- HOT *My Love [1]...Paul McCartney & Wings
- R&B I'm Gonna Love You Just A Little More Baby [2]...Barry White
- C&W Satin Sheets [2]...Jeanne Pruett
- A/C *My Love [1]...Paul McCartney & Wings

ALBUMS
- POP Red Rose Speedway [1]...Paul McCartney & Wings
- R&B Birth Day [1]...The New Birth
- C&W Entertainer Of The Year [1]...Loretta Lynn

June 9, 1973
SINGLES
- *HOT* My Love [2]...Paul McCartney & Wings
- *R&B* One Of A Kind (Love Affair) [1]...Spinners
- *C&W* You Always Come Back (To Hurting Me) [1]...Johnny Rodriguez
- *A/C* My Love [2]...Paul McCartney & Wings

ALBUMS
- *POP* Red Rose Speedway [2]...Paul McCartney & Wings
- *R&B* Call Me [1]...Al Green
- *C&W* The Rhymer And Other Five And Dimers [1]...Tom T. Hall

June 16, 1973
SINGLES
- *HOT* My Love [3]...Paul McCartney & Wings
- *R&B* One Of A Kind (Love Affair) [2]...Spinners
- *C&W* Kids Say The Darndest Things [1]...Tammy Wynette
- *A/C* My Love [3]...Paul McCartney & Wings

ALBUMS
- *POP* Red Rose Speedway [3]...Paul McCartney & Wings
- *R&B* Call Me [2]...Al Green
- *C&W* Behind Closed Doors [1]...Charlie Rich

June 23, 1973
SINGLES
- *HOT* My Love [4]...Paul McCartney & Wings
- *R&B* One Of A Kind (Love Affair) [3]...Spinners
- *C&W* Satin Sheets [3]...Jeanne Pruett
- *A/C* Boogie Woogie Bugle Boy [1]...Bette Midler

ALBUMS
- *POP* Living In The Material World [1]...George Harrison
- *R&B* Live At The Sahara Tahoe [1]...Isaac Hayes
- *C&W* Behind Closed Doors [2]...Charlie Rich

June 30, 1973
SINGLES
- *HOT* Give Me Love - (Give Me Peace On Earth) [1]...George Harrison
- *R&B* One Of A Kind (Love Affair) [4]...Spinners
- *C&W* Don't Fight The Feelings Of Love [1]...Charley Pride
- *A/C* Boogie Woogie Bugle Boy [2]...Bette Midler

ALBUMS
- *POP* Living In The Material World [2]...George Harrison
- *R&B* Live At The Sahara Tahoe [2]...Isaac Hayes
- *C&W* Behind Closed Doors [3]...Charlie Rich

July 7, 1973
SINGLES
- *HOT* Will It Go Round In Circles [1]...Billy Preston
- *R&B* Doing It To Death [1]...Fred Wesley & The J.B.'s
- *C&W* Why Me [1]...Kris Kristofferson
- *A/C* Yesterday Once More [1]...Carpenters

ALBUMS
- *POP* Living In The Material World [3]...George Harrison
- *R&B* I've Got So Much To Give [1]...Barry White
- *C&W* Good Time Charlie [1]...Charlie McCoy

July 14, 1973
SINGLES
- *HOT* Will It Go Round In Circles [2]...Billy Preston
- *R&B* Doing It To Death [2]...Fred Wesley & The J.B.'s
- *C&W* Love Is The Foundation [1]...Loretta Lynn
- *A/C* Yesterday Once More [2]...Carpenters

ALBUMS
- *POP* Living In The Material World [4]...George Harrison
- *R&B* I've Got So Much To Give [2]...Barry White
- *C&W* Behind Closed Doors [4]...Charlie Rich

July 21, 1973
SINGLES
- *HOT* Bad, Bad Leroy Brown [1]...Jim Croce
- *R&B* I Believe In You (You Believe In Me) [1]...Johnnie Taylor
- *C&W* Love Is The Foundation [2]...Loretta Lynn
- *A/C* Yesterday Once More [3]...Carpenters

ALBUMS
- *POP* Living In The Material World [5]...George Harrison
- *R&B* Back To The World [1]...Curtis Mayfield
- *C&W* Satin Sheets [1]...Jeanne Pruett

July 28, 1973
SINGLES
- *HOT* Bad, Bad Leroy Brown [2]...Jim Croce
- *R&B* I Believe In You (You Believe In Me) [2]...Johnnie Taylor
- *C&W* You Were Always There [1]...Donna Fargo
- *A/C* *Touch Me In The Morning [1]...Diana Ross

ALBUMS
- *POP* Chicago VI [1]...Chicago
- *R&B* Back To The World [2]...Curtis Mayfield
- *C&W* Satin Sheets [2]...Jeanne Pruett

August 4, 1973

SINGLES
- HOT The Morning After [1]...Maureen McGovern
- R&B Angel [1]...Aretha Franklin
- C&W Lord, Mr. Ford [1]...Jerry Reed
- A/C *Delta Dawn [1]...Helen Reddy

ALBUMS
- POP Chicago VI [2]...Chicago
- R&B Fresh [1]...Sly & The Family Stone
- C&W Satin Sheets [3]...Jeanne Pruett

August 11, 1973

SINGLES
- HOT The Morning After [2]...Maureen McGovern
- R&B Angel [2]...Aretha Franklin
- C&W Trip To Heaven [1]...Freddie Hart
- A/C Delta Dawn [2]...Helen Reddy

ALBUMS
- POP Chicago VI [3]...Chicago
- R&B Fresh [2]...Sly & The Family Stone
- C&W Satin Sheets [4]...Jeanne Pruett

August 18, 1973

SINGLES
- HOT Touch Me In The Morning [1]...Diana Ross
- R&B *Let's Get It On [1]...Marvin Gaye
- C&W Louisiana Woman, Mississippi Man [1]...
  Conway Twitty & Loretta Lynn
- A/C Say, Has Anybody Seen My Sweet Gypsy Rose [1]...Dawn featuring Tony Orlando

ALBUMS
- POP A Passion Play [1]...Jethro Tull
- R&B Fresh [3]...Sly & The Family Stone
- C&W Satin Sheets [5]...Jeanne Pruett

August 25, 1973

SINGLES
- HOT Brother Louie [1]...Stories
- R&B Let's Get It On [2]...Marvin Gaye
- C&W Everybody's Had The Blues [1]...Merle Haggard
- A/C Say, Has Anybody Seen My Sweet Gypsy Rose [2]...Dawn featuring Tony Orlando

ALBUMS
- POP Chicago VI [4]...Chicago
- R&B Touch Me In The Morning [1]...Diana Ross
- C&W Satin Sheets [6]...Jeanne Pruett

September 1, 1973

SINGLES
- HOT Brother Louie [2]...Stories
- R&B Let's Get It On [3]...Marvin Gaye
- C&W Everybody's Had The Blues [2]...Merle Haggard
- A/C Say, Has Anybody Seen My Sweet Gypsy Rose [3]...Dawn featuring Tony Orlando

ALBUMS
- POP Chicago VI [5]...Chicago
- R&B Touch Me In The Morning [2]...Diana Ross
- C&W Satin Sheets [7]...Jeanne Pruett

September 8, 1973

SINGLES
- HOT Let's Get It On [1]...Marvin Gaye
- R&B Let's Get It On [4]...Marvin Gaye
- C&W You've Never Been This Far Before [1]...
  Conway Twitty
- A/C Loves Me Like A Rock [1]...Paul Simon

ALBUMS
- POP Brothers And Sisters [1]...The Allman Brothers Band
- R&B Innervisions [1]...Stevie Wonder
- C&W Satin Sheets [8]...Jeanne Pruett

September 15, 1973

SINGLES
- HOT Delta Dawn [1]...Helen Reddy
- R&B Let's Get It On [5]...Marvin Gaye
- C&W You've Never Been This Far Before [2]...
  Conway Twitty
- A/C Loves Me Like A Rock [2]...Paul Simon

ALBUMS
- POP Brothers And Sisters [2]...The Allman Brothers Band
- R&B Innervisions [2]...Stevie Wonder
- C&W Louisiana Woman-Mississippi Man [1]...
  Conway Twitty-Loretta Lynn

September 22, 1973

SINGLES
- HOT Let's Get It On [2]...Marvin Gaye
- R&B Let's Get It On [6]...Marvin Gaye
- C&W You've Never Been This Far Before [3]...
  Conway Twitty
- A/C My Maria [1]...B.W. Stevenson

ALBUMS
- POP Brothers And Sisters [3]...The Allman Brothers Band
- R&B Deliver The Word [1]...War
- C&W I Love Dixie Blues...so I recorded "Live" in New Orleans [1]...Merle Haggard

September 29, 1973

SINGLES
- HOT We're An American Band [1]...Grand Funk
- R&B Higher Ground [1]...Stevie Wonder
- C&W Blood Red And Goin' Down [1]...Tanya Tucker
- A/C I'm Coming Home [1]...Johnny Mathis

ALBUMS
- POP Brothers And Sisters [4]...The Allman Brothers Band
- R&B Let's Get It On [1]...Marvin Gaye
- C&W I Love Dixie Blues...so I recorded "Live" in New Orleans [2]...Merle Haggard

October 6, 1973

SINGLES
- HOT Half-Breed [1]...Cher
- R&B *Keep On Truckin' (Part 1) [1]...Eddie Kendricks
- C&W You're The Best Thing That Ever Happened To Me [1]...Ray Price
- A/C All I Know [1]...Garfunkel

ALBUMS
- POP Brothers And Sisters [5]...The Allman Brothers Band
- R&B Let's Get It On [2]...Marvin Gaye
- C&W You've Never Been This Far Before/Baby's Gone [1]...Conway Twitty

October 13, 1973

SINGLES
- HOT Half-Breed [2]...Cher
- R&B Keep On Truckin' (Part 1) [2]...Eddie Kendricks
- C&W Ridin' My Thumb To Mexico [1]...Johnny Rodriguez
- A/C All I Know [2]...Garfunkel

ALBUMS
- POP Goats Head Soup [1]...The Rolling Stones
- R&B Let's Get It On [3]...Marvin Gaye
- C&W You've Never Been This Far Before/Baby's Gone [2]...Conway Twitty

October 20, 1973

SINGLES
- HOT Angie [1]...The Rolling Stones
- R&B *Midnight Train To Georgia [1]...Gladys Knight & The Pips
- C&W Ridin' My Thumb To Mexico [2]...Johnny Rodriguez
- A/C All I Know [3]...Garfunkel

ALBUMS
- POP Goats Head Soup [2]...The Rolling Stones
- R&B Let's Get It On [4]...Marvin Gaye
- C&W You've Never Been This Far Before/Baby's Gone [3]...Conway Twitty

October 27, 1973

SINGLES
- HOT Midnight Train To Georgia [1]...Gladys Knight & The Pips
- R&B Midnight Train To Georgia [2]...Gladys Knight & The Pips
- C&W We're Gonna Hold On [1]...George Jones & Tammy Wynette
- A/C All I Know [4]...Garfunkel

ALBUMS
- POP Goats Head Soup [3]...The Rolling Stones
- R&B Let's Get It On [5]...Marvin Gaye
- C&W Love Is The Foundation [1]...Loretta Lynn

November 3, 1973

SINGLES
- HOT Midnight Train To Georgia [2]...Gladys Knight & The Pips
- R&B Midnight Train To Georgia [3]...Gladys Knight & The Pips
- C&W We're Gonna Hold On [2]...George Jones & Tammy Wynette
- A/C *Paper Roses [1]...Marie Osmond

ALBUMS
- POP Goats Head Soup [4]...The Rolling Stones
- R&B Let's Get It On [6]...Marvin Gaye
- C&W Jesus Was A Capricorn [1]...Kris Kristofferson

November 10, 1973

SINGLES
- HOT Keep On Truckin' (Part 1) [1]...Eddie Kendricks
- R&B Midnight Train To Georgia [4]...Gladys Knight & The Pips
- C&W Paper Roses [1]...Marie Osmond
- A/C *The Most Beautiful Girl [1]...Charlie Rich

ALBUMS
- POP Goodbye Yellow Brick Road [1]...Elton John
- R&B Let's Get It On [7]...Marvin Gaye
- C&W Full Moon [1]...Kris Kristofferson & Rita Coolidge

November 17, 1973

SINGLES
- HOT Keep On Truckin' (Part 1) [2]...Eddie Kendricks
- R&B Space Race [1]...Billy Preston
- C&W Paper Roses [2]...Marie Osmond
- A/C The Most Beautiful Girl [2]...Charlie Rich

ALBUMS
- POP Goodbye Yellow Brick Road [2]...Elton John
- R&B Let's Get It On [8]...Marvin Gaye
- C&W Paper Roses [1]...Marie Osmond

November 24, 1973
SINGLES
- HOT   Photograph [1]...Ringo Starr
- R&B   The Love I Lost (Part 1) [1]...
        Harold Melvin & The Blue Notes
- C&W   The Most Beautiful Girl [1]...Charlie Rich
- A/C   The Most Beautiful Girl [3]...Charlie Rich

ALBUMS
- POP   Goodbye Yellow Brick Road [3]...Elton John
- R&B   Let's Get It On [9]...Marvin Gaye
- C&W   Paper Roses [2]...Marie Osmond

December 1, 1973
SINGLES
- HOT   Top Of The World [1]...Carpenters
- R&B   The Love I Lost (Part 1) [2]...
        Harold Melvin & The Blue Notes
- C&W   The Most Beautiful Girl [2]...Charlie Rich
- A/C   Leave Me Alone (Ruby Red Dress) [1]...Helen Reddy

ALBUMS
- POP   Goodbye Yellow Brick Road [4]...Elton John
- R&B   Let's Get It On [10]...Marvin Gaye
- C&W   Paper Roses [3]...Marie Osmond

December 8, 1973
SINGLES
- HOT   Top Of The World [2]...Carpenters
- R&B   If You're Ready (Come Go With Me) [1]...
        The Staple Singers
- C&W   The Most Beautiful Girl [3]...Charlie Rich
- A/C   Leave Me Alone (Ruby Red Dress) [2]...Helen Reddy

ALBUMS
- POP   Goodbye Yellow Brick Road [5]...Elton John
- R&B   Let's Get It On [11]...Marvin Gaye
- C&W   Primrose Lane/Don't Give Up On Me [1]...
        Jerry Wallace

December 15, 1973
SINGLES
- HOT   The Most Beautiful Girl [1]...Charlie Rich
- R&B   If You're Ready (Come Go With Me) [2]...
        The Staple Singers
- C&W   Amazing Love [1]...Charley Pride
- A/C   Leave Me Alone (Ruby Red Dress) [3]...Helen Reddy

ALBUMS
- POP   Goodbye Yellow Brick Road [6]...Elton John
- R&B   Imagination [1]...Gladys Knight & The Pips
- C&W   Behind Closed Doors [5]...Charlie Rich

December 22, 1973
SINGLES
- HOT   The Most Beautiful Girl [2]...Charlie Rich
- R&B   If You're Ready (Come Go With Me) [3]...
        The Staple Singers
- C&W   If We Make It Through December [1]...
        Merle Haggard
- A/C   Leave Me Alone (Ruby Red Dress) [4]...Helen Reddy

ALBUMS
- POP   Goodbye Yellow Brick Road [7]...Elton John
- R&B   Imagination [2]...Gladys Knight & The Pips
- C&W   Behind Closed Doors [6]...Charlie Rich

December 29, 1973
SINGLES
- HOT   *Time In A Bottle [1]...Jim Croce
- R&B   Living For The City [1]...Stevie Wonder
- C&W   If We Make It Through December [2]...
        Merle Haggard
- A/C   *Time In A Bottle [1]...Jim Croce

ALBUMS
- POP   Goodbye Yellow Brick Road [8]...Elton John
- R&B   Imagination [3]...Gladys Knight & The Pips
- C&W   Behind Closed Doors [7]...Charlie Rich

January 5, 1974
SINGLES
- HOT   Time In A Bottle [2]...Jim Croce
- R&B   Living For The City [2]...Stevie Wonder
- C&W   If We Make It Through December [3]...
        Merle Haggard
- A/C   Time In A Bottle [2]...Jim Croce

ALBUMS
- POP   The Singles 1969-1973 [1]...Carpenters
- R&B   Imagination [4]...Gladys Knight & The Pips
- C&W   Behind Closed Doors [8]...Charlie Rich

January 12, 1974
SINGLES
- HOT   The Joker [1]...Steve Miller Band
- R&B   Until You Come Back To Me (That's What I'm
        Gonna Do) [1]...Aretha Franklin
- C&W   If We Make It Through December [4]...
        Merle Haggard
- A/C   *The Way We Were [1]...Barbra Streisand

ALBUMS
- POP   You Don't Mess Around With Jim [1]...Jim Croce
- R&B   Imagination [5]...Gladys Knight & The Pips
- C&W   Behind Closed Doors [9]...Charlie Rich

January 19, 1974
SINGLES
- HOT   Show And Tell [1]...Al Wilson
- R&B   I've Got To Use My Imagination [1]...
         Gladys Knight & The Pips
- C&W   I Love [1]...Tom T. Hall
- A/C   The Way We Were [2]...Barbra Streisand

ALBUMS
- POP   You Don't Mess Around With Jim [2]...Jim Croce
- R&B   Imagination [6]...Gladys Knight & The Pips
- C&W   Behind Closed Doors [10]...Charlie Rich

January 26, 1974
SINGLES
- HOT   You're Sixteen [1]...Ringo Starr
- R&B   Livin' For You [1]...Al Green
- C&W   I Love [2]...Tom T. Hall
- A/C   *Love's Theme [1]...Love Unlimited Orchestra

ALBUMS
- POP   You Don't Mess Around With Jim [3]...Jim Croce
- R&B   Imagination [7]...Gladys Knight & The Pips
- C&W   Behind Closed Doors [11]...Charlie Rich

February 2, 1974
SINGLES
- HOT   The Way We Were [1]...Barbra Streisand
- R&B   Let Your Hair Down [1]...The Temptations
- C&W   Jolene [1]...Dolly Parton
- A/C   Love's Theme [2]...Love Unlimited Orchestra

ALBUMS
- POP   You Don't Mess Around With Jim [4]...Jim Croce
- R&B   Stone Gon' [1]...Barry White
- C&W   Behind Closed Doors [12]...Charlie Rich

February 9, 1974
SINGLES
- HOT   Love's Theme [1]...Love Unlimited Orchestra
- R&B   Boogie Down [1]...Eddie Kendricks
- C&W   World Of Make Believe [1]...Bill Anderson
- A/C   Love Song [1]...Anne Murray

ALBUMS
- POP   You Don't Mess Around With Jim [5]...Jim Croce
- R&B   Stone Gon' [2]...Barry White
- C&W   Behind Closed Doors [13]...Charlie Rich

February 16, 1974
SINGLES
- HOT   The Way We Were [2]...Barbra Streisand
- R&B   Boogie Down [2]...Eddie Kendricks
- C&W   That's The Way Love Goes [1]...Johnny Rodriguez
- A/C   Last Time I Saw Him [1]...Diana Ross

ALBUMS
- POP   Planet Waves [1]...Bob Dylan
- R&B   Ship Ahoy [1]...The O'Jays
- C&W   Amazing Love [1]...Charley Pride

February 23, 1974
SINGLES
- HOT   The Way We Were [3]...Barbra Streisand
- R&B   Boogie Down [3]...Eddie Kendricks
- C&W   Another Lonely Song [1]...Tammy Wynette
- A/C   Last Time I Saw Him [2]...Diana Ross

ALBUMS
- POP   Planet Waves [2]...Bob Dylan
- R&B   Livin' For You [1]...Al Green
- C&W   Amazing Love [2]...Charley Pride

March 2, 1974
SINGLES
- HOT   *Seasons In The Sun [1]...Terry Jacks
- R&B   Mighty Love-Pt. 1 [1]...Spinners
- C&W   Another Lonely Song [2]...Tammy Wynette
- A/C   Last Time I Saw Him [3]...Diana Ross

ALBUMS
- POP   Planet Waves [3]...Bob Dylan
- R&B   Ship Ahoy [2]...The O'Jays
- C&W   Let Me Be There [1]...Olivia Newton-John

March 9, 1974
SINGLES
- HOT   Seasons In The Sun [2]...Terry Jacks
- R&B   Mighty Love-Pt. 1 [2]...Spinners
- C&W   There Won't Be Anymore [1]...Charlie Rich
- A/C   Seasons In The Sun [1]...Terry Jacks

ALBUMS
- POP   Planet Waves [4]...Bob Dylan
- R&B   Ship Ahoy [3]...The O'Jays
- C&W   Let Me Be There [2]...Olivia Newton-John

March 16, 1974
SINGLES
- HOT   Seasons In The Sun [3]...Terry Jacks
- R&B   Lookin' For A Love [1]...Bobby Womack
- C&W   There Won't Be Anymore [2]...Charlie Rich
- A/C   *Sunshine On My Shoulders [1]...John Denver

ALBUMS
- POP   The Way We Were [1]...Barbra Streisand
- R&B   Love Is The Message [1]...MFSB
- C&W   Behind Closed Doors [14]...Charlie Rich

March 23, 1974
SINGLES
- HOT   Dark Lady [1]...Cher
- R&B   Lookin' For A Love [2]...Bobby Womack
- C&W   There's A Honky Tonk Angel (Who'll Take Me Back In) [1]...Conway Twitty
- A/C   Sunshine On My Shoulders [2]...John Denver

ALBUMS
- POP   The Way We Were [2]...Barbra Streisand
- R&B   Love Is The Message [2]...MFSB
- C&W   Behind Closed Doors [15]...Charlie Rich

March 30, 1974
SINGLES
- *HOT* Sunshine On My Shoulders [1]...John Denver
- *R&B* Lookin' For A Love [3]...Bobby Womack
- *C&W* Would You Lay With Me (In A Field Of Stone) [1]...Tanya Tucker
- *A/C* *A Very Special Love Song [1]...Charlie Rich

ALBUMS
- *POP* John Denver's Greatest Hits [1]...John Denver
- *R&B* Love Is The Message [3]...MFSB
- *C&W* Elvis-A Legendary Performer, Volume 1 [1]...Elvis Presley

April 6, 1974
SINGLES
- *HOT* Hooked On A Feeling [1]...Blue Swede
- *R&B* Best Thing That Ever Happened To Me [1]...Gladys Knight & The Pips
- *C&W* A Very Special Love Song [1]...Charlie Rich
- *A/C* A Very Special Love Song [2]...Charlie Rich

ALBUMS
- *POP* John Denver's Greatest Hits [2]...John Denver
- *R&B* Love Is The Message [4]...MFSB
- *C&W* Elvis-A Legendary Performer, Volume 1 [2]...Elvis Presley

April 13, 1974
SINGLES
- *HOT* Bennie And The Jets [1]...Elton John
- *R&B* Best Thing That Ever Happened To Me [2]...Gladys Knight & The Pips
- *C&W* A Very Special Love Song [2]...Charlie Rich
- *A/C* Keep On Singing [1]...Helen Reddy

ALBUMS
- *POP* Band On The Run [1]...Paul McCartney & Wings
- *R&B* Love Is The Message [5]...MFSB
- *C&W* There Won't Be Anymore [1]...Charlie Rich

April 20, 1974
SINGLES
- *HOT* *TSOP (The Sound Of Philadelphia) [1]...MFSB featuring The Three Degrees
- *R&B* *TSOP (The Sound Of Philadelphia) [1]...MFSB featuring The Three Degrees
- *C&W* A Very Special Love Song [3]...Charlie Rich
- *A/C* Keep On Singing [2]...Helen Reddy

ALBUMS
- *POP* John Denver's Greatest Hits [3]...John Denver
- *R&B* Love Is The Message [6]...MFSB
- *C&W* There Won't Be Anymore [2]...Charlie Rich

April 27, 1974
SINGLES
- *HOT* TSOP (The Sound Of Philadelphia) [2]...MFSB featuring The Three Degrees
- *R&B* The Payback (Part I) [1]...James Brown
- *C&W* Hello Love [1]...Hank Snow
- *A/C* I'll Have To Say I Love You In A Song [1]...Jim Croce

ALBUMS
- *POP* Chicago VII [1]...Chicago
- *R&B* Boogie Down! [1]...Eddie Kendricks
- *C&W* Very Special Love Songs [1]...Charlie Rich

May 4, 1974
SINGLES
- *HOT* The Loco-Motion [1]...Grand Funk
- *R&B* The Payback (Part I) [2]...James Brown
- *C&W* Things Aren't Funny Anymore [1]...Merle Haggard
- *A/C* TSOP (The Sound Of Philadelphia) [1]...MFSB featuring The Three Degrees

ALBUMS
- *POP* The Sting [1]...Soundtrack (Marvin Hamlisch)
- *R&B* The Payback [1]...James Brown
- *C&W* Very Special Love Songs [2]...Charlie Rich

May 11, 1974
SINGLES
- *HOT* The Loco-Motion [2]...Grand Funk
- *R&B* Dancing Machine [1]...Jackson 5
- *C&W* Is It Wrong (For Loving You) [1]...Sonny James
- *A/C* TSOP (The Sound Of Philadelphia) [2]...MFSB featuring The Three Degrees

ALBUMS
- *POP* The Sting [2]...Soundtrack (Marvin Hamlisch)
- *R&B* The Payback [2]...James Brown
- *C&W* Behind Closed Doors [16]...Charlie Rich

May 18, 1974
SINGLES
- *HOT* The Streak [1]...Ray Stevens
- *R&B* I'm In Love [1]...Aretha Franklin
- *C&W* Country Bumpkin [1]...Cal Smith
- *A/C* The Entertainer [1]...Marvin Hamlisch

ALBUMS
- *POP* The Sting [3]...Soundtrack (Marvin Hamlisch)
- *R&B* Let Me In Your Life [1]...Aretha Franklin
- *C&W* Behind Closed Doors [17]...Charlie Rich

May 25, 1974
SINGLES
- HOT The Streak [2]...Ray Stevens
- R&B I'm In Love [2]...Aretha Franklin
- C&W No Charge [1]...Melba Montgomery
- A/C Help Me [1]...Joni Mitchell

ALBUMS
- POP The Sting [4]...Soundtrack (Marvin Hamlisch)
- R&B Open Our Eyes [1]...Earth, Wind & Fire
- C&W Behind Closed Doors [18]...Charlie Rich

June 1, 1974
SINGLES
- HOT The Streak [3]...Ray Stevens
- R&B Be Thankful For What You Got [1]...William DeVaughn
- C&W Pure Love [1]...Ronnie Milsap
- A/C I Won't Last A Day Without You [1]...Carpenters

ALBUMS
- POP The Sting [5]...Soundtrack (Marvin Hamlisch)
- R&B Mighty Love [1]...Spinners
- C&W Honky Tonk Angel [1]...Conway Twitty

June 8, 1974
SINGLES
- HOT Band On The Run [1]...Paul McCartney & Wings
- R&B Hollywood Swinging [1]...Kool & The Gang
- C&W I Will Always Love You [1]...Dolly Parton
- A/C *Sundown [1]...Gordon Lightfoot

ALBUMS
- POP Band On The Run [2]...Paul McCartney & Wings
- R&B Ship Ahoy [4]...The O'Jays
- C&W Very Special Love Songs [3]...Charlie Rich

June 15, 1974
SINGLES
- HOT Billy, Don't Be A Hero [1]...Bo Donaldson & The Heywoods
- R&B Sideshow [1]...Blue Magic
- C&W I Don't See Me In Your Eyes Anymore [1]...Charlie Rich
- A/C Sundown [2]...Gordon Lightfoot

ALBUMS
- POP Band On The Run [3]...Paul McCartney & Wings
- R&B Ship Ahoy [5]...The O'Jays
- C&W Very Special Love Songs [4]...Charlie Rich

June 22, 1974
SINGLES
- HOT Billy, Don't Be A Hero [2]...Bo Donaldson & The Heywoods
- R&B Finally Got Myself Together (I'm A Changed Man) [1]...The Impressions
- C&W This Time [1]...Waylon Jennings
- A/C You Won't See Me [1]...Anne Murray

ALBUMS
- POP Sundown [1]...Gordon Lightfoot
- R&B War Live! [1]...War
- C&W Behind Closed Doors [19]...Charlie Rich

June 29, 1974
SINGLES
- HOT Sundown [1]...Gordon Lightfoot
- R&B Finally Got Myself Together (I'm A Changed Man) [2]...The Impressions
- C&W Room Full Of Roses [1]...Mickey Gilley
- A/C You Won't See Me [2]...Anne Murray

ALBUMS
- POP Sundown [2]...Gordon Lightfoot
- R&B War Live! [2]...War
- C&W Behind Closed Doors [20]...Charlie Rich

July 6, 1974
SINGLES
- HOT Rock The Boat [1]...The Hues Corporation
- R&B *Rock Your Baby [1]...George McCrae
- C&W He Thinks I Still Care [1]...Anne Murray
- A/C *Annie's Song [1]...John Denver

ALBUMS
- POP Band On The Run [4]...Paul McCartney & Wings
- R&B Body Heat [1]...Quincy Jones
- C&W Very Special Love Songs [5]...Charlie Rich

July 13, 1974
SINGLES
- HOT Rock Your Baby [1]...George McCrae
- R&B Rock Your Baby [2]...George McCrae
- C&W He Thinks I Still Care [2]...Anne Murray
- A/C Annie's Song [2]...John Denver

ALBUMS
- POP Caribou [1]...Elton John
- R&B Claudine [1]...Gladys Knight & The Pips
- C&W If You Love Me, Let Me Know [1]...Olivia Newton-John

July 20, 1974
SINGLES
- HOT Rock Your Baby [2]...George McCrae
- R&B My Thang [1]...James Brown
- C&W Marie Laveau [1]...Bobby Bare
- A/C Annie's Song [3]...John Denver

ALBUMS
- POP Caribou [2]...Elton John
- R&B Skin Tight [1]...Ohio Players
- C&W If You Love Me, Let Me Know [2]...Olivia Newton-John

July 27, 1974
SINGLES
- HOT Annie's Song [1]...John Denver
- R&B My Thang [2]...James Brown
- C&W You Can't Be A Beacon (If Your Light Don't Shine) [1]...Donna Fargo
- A/C You And Me Against The World [1]...Helen Reddy

ALBUMS
- POP Caribou [3]...Elton John
- R&B Skin Tight [2]...Ohio Players
- C&W If You Love Me, Let Me Know [3]...Olivia Newton-John

August 3, 1974
SINGLES
- HOT Annie's Song [2]...John Denver
- R&B *Feel Like Makin' Love [1]...Roberta Flack
- C&W Rub It In [1]...Billy "Crash" Craddock
- A/C Please Come To Boston [1]...Dave Loggins

ALBUMS
- POP Caribou [4]...Elton John
- R&B Skin Tight [3]...Ohio Players
- C&W If You Love Me, Let Me Know [4]...Olivia Newton-John

August 10, 1974
SINGLES
- HOT Feel Like Makin' Love [1]...Roberta Flack
- R&B Feel Like Makin' Love [2]...Roberta Flack
- C&W Rub It In [2]...Billy "Crash" Craddock
- A/C Feel Like Makin' Love [1]...Roberta Flack

ALBUMS
- POP Back Home Again [1]...John Denver
- R&B Skin Tight [4]...Ohio Players
- C&W If You Love Me, Let Me Know [5]...Olivia Newton-John

August 17, 1974
SINGLES
- HOT The Night Chicago Died [1]...Paper Lace
- R&B Feel Like Makin' Love [3]...Roberta Flack
- C&W As Soon As I Hang Up The Phone [1]...Conway Twitty & Loretta Lynn
- A/C Feel Like Makin' Love [2]...Roberta Flack

ALBUMS
- POP 461 Ocean Boulevard [1]...Eric Clapton
- R&B Skin Tight [5]...Ohio Players
- C&W Behind Closed Doors [21]...Charlie Rich

August 24, 1974
SINGLES
- HOT (You're) Having My Baby [1]...Paul Anka
- R&B Feel Like Makin' Love [4]...Roberta Flack
- C&W Old Man From The Mountain [1]...Merle Haggard
- A/C Call On Me [1]...Chicago

ALBUMS
- POP 461 Ocean Boulevard [2]...Eric Clapton
- R&B Skin Tight [6]...Ohio Players
- C&W Back Home Again [1]...John Denver

August 31, 1974
SINGLES
- HOT (You're) Having My Baby [2]...Paul Anka
- R&B Feel Like Makin' Love [5]...Roberta Flack
- C&W The Grand Tour [1]...George Jones
- A/C I'm Leaving It (All) Up To You [1]...Donny & Marie Osmond

ALBUMS
- POP 461 Ocean Boulevard [3]...Eric Clapton
- R&B Marvin Gaye Live! [1]...Marvin Gaye
- C&W Back Home Again [2]...John Denver

September 7, 1974
SINGLES
- HOT (You're) Having My Baby [3]...Paul Anka
- R&B *Can't Get Enough Of Your Love, Babe [1]...Barry White
- C&W Please Don't Tell Me How The Story Ends [1]...Ronnie Milsap
- A/C *I Love My Friend [1]...Charlie Rich

ALBUMS
- POP 461 Ocean Boulevard [4]...Eric Clapton
- R&B That Nigger's Crazy [1]...Richard Pryor
- C&W Back Home Again [3]...John Denver

September 14, 1974
SINGLES
- HOT I Shot The Sheriff [1]...Eric Clapton
- R&B Can't Get Enough Of Your Love, Babe [2]...Barry White
- C&W Please Don't Tell Me How The Story Ends [2]...Ronnie Milsap
- A/C *I Honestly Love You [1]...Olivia Newton-John

ALBUMS
- POP Fulfillingness' First Finale [1]...Stevie Wonder
- R&B That Nigger's Crazy [2]...Richard Pryor
- C&W Back Home Again [4]...John Denver

September 21, 1974
SINGLES
- HOT Can't Get Enough Of Your Love, Babe [1]...Barry White
- R&B Can't Get Enough Of Your Love, Babe [3]...Barry White
- C&W I Wouldn't Want To Live If You Didn't Love Me [1]...Don Williams
- A/C I Honestly Love You [2]...Olivia Newton-John

ALBUMS
- POP Fulfillingness' First Finale [2]...Stevie Wonder
- R&B That Nigger's Crazy [3]...Richard Pryor
- C&W Country Partners [1]...Conway Twitty & Loretta Lynn

September 28, 1974
SINGLES
- HOT Rock Me Gently [1]...Andy Kim
- R&B *You Haven't Done Nothin' [1]...Stevie Wonder
- C&W I'm A Ramblin' Man [1]...Waylon Jennings
- A/C I Honestly Love You [3]...Olivia Newton-John

ALBUMS
- POP Bad Company [1]...Bad Company
- R&B That Nigger's Crazy [4]...Richard Pryor
- C&W If You Love Me, Let Me Know [6]...Olivia Newton-John

October 5, 1974
SINGLES
- HOT I Honestly Love You [1]...Olivia Newton-John
- R&B You Haven't Done Nothin' [2]...Stevie Wonder
- C&W I Love My Friend [1]...Charlie Rich
- A/C Tin Man [1]...America

ALBUMS
- POP Endless Summer [1]...The Beach Boys
- R&B Fullfillingness' First Finale [1]...Stevie Wonder
- C&W If You Love Me, Let Me Know [7]...Olivia Newton-John

October 12, 1974
SINGLES
- HOT I Honestly Love You [2]...Olivia Newton-John
- R&B Papa Don't Take No Mess (Part I) [1]...James Brown
- C&W Please Don't Stop Loving Me [1]...Porter Wagoner & Dolly Parton
- A/C Stop And Smell The Roses [1]...Mac Davis

ALBUMS
- POP If You Love Me, Let Me Know [1]...Olivia Newton-John
- R&B Fullfillingness' First Finale [2]...Stevie Wonder
- C&W If You Love Me, Let Me Know [8]...Olivia Newton-John

October 19, 1974
SINGLES
- HOT Nothing From Nothing [1]...Billy Preston
- R&B Do It ('Til You're Satisfied) [1]...B.T. Express
- C&W I See The Want To In Your Eyes [1]...Conway Twitty
- A/C Carefree Highway [1]...Gordon Lightfoot

ALBUMS
- POP Not Fragile [1]...Bachman-Turner Overdrive
- R&B Fullfillingness' First Finale [3]...Stevie Wonder
- C&W Back Home Again [5]...John Denver

October 26, 1974
SINGLES
- HOT Then Came You [1]...Dionne Warwicke & Spinners
- R&B Higher Plane [1]...Kool & The Gang
- C&W I See The Want To In Your Eyes [2]...Conway Twitty
- A/C *Back Home Again [1]...John Denver

ALBUMS
- POP Can't Get Enough [1]...Barry White
- R&B Fullfillingness' First Finale [4]...Stevie Wonder
- C&W Back Home Again [6]...John Denver

November 2, 1974
SINGLES
- HOT You Haven't Done Nothin [1]...Stevie Wonder
- R&B Let's Straighten It Out [1]...Latimore
- C&W I Overlooked An Orchid [1]...Mickey Gilley
- A/C Back Home Again [2]...John Denver

ALBUMS
- POP So Far [1]...Crosby, Stills, Nash and Young
- R&B Fullfillingness' First Finale [5]...Stevie Wonder
- C&W Back Home Again [7]...John Denver

November 9, 1974
SINGLES
- HOT You Ain't Seen Nothing Yet [1]...Bachman-Turner Overdrive
- R&B Let's Straighten It Out [2]...Latimore
- C&W Love Is Like A Butterfly [1]...Dolly Parton
- A/C My Melody Of Love [1]...Bobby Vinton

ALBUMS
- POP Wrap Around Joy [1]...Carole King
- R&B Marvin Gaye Live! [2]...Marvin Gaye
- C&W Room Full Of Roses [1]...Mickey Gilley

November 16, 1974
SINGLES
- HOT Whatever Gets You Thru The Night [1]...John Lennon
- R&B Woman To Woman [1]...Shirley Brown
- C&W Country Is [1]...Tom T. Hall
- A/C Longfellow Serenade [1]...Neil Diamond

ALBUMS
- POP Walls And Bridges [1]...John Lennon
- R&B Live It Up [1]...The Isley Brothers
- C&W Back Home Again [8]...John Denver

November 23, 1974
SINGLES
- HOT *I Can Help [1]...Billy Swan
- R&B Woman To Woman [2]...Shirley Brown
- C&W Trouble In Paradise [1]...Loretta Lynn
- A/C *Laughter In The Rain [1]...Neil Sedaka

ALBUMS
- POP It's Only Rock 'N Roll [1]...The Rolling Stones
- R&B Can't Get Enough [1]...Barry White
- C&W Back Home Again [9]...John Denver

November 30, 1974
SINGLES
- HOT I Can Help [2]...Billy Swan
- R&B I Feel A Song (In My Heart) [1]...Gladys Knight & The Pips
- C&W Back Home Again [1]...John Denver
- A/C Laughter In The Rain [2]...Neil Sedaka

ALBUMS
- POP Elton John - Greatest Hits [1]...Elton John
- R&B Can't Get Enough [2]...Barry White
- C&W Merle Haggard Presents His 30th Album [1]...Merle Haggard

December 7, 1974
SINGLES
- HOT *Kung Fu Fighting [1]...Carl Douglas
- R&B I Feel A Song (In My Heart) [2]...Gladys Knight & The Pips
- C&W She Called Me Baby [1]...Charlie Rich
- A/C *Angie Baby [1]...Helen Reddy

ALBUMS
- POP Elton John - Greatest Hits [2]...Elton John
- R&B Fullfillingness' First Finale [6]...Stevie Wonder
- C&W Merle Haggard Presents His 30th Album [2]...Merle Haggard

December 14, 1974
SINGLES
- HOT Kung Fu Fighting [2]...Carl Douglas
- R&B You Got The Love [1]...Rufus Featuring Chaka Khan
- C&W I Can Help [1]...Billy Swan
- A/C When Will I See You Again [1]...The Three Degrees

ALBUMS
- POP Elton John - Greatest Hits [3]...Elton John
- R&B Fullfillingness' First Finale [7]...Stevie Wonder
- C&W Back Home Again [10]...John Denver

December 21, 1974
SINGLES
- HOT Cat's In The Cradle [1]...Harry Chapin
- R&B She's Gone [1]...Tavares
- C&W I Can Help [2]...Billy Swan
- A/C Wishing You Were Here [1]...Chicago

ALBUMS
- POP Elton John - Greatest Hits [4]...Elton John
- R&B Fullfillingness' First Finale [8]...Stevie Wonder
- C&W Back Home Again [11]...John Denver

December 28, 1974
SINGLES
- HOT Angie Baby [1]...Helen Reddy
- R&B Boogie On Reggae Woman [1]...Stevie Wonder
- C&W What A Man, My Man Is [1]...Lynn Anderson
- A/C *Mandy [1]...Barry Manilow

ALBUMS
- POP Elton John - Greatest Hits [5]...Elton John
- R&B I Feel A Song [1]...Gladys Knight & The Pips
- C&W Back Home Again [12]...John Denver

January 4, 1975
SINGLES
- HOT Lucy In The Sky With Diamonds [1]...Elton John
- R&B Boogie On Reggae Woman [2]...Stevie Wonder
- C&W The Door [1]...George Jones
- A/C Mandy [2]...Barry Manilow

ALBUMS
- POP Elton John - Greatest Hits [6]...Elton John
- R&B Fire [1]...Ohio Players
- C&W Back Home Again [13]...John Denver

January 11, 1975
SINGLES
- HOT Lucy In The Sky With Diamonds [2]...Elton John
- R&B Kung Fu Fighting [1]...Carl Douglas
- C&W Ruby, Baby [1]...Billy "Crash" Craddock
- A/C Only You [1]...Ringo Starr

ALBUMS
- POP Elton John - Greatest Hits [7]...Elton John
- R&B Fire [2]...Ohio Players
- C&W The Silver Fox [1]...Charlie Rich

January 18, 1975
SINGLES
- HOT Mandy [1]...Barry Manilow
- R&B You're The First, The Last, My Everything [1]...Barry White
- C&W Kentucky Gambler [1]...Merle Haggard
- A/C *Please Mr. Postman [1]...Carpenters

ALBUMS
- POP Elton John - Greatest Hits [8]...Elton John
- R&B Fire [3]...Ohio Players
- C&W I Can Help [1]...Billy Swan

January 25, 1975
SINGLES
- HOT Please Mr. Postman [1]...Carpenters
- R&B *Fire [1]...Ohio Players
- C&W (I'd Be) A Legend In My Time [1]...Ronnie Milsap
- A/C Morning Side Of The Mountain [1]...Donny & Marie Osmond

ALBUMS
- POP Elton John - Greatest Hits [9]...Elton John
- R&B Fire [4]...Ohio Players
- C&W I Can Help [2]...Billy Swan

February 1, 1975
SINGLES
- HOT Laughter In The Rain [1]...Neil Sedaka
- R&B Fire [2]...Ohio Players
- C&W City Lights [1]...Mickey Gilley
- A/C Best Of My Love [1]...Eagles

ALBUMS
- POP Elton John - Greatest Hits [10]...Elton John
- R&B Fire [5]...Ohio Players
- C&W City Lights [1]...Mickey Gilley

February 8, 1975
SINGLES
- HOT Fire [1]...Ohio Players
- R&B Happy People [1]...The Temptations
- C&W Then Who Am I [1]...Charley Pride
- A/C Sweet Surrender [1]...John Denver

ALBUMS
- POP Fire [1]...Ohio Players
- R&B Kung Fu Fighting And Other Great Love Songs [1]...Carl Douglas
- C&W Heart Like A Wheel [1]...Linda Ronstadt

February 15, 1975
SINGLES
- HOT You're No Good [1]...Linda Ronstadt
- R&B I Belong To You [1]...Love Unlimited
- C&W Devil In The Bottle [1]...T.G. Sheppard
- A/C Lonely People [1]...America

ALBUMS
- POP Heart Like A Wheel [1]...Linda Ronstadt
- R&B New And Improved [1]...Spinners
- C&W Heart Like A Wheel [2]...Linda Ronstadt

February 22, 1975
SINGLES
- HOT Pick Up The Pieces [1]...AWB
- R&B *Lady Marmalade [1]...LaBelle
- C&W I Care/Sneaky Snake [1]...Tom T. Hall
- A/C Nightingale [1]...Carole King

ALBUMS
- POP AWB [1]...Average White Band
- R&B Do It ('Til You're Satisfied) [1]...B.T. Express
- C&W Heart Like A Wheel [3]...Linda Ronstadt

March 1, 1975
SINGLES
- HOT Best Of My Love [1]...The Eagles
- R&B Shame, Shame, Shame [1]...Shirley & Company
- C&W It's Time To Pay The Fiddler [1]...Cal Smith
- A/C Poetry Man [1]...Phoebe Snow

ALBUMS
- POP Blood On The Tracks [1]...Bob Dylan
- R&B AWB [1]...Average White Band
- C&W Heart Like A Wheel [4]...Linda Ronstadt

March 8, 1975

SINGLES
- HOT *Have You Never Been Mellow [1]...Olivia Newton-John
- R&B Express [1]...B.T. Express
- C&W Linda On My Mind [1]...Conway Twitty
- A/C *Have You Never Been Mellow [1]...Olivia Newton-John

ALBUMS
- POP Blood On The Tracks [2]...Bob Dylan
- R&B AWB [2]...Average White Band
- C&W Promised Land [1]...Elvis Presley

March 15, 1975

SINGLES
- HOT Black Water [1]...The Doobie Brothers
- R&B Supernatural Thing - Part I [1]...Ben E. King
- C&W *Before The Next Teardrop Falls [1]...Freddy Fender
- A/C I've Been This Way Before [1]...Neil Diamond

ALBUMS
- POP Have You Never Been Mellow [1]...Olivia Newton-John
- R&B AWB [3]...Average White Band
- C&W Linda On My Mind [1]...Conway Twitty

March 22, 1975

SINGLES
- HOT My Eyes Adored You [1]...Frankie Valli
- R&B *Shining Star [1]...Earth, Wind & Fire
- C&W Before The Next Teardrop Falls [2]...Freddy Fender
- A/C *(Hey Won't You Play) Another Somebody Done Somebody Wrong Song [1]...B.J. Thomas

ALBUMS
- POP Physical Graffiti [1]...Led Zeppelin
- R&B Al Green Explores Your Mind [1]...Al Green
- C&W Have You Never Been Mellow [1]...Olivia Newton-John

March 29, 1975

SINGLES
- HOT Lady Marmalade [1]...LaBelle
- R&B Shining Star [2]...Earth, Wind & Fire
- C&W The Bargain Store [1]...Dolly Parton
- A/C Emotion [1]...Helen Reddy

ALBUMS
- POP Physical Graffiti [2]...Led Zeppelin
- R&B Perfect Angel [1]...Minnie Riperton
- C&W Have You Never Been Mellow [2]...Olivia Newton-John

April 5, 1975

SINGLES
- HOT Lovin' You [1]...Minnie Riperton
- R&B Shoeshine Boy [1]...Eddie Kendricks
- C&W I Just Can't Get Her Out Of My Mind [1]...Johnny Rodriguez
- A/C My Boy [1]...Elvis Presley

ALBUMS
- POP Physical Graffiti [3]...Led Zeppelin
- R&B Perfect Angel [2]...Minnie Riperton
- C&W Have You Never Been Mellow [3]...Olivia Newton-John

April 12, 1975

SINGLES
- HOT Philadelphia Freedom [1]...The Elton John Band
- R&B L-O-V-E (Love) [1]...Al Green
- C&W Always Wanting You [1]...Merle Haggard
- A/C The Last Farewell [1]...Roger Whittaker

ALBUMS
- POP Physical Graffiti [4]...Led Zeppelin
- R&B Perfect Angel [3]...Minnie Riperton
- C&W Have You Never Been Mellow [4]...Olivia Newton-John

April 19, 1975

SINGLES
- HOT Philadelphia Freedom [2]...The Elton John Band
- R&B L-O-V-E (Love) [2]...Al Green
- C&W Always Wanting You [2]...Merle Haggard
- A/C *He Don't Love You (Like I Love You) [1]...Tony Orlando & Dawn

ALBUMS
- POP Physical Graffiti [5]...Led Zeppelin
- R&B That's The Way Of The World [1]...Earth, Wind & Fire
- C&W Have You Never Been Mellow [5]...Olivia Newton-John

April 26, 1975

SINGLES
- HOT (Hey Won't You Play) Another Somebody Done Somebody Wrong Song [1]...B.J. Thomas
- R&B Shakey Ground [1]...The Temptations
- C&W Blanket On The Ground [1]...Billie Jo Spears
- A/C It's A Miracle [1]...Barry Manilow

ALBUMS
- POP Physical Graffiti [6]...Led Zeppelin
- R&B That's The Way Of The World [2]...Earth, Wind & Fire
- C&W Have You Never Been Mellow [6]...Olivia Newton-John

May 3, 1975
SINGLES
- HOT   He Don't Love You (Like I Love You) [1]...Tony Orlando & Dawn
- R&B   What Am I Gonna Do With You [1]...Barry White
- C&W   Roll On Big Mama [1]...Joe Stampley
- A/C   Only Yesterday [1]...Carpenters

ALBUMS
- POP   Chicago VIII [1]...Chicago
- R&B   A Song For You [1]...The Temptations
- C&W   An Evening With John Denver [1]...John Denver

May 10, 1975
SINGLES
- HOT   He Don't Love You (Like I Love You) [2]...Tony Orlando & Dawn
- R&B   Get Down, Get Down (Get On The Floor) [1]...Joe Simon
- C&W   She's Actin' Single (I'm Drinkin' Doubles) [1]...Gary Stewart
- A/C   The Immigrant [1]...Neil Sedaka

ALBUMS
- POP   Chicago VIII [2]...Chicago
- R&B   To Be True [1]...Harold Melvin & The Blue Notes
- C&W   An Evening With John Denver [2]...John Denver

May 17, 1975
SINGLES
- HOT   He Don't Love You (Like I Love You) [3]...Tony Orlando & Dawn
- R&B   Get Down, Get Down (Get On The Floor) [2]...Joe Simon
- C&W   (Hey Won't You Play) Another Somebody Done Somebody Wrong Song [1]...B.J. Thomas
- A/C   Rainy Day People [1]...Gordon Lightfoot

ALBUMS
- POP   That's The Way Of The World [1]...Earth, Wind & Fire/Soundtrack
- R&B   Mister Magic [1]...Grover Washington, Jr.
- C&W   Before The Next Teardrop Falls [1]...Freddy Fender

May 24, 1975
SINGLES
- HOT   Shining Star [1]...Earth, Wind & Fire
- R&B   Baby That's Backatcha [1]...Smokey Robinson
- C&W   I'm Not Lisa [1]...Jessi Colter
- A/C   99 Miles From L.A. [1]...Albert Hammond

ALBUMS
- POP   That's The Way Of The World [2]...Earth, Wind & Fire/Soundtrack
- R&B   Sun Goddess [1]...Ramsey Lewis
- C&W   Before The Next Teardrop Falls [2]...Freddy Fender

May 31, 1975
SINGLES
- HOT   Before The Next Teardrop Falls [1]...Freddy Fender
- R&B   Spirit Of The Boogie [1]...Kool & The Gang
- C&W   *Thank God I'm A Country Boy [1]...John Denver
- A/C   Wonderful Baby [1]...Don McLean

ALBUMS
- POP   That's The Way Of The World [3]...Earth, Wind & Fire/Soundtrack
- R&B   Just Another Way To Say I Love You [1]...Barry White
- C&W   Before The Next Teardrop Falls [3]...Freddy Fender

June 7, 1975
SINGLES
- HOT   Thank God I'm A Country Boy [1]...John Denver
- R&B   Love Won't Let Me Wait [1]...Major Harris
- C&W   Window Up Above [1]...Mickey Gilley
- A/C   *Love Will Keep Us Together [1]...Captain & Tennille

ALBUMS
- POP   Captain Fantastic And The Brown Dirt Cowboy [1]...Elton John
- R&B   Survival [1]...The O'Jays
- C&W   Before The Next Teardrop Falls [4]...Freddy Fender

June 14, 1975
SINGLES
- HOT   Sister Golden Hair [1]...America
- R&B   Rockin' Chair [1]...Gwen McCrae
- C&W   When Will I Be Loved [1]...Linda Ronstadt
- A/C   Wildfire [1]...Michael Murphey

ALBUMS
- POP   Captain Fantastic And The Brown Dirt Cowboy [2]...Elton John
- R&B   Survival [2]...The O'Jays
- C&W   Keep Movin' On [1]...Merle Haggard

June 21, 1975
SINGLES
- HOT   Love Will Keep Us Together [1]...Captain & Tennille
- R&B   Give The People What They Want [1]...The O'Jays
- C&W   You're My Best Friend [1]...Don Williams
- A/C   Midnight Blue [1]...Melissa Manchester

ALBUMS
- POP   Captain Fantastic And The Brown Dirt Cowboy [3]...Elton John
- R&B   That's The Way Of The World [3]...Earth, Wind & Fire
- C&W   Keep Movin' On [2]...Merle Haggard

June 28, 1975

SINGLES
- HOT Love Will Keep Us Together [2]...Captain & Tennille
- R&B Look At Me (I'm In Love) [1]...The Moments
- C&W Tryin' To Beat The Morning Home [1]...T.G. Sheppard
- A/C Midnight Blue [2]...Melissa Manchester

ALBUMS
- POP Captain Fantastic And The Brown Dirt Cowboy [4]...Elton John
- R&B That's The Way Of The World [4]...Earth, Wind & Fire
- C&W Keep Movin' On [3]...Merle Haggard

July 5, 1975

SINGLES
- HOT Love Will Keep Us Together [3]...Captain & Tennille
- R&B Slippery When Wet [1]...Commodores
- C&W Lizzie And The Rainman [1]...Tanya Tucker
- A/C Every Time You Touch Me (I Get High) [1]...Charlie Rich

ALBUMS
- POP Captain Fantastic And The Brown Dirt Cowboy [5]...Elton John
- R&B That's The Way Of The World [5]...Earth, Wind & Fire
- C&W Before The Next Teardrop Falls [5]...Freddy Fender

July 12, 1975

SINGLES
- HOT Love Will Keep Us Together [4]...Captain & Tennille
- R&B *The Hustle [1]...Van McCoy
- C&W Movin' On [1]...Merle Haggard
- A/C Please Mr. Please [1]...Olivia Newton-John

ALBUMS
- POP Captain Fantastic And The Brown Dirt Cowboy [6]...Elton John
- R&B Disco Baby [1]...Van McCoy
- C&W Before The Next Teardrop Falls [6]...Freddy Fender

July 19, 1975

SINGLES
- HOT Listen To What The Man Said [1]...Wings
- R&B Fight The Power (Part 1) [1]...The Isley Brothers
- C&W Touch The Hand [1]...Conway Twitty
- A/C Please Mr. Please [2]...Olivia Newton-John

ALBUMS
- POP Venus And Mars [1]...Wings
- R&B The Heat Is On [1]...The Isley Brothers
- C&W Keep Movin' On [4]...Merle Haggard

July 26, 1975

SINGLES
- HOT The Hustle [1]...Van McCoy
- R&B Fight The Power (Part 1) [2]...The Isley Brothers
- C&W Touch The Hand [2]...Conway Twitty
- A/C Please Mr. Please [3]...Olivia Newton-John

ALBUMS
- POP One Of These Nights [1]...Eagles
- R&B The Heat Is On [2]...The Isley Brothers
- C&W Before The Next Teardrop Falls [7]...Freddy Fender

August 2, 1975

SINGLES
- HOT One Of These Nights [1]...Eagles
- R&B Fight The Power (Part 1) [3]...The Isley Brothers
- C&W Just Get Up And Close The Door [1]...Johnny Rodriguez
- A/C *Rhinestone Cowboy [1]...Glen Campbell

ALBUMS
- POP One Of These Nights [2]...Eagles
- R&B The Heat Is On [3]...The Isley Brothers
- C&W Before The Next Teardrop Falls [8]...Freddy Fender

August 9, 1975

SINGLES
- HOT Jive Talkin' [1]...Bee Gees
- R&B Hope That We Can Be Together Soon [1]...Sharon Paige/Harold Melvin
- C&W Wasted Days And Wasted Nights [1]...Freddy Fender
- A/C At Seventeen [1]...Janis Ian

ALBUMS
- POP One Of These Nights [3]...Eagles
- R&B Chocolate Chip [1]...Isaac Hayes
- C&W Before The Next Teardrop Falls [9]...Freddy Fender

August 16, 1975

SINGLES
- HOT Jive Talkin' [2]...Bee Gees
- R&B Dream Merchant [1]...The New Birth
- C&W Wasted Days And Wasted Nights [2]...Freddy Fender
- A/C At Seventeen [2]...Janis Ian

ALBUMS
- POP One Of These Nights [4]...Eagles
- R&B Chocolate Chip [2]...Isaac Hayes
- C&W Feelins' [1]...Conway Twitty & Loretta Lynn

August 23, 1975

SINGLES
- HOT *Fallin' In Love [1]...Hamilton, Joe Frank & Reynolds
- R&B *Get Down Tonight [1]...KC & The Sunshine Band
- C&W Rhinestone Cowboy [1]...Glen Campbell
- A/C How Sweet It Is (To Be Loved By You) [1]...James Taylor

ALBUMS
- POP One Of These Nights [5]...Eagles
- R&B Cut The Cake [1]...Average White Band
- C&W Every Time You Touch Me (I Get High) [1]...Charlie Rich

August 30, 1975

SINGLES
- HOT Get Down Tonight [1]...K.C. & The Sunshine Band
- R&B Your Love [1]...Graham Central Station
- C&W Rhinestone Cowboy [2]...Glen Campbell
- A/C Fallin' In Love [1]...Hamilton, Joe Frank & Reynolds

ALBUMS
- POP Captain Fantastic And The Brown Dirt Cowboy [7]...Elton John
- R&B Why Can't We Be Friends? [1]...War
- C&W Every Time You Touch Me (I Get High) [2]...Charlie Rich

September 6, 1975

SINGLES
- HOT Rhinestone Cowboy [1]...Glen Campbell
- R&B How Long (Betcha' Got A Chick On The Side) [1]...Pointer Sisters
- C&W Feelins' [1]...Conway Twitty & Loretta Lynn
- A/C Solitaire [1]...Carpenters

ALBUMS
- POP Red Octopus [1]...Jefferson Starship
- R&B Non-Stop [1]...B.T. Express
- C&W Dreaming My Dreams [1]...Waylon Jennings

September 13, 1975

SINGLES
- HOT Rhinestone Cowboy [2]...Glen Campbell
- R&B How Long (Betcha' Got A Chick On The Side) [2]...Pointer Sisters
- C&W Rhinestone Cowboy [3]...Glen Campbell
- A/C The Proud One [1]...The Osmonds

ALBUMS
- POP The Heat Is On [1]...The Isley Brothers
- R&B Non-Stop [2]...B.T. Express
- C&W Rhinestone Cowboy [1]...Glen Campbell

September 20, 1975

SINGLES
- HOT Fame [1]...David Bowie
- R&B It Only Takes A Minute [1]...Tavares
- C&W Daydreams About Night Things [1]...Ronnie Milsap
- A/C *I'm Sorry [1]...John Denver

ALBUMS
- POP Between The Lines [1]...Janis Ian
- R&B The Heat Is On [4]...The Isley Brothers
- C&W Rhinestone Cowboy [2]...Glen Campbell

September 27, 1975

SINGLES
- HOT I'm Sorry [1]...John Denver
- R&B Do It Any Way You Wanna [1]...People's Choice
- C&W Daydreams About Night Things [2]...Ronnie Milsap
- A/C I'm Sorry [2]...John Denver

ALBUMS
- POP Red Octopus [2]...Jefferson Starship
- R&B Honey [1]...Ohio Players
- C&W Rhinestone Cowboy [3]...Glen Campbell

October 4, 1975

SINGLES
- HOT Fame [2]...David Bowie
- R&B This Will Be [1]...Natalie Cole
- C&W Blue Eyes Crying In The Rain [1]...Willie Nelson
- A/C Ain't No Way To Treat A Lady [1]...Helen Reddy

ALBUMS
- POP Wish You Were Here [1]...Pink Floyd
- R&B Honey [2]...Ohio Players
- C&W Red Headed Stranger [1]...Willie Nelson

October 11, 1975

SINGLES
- HOT Bad Blood [1]...Neil Sedaka
- R&B This Will Be [2]...Natalie Cole
- C&W Blue Eyes Crying In The Rain [2]...Willie Nelson
- A/C I Only Have Eyes For You [1]...Art Garfunkel

ALBUMS
- POP Wish You Were Here [2]...Pink Floyd
- R&B Is It Something I Said? [1]...Richard Pryor
- C&W Red Headed Stranger [2]...Willie Nelson

October 18, 1975
SINGLES
- HOT Bad Blood [2]...Neil Sedaka
- R&B They Just Can't Stop It the (Games People Play) [1]...Spinners
- C&W Hope You're Feelin' Me (Like I'm Feelin' You) [1]...Charley Pride
- A/C Something Better To Do [1]...Olivia Newton-John

ALBUMS
- POP Windsong [1]...John Denver
- R&B Is It Something I Said? [2]...Richard Pryor
- C&W Red Headed Stranger [3]...Willie Nelson

October 25, 1975
SINGLES
- HOT Bad Blood [3]...Neil Sedaka
- R&B To Each His Own [1]...Faith Hope & Charity
- C&W San Antonio Stroll [1]...Tanya Tucker
- A/C Something Better To Do [2]...Olivia Newton-John

ALBUMS
- POP Windsong [2]...John Denver
- R&B Honey [3]...Ohio Players
- C&W Windsong [1]...John Denver

November 1, 1975
SINGLES
- HOT Island Girl [1]...Elton John
- R&B Sweet Sticky Thing [1]...Ohio Players
- C&W (Turn Out The Light And) Love Me Tonight [1]...Don Williams
- A/C Something Better To Do [3]...Olivia Newton-John

ALBUMS
- POP Red Octopus [3]...Jefferson Starship
- R&B Al Green Is Love [1]...Al Green
- C&W Windsong [2]...John Denver

November 8, 1975
SINGLES
- HOT Island Girl [2]...Elton John
- R&B Low Rider [1]...War
- C&W I'm Sorry [1]...John Denver
- A/C The Way I Want To Touch You [1]...Captain & Tennille

ALBUMS
- POP Rock Of The Westies [1]...Elton John
- R&B Al Green Is Love [2]...Al Green
- C&W Windsong [3]...John Denver

November 15, 1975
SINGLES
- HOT Island Girl [3]...Elton John
- R&B *Fly, Robin, Fly [1]...Silver Convention
- C&W Are You Sure Hank Done It This Way/Bob Wills Is Still The King [1]...Waylon Jennings
- A/C The Way I Want To Touch You [2]...Captain & Tennille

ALBUMS
- POP Rock Of The Westies [2]...Elton John
- R&B KC And The Sunshine Band [1]...KC & The Sunshine Band
- C&W Windsong [4]...John Denver

November 22, 1975
SINGLES
- HOT *That's The Way (I Like It) [1]...KC & The Sunshine Band
- R&B *Let's Do It Again [1]...The Staple Singers
- C&W Rocky [1]...Dickey Lee
- A/C My Little Town [1]...Simon & Garfunkel

ALBUMS
- POP Rock Of The Westies [3]...Elton John
- R&B Inseparable [1]...Natalie Cole
- C&W Windsong [5]...John Denver

November 29, 1975
SINGLES
- HOT Fly, Robin, Fly [1]...Silver Convention
- R&B That's The Way (I Like It) [1]...KC & The Sunshine Band
- C&W It's All In The Movies [1]...Merle Haggard
- A/C My Little Town [2]...Simon & Garfunkel

ALBUMS
- POP Red Octopus [4]...Jefferson Starship
- R&B Save Me [1]...Silver Convention
- C&W Red Headed Stranger [4]...Willie Nelson

December 6, 1975
SINGLES
- HOT Fly, Robin, Fly [2]...Silver Convention
- R&B I Love Music (Part 1) [1]...The O'Jays
- C&W Secret Love [1]...Freddy Fender
- A/C *Theme From Mahogany (Do You Know Where You're Going To) [1]...Diana Ross

ALBUMS
- POP Still Crazy After All These Years [1]...Paul Simon
- R&B Let's Do It Again [1]...The Staple Singers
- C&W Red Headed Stranger [5]...Willie Nelson

December 13, 1975
SINGLES
- HOT Fly, Robin, Fly [3]...Silver Convention
- R&B Let's Do It Again [2]...The Staple Singers
- C&W Love Put A Song In My Heart [1]...Johnny Rodriguez
- A/C *I Write The Songs [1]...Barry Manilow

ALBUMS
- POP Chicago IX - Chicago's Greatest Hits [1]...Chicago
- R&B Let's Do It Again [2]...The Staple Singers
- C&W Are You Ready For Freddy [1]...Freddy Fender

December 20, 1975
SINGLES
- HOT That's The Way (I Like It) [2]...KC & The Sunshine Band
- R&B Full Of Fire [1]...Al Green
- C&W *Convoy [1]...C.W. McCall
- A/C I Write The Songs [2]...Barry Manilow

ALBUMS
- POP Chicago IX - Chicago's Greatest Hits [2]...Chicago
- R&B Feels So Good [1]...Grover Washington, Jr.
- C&W Are You Ready For Freddy [2]...Freddy Fender

December 27, 1975
SINGLES
- HOT Let's Do It Again [1]...The Staple Singers
- R&B *Love Rollercoaster [1]...Ohio Players
- C&W Convoy [2]...C.W. McCall
- A/C Country Boy (You Got Your Feet In L.A.) [1]...Glen Campbell

ALBUMS
- POP Chicago IX - Chicago's Greatest Hits [3]...Chicago
- R&B Family Reunion [1]...The O'Jays
- C&W Black Bear Road [1]...C.W. McCall

January 3, 1976
SINGLES
- HOT Saturday Night [1]...Bay City Rollers
- R&B Walk Away From Love [1]...David Ruffin
- C&W Convoy [3]...C.W. McCall
- A/C Times Of Your Life [1]...Paul Anka

ALBUMS
- POP Chicago IX - Chicago's Greatest Hits [4]...Chicago
- R&B Gratitude [1]...Earth, Wind & Fire
- C&W Black Bear Road [2]...C.W. McCall

January 10, 1976
SINGLES
- HOT Convoy [1]...C.W. McCall
- R&B Sing A Song [1]...Earth, Wind & Fire
- C&W Convoy [4]...C.W. McCall
- A/C Fly Away [1]...John Denver

ALBUMS
- POP Chicago IX - Chicago's Greatest Hits [5]...Chicago
- R&B Gratitude [2]...Earth, Wind & Fire
- C&W Black Bear Road [3]...C.W. McCall

January 17, 1976
SINGLES
- HOT I Write The Songs [1]...Barry Manilow
- R&B Wake Up Everybody (Part 1) [1]...Harold Melvin & The Blue Notes
- C&W Convoy [5]...C.W. McCall
- A/C Let It Shine/He Ain't Heavy...He's My Brother [1]...Olivia Newton-John

ALBUMS
- POP Gratitude [1]...Earth, Wind & Fire
- R&B Gratitude [3]...Earth, Wind & Fire
- C&W Black Bear Road [4]...C.W. McCall

January 24, 1976
SINGLES
- HOT Theme From Mahogany (Do You Know Where You're Going To) [1]...Diana Ross
- R&B Wake Up Everybody (Part 1) [2]...Harold Melvin & The Blue Notes
- C&W Convoy [6]...C.W. McCall
- A/C Let It Shine/He Ain't Heavy...He's My Brother [2]...Olivia Newton-John

ALBUMS
- POP Gratitude [2]...Earth, Wind & Fire
- R&B Wake Up Everybody [1]...Harold Melvin & The Blue Notes
- C&W Black Bear Road [5]...C.W. McCall

January 31, 1976
SINGLES
- HOT Love Rollercoaster [1]...Ohio Players
- R&B Sing A Song [2]...Earth, Wind & Fire
- C&W This Time I've Hurt Her More Than She Loves Me [1]...Conway Twitty
- A/C Fly Away [2]...John Denver

ALBUMS
- POP Gratitude [3]...Earth, Wind & Fire
- R&B Wake Up Everybody [2]...Harold Melvin & The Blue Notes
- C&W Black Bear Road [6]...C.W. McCall

February 7, 1976

SINGLES
- HOT *50 Ways To Leave Your Lover [1]...Paul Simon
- R&B Turning Point [1]...Tyrone Davis
- C&W Sometimes [1]...Bill Anderson & Mary Lou Turner
- A/C Breaking Up Is Hard To Do [1]...Neil Sedaka

ALBUMS
- POP Desire [1]...Bob Dylan
- R&B Gratitude [4]...Earth, Wind & Fire
- C&W Black Bear Road [7]...C.W. McCall

February 14, 1976

SINGLES
- HOT 50 Ways To Leave Your Lover [2]...Paul Simon
- R&B Inseparable [1]...Natalie Cole
- C&W The White Knight [1]...
  Cledus Maggard & The Citizen's Band
- A/C Paloma Blanca [1]...George Baker Selection

ALBUMS
- POP Desire [2]...Bob Dylan
- R&B Gratitude [5]...Earth, Wind & Fire
- C&W Black Bear Road [8]...C.W. McCall

February 21, 1976

SINGLES
- HOT 50 Ways To Leave Your Lover [3]...Paul Simon
- R&B Sweet Thing [1]...Rufus Featuring Chaka Khan
- C&W Good Hearted Woman [1]...Waylon & Willie
- A/C Break Away [1]...Art Garfunkel

ALBUMS
- POP Desire [3]...Bob Dylan
- R&B Gratitude [6]...Earth, Wind & Fire
- C&W Black Bear Road [9]...C.W. McCall

February 28, 1976

SINGLES
- HOT Theme From S.W.A.T. [1]...Rhythm Heritage
- R&B Sweet Thing [2]...Rufus Featuring Chaka Khan
- C&W Good Hearted Woman [2]...Waylon & Willie
- A/C 50 Ways To Leave Your Lover [1]...Paul Simon

ALBUMS
- POP Desire [4]...Bob Dylan
- R&B Rufus featuring Chaka Khan [1]...
  Rufus Featuring Chaka Khan
- C&W Wanted: The Outlaws [1]...
  Waylon Jennings, Willie Nelson, Jessi Colter, Tompall Glaser

March 6, 1976

SINGLES
- HOT Love Machine (Part 1) [1]...The Miracles
- R&B *Boogie Fever [1]...The Sylvers
- C&W Good Hearted Woman [3]...Waylon & Willie
- A/C 50 Ways To Leave Your Lover [2]...Paul Simon

ALBUMS
- POP Desire [5]...Bob Dylan
- R&B Rufus featuring Chaka Khan [2]...
  Rufus Featuring Chaka Khan
- C&W Wanted: The Outlaws [2]...
  Waylon Jennings, Willie Nelson, Jessi Colter, Tompall Glaser

March 13, 1976

SINGLES
- HOT December, 1963 (Oh, What a Night) [1]...
  The Four Seasons
- R&B *Disco Lady [1]...Johnnie Taylor
- C&W The Roots Of My Raising [1]...Merle Haggard
- A/C Lonely Night (Angel Face) [1]...Captain & Tennille

ALBUMS
- POP Eagles/Their Greatest Hits 1971-1975 [1]...Eagles
- R&B Rufus featuring Chaka Khan [3]...
  Rufus Featuring Chaka Khan
- C&W Wanted: The Outlaws [3]...
  Waylon Jennings, Willie Nelson, Jessi Colter, Tompall Glaser

March 20, 1976

SINGLES
- HOT December, 1963 (Oh, What a Night) [2]...
  The Four Seasons
- R&B Disco Lady [2]...Johnnie Taylor
- C&W Faster Horses (The Cowboy And The Poet) [1]...
  Tom T. Hall
- A/C Venus [1]...Frankie Avalon

ALBUMS
- POP Eagles/Their Greatest Hits 1971-1975 [2]...Eagles
- R&B Rufus featuring Chaka Khan [4]...
  Rufus Featuring Chaka Khan
- C&W Wanted: The Outlaws [4]...
  Waylon Jennings, Willie Nelson, Jessi Colter, Tompall Glaser

March 27, 1976

SINGLES
- HOT December, 1963 (Oh, What a Night) [3]...
  The Four Seasons
- R&B Disco Lady [3]...Johnnie Taylor
- C&W Til The Rivers All Run Dry [1]...Don Williams
- A/C Only Love Is Real [1]...Carole King

ALBUMS
- POP Eagles/Their Greatest Hits 1971-1975 [3]...Eagles
- R&B Rufus featuring Chaka Khan [5]...
  Rufus Featuring Chaka Khan
- C&W Wanted: The Outlaws [5]...
  Waylon Jennings, Willie Nelson, Jessi Colter, Tompall Glaser

April 3, 1976
SINGLES
- HOT Disco Lady [1]...Johnnie Taylor
- R&B Disco Lady [4]...Johnnie Taylor
- C&W You'll Lose A Good Thing [1]...Freddy Fender
- A/C There's A Kind Of Hush (All Over The World) [1]...Carpenters

ALBUMS
- POP Eagles/Their Greatest Hits 1971-1975 [4]...Eagles
- R&B Rufus featuring Chaka Khan [6]...Rufus Featuring Chaka Khan
- C&W Wanted: The Outlaws [6]...Waylon Jennings, Willie Nelson, Jessi Colter, Tompall Glaser

April 10, 1976
SINGLES
- HOT Disco Lady [2]...Johnnie Taylor
- R&B Disco Lady [5]...Johnnie Taylor
- C&W 'Til I Can Make It On My Own [1]...Tammy Wynette
- A/C There's A Kind Of Hush (All Over The World) [2]...Carpenters

ALBUMS
- POP Frampton Comes Alive! [1]...Peter Frampton
- R&B Eargasm [1]...Johnnie Taylor
- C&W Elite Hotel [1]...Emmylou Harris

April 17, 1976
SINGLES
- HOT Disco Lady [3]...Johnnie Taylor
- R&B Disco Lady [6]...Johnnie Taylor
- C&W Drinkin' My Baby (Off My Mind) [1]...Eddie Rabbitt
- A/C Looking For Space [1]...John Denver

ALBUMS
- POP Eagles/Their Greatest Hits 1971-1975 [5]...Eagles
- R&B Eargasm [2]...Johnnie Taylor
- C&W Elite Hotel [2]...Emmylou Harris

April 24, 1976
SINGLES
- HOT Disco Lady [4]...Johnnie Taylor
- R&B Livin' For The Weekend/Stairway To Heaven [1]...The O'Jays
- C&W Together Again [1]...Emmylou Harris
- A/C Come On Over [1]...Olivia Newton-John

ALBUMS
- POP Wings At The Speed Of Sound [1]...Wings
- R&B Brass Construction [1]...Brass Construction
- C&W The Sound In Your Mind [1]...Willie Nelson

May 1, 1976
SINGLES
- HOT Let Your Love Flow [1]...Bellamy Brothers
- R&B Livin' For The Weekend/Stairway To Heaven [2]...The O'Jays
- C&W Don't The Girls All Get Prettier At Closing Time [1]...Mickey Gilley
- A/C Tryin' To Get The Feeling Again [1]...Barry Manilow

ALBUMS
- POP Presence [1]...Led Zeppelin
- R&B Brass Construction [2]...Brass Construction
- C&W It's All In The Movies [1]...Merle Haggard

May 8, 1976
SINGLES
- HOT *Welcome Back [1]...John Sebastian
- R&B Movin' [1]...Brass Construction
- C&W My Eyes Can Only See As Far As You [1]...Charley Pride
- A/C Don't Pull Your Love/Then You Can Tell Me Goodbye [1]...Glen Campbell

ALBUMS
- POP Presence [2]...Led Zeppelin
- R&B Brass Construction [3]...Brass Construction
- C&W The Sound In Your Mind [2]...Willie Nelson

May 15, 1976
SINGLES
- HOT Boogie Fever [1]...Sylvers
- R&B *Love Hangover [1]...Diana Ross
- C&W What Goes On When The Sun Goes Down [1]...Ronnie Milsap
- A/C Welcome Back [1]...John Sebastian

ALBUMS
- POP Black And Blue [1]...The Rolling Stones
- R&B I Want You [1]...Marvin Gaye
- C&W The Sound In Your Mind [3]...Willie Nelson

May 22, 1976
SINGLES
- HOT *Silly Love Songs [1]...Wings
- R&B *Kiss And Say Goodbye [1]...Manhattans
- C&W After All The Good Is Gone [1]...Conway Twitty
- A/C Welcome Back [2]...John Sebastian

ALBUMS
- POP Black And Blue [2]...The Rolling Stones
- R&B Breezin' [1]...George Benson
- C&W The Sound In Your Mind [4]...Willie Nelson

May 29, 1976

SINGLES
- HOT Love Hangover [1]...Diana Ross
- R&B I Want You [1]...Marvin Gaye
- C&W One Piece At A Time [1]...Johnny Cash
- A/C Silly Love Songs [1]...Wings

ALBUMS
- POP Wings At The Speed Of Sound [2]...Wings
- R&B Look Out For #1 [1]...The Brothers Johnson
- C&W The Sound In Your Mind [5]...Willie Nelson

June 5, 1976

SINGLES
- HOT Love Hangover [2]...Diana Ross
- R&B Young Hearts Run Free [1]...Candi Staton
- C&W One Piece At A Time [2]...Johnny Cash
- A/C Shop Around [1]...Captain & Tennille

ALBUMS
- POP Black And Blue [3]...The Rolling Stones
- R&B Look Out For #1 [2]...The Brothers Johnson
- C&W The Sound In Your Mind [6]...Willie Nelson

June 12, 1976

SINGLES
- HOT Silly Love Songs [2]...Wings
- R&B I'll Be Good To You [1]...The Brothers Johnson
- C&W I'll Get Over You [1]...Crystal Gayle
- A/C Save Your Kisses For Me [1]...The Brotherhood Of Man

ALBUMS
- POP Black And Blue [4]...The Rolling Stones
- R&B Look Out For #1 [3]...The Brothers Johnson
- C&W The Sound In Your Mind [7]...Willie Nelson

June 19, 1976

SINGLES
- HOT Silly Love Songs [3]...Wings
- R&B Sophisticated Lady (She's A Different Lady) [1]...Natalie Cole
- C&W El Paso City [1]...Marty Robbins
- A/C Never Gonna Fall In Love Again [1]...Eric Carmen

ALBUMS
- POP Wings At The Speed Of Sound [3]...Wings
- R&B Look Out For #1 [4]...The Brothers Johnson
- C&W The Sound In Your Mind [8]...Willie Nelson

June 26, 1976

SINGLES
- HOT Silly Love Songs [4]...Wings
- R&B Something He Can Feel [1]...Aretha Franklin
- C&W El Paso City [2]...Marty Robbins
- A/C Today's The Day [1]...America

ALBUMS
- POP Wings At The Speed Of Sound [4]...Wings
- R&B Harvest For The World [1]...The Isley Brothers
- C&W Harmony [1]...Don Williams

July 4, 1976

SINGLES
- HOT Silly Love Songs [5]...Wings
- R&B Something He Can Feel [2]...Aretha Franklin
- C&W All These Things [1]...Joe Stampley
- A/C Today's The Day [2]...America

ALBUMS
- POP Wings At The Speed Of Sound [5]...Wings
- R&B Breezin' [2]...George Benson
- C&W Harmony [2]...Don Williams

July 10, 1976

SINGLES
- HOT Afternoon Delight [1]...Starland Vocal Band
- R&B Something He Can Feel [3]...Aretha Franklin
- C&W The Door Is Always Open [1]...Dave & Sugar
- A/C I Need To Be In Love [1]...Carpenters

ALBUMS
- POP Wings At The Speed Of Sound [6]...Wings
- R&B Breezin' [3]...George Benson
- C&W From Elvis Presley Boulevard, Memphis, Tennessee [1]...Elvis Presley

July 17, 1976

SINGLES
- HOT Afternoon Delight [2]...Starland Vocal Band
- R&B Something He Can Feel [4]...Aretha Franklin
- C&W Teddy Bear [1]...Red Sovine
- A/C If You Know What I Mean [1]...Neil Diamond

ALBUMS
- POP Wings At The Speed Of Sound [7]...Wings
- R&B Breezin' [4]...George Benson
- C&W From Elvis Presley Boulevard, Memphis, Tennessee [2]...Elvis Presley

July 24, 1976

SINGLES
- HOT Kiss And Say Goodbye [1]...Manhattans
- R&B *You'll Never Find Another Love Like Mine [1]...Lou Rawls
- C&W Teddy Bear [2]...Red Sovine
- A/C I'm Easy [1]...Keith Carradine

ALBUMS
- POP Frampton Comes Alive! [2]...Peter Frampton
- R&B Contradiction [1]...Ohio Players
- C&W From Elvis Presley Boulevard, Memphis, Tennessee [3]...Elvis Presley

July 31, 1976

SINGLES
- HOT Kiss And Say Goodbye [2]...Manhattans
- R&B You'll Never Find Another Love Like Mine [2]...Lou Rawls
- C&W Teddy Bear [3]...Red Sovine
- A/C You'll Never Find Another Love Like Mine [1]...Lou Rawls

ALBUMS
- POP Breezin' [1]...George Benson
- R&B Sparkle [1]...Aretha Franklin/Soundtrack
- C&W From Elvis Presley Boulevard, Memphis, Tennessee [4]...Elvis Presley

August 7, 1976

SINGLES
- HOT *Don't Go Breaking My Heart [1]...Elton John & Kiki Dee
- R&B Getaway [1]...Earth, Wind & Fire
- C&W Golden Ring [1]...George Jones & Tammy Wynette
- A/C Let 'Em In [1]...Wings

ALBUMS
- POP Breezin' [2]...George Benson
- R&B Breezin' [5]...George Benson
- C&W United Talent [1]...Conway Twitty & Loretta Lynn

August 14, 1976

SINGLES
- HOT Don't Go Breaking My Heart [2]...Elton John & Kiki Dee
- R&B Getaway [2]...Earth, Wind & Fire
- C&W Say It Again [1]...Don Williams
- A/C If You Know What I Mean [2]...Neil Diamond

ALBUMS
- POP Frampton Comes Alive! [3]...Peter Frampton
- R&B Breezin' [6]...George Benson
- C&W Are You Ready For The Country [1]...Waylon Jennings

August 21, 1976

SINGLES
- HOT Don't Go Breaking My Heart [3]...Elton John & Kiki Dee
- R&B Who'd She Coo? [1]...Ohio Players
- C&W Bring It On Home To Me [1]...Mickey Gilley
- A/C I'd Really Love To See You Tonight [1]...England Dan & John Ford Coley

ALBUMS
- POP Frampton Comes Alive! [4]...Peter Frampton
- R&B All Things In Time [1]...Lou Rawls
- C&W Are You Ready For The Country [2]...Waylon Jennings

August 28, 1976

SINGLES
- HOT Don't Go Breaking My Heart [4]...Elton John & Kiki Dee
- R&B *(Shake, Shake, Shake) Shake Your Booty [1]...KC & The Sunshine Band
- C&W (I'm A) Stand By My Woman Man [1]...Ronnie Milsap
- A/C Shower The People [1]...James Taylor

ALBUMS
- POP Frampton Comes Alive! [5]...Peter Frampton
- R&B Hot On The Tracks [1]...Commodores
- C&W Teddy Bear [1]...Red Sovine

September 4, 1976

SINGLES
- HOT You Should Be Dancing [1]...Bee Gees
- R&B *Play That Funky Music [1]...Wild Cherry
- C&W (I'm A) Stand By My Woman Man [2]...Ronnie Milsap
- A/C Summer [1]...War

ALBUMS
- POP Fleetwood Mac [1]...Fleetwood Mac
- R&B Hot On The Tracks [2]...Commodores
- C&W Are You Ready For The Country [3]...Waylon Jennings

September 11, 1976

SINGLES
- HOT (Shake, Shake, Shake) Shake Your Booty [1]...KC & The Sunshine Band
- R&B Play That Funky Music [2]...Wild Cherry
- C&W I Don't Want To Have To Marry You [1]...Jim Ed Brown/Helen Cornelius
- A/C Don't Go Breaking My Heart [1]...Elton John & Kiki Dee

ALBUMS
- POP Frampton Comes Alive! [6]...Peter Frampton
- R&B Wild Cherry [1]...Wild Cherry
- C&W Are You Ready For The Country [4]...Waylon Jennings

September 18, 1976

SINGLES
- HOT Play That Funky Music [1]...Wild Cherry
- R&B (Shake, Shake, Shake) Shake Your Booty [2]...KC & The Sunshine Band
- C&W I Don't Want To Have To Marry You [2]...Jim Ed Brown/Helen Cornelius
- A/C Don't Stop Believin' [1]...Olivia Newton-John

ALBUMS
- POP Frampton Comes Alive! [7]...Peter Frampton
- R&B Hot On The Tracks [3]...Commodores
- C&W Are You Ready For The Country [5]...Waylon Jennings

September 25, 1976

SINGLES
- HOT Play That Funky Music [2]...Wild Cherry
- R&B (Shake, Shake, Shake) Shake Your Booty [3]...KC & The Sunshine Band
- C&W If You've Got The Money I've Got The Time [1]...Willie Nelson
- A/C *If You Leave Me Now [1]...Chicago

ALBUMS
- POP Frampton Comes Alive! [8]...Peter Frampton
- R&B Hot On The Tracks [4]...Commodores
- C&W Are You Ready For The Country [6]...Waylon Jennings

October 2, 1976

SINGLES
- HOT Play That Funky Music [3]...Wild Cherry
- R&B (Shake, Shake, Shake) Shake Your Booty [4]...KC & The Sunshine Band
- C&W Here's Some Love [1]...Tanya Tucker
- A/C I Can't Hear You No More [1]...Helen Reddy

ALBUMS
- POP Frampton Comes Alive! [9]...Peter Frampton
- R&B Hot On The Tracks [5]...Commodores
- C&W Hasten Down The Wind [1]...Linda Ronstadt

October 9, 1976

SINGLES
- HOT A Fifth Of Beethoven [1]...Walter Murphy & The Big Apple Band
- R&B Just To Be Close To You [1]...Commodores
- C&W The Games That Daddies Play [1]...Conway Twitty
- A/C Like A Sad Song [1]...John Denver

ALBUMS
- POP Frampton Comes Alive! [10]...Peter Frampton
- R&B Hot On The Tracks [6]...Commodores
- C&W Hasten Down The Wind [2]...Linda Ronstadt

October 16, 1976

SINGLES
- HOT Disco Duck (Part 1) [1]...Rick Dees And His Cast Of Idiots
- R&B Just To Be Close To You [2]...Commodores
- C&W You And Me [1]...Tammy Wynette
- A/C Fernando [1]...Abba

ALBUMS
- POP Songs In The Key Of Life [1]...Stevie Wonder
- R&B Songs In The Key Of Life [1]...Stevie Wonder
- C&W Are You Ready For The Country [7]...Waylon Jennings

October 23, 1976

SINGLES
- HOT If You Leave Me Now [1]...Chicago
- R&B The Rubberband Man [1]...Spinners
- C&W You And Me [2]...Tammy Wynette
- A/C Fernando [2]...Abba

ALBUMS
- POP Songs In The Key Of Life [2]...Stevie Wonder
- R&B Songs In The Key Of Life [2]...Stevie Wonder
- C&W Hasten Down The Wind [3]...Linda Ronstadt

October 30, 1976

SINGLES
- HOT If You Leave Me Now [2]...Chicago
- R&B Message In Our Music [1]...The O'Jays
- C&W Among My Souvenirs [1]...Marty Robbins
- A/C Muskrat Love [1]...Captain & Tennille

ALBUMS
- POP Songs In The Key Of Life [3]...Stevie Wonder
- R&B Songs In The Key Of Life [3]...Stevie Wonder
- C&W Golden Ring [1]...Tammy Wynette

November 6, 1976

SINGLES
- HOT Rock'n Me [1]...Steve Miller
- R&B Love Ballad [1]...L.T.D.
- C&W Cherokee Maiden/What Have You Got Planned Tonight Diana [1]...Merle Haggard
- A/C Muskrat Love [2]...Captain & Tennille

ALBUMS
- POP Songs In The Key Of Life [4]...Stevie Wonder
- R&B Songs In The Key Of Life [4]...Stevie Wonder
- C&W Here's Some Love [1]...Tanya Tucker

November 13, 1976

SINGLES
- HOT Tonight's The Night (Gonna Be Alright) [1]...Rod Stewart
- R&B Love Ballad [2]...L.T.D.
- C&W Somebody Somewhere (Don't Know What He's Missin' Tonight) [1]...Loretta Lynn
- A/C This One's For You [1]...Barry Manilow

ALBUMS
- POP Songs In The Key Of Life [5]...Stevie Wonder
- R&B Songs In The Key Of Life [5]...Stevie Wonder
- C&W El Paso City [1]...Marty Robbins

November 20, 1976
SINGLES
- HOT Tonight's The Night (Gonna Be Alright) [2]...Rod Stewart
- R&B *You Don't Have To Be A Star (To Be In My Show) [1]...Marilyn McCoo & Billy Davis, Jr.
- C&W Somebody Somewhere (Don't Know What He's Missin' Tonight) [2]...Loretta Lynn
- A/C Muskrat Love [3]...Captain & Tennille

ALBUMS
- POP Songs In The Key Of Life [6]...Stevie Wonder
- R&B Songs In The Key Of Life [6]...Stevie Wonder
- C&W The Troublemaker [1]...Willie Nelson

November 27, 1976
SINGLES
- HOT Tonight's The Night (Gonna Be Alright) [3]...Rod Stewart
- R&B Dazz [1]...Brick
- C&W Good Woman Blues [1]...Mel Tillis
- A/C Muskrat Love [4]...Captain & Tennille

ALBUMS
- POP Songs In The Key Of Life [7]...Stevie Wonder
- R&B Songs In The Key Of Life [7]...Stevie Wonder
- C&W The Troublemaker [2]...Willie Nelson

December 4, 1976
SINGLES
- HOT Tonight's The Night (Gonna Be Alright) [4]...Rod Stewart
- R&B Dazz [2]...Brick
- C&W Good Woman Blues [2]...Mel Tillis
- A/C After The Lovin' [1]...Engelbert Humperdinck

ALBUMS
- POP Songs In The Key Of Life [8]...Stevie Wonder
- R&B Songs In The Key Of Life [8]...Stevie Wonder
- C&W The Troublemaker [3]...Willie Nelson

December 11, 1976
SINGLES
- HOT Tonight's The Night (Gonna Be Alright) [5]...Rod Stewart
- R&B Dazz [3]...Brick
- C&W Thinkin' Of A Rendezvous [1]...Johnny Duncan
- A/C After The Lovin' [2]...Engelbert Humperdinck

ALBUMS
- POP Songs In The Key Of Life [9]...Stevie Wonder
- R&B Songs In The Key Of Life [9]...Stevie Wonder
- C&W Somebody Somewhere [1]...Loretta Lynn

December 18, 1976
SINGLES
- HOT Tonight's The Night (Gonna Be Alright) [6]...Rod Stewart
- R&B Dazz [4]...Brick
- C&W Thinkin' Of A Rendezvous [2]...Johnny Duncan
- A/C Sorry Seems To Be The Hardest Word [1]...Elton John

ALBUMS
- POP Songs In The Key Of Life [10]...Stevie Wonder
- R&B Songs In The Key Of Life [10]...Stevie Wonder
- C&W Are You Ready For The Country [8]...Waylon Jennings

December 25, 1976
SINGLES
- HOT Tonight's The Night (Gonna Be Alright) [7]...Rod Stewart
- R&B *Car Wash [1]...Rose Royce
- C&W Sweet Dreams [1]...Emmylou Harris
- A/C *Torn Between Two Lovers [1]...Mary MacGregor

ALBUMS
- POP Songs In The Key Of Life [11]...Stevie Wonder
- R&B Songs In The Key Of Life [11]...Stevie Wonder
- C&W Are You Ready For The Country [9]...Waylon Jennings

January 1, 1977
SINGLES
- HOT Tonight's The Night (Gonna Be Alright) [8]...Rod Stewart
- R&B Car Wash [2]...Rose Royce
- C&W Sweet Dreams [2]...Emmylou Harris
- A/C Torn Between Two Lovers [2]...Mary MacGregor

ALBUMS
- POP Songs In The Key Of Life [12]...Stevie Wonder
- R&B Songs In The Key Of Life [12]...Stevie Wonder
- C&W Are You Ready For The Country [10]...Waylon Jennings

January 8, 1977
SINGLES
- HOT You Don't Have To Be A Star (To Be In My Show) [1]...Marilyn McCoo & Billy Davis, Jr.
- R&B Darlin' Darlin' Baby (Sweet, Tender, Love) [1]...The O'Jays
- C&W Broken Down In Tiny Pieces [1]...Billy "Crash" Craddock
- A/C Weekend In New England [1]...Barry Manilow

ALBUMS
- POP Songs In The Key Of Life [13]...Stevie Wonder
- R&B Good High [1]...Brick
- C&W Greatest Hits Vol. II [1]...Conway Twitty

January 15, 1977

SINGLES
- HOT You Make Me Feel Like Dancing [1]...Leo Sayer
- R&B *I Wish [1]...Stevie Wonder
- C&W You Never Miss A Real Good Thing (Till He Says Goodbye) [1]...Crystal Gayle
- A/C *Love Theme From "A Star Is Born" (Evergreen) [1]...Barbra Streisand

ALBUMS
- POP Hotel California [1]...Eagles
- R&B Songs In The Key Of Life [13]...Stevie Wonder
- C&W Waylon Live [1]...Waylon Jennings

January 22, 1977

SINGLES
- HOT I Wish [1]...Stevie Wonder
- R&B I Wish [2]...Stevie Wonder
- C&W I Can't Believe She Gives It All To Me [1]...Conway Twitty
- A/C Love Theme From "A Star Is Born" (Evergreen) [2]...Barbra Streisand

ALBUMS
- POP Wings Over America [1]...Wings
- R&B Songs In The Key Of Life [14]...Stevie Wonder
- C&W Waylon Live [2]...Waylon Jennings

January 29, 1977

SINGLES
- HOT Car Wash [1]...Rose Royce
- R&B I Wish [3]...Stevie Wonder
- C&W Let My Love Be Your Pillow [1]...Ronnie Milsap
- A/C Love Theme From "A Star Is Born" (Evergreen) [3]...Barbra Streisand

ALBUMS
- POP Songs In The Key Of Life [14]...Stevie Wonder
- R&B Songs In The Key Of Life [15]...Stevie Wonder
- C&W Waylon Live [3]...Waylon Jennings

February 5, 1977

SINGLES
- HOT Torn Between Two Lovers [1]...Mary MacGregor
- R&B I Wish [4]...Stevie Wonder
- C&W Near You [1]...George Jones & Tammy Wynette
- A/C Love Theme From "A Star Is Born" (Evergreen) [4]...Barbra Streisand

ALBUMS
- POP Hotel California [2]...Eagles
- R&B Songs In The Key Of Life [16]...Stevie Wonder
- C&W Waylon Live [4]...Waylon Jennings

February 12, 1977

SINGLES
- HOT Torn Between Two Lovers [2]...Mary MacGregor
- R&B I Wish [5]...Stevie Wonder
- C&W Near You [2]...George Jones & Tammy Wynette
- A/C Love Theme From "A Star Is Born" (Evergreen) [5]...Barbra Streisand

ALBUMS
- POP A Star Is Born [1]...Barbra Streisand/Soundtrack
- R&B Songs In The Key Of Life [17]...Stevie Wonder
- C&W Waylon Live [5]...Waylon Jennings

February 19, 1977

SINGLES
- HOT Blinded By The Light [1]...Manfred Mann's Earth Band
- R&B *Don't Leave Me This Way [1]...Thelma Houston
- C&W Moody Blue/She Thinks I Still Care [1]...Elvis Presley
- A/C Love Theme From "A Star Is Born" (Evergreen) [6]...Barbra Streisand

ALBUMS
- POP A Star Is Born [2]...Barbra Streisand/Soundtrack
- R&B Songs In The Key Of Life [18]...Stevie Wonder
- C&W Waylon Live [6]...Waylon Jennings

February 26, 1977

SINGLES
- HOT New Kid In Town [1]...Eagles
- R&B I've Got Love On My Mind [1]...Natalie Cole
- C&W Say You'll Stay Until Tomorrow [1]...Tom Jones
- A/C *Southern Nights [1]...Glen Campbell

ALBUMS
- POP A Star Is Born [3]...Barbra Streisand/Soundtrack
- R&B Songs In The Key Of Life [19]...Stevie Wonder
- C&W Luxury Liner [1]...Emmylou Harris

March 5, 1977

SINGLES
- HOT Love Theme From "A Star Is Born" (Evergreen) [1]...Barbra Streisand
- R&B I've Got Love On My Mind [2]...Natalie Cole
- C&W Heart Healer [1]...Mel Tillis
- A/C Southern Nights [2]...Glen Campbell

ALBUMS
- POP A Star Is Born [4]...Barbra Streisand/Soundtrack
- R&B Songs In The Key Of Life [20]...Stevie Wonder
- C&W Luxury Liner [2]...Emmylou Harris

March 12, 1977

SINGLES
- HOT Love Theme From "A Star Is Born" (Evergreen) [2]...Barbra Streisand
- R&B I've Got Love On My Mind [3]...Natalie Cole
- C&W She's Just An Old Love Turned Memory [1]...Charley Pride
- A/C Sam [1]...Olivia Newton-John

ALBUMS
- POP A Star Is Born [5]...Barbra Streisand/Soundtrack
- R&B Ask Rufus [1]...Rufus Featuring Chaka Khan
- C&W Luxury Liner [3]...Emmylou Harris

March 19, 1977

SINGLES
- HOT Love Theme From "A Star Is Born" (Evergreen) [3]...Barbra Streisand
- R&B I've Got Love On My Mind [4]...Natalie Cole
- C&W Southern Nights [1]...Glen Campbell
- A/C Sam [2]...Olivia Newton-John

ALBUMS
- POP A Star Is Born [6]...Barbra Streisand/Soundtrack
- R&B Ask Rufus [2]...Rufus Featuring Chaka Khan
- C&W Luxury Liner [4]...Emmylou Harris

March 26, 1977

SINGLES
- HOT Rich Girl [1]...Daryl Hall & John Oates
- R&B I've Got Love On My Mind [5]...Natalie Cole
- C&W Southern Nights [2]...Glen Campbell
- A/C Southern Nights [3]...Glen Campbell

ALBUMS
- POP Hotel California [3]...Eagles
- R&B Ask Rufus [3]...Rufus Featuring Chaka Khan
- C&W Luxury Liner [5]...Emmylou Harris

April 2, 1977

SINGLES
- HOT Rich Girl [2]...Daryl Hall & John Oates
- R&B Tryin' To Love Two [1]...William Bell
- C&W Lucille [1]...Kenny Rogers
- A/C Southern Nights [4]...Glen Campbell

ALBUMS
- POP Rumours [1]...Fleetwood Mac
- R&B Unpredictable [1]...Natalie Cole
- C&W Luxury Liner [6]...Emmylou Harris

April 9, 1977

SINGLES
- HOT Dancing Queen [1]...Abba
- R&B At Midnight (My Love Will Lift You Up) [1]...Rufus Featuring Chaka Khan
- C&W Lucille [2]...Kenny Rogers
- A/C *Don't Give Up On Us [1]...David Soul

ALBUMS
- POP Rumours [2]...Fleetwood Mac
- R&B Unpredictable [2]...Natalie Cole
- C&W Luxury Liner [7]...Emmylou Harris

April 16, 1977

SINGLES
- HOT Don't Give Up On Us [1]...David Soul
- R&B At Midnight (My Love Will Lift You Up) [2]...Rufus Featuring Chaka Khan
- C&W It Couldn't Have Been Any Better [1]...Johnny Duncan
- A/C Right Time Of The Night [1]...Jennifer Warnes

ALBUMS
- POP Hotel California [4]...Eagles
- R&B Unpredictable [3]...Natalie Cole
- C&W Luxury Liner [8]...Emmylou Harris

April 23, 1977

SINGLES
- HOT Don't Leave Me This Way [1]...Thelma Houston
- R&B The Pride (Part 1) [1]...The Isley Brothers
- C&W She's Got You [1]...Loretta Lynn
- A/C *When I Need You [1]...Leo Sayer

ALBUMS
- POP Hotel California [5]...Eagles
- R&B Ahh...The Name Is Bootsy, Baby! [1]...Bootsy's Rubber Band
- C&W Southern Nights [1]...Glen Campbell

April 30, 1977

SINGLES
- HOT Southern Nights [1]...Glen Campbell
- R&B *Got To Give It Up (Pt. I) [1]...Marvin Gaye
- C&W She's Pulling Me Back Again [1]...Mickey Gilley
- A/C Hello Stranger [1]...Yvonne Elliman

ALBUMS
- POP Hotel California [6]...Eagles
- R&B Marvin Gaye Live At The London Palladium [1]...Marvin Gaye
- C&W Southern Nights [2]...Glen Campbell

May 7, 1977
SINGLES
- HOT   Hotel California [1]...Eagles
- R&B   Got To Give It Up (Pt. I) [2]...Marvin Gaye
- C&W   Play, Guitar Play [1]...Conway Twitty
- A/C   Hello Stranger [2]...Yvonne Elliman

ALBUMS
- POP   Hotel California [7]...Eagles
- R&B   Marvin Gaye Live At The London Palladium [2]...Marvin Gaye
- C&W   Southern Nights [3]...Glen Campbell

May 14, 1977
SINGLES
- HOT   When I Need You [1]...Leo Sayer
- R&B   Got To Give It Up (Pt. I) [3]...Marvin Gaye
- C&W   Some Broken Hearts Never Mend [1]...Don Williams
- A/C   Hello Stranger [3]...Yvonne Elliman

ALBUMS
- POP   Hotel California [8]...Eagles
- R&B   Go For Your Guns [1]...The Isley Brothers
- C&W   New Harvest...First Gathering [1]...Dolly Parton

May 21, 1977
SINGLES
- HOT   *Sir Duke [1]...Stevie Wonder
- R&B   Whodunit [1]...Tavares
- C&W   Luckenbach, Texas (Back to the Basics of Love) [1]...Waylon Jennings
- A/C   Hello Stranger [4]...Yvonne Elliman

ALBUMS
- POP   Rumours [3]...Fleetwood Mac
- R&B   Commodores [1]...Commodores
- C&W   Kenny Rogers [1]...Kenny Rogers

May 28, 1977
SINGLES
- HOT   Sir Duke [2]...Stevie Wonder
- R&B   Sir Duke [1]...Stevie Wonder
- C&W   Luckenbach, Texas (Back to the Basics of Love) [2]...Waylon Jennings
- A/C   Margaritaville [1]...Jimmy Buffett

ALBUMS
- POP   Rumours [4]...Fleetwood Mac
- R&B   Commodores [2]...Commodores
- C&W   Kenny Rogers [2]...Kenny Rogers

June 4, 1977
SINGLES
- HOT   Sir Duke [3]...Stevie Wonder
- R&B   Got To Give It Up (Pt. I) [4]...Marvin Gaye
- C&W   Luckenbach, Texas (Back to the Basics of Love) [3]...Waylon Jennings
- A/C   *Looks Like We Made It [1]...Barry Manilow

ALBUMS
- POP   Rumours [5]...Fleetwood Mac
- R&B   Commodores [3]...Commodores
- C&W   Ol' Waylon [1]...Waylon Jennings

June 11, 1977
SINGLES
- HOT   I'm Your Boogie Man [1]...KC & The Sunshine Band
- R&B   Got To Give It Up (Pt. I) [5]...Marvin Gaye
- C&W   Luckenbach, Texas (Back to the Basics of Love) [4]...Waylon Jennings
- A/C   Looks Like We Made It [2]...Barry Manilow

ALBUMS
- POP   Rumours [6]...Fleetwood Mac
- R&B   Commodores [4]...Commodores
- C&W   Ol' Waylon [2]...Waylon Jennings

June 18, 1977
SINGLES
- HOT   Dreams [1]...Fleetwood Mac
- R&B   Break It To Me Gently [1]...Aretha Franklin
- C&W   Luckenbach, Texas (Back to the Basics of Love) [5]...Waylon Jennings
- A/C   Looks Like We Made It [3]...Barry Manilow

ALBUMS
- POP   Rumours [7]...Fleetwood Mac
- R&B   Commodores [5]...Commodores
- C&W   Ol' Waylon [3]...Waylon Jennings

June 25, 1977
SINGLES
- HOT   Got To Give It Up (Pt. I) [1]...Marvin Gaye
- R&B   *Best Of My Love [1]...Emotions
- C&W   Luckenbach, Texas (Back to the Basics of Love) [6]...Waylon Jennings
- A/C   It's Sad To Belong [1]...England Dan & John Ford Coley

ALBUMS
- POP   Rumours [8]...Fleetwood Mac
- R&B   Go For Your Guns [2]...The Isley Brothers
- C&W   Ol' Waylon [4]...Waylon Jennings

July 2, 1977
SINGLES
- *HOT* **Gonna Fly Now** [1]...Bill Conti
- *R&B* **Best Of My Love** [2]...Emotions
- *C&W* **That Was Yesterday** [1]...Donna Fargo
- *A/C* **It's Sad To Belong** [2]...England Dan & John Ford Coley

ALBUMS
- *POP* **Rumours** [9]...Fleetwood Mac
- *R&B* **Commodores** [6]...Commodores
- *C&W* **Ol' Waylon** [5]...Waylon Jennings

July 9, 1977
SINGLES
- *HOT* **Undercover Angel** [1]...Alan O'Day
- *R&B* **Best Of My Love** [3]...Emotions
- *C&W* **I'll Be Leaving Alone** [1]...Charley Pride
- *A/C* **It's Sad To Belong** [3]...England Dan & John Ford Coley

ALBUMS
- *POP* **Rumours** [10]...Fleetwood Mac
- *R&B* **Commodores** [7]...Commodores
- *C&W* **Ol' Waylon** [6]...Waylon Jennings

July 16, 1977
SINGLES
- *HOT* **Da Doo Ron Ron** [1]...Shaun Cassidy
- *R&B* **Easy** [1]...Commodores
- *C&W* **It Was Almost Like A Song** [1]...Ronnie Milsap
- *A/C* **It's Sad To Belong** [4]...England Dan & John Ford Coley

ALBUMS
- *POP* **Barry Manilow/Live** [1]...Barry Manilow
- *R&B* **Commodores** [8]...Commodores
- *C&W* **Ol' Waylon** [7]...Waylon Jennings

July 23, 1977
SINGLES
- *HOT* **Looks Like We Made It** [1]...Barry Manilow
- *R&B* **Best Of My Love** [4]...Emotions
- *C&W* **It Was Almost Like A Song** [2]...Ronnie Milsap
- *A/C* **It's Sad To Belong** [5]...England Dan & John Ford Coley

ALBUMS
- *POP* **Rumours** [11]...Fleetwood Mac
- *R&B* **Rejoice** [1]...Emotions
- *C&W* **Ol' Waylon** [8]...Waylon Jennings

July 30, 1977
SINGLES
- *HOT* **I Just Want To Be Your Everything** [1]...Andy Gibb
- *R&B* **Slide** [1]...Slave
- *C&W* **It Was Almost Like A Song** [3]...Ronnie Milsap
- *A/C* **My Heart Belongs To Me** [1]...Barbra Streisand

ALBUMS
- *POP* **Rumours** [12]...Fleetwood Mac
- *R&B* **Rejoice** [2]...Emotions
- *C&W* **Ol' Waylon** [9]...Waylon Jennings

August 6, 1977
SINGLES
- *HOT* **I Just Want To Be Your Everything** [2]...Andy Gibb
- *R&B* **Strawberry Letter 23** [1]...The Brothers Johnson
- *C&W* **Rollin' With The Flow** [1]...Charlie Rich
- *A/C* **My Heart Belongs To Me** [2]...Barbra Streisand

ALBUMS
- *POP* **Rumours** [13]...Fleetwood Mac
- *R&B* **Floaters** [1]...The Floaters
- *C&W* **Ol' Waylon** [10]...Waylon Jennings

August 13, 1977
SINGLES
- *HOT* **I Just Want To Be Your Everything** [3]...Andy Gibb
- *R&B* **Float On** [1]...The Floaters
- *C&W* **Rollin' With The Flow** [2]...Charlie Rich
- *A/C* **My Heart Belongs To Me** [3]...Barbra Streisand

ALBUMS
- *POP* **Rumours** [14]...Fleetwood Mac
- *R&B* **Floaters** [2]...The Floaters
- *C&W* **Ol' Waylon** [11]...Waylon Jennings

August 20, 1977
SINGLES
- *HOT* **Best Of My Love** [1]...Emotions
- *R&B* **Float On** [2]...The Floaters
- *C&W* **Way Down/Pledging My Love** [1]...Elvis Presley
- *A/C* **My Heart Belongs To Me** [4]...Barbra Streisand

ALBUMS
- *POP* **Rumours** [15]...Fleetwood Mac
- *R&B* **Floaters** [3]...The Floaters
- *C&W* **Ol' Waylon** [12]...Waylon Jennings

August 27, 1977
SINGLES
- *HOT* **Best Of My Love** [2]...Emotions
- *R&B* **Float On** [3]...The Floaters
- *C&W* **Don't It Make My Brown Eyes Blue** [1]...Crystal Gayle
- *A/C* **Sunflower** [1]...Glen Campbell

ALBUMS
- *POP* **Rumours** [16]...Fleetwood Mac
- *R&B* **Rejoice** [3]...The Emotions
- *C&W* **Ol' Waylon** [13]...Waylon Jennings

September 3, 1977
SINGLES
- *HOT* **Best Of My Love** [3]...Emotions
- *R&B* **Float On** [4]...The Floaters
- *C&W* **Don't It Make My Brown Eyes Blue** [2]...Crystal Gayle
- *A/C* **Handy Man** [1]...James Taylor

ALBUMS
- *POP* **Rumours** [17]...Fleetwood Mac
- *R&B* **Rejoice** [4]...The Emotions
- *C&W* **Moody Blue** [1]...Elvis Presley

September 10, 1977

SINGLES
- HOT Best Of My Love [4]...Emotions
- R&B Float On [5]...The Floaters
- C&W Don't It Make My Brown Eyes Blue [3]...Crystal Gayle
- A/C Nobody Does It Better [1]...Carly Simon

ALBUMS
- POP Rumours [18]...Fleetwood Mac
- R&B Rejoice [5]...The Emotions
- C&W Moody Blue [2]...Elvis Presley

September 17, 1977

SINGLES
- HOT I Just Want To Be Your Everything [4]...Andy Gibb
- R&B Float On [6]...The Floaters
- C&W Don't It Make My Brown Eyes Blue [4]...Crystal Gayle
- A/C Nobody Does It Better [2]...Carly Simon

ALBUMS
- POP Rumours [19]...Fleetwood Mac
- R&B Rejoice [6]...The Emotions
- C&W Moody Blue [3]...Elvis Presley

September 24, 1977

SINGLES
- HOT Best Of My Love [5]...Emotions
- R&B Keep It Comin' Love [1]...KC & The Sunshine Band
- C&W I've Already Loved You In My Mind [1]...Conway Twitty
- A/C Nobody Does It Better [3]...Carly Simon

ALBUMS
- POP Rumours [20]...Fleetwood Mac
- R&B Rejoice [7]...The Emotions
- C&W Moody Blue [4]...Elvis Presley

October 1, 1977

SINGLES
- HOT Star Wars Theme/Cantina Band [1]...Meco
- R&B It's Ecstasy When You Lay Down Next To Me [1]...Barry White
- C&W Daytime Friends [1]...Kenny Rogers
- A/C Nobody Does It Better [4]...Carly Simon

ALBUMS
- POP Rumours [21]...Fleetwood Mac
- R&B Rose Royce II/In Full Bloom [1]...Rose Royce
- C&W Moody Blue [5]...Elvis Presley

October 8, 1977

SINGLES
- HOT Star Wars Theme/Cantina Band [2]...Meco
- R&B It's Ecstasy When You Lay Down Next To Me [2]...Barry White
- C&W Heaven's Just A Sin Away [1]...The Kendalls
- A/C Nobody Does It Better [5]...Carly Simon

ALBUMS
- POP Rumours [22]...Fleetwood Mac
- R&B Something To Love [1]...L.T.D.
- C&W Moody Blue [6]...Elvis Presley

October 15, 1977

SINGLES
- HOT *You Light Up My Life [1]...Debby Boone
- R&B It's Ecstasy When You Lay Down Next To Me [3]...Barry White
- C&W Heaven's Just A Sin Away [2]...The Kendalls
- A/C Nobody Does It Better [6]...Carly Simon

ALBUMS
- POP Rumours [23]...Fleetwood Mac
- R&B Barry White Sings For Someone You Love [1]...Barry White
- C&W Moody Blue [7]...Elvis Presley

October 22, 1977

SINGLES
- HOT You Light Up My Life [2]...Debby Boone
- R&B It's Ecstasy When You Lay Down Next To Me [4]...Barry White
- C&W Heaven's Just A Sin Away [3]...The Kendalls
- A/C Nobody Does It Better [7]...Carly Simon

ALBUMS
- POP Rumours [24]...Fleetwood Mac
- R&B Barry White Sings For Someone You Love [2]...Barry White
- C&W Moody Blue [8]...Elvis Presley

October 29, 1977

SINGLES
- HOT You Light Up My Life [3]...Debby Boone
- R&B It's Ecstasy When You Lay Down Next To Me [5]...Barry White
- C&W Heaven's Just A Sin Away [4]...The Kendalls
- A/C Just Remember I Love You [1]...Firefall

ALBUMS
- POP Rumours [25]...Fleetwood Mac
- R&B Barry White Sings For Someone You Love [3]...Barry White
- C&W Moody Blue [9]...Elvis Presley

November 5, 1977
SINGLES
- HOT   You Light Up My Life [4]...Debby Boone
- R&B   (Every Time I Turn Around) Back In Love Again [1]...L.T.D.
- C&W   I'm Just A Country Boy [1]...Don Williams
- A/C   Just Remember I Love You [2]...Firefall

ALBUMS
- POP   Rumours [26]...Fleetwood Mac
- R&B   Barry White Sings For Someone You Love [4]...Barry White
- C&W   Moody Blue [10]...Elvis Presley

November 12, 1977
SINGLES
- HOT   You Light Up My Life [5]...Debby Boone
- R&B   (Every Time I Turn Around) Back In Love Again [2]...L.T.D.
- C&W   More To Me [1]...Charley Pride
- A/C   We're All Alone [1]...Rita Coolidge

ALBUMS
- POP   Rumours [27]...Fleetwood Mac
- R&B   Brick [1]...Brick
- C&W   Elvis In Concert [1]...Elvis Presley

November 19, 1977
SINGLES
- HOT   You Light Up My Life [6]...Debby Boone
- R&B   Serpentine Fire [1]...Earth, Wind & Fire
- C&W   The Wurlitzer Prize (I Don't Want To Get Over You)/Lookin' For A Feeling [1]...Waylon Jennings
- A/C   You Light Up My Life [1]...Debby Boone

ALBUMS
- POP   Rumours [28]...Fleetwood Mac
- R&B   Brick [2]...Brick
- C&W   Elvis In Concert [2]...Elvis Presley

November 26, 1977
SINGLES
- HOT   You Light Up My Life [7]...Debby Boone
- R&B   Serpentine Fire [2]...Earth, Wind & Fire
- C&W   The Wurlitzer Prize (I Don't Want To Get Over You)/Lookin' For A Feeling [2]...Waylon Jennings
- A/C   *How Deep Is Your Love [1]...Bee Gees

ALBUMS
- POP   Rumours [29]...Fleetwood Mac
- R&B   Barry White Sings For Someone You Love [5]...Barry White
- C&W   Elvis In Concert [3]...Elvis Presley

December 3, 1977
SINGLES
- HOT   You Light Up My Life [8]...Debby Boone
- R&B   Serpentine Fire [3]...Earth, Wind & Fire
- C&W   Here You Come Again [1]...Dolly Parton
- A/C   How Deep Is Your Love [2]...Bee Gees

ALBUMS
- POP   Simple Dreams [1]...Linda Ronstadt
- R&B   Rose Royce II/In Full Bloom [2]...Rose Royce
- C&W   Elvis In Concert [4]...Elvis Presley

December 10, 1977
SINGLES
- HOT   You Light Up My Life [9]...Debby Boone
- R&B   Serpentine Fire [4]...Earth, Wind & Fire
- C&W   Here You Come Again [2]...Dolly Parton
- A/C   How Deep Is Your Love [3]...Bee Gees

ALBUMS
- POP   Simple Dreams [2]...Linda Ronstadt
- R&B   Rose Royce II/In Full Bloom [3]...Rose Royce
- C&W   Elvis In Concert [5]...Elvis Presley

December 17, 1977
SINGLES
- HOT   You Light Up My Life [10]...Debby Boone
- R&B   Serpentine Fire [5]...Earth, Wind & Fire
- C&W   Here You Come Again [3]...Dolly Parton
- A/C   How Deep Is Your Love [4]...Bee Gees

ALBUMS
- POP   Simple Dreams [3]...Linda Ronstadt
- R&B   All 'N All [1]...Earth, Wind & Fire
- C&W   Simple Dreams [1]...Linda Ronstadt

December 24, 1977
SINGLES
- HOT   How Deep Is Your Love [1]...Bee Gees
- R&B   Serpentine Fire [6]...Earth, Wind & Fire
- C&W   Here You Come Again [4]...Dolly Parton
- A/C   How Deep Is Your Love [5]...Bee Gees

ALBUMS
- POP   Simple Dreams [4]...Linda Ronstadt
- R&B   All 'N All [2]...Earth, Wind & Fire
- C&W   Here You Come Again [1]...Dolly Parton

December 31, 1977
SINGLES
- HOT   How Deep Is Your Love [2]...Bee Gees
- R&B   Serpentine Fire [7]...Earth, Wind & Fire
- C&W   Here You Come Again [5]...Dolly Parton
- A/C   How Deep Is Your Love [6]...Bee Gees

ALBUMS
- POP   Simple Dreams [5]...Linda Ronstadt
- R&B   All 'N All [3]...Earth, Wind & Fire
- C&W   Here You Come Again [2]...Dolly Parton

January 7, 1978
SINGLES
- *HOT* How Deep Is Your Love [3]...Bee Gees
- *R&B* Ffun [1]...Con Funk Shun
- *C&W* Take This Job And Shove It [1]...Johnny Paycheck
- *A/C* Just The Way You Are [1]...Billy Joel

ALBUMS
- *POP* Rumours [30]...Fleetwood Mac
- *R&B* All 'N All [4]...Earth, Wind & Fire
- *C&W* Here You Come Again [3]...Dolly Parton

January 14, 1978
SINGLES
- *HOT* Baby Come Back [1]...Player
- *R&B* Ffun [2]...Con Funk Shun
- *C&W* Take This Job And Shove It [2]...Johnny Paycheck
- *A/C* Just The Way You Are [2]...Billy Joel

ALBUMS
- *POP* Rumours [31]...Fleetwood Mac
- *R&B* All 'N All [5]...Earth, Wind & Fire
- *C&W* Here You Come Again [4]...Dolly Parton

January 21, 1978
SINGLES
- *HOT* Baby Come Back [2]...Player
- *R&B* Our Love [1]...Natalie Cole
- *C&W* What A Difference You've Made In My Life [1]...Ronnie Milsap
- *A/C* Just The Way You Are [3]...Billy Joel

ALBUMS
- *POP* Saturday Night Fever [1]...Bee Gees/Soundtrack
- *R&B* All 'N All [6]...Earth, Wind & Fire
- *C&W* Here You Come Again [5]...Dolly Parton

January 28, 1978
SINGLES
- *HOT* Baby Come Back [3]...Player
- *R&B* Our Love [2]...Natalie Cole
- *C&W* Out Of My Head And Back In My Bed [1]...Loretta Lynn
- *A/C* Just The Way You Are [4]...Billy Joel

ALBUMS
- *POP* Saturday Night Fever [2]...Bee Gees/Soundtrack
- *R&B* All 'N All [7]...Earth, Wind & Fire
- *C&W* Here You Come Again [6]...Dolly Parton

February 4, 1978
SINGLES
- *HOT* Stayin' Alive [1]...Bee Gees
- *R&B* Theme Song From "Which Way Is Up" [1]...Stargard
- *C&W* Out Of My Head And Back In My Bed [2]...Loretta Lynn
- *A/C* Desiree [1]...Neil Diamond

ALBUMS
- *POP* Saturday Night Fever [3]...Bee Gees/Soundtrack
- *R&B* All 'N All [8]...Earth, Wind & Fire
- *C&W* Here You Come Again [7]...Dolly Parton

February 11, 1978
SINGLES
- *HOT* Stayin' Alive [2]...Bee Gees
- *R&B* Theme Song From "Which Way Is Up" [2]...Stargard
- *C&W* I Just Wish You Were Someone I Love [1]...Larry Gatlin with Brothers & Friends
- *A/C* (What A) Wonderful World [1]...Art Garfunkel with James Taylor & Paul Simon

ALBUMS
- *POP* Saturday Night Fever [4]...Bee Gees/Soundtrack
- *R&B* All 'N All [9]...Earth, Wind & Fire
- *C&W* Here You Come Again [8]...Dolly Parton

February 18, 1978
SINGLES
- *HOT* Stayin' Alive [3]...Bee Gees
- *R&B* Too Hot Ta Trot [1]...Commodores
- *C&W* Don't Break The Heart That Loves You [1]...Margo Smith
- *A/C* (What A) Wonderful World [2]...Art Garfunkel with James Taylor & Paul Simon

ALBUMS
- *POP* Saturday Night Fever [5]...Bee Gees/Soundtrack
- *R&B* Saturday Night Fever [1]...Bee Gees/Soundtrack
- *C&W* Here You Come Again [9]...Dolly Parton

February 25, 1978
SINGLES
- *HOT* Stayin' Alive [4]...Bee Gees
- *R&B* It's You That I Need [1]...Enchantment
- *C&W* Don't Break The Heart That Loves You [2]...Margo Smith
- *A/C* (What A) Wonderful World [3]...Art Garfunkel with James Taylor & Paul Simon

ALBUMS
- *POP* Saturday Night Fever [6]...Bee Gees/Soundtrack
- *R&B* Saturday Night Fever [2]...Bee Gees/Soundtrack
- *C&W* Waylon & Willie [1]...Waylon Jennings & Willie Nelson

March 4, 1978

SINGLES
- HOT (Love Is) Thicker Than Water [1]...Andy Gibb
- R&B Flash Light [1]...Parliament
- C&W Mammas Don't Let Your Babies Grow Up To Be Cowboys/I Can Get Off On You [1]...Waylon & Willie
- A/C (What A) Wonderful World [4]...Art Garfunkel with James Taylor & Paul Simon

ALBUMS
- POP Saturday Night Fever [7]...Bee Gees/Soundtrack
- R&B Saturday Night Fever [3]...Bee Gees/Soundtrack
- C&W Waylon & Willie [2]...Waylon Jennings & Willie Nelson

March 11, 1978

SINGLES
- HOT (Love Is) Thicker Than Water [2]...Andy Gibb
- R&B Flash Light [2]...Parliament
- C&W Mammas Don't Let Your Babies Grow Up To Be Cowboys/I Can Get Off On You [2]...Waylon & Willie
- A/C (What A) Wonderful World [5]...Art Garfunkel with James Taylor & Paul Simon

ALBUMS
- POP Saturday Night Fever [8]...Bee Gees/Soundtrack
- R&B Saturday Night Fever [4]...Bee Gees/Soundtrack
- C&W Waylon & Willie [3]...Waylon Jennings & Willie Nelson

March 18, 1978

SINGLES
- HOT Night Fever [1]...Bee Gees
- R&B Flash Light [3]...Parliament
- C&W Mammas Don't Let Your Babies Grow Up To Be Cowboys/I Can Get Off On You [3]...Waylon & Willie
- A/C Can't Smile Without You [1]...Barry Manilow

ALBUMS
- POP Saturday Night Fever [9]...Bee Gees/Soundtrack
- R&B Saturday Night Fever [5]...Bee Gees/Soundtrack
- C&W Waylon & Willie [4]...Waylon Jennings & Willie Nelson

March 25, 1978

SINGLES
- HOT Night Fever [2]...Bee Gees
- R&B Bootzilla [1]...Bootsy's Rubber Band
- C&W Mammas Don't Let Your Babies Grow Up To Be Cowboys/I Can Get Off On You [4]...Waylon & Willie
- A/C We'll Never Have To Say Goodbye Again [1]...England Dan & John Ford Coley

ALBUMS
- POP Saturday Night Fever [10]...Bee Gees/Soundtrack
- R&B Bootsy? Player Of The Year [1]...Bootsy's Rubber Band
- C&W Waylon & Willie [5]...Waylon Jennings & Willie Nelson

April 1, 1978

SINGLES
- HOT Night Fever [3]...Bee Gees
- R&B The Closer I Get To You [1]...Roberta Flack & Donny Hathaway
- C&W Ready For The Times To Get Better [1]...Crystal Gayle
- A/C We'll Never Have To Say Goodbye Again [2]...England Dan & John Ford Coley

ALBUMS
- POP Saturday Night Fever [11]...Bee Gees/Soundtrack
- R&B Bootsy? Player Of The Year [2]...Bootsy's Rubber Band
- C&W Waylon & Willie [6]...Waylon Jennings & Willie Nelson

April 8, 1978

SINGLES
- HOT Night Fever [4]...Bee Gees
- R&B The Closer I Get To You [2]...Roberta Flack & Donny Hathaway
- C&W Someone Loves You Honey [1]...Charley Pride
- A/C We'll Never Have To Say Goodbye Again [3]...England Dan & John Ford Coley

ALBUMS
- POP Saturday Night Fever [12]...Bee Gees/Soundtrack
- R&B Bootsy? Player Of The Year [3]...Bootsy's Rubber Band
- C&W Waylon & Willie [7]...Waylon Jennings & Willie Nelson

April 15, 1978

SINGLES
- HOT Night Fever [5]...Bee Gees
- R&B *Too Much, Too Little, Too Late [1]...Johnny Mathis/Deniece Williams
- C&W Someone Loves You Honey [2]...Charley Pride
- A/C We'll Never Have To Say Goodbye Again [4]...England Dan & John Ford Coley

ALBUMS
- POP Saturday Night Fever [13]...Bee Gees/Soundtrack
- R&B Street Player [1]...Rufus Featuring Chaka Khan
- C&W Ten Years Of Gold [1]...Kenny Rogers

April 22, 1978

SINGLES
- HOT Night Fever [6]...Bee Gees
- R&B Too Much, Too Little, Too Late [2]...Johnny Mathis/Deniece Williams
- C&W Every Time Two Fools Collide [1]...Kenny Rogers & Dottie West
- A/C We'll Never Have To Say Goodbye Again [5]...England Dan & John Ford Coley

ALBUMS
- POP Saturday Night Fever [14]...Bee Gees/Soundtrack
- R&B Saturday Night Fever [6]...Bee Gees/Soundtrack
- C&W Ten Years Of Gold [2]...Kenny Rogers

April 29, 1978
SINGLES
- HOT **Night Fever** [7]...Bee Gees
- R&B **Too Much, Too Little, Too Late** [3]...
  Johnny Mathis/Deniece Williams
- C&W **Every Time Two Fools Collide** [2]...
  Kenny Rogers & Dottie West
- A/C **We'll Never Have To Say Goodbye Again** [6]...
  England Dan & John Ford Coley

ALBUMS
- POP **Saturday Night Fever** [15]...Bee Gees/Soundtrack
- R&B **Weekend In L.A.** [1]...George Benson
- C&W **Waylon & Willie** [8]...Waylon Jennings & Willie Nelson

May 6, 1978
SINGLES
- HOT **Night Fever** [8]...Bee Gees
- R&B **Too Much, Too Little, Too Late** [4]...
  Johnny Mathis/Deniece Williams
- C&W **It's All Wrong, But It's All Right/Two Doors Down** [1]...Dolly Parton
- A/C **Can't Smile Without You** [2]...Barry Manilow

ALBUMS
- POP **Saturday Night Fever** [16]...Bee Gees/Soundtrack
- R&B **Weekend In L.A.** [2]...George Benson
- C&W **Waylon & Willie** [9]...Waylon Jennings & Willie Nelson

May 13, 1978
SINGLES
- HOT **If I Can't Have You** [1]...Yvonne Elliman
- R&B **Take Me To The Next Phase (Part 1)** [1]...
  The Isley Brothers
- C&W **It's All Wrong, But It's All Right/Two Doors Down** [2]...Dolly Parton
- A/C **Feels So Good** [1]...Chuck Mangione

ALBUMS
- POP **Saturday Night Fever** [17]...Bee Gees/Soundtrack
- R&B **Showdown** [1]...The Isley Brothers
- C&W **Waylon & Willie** [10]...Waylon Jennings & Willie Nelson

May 20, 1978
SINGLES
- HOT **With A Little Luck** [1]...Wings
- R&B **Take Me To The Next Phase (Part 1)** [2]...
  The Isley Brothers
- C&W **She Can Put Her Shoes Under My Bed (Anytime)** [1]...Johnny Duncan
- A/C **Too Much, Too Little, Too Late** [1]...
  Johnny Mathis/Deniece Williams

ALBUMS
- POP **Saturday Night Fever** [18]...Bee Gees/Soundtrack
- R&B **Showdown** [2]...The Isley Brothers
- C&W **Every Time Two Fools Collide** [1]...
  Kenny Rogers & Dottie West

May 27, 1978
SINGLES
- HOT **With A Little Luck** [2]...Wings
- R&B **Use Ta Be My Girl** [1]...The O'Jays
- C&W **Do You Know You Are My Sunshine** [1]...
  The Statler Brothers
- A/C **Even Now** [1]...Barry Manilow

ALBUMS
- POP **Saturday Night Fever** [19]...Bee Gees/Soundtrack
- R&B **Showdown** [3]...The Isley Brothers
- C&W **Every Time Two Fools Collide** [2]...
  Kenny Rogers & Dottie West

June 3, 1978
SINGLES
- HOT **Too Much, Too Little, Too Late** [1]...
  Johnny Mathis/Deniece Williams
- R&B **Use Ta Be My Girl** [2]...The O'Jays
- C&W **Do You Know You Are My Sunshine** [2]...
  The Statler Brothers
- A/C **Even Now** [2]...Barry Manilow

ALBUMS
- POP **Saturday Night Fever** [20]...Bee Gees/Soundtrack
- R&B **So Full Of Love** [1]...The O'Jays
- C&W **Waylon & Willie** [11]...Waylon Jennings & Willie Nelson

June 10, 1978
SINGLES
- HOT **You're The One That I Want** [1]...
  John Travolta & Olivia Newton-John
- R&B **Use Ta Be My Girl** [3]...The O'Jays
- C&W **Georgia On My Mind** [1]...Willie Nelson
- A/C **Even Now** [3]...Barry Manilow

ALBUMS
- POP **Saturday Night Fever** [21]...Bee Gees/Soundtrack
- R&B **So Full Of Love** [2]...The O'Jays
- C&W **Stardust** [1]...Willie Nelson

June 17, 1978
SINGLES
- HOT **Shadow Dancing** [1]...Andy Gibb
- R&B **Use Ta Be My Girl** [4]...The O'Jays
- C&W **Two More Bottles Of Wine** [1]...Emmylou Harris
- A/C **Bluer Than Blue** [1]...Michael Johnson

ALBUMS
- POP **Saturday Night Fever** [22]...Bee Gees/Soundtrack
- R&B **So Full Of Love** [3]...The O'Jays
- C&W **Stardust** [2]...Willie Nelson

June 24, 1978

SINGLES
- HOT Shadow Dancing [2]...Andy Gibb
- R&B Use Ta Be My Girl [5]...The O'Jays
- C&W I'll Be True To You [1]...The Oak Ridge Boys
- A/C Bluer Than Blue [2]...Michael Johnson

ALBUMS
- POP Saturday Night Fever [23]...Bee Gees/Soundtrack
- R&B Natural High [1]...Commodores
- C&W Stardust [3]...Willie Nelson

July 1, 1978

SINGLES
- HOT Shadow Dancing [3]...Andy Gibb
- R&B Stuff Like That [1]...Quincy Jones
- C&W It Only Hurts For A Little While [1]...Margo Smith
- A/C Bluer Than Blue [3]...Michael Johnson

ALBUMS
- POP Saturday Night Fever [24]...Bee Gees/Soundtrack
- R&B Natural High [2]...Commodores
- C&W Stardust [4]...Willie Nelson

July 8, 1978

SINGLES
- HOT Shadow Dancing [4]...Andy Gibb
- R&B Close The Door [1]...Teddy Pendergrass
- C&W I Believe In You [1]...Mel Tillis
- A/C If Ever I See You Again [1]...Roberta Flack

ALBUMS
- POP City to City [1]...Gerry Rafferty
- R&B Natural High [3]...Commodores
- C&W Stardust [5]...Willie Nelson

July 15, 1978

SINGLES
- HOT Shadow Dancing [5]...Andy Gibb
- R&B Close The Door [2]...Teddy Pendergrass
- C&W Only One Love In My Life [1]...Ronnie Milsap
- A/C If Ever I See You Again [2]...Roberta Flack

ALBUMS
- POP Some Girls [1]...The Rolling Stones
- R&B Natural High [4]...Commodores
- C&W Stardust [6]...Willie Nelson

July 22, 1978

SINGLES
- HOT Shadow Dancing [6]...Andy Gibb
- R&B You And I [1]...Rick James
- C&W Only One Love In My Life [2]...Ronnie Milsap
- A/C If Ever I See You Again [3]...Roberta Flack

ALBUMS
- POP Some Girls [2]...The Rolling Stones
- R&B Natural High [5]...Commodores
- C&W Stardust [7]...Willie Nelson

July 29, 1978

SINGLES
- HOT Shadow Dancing [7]...Andy Gibb
- R&B You And I [2]...Rick James
- C&W Only One Love In My Life [3]...Ronnie Milsap
- A/C Songbird [1]...Barbra Streisand

ALBUMS
- POP Grease [1]...Olivia Newton-John/Soundtrack
- R&B Natural High [6]...Commodores
- C&W Stardust [8]...Willie Nelson

August 5, 1978

SINGLES
- HOT Miss You [1]...The Rolling Stones
- R&B *Boogie Oogie Oogie [1]...A Taste Of Honey
- C&W Love Or Something Like It [1]...Kenny Rogers
- A/C Songbird [2]...Barbra Streisand

ALBUMS
- POP Grease [2]...Olivia Newton-John/Soundtrack
- R&B Natural High [7]...Commodores
- C&W Stardust [9]...Willie Nelson

August 12, 1978

SINGLES
- HOT *Three Times A Lady [1]...Commodores
- R&B *Three Times A Lady [1]...Commodores
- C&W You Don't Love Me Anymore [1]...Eddie Rabbitt
- A/C My Angel Baby [1]...Toby Beau

ALBUMS
- POP Grease [3]...Olivia Newton-John/Soundtrack
- R&B Life Is A Song Worth Singing [1]...Teddy Pendergrass
- C&W Stardust [10]...Willie Nelson

August 19, 1978

SINGLES
- HOT Three Times A Lady [2]...Commodores
- R&B Three Times A Lady [2]...Commodores
- C&W Talking In Your Sleep [1]...Crystal Gayle
- A/C Three Times A Lady [1]...Commodores

ALBUMS
- POP Grease [4]...Olivia Newton-John/Soundtrack
- R&B Life Is A Song Worth Singing [2]...Teddy Pendergrass
- C&W Stardust [11]...Willie Nelson

August 26, 1978

SINGLES
- HOT Grease [1]...Frankie Valli
- R&B Get Off [1]...Foxy
- C&W Talking In Your Sleep [2]...Crystal Gayle
- A/C Three Times A Lady [2]...Commodores

ALBUMS
- POP Grease [5]...Olivia Newton-John/Soundtrack
- R&B Natural High [8]...Commodores
- C&W Love Or Something Like It [1]...Kenny Rogers

September 2, 1978
SINGLES
- HOT   Grease [2]...Frankie Valli
- R&B   Get Off [2]...Foxy
- C&W   Blue Skies [1]...Willie Nelson
- A/C   Three Times A Lady [3]...Commodores

ALBUMS
- POP   Grease [6]...Olivia Newton-John/Soundtrack
- R&B   Blam!! [1]...The Brothers Johnson
- C&W   Love Or Something Like It [2]...Kenny Rogers

September 9, 1978
SINGLES
- HOT   Boogie Oogie Oogie [1]...A Taste Of Honey
- R&B   Holding On (When Love Is Gone) [1]...L.T.D.
- C&W   I've Always Been Crazy [1]...Waylon Jennings
- A/C   Fool (If You Think It's Over) [1]...Chris Rea

ALBUMS
- POP   Grease [7]...Olivia Newton-John/Soundtrack
- R&B   Blam!! [2]...The Brothers Johnson
- C&W   Heartbreaker [1]...Dolly Parton

September 16, 1978
SINGLES
- HOT   Boogie Oogie Oogie [2]...A Taste Of Honey
- R&B   Holding On (When Love Is Gone) [2]...L.T.D.
- C&W   I've Always Been Crazy [2]...Waylon Jennings
- A/C   Fool (If You Think It's Over) [2]...Chris Rea

ALBUMS
- POP   Don't Look Back [1]...Boston
- R&B   Blam!! [3]...The Brothers Johnson
- C&W   Heartbreaker [2]...Dolly Parton

September 23, 1978
SINGLES
- HOT   Boogie Oogie Oogie [3]...A Taste Of Honey
- R&B   Got To Get You Into My Life [1]...Earth, Wind & Fire
- C&W   I've Always Been Crazy [3]...Waylon Jennings
- A/C   Fool (If You Think It's Over) [3]...Chris Rea

ALBUMS
- POP   Grease [8]...Olivia Newton-John/Soundtrack
- R&B   Blam!! [4]...The Brothers Johnson
- C&W   Heartbreaker [3]...Dolly Parton

September 30, 1978
SINGLES
- HOT   Kiss You All Over [1]...Exile
- R&B   One Nation Under A Groove (Part 1) [1]...Funkadelic
- C&W   Heartbreaker [1]...Dolly Parton
- A/C   Right Down The Line [1]...Gerry Rafferty

ALBUMS
- POP   Grease [9]...Olivia Newton-John/Soundtrack
- R&B   Blam!! [5]...The Brothers Johnson
- C&W   Heartbreaker [4]...Dolly Parton

October 7, 1978
SINGLES
- HOT   Kiss You All Over [2]...Exile
- R&B   One Nation Under A Groove (Part 1) [2]...Funkadelic
- C&W   Heartbreaker [2]...Dolly Parton
- A/C   Love Is In The Air [1]...John Paul Young

ALBUMS
- POP   Don't Look Back [2]...Boston
- R&B   Blam!! [6]...The Brothers Johnson
- C&W   Heartbreaker [5]...Dolly Parton

October 14, 1978
SINGLES
- HOT   Kiss You All Over [3]...Exile
- R&B   One Nation Under A Groove (Part 1) [3]...Funkadelic
- C&W   Heartbreaker [3]...Dolly Parton
- A/C   Love Is In The Air [2]...John Paul Young

ALBUMS
- POP   Grease [10]...Olivia Newton-John/Soundtrack
- R&B   Blam!! [7]...The Brothers Johnson
- C&W   Heartbreaker [6]...Dolly Parton

October 21, 1978
SINGLES
- HOT   Kiss You All Over [4]...Exile
- R&B   One Nation Under A Groove (Part 1) [4]...Funkadelic
- C&W   Tear Time [1]...Dave & Sugar
- A/C   Right Down The Line [2]...Gerry Rafferty

ALBUMS
- POP   Grease [11]...Olivia Newton-John/Soundtrack
- R&B   Is It Still Good To Ya [1]...Ashford & Simpson
- C&W   Heartbreaker [7]...Dolly Parton

October 28, 1978
SINGLES
- HOT   Hot Child In The City [1]...Nick Gilder
- R&B   One Nation Under A Groove (Part 1) [5]...Funkadelic
- C&W   Let's Take The Long Way Around The World [1]...Ronnie Milsap
- A/C   Right Down The Line [3]...Gerry Rafferty

ALBUMS
- POP   Grease [12]...Olivia Newton-John/Soundtrack
- R&B   One Nation Under A Groove [1]...Funkadelic
- C&W   Heartbreaker [8]...Dolly Parton

November 4, 1978
SINGLES
- HOT You Needed Me [1]...Anne Murray
- R&B One Nation Under A Groove (Part 1) [6]...Funkadelic
- C&W Sleeping Single In A Double Bed [1]...Barbara Mandrell
- A/C Right Down The Line [4]...Gerry Rafferty

ALBUMS
- POP Living In The USA [1]...Linda Ronstadt
- R&B One Nation Under A Groove [2]...Funkadelic
- C&W Heartbreaker [9]...Dolly Parton

November 11, 1978
SINGLES
- HOT MacArthur Park [1]...Donna Summer
- R&B I'm Every Woman [1]...Chaka Khan
- C&W Sleeping Single In A Double Bed [2]...Barbara Mandrell
- A/C Time Passages [1]...Al Stewart

ALBUMS
- POP Live And More [1]...Donna Summer
- R&B One Nation Under A Groove [3]...Funkadelic
- C&W I've Always Been Crazy [1]...Waylon Jennings

November 18, 1978
SINGLES
- HOT MacArthur Park [2]...Donna Summer
- R&B I'm Every Woman [2]...Chaka Khan
- C&W Sleeping Single In A Double Bed [3]...Barbara Mandrell
- A/C Time Passages [2]...Al Stewart

ALBUMS
- POP 52nd Street [1]...Billy Joel
- R&B One Nation Under A Groove [4]...Funkadelic
- C&W I've Always Been Crazy [2]...Waylon Jennings

November 25, 1978
SINGLES
- HOT MacArthur Park [3]...Donna Summer
- R&B I'm Every Woman [3]...Chaka Khan
- C&W Sweet Desire/Old Fashioned Love [1]...The Kendalls
- A/C Time Passages [3]...Al Stewart

ALBUMS
- POP 52nd Street [2]...Billy Joel
- R&B Barry White The Man [1]...Barry White
- C&W I've Always Been Crazy [3]...Waylon Jennings

December 2, 1978
SINGLES
- HOT You Don't Bring Me Flowers [1]...Barbra Streisand & Neil Diamond
- R&B *Le Freak [1]...Chic
- C&W I Just Want To Love You [1]...Eddie Rabbitt
- A/C Time Passages [4]...Al Stewart

ALBUMS
- POP 52nd Street [3]...Billy Joel
- R&B Barry White The Man [2]...Barry White
- C&W I've Always Been Crazy [4]...Waylon Jennings

December 9, 1978
SINGLES
- HOT Le Freak [1]...Chic
- R&B Le Freak [2]...Chic
- C&W On My Knees [1]...Charlie Rich with Janie Fricke
- A/C Time Passages [5]...Al Stewart

ALBUMS
- POP 52nd Street [4]...Billy Joel
- R&B Barry White The Man [3]...Barry White
- C&W I've Always Been Crazy [5]...Waylon Jennings

December 16, 1978
SINGLES
- HOT You Don't Bring Me Flowers [2]...Barbra Streisand & Neil Diamond
- R&B Le Freak [3]...Chic
- C&W The Gambler [1]...Kenny Rogers
- A/C Time Passages [6]...Al Stewart

ALBUMS
- POP 52nd Street [5]...Billy Joel
- R&B C'est Chic [1]...Chic
- C&W I've Always Been Crazy [6]...Waylon Jennings

December 23, 1978
SINGLES
- HOT Le Freak [2]...Chic
- R&B Le Freak [4]...Chic
- C&W The Gambler [2]...Kenny Rogers
- A/C Time Passages [7]...Al Stewart

ALBUMS
- POP 52nd Street [6]...Billy Joel
- R&B C'est Chic [2]...Chic
- C&W I've Always Been Crazy [7]...Waylon Jennings

December 30, 1978

SINGLES
- HOT   Le Freak [3]...Chic
- R&B   Le Freak [5]...Chic
- C&W   The Gambler [3]...Kenny Rogers
- A/C   Time Passages [8]...Al Stewart

ALBUMS
- POP   52nd Street [7]...Billy Joel
- R&B   C'est Chic [3]...Chic
- C&W   I've Always Been Crazy [8]...Waylon Jennings

January 6, 1979

SINGLES
- HOT   Too Much Heaven [1]...Bee Gees
- R&B   Got To Be Real [1]...Cheryl Lynn
- C&W   Tulsa Time [1]...Don Williams
- A/C   Time Passages [9]...Al Stewart

ALBUMS
- POP   Barbra Streisand's Greatest Hits, Volume 2 [1]...Barbra Streisand
- R&B   C'est Chic [4]...Chic
- C&W   Willie and Family Live [1]...Willie Nelson

January 13, 1979

SINGLES
- HOT   Too Much Heaven [2]...Bee Gees
- R&B   September [1]...Earth, Wind & Fire
- C&W   Lady Lay Down [1]...John Conlee
- A/C   Time Passages [10]...Al Stewart

ALBUMS
- POP   Barbra Streisand's Greatest Hits, Volume 2 [2]...Barbra Streisand
- R&B   C'est Chic [5]...Chic
- C&W   Willie and Family Live [2]...Willie Nelson

January 20, 1979

SINGLES
- HOT   Le Freak [4]...Chic
- R&B   Aqua Boogie (A Psychoalphadiscobetabio-aquadoloop) [1]...Parliament
- C&W   I Really Got The Feeling/Baby I'm Burnin' [1]...Dolly Parton
- A/C   This Moment In Time [1]...Engelbert Humperdinck

ALBUMS
- POP   Barbra Streisand's Greatest Hits, Volume 2 [3]...Barbra Streisand
- R&B   C'est Chic [6]...Chic
- C&W   The Gambler [1]...Kenny Rogers

January 27, 1979

SINGLES
- HOT   Le Freak [5]...Chic
- R&B   Aqua Boogie (A Psychoalphadiscobetabio-aquadoloop) [2]...Parliament
- C&W   Why Have You Left The One You Left Me For [1]...Crystal Gayle
- A/C   This Moment In Time [2]...Engelbert Humperdinck

ALBUMS
- POP   52nd Street [8]...Billy Joel
- R&B   C'est Chic [7]...Chic
- C&W   The Gambler [2]...Kenny Rogers

February 3, 1979

SINGLES
- HOT   Le Freak [6]...Chic
- R&B   Aqua Boogie (A Psychoalphadiscobetabio-aquadoloop) [3]...Parliament
- C&W   Why Have You Left The One You Left Me For [2]...Crystal Gayle
- A/C   Lotta Love [1]...Nicolette Larson

ALBUMS
- POP   Briefcase Full Of Blues [1]...Blues Brothers
- R&B   C'est Chic [8]...Chic
- C&W   The Gambler [3]...Kenny Rogers

February 10, 1979

SINGLES
- HOT   Da Ya Think I'm Sexy? [1]...Rod Stewart
- R&B   Aqua Boogie (A Psychoalphadiscobetabio-aquadoloop) [4]...Parliament
- C&W   Every Which Way But Loose [1]...Eddie Rabbitt
- A/C   *I Just Fall In Love Again [1]...Anne Murray

ALBUMS
- POP   Blondes Have More Fun [1]...Rod Stewart
- R&B   C'est Chic [9]...Chic
- C&W   The Gambler [4]...Kenny Rogers

February 17, 1979

SINGLES
- HOT   Da Ya Think I'm Sexy? [2]...Rod Stewart
- R&B   Bustin' Loose, Part 1 [1]...Chuck Brown & The Soul Searchers
- C&W   Every Which Way But Loose [2]...Eddie Rabbitt
- A/C   I Just Fall In Love Again [2]...Anne Murray

ALBUMS
- POP   Blondes Have More Fun [2]...Rod Stewart
- R&B   C'est Chic [10]...Chic
- C&W   The Gambler [5]...Kenny Rogers

February 24, 1979
SINGLES
- HOT   Da Ya Think I'm Sexy? [3]...Rod Stewart
- R&B   Bustin' Loose, Part 1 [2]...
  Chuck Brown & The Soul Searchers
- C&W   Every Which Way But Loose [3]...Eddie Rabbitt
- A/C   I Just Fall In Love Again [3]...Anne Murray

ALBUMS
- POP   Blondes Have More Fun [3]...Rod Stewart
- R&B   C'est Chic [11]...Chic
- C&W   The Gambler [6]...Kenny Rogers

March 3, 1979
SINGLES
- HOT   Da Ya Think I'm Sexy? [4]...Rod Stewart
- R&B   Bustin' Loose, Part 1 [3]...
  Chuck Brown & The Soul Searchers
- C&W   Golden Tears [1]...Dave & Sugar
- A/C   I Just Fall In Love Again [4]...Anne Murray

ALBUMS
- POP   Spirits Having Flown [1]...Bee Gees
- R&B   2 Hot! [1]...Peaches & Herb
- C&W   The Gambler [7]...Kenny Rogers

March 10, 1979
SINGLES
- HOT   I Will Survive [1]...Gloria Gaynor
- R&B   Bustin' Loose, Part 1 [4]...
  Chuck Brown & The Soul Searchers
- C&W   Golden Tears [2]...Dave & Sugar
- A/C   Crazy Love [1]...Poco

ALBUMS
- POP   Spirits Having Flown [2]...Bee Gees
- R&B   2 Hot! [2]...Peaches & Herb
- C&W   The Gambler [8]...Kenny Rogers

March 17, 1979
SINGLES
- HOT   I Will Survive [2]...Gloria Gaynor
- R&B   I Got My Mind Made Up (You Can Get It Girl) [1]...Instant Funk
- C&W   Golden Tears [3]...Dave & Sugar
- A/C   Crazy Love [2]...Poco

ALBUMS
- POP   Spirits Having Flown [3]...Bee Gees
- R&B   2 Hot! [3]...Peaches & Herb
- C&W   The Gambler [9]...Kenny Rogers

March 24, 1979
SINGLES
- HOT   Tragedy [1]...Bee Gees
- R&B   I Got My Mind Made Up (You Can Get It Girl) [2]...Instant Funk
- C&W   I Just Fall In Love Again [1]...Anne Murray
- A/C   Crazy Love [3]...Poco

ALBUMS
- POP   Spirits Having Flown [4]...Bee Gees
- R&B   2 Hot! [4]...Peaches & Herb
- C&W   The Gambler [10]...Kenny Rogers

March 31, 1979
SINGLES
- HOT   Tragedy [2]...Bee Gees
- R&B   He's The Greatest Dancer [1]...Sister Sledge
- C&W   I Just Fall In Love Again [2]...Anne Murray
- A/C   Crazy Love [4]...Poco

ALBUMS
- POP   Spirits Having Flown [5]...Bee Gees
- R&B   Instant Funk [1]...Instant Funk
- C&W   The Gambler [11]...Kenny Rogers

April 7, 1979
SINGLES
- HOT   I Will Survive [3]...Gloria Gaynor
- R&B   I Got My Mind Made Up (You Can Get It Girl) [3]...Instant Funk
- C&W   I Just Fall In Love Again [3]...Anne Murray
- A/C   Crazy Love [5]...Poco

ALBUMS
- POP   Minute By Minute [1]...The Doobie Brothers
- R&B   We Are Family [1]...Sister Sledge
- C&W   The Gambler [12]...Kenny Rogers

April 14, 1979
SINGLES
- HOT   What A Fool Believes [1]...The Doobie Brothers
- R&B   Disco Nights (Rock-Freak) [1]...GQ
- C&W   (If Loving You Is Wrong) I Don't Want To Be Right [1]...Barbara Mandrell
- A/C   Crazy Love [6]...Poco

ALBUMS
- POP   Minute By Minute [2]...The Doobie Brothers
- R&B   2 Hot! [5]...Peaches & Herb
- C&W   The Gambler [13]...Kenny Rogers

April 21, 1979

SINGLES
- HOT Knock On Wood [1]...Amii Stewart
- R&B Disco Nights (Rock-Freak) [2]...GQ
- C&W All I Ever Need Is You [1]...
   Kenny Rogers & Dottie West
- A/C Crazy Love [7]...Poco

ALBUMS
- POP Spirits Having Flown [6]...Bee Gees
- R&B 2 Hot! [6]...Peaches & Herb
- C&W The Gambler [14]...Kenny Rogers

April 28, 1979

SINGLES
- HOT Heart Of Glass [1]...Blondie
- R&B *Reunited [1]...Peaches & Herb
- C&W Where Do I Put Her Memory [1]...Charley Pride
- A/C I Never Said I Love You [1]...Orsa Lia

ALBUMS
- POP Minute By Minute [3]...The Doobie Brothers
- R&B 2 Hot! [7]...Peaches & Herb
- C&W The Gambler [15]...Kenny Rogers

May 5, 1979

SINGLES
- HOT Reunited [1]...Peaches & Herb
- R&B Reunited [2]...Peaches & Herb
- C&W Backside Of Thirty [1]...John Conlee
- A/C Love Is The Answer [1]...
   England Dan & John Ford Coley

ALBUMS
- POP Minute By Minute [4]...The Doobie Brothers
- R&B 2 Hot! [8]...Peaches & Herb
- C&W The Gambler [16]...Kenny Rogers

May 12, 1979

SINGLES
- HOT Reunited [2]...Peaches & Herb
- R&B Reunited [3]...Peaches & Herb
- C&W Don't Take It Away [1]...Conway Twitty
- A/C Love Is The Answer [2]...
   England Dan & John Ford Coley

ALBUMS
- POP Minute By Minute [5]...The Doobie Brothers
- R&B We Are Family [2]...Sister Sledge
- C&W The Gambler [17]...Kenny Rogers

May 19, 1979

SINGLES
- HOT Reunited [3]...Peaches & Herb
- R&B Reunited [4]...Peaches & Herb
- C&W If I Said You Have A Beautiful Body Would You
   Hold It Against Me [1]...The Bellamy Brothers
- A/C Just When I Needed You Most [1]...Randy Vanwarmer

ALBUMS
- POP Breakfast In America [1]...Supertramp
- R&B We Are Family [3]...Sister Sledge
- C&W The Gambler [18]...Kenny Rogers

May 26, 1979

SINGLES
- HOT Reunited [4]...Peaches & Herb
- R&B I Wanna Be With You (Part 1) [1]...The Isley Brothers
- C&W If I Said You Have A Beautiful Body Would You
   Hold It Against Me [2]...The Bellamy Brothers
- A/C *She Believes In Me [1]...Kenny Rogers

ALBUMS
- POP Breakfast In America [2]...Supertramp
- R&B We Are Family [4]...Sister Sledge
- C&W The Gambler [19]...Kenny Rogers

June 2, 1979

SINGLES
- HOT Hot Stuff [1]...Donna Summer
- R&B Ain't No Stoppin' Us Now [1]...McFadden & Whitehead
- C&W If I Said You Have A Beautiful Body Would You
   Hold It Against Me [3]...The Bellamy Brothers
- A/C She Believes In Me [2]...Kenny Rogers

ALBUMS
- POP Breakfast In America [3]...Supertramp
- R&B We Are Family [5]...Sister Sledge
- C&W Greatest Hits [1]...Waylon Jennings

June 9, 1979

SINGLES
- HOT Love You Inside Out [1]...Bee Gees
- R&B We Are Family [1]...Sister Sledge
- C&W She Believes In Me [1]...Kenny Rogers
- A/C Just When I Needed You Most [2]...Randy Vanwarmer

ALBUMS
- POP Breakfast In America [4]...Supertramp
- R&B We Are Family [6]...Sister Sledge
- C&W The Gambler [20]...Kenny Rogers

June 16, 1979
SINGLES
- *HOT* Hot Stuff [2]...Donna Summer
- *R&B* *Ring My Bell [1]...Anita Ward
- *C&W* She Believes In Me [2]...Kenny Rogers
- *A/C* *Shadows In The Moonlight [1]...Anne Murray

ALBUMS
- *POP* Bad Girls [1]...Donna Summer
- *R&B* We Are Family [7]...Sister Sledge
- *C&W* The Gambler [21]...Kenny Rogers

June 23, 1979
SINGLES
- *HOT* Hot Stuff [3]...Donna Summer
- *R&B* Ring My Bell [2]...Anita Ward
- *C&W* Nobody Likes Sad Songs [1]...Ronnie Milsap
- *A/C* Shadows In The Moonlight [2]...Anne Murray

ALBUMS
- *POP* Breakfast In America [5]...Supertramp
- *R&B* Bad Girls [1]...Donna Summer
- *C&W* The Gambler [22]...Kenny Rogers

June 30, 1979
SINGLES
- *HOT* Ring My Bell [1]...Anita Ward
- *R&B* Ring My Bell [3]...Anita Ward
- *C&W* Amanda [1]...Waylon
- *A/C* Shadows In The Moonlight [3]...Anne Murray

ALBUMS
- *POP* Breakfast In America [6]...Supertramp
- *R&B* Bad Girls [2]...Donna Summer
- *C&W* The Gambler [23]...Kenny Rogers

July 7, 1979
SINGLES
- *HOT* Ring My Bell [2]...Anita Ward
- *R&B* Ring My Bell [4]...Anita Ward
- *C&W* Amanda [2]...Waylon
- *A/C* Lead Me On [1]...Maxine Nightingale

ALBUMS
- *POP* Bad Girls [2]...Donna Summer
- *R&B* Bad Girls [3]...Donna Summer
- *C&W* Greatest Hits [2]...Waylon Jennings

July 14, 1979
SINGLES
- *HOT* *Bad Girls [1]...Donna Summer
- *R&B* Ring My Bell [5]...Anita Ward
- *C&W* Amanda [3]...Waylon
- *A/C* Lead Me On [2]...Maxine Nightingale

ALBUMS
- *POP* Bad Girls [3]...Donna Summer
- *R&B* I Am [1]...Earth, Wind & Fire
- *C&W* Greatest Hits [3]...Waylon Jennings

July 21, 1979
SINGLES
- *HOT* Bad Girls [2]...Donna Summer
- *R&B* Bad Girls [1]...Donna Summer
- *C&W* Shadows In The Moonlight [1]...Anne Murray
- *A/C* Lead Me On [3]...Maxine Nightingale

ALBUMS
- *POP* Bad Girls [4]...Donna Summer
- *R&B* Teddy [1]...Teddy Pendergrass
- *C&W* Greatest Hits [4]...Waylon Jennings

July 28, 1979
SINGLES
- *HOT* Bad Girls [3]...Donna Summer
- *R&B* *Good Times [1]...Chic
- *C&W* You're The Only One [1]...Dolly Parton
- *A/C* Morning Dance [1]...Spyro Gyra

ALBUMS
- *POP* Bad Girls [5]...Donna Summer
- *R&B* Teddy [2]...Teddy Pendergrass
- *C&W* Greatest Hits [5]...Waylon Jennings

August 4, 1979
SINGLES
- *HOT* Bad Girls [4]...Donna Summer
- *R&B* Good Times [2]...Chic
- *C&W* You're The Only One [2]...Dolly Parton
- *A/C* Lead Me On [4]...Maxine Nightingale

ALBUMS
- *POP* Bad Girls [6]...Donna Summer
- *R&B* Teddy [3]...Teddy Pendergrass
- *C&W* Greatest Hits [6]...Waylon Jennings

August 11, 1979
SINGLES
- *HOT* Bad Girls [5]...Donna Summer
- *R&B* Good Times [3]...Chic
- *C&W* Suspicions [1]...Eddie Rabbitt
- *A/C* Lead Me On [5]...Maxine Nightingale

ALBUMS
- *POP* Get The Knack [1]...The Knack
- *R&B* Teddy [4]...Teddy Pendergrass
- *C&W* Greatest Hits [7]...Waylon Jennings

August 18, 1979
SINGLES
- *HOT* Good Times [1]...Chic
- *R&B* Good Times [4]...Chic
- *C&W* Coca Cola Cowboy [1]...Mel Tillis
- *A/C* Lead Me On [6]...Maxine Nightingale

ALBUMS
- *POP* Get The Knack [2]...The Knack
- *R&B* Teddy [5]...Teddy Pendergrass
- *C&W* Greatest Hits [8]...Waylon Jennings

August 25, 1979

SINGLES
- *HOT* My Sharona [1]...The Knack
- *R&B* Good Times [5]...Chic
- *C&W* The Devil Went Down To Georgia [1]...
  Charlie Daniels Band
- *A/C* Mama Can't Buy You Love [1]...Elton John

ALBUMS
- *POP* Get The Knack [3]...The Knack
- *R&B* Teddy [6]...Teddy Pendergrass
- *C&W* Greatest Hits [9]...Waylon Jennings

September 1, 1979

SINGLES
- *HOT* My Sharona [2]...The Knack
- *R&B* Good Times [6]...Chic
- *C&W* Heartbreak Hotel [1]...Willie Nelson & Leon Russell
- *A/C* Lead Me On [7]...Maxine Nightingale

ALBUMS
- *POP* Get The Knack [4]...The Knack
- *R&B* Teddy [7]...Teddy Pendergrass
- *C&W* Million Mile Reflections [1]...Charlie Daniels Band

September 8, 1979

SINGLES
- *HOT* My Sharona [3]...The Knack
- *R&B* *Don't Stop 'Til You Get Enough [1]...Michael Jackson
- *C&W* I May Never Get To Heaven [1]...Conway Twitty
- *A/C* Different Worlds [1]...Maureen McGovern

ALBUMS
- *POP* Get The Knack [5]...The Knack
- *R&B* Teddy [8]...Teddy Pendergrass
- *C&W* Greatest Hits [10]...Waylon Jennings

September 15, 1979

SINGLES
- *HOT* My Sharona [4]...The Knack
- *R&B* Don't Stop 'Til You Get Enough [2]...Michael Jackson
- *C&W* You're My Jamaica [1]...Charley Pride
- *A/C* Different Worlds [2]...Maureen McGovern

ALBUMS
- *POP* In Through The Out Door [1]...Led Zeppelin
- *R&B* Midnight Magic [1]...Commodores
- *C&W* Greatest Hits [11]...Waylon Jennings

September 22, 1979

SINGLES
- *HOT* My Sharona [5]...The Knack
- *R&B* Don't Stop 'Til You Get Enough [3]...Michael Jackson
- *C&W* Just Good Ol' Boys [1]...Moe Bandy & Joe Stampley
- *A/C* *Rise [1]...Herb Alpert

ALBUMS
- *POP* In Through The Out Door [2]...Led Zeppelin
- *R&B* Midnight Magic [2]...Commodores
- *C&W* Million Mile Reflections [2]...Charlie Daniels Band

September 29, 1979

SINGLES
- *HOT* My Sharona [6]...The Knack
- *R&B* Don't Stop 'Til You Get Enough [4]...Michael Jackson
- *C&W* It Must Be Love [1]...Don Williams
- *A/C* Where Were You When I Was Falling In Love [1]...Lobo

ALBUMS
- *POP* In Through The Out Door [3]...Led Zeppelin
- *R&B* Midnight Magic [3]...Commodores
- *C&W* Million Mile Reflections [3]...Charlie Daniels Band

October 6, 1979

SINGLES
- *HOT* Sad Eyes [1]...Robert John
- *R&B* Don't Stop 'Til You Get Enough [5]...Michael Jackson
- *C&W* Last Cheater's Waltz [1]...T.G. Sheppard
- *A/C* Where Were You When I Was Falling In Love [2]...Lobo

ALBUMS
- *POP* In Through The Out Door [4]...Led Zeppelin
- *R&B* Off The Wall [1]...Michael Jackson
- *C&W* Million Mile Reflections [4]...Charlie Daniels Band

October 13, 1979

SINGLES
- *HOT* Don't Stop 'Til You Get Enough [1]...Michael Jackson
- *R&B* (not just) Knee Deep - Part 1 [1]...Funkadelic
- *C&W* Last Cheater's Waltz [2]...T.G. Sheppard
- *A/C* *Broken Hearted Me [1]...Anne Murray

ALBUMS
- *POP* In Through The Out Door [5]...Led Zeppelin
- *R&B* Off The Wall [2]...Michael Jackson
- *C&W* Greatest Hits [12]...Waylon Jennings

October 20, 1979

SINGLES
- *HOT* Rise [1]...Herb Alpert
- *R&B* (not just) Knee Deep - Part 1 [2]...Funkadelic
- *C&W* All The Gold In California [1]...
  Larry Gatlin & The Gatlin Brothers Band
- *A/C* Broken Hearted Me [2]...Anne Murray

ALBUMS
- *POP* In Through The Out Door [6]...Led Zeppelin
- *R&B* Off The Wall [3]...Michael Jackson
- *C&W* Greatest Hits [13]...Waylon Jennings

October 27, 1979

SINGLES
- HOT Rise [2]...Herb Alpert
- R&B (not just) Knee Deep - Part 1 [3]...Funkadelic
- C&W All The Gold In California [2]...
   Larry Gatlin & The Gatlin Brothers Band
- A/C Broken Hearted Me [3]...Anne Murray

ALBUMS
- POP In Through The Out Door [7]...Led Zeppelin
- R&B Ladies' Night [1]...Kool & The Gang
- C&W Greatest Hits [14]...Waylon Jennings

November 3, 1979

SINGLES
- HOT Pop Muzik [1]...M
- R&B Ladies Night [1]...Kool & The Gang
- C&W You Decorated My Life [1]...Kenny Rogers
- A/C Broken Hearted Me [4]...Anne Murray

ALBUMS
- POP The Long Run [1]...Eagles
- R&B Ladies' Night [2]...Kool & The Gang
- C&W Greatest Hits [15]...Waylon Jennings

November 10, 1979

SINGLES
- HOT Heartache Tonight [1]...Eagles
- R&B Ladies Night [2]...Kool & The Gang
- C&W You Decorated My Life [2]...Kenny Rogers
- A/C Broken Hearted Me [5]...Anne Murray

ALBUMS
- POP The Long Run [2]...Eagles
- R&B Off The Wall [4]...Michael Jackson
- C&W Kenny [1]...Kenny Rogers

November 17, 1979

SINGLES
- HOT *Still [1]...Commodores
- R&B Ladies Night [3]...Kool & The Gang
- C&W Come With Me [1]...Waylon Jennings
- A/C You're Only Lonely [1]...J.D. Souther

ALBUMS
- POP The Long Run [3]...Eagles
- R&B Off The Wall [5]...Michael Jackson
- C&W Kenny [2]...Kenny Rogers

November 24, 1979

SINGLES
- HOT No More Tears (Enough Is Enough) [1]...
   Barbra Streisand/Donna Summer
- R&B Still [1]...Commodores
- C&W Come With Me [2]...Waylon Jennings
- A/C You're Only Lonely [2]...J.D. Souther

ALBUMS
- POP The Long Run [4]...Eagles
- R&B Off The Wall [6]...Michael Jackson
- C&W Kenny [3]...Kenny Rogers

December 1, 1979

SINGLES
- HOT No More Tears (Enough Is Enough) [2]...
   Barbra Streisand/Donna Summer
- R&B I Wanna Be Your Lover [1]...Prince
- C&W Broken Hearted Me [1]...Anne Murray
- A/C You're Only Lonely [3]...J.D. Souther

ALBUMS
- POP The Long Run [5]...Eagles
- R&B Off The Wall [7]...Michael Jackson
- C&W Kenny [4]...Kenny Rogers

December 8, 1979

SINGLES
- HOT Babe [1]...Styx
- R&B I Wanna Be Your Lover [2]...Prince
- C&W I Cheated Me Right Out Of You [1]...Moe Bandy
- A/C You're Only Lonely [4]...J.D. Souther

ALBUMS
- POP The Long Run [6]...Eagles
- R&B Off The Wall [8]...Michael Jackson
- C&W Kenny [5]...Kenny Rogers

December 15, 1979

SINGLES
- HOT Babe [2]...Styx
- R&B Do You Love What You Feel [1]...Rufus & Chaka Khan
- C&W Happy Birthday Darlin' [1]...Conway Twitty
- A/C You're Only Lonely [5]...J.D. Souther

ALBUMS
- POP The Long Run [7]...Eagles
- R&B Off The Wall [9]...Michael Jackson
- C&W Kenny [6]...Kenny Rogers

December 22, 1979

SINGLES
- HOT Escape (The Pina Colada Song) [1]...Rupert Holmes
- R&B Do You Love What You Feel [2]...Rufus & Chaka Khan
- C&W Happy Birthday Darlin' [2]...Conway Twitty
- A/C Send One Your Love [1]...Stevie Wonder

ALBUMS
- POP The Long Run [8]...Eagles
- R&B Masterjam [1]...Rufus Featuring Chaka Khan
- C&W Kenny [7]...Kenny Rogers

December 29, 1979

SINGLES
- HOT Escape (The Pina Colada Song) [2]...Rupert Holmes
- R&B Do You Love What You Feel [3]...Rufus & Chaka Khan
- C&W Happy Birthday Darlin' [3]...Conway Twitty
- A/C Send One Your Love [2]...Stevie Wonder

ALBUMS
- POP The Long Run [9]...Eagles
- R&B Masterjam [2]...Rufus Featuring Chaka Khan
- C&W Kenny [8]...Kenny Rogers

January 5, 1980

SINGLES
- HOT Please Don't Go [1]...K.C. & The Sunshine Band
- R&B *Rock With You [1]...Michael Jackson
- C&W Coward Of The County [1]...Kenny Rogers
- A/C Send One Your Love [3]...Stevie Wonder

ALBUMS
- POP On The Radio-Greatest Hits-Volumes I & II [1]...Donna Summer
- R&B Off The Wall [10]...Michael Jackson
- C&W Kenny [9]...Kenny Rogers

January 12, 1980

SINGLES
- HOT Escape (The Pina Colada Song) [3]...Rupert Holmes
- R&B Rock With You [2]...Michael Jackson
- C&W Coward Of The County [2]...Kenny Rogers
- A/C Send One Your Love [4]...Stevie Wonder

ALBUMS
- POP Bee Gees Greatest [1]...Bee Gees
- R&B Off The Wall [11]...Michael Jackson
- C&W Kenny [10]...Kenny Rogers

January 19, 1980

SINGLES
- HOT Rock With You [1]...Michael Jackson
- R&B Rock With You [3]...Michael Jackson
- C&W Coward Of The County [3]...Kenny Rogers
- A/C Deja Vu [1]...Dionne Warwick

ALBUMS
- POP The Wall [1]...Pink Floyd
- R&B Off The Wall [12]...Michael Jackson
- C&W Kenny [11]...Kenny Rogers

January 26, 1980

SINGLES
- HOT Rock With You [2]...Michael Jackson
- R&B Rock With You [4]...Michael Jackson
- C&W I'll Be Coming Back For More [1]...T.G. Sheppard
- A/C Yes, I'm Ready [1]...Teri DeSario with K.C.

ALBUMS
- POP The Wall [2]...Pink Floyd
- R&B Off The Wall [13]...Michael Jackson
- C&W Kenny [12]...Kenny Rogers

February 2, 1980

SINGLES
- HOT Rock With You [3]...Michael Jackson
- R&B Rock With You [5]...Michael Jackson
- C&W I'll Be Coming Back For More [2]...T.G. Sheppard
- A/C Yes, I'm Ready [2]...Teri DeSario with K.C.

ALBUMS
- POP The Wall [3]...Pink Floyd
- R&B Off The Wall [14]...Michael Jackson
- C&W Kenny [13]...Kenny Rogers

February 9, 1980

SINGLES
- HOT Rock With You [4]...Michael Jackson
- R&B Rock With You [6]...Michael Jackson
- C&W Leaving Louisiana In The Broad Daylight [1]...The Oak Ridge Boys
- A/C Longer [1]...Dan Fogelberg

ALBUMS
- POP The Wall [4]...Pink Floyd
- R&B Off The Wall [15]...Michael Jackson
- C&W Kenny [14]...Kenny Rogers

February 16, 1980

SINGLES
- HOT Do That To Me One More Time [1]...Captain & Tennille
- R&B The Second Time Around [1]...Shalamar
- C&W Love Me Over Again [1]...Don Williams
- A/C When I Wanted You [1]...Barry Manilow

ALBUMS
- POP The Wall [5]...Pink Floyd
- R&B Off The Wall [16]...Michael Jackson
- C&W Kenny [15]...Kenny Rogers

February 23, 1980

SINGLES
- *HOT* **Crazy Little Thing Called Love** [1]...Queen
- *R&B* **Special Lady** [1]...Ray, Goodman & Brown
- *C&W* **Years** [1]...Barbara Mandrell
- *A/C* **Give It All You Got** [1]...Chuck Mangione

ALBUMS
- *POP* **The Wall** [6]...Pink Floyd
- *R&B* **The Whispers** [1]...The Whispers
- *C&W* **Kenny** [16]...Kenny Rogers

March 1, 1980

SINGLES
- *HOT* **Crazy Little Thing Called Love** [2]...Queen
- *R&B* **And The Beat Goes On** [1]...The Whispers
- *C&W* **I Ain't Living Long Like This** [1]...Waylon Jennings
- *A/C* **Daydream Believer** [1]...Anne Murray

ALBUMS
- *POP* **The Wall** [7]...Pink Floyd
- *R&B* **The Whispers** [2]...The Whispers
- *C&W* **Kenny** [17]...Kenny Rogers

March 8, 1980

SINGLES
- *HOT* **Crazy Little Thing Called Love** [3]...Queen
- *R&B* **And The Beat Goes On** [2]...The Whispers
- *C&W* **My Heroes Have Always Been Cowboys** [1]...Willie Nelson
- *A/C* **Give It All You Got** [2]...Chuck Mangione

ALBUMS
- *POP* **The Wall** [8]...Pink Floyd
- *R&B* **The Whispers** [3]...The Whispers
- *C&W* **Kenny** [18]...Kenny Rogers

March 15, 1980

SINGLES
- *HOT* **Crazy Little Thing Called Love** [4]...Queen
- *R&B* **And The Beat Goes On** [3]...The Whispers
- *C&W* **My Heroes Have Always Been Cowboys** [2]...Willie Nelson
- *A/C* **Give It All You Got** [3]...Chuck Mangione

ALBUMS
- *POP* **The Wall** [9]...Pink Floyd
- *R&B* **The Whispers** [4]...The Whispers
- *C&W* **Kenny** [19]...Kenny Rogers

March 22, 1980

SINGLES
- *HOT* **Another Brick In The Wall (Part II)** [1]...Pink Floyd
- *R&B* **And The Beat Goes On** [4]...The Whispers
- *C&W* **Why Don't You Spend The Night** [1]...Ronnie Milsap
- *A/C* **Lost In Love** [1]...Air Supply

ALBUMS
- *POP* **The Wall** [10]...Pink Floyd
- *R&B* **The Whispers** [5]...The Whispers
- *C&W* **Kenny** [20]...Kenny Rogers

March 29, 1980

SINGLES
- *HOT* **Another Brick In The Wall (Part II)** [2]...Pink Floyd
- *R&B* **And The Beat Goes On** [5]...The Whispers
- *C&W* **I'd Love To Lay You Down** [1]...Conway Twitty
- *A/C* **Three Times In Love** [1]...Tommy James

ALBUMS
- *POP* **The Wall** [11]...Pink Floyd
- *R&B* **The Whispers** [6]...The Whispers
- *C&W* **Kenny** [21]...Kenny Rogers

April 5, 1980

SINGLES
- *HOT* **Another Brick In The Wall (Part II)** [3]...Pink Floyd
- *R&B* **Stomp!** [1]...The Brothers Johnson
- *C&W* **Sugar Daddy** [1]...The Bellamy Brothers
- *A/C* **Lost In Love** [2]...Air Supply

ALBUMS
- *POP* **The Wall** [12]...Pink Floyd
- *R&B* **The Whispers** [7]...The Whispers
- *C&W* **Kenny** [22]...Kenny Rogers

April 12, 1980

SINGLES
- *HOT* **Another Brick In The Wall (Part II)** [4]...Pink Floyd
- *R&B* **Stomp!** [2]...The Brothers Johnson
- *C&W* **Honky Tonk Blues** [1]...Charley Pride
- *A/C* **Lost In Love** [3]...Air Supply

ALBUMS
- *POP* **The Wall** [13]...Pink Floyd
- *R&B* **The Whispers** [8]...The Whispers
- *C&W* **Kenny** [23]...Kenny Rogers

April 19, 1980

SINGLES
- *HOT* **Call Me** [1]...Blondie
- *R&B* **Don't Say Goodnight (It's Time For Love) (Parts 1 & 2)** [1]...The Isley Brothers
- *C&W* **It's Like We Never Said Goodbye** [1]...Crystal Gayle
- *A/C* **Lost In Love** [4]...Air Supply

ALBUMS
- *POP* **The Wall** [14]...Pink Floyd
- *R&B* **Light Up The Night** [1]...The Brothers Johnson
- *C&W* **Kenny** [24]...Kenny Rogers

April 26, 1980

SINGLES
- HOT   Call Me [2]...Blondie
- R&B   Don't Say Goodnight (It's Time For Love) (Parts 1 & 2) [2]...The Isley Brothers
- C&W   A Lesson In Leavin' [1]...Dottie West
- A/C   Lost In Love [5]...Air Supply

ALBUMS
- POP   The Wall [15]...Pink Floyd
- R&B   Light Up The Night [2]...The Brothers Johnson
- C&W   Kenny [25]...Kenny Rogers

May 3, 1980

SINGLES
- HOT   Call Me [3]...Blondie
- R&B   Don't Say Goodnight (It's Time For Love) (Parts 1 & 2) [3]...The Isley Brothers
- C&W   Are You On The Road To Lovin' Me Again [1]...Debby Boone
- A/C   Lost In Love [6]...Air Supply

ALBUMS
- POP   Against The Wind [1]...Bob Seger & The Silver Bullet Band
- R&B   Go All The Way [1]...The Isley Brothers
- C&W   There's A Little Bit Of Hank In Me [1]...Charley Pride

May 10, 1980

SINGLES
- HOT   Call Me [4]...Blondie
- R&B   Don't Say Goodnight (It's Time For Love) (Parts 1 & 2) [4]...The Isley Brothers
- C&W   Beneath Still Waters [1]...Emmylou Harris
- A/C   The Rose [1]...Bette Midler

ALBUMS
- POP   Against The Wind [2]...Bob Seger & The Silver Bullet Band
- R&B   Go All The Way [2]...The Isley Brothers
- C&W   Gideon [1]...Kenny Rogers

May 17, 1980

SINGLES
- HOT   Call Me [5]...Blondie
- R&B   Let's Get Serious [1]...Jermaine Jackson
- C&W   Gone Too Far [1]...Eddie Rabbitt
- A/C   The Rose [2]...Bette Midler

ALBUMS
- POP   Against The Wind [3]...Bob Seger & The Silver Bullet Band
- R&B   Go All The Way [3]...The Isley Brothers
- C&W   There's A Little Bit Of Hank In Me [2]...Charley Pride

May 24, 1980

SINGLES
- HOT   Call Me [6]...Blondie
- R&B   Let's Get Serious [2]...Jermaine Jackson
- C&W   Starting Over Again [1]...Dolly Parton
- A/C   The Rose [3]...Bette Midler

ALBUMS
- POP   Against The Wind [4]...Bob Seger & The Silver Bullet Band
- R&B   Go All The Way [4]...The Isley Brothers
- C&W   Gideon [2]...Kenny Rogers

May 31, 1980

SINGLES
- HOT   Funkytown [1]...Lipps, Inc.
- R&B   Let's Get Serious [3]...Jermaine Jackson
- C&W   My Heart/Silent Night (After The Fight) [1]...Ronnie Milsap
- A/C   The Rose [4]...Bette Midler

ALBUMS
- POP   Against The Wind [5]...Bob Seger & The Silver Bullet Band
- R&B   Go All The Way [5]...The Isley Brothers
- C&W   Greatest Hits [16]...Waylon Jennings

June 7, 1980

SINGLES
- HOT   Funkytown [2]...Lipps, Inc.
- R&B   Let's Get Serious [4]...Jermaine Jackson
- C&W   My Heart/Silent Night (After The Fight) [2]...Ronnie Milsap
- A/C   The Rose [5]...Bette Midler

ALBUMS
- POP   Against The Wind [6]...Bob Seger & The Silver Bullet Band
- R&B   Let's Get Serious [1]...Jermaine Jackson
- C&W   Gideon [3]...Kenny Rogers

June 14, 1980

SINGLES
- HOT   Funkytown [3]...Lipps, Inc.
- R&B   Let's Get Serious [5]...Jermaine Jackson
- C&W   My Heart/Silent Night (After The Fight) [3]...Ronnie Milsap
- A/C   Little Jeannie [1]...Elton John

ALBUMS
- POP   Glass Houses [1]...Billy Joel
- R&B   Let's Get Serious [2]...Jermaine Jackson
- C&W   Gideon [4]...Kenny Rogers

June 21, 1980

SINGLES
- *HOT* Funkytown [4]...Lipps, Inc.
- *R&B* Let's Get Serious [6]...Jermaine Jackson
- *C&W* One Day At A Time [1]...Cristy Lane
- *A/C* Little Jeannie [2]...Elton John

ALBUMS
- *POP* Glass Houses [2]...Billy Joel
- *R&B* Let's Get Serious [3]...Jermaine Jackson
- *C&W* Gideon [5]...Kenny Rogers

June 28, 1980

SINGLES
- *HOT* Coming Up (Live at Glasgow) [1]...Paul McCartney & Wings
- *R&B* Take Your Time (Do It Right) Part 1 [1]...The S.O.S. Band
- *C&W* Trying To Love Two Women [1]...The Oak Ridge Boys
- *A/C* Let Me Love You Tonight [1]...Pure Prairie League

ALBUMS
- *POP* Glass Houses [3]...Billy Joel
- *R&B* Let's Get Serious [4]...Jermaine Jackson
- *C&W* Gideon [6]...Kenny Rogers

July 5, 1980

SINGLES
- *HOT* Coming Up (Live at Glasgow) [2]...Paul McCartney & Wings
- *R&B* Take Your Time (Do It Right) Part 1 [2]...The S.O.S. Band
- *C&W* He Stopped Loving Her Today [1]...George Jones
- *A/C* Let Me Love You Tonight [2]...Pure Prairie League

ALBUMS
- *POP* Glass Houses [4]...Billy Joel
- *R&B* Let's Get Serious [5]...Jermaine Jackson
- *C&W* Gideon [7]...Kenny Rogers

July 12, 1980

SINGLES
- *HOT* Coming Up (Live at Glasgow) [3]...Paul McCartney & Wings
- *R&B* Take Your Time (Do It Right) Part 1 [3]...The S.O.S. Band
- *C&W* You Win Again [1]...Charley Pride
- *A/C* Let Me Love You Tonight [3]...Pure Prairie League

ALBUMS
- *POP* Glass Houses [5]...Billy Joel
- *R&B* Cameosis [1]...Cameo
- *C&W* Music Man [1]...Waylon Jennings

July 19, 1980

SINGLES
- *HOT* It's Still Rock And Roll To Me [1]...Billy Joel
- *R&B* Take Your Time (Do It Right) Part 1 [4]...The S.O.S. Band
- *C&W* True Love Ways [1]...Mickey Gilley
- *A/C* *Magic [1]...Olivia Newton-John

ALBUMS
- *POP* Glass Houses [6]...Billy Joel
- *R&B* Cameosis [2]...Cameo
- *C&W* Music Man [2]...Waylon Jennings

July 26, 1980

SINGLES
- *HOT* It's Still Rock And Roll To Me [2]...Billy Joel
- *R&B* Take Your Time (Do It Right) Part 1 [5]...The S.O.S. Band
- *C&W* Bar Room Buddies [1]...Merle Haggard & Clint Eastwood
- *A/C* Magic [2]...Olivia Newton-John

ALBUMS
- *POP* Emotional Rescue [1]...The Rolling Stones
- *R&B* Diana [1]...Diana Ross
- *C&W* Music Man [3]...Waylon Jennings

August 2, 1980

SINGLES
- *HOT* Magic [1]...Olivia Newton-John
- *R&B* One In A Million You [1]...Larry Graham
- *C&W* Dancin' Cowboys [1]...The Bellamy Brothers
- *A/C* Magic [3]...Olivia Newton-John

ALBUMS
- *POP* Emotional Rescue [2]...The Rolling Stones
- *R&B* Diana [2]...Diana Ross
- *C&W* Urban Cowboy [1]...Soundtrack

August 9, 1980

SINGLES
- *HOT* Magic [2]...Olivia Newton-John
- *R&B* One In A Million You [2]...Larry Graham
- *C&W* Stand By Me [1]...Mickey Gilley
- *A/C* Magic [4]...Olivia Newton-John

ALBUMS
- *POP* Emotional Rescue [3]...The Rolling Stones
- *R&B* Diana [3]...Diana Ross
- *C&W* Urban Cowboy [2]...Soundtrack

August 16, 1980

SINGLES
- HOT   Magic [3]...Olivia Newton-John
- R&B   *Upside Down [1]...Diana Ross
- C&W   Tennessee River [1]...Alabama
- A/C   Magic [5]...Olivia Newton-John

ALBUMS
- POP   Emotional Rescue [4]...The Rolling Stones
- R&B   Diana [4]...Diana Ross
- C&W   Urban Cowboy [3]...Soundtrack

August 23, 1980

SINGLES
- HOT   Magic [4]...Olivia Newton-John
- R&B   Upside Down [2]...Diana Ross
- C&W   Drivin' My Life Away [1]...Eddie Rabbitt
- A/C   Why Not Me [1]...Fred Knoblock

ALBUMS
- POP   Emotional Rescue [5]...The Rolling Stones
- R&B   Diana [5]...Diana Ross
- C&W   Urban Cowboy [4]...Soundtrack

August 30, 1980

SINGLES
- HOT   Sailing [1]...Christopher Cross
- R&B   Upside Down [3]...Diana Ross
- C&W   Cowboys And Clowns/Misery Loves Company [1]...Ronnie Milsap
- A/C   Why Not Me [2]...Fred Knoblock

ALBUMS
- POP   Emotional Rescue [6]...The Rolling Stones
- R&B   Diana [6]...Diana Ross
- C&W   Urban Cowboy [5]...Soundtrack

September 6, 1980

SINGLES
- HOT   Upside Down [1]...Diana Ross
- R&B   Upside Down [4]...Diana Ross
- C&W   Lookin' For Love [1]...Johnny Lee
- A/C   Don't Ask Me Why [1]...Billy Joel

ALBUMS
- POP   Emotional Rescue [7]...The Rolling Stones
- R&B   Diana [7]...Diana Ross
- C&W   Urban Cowboy [6]...Soundtrack

September 13, 1980

SINGLES
- HOT   Upside Down [2]...Diana Ross
- R&B   Give Me The Night [1]...George Benson
- C&W   Lookin' For Love [2]...Johnny Lee
- A/C   Don't Ask Me Why [2]...Billy Joel

ALBUMS
- POP   Hold Out [1]...Jackson Browne
- R&B   Diana [8]...Diana Ross
- C&W   Horizon [1]...Eddie Rabbitt

September 20, 1980

SINGLES
- HOT   Upside Down [3]...Diana Ross
- R&B   Give Me The Night [2]...George Benson
- C&W   Lookin' For Love [3]...Johnny Lee
- A/C   No Night So Long [1]...Dionne Warwick

ALBUMS
- POP   The Game [1]...Queen
- R&B   Give Me The Night [1]...George Benson
- C&W   Urban Cowboy [7]...Soundtrack

September 27, 1980

SINGLES
- HOT   Upside Down [4]...Diana Ross
- R&B   Give Me The Night [3]...George Benson
- C&W   Old Flames Can't Hold A Candle To You [1]...Dolly Parton
- A/C   No Night So Long [2]...Dionne Warwick

ALBUMS
- POP   The Game [2]...Queen
- R&B   Give Me The Night [2]...George Benson
- C&W   Urban Cowboy [8]...Soundtrack

October 4, 1980

SINGLES
- HOT   Another One Bites The Dust [1]...Queen
- R&B   Funkin' For Jamaica (N.Y.) [1]...Tom Browne
- C&W   Do You Wanna Go To Heaven [1]...T.G. Sheppard
- A/C   No Night So Long [3]...Dionne Warwick

ALBUMS
- POP   The Game [3]...Queen
- R&B   Give Me The Night [3]...George Benson
- C&W   Honeysuckle Rose [1]...Willie Nelson & Family/Soundtrack

October 11, 1980

SINGLES
- HOT   Another One Bites The Dust [2]...Queen
- R&B   Funkin' For Jamaica (N.Y.) [2]...Tom Browne
- C&W   Loving Up A Storm [1]...Razzy Bailey
- A/C   *Woman In Love [1]...Barbra Streisand

ALBUMS
- POP   The Game [4]...Queen
- R&B   Give Me The Night [4]...George Benson
- C&W   Honeysuckle Rose [2]...Willie Nelson & Family/Soundtrack

October 18, 1980

SINGLES
- HOT Another One Bites The Dust [3]...Queen
- R&B Funkin' For Jamaica (N.Y.) [3]...Tom Browne
- C&W I Believe In You [1]...Don Williams
- A/C Woman In Love [2]...Barbra Streisand

ALBUMS
- POP The Game [5]...Queen
- R&B Love Approach [1]...Tom Browne
- C&W Honeysuckle Rose [3]...
  Willie Nelson & Family/Soundtrack

October 25, 1980

SINGLES
- HOT Woman In Love [1]...Barbra Streisand
- R&B Funkin' For Jamaica (N.Y.) [4]...Tom Browne
- C&W I Believe In You [2]...Don Williams
- A/C Woman In Love [3]...Barbra Streisand

ALBUMS
- POP Guilty [1]...Barbra Streisand
- R&B Zapp [1]...Zapp
- C&W Honeysuckle Rose [4]...
  Willie Nelson & Family/Soundtrack

November 1, 1980

SINGLES
- HOT Woman In Love [2]...Barbra Streisand
- R&B Master Blaster (Jammin') [1]...Stevie Wonder
- C&W Theme From The Dukes Of Hazzard (Good Ol' Boys) [1]...Waylon Jennings
- A/C Woman In Love [4]...Barbra Streisand

ALBUMS
- POP Guilty [2]...Barbra Streisand
- R&B Zapp [2]...Zapp
- C&W Honeysuckle Rose [5]...
  Willie Nelson & Family/Soundtrack

November 8, 1980

SINGLES
- HOT Woman In Love [3]...Barbra Streisand
- R&B Master Blaster (Jammin') [2]...Stevie Wonder
- C&W On The Road Again [1]...Willie Nelson
- A/C Woman In Love [5]...Barbra Streisand

ALBUMS
- POP The River [1]...Bruce Springsteen
- R&B Triumph [1]...Jacksons
- C&W Honeysuckle Rose [6]...
  Willie Nelson & Family/Soundtrack

November 15, 1980

SINGLES
- HOT *Lady [1]...Kenny Rogers
- R&B Master Blaster (Jammin') [3]...Stevie Wonder
- C&W Could I Have This Dance [1]...Anne Murray
- A/C *Lady [1]...Kenny Rogers

ALBUMS
- POP The River [2]...Bruce Springsteen
- R&B Triumph [2]...Jacksons
- C&W Kenny Rogers' Greatest Hits [1]...Kenny Rogers

November 22, 1980

SINGLES
- HOT Lady [2]...Kenny Rogers
- R&B Master Blaster (Jammin') [4]...Stevie Wonder
- C&W Lady [1]...Kenny Rogers
- A/C Lady [2]...Kenny Rogers

ALBUMS
- POP The River [3]...Bruce Springsteen
- R&B Hotter Than July [1]...Stevie Wonder
- C&W Kenny Rogers' Greatest Hits [2]...Kenny Rogers

November 29, 1980

SINGLES
- HOT Lady [3]...Kenny Rogers
- R&B Master Blaster (Jammin') [5]...Stevie Wonder
- C&W If You Ever Change Your Mind [1]...Crystal Gayle
- A/C Lady [3]...Kenny Rogers

ALBUMS
- POP The River [4]...Bruce Springsteen
- R&B Hotter Than July [2]...Stevie Wonder
- C&W Kenny Rogers' Greatest Hits [3]...Kenny Rogers

December 6, 1980

SINGLES
- HOT Lady [4]...Kenny Rogers
- R&B Master Blaster (Jammin') [6]...Stevie Wonder
- C&W *Smoky Mountain Rain [1]...Ronnie Milsap
- A/C Lady [4]...Kenny Rogers

ALBUMS
- POP Guilty [3]...Barbra Streisand
- R&B Hotter Than July [3]...Stevie Wonder
- C&W Kenny Rogers' Greatest Hits [4]...Kenny Rogers

December 13, 1980

SINGLES
- HOT Lady [5]...Kenny Rogers
- R&B Master Blaster (Jammin') [7]...Stevie Wonder
- C&W Why Lady Why [1]...Alabama
- A/C Never Be The Same [1]...Christopher Cross

ALBUMS
- POP Kenny Rogers' Greatest Hits [1]...Kenny Rogers
- R&B Hotter Than July [4]...Stevie Wonder
- C&W Kenny Rogers' Greatest Hits [5]...Kenny Rogers

December 20, 1980
SINGLES
- *HOT*   Lady [6]...Kenny Rogers
- *R&B*   *Celebration [1]...Kool & The Gang
- *C&W*   That's All That Matters [1]...Mickey Gilley
- *A/C*   Never Be The Same [2]...Christopher Cross

ALBUMS
- *POP*   Kenny Rogers' Greatest Hits [2]...Kenny Rogers
- *R&B*   Hotter Than July [5]...Stevie Wonder
- *C&W*   Greatest Hits [1]...Ronnie Milsap

December 27, 1980
SINGLES
- *HOT*   (Just Like) Starting Over [1]...John Lennon
- *R&B*   Celebration [2]...Kool & The Gang
- *C&W*   One In A Million [1]...Johnny Lee
- *A/C*   More Than I Can Say [1]...Leo Sayer

ALBUMS
- *POP*   Double Fantasy [1]...John Lennon/Yoko Ono
- *R&B*   Hotter Than July [6]...Stevie Wonder
- *C&W*   Kenny Rogers' Greatest Hits [6]...Kenny Rogers

January 3, 1981
SINGLES
- *HOT*   (Just Like) Starting Over [2]...John Lennon
- *R&B*   Celebration [3]...Kool & The Gang
- *C&W*   One In A Million [2]...Johnny Lee
- *A/C*   More Than I Can Say [2]...Leo Sayer

ALBUMS
- *POP*   Double Fantasy [2]...John Lennon/Yoko Ono
- *R&B*   Hotter Than July [7]...Stevie Wonder
- *C&W*   Kenny Rogers' Greatest Hits [7]...Kenny Rogers

January 10, 1981
SINGLES
- *HOT*   (Just Like) Starting Over [3]...John Lennon
- *R&B*   Celebration [4]...Kool & The Gang
- *C&W*   I Think I'll Just Stay Here And Drink [1]...Merle Haggard
- *A/C*   More Than I Can Say [3]...Leo Sayer

ALBUMS
- *POP*   Double Fantasy [3]...John Lennon/Yoko Ono
- *R&B*   Hotter Than July [8]...Stevie Wonder
- *C&W*   Kenny Rogers' Greatest Hits [8]...Kenny Rogers

January 17, 1981
SINGLES
- *HOT*   (Just Like) Starting Over [4]...John Lennon
- *R&B*   Celebration [5]...Kool & The Gang
- *C&W*   *I Love A Rainy Night [1]...Eddie Rabbitt
- *A/C*   *I Love A Rainy Night [1]...Eddie Rabbitt

ALBUMS
- *POP*   Double Fantasy [4]...John Lennon/Yoko Ono
- *R&B*   Hotter Than July [9]...Stevie Wonder
- *C&W*   Kenny Rogers' Greatest Hits [9]...Kenny Rogers

January 24, 1981
SINGLES
- *HOT*   (Just Like) Starting Over [5]...John Lennon
- *R&B*   Celebration [6]...Kool & The Gang
- *C&W*   *9 To 5 [1]...Dolly Parton
- *A/C*   I Love A Rainy Night [2]...Eddie Rabbitt

ALBUMS
- *POP*   Double Fantasy [5]...John Lennon/Yoko Ono
- *R&B*   Hotter Than July [10]...Stevie Wonder
- *C&W*   Greatest Hits [2]...Ronnie Milsap

January 31, 1981
SINGLES
- *HOT*   The Tide Is High [1]...Blondie
- *R&B*   Fantastic Voyage [1]...Lakeside
- *C&W*   I Feel Like Loving You Again [1]...T.G. Sheppard
- *A/C*   I Love A Rainy Night [3]...Eddie Rabbitt

ALBUMS
- *POP*   Double Fantasy [6]...John Lennon/Yoko Ono
- *R&B*   Hotter Than July [11]...Stevie Wonder
- *C&W*   Kenny Rogers' Greatest Hits [10]...Kenny Rogers

February 7, 1981
SINGLES
- *HOT*   Celebration [1]...Kool & The Gang
- *R&B*   Fantastic Voyage [2]...Lakeside
- *C&W*   I Keep Coming Back/True Life Country Music [1]...Razzy Bailey
- *A/C*   The Winner Takes It All [1]...Abba

ALBUMS
- *POP*   Double Fantasy [7]...John Lennon/Yoko Ono
- *R&B*   Hotter Than July [12]...Stevie Wonder
- *C&W*   Kenny Rogers' Greatest Hits [11]...Kenny Rogers

February 14, 1981
SINGLES
- *HOT*   Celebration [2]...Kool & The Gang
- *R&B*   Burn Rubber (Why You Wanna Hurt Me) [1]...The Gap Band
- *C&W*   Who's Cheatin' Who [1]...Charly McClain
- *A/C*   The Winner Takes It All [2]...Abba

ALBUMS
- *POP*   Double Fantasy [8]...John Lennon/Yoko Ono
- *R&B*   Hotter Than July [13]...Stevie Wonder
- *C&W*   9 To 5 and Odd Jobs [1]...Dolly Parton

February 21, 1981

SINGLES
- HOT 9 To 5 [1]...Dolly Parton
- R&B Burn Rubber (Why You Wanna Hurt Me) [2]...The Gap Band
- C&W Southern Rains [1]...Mel Tillis
- A/C Smoky Mountain Rain [1]...Ronnie Milsap

ALBUMS
- POP Hi Infidelity [1]...REO Speedwagon
- R&B The Gap Band III [1]...The Gap Band
- C&W 9 To 5 and Odd Jobs [2]...Dolly Parton

February 28, 1981

SINGLES
- HOT I Love A Rainy Night [1]...Eddie Rabbitt
- R&B Don't Stop The Music [1]...Yarbrough & Peoples
- C&W Are You Happy Baby? [1]...Dottie West
- A/C 9 To 5 [1]...Dolly Parton

ALBUMS
- POP Hi Infidelity [2]...REO Speedwagon
- R&B The Gap Band III [2]...The Gap Band
- C&W 9 To 5 and Odd Jobs [3]...Dolly Parton

March 7, 1981

SINGLES
- HOT I Love A Rainy Night [2]...Eddie Rabbitt
- R&B Don't Stop The Music [2]...Yarbrough & Peoples
- C&W Do You Love As Good As You Look [1]...The Bellamy Brothers
- A/C 9 To 5 [2]...Dolly Parton

ALBUMS
- POP Hi Infidelity [3]...REO Speedwagon
- R&B The Two Of Us [1]...Yarbrough & Peoples
- C&W 9 To 5 and Odd Jobs [4]...Dolly Parton

March 14, 1981

SINGLES
- HOT 9 To 5 [2]...Dolly Parton
- R&B Don't Stop The Music [3]...Yarbrough & Peoples
- C&W Guitar Man [1]...Elvis Presley
- A/C What Kind Of Fool [1]...Barbra Streisand & Barry Gibb

ALBUMS
- POP Hi Infidelity [4]...REO Speedwagon
- R&B The Two Of Us [2]...Yarbrough & Peoples
- C&W 9 To 5 and Odd Jobs [5]...Dolly Parton

March 21, 1981

SINGLES
- HOT Keep On Loving You [1]...REO Speedwagon
- R&B Don't Stop The Music [4]...Yarbrough & Peoples
- C&W Angel Flying Too Close To The Ground [1]...Willie Nelson
- A/C What Kind Of Fool [2]...Barbra Streisand & Barry Gibb

ALBUMS
- POP Hi Infidelity [5]...REO Speedwagon
- R&B The Gap Band III [3]...The Gap Band
- C&W 9 To 5 and Odd Jobs [6]...Dolly Parton

March 28, 1981

SINGLES
- HOT Rapture [1]...Blondie
- R&B Don't Stop The Music [5]...Yarbrough & Peoples
- C&W Texas Women [1]...Hank Williams, Jr.
- A/C What Kind Of Fool [3]...Barbra Streisand & Barry Gibb

ALBUMS
- POP Hi Infidelity [6]...REO Speedwagon
- R&B The Gap Band III [4]...The Gap Band
- C&W 9 To 5 and Odd Jobs [7]...Dolly Parton

April 4, 1981

SINGLES
- HOT Rapture [2]...Blondie
- R&B Being With You [1]...Smokey Robinson
- C&W Drifter [1]...Sylvia
- A/C What Kind Of Fool [4]...Barbra Streisand & Barry Gibb

ALBUMS
- POP Paradise Theater [1]...Styx
- R&B The Gap Band III [5]...The Gap Band
- C&W 9 To 5 and Odd Jobs [8]...Dolly Parton

April 11, 1981

SINGLES
- HOT Kiss On My List [1]...Daryl Hall & John Oates
- R&B Being With You [2]...Smokey Robinson
- C&W You're The Reason God Made Oklahoma [1]...David Frizzell & Shelly West
- A/C Angel Of The Morning [1]...Juice Newton

ALBUMS
- POP Paradise Theater [2]...Styx
- R&B The Gap Band III [6]...The Gap Band
- C&W 9 To 5 and Odd Jobs [9]...Dolly Parton

April 18, 1981
SINGLES
- *HOT*   Kiss On My List [2]...Daryl Hall & John Oates
- *R&B*   Being With You [3]...Smokey Robinson
- *C&W*   Old Flame [1]...Alabama
- *A/C*   Angel Of The Morning [2]...Juice Newton

ALBUMS
- *POP*   Hi Infidelity [7]...REO Speedwagon
- *R&B*   Being With You [1]...Smokey Robinson
- *C&W*   9 To 5 and Odd Jobs [10]...Dolly Parton

April 25, 1981
SINGLES
- *HOT*   Kiss On My List [3]...Daryl Hall & John Oates
- *R&B*   Being With You [4]...Smokey Robinson
- *C&W*   A Headache Tomorrow (Or A Heartache Tonight) [1]...Mickey Gilley
- *A/C*   Angel Of The Morning [3]...Juice Newton

ALBUMS
- *POP*   Hi Infidelity [8]...REO Speedwagon
- *R&B*   Being With You [2]...Smokey Robinson
- *C&W*   Horizon [2]...Eddie Rabbitt

May 2, 1981
SINGLES
- *HOT*   *Morning Train (Nine To Five) [1]...Sheena Easton
- *R&B*   Being With You [5]...Smokey Robinson
- *C&W*   Rest Your Love On Me/I Am The Dreamer (You Are The Dream) [1]...Conway Twitty
- *A/C*   *Morning Train (Nine To Five) [1]...Sheena Easton

ALBUMS
- *POP*   Hi Infidelity [9]...REO Speedwagon
- *R&B*   Being With You [3]...Smokey Robinson
- *C&W*   Somewhere Over The Rainbow [1]...Willie Nelson

May 9, 1981
SINGLES
- *HOT*   Morning Train (Nine To Five) [2]...Sheena Easton
- *R&B*   *Sukiyaki [1]...A Taste Of Honey
- *C&W*   Am I Losing You [1]...Ronnie Milsap
- *A/C*   Morning Train (Nine To Five) [2]...Sheena Easton

ALBUMS
- *POP*   Paradise Theater [3]...Styx
- *R&B*   Being With You [4]...Smokey Robinson
- *C&W*   Somewhere Over The Rainbow [2]...Willie Nelson

May 16, 1981
SINGLES
- *HOT*   Bette Davis Eyes [1]...Kim Carnes
- *R&B*   A Woman Needs Love (Just Like You Do) [1]...Ray Parker Jr. & Raydio
- *C&W*   I Loved 'Em Every One [1]...T.G. Sheppard
- *A/C*   Sukiyaki [1]...A Taste Of Honey

ALBUMS
- *POP*   Hi Infidelity [10]...REO Speedwagon
- *R&B*   Being With You [5]...Smokey Robinson
- *C&W*   Somewhere Over The Rainbow [3]...Willie Nelson

May 23, 1981
SINGLES
- *HOT*   Bette Davis Eyes [2]...Kim Carnes
- *R&B*   A Woman Needs Love (Just Like You Do) [2]...Ray Parker Jr. & Raydio
- *C&W*   Seven Year Ache [1]...Rosanne Cash
- *A/C*   Sukiyaki [2]...A Taste Of Honey

ALBUMS
- *POP*   Hi Infidelity [11]...REO Speedwagon
- *R&B*   A Woman Needs Love [1]...Ray Parker Jr. & Raydio
- *C&W*   Feels So Right [1]...Alabama

May 30, 1981
SINGLES
- *HOT*   Bette Davis Eyes [3]...Kim Carnes
- *R&B*   What Cha' Gonna Do For Me [1]...Chaka Khan
- *C&W*   Elvira [1]...The Oak Ridge Boys
- *A/C*   How 'Bout Us [1]...Champaign

ALBUMS
- *POP*   Hi Infidelity [12]...REO Speedwagon
- *R&B*   A Woman Needs Love [2]...Ray Parker Jr. & Raydio
- *C&W*   Feels So Right [2]...Alabama

June 6, 1981
SINGLES
- *HOT*   Bette Davis Eyes [4]...Kim Carnes
- *R&B*   What Cha' Gonna Do For Me [2]...Chaka Khan
- *C&W*   Friends/Anywhere There's A Jukebox [1]...Razzy Bailey
- *A/C*   How 'Bout Us [2]...Champaign

ALBUMS
- *POP*   Hi Infidelity [13]...REO Speedwagon
- *R&B*   Street Songs [1]...Rick James
- *C&W*   Seven Year Ache [1]...Rosanne Cash

June 13, 1981

SINGLES
- HOT Bette Davis Eyes [5]...Kim Carnes
- R&B Give It To Me Baby [1]...Rick James
- C&W What Are We Doin' In Love [1]... Kenny Rogers & Dottie West
- A/C America [1]...Neil Diamond

ALBUMS
- POP Hi Infidelity [14]...REO Speedwagon
- R&B Street Songs [2]...Rick James
- C&W Seven Year Ache [2]...Rosanne Cash

June 20, 1981

SINGLES
- HOT Stars on 45 [1]...Stars on 45
- R&B Give It To Me Baby [2]...Rick James
- C&W But You Know I Love You [1]...Dolly Parton
- A/C America [2]...Neil Diamond

ALBUMS
- POP Hi Infidelity [15]...REO Speedwagon
- R&B Street Songs [3]...Rick James
- C&W Feels So Right [3]...Alabama

June 27, 1981

SINGLES
- HOT Bette Davis Eyes [6]...Kim Carnes
- R&B Give It To Me Baby [3]...Rick James
- C&W Blessed Are The Believers [1]...Anne Murray
- A/C America [3]...Neil Diamond

ALBUMS
- POP Mistaken Identity [1]...Kim Carnes
- R&B Street Songs [4]...Rick James
- C&W Feels So Right [4]...Alabama

July 4, 1981

SINGLES
- HOT Bette Davis Eyes [7]...Kim Carnes
- R&B Give It To Me Baby [4]...Rick James
- C&W I Was Country When Country Wasn't Cool [1]... Barbara Mandrell
- A/C All Those Years Ago [1]...George Harrison

ALBUMS
- POP Mistaken Identity [2]...Kim Carnes
- R&B Street Songs [5]...Rick James
- C&W Feels So Right [5]...Alabama

July 11, 1981

SINGLES
- HOT Bette Davis Eyes [8]...Kim Carnes
- R&B Give It To Me Baby [5]...Rick James
- C&W Fire & Smoke [1]...Earl Thomas Conley
- A/C *I Don't Need You [1]...Kenny Rogers

ALBUMS
- POP Mistaken Identity [3]...Kim Carnes
- R&B Street Songs [6]...Rick James
- C&W Feels So Right [6]...Alabama

July 18, 1981

SINGLES
- HOT Bette Davis Eyes [9]...Kim Carnes
- R&B Double Dutch Bus [1]...Frankie Smith
- C&W Feels So Right [1]...Alabama
- A/C I Don't Need You [2]...Kenny Rogers

ALBUMS
- POP Mistaken Identity [4]...Kim Carnes
- R&B Street Songs [7]...Rick James
- C&W Fancy Free [1]...Oak Ridge Boys

July 25, 1981

SINGLES
- HOT The One That You Love [1]...Air Supply
- R&B Double Dutch Bus [2]...Frankie Smith
- C&W Feels So Right [2]...Alabama
- A/C I Don't Need You [3]...Kenny Rogers

ALBUMS
- POP Long Distance Voyager [1]...The Moody Blues
- R&B Street Songs [8]...Rick James
- C&W Feels So Right [7]...Alabama

August 1, 1981

SINGLES
- HOT Jessie's Girl [1]...Rick Springfield
- R&B Double Dutch Bus [3]...Frankie Smith
- C&W Dixie On My Mind [1]...Hank Williams, Jr.
- A/C I Don't Need You [4]...Kenny Rogers

ALBUMS
- POP Long Distance Voyager [2]...The Moody Blues
- R&B Street Songs [9]...Rick James
- C&W Fancy Free [2]...Oak Ridge Boys

August 8, 1981

SINGLES
- HOT Jessie's Girl [2]...Rick Springfield
- R&B Double Dutch Bus [4]...Frankie Smith
- C&W Too Many Lovers [1]...Crystal Gayle
- A/C I Don't Need You [5]...Kenny Rogers

ALBUMS
- POP Long Distance Voyager [3]...The Moody Blues
- R&B Street Songs [10]...Rick James
- C&W Feels So Right [8]...Alabama

August 15, 1981
SINGLES
- HOT *Endless Love [1]...Diana Ross & Lionel Richie
- R&B I'm In Love [1]...Evelyn King
- C&W I Don't Need You [1]...Kenny Rogers
- A/C I Don't Need You [6]...Kenny Rogers

ALBUMS
- POP Precious Time [1]...Pat Benatar
- R&B Street Songs [11]...Rick James
- C&W Feels So Right [9]...Alabama

August 22, 1981
SINGLES
- HOT Endless Love [2]...Diana Ross & Lionel Richie
- R&B Endless Love [1]...Diana Ross & Lionel Richie
- C&W I Don't Need You [2]...Kenny Rogers
- A/C Touch Me When We're Dancing [1]...Carpenters

ALBUMS
- POP 4 [1]...Foreigner
- R&B Street Songs [12]...Rick James
- C&W Feels So Right [10]...Alabama

August 29, 1981
SINGLES
- HOT Endless Love [3]...Diana Ross & Lionel Richie
- R&B Endless Love [2]...Diana Ross & Lionel Richie
- C&W (There's) No Gettin' Over Me [1]...Ronnie Milsap
- A/C Touch Me When We're Dancing [2]...Carpenters

ALBUMS
- POP 4 [2]...Foreigner
- R&B Street Songs [13]...Rick James
- C&W Share Your Love [1]...Kenny Rogers

September 5, 1981
SINGLES
- HOT Endless Love [4]...Diana Ross & Lionel Richie
- R&B Endless Love [3]...Diana Ross & Lionel Richie
- C&W (There's) No Gettin' Over Me [2]...Ronnie Milsap
- A/C Endless Love [1]...Diana Ross & Lionel Richie

ALBUMS
- POP Bella Donna [1]...Stevie Nicks
- R&B Street Songs [14]...Rick James
- C&W Share Your Love [2]...Kenny Rogers

September 12, 1981
SINGLES
- HOT Endless Love [5]...Diana Ross & Lionel Richie
- R&B Endless Love [4]...Diana Ross & Lionel Richie
- C&W Older Women [1]...Ronnie McDowell
- A/C Endless Love [2]...Diana Ross & Lionel Richie

ALBUMS
- POP Escape [1]...Journey
- R&B Street Songs [15]...Rick James
- C&W Feels So Right [11]...Alabama

September 19, 1981
SINGLES
- HOT Endless Love [6]...Diana Ross & Lionel Richie
- R&B Endless Love [5]...Diana Ross & Lionel Richie
- C&W You Don't Know Me [1]...Mickey Gilley
- A/C Endless Love [3]...Diana Ross & Lionel Richie

ALBUMS
- POP Tattoo You [1]...The Rolling Stones
- R&B Street Songs [16]...Rick James
- C&W Feels So Right [12]...Alabama

September 26, 1981
SINGLES
- HOT Endless Love [7]...Diana Ross & Lionel Richie
- R&B Endless Love [6]...Diana Ross & Lionel Richie
- C&W Tight Fittin' Jeans [1]...Conway Twitty
- A/C *Arthur's Theme (Best That You Can Do) [1]...Christopher Cross

ALBUMS
- POP Tattoo You [2]...The Rolling Stones
- R&B Street Songs [17]...Rick James
- C&W Step By Step [1]...Eddie Rabbitt

October 3, 1981
SINGLES
- HOT Endless Love [8]...Diana Ross & Lionel Richie
- R&B Endless Love [7]...Diana Ross & Lionel Richie
- C&W Midnight Hauler/Scratch My Back (And Whisper in My Ear) [1]...Razzy Bailey
- A/C Arthur's Theme (Best That You Can Do) [2]...Christopher Cross

ALBUMS
- POP Tattoo You [3]...The Rolling Stones
- R&B Street Songs [18]...Rick James
- C&W Step By Step [2]...Eddie Rabbitt

October 10, 1981
SINGLES
- HOT Endless Love [9]...Diana Ross & Lionel Richie
- R&B When She Was My Girl [1]...Four Tops
- C&W Party Time [1]...T.G. Sheppard
- A/C Arthur's Theme (Best That You Can Do) [3]...Christopher Cross

ALBUMS
- POP Tattoo You [4]...The Rolling Stones
- R&B Street Songs [19]...Rick James
- C&W Step By Step [3]...Eddie Rabbitt

October 17, 1981

SINGLES
- HOT Arthur's Theme (Best That You Can Do) [1]...Christopher Cross
- R&B When She Was My Girl [2]...Four Tops
- C&W Step By Step [1]...Eddie Rabbitt
- A/C Arthur's Theme (Best That You Can Do) [4]...Christopher Cross

ALBUMS
- POP Tattoo You [5]...The Rolling Stones
- R&B Street Songs [20]...Rick James
- C&W There's No Gettin' Over Me [1]...Ronnie Milsap

October 24, 1981

SINGLES
- HOT Arthur's Theme (Best That You Can Do) [2]...Christopher Cross
- R&B Never Too Much [1]...Luther Vandross
- C&W Never Been So Loved (In All My Life) [1]...Charley Pride
- A/C Share Your Love With Me [1]...Kenny Rogers

ALBUMS
- POP Tattoo You [6]...The Rolling Stones
- R&B Breakin' Away [1]...Al Jarreau
- C&W There's No Gettin' Over Me [2]...Ronnie Milsap

October 31, 1981

SINGLES
- HOT Arthur's Theme (Best That You Can Do) [3]...Christopher Cross
- R&B Never Too Much [2]...Luther Vandross
- C&W Never Been So Loved (In All My Life) [2]...Charley Pride
- A/C Share Your Love With Me [2]...Kenny Rogers

ALBUMS
- POP Tattoo You [7]...The Rolling Stones
- R&B Breakin' Away [2]...Al Jarreau
- C&W Feels So Right [13]...Alabama

November 7, 1981

SINGLES
- HOT Private Eyes [1]...Daryl Hall & John Oates
- R&B I Heard It Through The Grapevine [1]...Roger
- C&W Fancy Free [1]...The Oak Ridge Boys
- A/C Here I Am (Just When I Thought I Was Over You) [1]...Air Supply

ALBUMS
- POP Tattoo You [8]...The Rolling Stones
- R&B The Many Facets Of Roger [1]...Roger
- C&W Feels So Right [14]...Alabama

November 14, 1981

SINGLES
- HOT Private Eyes [2]...Daryl Hall & John Oates
- R&B I Heard It Through The Grapevine [2]...Roger
- C&W My Baby Thinks He's A Train [1]...Rosanne Cash
- A/C Here I Am (Just When I Thought I Was Over You) [2]...Air Supply

ALBUMS
- POP Tattoo You [9]...The Rolling Stones
- R&B Never Too Much [1]...Luther Vandross
- C&W Feels So Right [15]...Alabama

November 21, 1981

SINGLES
- HOT Physical [1]...Olivia Newton-John
- R&B Take My Heart (You Can Have It If You Want It) [1]...Kool & The Gang
- C&W All My Rowdy Friends (Have Settled Down) [1]...Hank Williams, Jr.
- A/C Here I Am (Just When I Thought I Was Over You) [3]...Air Supply

ALBUMS
- POP 4 [3]...Foreigner
- R&B Something Special [1]...Kool & The Gang
- C&W There's No Gettin' Over Me [3]...Ronnie Milsap

November 28, 1981

SINGLES
- HOT Physical [2]...Olivia Newton-John
- R&B Let's Groove [1]...Earth, Wind & Fire
- C&W My Favorite Memory [1]...Merle Haggard
- A/C The Old Songs [1]...Barry Manilow

ALBUMS
- POP 4 [4]...Foreigner
- R&B Raise! [1]...Earth, Wind & Fire
- C&W Feels So Right [16]...Alabama

December 5, 1981

SINGLES
- HOT Physical [3]...Olivia Newton-John
- R&B Let's Groove [2]...Earth, Wind & Fire
- C&W Bet Your Heart On Me [1]...Johnny Lee
- A/C The Old Songs [2]...Barry Manilow

ALBUMS
- POP 4 [5]...Foreigner
- R&B Raise! [2]...Earth, Wind & Fire
- C&W Willie Nelson's Greatest Hits (& Some That Will Be) [1]...Willie Nelson

December 12, 1981
SINGLES
- HOT Physical [4]...Olivia Newton-John
- R&B Let's Groove [3]...Earth, Wind & Fire
- C&W Still Doin' Time [1]...George Jones
- A/C The Old Songs [3]...Barry Manilow

ALBUMS
- POP 4 [6]...Foreigner
- R&B Raise! [3]...Earth, Wind & Fire
- C&W Willie Nelson's Greatest Hits (& Some That Will Be) [2]...Willie Nelson

December 19, 1981
SINGLES
- HOT Physical [5]...Olivia Newton-John
- R&B Let's Groove [4]...Earth, Wind & Fire
- C&W All Roads Lead To You [1]...Steve Wariner
- A/C Yesterday's Songs [1]...Neil Diamond

ALBUMS
- POP 4 [7]...Foreigner
- R&B Raise! [4]...Earth, Wind & Fire
- C&W Willie Nelson's Greatest Hits (& Some That Will Be) [3]...Willie Nelson

December 26, 1981
SINGLES
- HOT Physical [6]...Olivia Newton-John
- R&B Let's Groove [5]...Earth, Wind & Fire
- C&W Love In The First Degree [1]...Alabama
- A/C Yesterday's Songs [2]...Neil Diamond

ALBUMS
- POP For Those About To Rock We Salute You [1]...AC/DC
- R&B Raise! [5]...Earth, Wind & Fire
- C&W Feels So Right [17]...Alabama

January 2, 1982
SINGLES
- HOT Physical [7]...Olivia Newton-John
- R&B Let's Groove [6]...Earth, Wind & Fire
- C&W Love In The First Degree [2]...Alabama
- A/C Yesterday's Songs [3]...Neil Diamond

ALBUMS
- POP For Those About To Rock We Salute You [2]...AC/DC
- R&B Raise! [6]...Earth, Wind & Fire
- C&W Feels So Right [18]...Alabama

January 9, 1982
SINGLES
- HOT Physical [8]...Olivia Newton-John
- R&B Let's Groove [7]...Earth, Wind & Fire
- C&W Fourteen Carat Mind [1]...Gene Watson
- A/C Yesterday's Songs [4]...Neil Diamond

ALBUMS
- POP For Those About To Rock We Salute You [3]...AC/DC
- R&B Raise! [7]...Earth, Wind & Fire
- C&W Feels So Right [19]...Alabama

January 16, 1982
SINGLES
- HOT Physical [9]...Olivia Newton-John
- R&B Let's Groove [8]...Earth, Wind & Fire
- C&W I Wouldn't Have Missed It For The World [1]...Ronnie Milsap
- A/C Yesterday's Songs [5]...Neil Diamond

ALBUMS
- POP 4 [8]...Foreigner
- R&B Raise! [8]...Earth, Wind & Fire
- C&W Willie Nelson's Greatest Hits (& Some That Will Be) [4]...Willie Nelson

January 23, 1982
SINGLES
- HOT Physical [10]...Olivia Newton-John
- R&B Turn Your Love Around [1]...George Benson
- C&W Red Neckin' Love Makin' Night [1]...Conway Twitty
- A/C Yesterday's Songs [6]...Neil Diamond

ALBUMS
- POP 4 [9]...Foreigner
- R&B Raise! [9]...Earth, Wind & Fire
- C&W Feels So Right [20]...Alabama

January 30, 1982
SINGLES
- HOT *I Can't Go For That (No Can Do) [1]...Daryl Hall & John Oates
- R&B *I Can't Go For That (No Can Do) [1]...Daryl Hall & John Oates
- C&W *The Sweetest Thing (I've Ever Known) [1]...Juice Newton
- A/C *The Sweetest Thing (I've Ever Known) [1]...Juice Newton

ALBUMS
- POP 4 [10]...Foreigner
- R&B Raise! [10]...Earth, Wind & Fire
- C&W Feels So Right [21]...Alabama

February 6, 1982

SINGLES
- *HOT* Centerfold [1]...The J. Geils Band
- *R&B* Call Me [1]...Skyy
- *C&W* Lonely Nights [1]...Mickey Gilley
- *A/C* Leader Of The Band [1]...Dan Fogelberg

ALBUMS
- *POP* Freeze-Frame [1]...The J. Geils Band
- *R&B* Raise! [11]...Earth, Wind & Fire
- *C&W* Feels So Right [22]...Alabama

February 13, 1982

SINGLES
- *HOT* Centerfold [2]...The J. Geils Band
- *R&B* Call Me [2]...Skyy
- *C&W* Someone Could Lose A Heart Tonight [1]...Eddie Rabbitt
- *A/C* Leader Of The Band [2]...Dan Fogelberg

ALBUMS
- *POP* Freeze-Frame [2]...The J. Geils Band
- *R&B* Skyy Line [1]...Skyy
- *C&W* Feels So Right [23]...Alabama

February 20, 1982

SINGLES
- *HOT* Centerfold [3]...The J. Geils Band
- *R&B* That Girl [1]...Stevie Wonder
- *C&W* Only One You [1]...T.G. Sheppard
- *A/C* Somewhere Down The Road [1]...Barry Manilow

ALBUMS
- *POP* Freeze-Frame [3]...The J. Geils Band
- *R&B* The Poet [1]...Bobby Womack
- *C&W* Feels So Right [24]...Alabama

February 27, 1982

SINGLES
- *HOT* Centerfold [4]...The J. Geils Band
- *R&B* That Girl [2]...Stevie Wonder
- *C&W* Lord, I Hope This Day Is Good [1]...Don Williams
- *A/C* Somewhere Down The Road [2]...Barry Manilow

ALBUMS
- *POP* Freeze-Frame [4]...The J. Geils Band
- *R&B* The Poet [2]...Bobby Womack
- *C&W* Feels So Right [25]...Alabama

March 6, 1982

SINGLES
- *HOT* Centerfold [5]...The J. Geils Band
- *R&B* That Girl [3]...Stevie Wonder
- *C&W* You're The Best Break This Old Heart Ever Had [1]...Ed Bruce
- *A/C* Through The Years [1]...Kenny Rogers

ALBUMS
- *POP* Beauty And The Beat [1]...Go-Go's
- *R&B* The Poet [3]...Bobby Womack
- *C&W* Feels So Right [26]...Alabama

March 13, 1982

SINGLES
- *HOT* Centerfold [6]...The J. Geils Band
- *R&B* That Girl [4]...Stevie Wonder
- *C&W* Blue Moon With Heartache [1]...Rosanne Cash
- *A/C* Through The Years [2]...Kenny Rogers

ALBUMS
- *POP* Beauty And The Beat [2]...Go-Go's
- *R&B* The Poet [4]...Bobby Womack
- *C&W* Feels So Right [27]...Alabama

March 20, 1982

SINGLES
- *HOT* I Love Rock 'N Roll [1]...Joan Jett & The Blackhearts
- *R&B* That Girl [5]...Stevie Wonder
- *C&W* Mountain Of Love [1]...Charley Pride
- *A/C* Key Largo [1]...Bertie Higgins

ALBUMS
- *POP* Beauty And The Beat [3]...Go-Go's
- *R&B* The Poet [5]...Bobby Womack
- *C&W* Feels So Right [28]...Alabama

March 27, 1982

SINGLES
- *HOT* I Love Rock 'N Roll [2]...Joan Jett & The Blackhearts
- *R&B* That Girl [6]...Stevie Wonder
- *C&W* She Left Love All Over Me [1]...Razzy Bailey
- *A/C* Key Largo [2]...Bertie Higgins

ALBUMS
- *POP* Beauty And The Beat [4]...Go-Go's
- *R&B* Skyy Line [2]...Skyy
- *C&W* Bobbie Sue [1]...Oak Ridge Boys

April 3, 1982

SINGLES
- *HOT* I Love Rock 'N Roll [3]...Joan Jett & The Blackhearts
- *R&B* That Girl [7]...Stevie Wonder
- *C&W* Bobbie Sue [1]...The Oak Ridge Boys
- *A/C* *Chariots Of Fire - Titles [1]...Vangelis

ALBUMS
- *POP* Beauty And The Beat [5]...Go-Go's
- *R&B* Skyy Line [3]...Skyy
- *C&W* Bobbie Sue [2]...Oak Ridge Boys

April 10, 1982

SINGLES
- HOT I Love Rock 'N Roll [4]...Joan Jett & The Blackhearts
- R&B That Girl [8]...Stevie Wonder
- C&W Big City [1]...Merle Haggard
- A/C Chariots Of Fire - Titles [2]...Vangelis

ALBUMS
- POP Beauty And The Beat [6]...Go-Go's
- R&B Skyy Line [4]...Skyy
- C&W Bobbie Sue [3]...Oak Ridge Boys

April 17, 1982

SINGLES
- HOT I Love Rock 'N Roll [5]...Joan Jett & The Blackhearts
- R&B That Girl [9]...Stevie Wonder
- C&W The Clown [1]...Conway Twitty
- A/C Chariots Of Fire - Titles [3]...Vangelis

ALBUMS
- POP Chariots Of Fire [1]...Vangelis/Soundtrack
- R&B Love Is Where You Find It [1]...The Whispers
- C&W Mountain Music [1]...Alabama

April 24, 1982

SINGLES
- HOT I Love Rock 'N Roll [6]...Joan Jett & The Blackhearts
- R&B If It Ain't One Thing...It's Another [1]...
  Richard "Dimples" Fields
- C&W Crying My Heart Out Over You [1]...Ricky Skaggs
- A/C Chariots Of Fire - Titles [4]...Vangelis

ALBUMS
- POP Chariots Of Fire [2]...Vangelis/Soundtrack
- R&B Friends [1]...Shalamar
- C&W Mountain Music [2]...Alabama

May 1, 1982

SINGLES
- HOT I Love Rock 'N Roll [7]...Joan Jett & The Blackhearts
- R&B If It Ain't One Thing...It's Another [2]...
  Richard "Dimples" Fields
- C&W Mountain Music [1]...Alabama
- A/C Chariots Of Fire - Titles [5]...Vangelis

ALBUMS
- POP Chariots Of Fire [3]...Vangelis/Soundtrack
- R&B Friends [2]...Shalamar
- C&W Mountain Music [3]...Alabama

May 8, 1982

SINGLES
- HOT Chariots Of Fire - Titles [1]...Vangelis
- R&B If It Ain't One Thing...It's Another [3]...
  Richard "Dimples" Fields
- C&W Always On My Mind [1]...Willie Nelson
- A/C Shanghai Breezes [1]...John Denver

ALBUMS
- POP Chariots Of Fire [4]...Vangelis/Soundtrack
- R&B Brillance [1]...Atlantic Starr
- C&W Mountain Music [4]...Alabama

May 15, 1982

SINGLES
- HOT *Ebony And Ivory [1]...
  Paul McCartney with Stevie Wonder
- R&B It's Gonna Take A Miracle [1]...Deniece Williams
- C&W Always On My Mind [2]...Willie Nelson
- A/C *Ebony And Ivory [1]...
  Paul McCartney with Stevie Wonder

ALBUMS
- POP Asia [1]...Asia
- R&B Brillance [2]...Atlantic Starr
- C&W Mountain Music [5]...Alabama

May 22, 1982

SINGLES
- HOT Ebony And Ivory [2]...
  Paul McCartney with Stevie Wonder
- R&B It's Gonna Take A Miracle [2]...Deniece Williams
- C&W Just To Satisfy You [1]...
  Waylon Jennings & Willie Nelson
- A/C Ebony And Ivory [2]...
  Paul McCartney with Stevie Wonder

ALBUMS
- POP Asia [2]...Asia
- R&B Brillance [3]...Atlantic Starr
- C&W Always On My Mind [1]...Willie Nelson

May 29, 1982

SINGLES
- HOT Ebony And Ivory [3]...
  Paul McCartney with Stevie Wonder
- R&B Let It Whip [1]...Dazz Band
- C&W Just To Satisfy You [2]...
  Waylon Jennings & Willie Nelson
- A/C Ebony And Ivory [3]...
  Paul McCartney with Stevie Wonder

ALBUMS
- POP Tug Of War [1]...Paul McCartney
- R&B The Other Woman [1]...Ray Parker Jr.
- C&W Always On My Mind [2]...Willie Nelson

June 5, 1982
SINGLES
- *HOT* Ebony And Ivory [4]...
  Paul McCartney with Stevie Wonder
- *R&B* Let It Whip [2]...Dazz Band
- *C&W* Finally [1]...T.G. Sheppard
- *A/C* Ebony And Ivory [4]...
  Paul McCartney with Stevie Wonder

ALBUMS
- *POP* Tug Of War [2]...Paul McCartney
- *R&B* Stevie Wonder's Original Musiquarium I [1]...
  Stevie Wonder
- *C&W* Mountain Music [6]...Alabama

June 12, 1982
SINGLES
- *HOT* Ebony And Ivory [5]...
  Paul McCartney with Stevie Wonder
- *R&B* Let It Whip [3]...Dazz Band
- *C&W* For All The Wrong Reasons [1]...The Bellamy Brothers
- *A/C* Ebony And Ivory [5]...
  Paul McCartney with Stevie Wonder

ALBUMS
- *POP* Tug Of War [3]...Paul McCartney
- *R&B* Stevie Wonder's Original Musiquarium I [2]...
  Stevie Wonder
- *C&W* Always On My Mind [3]...Willie Nelson

June 19, 1982
SINGLES
- *HOT* Ebony And Ivory [6]...
  Paul McCartney with Stevie Wonder
- *R&B* Let It Whip [4]...Dazz Band
- *C&W* Slow Hand [1]...Conway Twitty
- *A/C* *Any Day Now [1]...Ronnie Milsap

ALBUMS
- *POP* Asia [3]...Asia
- *R&B* Keep It Live [1]...Dazz Band
- *C&W* Always On My Mind [4]...Willie Nelson

June 26, 1982
SINGLES
- *HOT* Ebony And Ivory [7]...
  Paul McCartney with Stevie Wonder
- *R&B* Early In The Morning [1]...The Gap Band
- *C&W* Slow Hand [2]...Conway Twitty
- *A/C* Any Day Now [2]...Ronnie Milsap

ALBUMS
- *POP* Asia [4]...Asia
- *R&B* Stevie Wonder's Original Musiquarium I [3]...
  Stevie Wonder
- *C&W* Mountain Music [7]...Alabama

July 3, 1982
SINGLES
- *HOT* Don't You Want Me [1]...The Human League
- *R&B* Let It Whip [5]...Dazz Band
- *C&W* Any Day Now [1]...Ronnie Milsap
- *A/C* Any Day Now [3]...Ronnie Milsap

ALBUMS
- *POP* Asia [5]...Asia
- *R&B* Gap Band IV [1]...The Gap Band
- *C&W* Mountain Music [8]...Alabama

July 10, 1982
SINGLES
- *HOT* Don't You Want Me [2]...The Human League
- *R&B* Early In The Morning [2]...The Gap Band
- *C&W* Don't Worry 'Bout Me Baby [1]...Janie Fricke
- *A/C* Any Day Now [4]...Ronnie Milsap

ALBUMS
- *POP* Asia [6]...Asia
- *R&B* Gap Band IV [2]...The Gap Band
- *C&W* Mountain Music [9]...Alabama

July 17, 1982
SINGLES
- *HOT* Don't You Want Me [3]...The Human League
- *R&B* Early In The Morning [3]...The Gap Band
- *C&W* 'Till You're Gone [1]...Barbara Mandrell
- *A/C* Any Day Now [5]...Ronnie Milsap

ALBUMS
- *POP* Asia [7]...Asia
- *R&B* Gap Band IV [3]...The Gap Band
- *C&W* Always On My Mind [5]...Willie Nelson

July 24, 1982
SINGLES
- *HOT* Eye Of The Tiger [1]...Survivor
- *R&B* And I Am Telling You I'm Not Going [1]...
  Jennifer Holliday
- *C&W* Take Me Down [1]...Alabama
- *A/C* Even The Nights Are Better [1]...Air Supply

ALBUMS
- *POP* Asia [8]...Asia
- *R&B* Gap Band IV [4]...The Gap Band
- *C&W* Always On My Mind [6]...Willie Nelson

July 31, 1982

SINGLES
- HOT Eye Of The Tiger [2]...Survivor
- R&B And I Am Telling You I'm Not Going [2]...Jennifer Holliday
- C&W I Don't Care [1]...Ricky Skaggs
- A/C Even The Nights Are Better [2]...Air Supply

ALBUMS
- POP Asia [9]...Asia
- R&B Gap Band IV [5]...The Gap Band
- C&W Always On My Mind [7]...Willie Nelson

August 7, 1982

SINGLES
- HOT Eye Of The Tiger [3]...Survivor
- R&B And I Am Telling You I'm Not Going [3]...Jennifer Holliday
- C&W Honky Tonkin' [1]...Hank Williams, Jr.
- A/C Even The Nights Are Better [3]...Air Supply

ALBUMS
- POP Mirage [1]...Fleetwood Mac
- R&B Gap Band IV [6]...The Gap Band
- C&W Always On My Mind [8]...Willie Nelson

August 14, 1982

SINGLES
- HOT Eye Of The Tiger [4]...Survivor
- R&B And I Am Telling You I'm Not Going [4]...Jennifer Holliday
- C&W I'm Gonna Hire A Wino To Decorate Our Home [1]...David Frizzell
- A/C Even The Nights Are Better [4]...Air Supply

ALBUMS
- POP Mirage [2]...Fleetwood Mac
- R&B Gap Band IV [7]...The Gap Band
- C&W Always On My Mind [9]...Willie Nelson

August 21, 1982

SINGLES
- HOT Eye Of The Tiger [5]...Survivor
- R&B Dance Floor (Part I) [1]...Zapp
- C&W Nobody [1]...Sylvia
- A/C *Hard To Say I'm Sorry [1]...Chicago

ALBUMS
- POP Mirage [3]...Fleetwood Mac
- R&B Gap Band IV [8]...The Gap Band
- C&W Always On My Mind [10]...Willie Nelson

August 28, 1982

SINGLES
- HOT Eye Of The Tiger [6]...Survivor
- R&B Dance Floor (Part I) [2]...Zapp
- C&W Fool Hearted Memory [1]...George Strait
- A/C Hard To Say I'm Sorry [2]...Chicago

ALBUMS
- POP Mirage [4]...Fleetwood Mac
- R&B Gap Band IV [9]...The Gap Band
- C&W Always On My Mind [11]...Willie Nelson

September 4, 1982

SINGLES
- HOT Abracadabra [1]...Steve Miller Band
- R&B Jump To It [1]...Aretha Franklin
- C&W *Love Will Turn You Around [1]...Kenny Rogers
- A/C Hard To Say I'm Sorry [3]...Chicago

ALBUMS
- POP Mirage [5]...Fleetwood Mac
- R&B Jump To It [1]...Aretha Franklin
- C&W Always On My Mind [12]...Willie Nelson

September 11, 1982

SINGLES
- HOT Hard To Say I'm Sorry [1]...Chicago
- R&B Jump To It [2]...Aretha Franklin
- C&W She Got The Goldmine (I Got The Shaft) [1]...Jerry Reed
- A/C Blue Eyes [1]...Elton John

ALBUMS
- POP American Fool [1]...John Cougar
- R&B Jump To It [2]...Aretha Franklin
- C&W Always On My Mind [13]...Willie Nelson

September 18, 1982

SINGLES
- HOT Hard To Say I'm Sorry [2]...Chicago
- R&B Jump To It [3]...Aretha Franklin
- C&W She Got The Goldmine (I Got The Shaft) [2]...Jerry Reed
- A/C Blue Eyes [2]...Elton John

ALBUMS
- POP American Fool [2]...John Cougar
- R&B Jump To It [3]...Aretha Franklin
- C&W Always On My Mind [14]...Willie Nelson

September 25, 1982

SINGLES
- *HOT*   Abracadabra [2]...Steve Miller Band
- *R&B*   Jump To It [4]...Aretha Franklin
- *C&W*   What's Forever For [1]...Michael Martin Murphey
- *A/C*   Love Will Turn You Around [1]...Kenny Rogers

ALBUMS
- *POP*   American Fool [3]...John Cougar
- *R&B*   Jump To It [4]...Aretha Franklin
- *C&W*   Always On My Mind [15]...Willie Nelson

October 2, 1982

SINGLES
- *HOT*   Jack & Diane [1]...John Cougar
- *R&B*   Love Come Down [1]...Evelyn King
- *C&W*   Put Your Dreams Away [1]...Mickey Gilley
- *A/C*   Love Will Turn You Around [2]...Kenny Rogers

ALBUMS
- *POP*   American Fool [4]...John Cougar
- *R&B*   Jump To It [5]...Aretha Franklin
- *C&W*   Always On My Mind [16]...Willie Nelson

October 9, 1982

SINGLES
- *HOT*   Jack & Diane [2]...John Cougar
- *R&B*   Love Come Down [2]...Evelyn King
- *C&W*   Yesterday's Wine [1]...George Jones/Merle Haggard
- *A/C*   Break It To Me Gently [1]...Juice Newton

ALBUMS
- *POP*   American Fool [5]...John Cougar
- *R&B*   Jump To It [6]...Aretha Franklin
- *C&W*   Always On My Mind [17]...Willie Nelson

October 16, 1982

SINGLES
- *HOT*   Jack & Diane [3]...John Cougar
- *R&B*   Love Come Down [3]...Evelyn King
- *C&W*   I Will Always Love You/Do I Ever Cross Your Mind [2]...Dolly Parton
  new version of #1 hit in 1974
- *A/C*   Break It To Me Gently [2]...Juice Newton

ALBUMS
- *POP*   American Fool [6]...John Cougar
- *R&B*   Jump To It [7]...Aretha Franklin
- *C&W*   Always On My Mind [18]...Willie Nelson

October 23, 1982

SINGLES
- *HOT*   Jack & Diane [4]...John Cougar
- *R&B*   Love Come Down [4]...Evelyn King
- *C&W*   He Got You [1]...Ronnie Milsap
- *A/C*   Heartlight [1]...Neil Diamond

ALBUMS
- *POP*   American Fool [7]...John Cougar
- *R&B*   Get Loose [1]...Evelyn "Champagne" King
- *C&W*   Always On My Mind [19]...Willie Nelson

October 30, 1982

SINGLES
- *HOT*   Who Can It Be Now? [1]...Men At Work
- *R&B*   Love Come Down [5]...Evelyn King
- *C&W*   Close Enough To Perfect [1]...Alabama
- *A/C*   Heartlight [2]...Neil Diamond

ALBUMS
- *POP*   American Fool [8]...John Cougar
- *R&B*   Get Loose [2]...Evelyn "Champagne" King
- *C&W*   Always On My Mind [20]...Willie Nelson

November 6, 1982

SINGLES
- *HOT*   Up Where We Belong [1]...Joe Cocker & Jennifer Warnes
- *R&B*   Sexual Healing [1]...Marvin Gaye
- *C&W*   You're So Good When You're Bad [1]...Charley Pride
- *A/C*   Heartlight [3]...Neil Diamond

ALBUMS
- *POP*   American Fool [9]...John Cougar
- *R&B*   Forever, For Always, For Love [1]...Luther Vandross
- *C&W*   Always On My Mind [21]...Willie Nelson

November 13, 1982

SINGLES
- *HOT*   Up Where We Belong [2]...Joe Cocker & Jennifer Warnes
- *R&B*   Sexual Healing [2]...Marvin Gaye
- *C&W*   Heartbroke [1]...Ricky Skaggs
- *A/C*   Heartlight [4]...Neil Diamond

ALBUMS
- *POP*   Business As Usual [1]...Men At Work
- *R&B*   Forever, For Always, For Love [2]...Luther Vandross
- *C&W*   Always On My Mind [22]...Willie Nelson

November 20, 1982

SINGLES
- *HOT*   Up Where We Belong [3]...Joe Cocker & Jennifer Warnes
- *R&B*   Sexual Healing [3]...Marvin Gaye
- *C&W*   War Is Hell (On The Homefront Too) [1]...T.G. Sheppard
- *A/C*   *Truly [1]...Lionel Richie

ALBUMS
- *POP*   Business As Usual [2]...Men At Work
- *R&B*   Forever, For Always, For Love [3]...Luther Vandross
- *C&W*   Highways & Heartaches [1]...Ricky Skaggs

November 27, 1982
SINGLES
- HOT   Truly [1]...Lionel Richie
- R&B   Sexual Healing [4]...Marvin Gaye
- C&W   It Ain't Easy Bein' Easy [1]...Janie Fricke
- A/C   Truly [2]...Lionel Richie

ALBUMS
- POP   Business As Usual [3]...Men At Work
- R&B   Lionel Richie [1]...Lionel Richie
- C&W   Mountain Music [10]...Alabama

December 4, 1982
SINGLES
- HOT   Truly [2]...Lionel Richie
- R&B   Sexual Healing [5]...Marvin Gaye
- C&W   You And I [1]...Eddie Rabbitt with Crystal Gayle
- A/C   Truly [3]...Lionel Richie

ALBUMS
- POP   Business As Usual [4]...Men At Work
- R&B   Midnight Love [1]...Marvin Gaye
- C&W   Mountain Music [11]...Alabama

December 11, 1982
SINGLES
- HOT   Mickey [1]...Toni Basil
- R&B   Sexual Healing [6]...Marvin Gaye
- C&W   Redneck Girl [1]...The Bellamy Brothers
- A/C   Truly [4]...Lionel Richie

ALBUMS
- POP   Business As Usual [5]...Men At Work
- R&B   Midnight Love [2]...Marvin Gaye
- C&W   Mountain Music [12]...Alabama

December 18, 1982
SINGLES
- HOT   Maneater [1]...Daryl Hall & John Oates
- R&B   Sexual Healing [7]...Marvin Gaye
- C&W   Somewhere Between Right And Wrong [1]...Earl Thomas Conley
- A/C   Heartbreaker [1]...Dionne Warwick

ALBUMS
- POP   Business As Usual [6]...Men At Work
- R&B   Midnight Love [3]...Marvin Gaye
- C&W   Mountain Music [13]...Alabama

December 25, 1982
SINGLES
- HOT   Maneater [2]...Daryl Hall & John Oates
- R&B   Sexual Healing [8]...Marvin Gaye
- C&W   Wild And Blue [1]...John Anderson
- A/C   *The Girl Is Mine [1]...Michael Jackson/Paul McCartney

ALBUMS
- POP   Business As Usual [7]...Men At Work
- R&B   Midnight Love [4]...Marvin Gaye
- C&W   Mountain Music [14]...Alabama

January 1, 1983
SINGLES
- HOT   Maneater [3]...Daryl Hall & John Oates
- R&B   Sexual Healing [9]...Marvin Gaye
- C&W   Wild And Blue [2]...John Anderson
- A/C   The Girl Is Mine [2]...Michael Jackson/Paul McCartney

ALBUMS
- POP   Business As Usual [8]...Men At Work
- R&B   Midnight Love [5]...Marvin Gaye
- C&W   Mountain Music [15]...Alabama

January 8, 1983
SINGLES
- HOT   Maneater [4]...Daryl Hall & John Oates
- R&B   Sexual Healing [10]...Marvin Gaye
- C&W   Can't Even Get The Blues [1]...Reba McEntire
- A/C   The Girl Is Mine [3]...Michael Jackson/Paul McCartney

ALBUMS
- POP   Business As Usual [9]...Men At Work
- R&B   Midnight Love [6]...Marvin Gaye
- C&W   Mountain Music [16]...Alabama

January 15, 1983
SINGLES
- HOT   Down Under [1]...Men At Work
- R&B   The Girl Is Mine [1]...Michael Jackson/Paul McCartney
- C&W   Going Where The Lonely Go [1]...Merle Haggard
- A/C   The Girl Is Mine [4]...Michael Jackson/Paul McCartney

ALBUMS
- POP   Business As Usual [10]...Men At Work
- R&B   Midnight Love [7]...Marvin Gaye
- C&W   Mountain Music [17]...Alabama

January 22, 1983
SINGLES
- HOT   Down Under [2]...Men At Work
- R&B   The Girl Is Mine [2]...Michael Jackson/Paul McCartney
- C&W   (Lost His Love) On Our Last Date [1]...Emmylou Harris
- A/C   *Baby, Come To Me [1]...Patti Austin with James Ingram

ALBUMS
- POP   Business As Usual [11]...Men At Work
- R&B   Midnight Love [8]...Marvin Gaye
- C&W   Mountain Music [18]...Alabama

January 29, 1983
SINGLES
- HOT   Down Under [3]...Men At Work
- R&B   The Girl Is Mine [3]...Michael Jackson/Paul McCartney
- C&W   Talk To Me [1]...Mickey Gilley
- A/C   Baby, Come To Me [2]...Patti Austin with James Ingram

ALBUMS
- POP   Business As Usual [12]...Men At Work
- R&B   Thriller [1]...Michael Jackson
- C&W   Mountain Music [19]...Alabama

February 5, 1983

SINGLES
- HOT Africa [1]...Toto
- R&B Outstanding [1]...The Gap Band
- C&W Inside/Carolina Dreams [1]...Ronnie Milsap
- A/C Baby, Come To Me [3]...Patti Austin with James Ingram

ALBUMS
- POP Business As Usual [13]...Men At Work
- R&B Thriller [2]...Michael Jackson
- C&W Mountain Music [20]...Alabama

February 12, 1983

SINGLES
- HOT Down Under [4]...Men At Work
- R&B *Billie Jean [1]...Michael Jackson
- C&W 'Til I Gain Control Again [1]...Crystal Gayle
- A/C Shame On The Moon [1]...
  Bob Seger & The Silver Bullet Band

ALBUMS
- POP Business As Usual [14]...Men At Work
- R&B Thriller [3]...Michael Jackson
- C&W Mountain Music [21]...Alabama

February 19, 1983

SINGLES
- HOT Baby, Come To Me [1]...Patti Austin with James Ingram
- R&B Billie Jean [2]...Michael Jackson
- C&W Faking Love [1]...T.G. Sheppard & Karen Brooks
- A/C Shame On The Moon [2]...
  Bob Seger & The Silver Bullet Band

ALBUMS
- POP Business As Usual [15]...Men At Work
- R&B Thriller [4]...Michael Jackson
- C&W Mountain Music [22]...Alabama

February 26, 1983

SINGLES
- HOT Baby, Come To Me [2]...Patti Austin with James Ingram
- R&B Billie Jean [3]...Michael Jackson
- C&W Why Baby Why [1]...Charley Pride
- A/C You Are [1]...Lionel Richie

ALBUMS
- POP Thriller [1]...Michael Jackson
- R&B Thriller [5]...Michael Jackson
- C&W Mountain Music [23]...Alabama

March 5, 1983

SINGLES
- HOT Billie Jean [1]...Michael Jackson
- R&B Billie Jean [4]...Michael Jackson
- C&W If Hollywood Don't Need You [1]...Don Williams
- A/C You Are [2]...Lionel Richie

ALBUMS
- POP Thriller [2]...Michael Jackson
- R&B Thriller [6]...Michael Jackson
- C&W Mountain Music [24]...Alabama

March 12, 1983

SINGLES
- HOT Billie Jean [2]...Michael Jackson
- R&B Billie Jean [5]...Michael Jackson
- C&W The Rose [1]...Conway Twitty
- A/C You Are [3]...Lionel Richie

ALBUMS
- POP Thriller [3]...Michael Jackson
- R&B Thriller [7]...Michael Jackson
- C&W Mountain Music [25]...Alabama

March 19, 1983

SINGLES
- HOT Billie Jean [3]...Michael Jackson
- R&B Billie Jean [6]...Michael Jackson
- C&W I Wouldn't Change You If I Could [1]...Ricky Skaggs
- A/C You Are [4]...Lionel Richie

ALBUMS
- POP Thriller [4]...Michael Jackson
- R&B Thriller [8]...Michael Jackson
- C&W Mountain Music [26]...Alabama

March 26, 1983

SINGLES
- HOT Billie Jean [4]...Michael Jackson
- R&B Billie Jean [7]...Michael Jackson
- C&W Swingin' [1]...John Anderson
- A/C You Are [5]...Lionel Richie

ALBUMS
- POP Thriller [5]...Michael Jackson
- R&B Thriller [9]...Michael Jackson
- C&W Mountain Music [27]...Alabama

April 2, 1983

SINGLES
- HOT Billie Jean [5]...Michael Jackson
- R&B Billie Jean [8]...Michael Jackson
- C&W When I'm Away From You [1]...The Bellamy Brothers
- A/C You Are [6]...Lionel Richie

ALBUMS
- POP Thriller [6]...Michael Jackson
- R&B Thriller [10]...Michael Jackson
- C&W Mountain Music [28]...Alabama

April 9, 1983

SINGLES
- *HOT* Billie Jean [6]...Michael Jackson
- *R&B* Billie Jean [9]...Michael Jackson
- *C&W* We've Got Tonight [1]...Kenny Rogers & Sheena Easton
- *A/C* Make Love Stay [1]...Dan Fogelberg

ALBUMS
- *POP* Thriller [7]...Michael Jackson
- *R&B* Thriller [11]...Michael Jackson
- *C&W* Poncho & Lefty [1]...Merle Haggard & Willie Nelson

April 16, 1983

SINGLES
- *HOT* Billie Jean [7]...Michael Jackson
- *R&B* Atomic Dog [1]...George Clinton
- *C&W* Dixieland Delight [1]...Alabama
- *A/C* It Might Be You [1]...Stephen Bishop

ALBUMS
- *POP* Thriller [8]...Michael Jackson
- *R&B* Thriller [12]...Michael Jackson
- *C&W* The Closer You Get... [1]...Alabama

April 23, 1983

SINGLES
- *HOT* Come On Eileen [1]...Dexys Midnight Runners
- *R&B* Atomic Dog [2]...George Clinton
- *C&W* American Made [1]...The Oak Ridge Boys
- *A/C* It Might Be You [2]...Stephen Bishop

ALBUMS
- *POP* Thriller [9]...Michael Jackson
- *R&B* Thriller [13]...Michael Jackson
- *C&W* The Closer You Get... [2]...Alabama

April 30, 1983

SINGLES
- *HOT* *Beat It [1]...Michael Jackson
- *R&B* Atomic Dog [3]...George Clinton
- *C&W* You're The First Time I've Thought About Leaving [1]...Reba McEntire
- *A/C* I Won't Hold You Back [1]...Toto

ALBUMS
- *POP* Thriller [10]...Michael Jackson
- *R&B* Thriller [14]...Michael Jackson
- *C&W* The Closer You Get... [3]...Alabama

May 7, 1983

SINGLES
- *HOT* Beat It [2]...Michael Jackson
- *R&B* Atomic Dog [4]...George Clinton
- *C&W* Jose Cuervo [1]...Shelly West
- *A/C* I Won't Hold You Back [2]...Toto

ALBUMS
- *POP* Thriller [11]...Michael Jackson
- *R&B* Thriller [15]...Michael Jackson
- *C&W* The Closer You Get... [4]...Alabama

May 14, 1983

SINGLES
- *HOT* Beat It [3]...Michael Jackson
- *R&B* Candy Girl [1]...New Edition
- *C&W* Whatever Happened To Old Fashioned Love [1]...B.J. Thomas
- *A/C* I Won't Hold You Back [3]...Toto

ALBUMS
- *POP* Thriller [12]...Michael Jackson
- *R&B* Thriller [16]...Michael Jackson
- *C&W* The Closer You Get... [5]...Alabama

May 21, 1983

SINGLES
- *HOT* Let's Dance [1]...David Bowie
- *R&B* Beat It [1]...Michael Jackson
- *C&W* Common Man [1]...John Conlee
- *A/C* My Love [1]...Lionel Richie

ALBUMS
- *POP* Thriller [13]...Michael Jackson
- *R&B* Thriller [17]...Michael Jackson
- *C&W* The Closer You Get... [6]...Alabama

May 28, 1983

SINGLES
- *HOT* Flashdance...What A Feeling [1]...Irene Cara
- *R&B* Save The Overtime (For Me) [1]...Gladys Knight & The Pips
- *C&W* You Take Me For Granted [1]...Merle Haggard
- *A/C* My Love [2]...Lionel Richie

ALBUMS
- *POP* Thriller [14]...Michael Jackson
- *R&B* Thriller [18]...Michael Jackson
- *C&W* The Closer You Get... [7]...Alabama

June 4, 1983

SINGLES
- *HOT* Flashdance...What A Feeling [2]...Irene Cara
- *R&B* Juicy Fruit [1]...Mtume
- *C&W* Lucille (You Won't Do Your Daddy's Will) [1]...Waylon Jennings
- *A/C* My Love [3]...Lionel Richie

ALBUMS
- *POP* Thriller [15]...Michael Jackson
- *R&B* Thriller [19]...Michael Jackson
- *C&W* The Closer You Get... [8]...Alabama

June 11, 1983
SINGLES
- *HOT* Flashdance...What A Feeling [3]...Irene Cara
- *R&B* Juicy Fruit [2]...Mtume
- *C&W* Our Love Is On The Faultline [1]...Crystal Gayle
- *A/C* My Love [4]...Lionel Richie

ALBUMS
- *POP* Thriller [16]...Michael Jackson
- *R&B* Thriller [20]...Michael Jackson
- *C&W* The Closer You Get... [9]...Alabama

June 18, 1983
SINGLES
- *HOT* Flashdance...What A Feeling [4]...Irene Cara
- *R&B* Juicy Fruit [3]...Mtume
- *C&W* You Can't Run From Love [1]...Eddie Rabbitt
- *A/C* Never Gonna Let You Go [1]...Sergio Mendes

ALBUMS
- *POP* Thriller [17]...Michael Jackson
- *R&B* Thriller [21]...Michael Jackson
- *C&W* The Closer You Get... [10]...Alabama

June 25, 1983
SINGLES
- *HOT* Flashdance...What A Feeling [5]...Irene Cara
- *R&B* Juicy Fruit [4]...Mtume
- *C&W* Fool For Your Love [1]...Mickey Gilley
- *A/C* Never Gonna Let You Go [2]...Sergio Mendes

ALBUMS
- *POP* Flashdance [1]...Soundtrack
- *R&B* Thriller [22]...Michael Jackson
- *C&W* The Closer You Get... [11]...Alabama

July 2, 1983
SINGLES
- *HOT* Flashdance...What A Feeling [6]...Irene Cara
- *R&B* Juicy Fruit [5]...Mtume
- *C&W* Love Is On A Roll [1]...Don Williams
- *A/C* Never Gonna Let You Go [3]...Sergio Mendes

ALBUMS
- *POP* Flashdance [2]...Soundtrack
- *R&B* Thriller [23]...Michael Jackson
- *C&W* The Closer You Get... [12]...Alabama

July 9, 1983
SINGLES
- *HOT* Every Breath You Take [1]...The Police
- *R&B* Juicy Fruit [6]...Mtume
- *C&W* Highway 40 Blues [1]...Ricky Skaggs
- *A/C* Never Gonna Let You Go [4]...Sergio Mendes

ALBUMS
- *POP* Thriller [18]...Michael Jackson
- *R&B* Thriller [24]...Michael Jackson
- *C&W* Poncho & Lefty [2]...Merle Haggard & Willie Nelson

July 16, 1983
SINGLES
- *HOT* Every Breath You Take [2]...The Police
- *R&B* Juicy Fruit [7]...Mtume
- *C&W* The Closer You Get [1]...Alabama
- *A/C* All This Love [1]...DeBarge

ALBUMS
- *POP* Thriller [19]...Michael Jackson
- *R&B* Thriller [25]...Michael Jackson
- *C&W* The Closer You Get... [13]...Alabama

July 23, 1983
SINGLES
- *HOT* Every Breath You Take [3]...The Police
- *R&B* Juicy Fruit [8]...Mtume
- *C&W* Pancho And Lefty [1]...Willie Nelson & Merle Haggard
- *A/C* All This Love [2]...DeBarge

ALBUMS
- *POP* Synchronicity [1]...The Police
- *R&B* Between The Sheets [1]...The Isley Brothers
- *C&W* Poncho & Lefty [3]...Merle Haggard & Willie Nelson

July 30, 1983
SINGLES
- *HOT* Every Breath You Take [4]...The Police
- *R&B* She Works Hard For The Money [1]...Donna Summer
- *C&W* I Always Get Lucky With You [1]...George Jones
- *A/C* All This Love [3]...DeBarge

ALBUMS
- *POP* Synchronicity [2]...The Police
- *R&B* Thriller [26]...Michael Jackson
- *C&W* Poncho & Lefty [4]...Merle Haggard & Willie Nelson

August 6, 1983
SINGLES
- *HOT* Every Breath You Take [5]...The Police
- *R&B* She Works Hard For The Money [2]...Donna Summer
- *C&W* Your Love's On The Line [1]...Earl Thomas Conley
- *A/C* All Time High [1]...Rita Coolidge

ALBUMS
- *POP* Synchronicity [3]...The Police
- *R&B* Thriller [27]...Michael Jackson
- *C&W* The Closer You Get... [14]...Alabama

August 13, 1983
SINGLES
- *HOT* Every Breath You Take [6]...The Police
- *R&B* She Works Hard For The Money [3]...Donna Summer
- *C&W* He's A Heartache (Looking For A Place To Happen) [1]...Janie Fricke
- *A/C* All Time High [2]...Rita Coolidge

ALBUMS
- *POP* Synchronicity [4]...The Police
- *R&B* Thriller [28]...Michael Jackson
- *C&W* The Closer You Get... [15]...Alabama

August 20, 1983

SINGLES
- HOT Every Breath You Take [7]...The Police
- R&B Get It Right [1]...Aretha Franklin
- C&W Love Song [1]...The Oak Ridge Boys
- A/C All Time High [3]...Rita Coolidge

ALBUMS
- POP Synchronicity [5]...The Police
- R&B Thriller [29]...Michael Jackson
- C&W The Closer You Get... [16]...Alabama

August 27, 1983

SINGLES
- HOT Every Breath You Take [8]...The Police
- R&B Get It Right [2]...Aretha Franklin
- C&W You're Gonna Ruin My Bad Reputation [1]...Ronnie McDowell
- A/C All Time High [4]...Rita Coolidge

ALBUMS
- POP Synchronicity [6]...The Police
- R&B Thriller [30]...Michael Jackson
- C&W The Closer You Get... [17]...Alabama

September 3, 1983

SINGLES
- HOT Sweet Dreams (Are Made of This) [1]...Eurythmics
- R&B Cold Blooded [1]...Rick James
- C&W A Fire I Can't Put Out [1]...George Strait
- A/C How Am I Supposed To Live Without You [1]...Laura Branigan

ALBUMS
- POP Synchronicity [7]...The Police
- R&B Thriller [31]...Michael Jackson
- C&W Poncho & Lefty [5]...Merle Haggard & Willie Nelson

September 10, 1983

SINGLES
- HOT Maniac [1]...Michael Sembello
- R&B Cold Blooded [2]...Rick James
- C&W I'm Only In It For The Love [1]...John Conlee
- A/C How Am I Supposed To Live Without You [2]...Laura Branigan

ALBUMS
- POP Thriller [20]...Michael Jackson
- R&B Thriller [32]...Michael Jackson
- C&W Poncho & Lefty [6]...Merle Haggard & Willie Nelson

September 17, 1983

SINGLES
- HOT Maniac [2]...Michael Sembello
- R&B Cold Blooded [3]...Rick James
- C&W Night Games [1]...Charley Pride
- A/C How Am I Supposed To Live Without You [3]...Laura Branigan

ALBUMS
- POP Synchronicity [8]...The Police
- R&B Cold Blooded [1]...Rick James
- C&W Poncho & Lefty [7]...Merle Haggard & Willie Nelson

September 24, 1983

SINGLES
- HOT *Tell Her About It [1]...Billy Joel
- R&B Cold Blooded [4]...Rick James
- C&W Baby, What About You [1]...Crystal Gayle
- A/C *Tell Her About It [1]...Billy Joel

ALBUMS
- POP Synchronicity [9]...The Police
- R&B Cold Blooded [2]...Rick James
- C&W The Closer You Get... [18]...Alabama

October 1, 1983

SINGLES
- HOT Total Eclipse Of The Heart [1]...Bonnie Tyler
- R&B Cold Blooded [5]...Rick James
- C&W New Looks From An Old Lover [1]...B.J. Thomas
- A/C Tell Her About It [2]...Billy Joel

ALBUMS
- POP Synchronicity [10]...The Police
- R&B Cold Blooded [3]...Rick James
- C&W Poncho & Lefty [8]...Merle Haggard & Willie Nelson

October 8, 1983

SINGLES
- HOT Total Eclipse Of The Heart [2]...Bonnie Tyler
- R&B Cold Blooded [6]...Rick James
- C&W Don't You Know How Much I Love You [1]...Ronnie Milsap
- A/C True [1]...Spandau Ballet

ALBUMS
- POP Synchronicity [11]...The Police
- R&B Cold Blooded [4]...Rick James
- C&W The Closer You Get... [19]...Alabama

October 15, 1983
SINGLES
- *HOT* Total Eclipse Of The Heart [3]...Bonnie Tyler
- *R&B* Ain't Nobody [1]...Rufus & Chaka Khan
- *C&W* Paradise Tonight [1]...Charly McClain & Mickey Gilley
- *A/C* *Islands In The Stream [1]...
  Kenny Rogers with Dolly Parton

ALBUMS
- *POP* Synchronicity [12]...The Police
- *R&B* Cold Blooded [5]...Rick James
- *C&W* The Closer You Get... [20]...Alabama

October 22, 1983
SINGLES
- *HOT* Total Eclipse Of The Heart [4]...Bonnie Tyler
- *R&B* *All Night Long (All Night) [1]...Lionel Richie
- *C&W* Lady Down On Love [1]...Alabama
- *A/C* Islands In The Stream [2]...
  Kenny Rogers with Dolly Parton

ALBUMS
- *POP* Synchronicity [13]...The Police
- *R&B* Cold Blooded [6]...Rick James
- *C&W* The Closer You Get... [21]...Alabama

October 29, 1983
SINGLES
- *HOT* Islands In The Stream [1]...
  Kenny Rogers with Dolly Parton
- *R&B* All Night Long (All Night) [2]...Lionel Richie
- *C&W* Islands In The Stream [1]...
  Kenny Rogers with Dolly Parton
- *A/C* Islands In The Stream [3]...
  Kenny Rogers with Dolly Parton

ALBUMS
- *POP* Synchronicity [14]...The Police
- *R&B* Cold Blooded [7]...Rick James
- *C&W* Eyes That See In The Dark [1]...Kenny Rogers

November 5, 1983
SINGLES
- *HOT* Islands In The Stream [2]...
  Kenny Rogers with Dolly Parton
- *R&B* All Night Long (All Night) [3]...Lionel Richie
- *C&W* Islands In The Stream [2]...
  Kenny Rogers with Dolly Parton
- *A/C* Islands In The Stream [4]...
  Kenny Rogers with Dolly Parton

ALBUMS
- *POP* Synchronicity [15]...The Police
- *R&B* Cold Blooded [8]...Rick James
- *C&W* Eyes That See In The Dark [2]...Kenny Rogers

November 12, 1983
SINGLES
- *HOT* All Night Long (All Night) [1]...Lionel Richie
- *R&B* All Night Long (All Night) [4]...Lionel Richie
- *C&W* Somebody's Gonna Love You [1]...Lee Greenwood
- *A/C* All Night Long (All Night) [1]...Lionel Richie

ALBUMS
- *POP* Synchronicity [16]...The Police
- *R&B* Cold Blooded [9]...Rick James
- *C&W* Eyes That See In The Dark [3]...Kenny Rogers

November 19, 1983
SINGLES
- *HOT* All Night Long (All Night) [2]...Lionel Richie
- *R&B* All Night Long (All Night) [5]...Lionel Richie
- *C&W* One Of A Kind Pair Of Fools [1]...Barbara Mandrell
- *A/C* All Night Long (All Night) [2]...Lionel Richie

ALBUMS
- *POP* Synchronicity [17]...The Police
- *R&B* Cold Blooded [10]...Rick James
- *C&W* Eyes That See In The Dark [4]...Kenny Rogers

November 26, 1983
SINGLES
- *HOT* All Night Long (All Night) [3]...Lionel Richie
- *R&B* All Night Long (All Night) [6]...Lionel Richie
- *C&W* Holding Her And Loving You [1]...
  Earl Thomas Conley
- *A/C* All Night Long (All Night) [3]...Lionel Richie

ALBUMS
- *POP* Metal Health [1]...Quiet Riot
- *R&B* Can't Slow Down [1]...Lionel Richie
- *C&W* Eyes That See In The Dark [5]...Kenny Rogers

December 3, 1983
SINGLES
- *HOT* All Night Long (All Night) [4]...Lionel Richie
- *R&B* All Night Long (All Night) [7]...Lionel Richie
- *C&W* A Little Good News [1]...Anne Murray
- *A/C* All Night Long (All Night) [4]...Lionel Richie

ALBUMS
- *POP* Can't Slow Down [1]...Lionel Richie
- *R&B* Can't Slow Down [2]...Lionel Richie
- *C&W* Eyes That See In The Dark [6]...Kenny Rogers

December 10, 1983
SINGLES
- *HOT* Say Say Say [1]...Paul McCartney & Michael Jackson
- *R&B* Time Will Reveal [1]...DeBarge
- *C&W* Tell Me A Lie [1]...Janie Fricke
- *A/C* The Way He Makes Me Feel [1]...Barbra Streisand

ALBUMS
- *POP* Can't Slow Down [2]...Lionel Richie
- *R&B* Can't Slow Down [3]...Lionel Richie
- *C&W* Eyes That See In The Dark [7]...Kenny Rogers

December 17, 1983

SINGLES
- HOT   Say Say Say [2]...Paul McCartney & Michael Jackson
- R&B   Time Will Reveal [2]...DeBarge
- C&W   Black Sheep [1]...John Anderson
- A/C   The Way He Makes Me Feel [2]...Barbra Streisand

ALBUMS
- POP   Can't Slow Down [3]...Lionel Richie
- R&B   Can't Slow Down [4]...Lionel Richie
- C&W   Eyes That See In The Dark [8]...Kenny Rogers

December 24, 1983

SINGLES
- HOT   Say Say Say [3]...Paul McCartney & Michael Jackson
- R&B   Time Will Reveal [3]...DeBarge
- C&W   Houston (Means I'm One Day Closer To You) [1]...
        Larry Gatlin & The Gatlin Brothers Band
- A/C   Read 'Em And Weep [1]...Barry Manilow

ALBUMS
- POP   Thriller [21]...Michael Jackson
- R&B   Can't Slow Down [5]...Lionel Richie
- C&W   Eyes That See In The Dark [9]...Kenny Rogers

December 31, 1983

SINGLES
- HOT   Say Say Say [4]...Paul McCartney & Michael Jackson
- R&B   Time Will Reveal [4]...DeBarge
- C&W   Houston (Means I'm One Day Closer To You) [2]...
        Larry Gatlin & The Gatlin Brothers Band
- A/C   Read 'Em And Weep [2]...Barry Manilow

ALBUMS
- POP   Thriller [22]...Michael Jackson
- R&B   Can't Slow Down [6]...Lionel Richie
- C&W   Eyes That See In The Dark [10]...Kenny Rogers

January 7, 1984

SINGLES
- HOT   Say Say Say [5]...Paul McCartney & Michael Jackson
- R&B   Time Will Reveal [5]...DeBarge
- C&W   You Look So Good In Love [1]...George Strait
- A/C   Read 'Em And Weep [3]...Barry Manilow

ALBUMS
- POP   Thriller [23]...Michael Jackson
- R&B   Can't Slow Down [7]...Lionel Richie
- C&W   Eyes That See In The Dark [11]...Kenny Rogers

January 14, 1984

SINGLES
- HOT   Say Say Say [6]...Paul McCartney & Michael Jackson
- R&B   Joanna [1]...Kool & The Gang
- C&W   Slow Burn [1]...T.G. Sheppard
- A/C   Read 'Em And Weep [4]...Barry Manilow

ALBUMS
- POP   Thriller [24]...Michael Jackson
- R&B   Can't Slow Down [8]...Lionel Richie
- C&W   Eyes That See In The Dark [12]...Kenny Rogers

January 21, 1984

SINGLES
- HOT   Owner Of A Lonely Heart [1]...Yes
- R&B   Joanna [2]...Kool & The Gang
- C&W   In My Eyes [1]...John Conlee
- A/C   Read 'Em And Weep [5]...Barry Manilow

ALBUMS
- POP   Thriller [25]...Michael Jackson
- R&B   Can't Slow Down [9]...Lionel Richie
- C&W   Eyes That See In The Dark [13]...Kenny Rogers

January 28, 1984

SINGLES
- HOT   Owner Of A Lonely Heart [2]...Yes
- R&B   If Only You Knew [1]...Patti LaBelle
- C&W   The Sound Of Goodbye [1]...Crystal Gayle
- A/C   Read 'Em And Weep [6]...Barry Manilow

ALBUMS
- POP   Thriller [26]...Michael Jackson
- R&B   Can't Slow Down [10]...Lionel Richie
- C&W   Eyes That See In The Dark [14]...Kenny Rogers

February 4, 1984

SINGLES
- HOT   Karma Chameleon [1]...Culture Club
- R&B   If Only You Knew [2]...Patti LaBelle
- C&W   Show Her [1]...Ronnie Milsap
- A/C   Think Of Laura [1]...Christopher Cross

ALBUMS
- POP   Thriller [27]...Michael Jackson
- R&B   Can't Slow Down [11]...Lionel Richie
- C&W   Eyes That See In The Dark [15]...Kenny Rogers

February 11, 1984

SINGLES
- HOT   Karma Chameleon [2]...Culture Club
- R&B   If Only You Knew [3]...Patti LaBelle
- C&W   That's The Way Love Goes [1]...Merle Haggard
- A/C   Think Of Laura [2]...Christopher Cross

ALBUMS
- POP   Thriller [28]...Michael Jackson
- R&B   Can't Slow Down [12]...Lionel Richie
- C&W   Eyes That See In The Dark [16]...Kenny Rogers

February 18, 1984
SINGLES
- *HOT* Karma Chameleon [3]...Culture Club
- *R&B* If Only You Knew [4]...Patti LaBelle
- *C&W* Don't Cheat In Our Hometown [1]...Ricky Skaggs
- *A/C* Think Of Laura [3]...Christopher Cross

ALBUMS
- *POP* Thriller [29]...Michael Jackson
- *R&B* Can't Slow Down [13]...Lionel Richie
- *C&W* Right Or Wrong [1]...George Strait

February 25, 1984
SINGLES
- *HOT* Jump [1]...Van Halen
- *R&B* Encore [1]...Cheryl Lynn
- *C&W* Stay Young [1]...Don Williams
- *A/C* Think Of Laura [4]...Christopher Cross

ALBUMS
- *POP* Thriller [30]...Michael Jackson
- *R&B* Can't Slow Down [14]...Lionel Richie
- *C&W* Don't Cheat In Our Hometown [1]...Ricky Skaggs

March 3, 1984
SINGLES
- *HOT* Jump [2]...Van Halen
- *R&B* Somebody's Watching Me [1]...Rockwell
- *C&W* Woke Up In Love [1]...Exile
- *A/C* An Innocent Man [1]...Billy Joel

ALBUMS
- *POP* Thriller [31]...Michael Jackson
- *R&B* Can't Slow Down [15]...Lionel Richie
- *C&W* Right Or Wrong [2]...George Strait

March 10, 1984
SINGLES
- *HOT* Jump [3]...Van Halen
- *R&B* Somebody's Watching Me [2]...Rockwell
- *C&W* Going, Going, Gone [1]...Lee Greenwood
- *A/C* Got A Hold On Me [1]...Christine McVie

ALBUMS
- *POP* Thriller [32]...Michael Jackson
- *R&B* Thriller [33]...Michael Jackson
- *C&W* Right Or Wrong [3]...George Strait

March 17, 1984
SINGLES
- *HOT* Jump [4]...Van Halen
- *R&B* Somebody's Watching Me [3]...Rockwell
- *C&W* Elizabeth [1]...The Statler Brothers
- *A/C* Got A Hold On Me [2]...Christine McVie

ALBUMS
- *POP* Thriller [33]...Michael Jackson
- *R&B* Thriller [34]...Michael Jackson
- *C&W* Roll On [1]...Alabama

March 24, 1984
SINGLES
- *HOT* Jump [5]...Van Halen
- *R&B* Somebody's Watching Me [4]...Rockwell
- *C&W* Roll On (Eighteen Wheeler) [1]...Alabama
- *A/C* Got A Hold On Me [3]...Christine McVie

ALBUMS
- *POP* Thriller [34]...Michael Jackson
- *R&B* Thriller [35]...Michael Jackson
- *C&W* Roll On [2]...Alabama

March 31, 1984
SINGLES
- *HOT* Footloose [1]...Kenny Loggins
- *R&B* Somebody's Watching Me [5]...Rockwell
- *C&W* Let's Stop Talkin' About It [1]...Janie Fricke
- *A/C* Got A Hold On Me [4]...Christine McVie

ALBUMS
- *POP* Thriller [35]...Michael Jackson
- *R&B* Thriller [36]...Michael Jackson
- *C&W* Roll On [3]...Alabama

April 7, 1984
SINGLES
- *HOT* Footloose [2]...Kenny Loggins
- *R&B* She's Strange [1]...Cameo
- *C&W* Don't Make It Easy For Me [1]...Earl Thomas Conley
- *A/C* *Hello [1]...Lionel Richie

ALBUMS
- *POP* Thriller [36]...Michael Jackson
- *R&B* Thriller [37]...Michael Jackson
- *C&W* Roll On [4]...Alabama

April 14, 1984
SINGLES
- *HOT* Footloose [3]...Kenny Loggins
- *R&B* She's Strange [2]...Cameo
- *C&W* Thank God For The Radio [1]...The Kendalls
- *A/C* Hello [2]...Lionel Richie

ALBUMS
- *POP* Thriller [37]...Michael Jackson
- *R&B* Busy Body [1]...Luther Vandross
- *C&W* Roll On [5]...Alabama

April 21, 1984
SINGLES
- *HOT* Against All Odds (Take A Look At Me Now) [1]...Phil Collins
- *R&B* She's Strange [3]...Cameo
- *C&W* The Yellow Rose [1]...Johnny Lee with Lane Brody
- *A/C* Hello [3]...Lionel Richie

ALBUMS
- *POP* Footloose [1]...Soundtrack
- *R&B* Busy Body [2]...Luther Vandross
- *C&W* Roll On [6]...Alabama

April 28, 1984

SINGLES
- *HOT* **Against All Odds (Take A Look At Me Now)** [2]...Phil Collins
- *R&B* **She's Strange** [4]...Cameo
- *C&W* **Right Or Wrong** [1]...George Strait
- *A/C* **Hello** [4]...Lionel Richie

ALBUMS
- *POP* **Footloose** [2]...Soundtrack
- *R&B* **She's Strange** [1]...Cameo
- *C&W* **Deliver** [1]...Oak Ridge Boys

May 5, 1984

SINGLES
- *HOT* **Against All Odds (Take A Look At Me Now)** [3]...Phil Collins
- *R&B* **Hello** [1]...Lionel Richie
- *C&W* **I Guess It Never Hurts To Hurt Sometimes** [1]...The Oak Ridge Boys
- *A/C* **Hello** [5]...Lionel Richie

ALBUMS
- *POP* **Footloose** [3]...Soundtrack
- *R&B* **She's Strange** [2]...Cameo
- *C&W* **Deliver** [2]...Oak Ridge Boys

May 12, 1984

SINGLES
- *HOT* **Hello** [1]...Lionel Richie
- *R&B* **Hello** [2]...Lionel Richie
- *C&W* **To All The Girls I've Loved Before** [1]...Julio Iglesias & Willie Nelson
- *A/C* **Hello** [6]...Lionel Richie

ALBUMS
- *POP* **Footloose** [4]...Soundtrack
- *R&B* **Can't Slow Down** [16]...Lionel Richie
- *C&W* **Deliver** [3]...Oak Ridge Boys

May 19, 1984

SINGLES
- *HOT* **Hello** [2]...Lionel Richie
- *R&B* **Hello** [3]...Lionel Richie
- *C&W* **To All The Girls I've Loved Before** [2]...Julio Iglesias & Willie Nelson
- *A/C* **The Longest Time** [1]...Billy Joel

ALBUMS
- *POP* **Footloose** [5]...Soundtrack
- *R&B* **Can't Slow Down** [17]...Lionel Richie
- *C&W* **Deliver** [4]...Oak Ridge Boys

May 26, 1984

SINGLES
- *HOT* ***Let's Hear It For The Boy** [1]...Deniece Williams
- *R&B* **Don't Waste Your Time** [1]...Yarbrough & Peoples
- *C&W* **As Long As I'm Rockin' With You** [1]...John Conlee
- *A/C* **The Longest Time** [2]...Billy Joel

ALBUMS
- *POP* **Footloose** [6]...Soundtrack
- *R&B* **Can't Slow Down** [18]...Lionel Richie
- *C&W* **Deliver** [5]...Oak Ridge Boys

June 2, 1984

SINGLES
- *HOT* **Let's Hear It For The Boy** [2]...Deniece Williams
- *R&B* **Let's Hear It For The Boy** [1]...Deniece Williams
- *C&W* **Honey (Open That Door)** [1]...Ricky Skaggs
- *A/C* ***Time After Time** [1]...Cyndi Lauper

ALBUMS
- *POP* **Footloose** [7]...Soundtrack
- *R&B* **Can't Slow Down** [19]...Lionel Richie
- *C&W* **Roll On** [7]...Alabama

June 9, 1984

SINGLES
- *HOT* **Time After Time** [1]...Cyndi Lauper
- *R&B* **Let's Hear It For The Boy** [2]...Deniece Williams
- *C&W* **Someday When Things Are Good** [1]...Merle Haggard
- *A/C* **Time After Time** [2]...Cyndi Lauper

ALBUMS
- *POP* **Footloose** [8]...Soundtrack
- *R&B* **Can't Slow Down** [20]...Lionel Richie
- *C&W* **Roll On** [8]...Alabama

June 16, 1984

SINGLES
- *HOT* **Time After Time** [2]...Cyndi Lauper
- *R&B* **Let's Hear It For The Boy** [3]...Deniece Williams
- *C&W* **I Got Mexico** [1]...Eddy Raven
- *A/C* **Time After Time** [3]...Cyndi Lauper

ALBUMS
- *POP* **Footloose** [9]...Soundtrack
- *R&B* **Can't Slow Down** [21]...Lionel Richie
- *C&W* **Roll On** [9]...Alabama

June 23, 1984

SINGLES
- *HOT* **The Reflex** [1]...Duran Duran
- *R&B* **Lovelite** [1]...O'Bryan
- *C&W* **When We Make Love** [1]...Alabama
- *A/C* **Believe In Me** [1]...Dan Fogelberg

ALBUMS
- *POP* **Footloose** [10]...Soundtrack
- *R&B* **Can't Slow Down** [22]...Lionel Richie
- *C&W* **Roll On** [10]...Alabama

June 30, 1984

SINGLES
- HOT The Reflex [2]...Duran Duran
- R&B *When Doves Cry [1]...Prince
- C&W I Can Tell By The Way You Dance (You're Gonna Love Me Tonight) [1]...Vern Gosdin
- A/C Almost Paradise...Love Theme From Footloose [1]...Mike Reno and Ann Wilson

ALBUMS
- POP Sports [1]...Huey Lewis & The News
- R&B Can't Slow Down [23]...Lionel Richie
- C&W Roll On [11]...Alabama

July 7, 1984

SINGLES
- HOT When Doves Cry [1]...Prince
- R&B When Doves Cry [2]...Prince
- C&W Somebody's Needin' Somebody [1]...Conway Twitty
- A/C If Ever You're In My Arms Again [1]...Peabo Bryson

ALBUMS
- POP Born In The U.S.A. [1]...Bruce Springsteen
- R&B Jermaine Jackson [1]...Jermaine Jackson
- C&W Roll On [12]...Alabama

July 14, 1984

SINGLES
- HOT When Doves Cry [2]...Prince
- R&B When Doves Cry [3]...Prince
- C&W I Don't Want To Be A Memory [1]...Exile
- A/C If Ever You're In My Arms Again [2]...Peabo Bryson

ALBUMS
- POP Born In The U.S.A. [2]...Bruce Springsteen
- R&B Lady [1]...One Way
- C&W Roll On [13]...Alabama

July 21, 1984

SINGLES
- HOT When Doves Cry [3]...Prince
- R&B When Doves Cry [4]...Prince
- C&W Just Another Woman In Love [1]...Anne Murray
- A/C If Ever You're In My Arms Again [3]...Peabo Bryson

ALBUMS
- POP Born In The U.S.A. [3]...Bruce Springsteen
- R&B Private Dancer [1]...Tina Turner
- C&W Major Moves [1]...Hank Williams, Jr.

July 28, 1984

SINGLES
- HOT When Doves Cry [4]...Prince
- R&B When Doves Cry [5]...Prince
- C&W Angel In Disguise [1]...Earl Thomas Conley
- A/C If Ever You're In My Arms Again [4]...Peabo Bryson

ALBUMS
- POP Born In The U.S.A. [4]...Bruce Springsteen
- R&B Purple Rain [1]...Prince and The Revolution/Soundtrack
- C&W Major Moves [2]...Hank Williams, Jr.

August 4, 1984

SINGLES
- HOT When Doves Cry [5]...Prince
- R&B When Doves Cry [6]...Prince
- C&W Mama He's Crazy [1]...The Judds
- A/C Stuck On You [1]...Lionel Richie

ALBUMS
- POP Purple Rain [1]...Prince and The Revolution/Soundtrack
- R&B Purple Rain [2]...Prince and The Revolution/Soundtrack
- C&W Major Moves [3]...Hank Williams, Jr.

August 11, 1984

SINGLES
- HOT *Ghostbusters [1]...Ray Parker Jr.
- R&B When Doves Cry [7]...Prince
- C&W That's The Thing About Love [1]...Don Williams
- A/C Stuck On You [2]...Lionel Richie

ALBUMS
- POP Purple Rain [2]...Prince and The Revolution/Soundtrack
- R&B Purple Rain [3]...Prince and The Revolution/Soundtrack
- C&W Major Moves [4]...Hank Williams, Jr.

August 18, 1984

SINGLES
- HOT Ghostbusters [2]...Ray Parker Jr.
- R&B When Doves Cry [8]...Prince
- C&W Still Losing You [1]...Ronnie Milsap
- A/C Stuck On You [3]...Lionel Richie

ALBUMS
- POP Purple Rain [3]...Prince and The Revolution/Soundtrack
- R&B Purple Rain [4]...Prince and The Revolution/Soundtrack
- C&W Major Moves [5]...Hank Williams, Jr.

August 25, 1984

SINGLES
- HOT Ghostbusters [3]...Ray Parker Jr.
- R&B Ghostbusters [1]...Ray Parker Jr.
- C&W Long Hard Road (The Sharecropper's Dream) [1]...Nitty Gritty Dirt Band
- A/C Stuck On You [4]...Lionel Richie

ALBUMS
- POP Purple Rain [4]...Prince and The Revolution/Soundtrack
- R&B Purple Rain [5]...Prince and The Revolution/Soundtrack
- C&W Major Moves [6]...Hank Williams, Jr.

September 1, 1984
SINGLES
- HOT   What's Love Got To Do With It [1]...Tina Turner
- R&B   Ghostbusters [2]...Ray Parker Jr.
- C&W   Let's Fall To Pieces Together [1]...George Strait
- A/C   Stuck On You [5]...Lionel Richie

ALBUMS
- POP   Purple Rain [5]...Prince and The Revolution/Soundtrack
- R&B   Purple Rain [6]...Prince and The Revolution/Soundtrack
- C&W   Right Or Wrong [4]...George Strait

September 8, 1984
SINGLES
- HOT   What's Love Got To Do With It [2]...Tina Turner
- R&B   *Caribbean Queen (No More Love On The Run) [1]...Billy Ocean
- C&W   Tennessee Homesick Blues [1]...Dolly Parton
- A/C   Leave A Tender Moment Alone [1]...Billy Joel

ALBUMS
- POP   Purple Rain [6]...Prince and The Revolution/Soundtrack
- R&B   Purple Rain [7]...Prince and The Revolution/Soundtrack
- C&W   Right Or Wrong [5]...George Strait

September 15, 1984
SINGLES
- HOT   What's Love Got To Do With It [3]...Tina Turner
- R&B   Caribbean Queen (No More Love On The Run) [2]...Billy Ocean
- C&W   You're Gettin' To Me Again [1]...Jim Glaser
- A/C   Leave A Tender Moment Alone [2]...Billy Joel

ALBUMS
- POP   Purple Rain [7]...Prince and The Revolution/Soundtrack
- R&B   Purple Rain [8]...Prince and The Revolution/Soundtrack
- C&W   Major Moves [7]...Hank Williams, Jr.

September 22, 1984
SINGLES
- HOT   Missing You [1]...John Waite
- R&B   Caribbean Queen (No More Love On The Run) [3]...Billy Ocean
- C&W   Let's Chase Each Other Around The Room [1]...Merle Haggard
- A/C   Drive [1]...The Cars

ALBUMS
- POP   Purple Rain [8]...Prince and The Revolution/Soundtrack
- R&B   Purple Rain [9]...Prince and The Revolution/Soundtrack
- C&W   It's All In The Game [1]...Merle Haggard

September 29, 1984
SINGLES
- HOT   *Let's Go Crazy [1]...Prince and The Revolution
- R&B   Caribbean Queen (No More Love On The Run) [4]...Billy Ocean
- C&W   Turning Away [1]...Crystal Gayle
- A/C   Drive [2]...The Cars

ALBUMS
- POP   Purple Rain [9]...Prince and The Revolution/Soundtrack
- R&B   Purple Rain [10]...Prince and The Revolution/Soundtrack
- C&W   City Of New Orleans [1]...Willie Nelson

October 6, 1984
SINGLES
- HOT   Let's Go Crazy [2]...Prince and The Revolution
- R&B   Let's Go Crazy [1]...Prince and The Revolution
- C&W   Everyday [1]...The Oak Ridge Boys
- A/C   Drive [3]...The Cars

ALBUMS
- POP   Purple Rain [10]...Prince and The Revolution/Soundtrack
- R&B   Purple Rain [11]...Prince and The Revolution/Soundtrack
- C&W   City Of New Orleans [2]...Willie Nelson

October 13, 1984
SINGLES
- HOT   *I Just Called To Say I Love You [1]...Stevie Wonder
- R&B   *I Just Called To Say I Love You [1]...Stevie Wonder
- C&W   Uncle Pen [1]...Ricky Skaggs
- A/C   *I Just Called To Say I Love You [1]...Stevie Wonder

ALBUMS
- POP   Purple Rain [11]...Prince and The Revolution/Soundtrack
- R&B   Purple Rain [12]...Prince and The Revolution/Soundtrack
- C&W   City Of New Orleans [3]...Willie Nelson

October 20, 1984
SINGLES
- HOT   I Just Called To Say I Love You [2]...Stevie Wonder
- R&B   I Just Called To Say I Love You [2]...Stevie Wonder
- C&W   I Don't Know A Thing About Love (The Moon Song) [1]...Conway Twitty
- A/C   I Just Called To Say I Love You [2]...Stevie Wonder

ALBUMS
- POP   Purple Rain [12]...Prince and The Revolution/Soundtrack
- R&B   Purple Rain [13]...Prince and The Revolution/Soundtrack
- C&W   City Of New Orleans [4]...Willie Nelson

October 27, 1984

SINGLES
- HOT   I Just Called To Say I Love You [3]...Stevie Wonder
- R&B   I Just Called To Say I Love You [3]...Stevie Wonder
- C&W   If You're Gonna Play In Texas (You Gotta Have A Fiddle In The Band) [1]...Alabama
- A/C   I Just Called To Say I Love You [3]...Stevie Wonder

ALBUMS
- POP   Purple Rain [13]...Prince and The Revolution/Soundtrack
- R&B   Purple Rain [14]...Prince and The Revolution/Soundtrack
- C&W   City Of New Orleans [5]...Willie Nelson

November 3, 1984

SINGLES
- HOT   Caribbean Queen (No More Love On The Run) [1]...Billy Ocean
- R&B   I Feel For You [1]...Chaka Khan
- C&W   City Of New Orleans [1]...Willie Nelson
- A/C   What About Me? [1]... Kenny Rogers with Kim Carnes and James Ingram

ALBUMS
- POP   Purple Rain [14]...Prince and The Revolution/Soundtrack
- R&B   Purple Rain [15]...Prince and The Revolution/Soundtrack
- C&W   City Of New Orleans [6]...Willie Nelson

November 10, 1984

SINGLES
- HOT   Caribbean Queen (No More Love On The Run) [2]...Billy Ocean
- R&B   I Feel For You [2]...Chaka Khan
- C&W   I've Been Around Enough To Know [1]...John Schneider
- A/C   What About Me? [2]... Kenny Rogers with Kim Carnes and James Ingram

ALBUMS
- POP   Purple Rain [15]...Prince and The Revolution/Soundtrack
- R&B   Purple Rain [16]...Prince and The Revolution/Soundtrack
- C&W   City Of New Orleans [7]...Willie Nelson

November 17, 1984

SINGLES
- HOT   Wake Me Up Before You Go-Go [1]...Wham!
- R&B   I Feel For You [3]...Chaka Khan
- C&W   Give Me One More Chance [1]...Exile
- A/C   Penny Lover [1]...Lionel Richie

ALBUMS
- POP   Purple Rain [16]...Prince and The Revolution/Soundtrack
- R&B   Purple Rain [17]...Prince and The Revolution/Soundtrack
- C&W   City Of New Orleans [8]...Willie Nelson

November 24, 1984

SINGLES
- HOT   Wake Me Up Before You Go-Go [2]...Wham!
- R&B   Cool It Now [1]...New Edition
- C&W   You Could've Heard A Heart Break [1]...Johnny Lee
- A/C   Penny Lover [2]...Lionel Richie

ALBUMS
- POP   Purple Rain [17]...Prince and The Revolution/Soundtrack
- R&B   Purple Rain [18]...Prince and The Revolution/Soundtrack
- C&W   City Of New Orleans [9]...Willie Nelson

December 1, 1984

SINGLES
- HOT   Wake Me Up Before You Go-Go [3]...Wham!
- R&B   Solid [1]...Ashford & Simpson
- C&W   Your Heart's Not In It [1]...Janie Fricke
- A/C   Penny Lover [3]...Lionel Richie

ALBUMS
- POP   Purple Rain [18]...Prince and The Revolution/Soundtrack
- R&B   Purple Rain [19]...Prince and The Revolution/Soundtrack
- C&W   City Of New Orleans [10]...Willie Nelson

December 8, 1984

SINGLES
- HOT   Out Of Touch [1]...Daryl Hall John Oates
- R&B   Solid [2]...Ashford & Simpson
- C&W   Chance Of Lovin' You [1]...Earl Thomas Conley
- A/C   Penny Lover [4]...Lionel Richie

ALBUMS
- POP   Purple Rain [19]...Prince and The Revolution/Soundtrack
- R&B   The Woman In Red [1]...Stevie Wonder/Soundtrack
- C&W   City Of New Orleans [11]...Willie Nelson

December 15, 1984

SINGLES
- HOT   Out Of Touch [2]...Daryl Hall John Oates
- R&B   Solid [3]...Ashford & Simpson
- C&W   Nobody Loves Me Like You Do [1]... Anne Murray with Dave Loggins
- A/C   Sea Of Love [1]...The Honeydrippers

ALBUMS
- POP   Purple Rain [20]...Prince and The Revolution/Soundtrack
- R&B   The Woman In Red [2]...Stevie Wonder/Soundtrack
- C&W   City Of New Orleans [12]...Willie Nelson

December 22, 1984

SINGLES
- HOT   Like A Virgin [1]...Madonna
- R&B   Operator [1]...Midnight Star
- C&W   Why Not Me [1]...The Judds
- A/C   Do What You Do [1]...Jermaine Jackson

ALBUMS
- POP   Purple Rain [21]...Prince and The Revolution/Soundtrack
- R&B   The Woman In Red [3]...Stevie Wonder/Soundtrack
- C&W   Kentucky Hearts [1]...Exile

December 29, 1984
SINGLES
- HOT Like A Virgin [2]...Madonna
- R&B Operator [2]...Midnight Star
- C&W Why Not Me [2]...The Judds
- A/C Do What You Do [2]...Jermaine Jackson

ALBUMS
- POP Purple Rain [22]...Prince and The Revolution/Soundtrack
- R&B The Woman In Red [4]...Stevie Wonder/Soundtrack
- C&W Kentucky Hearts [2]...Exile

January 5, 1985
SINGLES
- HOT Like A Virgin [3]...Madonna
- R&B Operator [3]...Midnight Star
- C&W Does Fort Worth Ever Cross Your Mind [1]...George Strait
- A/C Do What You Do [3]...Jermaine Jackson

ALBUMS
- POP Purple Rain [23]...Prince and The Revolution/Soundtrack
- R&B New Edition [1]...New Edition
- C&W Kentucky Hearts [3]...Exile

January 12, 1985
SINGLES
- HOT Like A Virgin [4]...Madonna
- R&B Operator [4]...Midnight Star
- C&W The Best Year Of My Life [1]...Eddie Rabbitt
- A/C All I Need [1]...Jack Wagner

ALBUMS
- POP Purple Rain [24]...Prince and The Revolution/Soundtrack
- R&B New Edition [2]...New Edition
- C&W Kentucky Hearts [4]...Exile

January 19, 1985
SINGLES
- HOT Like A Virgin [5]...Madonna
- R&B Operator [5]...Midnight Star
- C&W How Blue [1]...Reba McEntire
- A/C All I Need [2]...Jack Wagner

ALBUMS
- POP Born In The U.S.A. [5]...Bruce Springsteen
- R&B New Edition [3]...New Edition
- C&W Does Fort Worth Ever Cross Your Mind [1]...George Strait

January 26, 1985
SINGLES
- HOT Like A Virgin [6]...Madonna
- R&B Gotta Get You Home Tonight [1]...Eugene Wilde
- C&W (There's A) Fire In The Night [1]...Alabama
- A/C You're The Inspiration [1]...Chicago

ALBUMS
- POP Born In The U.S.A. [6]...Bruce Springsteen
- R&B New Edition [4]...New Edition
- C&W Does Fort Worth Ever Cross Your Mind [2]...George Strait

February 2, 1985
SINGLES
- HOT I Want To Know What Love Is [1]...Foreigner
- R&B Mr. Telephone Man [1]...New Edition
- C&W A Place To Fall Apart [1]...Merle Haggard with Janie Fricke
- A/C You're The Inspiration [2]...Chicago

ALBUMS
- POP Born In The U.S.A. [7]...Bruce Springsteen
- R&B New Edition [5]...New Edition
- C&W Why Not Me [1]...The Judds

February 9, 1985
SINGLES
- HOT I Want To Know What Love Is [2]...Foreigner
- R&B Mr. Telephone Man [2]...New Edition
- C&W Ain't She Somethin' Else [1]...Conway Twitty
- A/C *Careless Whisper [1]...Wham! featuring George Michael

ALBUMS
- POP Like A Virgin [1]...Madonna
- R&B Solid [1]...Ashford & Simpson
- C&W Why Not Me [2]...The Judds

February 16, 1985
SINGLES
- HOT Careless Whisper [1]...Wham! featuring George Michael
- R&B Mr. Telephone Man [3]...New Edition
- C&W Make My Life With You [1]...Oak Ridge Boys
- A/C Careless Whisper [2]...Wham! featuring George Michael

ALBUMS
- POP Like A Virgin [2]...Madonna
- R&B Solid [2]...Ashford & Simpson
- C&W Why Not Me [3]...The Judds

February 23, 1985
SINGLES
- *HOT* **Careless Whisper** [2]...Wham! featuring George Michael
- *R&B* **Missing You** [1]...Diana Ross
- *C&W* **Baby's Got Her Blue Jeans On** [1]...Mel McDaniel
- *A/C* **Careless Whisper** [3]...Wham! featuring George Michael

ALBUMS
- *POP* **Like A Virgin** [3]...Madonna
- *R&B* **Solid** [3]...Ashford & Simpson
- *C&W* **Country Boy** [1]...Ricky Skaggs

March 2, 1985
SINGLES
- *HOT* **Careless Whisper** [3]...Wham! featuring George Michael
- *R&B* **Missing You** [2]...Diana Ross
- *C&W* **Baby Bye Bye** [1]...Gary Morris
- *A/C* **Careless Whisper** [4]...Wham! featuring George Michael

ALBUMS
- *POP* **Make It Big** [1]...Wham!
- *R&B* **Solid** [4]...Ashford & Simpson
- *C&W* **Country Boy** [2]...Ricky Skaggs

March 9, 1985
SINGLES
- *HOT* **Can't Fight This Feeling** [1]...REO Speedwagon
- *R&B* **Missing You** [3]...Diana Ross
- *C&W* **My Only Love** [1]...The Statler Brothers
- *A/C* **Careless Whisper** [5]...Wham! featuring George Michael

ALBUMS
- *POP* **Make It Big** [2]...Wham!
- *R&B* **Gap Band VI** [1]...The Gap Band
- *C&W* **Country Boy** [3]...Ricky Skaggs

March 16, 1985
SINGLES
- *HOT* **Can't Fight This Feeling** [2]...REO Speedwagon
- *R&B* **Nightshift** [1]...Commodores
- *C&W* **Crazy For Your Love** [1]...Exile
- *A/C* **Too Late For Goodbyes** [1]...Julian Lennon

ALBUMS
- *POP* **Make It Big** [3]...Wham!
- *R&B* **Gap Band VI** [2]...The Gap Band
- *C&W* **Does Fort Worth Ever Cross Your Mind** [3]...George Strait

March 23, 1985
SINGLES
- *HOT* **Can't Fight This Feeling** [3]...REO Speedwagon
- *R&B* **Nightshift** [2]...Commodores
- *C&W* **Seven Spanish Angels** [1]...Ray Charles with Willie Nelson
- *A/C* **Too Late For Goodbyes** [2]...Julian Lennon

ALBUMS
- *POP* **Centerfield** [1]...John Fogerty
- *R&B* **Private Dancer** [2]...Tina Turner
- *C&W* **Friendship** [1]...Ray Charles

March 30, 1985
SINGLES
- *HOT* ***One More Night** [1]...Phil Collins
- *R&B* **Nightshift** [3]...Commodores
- *C&W* **Crazy** [1]...Kenny Rogers
- *A/C* ***One More Night** [1]...Phil Collins

ALBUMS
- *POP* **No Jacket Required** [1]...Phil Collins
- *R&B* **Private Dancer** [3]...Tina Turner
- *C&W* **40 Hour Week** [1]...Alabama

April 6, 1985
SINGLES
- *HOT* **One More Night** [2]...Phil Collins
- *R&B* **Nightshift** [4]...Commodores
- *C&W* **Country Girls** [1]...John Schneider
- *A/C* **One More Night** [2]...Phil Collins

ALBUMS
- *POP* **No Jacket Required** [2]...Phil Collins
- *R&B* **Nightshift** [1]...Commodores
- *C&W* **40 Hour Week** [2]...Alabama

April 13, 1985
SINGLES
- *HOT* ***We Are The World** [1]...USA for Africa
- *R&B* **Back In Stride** [1]...Maze Featuring Frankie Beverly
- *C&W* **Honor Bound** [1]...Earl Thomas Conley
- *A/C* **One More Night** [3]...Phil Collins

ALBUMS
- *POP* **No Jacket Required** [3]...Phil Collins
- *R&B* **Nightshift** [2]...Commodores
- *C&W* **40 Hour Week** [3]...Alabama

April 20, 1985
SINGLES
- *HOT* **We Are The World** [2]...USA for Africa
- *R&B* **Back In Stride** [2]...Maze Featuring Frankie Beverly
- *C&W* **I Need More Of You** [1]...The Bellamy Brothers
- *A/C* **We Are The World** [1]...USA for Africa

ALBUMS
- *POP* **No Jacket Required** [4]...Phil Collins
- *R&B* **Nightshift** [3]...Commodores
- *C&W* **40 Hour Week** [4]...Alabama

April 27, 1985
SINGLES
- HOT We Are The World [3]...USA for Africa
- R&B *Rhythm Of The Night [1]...DeBarge
- C&W Girls Night Out [1]...The Judds
- A/C We Are The World [2]...USA for Africa

ALBUMS
- POP We Are The World [1]...USA for Africa
- R&B Can't Stop The Love [1]...
        Maze Featuring Frankie Beverly
- C&W 40 Hour Week [5]...Alabama

May 4, 1985
SINGLES
- HOT We Are The World [4]...USA for Africa
- R&B We Are The World [1]...USA for Africa
- C&W There's No Way [1]...Alabama
- A/C Rhythm Of The Night [1]...DeBarge

ALBUMS
- POP We Are The World [2]...USA for Africa
- R&B The Night I Fell In Love [1]...Luther Vandross
- C&W 40 Hour Week [6]...Alabama

May 11, 1985
SINGLES
- HOT Crazy For You [1]...Madonna
- R&B We Are The World [2]...USA for Africa
- C&W Somebody Should Leave [1]...Reba McEntire
- A/C Smooth Operator [1]...Sade

ALBUMS
- POP We Are The World [3]...USA for Africa
- R&B The Night I Fell In Love [2]...Luther Vandross
- C&W 40 Hour Week [7]...Alabama

May 18, 1985
SINGLES
- HOT Don't You (Forget About Me) [1]...Simple Minds
- R&B Fresh [1]...Kool & The Gang
- C&W Step That Step [1]...Sawyer Brown
- A/C Smooth Operator [2]...Sade

ALBUMS
- POP No Jacket Required [5]...Phil Collins
- R&B The Night I Fell In Love [3]...Luther Vandross
- C&W 40 Hour Week [8]...Alabama

May 25, 1985
SINGLES
- HOT Everything She Wants [1]...Wham!
- R&B You Give Good Love [1]...Whitney Houston
- C&W Radio Heart [1]...Charly McClain
- A/C Suddenly [1]...Billy Ocean

ALBUMS
- POP No Jacket Required [6]...Phil Collins
- R&B The Night I Fell In Love [4]...Luther Vandross
- C&W 40 Hour Week [9]...Alabama

June 1, 1985
SINGLES
- HOT Everything She Wants [2]...Wham!
- R&B Rock Me Tonight (For Old Times Sake) [1]...
        Freddie Jackson
- C&W Don't Call Him A Cowboy [1]...Conway Twitty
- A/C Suddenly [2]...Billy Ocean

ALBUMS
- POP Around the World in a Day [1]...
        Prince & The Revolution
- R&B The Night I Fell In Love [5]...Luther Vandross
- C&W 40 Hour Week [10]...Alabama

June 8, 1985
SINGLES
- HOT Everybody Wants To Rule The World [1]...
        Tears For Fears
- R&B Rock Me Tonight (For Old Times Sake) [2]...
        Freddie Jackson
- C&W Natural High [1]...Merle Haggard
- A/C Axel F [1]...Harold Faltermeyer

ALBUMS
- POP Around the World in a Day [2]...
        Prince & The Revolution
- R&B The Night I Fell In Love [6]...Luther Vandross
- C&W 40 Hour Week [11]...Alabama

June 15, 1985
SINGLES
- HOT Everybody Wants To Rule The World [2]...
        Tears For Fears
- R&B Rock Me Tonight (For Old Times Sake) [3]...
        Freddie Jackson
- C&W Country Boy [1]...Ricky Skaggs
- A/C Axel F [2]...Harold Faltermeyer

ALBUMS
- POP Around the World in a Day [3]...
        Prince & The Revolution
- R&B The Night I Fell In Love [7]...Luther Vandross
- C&W 40 Hour Week [12]...Alabama

June 22, 1985
SINGLES
- HOT Heaven [1]...Bryan Adams
- R&B Rock Me Tonight (For Old Times Sake) [4]...
        Freddie Jackson
- C&W Little Things [1]...The Oak Ridge Boys
- A/C The Search Is Over [1]...Survivor

ALBUMS
- POP Beverly Hills Cop [1]...Soundtrack
- R&B Whitney Houston [1]...Whitney Houston
- C&W Five-O [1]...Hank Williams, Jr.

June 29, 1985
SINGLES
- HOT Heaven [2]...Bryan Adams
- R&B Rock Me Tonight (For Old Times Sake) [5]...Freddie Jackson
- C&W She Keeps The Home Fires Burning [1]...Ronnie Milsap
- A/C The Search Is Over [2]...Survivor

ALBUMS
- POP Beverly Hills Cop [2]...Soundtrack
- R&B Rock Me Tonight [1]...Freddie Jackson
- C&W Five-O [2]...Hank Williams, Jr.

July 6, 1985
SINGLES
- HOT Sussudio [1]...Phil Collins
- R&B Rock Me Tonight (For Old Times Sake) [6]...Freddie Jackson
- C&W She's A Miracle [1]...Exile
- A/C The Search Is Over [3]...Survivor

ALBUMS
- POP No Jacket Required [7]...Phil Collins
- R&B Rock Me Tonight [2]...Freddie Jackson
- C&W Five-O [3]...Hank Williams, Jr.

July 13, 1985
SINGLES
- HOT A View To A Kill [1]...Duran Duran
- R&B Hangin' On A String (Contemplating) [1]...Loose Ends
- C&W Forgiving You Was Easy [1]...Willie Nelson
- A/C The Search Is Over [4]...Survivor

ALBUMS
- POP Songs From The Big Chair [1]...Tears For Fears
- R&B Rock Me Tonight [3]...Freddie Jackson
- C&W Five-O [4]...Hank Williams, Jr.

July 20, 1985
SINGLES
- HOT A View To A Kill [2]...Duran Duran
- R&B Save Your Love (For #1) [1]...Rene & Angela
- C&W Dixie Road [1]...Lee Greenwood
- A/C Who's Holding Donna Now [1]...DeBarge

ALBUMS
- POP Songs From The Big Chair [2]...Tears For Fears
- R&B Rock Me Tonight [4]...Freddie Jackson
- C&W Five-O [5]...Hank Williams, Jr.

July 27, 1985
SINGLES
- HOT *Everytime You Go Away [1]...Paul Young
- R&B Save Your Love (For #1) [2]...Rene & Angela
- C&W Love Don't Care (Whose Heart It Breaks) [1]...Earl Thomas Conley
- A/C Who's Holding Donna Now [2]...DeBarge

ALBUMS
- POP Songs From The Big Chair [3]...Tears For Fears
- R&B Rock Me Tonight [5]...Freddie Jackson
- C&W Five-O [6]...Hank Williams, Jr.

August 3, 1985
SINGLES
- HOT Shout [1]...Tears For Fears
- R&B Freeway Of Love [1]...Aretha Franklin
- C&W Forty Hour Week (For A Livin') [1]...Alabama
- A/C Who's Holding Donna Now [3]...DeBarge

ALBUMS
- POP Songs From The Big Chair [4]...Tears For Fears
- R&B Rock Me Tonight [6]...Freddie Jackson
- C&W 40 Hour Week [13]...Alabama

August 10, 1985
SINGLES
- HOT Shout [2]...Tears For Fears
- R&B Freeway Of Love [2]...Aretha Franklin
- C&W I'm For Love [1]...Hank Williams, Jr.
- A/C Everytime You Go Away [1]...Paul Young

ALBUMS
- POP Reckless [1]...Bryan Adams
- R&B Rock Me Tonight [7]...Freddie Jackson
- C&W 40 Hour Week [14]...Alabama

August 17, 1985
SINGLES
- HOT Shout [3]...Tears For Fears
- R&B Freeway Of Love [3]...Aretha Franklin
- C&W Highwayman [1]...Waylon Jennings/Willie Nelson/Johnny Cash/Kris Kristofferson
- A/C Everytime You Go Away [2]...Paul Young

ALBUMS
- POP Reckless [2]...Bryan Adams
- R&B Rock Me Tonight [8]...Freddie Jackson
- C&W Five-O [7]...Hank Williams, Jr.

August 24, 1985

SINGLES
- HOT   The Power Of Love [1]...Huey Lewis and The News
- R&B   Freeway Of Love [4]...Aretha Franklin
- C&W   Real Love [1]...Kenny Rogers & Dolly Parton
- A/C   *Cherish [1]...Kool & The Gang

ALBUMS
- POP   Songs From The Big Chair [5]...Tears For Fears
- R&B   Rock Me Tonight [9]...Freddie Jackson
- C&W   Five-O [8]...Hank Williams, Jr.

August 31, 1985

SINGLES
- HOT   The Power Of Love [2]...Huey Lewis and The News
- R&B   Freeway Of Love [5]...Aretha Franklin
- C&W   Love Is Alive [1]...The Judds
- A/C   Cherish [2]...Kool & The Gang

ALBUMS
- POP   Brothers In Arms [1]...Dire Straits
- R&B   Rock Me Tonight [10]...Freddie Jackson
- C&W   Five-O [9]...Hank Williams, Jr.

September 7, 1985

SINGLES
- HOT   St. Elmo's Fire (Man In Motion) [1]...John Parr
- R&B   *Saving All My Love For You [1]...Whitney Houston
- C&W   I Don't Know Why You Don't Want Me [1]...Rosanne Cash
- A/C   Cherish [3]...Kool & The Gang

ALBUMS
- POP   Brothers In Arms [2]...Dire Straits
- R&B   Whitney Houston [2]...Whitney Houston
- C&W   Greatest Hits, Vol. 2 [1]...Ronnie Milsap

September 14, 1985

SINGLES
- HOT   St. Elmo's Fire (Man In Motion) [2]...John Parr
- R&B   Cherish [1]...Kool & The Gang
- C&W   Modern Day Romance [1]...Nitty Gritty Dirt Band
- A/C   Cherish [4]...Kool & The Gang

ALBUMS
- POP   Brothers In Arms [3]...Dire Straits
- R&B   Whitney Houston [3]...Whitney Houston
- C&W   Greatest Hits, Vol. 2 [2]...Ronnie Milsap

September 21, 1985

SINGLES
- HOT   Money For Nothing [1]...Dire Straits
- R&B   *Oh Sheila [1]...Ready For The World
- C&W   I Fell In Love Again Last Night [1]...The Forester Sisters
- A/C   Cherish [5]...Kool & The Gang

ALBUMS
- POP   Brothers In Arms [4]...Dire Straits
- R&B   Whitney Houston [4]...Whitney Houston
- C&W   Greatest Hits, Vol. 2 [3]...Ronnie Milsap

September 28, 1985

SINGLES
- HOT   Money For Nothing [2]...Dire Straits
- R&B   Oh Sheila [2]...Ready For The World
- C&W   Lost In The Fifties Tonight (In the Still of the Night) [1]...Ronnie Milsap
- A/C   Cherish [6]...Kool & The Gang

ALBUMS
- POP   Brothers In Arms [5]...Dire Straits
- R&B   Whitney Houston [5]...Whitney Houston
- C&W   Highwayman [1]...Waylon Jennings/Willie Nelson/Johnny Cash/Kris Kristofferson

October 5, 1985

SINGLES
- HOT   Money For Nothing [3]...Dire Straits
- R&B   You Are My Lady [1]...Freddie Jackson
- C&W   Lost In The Fifties Tonight (In the Still of the Night) [2]...Ronnie Milsap
- A/C   Saving All My Love For You [1]...Whitney Houston

ALBUMS
- POP   Brothers In Arms [6]...Dire Straits
- R&B   Whitney Houston [6]...Whitney Houston
- C&W   Greatest Hits, Vol. 2 [4]...Ronnie Milsap

October 12, 1985

SINGLES
- HOT   Oh Sheila [1]...Ready For The World
- R&B   You Are My Lady [2]...Freddie Jackson
- C&W   Meet Me In Montana [1]...Marie Osmond with Dan Seals
- A/C   Saving All My Love For You [2]...Whitney Houston

ALBUMS
- POP   Brothers In Arms [7]...Dire Straits
- R&B   Rock Me Tonight [11]...Freddie Jackson
- C&W   Greatest Hits, Vol. 2 [5]...Ronnie Milsap

October 19, 1985
SINGLES
- HOT Take On Me [1]...a-ha
- R&B *Part-Time Lover [1]...Stevie Wonder
- C&W You Make Me Want To Make You Mine [1]...Juice Newton
- A/C Saving All My Love For You [3]...Whitney Houston

ALBUMS
- POP Brothers In Arms [8]...Dire Straits
- R&B Rock Me Tonight [12]...Freddie Jackson
- C&W Pardners in Rhyme [1]...The Statler Brothers

October 26, 1985
SINGLES
- HOT Saving All My Love For You [1]...Whitney Houston
- R&B Part-Time Lover [2]...Stevie Wonder
- C&W Touch A Hand, Make A Friend [1]...The Oak Ridge Boys
- A/C Part-Time Lover [1]...Stevie Wonder

ALBUMS
- POP Brothers In Arms [9]...Dire Straits
- R&B Rock Me Tonight [13]...Freddie Jackson
- C&W Greatest Hits, Vol. 2 [6]...Ronnie Milsap

November 2, 1985
SINGLES
- HOT Part-Time Lover [1]...Stevie Wonder
- R&B Part-Time Lover [3]...Stevie Wonder
- C&W Some Fools Never Learn [1]...Steve Wariner
- A/C Part-Time Lover [2]...Stevie Wonder

ALBUMS
- POP Miami Vice [1]...TV Soundtrack
- R&B Rock Me Tonight [14]...Freddie Jackson
- C&W Greatest Hits, Vol. 2 [7]...Ronnie Milsap

November 9, 1985
SINGLES
- HOT Miami Vice Theme [1]...Jan Hammer
- R&B Part-Time Lover [4]...Stevie Wonder
- C&W Can't Keep A Good Man Down [1]...Alabama
- A/C Part-Time Lover [3]...Stevie Wonder

ALBUMS
- POP Miami Vice [2]...TV Soundtrack
- R&B In Square Circle [1]...Stevie Wonder
- C&W Greatest Hits, Vol. 2 [8]...Ronnie Milsap

November 16, 1985
SINGLES
- HOT We Built This City [1]...Starship
- R&B Part-Time Lover [5]...Stevie Wonder
- C&W Hang On To Your Heart [1]...Exile
- A/C *Separate Lives [1]...Phil Collins & Marilyn Martin

ALBUMS
- POP Miami Vice [3]...TV Soundtrack
- R&B In Square Circle [2]...Stevie Wonder
- C&W Greatest Hits, Vol. 2 [9]...Ronnie Milsap

November 23, 1985
SINGLES
- HOT We Built This City [2]...Starship
- R&B Part-Time Lover [6]...Stevie Wonder
- C&W I'll Never Stop Loving You [1]...Gary Morris
- A/C Separate Lives [2]...Phil Collins & Marilyn Martin

ALBUMS
- POP Miami Vice [4]...TV Soundtrack
- R&B In Square Circle [3]...Stevie Wonder
- C&W Greatest Hits, Vol. 2 [10]...Ronnie Milsap

November 30, 1985
SINGLES
- HOT Separate Lives [1]...Phil Collins & Marilyn Martin
- R&B Caravan Of Love [1]...Isley, Jasper, Isley
- C&W Too Much On My Heart [1]...The Statler Brothers
- A/C Separate Lives [3]...Phil Collins & Marilyn Martin

ALBUMS
- POP Miami Vice [5]...TV Soundtrack
- R&B In Square Circle [4]...Stevie Wonder
- C&W Greatest Hits, Vol. 2 [11]...Ronnie Milsap

December 7, 1985
SINGLES
- HOT Broken Wings [1]...Mr. Mister
- R&B Caravan Of Love [2]...Isley, Jasper, Isley
- C&W I Don't Mind The Thorns (If You're The Rose) [1]...Lee Greenwood
- A/C *Say You, Say Me [1]...Lionel Richie

ALBUMS
- POP Miami Vice [6]...TV Soundtrack
- R&B In Square Circle [5]...Stevie Wonder
- C&W Rhythm And Romance [1]...Rosanne Cash

December 14, 1985
SINGLES
- HOT Broken Wings [2]...Mr. Mister
- R&B Caravan Of Love [3]...Isley, Jasper, Isley
- C&W Nobody Falls Like A Fool [1]...Earl Thomas Conley
- A/C Say You, Say Me [2]...Lionel Richie

ALBUMS
- POP Miami Vice [7]...TV Soundtrack
- R&B In Square Circle [6]...Stevie Wonder
- C&W Something Special [1]...George Strait

December 21, 1985
SINGLES
- HOT   Say You, Say Me [1]...Lionel Richie
- R&B   Don't Say No Tonight [1]...Eugene Wilde
- C&W   The Chair [1]...George Strait
- A/C   Say You, Say Me [3]...Lionel Richie

ALBUMS
- POP   Heart [1]...Heart
- R&B   In Square Circle [7]...Stevie Wonder
- C&W   Anything Goes... [1]...Gary Morris

December 28, 1985
SINGLES
- HOT   Say You, Say Me [2]...Lionel Richie
- R&B   Don't Say No Tonight [2]...Eugene Wilde
- C&W   Have Mercy [1]...The Judds
- A/C   Say You, Say Me [4]...Lionel Richie

ALBUMS
- POP   Miami Vice [8]...TV Soundtrack
- R&B   In Square Circle [8]...Stevie Wonder
- C&W   The Heart Of The Matter [1]...Kenny Rogers

January 4, 1986
SINGLES
- HOT   Say You, Say Me [3]...Lionel Richie
- R&B   Don't Say No Tonight [3]...Eugene Wilde
- C&W   Have Mercy [2]...The Judds
- A/C   Say You, Say Me [5]...Lionel Richie

ALBUMS
- POP   Miami Vice [9]...TV Soundtrack
- R&B   In Square Circle [9]...Stevie Wonder
- C&W   The Heart Of The Matter [2]...Kenny Rogers

January 11, 1986
SINGLES
- HOT   Say You, Say Me [4]...Lionel Richie
- R&B   Say You, Say Me [1]...Lionel Richie
- C&W   Morning Desire [1]...Kenny Rogers
- A/C   *That's What Friends Are For [1]...Dionne & Friends

ALBUMS
- POP   Miami Vice [10]...TV Soundtrack
- R&B   In Square Circle [10]...Stevie Wonder
- C&W   The Heart Of The Matter [3]...Kenny Rogers

January 18, 1986
SINGLES
- HOT   That's What Friends Are For [1]...Dionne & Friends
- R&B   Say You, Say Me [2]...Lionel Richie
- C&W   Bop [1]...Dan Seals
- A/C   That's What Friends Are For [2]...Dionne & Friends

ALBUMS
- POP   Miami Vice [11]...TV Soundtrack
- R&B   In Square Circle [11]...Stevie Wonder
- C&W   The Heart Of The Matter [4]...Kenny Rogers

January 25, 1986
SINGLES
- HOT   That's What Friends Are For [2]...Dionne & Friends
- R&B   That's What Friends Are For [1]...Dionne & Friends
- C&W   Never Be You [1]...Rosanne Cash
- A/C   Go Home [1]...Stevie Wonder

ALBUMS
- POP   The Broadway Album [1]...Barbra Streisand
- R&B   In Square Circle [12]...Stevie Wonder
- C&W   The Heart Of The Matter [5]...Kenny Rogers

February 1, 1986
SINGLES
- HOT   That's What Friends Are For [3]...Dionne & Friends
- R&B   That's What Friends Are For [2]...Dionne & Friends
- C&W   Just In Case [1]...The Forester Sisters
- A/C   My Hometown [1]...Bruce Springsteen

ALBUMS
- POP   The Broadway Album [2]...Barbra Streisand
- R&B   Promise [1]...Sade
- C&W   The Heart Of The Matter [6]...Kenny Rogers

February 8, 1986
SINGLES
- HOT   That's What Friends Are For [4]...Dionne & Friends
- R&B   That's What Friends Are For [3]...Dionne & Friends
- C&W   Hurt [1]...Juice Newton
- A/C   The Sweetest Taboo [1]...Sade

ALBUMS
- POP   The Broadway Album [3]...Barbra Streisand
- R&B   Promise [2]...Sade
- C&W   Greatest Hits - Volume 2 [1]...Hank Williams, Jr.

February 15, 1986
SINGLES
- HOT   *How Will I Know [1]...Whitney Houston
- R&B   Do Me Baby [1]...Meli'sa Morgan
- C&W   Makin' Up For Lost Time (The Dallas Lovers' Song) [1]...Crystal Gayle & Gary Morris
- A/C   *How Will I Know [1]...Whitney Houston

ALBUMS
- POP   Promise [1]...Sade
- R&B   Promise [3]...Sade
- C&W   Greatest Hits - Volume 2 [2]...Hank Williams, Jr.

February 22, 1986
SINGLES
- HOT   How Will I Know [2]...Whitney Houston
- R&B   Do Me Baby [2]...Meli'sa Morgan
- C&W   There's No Stopping Your Heart [1]...Marie Osmond
- A/C   *Sara [1]...Starship

ALBUMS
- POP   Promise [2]...Sade
- R&B   Promise [4]...Sade
- C&W   Streamline [1]...Lee Greenwood

March 1, 1986
SINGLES
- *HOT* Kyrie [1]...Mr. Mister
- *R&B* Do Me Baby [3]...Meli'sa Morgan
- *C&W* You Can Dream Of Me [1]...Steve Wariner
- *A/C* Sara [2]...Starship

ALBUMS
- *POP* Welcome To The Real World [1]...Mr. Mister
- *R&B* Promise [5]...Sade
- *C&W* Rockin' With The Rhythm [1]...The Judds

March 8, 1986
SINGLES
- *HOT* Kyrie [2]...Mr. Mister
- *R&B* How Will I Know [1]...Whitney Houston
- *C&W* Think About Love [1]...Dolly Parton
- *A/C* Sara [3]...Starship

ALBUMS
- *POP* Whitney Houston [1]...Whitney Houston
- *R&B* Promise [6]...Sade
- *C&W* Won't Be Blue Anymore [1]...Dan Seals

March 15, 1986
SINGLES
- *HOT* Sara [1]...Starship
- *R&B* Your Smile [1]...Rene & Angela
- *C&W* I Could Get Used To You [1]...Exile
- *A/C* *These Dreams [1]...Heart

ALBUMS
- *POP* Whitney Houston [2]...Whitney Houston
- *R&B* Promise [7]...Sade
- *C&W* I Have Returned [1]...Ray Stevens

March 22, 1986
SINGLES
- *HOT* These Dreams [1]...Heart
- *R&B* What Have You Done For Me Lately [1]...Janet Jackson
- *C&W* What's A Memory Like You (Doing In A Love Like This) [1]...John Schneider
- *A/C* These Dreams [2]...Heart

ALBUMS
- *POP* Whitney Houston [3]...Whitney Houston
- *R&B* Promise [8]...Sade
- *C&W* Greatest Hits [1]...Earl Thomas Conley

March 29, 1986
SINGLES
- *HOT* Rock Me Amadeus [1]...Falco
- *R&B* What Have You Done For Me Lately [2]...Janet Jackson
- *C&W* Don't Underestimate My Love For You [1]...Lee Greenwood
- *A/C* These Dreams [3]...Heart

ALBUMS
- *POP* Whitney Houston [4]...Whitney Houston
- *R&B* Promise [9]...Sade
- *C&W* Live In London [1]...Ricky Skaggs

April 5, 1986
SINGLES
- *HOT* Rock Me Amadeus [2]...Falco
- *R&B* *Kiss [1]...Prince and The Revolution
- *C&W* 100% Chance Of Rain [1]...Gary Morris
- *A/C* Secret Lovers [1]...Atlantic Starr

ALBUMS
- *POP* Whitney Houston [5]...Whitney Houston
- *R&B* Promise [10]...Sade
- *C&W* Greatest Hits [1]...Alabama

April 12, 1986
SINGLES
- *HOT* Rock Me Amadeus [3]...Falco
- *R&B* Kiss [2]...Prince and The Revolution
- *C&W* She And I [1]...Alabama
- *A/C* Overjoyed [1]...Stevie Wonder

ALBUMS
- *POP* Whitney Houston [6]...Whitney Houston
- *R&B* Promise [11]...Sade
- *C&W* Greatest Hits [2]...Alabama

April 19, 1986
SINGLES
- *HOT* Kiss [1]...Prince and The Revolution
- *R&B* Kiss [3]...Prince and The Revolution
- *C&W* Cajun Moon [1]...Ricky Skaggs
- *A/C* Overjoyed [2]...Stevie Wonder

ALBUMS
- *POP* Whitney Houston [7]...Whitney Houston
- *R&B* Control [1]...Janet Jackson
- *C&W* A Memory Like You [1]...John Schneider

April 26, 1986

SINGLES
- *HOT* Kiss [2]...Prince and The Revolution
- *R&B* Kiss [4]...Prince and The Revolution
- *C&W* Now And Forever (You And Me) [1]...Anne Murray
- *A/C* *Greatest Love Of All [1]...Whitney Houston

ALBUMS
- *POP* 5150 [1]...Van Halen
- *R&B* Control [2]...Janet Jackson
- *C&W* Greatest Hits [3]...Alabama

May 3, 1986

SINGLES
- *HOT* Addicted To Love [1]...Robert Palmer
- *R&B* I Have Learned To Respect The Power Of Love [1]...Stephanie Mills
- *C&W* Once In A Blue Moon [1]...Earl Thomas Conley
- *A/C* Greatest Love Of All [2]...Whitney Houston

ALBUMS
- *POP* 5150 [2]...Van Halen
- *R&B* Control [3]...Janet Jackson
- *C&W* Greatest Hits [4]...Alabama

May 10, 1986

SINGLES
- *HOT* West End Girls [1]...Pet Shop Boys
- *R&B* I Have Learned To Respect The Power Of Love [2]...Stephanie Mills
- *C&W* Grandpa (Tell Me 'Bout The Good Old Days) [1]...The Judds
- *A/C* Greatest Love Of All [3]...Whitney Houston

ALBUMS
- *POP* 5150 [3]...Van Halen
- *R&B* Control [4]...Janet Jackson
- *C&W* Greatest Hits [5]...Alabama

May 17, 1986

SINGLES
- *HOT* Greatest Love Of All [1]...Whitney Houston
- *R&B* *On My Own [1]...Patti LaBelle & Michael McDonald
- *C&W* Ain't Misbehavin' [1]...Hank Williams, Jr.
- *A/C* Greatest Love Of All [4]...Whitney Houston

ALBUMS
- *POP* Whitney Houston [8]...Whitney Houston
- *R&B* Control [5]...Janet Jackson
- *C&W* Five-O [10]...Hank Williams, Jr.

May 24, 1986

SINGLES
- *HOT* Greatest Love Of All [2]...Whitney Houston
- *R&B* On My Own [2]...Patti LaBelle & Michael McDonald
- *C&W* Tomb Of The Unknown Love [1]...Kenny Rogers
- *A/C* Greatest Love Of All [5]...Whitney Houston

ALBUMS
- *POP* Whitney Houston [9]...Whitney Houston
- *R&B* Control [6]...Janet Jackson
- *C&W* Whoever's In New England [1]...Reba McEntire

May 31, 1986

SINGLES
- *HOT* Greatest Love Of All [3]...Whitney Houston
- *R&B* On My Own [3]...Patti LaBelle & Michael McDonald
- *C&W* Whoever's In New England [1]...Reba McEntire
- *A/C* *Live To Tell [1]...Madonna

ALBUMS
- *POP* Whitney Houston [10]...Whitney Houston
- *R&B* Control [7]...Janet Jackson
- *C&W* The Promiseland [1]...Willie Nelson

June 7, 1986

SINGLES
- *HOT* Live To Tell [1]...Madonna
- *R&B* On My Own [4]...Patti LaBelle & Michael McDonald
- *C&W* Happy, Happy Birthday Baby [1]...Ronnie Milsap
- *A/C* Live To Tell [2]...Madonna

ALBUMS
- *POP* Whitney Houston [11]...Whitney Houston
- *R&B* Control [8]...Janet Jackson
- *C&W* The Promiseland [2]...Willie Nelson

June 14, 1986

SINGLES
- *HOT* On My Own [1]...Patti LaBelle & Michael McDonald
- *R&B* Nasty [1]...Janet Jackson
- *C&W* Life's Highway [1]...Steve Wariner
- *A/C* Live To Tell [3]...Madonna

ALBUMS
- *POP* Whitney Houston [12]...Whitney Houston
- *R&B* Winner In You [1]...Patti LaBelle
- *C&W* Will The Wolf Survive [1]...Waylon Jennings

June 21, 1986

SINGLES
- *HOT* On My Own [2]...Patti LaBelle & Michael McDonald
- *R&B* Nasty [2]...Janet Jackson
- *C&W* Mama's Never Seen Those Eyes [1]...The Forester Sisters
- *A/C* *There'll Be Sad Songs (To Make You Cry) [1]...Billy Ocean

ALBUMS
- *POP* Whitney Houston [13]...Whitney Houston
- *R&B* Winner In You [2]...Patti LaBelle
- *C&W* Lost In The Fifties Tonight [1]...Ronnie Milsap

June 28, 1986

SINGLES
- *HOT* On My Own [3]...Patti LaBelle & Michael McDonald
- *R&B* There'll Be Sad Songs (To Make You Cry) [1]...Billy Ocean
- *C&W* Living In The Promiseland [1]...Willie Nelson
- *A/C* No One Is To Blame [1]...Howard Jones

ALBUMS
- *POP* Whitney Houston [14]...Whitney Houston
- *R&B* Winner In You [3]...Patti LaBelle
- *C&W* Guitars, Cadillacs, Ect., Etc. [1]...Dwight Yoakam

July 5, 1986

SINGLES
- *HOT* There'll Be Sad Songs (To Make You Cry) [1]...Billy Ocean
- *R&B* There'll Be Sad Songs (To Make You Cry) [2]...Billy Ocean
- *C&W* Everything That Glitters (Is Not Gold) [1]...Dan Seals
- *A/C* Your Wildest Dreams [1]...The Moody Blues

ALBUMS
- *POP* Control [1]...Janet Jackson
- *R&B* Winner In You [4]...Patti LaBelle
- *C&W* Guitars, Cadillacs, Ect., Etc. [2]...Dwight Yoakam

July 12, 1986

SINGLES
- *HOT* Holding Back The Years [1]...Simply Red
- *R&B* Who's Johnny [1]...El DeBarge
- *C&W* Hearts Aren't Made To Break (They're Made To Love) [1]...Lee Greenwood
- *A/C* Your Wildest Dreams [2]...The Moody Blues

ALBUMS
- *POP* Control [2]...Janet Jackson
- *R&B* Winner In You [5]...Patti LaBelle
- *C&W* #7 [1]...George Strait

July 19, 1986

SINGLES
- *HOT* Invisible Touch [1]...Genesis
- *R&B* Rumors [1]...Timex Social Club
- *C&W* Until I Met You [1]...Judy Rodman
- *A/C* *Glory Of Love [1]...Peter Cetera

ALBUMS
- *POP* Winner In You [1]...Patti LaBelle
- *R&B* Winner In You [6]...Patti LaBelle
- *C&W* #7 [2]...George Strait

July 26, 1986

SINGLES
- *HOT* Sledgehammer [1]...Peter Gabriel
- *R&B* Rumors [2]...Timex Social Club
- *C&W* On The Other Hand [1]...Randy Travis
- *A/C* Glory Of Love [2]...Peter Cetera

ALBUMS
- *POP* Top Gun [1]...Soundtrack
- *R&B* Winner In You [7]...Patti LaBelle
- *C&W* #7 [3]...George Strait

August 2, 1986

SINGLES
- *HOT* Glory Of Love [1]...Peter Cetera
- *R&B* Closer Than Close [1]...Jean Carne
- *C&W* Nobody In His Right Mind Would've Left Her [1]...George Strait
- *A/C* Glory Of Love [3]...Peter Cetera

ALBUMS
- *POP* Top Gun [2]...Soundtrack
- *R&B* Winner In You [8]...Patti LaBelle
- *C&W* #7 [4]...George Strait

August 9, 1986

SINGLES
- *HOT* Glory Of Love [2]...Peter Cetera
- *R&B* Closer Than Close [2]...Jean Carne
- *C&W* Rockin' With The Rhythm Of The Rain [1]...The Judds
- *A/C* Glory Of Love [4]...Peter Cetera

ALBUMS
- *POP* Top Gun [3]...Soundtrack
- *R&B* Love Zone [1]...Billy Ocean
- *C&W* Storms Of Life [1]...Randy Travis

August 16, 1986
SINGLES
- HOT   Papa Don't Preach [1]...Madonna
- R&B   Do You Get Enough Love [1]...Shirley Jones
- C&W   You're The Last Thing I Needed Tonight [1]...John Schneider
- A/C   Glory Of Love [5]...Peter Cetera

ALBUMS
- POP   True Blue [1]...Madonna
- R&B   Raising Hell [1]...Run-D.M.C.
- C&W   Storms Of Life [2]...Randy Travis

August 23, 1986
SINGLES
- HOT   Papa Don't Preach [2]...Madonna
- R&B   Do You Get Enough Love [2]...Shirley Jones
- C&W   Strong Heart [1]...T.G. Sheppard
- A/C   Words Get In The Way [1]...Miami Sound Machine

ALBUMS
- POP   True Blue [2]...Madonna
- R&B   Raising Hell [2]...Run-D.M.C.
- C&W   Storms Of Life [3]...Randy Travis

August 30, 1986
SINGLES
- HOT   Higher Love [1]...Steve Winwood
- R&B   Love Zone [1]...Billy Ocean
- C&W   Heartbeat In The Darkness [1]...Don Williams
- A/C   Words Get In The Way [2]...Miami Sound Machine

ALBUMS
- POP   True Blue [3]...Madonna
- R&B   Raising Hell [3]...Run-D.M.C.
- C&W   Storms Of Life [4]...Randy Travis

September 6, 1986
SINGLES
- HOT   Venus [1]...Bananarama
- R&B   Ain't Nothin' Goin' On But The Rent [1]...Gwen Guthrie
- C&W   Desperado Love [1]...Conway Twitty
- A/C   Friends And Lovers [1]...Gloria Loring & Carl Anderson

ALBUMS
- POP   True Blue [4]...Madonna
- R&B   Raising Hell [4]...Run-D.M.C.
- C&W   Montana Cafe [1]...Hank Williams, Jr.

September 13, 1986
SINGLES
- HOT   Take My Breath Away [1]...Berlin
- R&B   (Pop, Pop, Pop, Pop) Goes My Mind [1]...Levert
- C&W   Little Rock [1]...Reba McEntire
- A/C   Friends And Lovers [2]...Gloria Loring & Carl Anderson

ALBUMS
- POP   True Blue [5]...Madonna
- R&B   Raising Hell [5]...Run-D.M.C.
- C&W   Montana Cafe [2]...Hank Williams, Jr.

September 20, 1986
SINGLES
- HOT   *Stuck With You [1]...Huey Lewis and the News
- R&B   The Rain [1]...Oran "Juice" Jones
- C&W   Got My Heart Set On You [1]...John Conlee
- A/C   *Stuck With You [1]...Huey Lewis and the News

ALBUMS
- POP   Top Gun [4]...Soundtrack
- R&B   Rapture [1]...Anita Baker
- C&W   Montana Cafe [3]...Hank Williams, Jr.

September 27, 1986
SINGLES
- HOT   Stuck With You [2]...Huey Lewis and the News
- R&B   The Rain [2]...Oran "Juice" Jones
- C&W   In Love [1]...Ronnie Milsap
- A/C   Stuck With You [2]...Huey Lewis and the News

ALBUMS
- POP   Dancing On The Ceiling [1]...Lionel Richie
- R&B   Raising Hell [6]...Run-D.M.C.
- C&W   Montana Cafe [4]...Hank Williams, Jr.

October 4, 1986
SINGLES
- HOT   Stuck With You [3]...Huey Lewis and the News
- R&B   Word Up [1]...Cameo
- C&W   Always Have Always Will [1]...Janie Frickie
- A/C   Stuck With You [3]...Huey Lewis and the News

ALBUMS
- POP   Dancing On The Ceiling [2]...Lionel Richie
- R&B   Rapture [2]...Anita Baker
- C&W   Black & White [1]...Janie Frickie

October 11, 1986
SINGLES
- HOT   When I Think Of You [1]...Janet Jackson
- R&B   Word Up [2]...Cameo
- C&W   Both To Each Other (Friends & Lovers) [1]...Eddie Rabbitt & Juice Newton
- A/C   Throwing It All Away [1]...Genesis

ALBUMS
- POP   Top Gun [5]...Soundtrack
- R&B   Raising Hell [7]...Run-D.M.C.
- C&W   Storms Of Life [5]...Randy Travis

October 18, 1986
SINGLES
- HOT When I Think Of You [2]...Janet Jackson
- R&B Word Up [3]...Cameo
- C&W Just Another Love [1]...Tanya Tucker
- A/C Throwing It All Away [2]...Genesis

ALBUMS
- POP Fore! [1]...Huey Lewis and the News
- R&B Rapture [3]...Anita Baker
- C&W Storms Of Life [6]...Randy Travis

October 25, 1986
SINGLES
- HOT True Colors [1]...Cyndi Lauper
- R&B *Shake You Down [1]...Gregory Abbott
- C&W Cry [1]...Crystal Gayle
- A/C I'll Be Over You [1]...Toto

ALBUMS
- POP Slippery When Wet [1]...Bon Jovi
- R&B Word Up! [1]...Cameo
- C&W Storms Of Life [7]...Randy Travis

November 1, 1986
SINGLES
- HOT True Colors [2]...Cyndi Lauper
- R&B Shake You Down [2]...Gregory Abbott
- C&W It'll Be Me [1]...Exile
- A/C I'll Be Over You [2]...Toto

ALBUMS
- POP Third Stage [1]...Boston
- R&B Word Up! [2]...Cameo
- C&W Storms Of Life [8]...Randy Travis

November 8, 1986
SINGLES
- HOT Amanda [1]...Boston
- R&B A Little Bit More [1]...Melba Moore with Freddie Jackson
- C&W Diggin' Up Bones [1]...Randy Travis
- A/C *The Next Time I Fall [1]...Peter Cetera W/Amy Grant

ALBUMS
- POP Third Stage [2]...Boston
- R&B Word Up! [3]...Cameo
- C&W Guitar Town [1]...Steve Earle

November 15, 1986
SINGLES
- HOT Amanda [2]...Boston
- R&B Tasty Love [1]...Freddie Jackson
- C&W That Rock Won't Roll [1]...Restless Heart
- A/C The Next Time I Fall [2]...Peter Cetera W/Amy Grant

ALBUMS
- POP Third Stage [3]...Boston
- R&B Word Up! [4]...Cameo
- C&W The Touch [1]...Alabama

November 22, 1986
SINGLES
- HOT Human [1]...Human League
- R&B Tasty Love [2]...Freddie Jackson
- C&W You're Still New To Me [1]...Marie Osmond with Paul Davis
- A/C Love Will Conquer All [1]...Lionel Richie

ALBUMS
- POP Third Stage [4]...Boston
- R&B Word Up! [5]...Cameo
- C&W The Touch [2]...Alabama

November 29, 1986
SINGLES
- HOT You Give Love A Bad Name [1]...Bon Jovi
- R&B Tasty Love [3]...Freddie Jackson
- C&W Touch Me When We're Dancing [1]...Alabama
- A/C Love Will Conquer All [2]...Lionel Richie

ALBUMS
- POP Bruce Springsteen & The E Street Band Live/1975-85 [1]...Bruce Springsteen
- R&B Give Me The Reason [1]...Luther Vandross
- C&W The Touch [3]...Alabama

December 6, 1986
SINGLES
- HOT The Next Time I Fall [1]...Peter Cetera W/Amy Grant
- R&B Tasty Love [4]...Freddie Jackson
- C&W It Ain't Cool To Be Crazy About You [1]...George Strait
- A/C *The Way It Is [1]...Bruce Hornsby & The Range

ALBUMS
- POP Bruce Springsteen & The E Street Band Live/1975-85 [2]...Bruce Springsteen
- R&B Just Like The First Time [1]...Freddie Jackson
- C&W The Touch [4]...Alabama

December 13, 1986
SINGLES
- HOT The Way It Is [1]...Bruce Hornsby & The Range
- R&B Love You Down [1]...Ready For The World
- C&W Hell And High Water [1]...T. Graham Brown
- A/C The Way It Is [2]...Bruce Hornsby & The Range

ALBUMS
- POP Bruce Springsteen & The E Street Band Live/1975-85 [3]...Bruce Springsteen
- R&B Just Like The First Time [2]...Freddie Jackson
- C&W The Touch [5]...Alabama

December 20, 1986
SINGLES
- HOT Walk Like An Egyptian [1]...Bangles
- R&B Love You Down [2]...Ready For The World
- C&W Too Much Is Not Enough [1]...
  The Bellamy Brothers with The Forester Sisters
- A/C Love Is Forever [1]...Billy Ocean

ALBUMS
- POP Bruce Springsteen & The E Street Band
  Live/1975-85 [4]...Bruce Springsteen
- R&B Just Like The First Time [3]...Freddie Jackson
- C&W The Touch [6]...Alabama

December 27, 1986
SINGLES
- HOT Walk Like An Egyptian [2]...Bangles
- R&B Girlfriend [1]...Bobby Brown
- C&W Mind Your Own Business [1]...Hank Williams, Jr.
- A/C Love Is Forever [2]...Billy Ocean

ALBUMS
- POP Bruce Springsteen & The E Street Band
  Live/1975-85 [5]...Bruce Springsteen
- R&B Just Like The First Time [4]...Freddie Jackson
- C&W The Touch [7]...Alabama

January 3, 1987
SINGLES
- HOT Walk Like An Egyptian [3]...Bangles
- R&B Girlfriend [2]...Bobby Brown
- C&W Mind Your Own Business [2]...Hank Williams, Jr.
- A/C Love Is Forever [3]...Billy Ocean

ALBUMS
- POP Bruce Springsteen & The E Street Band
  Live/1975-85 [6]...Bruce Springsteen
- R&B Just Like The First Time [5]...Freddie Jackson
- C&W The Touch [8]...Alabama

January 10, 1987
SINGLES
- HOT Walk Like An Egyptian [4]...Bangles
- R&B Control [1]...Janet Jackson
- C&W Give Me Wings [1]...Michael Johnson
- A/C This Is The Time [1]...Billy Joel

ALBUMS
- POP Bruce Springsteen & The E Street Band
  Live/1975-85 [7]...Bruce Springsteen
- R&B Just Like The First Time [6]...Freddie Jackson
- C&W The Touch [9]...Alabama

January 17, 1987
SINGLES
- HOT Shake You Down [1]...Gregory Abbott
- R&B Stop To Love [1]...Luther Vandross
- C&W What Am I Gonna Do About You [1]...Reba McEntire
- A/C This Is The Time [2]...Billy Joel

ALBUMS
- POP Slippery When Wet [2]...Bon Jovi
- R&B Just Like The First Time [7]...Freddie Jackson
- C&W The Touch [10]...Alabama

January 24, 1987
SINGLES
- HOT *At This Moment [1]...Billy Vera & The Beaters
- R&B Stop To Love [2]...Luther Vandross
- C&W Cry Myself To Sleep [1]...The Judds
- A/C This Is The Time [3]...Billy Joel

ALBUMS
- POP Slippery When Wet [3]...Bon Jovi
- R&B Just Like The First Time [8]...Freddie Jackson
- C&W What Am I Gonna Do About You [1]...Reba McEntire

January 31, 1987
SINGLES
- HOT At This Moment [2]...Billy Vera & The Beaters
- R&B Candy [1]...Cameo
- C&W You Still Move Me [1]...Dan Seals
- A/C At This Moment [1]...Billy Vera & The Beaters

ALBUMS
- POP Slippery When Wet [4]...Bon Jovi
- R&B Just Like The First Time [9]...Freddie Jackson
- C&W What Am I Gonna Do About You [2]...Reba McEntire

February 7, 1987
SINGLES
- HOT Open Your Heart [1]...Madonna
- R&B Candy [2]...Cameo
- C&W Leave Me Lonely [1]...Gary Morris
- A/C Ballerina Girl [1]...Lionel Richie

ALBUMS
- POP Slippery When Wet [5]...Bon Jovi
- R&B Just Like The First Time [10]...Freddie Jackson
- C&W What Am I Gonna Do About You [3]...Reba McEntire

February 14, 1987
SINGLES
- HOT Livin' On A Prayer [1]...Bon Jovi
- R&B Falling [1]...Melba Moore
- C&W How Do I Turn You On [1]...Ronnie Milsap
- A/C Ballerina Girl [2]...Lionel Richie

ALBUMS
- POP Slippery When Wet [6]...Bon Jovi
- R&B Just Like The First Time [11]...Freddie Jackson
- C&W Ocean Front Property [1]...George Strait

February 21, 1987
SINGLES
- HOT   Livin' On A Prayer [2]...Bon Jovi
- R&B   Have You Ever Loved Somebody [1]...Freddie Jackson
- C&W   Straight To The Heart [1]...Crystal Gayle
- A/C   Ballerina Girl [3]...Lionel Richie

ALBUMS
- POP   Slippery When Wet [7]...Bon Jovi
- R&B   Just Like The First Time [12]...Freddie Jackson
- C&W   Ocean Front Property [2]...George Strait

February 28, 1987
SINGLES
- HOT   Livin' On A Prayer [3]...Bon Jovi
- R&B   Have You Ever Loved Somebody [2]...Freddie Jackson
- C&W   I Can't Win For Losin' You [1]...Earl Thomas Conley
- A/C   Ballerina Girl [4]...Lionel Richie

ALBUMS
- POP   Slippery When Wet [8]...Bon Jovi
- R&B   Just Like The First Time [13]...Freddie Jackson
- C&W   Ocean Front Property [3]...George Strait

March 7, 1987
SINGLES
- HOT   Livin' On A Prayer [4]...Bon Jovi
- R&B   Slow Down [1]...Loose Ends
- C&W   Mornin' Ride [1]...Lee Greenwood
- A/C   You Got It All [1]...The Jets

ALBUMS
- POP   Licensed To Ill [1]...Beastie Boys
- R&B   Just Like The First Time [14]...Freddie Jackson
- C&W   Ocean Front Property [4]...George Strait

March 14, 1987
SINGLES
- HOT   Jacob's Ladder [1]...Huey Lewis and the News
- R&B   Let's Wait Awhile [1]...Janet Jackson
- C&W   Baby's Got A New Baby [1]...S-K-O
- A/C   You Got It All [2]...The Jets

ALBUMS
- POP   Licensed To Ill [2]...Beastie Boys
- R&B   Just Like The First Time [15]...Freddie Jackson
- C&W   Ocean Front Property [5]...George Strait

March 21, 1987
SINGLES
- HOT   Lean On Me [1]...Club Nouveau
- R&B   Looking For A New Love [1]...Jody Watley
- C&W   I'll Still Be Loving You [1]...Restless Heart
- A/C   Mandolin Rain [1]...Bruce Hornsby & The Range

ALBUMS
- POP   Licensed To Ill [3]...Beastie Boys
- R&B   Just Like The First Time [16]...Freddie Jackson
- C&W   Heartland [1]...The Judds

March 28, 1987
SINGLES
- HOT   Lean On Me [2]...Club Nouveau
- R&B   Looking For A New Love [2]...Jody Watley
- C&W   Small Town Girl [1]...Steve Wariner
- A/C   Mandolin Rain [2]...Bruce Hornsby & The Range

ALBUMS
- POP   Licensed To Ill [4]...Beastie Boys
- R&B   Just Like The First Time [17]...Freddie Jackson
- C&W   Heartland [2]...The Judds

April 4, 1987
SINGLES
- HOT   *Nothing's Gonna Stop Us Now [1]...Starship
- R&B   Looking For A New Love [3]...Jody Watley
- C&W   Ocean Front Property [1]...George Strait
- A/C   Mandolin Rain [3]...Bruce Hornsby & The Range

ALBUMS
- POP   Licensed To Ill [5]...Beastie Boys
- R&B   Just Like The First Time [18]...Freddie Jackson
- C&W   Heartland [3]...The Judds

April 11, 1987
SINGLES
- HOT   Nothing's Gonna Stop Us Now [2]...Starship
- R&B   Sign 'O' The Times [1]...Prince
- C&W   "You've Got" The Touch [1]...Alabama
- A/C   Nothing's Gonna Stop Us Now [1]...Starship

ALBUMS
- POP   Licensed To Ill [6]...Beastie Boys
- R&B   Just Like The First Time [19]...Freddie Jackson
- C&W   Hank "Live" [1]...Hank Williams, Jr.

April 18, 1987
SINGLES
- HOT   I Knew You Were Waiting (For Me) [1]...Aretha Franklin & George Michael
- R&B   Sign 'O' The Times [2]...Prince
- C&W   Kids Of The Baby Boom [1]...The Bellamy Brothers
- A/C   Nothing's Gonna Stop Us Now [2]...Starship

ALBUMS
- POP   Licensed To Ill [7]...Beastie Boys
- R&B   Just Like The First Time [20]...Freddie Jackson
- C&W   Wheels [1]...Restless Heart

April 25, 1987
SINGLES
- HOT I Knew You Were Waiting (For Me) [2]...Aretha Franklin & George Michael
- R&B Sign 'O' The Times [3]...Prince
- C&W Rose In Paradise [1]...Waylon Jennings
- A/C The Finer Things [1]...Steve Winwood

ALBUMS
- POP The Joshua Tree [1]...U2
- R&B Just Like The First Time [21]...Freddie Jackson
- C&W Ocean Front Property [6]...George Strait

May 2, 1987
SINGLES
- HOT (I Just) Died In Your Arms [1]...Cutting Crew
- R&B Don't Disturb This Groove [1]...The System
- C&W Don't Go To Strangers [1]...T. Graham Brown
- A/C The Finer Things [2]...Steve Winwood

ALBUMS
- POP The Joshua Tree [2]...U2
- R&B Just Like The First Time [22]...Freddie Jackson
- C&W Trio [1]...Dolly Parton, Linda Ronstadt, Emmylou Harris

May 9, 1987
SINGLES
- HOT (I Just) Died In Your Arms [2]...Cutting Crew
- R&B There's Nothing Better Than Love [1]...Luther Vandross with Gregory Hines
- C&W The Moon Is Still Over Her Shoulder [1]...Michael Johnson
- A/C The Finer Things [3]...Steve Winwood

ALBUMS
- POP The Joshua Tree [3]...U2
- R&B Just Like The First Time [23]...Freddie Jackson
- C&W Trio [2]...Dolly Parton, Linda Ronstadt, Emmylou Harris

May 16, 1987
SINGLES
- HOT With Or Without You [1]...U2
- R&B *Always [1]...Atlantic Starr
- C&W To Know Him Is To Love Him [1]...Dolly Parton, Linda Ronstadt, Emmylou Harris
- A/C Just To See Her [1]...Smokey Robinson

ALBUMS
- POP The Joshua Tree [4]...U2
- R&B Give Me The Reason [2]...Luther Vandross
- C&W Trio [3]...Dolly Parton, Linda Ronstadt, Emmylou Harris

May 23, 1987
SINGLES
- HOT With Or Without You [2]...U2
- R&B Always [2]...Atlantic Starr
- C&W Can't Stop My Heart From Loving You [1]...The O'Kanes
- A/C La Isla Bonita [1]...Madonna

ALBUMS
- POP The Joshua Tree [5]...U2
- R&B Just Like The First Time [24]...Freddie Jackson
- C&W Trio [4]...Dolly Parton, Linda Ronstadt, Emmylou Harris

May 30, 1987
SINGLES
- HOT With Or Without You [3]...U2
- R&B *Head To Toe [1]...Lisa Lisa & Cult Jam
- C&W It Takes A Little Rain (To Make Love Grow) [1]...The Oak Ridge Boys
- A/C Always [1]...Atlantic Starr

ALBUMS
- POP The Joshua Tree [6]...U2
- R&B Just Like The First Time [25]...Freddie Jackson
- C&W Trio [5]...Dolly Parton, Linda Ronstadt, Emmylou Harris

June 6, 1987
SINGLES
- HOT You Keep Me Hangin' On [1]...Kim Wilde
- R&B Head To Toe [2]...Lisa Lisa & Cult Jam
- C&W I Will Be There [1]...Dan Seals
- A/C Always [2]...Atlantic Starr

ALBUMS
- POP The Joshua Tree [7]...U2
- R&B Jody Watley [1]...Jody Watley
- C&W Hillbilly Deluxe [1]...Dwight Yoakam

June 13, 1987
SINGLES
- HOT Always [1]...Atlantic Starr
- R&B Rock Steady [1]...The Whispers
- C&W Forever And Ever, Amen [1]...Randy Travis
- A/C In Too Deep [1]...Genesis

ALBUMS
- POP The Joshua Tree [8]...U2
- R&B Just Like The First Time [26]...Freddie Jackson
- C&W Hillbilly Deluxe [2]...Dwight Yoakam

June 20, 1987
SINGLES
- HOT Head To Toe [1]...Lisa Lisa & Cult Jam
- R&B Diamonds [1]...Herb Alpert
- C&W Forever And Ever, Amen [2]...Randy Travis
- A/C In Too Deep [2]...Genesis

ALBUMS
- POP The Joshua Tree [9]...U2
- R&B Jody Watley [2]...Jody Watley
- C&W Always & Forever [1]...Randy Travis

June 27, 1987
SINGLES
- HOT *I Wanna Dance With Somebody (Who Loves Me) [1]...Whitney Houston
- R&B Diamonds [2]...Herb Alpert
- C&W Forever And Ever, Amen [3]...Randy Travis
- A/C In Too Deep [3]...Genesis

ALBUMS
- POP Whitney [1]...Whitney Houston
- R&B Jody Watley [3]...Jody Watley
- C&W Always & Forever [2]...Randy Travis

July 4, 1987
SINGLES
- HOT I Wanna Dance With Somebody (Who Loves Me) [2]...Whitney Houston
- R&B I Feel Good All Over [1]...Stephanie Mills
- C&W That Was A Close One [1]...Earl Thomas Conley
- A/C I Wanna Dance With Somebody (Who Loves Me) [1]...Whitney Houston

ALBUMS
- POP Whitney [2]...Whitney Houston
- R&B One Heartbeat [1]...Smokey Robinson
- C&W Always & Forever [3]...Randy Travis

July 11, 1987
SINGLES
- HOT Alone [1]...Heart
- R&B I Feel Good All Over [2]...Stephanie Mills
- C&W All My Ex's Live In Texas [1]...George Strait
- A/C I Wanna Dance With Somebody (Who Loves Me) [2]...Whitney Houston

ALBUMS
- POP Whitney [3]...Whitney Houston
- R&B Bigger And Deffer [1]...L.L. Cool J
- C&W Always & Forever [4]...Randy Travis

July 18, 1987
SINGLES
- HOT Alone [2]...Heart
- R&B I Feel Good All Over [3]...Stephanie Mills
- C&W I Know Where I'm Going [1]...The Judds
- A/C I Wanna Dance With Somebody (Who Loves Me) [3]...Whitney Houston

ALBUMS
- POP Whitney [4]...Whitney Houston
- R&B Bigger And Deffer [2]...L.L. Cool J
- C&W Always & Forever [5]...Randy Travis

July 25, 1987
SINGLES
- HOT Alone [3]...Heart
- R&B Fake [1]...Alexander O'Neal
- C&W The Weekend [1]...Steve Wariner
- A/C Moonlighting [1]...Al Jarreau

ALBUMS
- POP Whitney [5]...Whitney Houston
- R&B Bigger And Deffer [3]...L.L. Cool J
- C&W Always & Forever [6]...Randy Travis

August 1, 1987
SINGLES
- HOT Shakedown [1]...Bob Seger
- R&B Fake [2]...Alexander O'Neal
- C&W Snap Your Fingers [1]...Ronnie Milsap
- A/C Back In The High Life Again [1]...Steve Winwood

ALBUMS
- POP Whitney [6]...Whitney Houston
- R&B Bigger And Deffer [4]...L.L. Cool J
- C&W Always & Forever [7]...Randy Travis

August 8, 1987
SINGLES
- HOT I Still Haven't Found What I'm Looking For [1]...U2
- R&B The Pleasure Principle [1]...Janet Jackson
- C&W One Promise Too Late [1]...Reba McEntire
- A/C Back In The High Life Again [2]...Steve Winwood

ALBUMS
- POP Whitney [7]...Whitney Houston
- R&B Bigger And Deffer [5]...L.L. Cool J
- C&W Always & Forever [8]...Randy Travis

August 15, 1987
SINGLES
- HOT I Still Haven't Found What I'm Looking For [2]...U2
- R&B Jam Tonight [1]...Freddie Jackson
- C&W A Long Line Of Love [1]...Michael Martin Murphey
- A/C Back In The High Life Again [3]...Steve Winwood

ALBUMS
- POP Whitney [8]...Whitney Houston
- R&B Bigger And Deffer [6]...L.L. Cool J
- C&W Always & Forever [9]...Randy Travis

August 22, 1987
SINGLES
- HOT   Who's That Girl [1]...Madonna
- R&B   Casanova [1]...Levert
- C&W   Why Does It Have To Be (Wrong or Right) [1]...Restless Heart
- A/C   Love Power [1]...Dionne Warwick & Jeffrey Osborne

ALBUMS
- POP   Whitney [9]...Whitney Houston
- R&B   Bigger And Deffer [7]...L.L. Cool J
- C&W   Always & Forever [10]...Randy Travis

August 29, 1987
SINGLES
- HOT   La Bamba [1]...Los Lobos
- R&B   Casanova [2]...Levert
- C&W   Born To Boogie [1]...Hank Williams, Jr.
- A/C   *I Just Can't Stop Loving You [1]...Michael Jackson

ALBUMS
- POP   Whitney [10]...Whitney Houston
- R&B   Bigger And Deffer [8]...L.L. Cool J
- C&W   Born To Boogie [1]...Hank Williams, Jr.

September 5, 1987
SINGLES
- HOT   La Bamba [2]...Los Lobos
- R&B   Love Is A House [1]...Force M.D.'s
- C&W   She's Too Good To Be True [1]...Exile
- A/C   I Just Can't Stop Loving You [2]...Michael Jackson

ALBUMS
- POP   Whitney [11]...Whitney Houston
- R&B   If I Were Your Woman [1]...Stephanie Mills
- C&W   Always & Forever [11]...Randy Travis

September 12, 1987
SINGLES
- HOT   La Bamba [3]...Los Lobos
- R&B   Love Is A House [2]...Force M.D.'s
- C&W   Make No Mistake, She's Mine [1]...Ronnie Milsap & Kenny Rogers
- A/C   I Just Can't Stop Loving You [3]...Michael Jackson

ALBUMS
- POP   La Bamba [1]...Los Lobos/Soundtrack
- R&B   Bigger And Deffer [9]...L.L. Cool J
- C&W   Always & Forever [12]...Randy Travis

September 19, 1987
SINGLES
- HOT   I Just Can't Stop Loving You [1]...Michael Jackson
- R&B   I Just Can't Stop Loving You [1]...Michael Jackson
- C&W   This Crazy Love [1]...The Oak Ridge Boys
- A/C   *Didn't We Almost Have It All [1]...Whitney Houston

ALBUMS
- POP   La Bamba [2]...Los Lobos/Soundtrack
- R&B   Bigger And Deffer [10]...L.L. Cool J
- C&W   Always & Forever [13]...Randy Travis

September 26, 1987
SINGLES
- HOT   Didn't We Almost Have It All [1]...Whitney Houston
- R&B   I Need Love [1]...L.L. Cool J
- C&W   Three Time Loser [1]...Dan Seals
- A/C   Didn't We Almost Have It All [2]...Whitney Houston

ALBUMS
- POP   Bad [1]...Michael Jackson
- R&B   Bigger And Deffer [11]...L.L. Cool J
- C&W   Always & Forever [14]...Randy Travis

October 3, 1987
SINGLES
- HOT   Didn't We Almost Have It All [2]...Whitney Houston
- R&B   *Lost In Emotion [1]...Lisa Lisa & Cult Jam
- C&W   You Again [1]...The Forester Sisters
- A/C   Didn't We Almost Have It All [3]...Whitney Houston

ALBUMS
- POP   Bad [2]...Michael Jackson
- R&B   Bad [1]...Michael Jackson
- C&W   Always & Forever [15]...Randy Travis

October 10, 1987
SINGLES
- HOT   Here I Go Again [1]...Whitesnake
- R&B   (You're Puttin') A Rush On Me [1]...Stephanie Mills
- C&W   The Way We Make A Broken Heart [1]...Rosanne Cash
- A/C   Little Lies [1]...Fleetwood Mac

ALBUMS
- POP   Bad [3]...Michael Jackson
- R&B   Bad [2]...Michael Jackson
- C&W   Always & Forever [16]...Randy Travis

October 17, 1987
SINGLES
- HOT   Lost In Emotion [1]...Lisa Lisa & Cult Jam
- R&B   *Bad [1]...Michael Jackson
- C&W   Fishin' In The Dark [1]...Nitty Gritty Dirt Band
- A/C   Little Lies [2]...Fleetwood Mac

ALBUMS
- POP   Bad [4]...Michael Jackson
- R&B   Bad [3]...Michael Jackson
- C&W   Always & Forever [17]...Randy Travis

October 24, 1987

SINGLES
- HOT Bad [1]...Michael Jackson
- R&B Bad [2]...Michael Jackson
- C&W Shine, Shine, Shine [1]...Eddy Raven
- A/C Little Lies [3]...Fleetwood Mac

ALBUMS
- POP Bad [5]...Michael Jackson
- R&B Bad [4]...Michael Jackson
- C&W Always & Forever [18]...Randy Travis

October 31, 1987

SINGLES
- HOT Bad [2]...Michael Jackson
- R&B Bad [3]...Michael Jackson
- C&W Right From The Start [1]...Earl Thomas Conley
- A/C Little Lies [4]...Fleetwood Mac

ALBUMS
- POP Bad [6]...Michael Jackson
- R&B Bad [5]...Michael Jackson
- C&W Always & Forever [19]...Randy Travis

November 7, 1987

SINGLES
- HOT I Think We're Alone Now [1]...Tiffany
- R&B Lovin' You [1]...The O'Jays
- C&W Am I Blue [1]...George Strait
- A/C Breakout [1]...Swing Out Sister

ALBUMS
- POP Tunnel of Love [1]...Bruce Springsteen
- R&B Bad [6]...Michael Jackson
- C&W Greatest Hits, Volume Two [1]...George Strait

November 14, 1987

SINGLES
- HOT I Think We're Alone Now [2]...Tiffany
- R&B Angel [1]...Angela Winbush
- C&W Maybe Your Baby's Got The Blues [1]...The Judds
- A/C Breakout [2]...Swing Out Sister

ALBUMS
- POP Dirty Dancing [1]...Soundtrack
- R&B Bad [7]...Michael Jackson
- C&W Always & Forever [20]...Randy Travis

November 21, 1987

SINGLES
- HOT Mony Mony "Live" [1]...Billy Idol
- R&B Angel [2]...Angela Winbush
- C&W I Won't Need You Anymore (Always And Forever) [1]...Randy Travis
- A/C *(I've Had) The Time Of My Life [1]...Bill Medley & Jennifer Warnes

ALBUMS
- POP Dirty Dancing [2]...Soundtrack
- R&B Bad [8]...Michael Jackson
- C&W Just Us [1]...Alabama

November 28, 1987

SINGLES
- HOT (I've Had) The Time Of My Life [1]...Bill Medley & Jennifer Warnes
- R&B Skeletons [1]...Stevie Wonder
- C&W Lynda [1]...Steve Wariner
- A/C (I've Had) The Time Of My Life [2]...Bill Medley & Jennifer Warnes

ALBUMS
- POP Dirty Dancing [3]...Soundtrack
- R&B Bad [9]...Michael Jackson
- C&W Always & Forever [21]...Randy Travis

December 5, 1987

SINGLES
- HOT Heaven Is A Place On Earth [1]...Belinda Carlisle
- R&B Skeletons [2]...Stevie Wonder
- C&W Somebody Lied [1]...Ricky Van Shelton
- A/C (I've Had) The Time Of My Life [3]...Bill Medley & Jennifer Warnes

ALBUMS
- POP Dirty Dancing [4]...Soundtrack
- R&B Bad [10]...Michael Jackson
- C&W Always & Forever [22]...Randy Travis

December 12, 1987

SINGLES
- HOT Faith [1]...George Michael
- R&B System Of Survival [1]...Earth, Wind & Fire
- C&W The Last One To Know [1]...Reba McEntire
- A/C (I've Had) The Time Of My Life [4]...Bill Medley & Jennifer Warnes

ALBUMS
- POP Dirty Dancing [5]...Soundtrack
- R&B Bad [11]...Michael Jackson
- C&W Always & Forever [23]...Randy Travis

December 19, 1987
SINGLES
- HOT   Faith [2]...George Michael
- R&B   I Want To Be Your Man [1]...Roger
- C&W   Do Ya' [1]...K.T. Oslin
- A/C   *Got My Mind Set On You [1]...George Harrison

ALBUMS
- POP   Dirty Dancing [6]...Soundtrack
- R&B   Characters [1]...Stevie Wonder
- C&W   Always & Forever [24]...Randy Travis

December 26, 1987
SINGLES
- HOT   Faith [3]...George Michael
- R&B   *The Way You Make Me Feel [1]...Michael Jackson
- C&W   Somewhere Tonight [1]...Highway 101
- A/C   Got My Mind Set On You [2]...George Harrison

ALBUMS
- POP   Dirty Dancing [7]...Soundtrack
- R&B   Bad [12]...Michael Jackson
- C&W   Always & Forever [25]...Randy Travis

January 2, 1988
SINGLES
- HOT   Faith [4]...George Michael
- R&B   The Way You Make Me Feel [2]...Michael Jackson
- C&W   Somewhere Tonight [2]...Highway 101
- A/C   Got My Mind Set On You [3]...George Harrison

ALBUMS
- POP   Dirty Dancing [8]...Soundtrack
- R&B   Bad [13]...Michael Jackson
- C&W   Always & Forever [26]...Randy Travis

January 9, 1988
SINGLES
- HOT   So Emotional [1]...Whitney Houston
- R&B   The Way You Make Me Feel [3]...Michael Jackson
- C&W   I Can't Get Close Enough [1]...Exile
- A/C   Got My Mind Set On You [4]...George Harrison

ALBUMS
- POP   Dirty Dancing [9]...Soundtrack
- R&B   Bad [14]...Michael Jackson
- C&W   Always & Forever [27]...Randy Travis

January 16, 1988
SINGLES
- HOT   Got My Mind Set On You [1]...George Harrison
- R&B   The Way You Make Me Feel [4]...Michael Jackson
- C&W   One Friend [1]...Dan Seals
- A/C   Everywhere [1]...Fleetwood Mac

ALBUMS
- POP   Faith [1]...George Michael
- R&B   Bad [15]...Michael Jackson
- C&W   Always & Forever [28]...Randy Travis

January 23, 1988
SINGLES
- HOT   The Way You Make Me Feel [1]...Michael Jackson
- R&B   Love Overboard [1]...Gladys Knight & The Pips
- C&W   Where Do The Nights Go [1]...Ronnie Milsap
- A/C   Everywhere [2]...Fleetwood Mac

ALBUMS
- POP   Tiffany [1]...Tiffany
- R&B   Characters [2]...Stevie Wonder
- C&W   Always & Forever [29]...Randy Travis

January 30, 1988
SINGLES
- HOT   Need You Tonight [1]...INXS
- R&B   I Want Her [1]...Keith Sweat
- C&W   Goin' Gone [1]...Kathy Mattea
- A/C   Everywhere [3]...Fleetwood Mac

ALBUMS
- POP   Tiffany [2]...Tiffany
- R&B   Characters [3]...Stevie Wonder
- C&W   Always & Forever [30]...Randy Travis

February 6, 1988
SINGLES
- HOT   *Could've Been [1]...Tiffany
- R&B   I Want Her [2]...Keith Sweat
- C&W   Wheels [1]...Restless Heart
- A/C   *Could've Been [1]...Tiffany

ALBUMS
- POP   Faith [2]...George Michael
- R&B   Characters [4]...Stevie Wonder
- C&W   Always & Forever [31]...Randy Travis

February 13, 1988
SINGLES
- HOT   Could've Been [2]...Tiffany
- R&B   I Want Her [3]...Keith Sweat
- C&W   Tennessee Flat Top Box [1]...Rosanne Cash
- A/C   Can't Stay Away From You [1]...
         Gloria Estefan & Miami Sound Machine

ALBUMS
- POP   Faith [3]...George Michael
- R&B   Characters [5]...Stevie Wonder
- C&W   Always & Forever [32]...Randy Travis

February 20, 1988
SINGLES
- HOT   *Seasons Change [1]...Expose
- R&B   Girlfriend [1]...Pebbles
- C&W   Twinkle, Twinkle Lucky Star [1]...Merle Haggard
- A/C   *Seasons Change [1]...Expose

ALBUMS
- POP   Faith [4]...George Michael
- R&B   Characters [6]...Stevie Wonder
- C&W   Always & Forever [33]...Randy Travis

February 27, 1988

SINGLES
- *HOT* Father Figure [1]...George Michael
- *R&B* Girlfriend [2]...Pebbles
- *C&W* I Won't Take Less Than Your Love [1]...
  Tanya Tucker with Paul Davis & Paul Overstreet
- *A/C* She's Like The Wind [1]...
  Patrick Swayze featuring Wendy Fraser

ALBUMS
- *POP* Faith [5]...George Michael
- *R&B* All Our Love [1]...Gladys Knight & The Pips
- *C&W* 80's Ladies [1]...K.T. Oslin

March 5, 1988

SINGLES
- *HOT* Father Figure [2]...George Michael
- *R&B* You Will Know [1]...Stevie Wonder
- *C&W* Face To Face [1]...Alabama
- *A/C* She's Like The Wind [2]...
  Patrick Swayze featuring Wendy Fraser

ALBUMS
- *POP* Faith [6]...George Michael
- *R&B* All Our Love [2]...Gladys Knight & The Pips
- *C&W* Wild-Eyed Dream [1]...Ricky Van Shelton

March 12, 1988

SINGLES
- *HOT* *Never Gonna Give You Up [1]...Rick Astley
- *R&B* Fishnet [1]...Morris Day
- *C&W* Too Gone Too Long [1]...Randy Travis
- *A/C* *Never Gonna Give You Up [1]...Rick Astley

ALBUMS
- *POP* Dirty Dancing [10]...Soundtrack
- *R&B* Characters [7]...Stevie Wonder
- *C&W* Always & Forever [34]...Randy Travis

March 19, 1988

SINGLES
- *HOT* Never Gonna Give You Up [2]...Rick Astley
- *R&B* Fishnet [2]...Morris Day
- *C&W* Life Turned Her That Way [1]...Ricky Van Shelton
- *A/C* Never Gonna Give You Up [2]...Rick Astley

ALBUMS
- *POP* Dirty Dancing [11]...Soundtrack
- *R&B* Make It Last Forever [1]...Keith Sweat
- *C&W* Always & Forever [35]...Randy Travis

March 26, 1988

SINGLES
- *HOT* *Man In The Mirror [1]...Michael Jackson
- *R&B* *Man In The Mirror [1]...Michael Jackson
- *C&W* Turn It Loose [1]...The Judds
- *A/C* Never Gonna Give You Up [3]...Rick Astley

ALBUMS
- *POP* Dirty Dancing [12]...Soundtrack
- *R&B* Make It Last Forever [2]...Keith Sweat
- *C&W* Always & Forever [36]...Randy Travis

April 2, 1988

SINGLES
- *HOT* Man In The Mirror [2]...Michael Jackson
- *R&B* *Wishing Well [1]...Terence Trent D'Arby
- *C&W* Love Will Find Its Way To You [1]...Reba McEntire
- *A/C* *Where Do Broken Hearts Go [1]...Whitney Houston

ALBUMS
- *POP* Dirty Dancing [13]...Soundtrack
- *R&B* Make It Last Forever [3]...Keith Sweat
- *C&W* Always & Forever [37]...Randy Travis

April 9, 1988

SINGLES
- *HOT* *Get Outta My Dreams, Get Into My Car [1]...
  Billy Ocean
- *R&B* Ooo La La La [1]...Teena Marie
- *C&W* Famous Last Words Of A Fool [1]...George Strait
- *A/C* Where Do Broken Hearts Go [2]...Whitney Houston

ALBUMS
- *POP* Dirty Dancing [14]...Soundtrack
- *R&B* Bad [16]...Michael Jackson
- *C&W* Always & Forever [38]...Randy Travis

April 16, 1988

SINGLES
- *HOT* Get Outta My Dreams, Get Into My Car [2]...
  Billy Ocean
- *R&B* Get Outta My Dreams, Get Into My Car [1]...
  Billy Ocean
- *C&W* I Wanna Dance With You [1]...Eddie Rabbitt
- *A/C* Where Do Broken Hearts Go [3]...Whitney Houston

ALBUMS
- *POP* Dirty Dancing [15]...Soundtrack
- *R&B* Bad [17]...Michael Jackson
- *C&W* Wild-Eyed Dream [2]...Ricky Van Shelton

April 23, 1988

SINGLES
- HOT Where Do Broken Hearts Go [1]...Whitney Houston
- R&B Da'Butt [1]...E.U.
- C&W I'll Always Come Back [1]...K.T. Oslin
- A/C *Anything For You [1]...
  Gloria Estefan & Miami Sound Machine

ALBUMS
- POP Dirty Dancing [16]...Soundtrack
- R&B Bad [18]...Michael Jackson
- C&W If You Ain't Lovin' You Ain't Livin' [1]...
  George Strait

April 30, 1988

SINGLES
- HOT Where Do Broken Hearts Go [2]...Whitney Houston
- R&B Nite And Day [1]...Al B. Sure!
- C&W It's Such A Small World [1]...
  Rodney Crowell & Rosanne Cash
- A/C Anything For You [2]...
  Gloria Estefan & Miami Sound Machine

ALBUMS
- POP Dirty Dancing [17]...Soundtrack
- R&B Introducing The Hardline According To Terence Trent D'Arby [1]...Terence Trent D'Arby
- C&W If You Ain't Lovin' You Ain't Livin' [2]...
  George Strait

May 7, 1988

SINGLES
- HOT Wishing Well [1]...Terence Trent D'Arby
- R&B Nite And Day [2]...Al B. Sure!
- C&W Cry, Cry, Cry [1]...Highway 101
- A/C Anything For You [3]...
  Gloria Estefan & Miami Sound Machine

ALBUMS
- POP Dirty Dancing [18]...Soundtrack
- R&B Introducing The Hardline According To Terence Trent D'Arby [2]...Terence Trent D'Arby
- C&W Always & Forever [39]...Randy Travis

May 14, 1988

SINGLES
- HOT Anything For You [1]...
  Gloria Estefan & Miami Sound Machine
- R&B Nite And Day [3]...Al B. Sure!
- C&W I'm Gonna Get You [1]...Eddy Raven
- A/C I Don't Want To Live Without You [1]...Foreigner

ALBUMS
- POP Faith [7]...George Michael
- R&B Introducing The Hardline According To Terence Trent D'Arby [3]...Terence Trent D'Arby
- C&W Always & Forever [40]...Randy Travis

May 21, 1988

SINGLES
- HOT Anything For You [2]...
  Gloria Estefan & Miami Sound Machine
- R&B Mercedes Boy [1]...Pebbles
- C&W Eighteen Wheels And A Dozen Roses [1]...
  Kathy Mattea
- A/C Shattered Dreams [1]...Johnny Hates Jazz

ALBUMS
- POP Faith [8]...George Michael
- R&B Faith [1]...George Michael
- C&W Always & Forever [41]...Randy Travis

May 28, 1988

SINGLES
- HOT *One More Try [1]...George Michael
- R&B Just Got Paid [1]...Johnny Kemp
- C&W Eighteen Wheels And A Dozen Roses [2]...
  Kathy Mattea
- A/C *One More Try [1]...George Michael

ALBUMS
- POP Faith [9]...George Michael
- R&B Faith [2]...George Michael
- C&W Always & Forever [42]...Randy Travis

June 4, 1988

SINGLES
- HOT One More Try [2]...George Michael
- R&B Just Got Paid [2]...Johnny Kemp
- C&W What She Is (Is A Woman In Love) [1]...
  Earl Thomas Conley
- A/C One More Try [2]...George Michael

ALBUMS
- POP Faith [10]...George Michael
- R&B Faith [3]...George Michael
- C&W Always & Forever [43]...Randy Travis

June 11, 1988

SINGLES
- HOT One More Try [3]...George Michael
- R&B Little Walter [1]...Tony! Toni! Tone!
- C&W I Told You So [1]...Randy Travis
- A/C One More Try [3]...George Michael

ALBUMS
- POP Faith [11]...George Michael
- R&B Faith [4]...George Michael
- C&W Reba [1]...Reba McEntire

June 18, 1988
SINGLES
- HOT Together Forever [1]...Rick Astley
- R&B One More Try [1]...George Michael
- C&W I Told You So [2]...Randy Travis
- A/C The Valley Road [1]...Bruce Hornsby & The Range

ALBUMS
- POP Faith [12]...George Michael
- R&B Faith [5]...George Michael
- C&W Reba [2]...Reba McEntire

June 25, 1988
SINGLES
- HOT Foolish Beat [1]...Debbie Gibson
- R&B Joy [1]...Teddy Pendergrass
- C&W He's Back And I'm Blue [1]...The Desert Rose Band
- A/C Make It Real [1]...The Jets

ALBUMS
- POP OU812 [1]...Van Halen
- R&B Faith [6]...George Michael
- C&W Reba [3]...Reba McEntire

July 2, 1988
SINGLES
- HOT Dirty Diana [1]...Michael Jackson
- R&B Joy [2]...Teddy Pendergrass
- C&W If It Don't Come Easy [1]...Tanya Tucker
- A/C Make It Real [2]...The Jets

ALBUMS
- POP OU812 [2]...Van Halen
- R&B In Effect Mode [1]...Al B. Sure!
- C&W Reba [4]...Reba McEntire

July 9, 1988
SINGLES
- HOT The Flame [1]...Cheap Trick
- R&B Paradise [1]...Sade
- C&W Fallin' Again [1]...Alabama
- A/C Make It Real [3]...The Jets

ALBUMS
- POP OU812 [3]...Van Halen
- R&B In Effect Mode [2]...Al B. Sure!
- C&W Reba [5]...Reba McEntire

July 16, 1988
SINGLES
- HOT The Flame [2]...Cheap Trick
- R&B Roses Are Red [1]...Mac Band/McCampbell Brothers
- C&W If You Change Your Mind [1]...Rosanne Cash
- A/C Make Me Lose Control [1]...Eric Carmen

ALBUMS
- POP OU812 [4]...Van Halen
- R&B In Effect Mode [3]...Al B. Sure!
- C&W Reba [6]...Reba McEntire

July 23, 1988
SINGLES
- HOT Hold On To The Nights [1]...Richard Marx
- R&B Don't Be Cruel [1]...Bobby Brown
- C&W Set 'Em Up Joe [1]...Vern Gosdin
- A/C Make Me Lose Control [2]...Eric Carmen

ALBUMS
- POP Hysteria [1]...Def Leppard
- R&B In Effect Mode [4]...Al B. Sure!
- C&W Reba [7]...Reba McEntire

July 30, 1988
SINGLES
- HOT *Roll With It [1]...Steve Winwood
- R&B Don't Be Cruel [2]...Bobby Brown
- C&W Don't We All Have The Right [1]...Ricky Van Shelton
- A/C Make Me Lose Control [3]...Eric Carmen

ALBUMS
- POP Hysteria [2]...Def Leppard
- R&B In Effect Mode [5]...Al B. Sure!
- C&W Reba [8]...Reba McEntire

August 6, 1988
SINGLES
- HOT Roll With It [2]...Steve Winwood
- R&B Off On Your Own (Girl) [1]...Al B. Sure!
- C&W Baby Blue [1]...George Strait
- A/C Roll With It [1]...Steve Winwood

ALBUMS
- POP Appetite For Destruction [1]...Guns N' Roses
- R&B In Effect Mode [6]...Al B. Sure!
- C&W Alabama Live [1]...Alabama

August 13, 1988
SINGLES
- HOT Roll With It [3]...Steve Winwood
- R&B Off On Your Own (Girl) [2]...Al B. Sure!
- C&W Don't Close Your Eyes [1]...Keith Whitley
- A/C Roll With It [2]...Steve Winwood

ALBUMS
- POP Hysteria [3]...Def Leppard
- R&B In Effect Mode [7]...Al B. Sure!
- C&W Wild Streak [1]...Hank Williams, Jr.

August 20, 1988
SINGLES
- HOT Roll With It [4]...Steve Winwood
- R&B Loosey's Rap [1]...Rick James/Roxanne Shante
- C&W Bluest Eyes In Texas [1]...Restless Heart
- A/C I Don't Wanna Go On With You Like That [1]...Elton John

ALBUMS
- POP Roll With It [1]...Steve Winwood
- R&B Strictly Business [1]...EPMD
- C&W Wild Streak [2]...Hank Williams, Jr.

August 27, 1988
SINGLES
- HOT   Monkey [1]...George Michael
- R&B   Nice 'N' Slow [1]...Freddie Jackson
- C&W   The Wanderer [1]...Eddie Rabbitt
- A/C   1-2-3 [1]...Gloria Estefan & Miami Sound Machine

ALBUMS
- POP   Tracy Chapman [1]...Tracy Chapman
- R&B   Strictly Business [2]...EPMD
- C&W   Old 8x10 [1]...Randy Travis

September 3, 1988
SINGLES
- HOT   Monkey [2]...George Michael
- R&B   Nice 'N' Slow [2]...Freddie Jackson
- C&W   I Couldn't Leave You If I Tried [1]...Rodney Crowell
- A/C   One Good Woman [1]...Peter Cetera

ALBUMS
- POP   Hysteria [4]...Def Leppard
- R&B   Strictly Business [3]...EPMD
- C&W   Old 8x10 [2]...Randy Travis

September 10, 1988
SINGLES
- HOT   Sweet Child O' Mine [1]...Guns N' Roses
- R&B   Nice 'N' Slow [3]...Freddie Jackson
- C&W   (Do You Love Me) Just Say Yes [1]...Highway 101
- A/C   One Good Woman [2]...Peter Cetera

ALBUMS
- POP   Hysteria [5]...Def Leppard
- R&B   Don't Be Cruel [1]...Bobby Brown
- C&W   Old 8x10 [3]...Randy Travis

September 17, 1988
SINGLES
- HOT   Sweet Child O' Mine [2]...Guns N' Roses
- R&B   Another Part Of Me [1]...Michael Jackson
- C&W   Joe Knows How To Live [1]...Eddy Raven
- A/C   One Good Woman [3]...Peter Cetera

ALBUMS
- POP   Hysteria [6]...Def Leppard
- R&B   Don't Be Cruel [2]...Bobby Brown
- C&W   Old 8x10 [4]...Randy Travis

September 24, 1988
SINGLES
- HOT   Don't Worry Be Happy [1]...Bobby McFerrin
- R&B   She's On The Left [1]...Jeffrey Osborne
- C&W   Addicted [1]...Dan Seals
- A/C   One Good Woman [4]...Peter Cetera

ALBUMS
- POP   Appetite For Destruction [2]...Guns N' Roses
- R&B   It Takes A Nation Of Millions To Hold Us Back [1]...Public Enemy
- C&W   Old 8x10 [5]...Randy Travis

October 1, 1988
SINGLES
- HOT   Don't Worry Be Happy [2]...Bobby McFerrin
- R&B   Addicted To You [1]...Levert
- C&W   We Believe In Happy Endings [1]...Earl Thomas Conley with Emmylou Harris
- A/C   It Would Take A Strong Strong Man [1]...Rick Astley

ALBUMS
- POP   Appetite For Destruction [3]...Guns N' Roses
- R&B   Don't Be Cruel [3]...Bobby Brown
- C&W   Old 8x10 [6]...Randy Travis

October 8, 1988
SINGLES
- HOT   Love Bites [1]...Def Leppard
- R&B   Addicted To You [2]...Levert
- C&W   Honky Tonk Moon [1]...Randy Travis
- A/C   *Groovy Kind Of Love [1]...Phil Collins

ALBUMS
- POP   Appetite For Destruction [4]...Guns N' Roses
- R&B   Don't Be Cruel [4]...Bobby Brown
- C&W   Old 8x10 [7]...Randy Travis

October 15, 1988
SINGLES
- HOT   Red Red Wine [1]...UB40
- R&B   *My Prerogative [1]...Bobby Brown
- C&W   Streets Of Bakersfield [1]...Dwight Yoakam & Buck Owens
- A/C   Groovy Kind Of Love [2]...Phil Collins

ALBUMS
- POP   New Jersey [1]...Bon Jovi
- R&B   Don't Let Love Slip Away [1]...Freddie Jackson
- C&W   Old 8x10 [8]...Randy Travis

October 22, 1988
SINGLES
- HOT   Groovy Kind Of Love [1]...Phil Collins
- R&B   My Prerogative [2]...Bobby Brown
- C&W   Strong Enough To Bend [1]...Tanya Tucker
- A/C   Groovy Kind Of Love [3]...Phil Collins

ALBUMS
- POP   New Jersey [2]...Bon Jovi
- R&B   Don't Be Cruel [5]...Bobby Brown
- C&W   Buenas Noches From A Lonely Room [1]...Dwight Yoakam

October 29, 1988
SINGLES
- HOT Groovy Kind Of Love [2]...Phil Collins
- R&B The Way You Love Me [1]...Karyn White
- C&W Gonna Take A Lot Of River [1]...The Oak Ridge Boys
- A/C One Moment In Time [1]...Whitney Houston

ALBUMS
- POP New Jersey [3]...Bon Jovi
- R&B Don't Be Cruel [6]...Bobby Brown
- C&W Greatest Hits [1]...The Judds

November 5, 1988
SINGLES
- HOT Kokomo [1]...The Beach Boys
- R&B Any Love [1]...Luther Vandross
- C&W Darlene [1]...T. Graham Brown
- A/C One Moment In Time [2]...Whitney Houston

ALBUMS
- POP New Jersey [4]...Bon Jovi
- R&B Don't Be Cruel [7]...Bobby Brown
- C&W Loving Proof [1]...Ricky Van Shelton

November 12, 1988
SINGLES
- HOT Wild, Wild West [1]...The Escape Club
- R&B *Giving You The Best That I Got [1]...Anita Baker
- C&W Runaway Train [1]...Rosanne Cash
- A/C How Can I Fall? [1]...Breathe

ALBUMS
- POP Rattle And Hum [1]...U2/Soundtrack
- R&B Don't Be Cruel [8]...Bobby Brown
- C&W Loving Proof [2]...Ricky Van Shelton

November 19, 1988
SINGLES
- HOT Bad Medicine [1]...Bon Jovi
- R&B Giving You The Best That I Got [2]...Anita Baker
- C&W I'll Leave This World Loving You [1]...Ricky Van Shelton
- A/C How Can I Fall? [2]...Breathe

ALBUMS
- POP Rattle And Hum [2]...U2/Soundtrack
- R&B Giving You The Best That I Got [1]...Anita Baker
- C&W Loving Proof [3]...Ricky Van Shelton

November 26, 1988
SINGLES
- HOT Bad Medicine [2]...Bon Jovi
- R&B Thanks For My Child [1]...Cheryl Pepsii Riley
- C&W I'll Leave This World Loving You [2]...Ricky Van Shelton
- A/C Kissing A Fool [1]...George Michael

ALBUMS
- POP Rattle And Hum [3]...U2/Soundtrack
- R&B Any Love [1]...Luther Vandross
- C&W Loving Proof [4]...Ricky Van Shelton

December 3, 1988
SINGLES
- HOT Baby, I Love Your Way/Freebird Medley (Free Baby) [1]...Will To Power
- R&B Hey Lover [1]...Freddie Jackson
- C&W I Know How He Feels [1]...Reba McEntire
- A/C *Look Away [1]...Chicago

ALBUMS
- POP Rattle And Hum [4]...U2/Soundtrack
- R&B Any Love [2]...Luther Vandross
- C&W Loving Proof [5]...Ricky Van Shelton

December 10, 1988
SINGLES
- HOT Look Away [1]...Chicago
- R&B Dial My Heart [1]...The Boys
- C&W If You Ain't Lovin' (You Ain't Livin') [1]...George Strait
- A/C Giving You The Best That I Got [1]...Anita Baker

ALBUMS
- POP Rattle And Hum [5]...U2/Soundtrack
- R&B Giving You The Best That I Got [2]...Anita Baker
- C&W Loving Proof [6]...Ricky Van Shelton

December 17, 1988
SINGLES
- HOT Look Away [2]...Chicago
- R&B Everything I Miss At Home [1]...Cherrelle
- C&W A Tender Lie [1]...Restless Heart
- A/C Waiting For A Star To Fall [1]...Boy Meets Girl

ALBUMS
- POP Rattle And Hum [6]...U2/Soundtrack
- R&B Giving You The Best That I Got [3]...Anita Baker
- C&W Loving Proof [7]...Ricky Van Shelton

December 24, 1988
SINGLES
- HOT Every Rose Has Its Thorn [1]...Poison
- R&B Tumblin' Down [1]...Ziggy Marley & The Melody Makers
- C&W When You Say Nothing At All [1]...Keith Whitley
- A/C *Two Hearts [1]...Phil Collins

ALBUMS
- POP Giving You The Best That I Got [1]...Anita Baker
- R&B Giving You The Best That I Got [4]...Anita Baker
- C&W Loving Proof [8]...Ricky Van Shelton

December 31, 1988
SINGLES
- HOT Every Rose Has Its Thorn [2]...Poison
- R&B Tumblin' Down [2]...Ziggy Marley & The Melody Makers
- C&W When You Say Nothing At All [2]...Keith Whitley
- A/C Two Hearts [2]...Phil Collins

ALBUMS
- POP Giving You The Best That I Got [2]...Anita Baker
- R&B Giving You The Best That I Got [5]...Anita Baker
- C&W Loving Proof [9]...Ricky Van Shelton

January 7, 1989
SINGLES
- HOT Every Rose Has Its Thorn [3]...Poison
- R&B Oasis [1]...Roberta Flack
- C&W Hold Me [1]...K.T. Oslin
- A/C Two Hearts [3]...Phil Collins

ALBUMS
- POP Giving You The Best That I Got [3]...Anita Baker
- R&B Giving You The Best That I Got [6]...Anita Baker
- C&W Old 8x10 [9]...Randy Travis

January 14, 1989
SINGLES
- HOT My Prerogative [1]...Bobby Brown
- R&B Superwoman [1]...Karyn White
- C&W Change Of Heart [1]...The Judds
- A/C Two Hearts [4]...Phil Collins

ALBUMS
- POP Giving You The Best That I Got [4]...Anita Baker
- R&B Giving You The Best That I Got [7]...Anita Baker
- C&W Old 8x10 [10]...Randy Travis

January 21, 1989
SINGLES
- HOT Two Hearts [1]...Phil Collins
- R&B Superwoman [2]...Karyn White
- C&W She's Crazy For Leavin' [1]...Rodney Crowell
- A/C Two Hearts [5]...Phil Collins

ALBUMS
- POP Don't Be Cruel [1]...Bobby Brown
- R&B Giving You The Best That I Got [8]...Anita Baker
- C&W Old 8x10 [11]...Randy Travis

January 28, 1989
SINGLES
- HOT Two Hearts [2]...Phil Collins
- R&B Superwoman [3]...Karyn White
- C&W Deeper Than The Holler [1]...Randy Travis
- A/C As Long As You Follow [1]...Fleetwood Mac

ALBUMS
- POP Don't Be Cruel [2]...Bobby Brown
- R&B Karyn White [1]...Karyn White
- C&W Old 8x10 [12]...Randy Travis

February 4, 1989
SINGLES
- HOT *When I'm With You [1]...Sheriff
- R&B Can You Stand The Rain [1]...New Edition
- C&W What I'd Say [1]...Earl Thomas Conley
- A/C Holding On [1]...Steve Winwood

ALBUMS
- POP Don't Be Cruel [3]...Bobby Brown
- R&B Karyn White [2]...Karyn White
- C&W Old 8x10 [13]...Randy Travis

February 11, 1989
SINGLES
- HOT Straight Up [1]...Paula Abdul
- R&B Can You Stand The Rain [2]...New Edition
- C&W Song Of The South [1]...Alabama
- A/C Holding On [2]...Steve Winwood

ALBUMS
- POP Appetite For Destruction [5]...Guns N' Roses
- R&B Karyn White [3]...Karyn White
- C&W Old 8x10 [14]...Randy Travis

February 18, 1989
SINGLES
- HOT Straight Up [2]...Paula Abdul
- R&B Dreamin' [1]...Vanessa Williams
- C&W Big Wheels In The Moonlight [1]...Dan Seals
- A/C When I'm With You [1]...Sheriff

ALBUMS
- POP Don't Be Cruel [4]...Bobby Brown
- R&B Karyn White [4]...Karyn White
- C&W Old 8x10 [15]...Randy Travis

February 25, 1989
SINGLES
- HOT Straight Up [3]...Paula Abdul
- R&B Dreamin' [2]...Vanessa Williams
- C&W I Sang Dixie [1]...Dwight Yoakam
- A/C *The Living Years [1]...Mike & The Mechanics

ALBUMS
- POP Don't Be Cruel [5]...Bobby Brown
- R&B Karyn White [5]...Karyn White
- C&W Old 8x10 [16]...Randy Travis

March 4, 1989
SINGLES
- HOT Lost In Your Eyes [1]...Debbie Gibson
- R&B Just Because [1]...Anita Baker
- C&W I Still Believe In You [1]...The Desert Rose Band
- A/C The Living Years [2]...Mike & The Mechanics

ALBUMS
- POP Don't Be Cruel [6]...Bobby Brown
- R&B Karyn White [6]...Karyn White
- C&W Loving Proof [10]...Ricky Van Shelton

March 11, 1989
SINGLES
- HOT Lost In Your Eyes [2]...Debbie Gibson
- R&B Just Coolin' [1]...Levert
- C&W Don't You Ever Get Tired (Of Hurting Me) [1]...Ronnie Milsap
- A/C The Living Years [3]...Mike & The Mechanics

ALBUMS
- POP Electric Youth [1]...Debbie Gibson
- R&B Karyn White [7]...Karyn White
- C&W Southern Star [1]...Alabama

March 18, 1989
SINGLES
- HOT Lost In Your Eyes [3]...Debbie Gibson
- R&B Closer Than Friends [1]...Surface
- C&W From A Jack To A King [1]...Ricky Van Shelton
- A/C The Living Years [4]...Mike & The Mechanics

ALBUMS
- POP Electric Youth [2]...Debbie Gibson
- R&B Don't Be Cruel [9]...Bobby Brown
- C&W Southern Star [2]...Alabama

March 25, 1989
SINGLES
- HOT The Living Years [1]...Mike & The Mechanics
- R&B Closer Than Friends [2]...Surface
- C&W New Fool At An Old Game [1]...Reba McEntire
- A/C You Got It [1]...Roy Orbison

ALBUMS
- POP Electric Youth [3]...Debbie Gibson
- R&B Don't Be Cruel [10]...Bobby Brown
- C&W Southern Star [3]...Alabama

April 1, 1989
SINGLES
- HOT *Eternal Flame [1]...Bangles
- R&B Lucky Charm [1]...The Boys
- C&W Baby's Gotten Good At Goodbye [1]...George Strait
- A/C You Got It [2]...Roy Orbison

ALBUMS
- POP Electric Youth [4]...Debbie Gibson
- R&B Don't Be Cruel [11]...Bobby Brown
- C&W Greatest Hits III [1]...Hank Williams, Jr.

April 8, 1989
SINGLES
- HOT The Look [1]...Roxette
- R&B Girl I Got My Eyes On You [1]...Today
- C&W I'm No Stranger To The Rain [1]...Keith Whitley
- A/C Eternal Flame [1]...Bangles

ALBUMS
- POP Electric Youth [5]...Debbie Gibson
- R&B Let's Get It Started [1]...M.C. Hammer
- C&W Greatest Hits III [2]...Hank Williams, Jr.

April 15, 1989
SINGLES
- HOT She Drives Me Crazy [1]...Fine Young Cannibals
- R&B Every Little Step [1]...Bobby Brown
- C&W I'm No Stranger To The Rain [2]...Keith Whitley
- A/C Eternal Flame [2]...Bangles

ALBUMS
- POP Loc-Ed After Dark [1]...Tone Loc
- R&B Guy [1]...Guy
- C&W Greatest Hits III [3]...Hank Williams, Jr.

April 22, 1989
SINGLES
- HOT Like A Prayer [1]...Madonna
- R&B Love Saw It [1]...Karyn White
- C&W The Church On Cumberland Road [1]...Shenandoah
- A/C After All [1]...Cher & Peter Cetera

ALBUMS
- POP Like A Prayer [1]...Madonna
- R&B Guy [2]...Guy
- C&W Greatest Hits III [4]...Hank Williams, Jr.

April 29, 1989
SINGLES
- HOT Like A Prayer [2]...Madonna
- R&B Love Saw It [2]...Karyn White
- C&W The Church On Cumberland Road [2]...Shenandoah
- A/C After All [2]...Cher & Peter Cetera

ALBUMS
- POP Like A Prayer [2]...Madonna
- R&B Guy [3]...Guy
- C&W Beyond The Blue Neon [1]...George Strait

May 6, 1989
SINGLES
- HOT Like A Prayer [3]...Madonna
- R&B Real Love [1]...Jody Watley
- C&W Young Love [1]...The Judds
- A/C After All [3]...Cher & Peter Cetera

ALBUMS
- POP Like A Prayer [3]...Madonna
- R&B Guy [4]...Guy
- C&W Greatest Hits III [5]...Hank Williams, Jr.

May 13, 1989
SINGLES
- HOT I'll Be There For You [1]...Bon Jovi
- R&B Start Of A Romance [1]...Skyy
- C&W Is It Still Over? [1]...Randy Travis
- A/C After All [4]...Cher & Peter Cetera

ALBUMS
- POP Like A Prayer [4]...Madonna
- R&B The Great Adventures Of Slick Rick [1]...Slick Rick
- C&W Greatest Hits III [6]...Hank Williams, Jr.

May 20, 1989
SINGLES
- HOT Forever Your Girl [1]...Paula Abdul
- R&B Start Of A Romance [2]...Skyy
- C&W If I Had You [1]...Alabama
- A/C Second Chance [1]...Thirty Eight Special

ALBUMS
- POP Like A Prayer [5]...Madonna
- R&B Guy [5]...Guy
- C&W Greatest Hits III [7]...Hank Williams, Jr.

May 27, 1989
SINGLES
- HOT Forever Your Girl [2]...Paula Abdul
- R&B My First Love [1]...Atlantic Starr
- C&W After All This Time [1]...Rodney Crowell
- A/C Second Chance [2]...Thirty Eight Special

ALBUMS
- POP Like A Prayer [6]...Madonna
- R&B 3 Feet High And Rising [1]...De La Soul
- C&W Greatest Hits III [8]...Hank Williams, Jr.

June 3, 1989
SINGLES
- HOT Rock On [1]...Michael Damian
- R&B *Miss You Like Crazy [1]...Natalie Cole
- C&W Where Did I Go Wrong [1]...Steve Wariner
- A/C *Miss You Like Crazy [1]...Natalie Cole

ALBUMS
- POP The Raw & The Cooked [1]...Fine Young Cannibals
- R&B 3 Feet High And Rising [2]...De La Soul
- C&W Greatest Hits III [9]...Hank Williams, Jr.

June 10, 1989
SINGLES
- HOT Wind Beneath My Wings [1]...Bette Midler
- R&B Me Myself And I [1]...De La Soul
- C&W Better Man [1]...Clint Black
- A/C Everlasting Love [1]...Howard Jones

ALBUMS
- POP The Raw & The Cooked [2]...Fine Young Cannibals
- R&B 3 Feet High And Rising [3]...De La Soul
- C&W Greatest Hits III [10]...Hank Williams, Jr.

June 17, 1989
SINGLES
- HOT I'll Be Loving You (Forever) [1]...New Kids On The Block
- R&B Have You Had Your Love Today [1]...The O'Jays
- C&W Love Out Loud [1]...Earl Thomas Conley
- A/C Everlasting Love [2]...Howard Jones

ALBUMS
- POP The Raw & The Cooked [3]...Fine Young Cannibals
- R&B 3 Feet High And Rising [4]...De La Soul
- C&W Greatest Hits III [11]...Hank Williams, Jr.

June 24, 1989
SINGLES
- HOT Satisfied [1]...Richard Marx
- R&B Have You Had Your Love Today [2]...The O'Jays
- C&W I Don't Want To Spoil The Party [1]...Rosanne Cash
- A/C *If You Don't Know Me By Now [1]...Simply Red

ALBUMS
- POP The Raw & The Cooked [4]...Fine Young Cannibals
- R&B 3 Feet High And Rising [5]...De La Soul
- C&W Sweet Sixteen [1]...Reba McEntire

July 1, 1989
SINGLES
- HOT Baby Don't Forget My Number [1]...Milli Vanilli
- R&B Show & Tell [1]...Peabo Bryson
- C&W Come From The Heart [1]...Kathy Mattea
- A/C If You Don't Know Me By Now [2]...Simply Red

ALBUMS
- POP The Raw & The Cooked [5]...Fine Young Cannibals
- R&B The Great Adventures Of Slick Rick [2]...Slick Rick
- C&W Sweet Sixteen [2]...Reba McEntire

July 8, 1989
SINGLES
- HOT Good Thing [1]...Fine Young Cannibals
- R&B Keep On Movin' [1]...Soul II Soul
- C&W Lovin' Only Me [1]...Ricky Skaggs
- A/C If You Don't Know Me By Now [3]...Simply Red

ALBUMS
- POP The Raw & The Cooked [6]...Fine Young Cannibals
- R&B The Great Adventures Of Slick Rick [3]...Slick Rick
- C&W Sweet Sixteen [3]...Reba McEntire

July 15, 1989
SINGLES
- HOT If You Don't Know Me By Now [1]...Simply Red
- R&B Keep On Movin' [2]...Soul II Soul
- C&W In A Letter To You [1]...Eddy Raven
- A/C If You Don't Know Me By Now [4]...Simply Red

ALBUMS
- POP The Raw & The Cooked [7]...Fine Young Cannibals
- R&B The Great Adventures Of Slick Rick [4]...Slick Rick
- C&W Sweet Sixteen [4]...Reba McEntire

July 22, 1989

SINGLES
- HOT Toy Soldiers [1]...Martika
- R&B Turned Away [1]...Chuckii Booker
- C&W What's Going On In Your World [1]...George Strait
- A/C If You Don't Know Me By Now [5]...Simply Red

ALBUMS
- POP Batman [1]...Prince/Soundtrack
- R&B Walking With A Panther [1]...L.L. Cool J
- C&W Sweet Sixteen [5]...Reba McEntire

July 29, 1989

SINGLES
- HOT Toy Soldiers [2]...Martika
- R&B Shower Me With Your Love [1]...Surface
- C&W Cathy's Clown [1]...Reba McEntire
- A/C If You Don't Know Me By Now [6]...Simply Red

ALBUMS
- POP Batman [2]...Prince/Soundtrack
- R&B Walking With A Panther [2]...L.L. Cool J
- C&W Sweet Sixteen [6]...Reba McEntire

August 5, 1989

SINGLES
- HOT *Batdance [1]...Prince
- R&B On Our Own [1]...Bobby Brown
- C&W Why'd You Come In Here Lookin' Like That [1]...Dolly Parton
- A/C *Right Here Waiting [1]...Richard Marx

ALBUMS
- POP Batman [3]...Prince/Soundtrack
- R&B Walking With A Panther [3]...L.L. Cool J
- C&W Sweet Sixteen [7]...Reba McEntire

August 12, 1989

SINGLES
- HOT Right Here Waiting [1]...Richard Marx
- R&B Batdance [1]...Prince
- C&W Timber, I'm Falling In Love [1]...Patty Loveless
- A/C Right Here Waiting [2]...Richard Marx

ALBUMS
- POP Batman [4]...Prince/Soundtrack
- R&B Walking With A Panther [4]...L.L. Cool J
- C&W Sweet Sixteen [8]...Reba McEntire

August 19, 1989

SINGLES
- HOT Right Here Waiting [2]...Richard Marx
- R&B Something In The Way (You Make Me Feel) [1]...Stephanie Mills
- C&W Sunday In The South [1]...Shenandoah
- A/C Right Here Waiting [3]...Richard Marx

ALBUMS
- POP Batman [5]...Prince/Soundtrack
- R&B Walking With A Panther [5]...L.L. Cool J
- C&W Sweet Sixteen [9]...Reba McEntire

August 26, 1989

SINGLES
- HOT Right Here Waiting [3]...Richard Marx
- R&B It's No Crime [1]...Babyface
- C&W Are You Ever Gonna Love Me [1]...Holly Dunn
- A/C Right Here Waiting [4]...Richard Marx

ALBUMS
- POP Batman [6]...Prince/Soundtrack
- R&B Big Tyme [1]...Heavy D. & The Boyz
- C&W Sweet Sixteen [10]...Reba McEntire

September 2, 1989

SINGLES
- HOT Cold Hearted [1]...Paula Abdul
- R&B It's No Crime [2]...Babyface
- C&W I'm Still Crazy [1]...Vern Gosdin
- A/C Right Here Waiting [5]...Richard Marx

ALBUMS
- POP Repeat Offender [1]...Richard Marx
- R&B Keep On Movin' [1]...Soul II Soul
- C&W Sweet Sixteen [11]...Reba McEntire

September 9, 1989

SINGLES
- HOT Hangin' Tough [1]...New Kids On The Block
- R&B My Fantasy [1]...Teddy Riley Featuring Guy
- C&W I Wonder Do You Think Of Me [1]...Keith Whitley
- A/C Right Here Waiting [6]...Richard Marx

ALBUMS
- POP Hangin' Tough [1]...New Kids On The Block
- R&B Big Tyme [2]...Heavy D. & The Boyz
- C&W Sweet Sixteen [12]...Reba McEntire

September 16, 1989

SINGLES
- HOT Don't Wanna Lose You [1]...Gloria Estefan
- R&B Remember (The First Time) [1]...Eric Gable
- C&W Nothing I Can Do About It Now [1]...Willie Nelson
- A/C One [1]...Bee Gees

ALBUMS
- POP Hangin' Tough [2]...New Kids On The Block
- R&B Unfinished Business [1]...EPMD
- C&W Sweet Sixteen [13]...Reba McEntire

September 23, 1989

SINGLES
- HOT Girl I'm Gonna Miss You [1]...Milli Vanilli
- R&B Can't Get Over You [1]...Maze Featuring Frankie Beverly
- C&W Above And Beyond [1]...Rodney Crowell
- A/C One [2]...Bee Gees

ALBUMS
- POP Girl You Know It's True [1]...Milli Vanilli
- R&B Unfinished Business [2]...EPMD
- C&W Killin' Time [1]...Clint Black

September 30, 1989

SINGLES
- HOT Girl I'm Gonna Miss You [2]...Milli Vanilli
- R&B Can't Get Over You [2]...Maze Featuring Frankie Beverly
- C&W Let Me Tell You About Love [1]...The Judds
- A/C If I Could Turn Back Time [1]...Cher

ALBUMS
- POP Girl You Know It's True [2]...Milli Vanilli
- R&B No One Can Do It Better [1]...The D.O.C.
- C&W Killin' Time [2]...Clint Black

October 7, 1989

SINGLES
- HOT *Miss You Much [1]...Janet Jackson
- R&B Back To Life (However Do You Want Me) [1]...Soul II Soul
- C&W I Got Dreams [1]...Steve Wariner
- A/C Cherish [1]...Madonna

ALBUMS
- POP Forever Your Girl [1]...Paula Abdul
- R&B No One Can Do It Better [2]...The D.O.C.
- C&W Killin' Time [3]...Clint Black

October 14, 1989

SINGLES
- HOT Miss You Much [2]...Janet Jackson
- R&B Miss You Much [1]...Janet Jackson
- C&W Killin' Time [1]...Clint Black
- A/C Cherish [2]...Madonna

ALBUMS
- POP Dr. Feelgood [1]...Motley Crue
- R&B Tender Lover [1]...Babyface
- C&W Killin' Time [4]...Clint Black

October 21, 1989

SINGLES
- HOT Miss You Much [3]...Janet Jackson
- R&B Miss You Much [2]...Janet Jackson
- C&W Living Proof [1]...Ricky Van Shelton
- A/C Healing Hands [1]...Elton John

ALBUMS
- POP Dr. Feelgood [2]...Motley Crue
- R&B Tender Lover [2]...Babyface
- C&W Killin' Time [5]...Clint Black

October 28, 1989

SINGLES
- HOT Miss You Much [4]...Janet Jackson
- R&B Baby Come To Me [1]...Regina Belle
- C&W High Cotton [1]...Alabama
- A/C Don't Know Much [1]...Linda Ronstadt/Aaron Neville

ALBUMS
- POP Janet Jackson's Rhythm Nation 1814 [1]...Janet Jackson
- R&B Tender Lover [3]...Babyface
- C&W Killin' Time [6]...Clint Black

November 4, 1989

SINGLES
- HOT Listen To Your Heart [1]...Roxette
- R&B You Are My Everything [1]...Surface
- C&W Ace In The Hole [1]...George Strait
- A/C Don't Know Much [2]...Linda Ronstadt/Aaron Neville

ALBUMS
- POP Janet Jackson's Rhythm Nation 1814 [2]...Janet Jackson
- R&B Tender Lover [4]...Babyface
- C&W No Holdin' Back [1]...Randy Travis

November 11, 1989

SINGLES
- HOT When I See You Smile [1]...Bad English
- R&B You Are My Everything [2]...Surface
- C&W Burnin' Old Memories [1]...Kathy Mattea
- A/C Don't Know Much [3]...Linda Ronstadt/Aaron Neville

ALBUMS
- POP Janet Jackson's Rhythm Nation 1814 [3]...Janet Jackson
- R&B Silky Soul [1]...Maze Featuring Frankie Beverly
- C&W No Holdin' Back [2]...Randy Travis

November 18, 1989

SINGLES
- HOT When I See You Smile [2]...Bad English
- R&B Don't Take It Personal [1]...Jermaine Jackson
- C&W Bayou Boys [1]...Eddy Raven
- A/C Don't Know Much [4]...Linda Ronstadt/Aaron Neville

ALBUMS
- POP Janet Jackson's Rhythm Nation 1814 [4]...Janet Jackson
- R&B Janet Jackson's Rhythm Nation 1814 [1]...Janet Jackson
- C&W No Holdin' Back [3]...Randy Travis

November 25, 1989
SINGLES
- HOT Blame It On The Rain [1]...Milli Vanilli
- R&B Home [1]...Stephanie Mills
- C&W Yellow Roses [1]...Dolly Parton
- A/C Don't Know Much [5]...Linda Ronstadt/Aaron Neville

ALBUMS
- POP Girl You Know It's True [3]...Milli Vanilli
- R&B Janet Jackson's Rhythm Nation 1814 [2]...Janet Jackson
- C&W No Holdin' Back [4]...Randy Travis

December 2, 1989
SINGLES
- HOT Blame It On The Rain [2]...Milli Vanilli
- R&B Here And Now [1]...Luther Vandross
- C&W It's Just A Matter Of Time [1]...Randy Travis
- A/C *Another Day In Paradise [1]...Phil Collins

ALBUMS
- POP Girl You Know It's True [4]...Milli Vanilli
- R&B Stay With Me [1]...Regina Belle
- C&W No Holdin' Back [5]...Randy Travis

December 9, 1989
SINGLES
- HOT We Didn't Start The Fire [1]...Billy Joel
- R&B Here And Now [2]...Luther Vandross
- C&W If Tomorrow Never Comes [1]...Garth Brooks
- A/C Another Day In Paradise [2]...Phil Collins

ALBUMS
- POP Girl You Know It's True [5]...Milli Vanilli
- R&B Janet Jackson's Rhythm Nation 1814 [3]...Janet Jackson
- C&W No Holdin' Back [6]...Randy Travis

December 16, 1989
SINGLES
- HOT We Didn't Start The Fire [2]...Billy Joel
- R&B Ain't Nuthin' In The World [1]...Miki Howard
- C&W Two Dozen Roses [1]...Shenandoah
- A/C Another Day In Paradise [3]...Phil Collins

ALBUMS
- POP Storm Front [1]...Billy Joel
- R&B Tender Lover [5]...Babyface
- C&W No Holdin' Back [7]...Randy Travis

December 23, 1989
SINGLES
- HOT Another Day In Paradise [1]...Phil Collins
- R&B All Of My Love [1]...The Gap Band
- C&W A Woman In Love [1]...Ronnie Milsap
- A/C Another Day In Paradise [4]...Phil Collins

ALBUMS
- POP Girl You Know It's True [6]...Milli Vanilli
- R&B Tender Lover [6]...Babyface
- C&W No Holdin' Back [8]...Randy Travis

December 30, 1989
SINGLES
- HOT Another Day In Paradise [2]...Phil Collins
- R&B All Of My Love [2]...The Gap Band
- C&W A Woman In Love [2]...Ronnie Milsap
- A/C Another Day In Paradise [5]...Phil Collins

ALBUMS
- POP Girl You Know It's True [7]...Milli Vanilli
- R&B Tender Lover [7]...Babyface
- C&W No Holdin' Back [9]...Randy Travis

January 6, 1990
SINGLES
- HOT Another Day In Paradise [3]...Phil Collins
- R&B Tender Lover [1]...Babyface
- C&W Who's Lonely Now [1]...Highway 101
- A/C *How Am I Supposed To Live Without You [1]...Michael Bolton

ALBUMS
- POP ...But Seriously [1]...Phil Collins
- R&B Tender Lover [8]...Babyface
- C&W No Holdin' Back [10]...Randy Travis

January 13, 1990
SINGLES
- HOT Another Day In Paradise [4]...Phil Collins
- R&B Rhythm Nation [1]...Janet Jackson
- C&W It Ain't Nothin' [1]...Keith Whitley
- A/C How Am I Supposed To Live Without You [2]...Michael Bolton

ALBUMS
- POP Girl You Know It's True [8]...Milli Vanilli
- R&B Tender Lover [9]...Babyface
- C&W No Holdin' Back [11]...Randy Travis

January 20, 1990

SINGLES
- *HOT* How Am I Supposed To Live Without You [1]...Michael Bolton
- *R&B* I'll Be Good To You [1]...Quincy Jones Feat. Ray Charles & Chaka Khan
- *C&W* Nobody's Home [1]...Clint Black
- *A/C* Downtown Train [1]...Rod Stewart

ALBUMS
- *POP* ...But Seriously [2]...Phil Collins
- *R&B* Tender Lover [10]...Babyface
- *C&W* No Holdin' Back [12]...Randy Travis

January 27, 1990

SINGLES
- *HOT* How Am I Supposed To Live Without You [2]...Michael Bolton
- *R&B* I'll Be Good To You [2]...Quincy Jones Feat. Ray Charles & Chaka Khan
- *C&W* Nobody's Home [2]...Clint Black
- *A/C* Here We Are [1]...Gloria Estefan

ALBUMS
- *POP* ...But Seriously [3]...Phil Collins
- *R&B* Back On The Block [1]...Quincy Jones
- *C&W* Killin' Time [7]...Clint Black

February 3, 1990

SINGLES
- *HOT* How Am I Supposed To Live Without You [3]...Michael Bolton
- *R&B* Make It Like It Was [1]...Regina Belle
- *C&W* Nobody's Home [3]...Clint Black
- *A/C* Here We Are [2]...Gloria Estefan

ALBUMS
- *POP* Forever Your Girl [2]...Paula Abdul
- *R&B* Back On The Block [2]...Quincy Jones
- *C&W* Killin' Time [8]...Clint Black

February 10, 1990

SINGLES
- *HOT* Opposites Attract [1]...Paula Abdul with The Wild Pair
- *R&B* Real Love [1]...Skyy
- *C&W* Southern Star [1]...Alabama
- *A/C* Here We Are [3]...Gloria Estefan

ALBUMS
- *POP* Forever Your Girl [3]...Paula Abdul
- *R&B* Back On The Block [3]...Quincy Jones
- *C&W* Killin' Time [9]...Clint Black

February 17, 1990

SINGLES
- *HOT* Opposites Attract [2]...Paula Abdul with The Wild Pair
- *R&B* It's Gonna Be Alright [1]...Ruby Turner
- *C&W* On Second Thought [1]...Eddie Rabbitt
- *A/C* Here We Are [4]...Gloria Estefan

ALBUMS
- *POP* Forever Your Girl [4]...Paula Abdul
- *R&B* Back On The Block [4]...Quincy Jones
- *C&W* Killin' Time [10]...Clint Black

February 24, 1990

SINGLES
- *HOT* Opposites Attract [3]...Paula Abdul with The Wild Pair
- *R&B* Where Do We Go From Here [1]...Stacy Lattisaw with Johnny Gill
- *C&W* On Second Thought [2]...Eddie Rabbitt
- *A/C* Here We Are [5]...Gloria Estefan

ALBUMS
- *POP* Forever Your Girl [5]...Paula Abdul
- *R&B* Back On The Block [5]...Quincy Jones
- *C&W* Killin' Time [11]...Clint Black

March 3, 1990

SINGLES
- *HOT* *Escapade [1]...Janet Jackson
- *R&B* Where Do We Go From Here [2]...Stacy Lattisaw with Johnny Gill
- *C&W* No Matter How High [1]...Oak Ridge Boys
- *A/C* All My Life [1]...Linda Ronstadt/Aaron Neville

ALBUMS
- *POP* Forever Your Girl [6]...Paula Abdul
- *R&B* Back On The Block [6]...Quincy Jones
- *C&W* RVS III [1]...Ricky Van Shelton

March 10, 1990

SINGLES
- *HOT* Escapade [2]...Janet Jackson
- *R&B* Escapade [1]...Janet Jackson
- *C&W* Chains [1]...Patty Loveless
- *A/C* All My Life [2]...Linda Ronstadt/Aaron Neville

ALBUMS
- *POP* Forever Your Girl [7]...Paula Abdul
- *R&B* Back On The Block [7]...Quincy Jones
- *C&W* RVS III [2]...Ricky Van Shelton

March 17, 1990
SINGLES
- HOT Escapade [3]...Janet Jackson
- R&B The Secret Garden (Sweet Seduction Suite) [1]...
  Quincy Jones/Al B. Sure!/James Ingram/
  El DeBarge/Barry White
- C&W Hard Rock Bottom Of Your Heart [1]...Randy Travis
- A/C All My Life [3]...Linda Ronstadt/Aaron Neville

ALBUMS
- POP Forever Your Girl [8]...Paula Abdul
- R&B Back On The Block [8]...Quincy Jones
- C&W RVS III [3]...Ricky Van Shelton

March 24, 1990
SINGLES
- HOT Black Velvet [1]...Alannah Myles
- R&B All Around The World [1]...Lisa Stansfield
- C&W Hard Rock Bottom Of Your Heart [2]...Randy Travis
- A/C *Love Will Lead You Back [1]...Taylor Dayne

ALBUMS
- POP Forever Your Girl [9]...Paula Abdul
- R&B Back On The Block [9]...Quincy Jones
- C&W RVS III [4]...Ricky Van Shelton

March 31, 1990
SINGLES
- HOT Black Velvet [2]...Alannah Myles
- R&B All Around The World [2]...Lisa Stansfield
- C&W Hard Rock Bottom Of Your Heart [3]...Randy Travis
- A/C Love Will Lead You Back [2]...Taylor Dayne

ALBUMS
- POP Forever Your Girl [10]...Paula Abdul
- R&B Back On The Block [10]...Quincy Jones
- C&W RVS III [5]...Ricky Van Shelton

April 7, 1990
SINGLES
- HOT Love Will Lead You Back [1]...Taylor Dayne
- R&B Spread My Wings [1]...Troop
- C&W Hard Rock Bottom Of Your Heart [4]...Randy Travis
- A/C Love Will Lead You Back [3]...Taylor Dayne

ALBUMS
- POP Nick Of Time [1]...Bonnie Raitt
- R&B Back On The Block [11]...Quincy Jones
- C&W RVS III [6]...Ricky Van Shelton

April 14, 1990
SINGLES
- HOT I'll Be Your Everything [1]...Tommy Page
- R&B Spread My Wings [2]...Troop
- C&W Five Minutes [1]...Lorrie Morgan
- A/C Love Will Lead You Back [4]...Taylor Dayne

ALBUMS
- POP Nick Of Time [2]...Bonnie Raitt
- R&B Back On The Block [12]...Quincy Jones
- C&W RVS III [7]...Ricky Van Shelton

April 21, 1990
SINGLES
- HOT Nothing Compares 2 U [1]...Sinead O'Connor
- R&B Ready or Not [1]...After 7
- C&W Love On Arrival [1]...Dan Seals
- A/C This Old Heart Of Mine [1]...
  Rod Stewart with Ronald Isley

ALBUMS
- POP Nick Of Time [3]...Bonnie Raitt
- R&B Tender Lover [11]...Babyface
- C&W RVS III [8]...Ricky Van Shelton

April 28, 1990
SINGLES
- HOT Nothing Compares 2 U [2]...Sinead O'Connor
- R&B Ready or Not [2]...After 7
- C&W Love On Arrival [2]...Dan Seals
- A/C This Old Heart Of Mine [2]...
  Rod Stewart with Ronald Isley

ALBUMS
- POP I Do Not Want What I Haven't Got [1]...
  Sinead O'Connor
- R&B Please Hammer Don't Hurt 'Em [1]...M.C. Hammer
- C&W RVS III [9]...Ricky Van Shelton

May 5, 1990
SINGLES
- HOT Nothing Compares 2 U [3]...Sinead O'Connor
- R&B Poison [1]...Bell Biv DeVoe
- C&W Love On Arrival [3]...Dan Seals
- A/C This Old Heart Of Mine [3]...
  Rod Stewart with Ronald Isley

ALBUMS
- POP I Do Not Want What I Haven't Got [2]...
  Sinead O'Connor
- R&B Please Hammer Don't Hurt 'Em [2]...M.C. Hammer
- C&W Killin' Time [12]...Clint Black

May 12, 1990
SINGLES
- HOT Nothing Compares 2 U [4]...Sinead O'Connor
- R&B Poison [2]...Bell Biv DeVoe
- C&W Help Me Hold On [1]...Travis Tritt
- A/C This Old Heart Of Mine [4]...
  Rod Stewart with Ronald Isley

ALBUMS
- POP I Do Not Want What I Haven't Got [3]...
  Sinead O'Connor
- R&B Please Hammer Don't Hurt 'Em [3]...M.C. Hammer
- C&W Killin' Time [13]...Clint Black

May 19, 1990
SINGLES
- HOT Vogue [1]...Madonna
- R&B Rub You The Right Way [1]...Johnny Gill
- C&W Walkin' Away [1]...Clint Black
- A/C This Old Heart Of Mine [5]...
  Rod Stewart with Ronald Isley

ALBUMS
- POP I Do Not Want What I Haven't Got [4]...
  Sinead O'Connor
- R&B Please Hammer Don't Hurt 'Em [4]...M.C. Hammer
- C&W Killin' Time [14]...Clint Black

May 26, 1990
SINGLES
- HOT Vogue [2]...Madonna
- R&B Hold On [1]...En Vogue
- C&W Walkin' Away [2]...Clint Black
- A/C *Hold On [1]...Wilson Phillips

ALBUMS
- POP I Do Not Want What I Haven't Got [5]...
  Sinead O'Connor
- R&B Please Hammer Don't Hurt 'Em [5]...M.C. Hammer
- C&W Killin' Time [15]...Clint Black

June 2, 1990
SINGLES
- HOT Vogue [3]...Madonna
- R&B Hold On [2]...En Vogue
- C&W I've Cried My Last Tear For You [1]...
  Ricky Van Shelton
- A/C Do You Remember? [1]...Phil Collins

ALBUMS
- POP I Do Not Want What I Haven't Got [6]...
  Sinead O'Connor
- R&B Poison [1]...Bell Biv DeVoe
- C&W Killin' Time [16]...Clint Black

June 9, 1990
SINGLES
- HOT Hold On [1]...Wilson Phillips
- R&B The Blues [1]...Tony! Toni! Tone!
- C&W Love Without End, Amen [1]...George Strait
- A/C Do You Remember? [2]...Phil Collins

ALBUMS
- POP Please Hammer Don't Hurt 'Em [1]...M.C. Hammer
- R&B Please Hammer Don't Hurt 'Em [6]...M.C. Hammer
- C&W Killin' Time [17]...Clint Black

June 16, 1990
SINGLES
- HOT It Must Have Been Love [1]...Roxette
- R&B Tomorrow (A Better You, A Better Me) [1]...
  Quincy Jones Featuring Tevin Campbell
- C&W Love Without End, Amen [2]...George Strait
- A/C Do You Remember? [3]...Phil Collins

ALBUMS
- POP Please Hammer Don't Hurt 'Em [2]...M.C. Hammer
- R&B Please Hammer Don't Hurt 'Em [7]...M.C. Hammer
- C&W Killin' Time [18]...Clint Black

June 23, 1990
SINGLES
- HOT It Must Have Been Love [2]...Roxette
- R&B U Can't Touch This [1]...M.C. Hammer
- C&W Love Without End, Amen [3]...George Strait
- A/C Do You Remember? [4]...Phil Collins

ALBUMS
- POP Please Hammer Don't Hurt 'Em [3]...M.C. Hammer
- R&B Please Hammer Don't Hurt 'Em [8]...M.C. Hammer
- C&W Killin' Time [19]...Clint Black

June 30, 1990
SINGLES
- HOT Step By Step [1]...New Kids On The Block
- R&B All I Do Is Think Of You [1]...Troop
- C&W Love Without End, Amen [4]...George Strait
- A/C Do You Remember? [5]...Phil Collins

ALBUMS
- POP Step By Step [1]...New Kids On The Block
- R&B Johnny Gill [1]...Johnny Gill
- C&W Killin' Time [20]...Clint Black

July 7, 1990
SINGLES
- HOT Step By Step [2]...New Kids On The Block
- R&B You Can't Deny It [1]...Lisa Stansfield
- C&W Love Without End, Amen [5]...George Strait
- A/C When I'm Back On My Feet Again [1]...Michael Bolton

ALBUMS
- POP Please Hammer Don't Hurt 'Em [4]...M.C. Hammer
- R&B Please Hammer Don't Hurt 'Em [9]...M.C. Hammer
- C&W Killin' Time [21]...Clint Black

July 14, 1990
SINGLES
- *HOT* Step By Step [3]...New Kids On The Block
- *R&B* My, My, My [1]...Johnny Gill
- *C&W* The Dance [1]...Garth Brooks
- *A/C* When I'm Back On My Feet Again [2]...Michael Bolton

ALBUMS
- *POP* Please Hammer Don't Hurt 'Em [5]...M.C. Hammer
- *R&B* Please Hammer Don't Hurt 'Em [10]...M.C. Hammer
- *C&W* Livin' It Up [1]...George Strait

July 21, 1990
SINGLES
- *HOT* She Ain't Worth It [1]...Glenn Medeiros & Bobby Brown
- *R&B* My, My, My [2]...Johnny Gill
- *C&W* The Dance [2]...Garth Brooks
- *A/C* When I'm Back On My Feet Again [3]...Michael Bolton

ALBUMS
- *POP* Please Hammer Don't Hurt 'Em [6]...M.C. Hammer
- *R&B* Please Hammer Don't Hurt 'Em [11]...M.C. Hammer
- *C&W* Livin' It Up [2]...George Strait

July 28, 1990
SINGLES
- *HOT* She Ain't Worth It [2]...Glenn Medeiros & Bobby Brown
- *R&B* Make You Sweat [1]...Keith Sweat
- *C&W* The Dance [3]...Garth Brooks
- *A/C* Cuts Both Ways [1]...Gloria Estefan

ALBUMS
- *POP* Please Hammer Don't Hurt 'Em [7]...M.C. Hammer
- *R&B* Please Hammer Don't Hurt 'Em [12]...M.C. Hammer
- *C&W* Livin' It Up [3]...George Strait

August 4, 1990
SINGLES
- *HOT* *Vision Of Love [1]...Mariah Carey
- *R&B* Can't Stop [1]...After 7
- *C&W* Good Times [1]...Dan Seals
- *A/C* *Vision Of Love [1]...Mariah Carey

ALBUMS
- *POP* Please Hammer Don't Hurt 'Em [8]...M.C. Hammer
- *R&B* Johnny Gill [2]...Johnny Gill
- *C&W* Killin' Time [22]...Clint Black

August 11, 1990
SINGLES
- *HOT* Vision Of Love [2]...Mariah Carey
- *R&B* Vision Of Love [1]...Mariah Carey
- *C&W* Good Times [2]...Dan Seals
- *A/C* Vision Of Love [2]...Mariah Carey

ALBUMS
- *POP* Please Hammer Don't Hurt 'Em [9]...M.C. Hammer
- *R&B* Johnny Gill [3]...Johnny Gill
- *C&W* Killin' Time [23]...Clint Black

August 18, 1990
SINGLES
- *HOT* Vision Of Love [3]...Mariah Carey
- *R&B* Vision Of Love [2]...Mariah Carey
- *C&W* Next To You, Next To Me [1]...Shenandoah
- *A/C* Vision Of Love [3]...Mariah Carey

ALBUMS
- *POP* Please Hammer Don't Hurt 'Em [10]...M.C. Hammer
- *R&B* Please Hammer Don't Hurt 'Em [13]...M.C. Hammer
- *C&W* Killin' Time [24]...Clint Black

August 25, 1990
SINGLES
- *HOT* Vision Of Love [4]...Mariah Carey
- *R&B* Jerk-Out [1]...The Time
- *C&W* Next To You, Next To Me [2]...Shenandoah
- *A/C* Come Back To Me [1]...Janet Jackson

ALBUMS
- *POP* Please Hammer Don't Hurt 'Em [11]...M.C. Hammer
- *R&B* I'll Give All My Love To You [1]...Keith Sweat
- *C&W* Killin' Time [25]...Clint Black

September 1, 1990
SINGLES
- *HOT* If Wishes Came True [1]...Sweet Sensation
- *R&B* Feels Good [1]...Tony! Toni! Tone!
- *C&W* Next To You, Next To Me [3]...Shenandoah
- *A/C* Come Back To Me [2]...Janet Jackson

ALBUMS
- *POP* Please Hammer Don't Hurt 'Em [12]...M.C. Hammer
- *R&B* Please Hammer Don't Hurt 'Em [14]...M.C. Hammer
- *C&W* Killin' Time [26]...Clint Black

September 8, 1990
SINGLES
- *HOT* Blaze Of Glory [1]...Jon Bon Jovi
- *R&B* Feels Good [2]...Tony! Toni! Tone!
- *C&W* Jukebox In My Mind [1]...Alabama
- *A/C* Come Back To Me [3]...Janet Jackson

ALBUMS
- *POP* Please Hammer Don't Hurt 'Em [13]...M.C. Hammer
- *R&B* Please Hammer Don't Hurt 'Em [15]...M.C. Hammer
- *C&W* Killin' Time [27]...Clint Black

September 15, 1990
SINGLES
- *HOT* *Release Me [1]...Wilson Phillips
- *R&B* Lies [1]...En Vogue
- *C&W* Jukebox In My Mind [2]...Alabama
- *A/C* *Release Me [1]...Wilson Phillips

ALBUMS
- *POP* Please Hammer Don't Hurt 'Em [14]...M.C. Hammer
- *R&B* Please Hammer Don't Hurt 'Em [16]...M.C. Hammer
- *C&W* Killin' Time [28]...Clint Black

September 22, 1990
SINGLES
- HOT Release Me [2]...Wilson Phillips
- R&B Crazy [1]...The Boys
- C&W Jukebox In My Mind [3]...Alabama
- A/C Oh Girl [1]...Paul Young

ALBUMS
- POP Please Hammer Don't Hurt 'Em [15]...M.C. Hammer
- R&B Please Hammer Don't Hurt 'Em [17]...M.C. Hammer
- C&W Killin' Time [29]...Clint Black

September 29, 1990
SINGLES
- HOT (Can't Live Without Your) Love And Affection [1]...Nelson
- R&B Thieves In The Temple [1]...Prince
- C&W Jukebox In My Mind [4]...Alabama
- A/C Oh Girl [2]...Paul Young

ALBUMS
- POP Please Hammer Don't Hurt 'Em [16]...M.C. Hammer
- R&B Please Hammer Don't Hurt 'Em [18]...M.C. Hammer
- C&W Killin' Time [30]...Clint Black

October 6, 1990
SINGLES
- HOT Close To You [1]...Maxi Priest
- R&B Giving You The Benefit [1]...Pebbles
- C&W Friends In Low Places [1]...Garth Brooks
- A/C Oh Girl [3]...Paul Young

ALBUMS
- POP Please Hammer Don't Hurt 'Em [17]...M.C. Hammer
- R&B Please Hammer Don't Hurt 'Em [19]...M.C. Hammer
- C&W Killin' Time [31]...Clint Black

October 13, 1990
SINGLES
- HOT Praying For Time [1]...George Michael
- R&B Giving You The Benefit [2]...Pebbles
- C&W Friends In Low Places [2]...Garth Brooks
- A/C Unchained Melody [1]...The Righteous Brothers

ALBUMS
- POP Please Hammer Don't Hurt 'Em [18]...M.C. Hammer
- R&B Please Hammer Don't Hurt 'Em [20]...M.C. Hammer
- C&W No Fences [1]...Garth Brooks

October 20, 1990
SINGLES
- HOT I Don't Have The Heart [1]...James Ingram
- R&B Giving You The Benefit [3]...Pebbles
- C&W Friends In Low Places [3]...Garth Brooks
- A/C Unchained Melody [2]...The Righteous Brothers

ALBUMS
- POP Please Hammer Don't Hurt 'Em [19]...M.C. Hammer
- R&B Please Hammer Don't Hurt 'Em [21]...M.C. Hammer
- C&W No Fences [2]...Garth Brooks

October 27, 1990
SINGLES
- HOT Black Cat [1]...Janet Jackson
- R&B So You Like What You See [1]...Samuelle
- C&W Friends In Low Places [4]...Garth Brooks
- A/C *Love Takes Time [1]...Mariah Carey

ALBUMS
- POP Please Hammer Don't Hurt 'Em [20]...M.C. Hammer
- R&B Please Hammer Don't Hurt 'Em [22]...M.C. Hammer
- C&W No Fences [3]...Garth Brooks

November 3, 1990
SINGLES
- HOT Ice Ice Baby [1]...Vanilla Ice
- R&B So You Like What You See [2]...Samuelle
- C&W You Lie [1]...Reba McEntire
- A/C From A Distance [1]...Bette Midler

ALBUMS
- POP Please Hammer Don't Hurt 'Em [21]...M.C. Hammer
- R&B Please Hammer Don't Hurt 'Em [23]...M.C. Hammer
- C&W No Fences [4]...Garth Brooks

November 10, 1990
SINGLES
- HOT Love Takes Time [1]...Mariah Carey
- R&B Love Takes Time [1]...Mariah Carey
- C&W Home [1]...Joe Diffie
- A/C From A Distance [2]...Bette Midler

ALBUMS
- POP To The Extreme [1]...Vanilla Ice
- R&B Please Hammer Don't Hurt 'Em [24]...M.C. Hammer
- C&W No Fences [5]...Garth Brooks

November 17, 1990
SINGLES
- HOT Love Takes Time [2]...Mariah Carey
- R&B B.B.D. (I Thought It Was Me)? [1]...Bell Biv DeVoe
- C&W You Really Had Me Going [1]...Holly Dunn
- A/C From A Distance [3]...Bette Midler

ALBUMS
- POP To The Extreme [2]...Vanilla Ice
- R&B Please Hammer Don't Hurt 'Em [25]...M.C. Hammer
- C&W No Fences [6]...Garth Brooks

November 24, 1990
SINGLES
- HOT Love Takes Time [3]...Mariah Carey
- R&B Missunderstanding [1]...Al B. Sure!
- C&W Come Next Monday [1]...K.T. Oslin
- A/C From A Distance [4]...Bette Midler

ALBUMS
- POP To The Extreme [3]...Vanilla Ice
- R&B Please Hammer Don't Hurt 'Em [26]...M.C. Hammer
- C&W Heroes And Friends [1]...Randy Travis

December 1, 1990
SINGLES
- HOT *I'm Your Baby Tonight [1]...Whitney Houston
- R&B *I'm Your Baby Tonight [1]...Whitney Houston
- C&W Come Next Monday [2]...K.T. Oslin
- A/C From A Distance [5]...Bette Midler

ALBUMS
- POP To The Extreme [4]...Vanilla Ice
- R&B Please Hammer Don't Hurt 'Em [27]...M.C. Hammer
- C&W No Fences [7]...Garth Brooks

December 8, 1990
SINGLES
- HOT *Because I Love You (The Postman Song) [1]...Stevie B
- R&B I'm Your Baby Tonight [2]...Whitney Houston
- C&W I've Come To Expect It From You [1]...George Strait
- A/C From A Distance [6]...Bette Midler

ALBUMS
- POP To The Extreme [5]...Vanilla Ice
- R&B Please Hammer Don't Hurt 'Em [28]...M.C. Hammer
- C&W No Fences [8]...Garth Brooks

December 15, 1990
SINGLES
- HOT Because I Love You (The Postman Song) [2]...Stevie B
- R&B Sensitivity [1]...Ralph Tresvant
- C&W I've Come To Expect It From You [2]...George Strait
- A/C You Gotta Love Someone [1]...Elton John

ALBUMS
- POP To The Extreme [6]...Vanilla Ice
- R&B Please Hammer Don't Hurt 'Em [29]...M.C. Hammer
- C&W No Fences [9]...Garth Brooks

December 22, 1990
SINGLES
- HOT Because I Love You (The Postman Song) [3]...Stevie B
- R&B It Never Rains (In Southern California) [1]...Tony! Toni! Tone!
- C&W I've Come To Expect It From You [3]...George Strait
- A/C You Gotta Love Someone [2]...Elton John

ALBUMS
- POP To The Extreme [7]...Vanilla Ice
- R&B I'm Your Baby Tonight [1]...Whitney Houston
- C&W Put Yourself In My Shoes [1]...Clint Black

December 29, 1990
SINGLES
- HOT Because I Love You (The Postman Song) [4]...Stevie B
- R&B It Never Rains (In Southern California) [2]...Tony! Toni! Tone!
- C&W I've Come To Expect It From You [4]...George Strait
- A/C You Gotta Love Someone [3]...Elton John

ALBUMS
- POP To The Extreme [8]...Vanilla Ice
- R&B I'm Your Baby Tonight [2]...Whitney Houston
- C&W Put Yourself In My Shoes [2]...Clint Black

January 5, 1991
SINGLES
- HOT Justify My Love [1]...Madonna
- R&B Love Me Down [1]...Freddie Jackson
- C&W I've Come To Expect It From You [5]...George Strait
- A/C You Gotta Love Someone [4]...Elton John

ALBUMS
- POP To The Extreme [9]...Vanilla Ice
- R&B I'm Your Baby Tonight [3]...Whitney Houston
- C&W Put Yourself In My Shoes [3]...Clint Black

January 12, 1991
SINGLES
- HOT Justify My Love [2]...Madonna
- R&B Love Me Down [2]...Freddie Jackson
- C&W Unanswered Prayers [1]...Garth Brooks
- A/C You Gotta Love Someone [5]...Elton John

ALBUMS
- POP To The Extreme [10]...Vanilla Ice
- R&B I'm Your Baby Tonight [4]...Whitney Houston
- C&W Put Yourself In My Shoes [4]...Clint Black

January 19, 1991
SINGLES
- HOT Love Will Never Do (Without You) [1]...Janet Jackson
- R&B *The First Time [1]...Surface
- C&W Unanswered Prayers [2]...Garth Brooks
- A/C Because I Love You (The Postman Song) [1]...Stevie B

ALBUMS
- POP To The Extreme [11]...Vanilla Ice
- R&B I'm Your Baby Tonight [5]...Whitney Houston
- C&W Put Yourself In My Shoes [5]...Clint Black

January 26, 1991
SINGLES
- HOT The First Time [1]...Surface
- R&B Love Makes Things Happen [1]...Pebbles
- C&W Forever's As Far As I'll Go [1]...Alabama
- A/C Because I Love You (The Postman Song) [2]...Stevie B

ALBUMS
- POP To The Extreme [12]...Vanilla Ice
- R&B I'm Your Baby Tonight [6]...Whitney Houston
- C&W Put Yourself In My Shoes [6]...Clint Black

February 2, 1991
SINGLES
- HOT   The First Time [2]...Surface
- R&B   Love Makes Things Happen [2]...Pebbles
- C&W   Daddy's Come Around [1]...Paul Overstreet
- A/C   The First Time [1]...Surface

ALBUMS
- POP   To The Extreme [13]...Vanilla Ice
- R&B   The Future [1]...Guy
- C&W   Put Yourself In My Shoes [7]...Clint Black

February 9, 1991
SINGLES
- HOT   *Gonna Make You Sweat (Everybody Dance Now) [1]...C & C Music Factory Featuring Freedom Williams
- R&B   You Don't Have To Worry [1]...En Vogue
- C&W   Brother Jukebox [1]...Mark Chesnutt
- A/C   The First Time [2]...Surface

ALBUMS
- POP   To The Extreme [14]...Vanilla Ice
- R&B   The Future [2]...Guy
- C&W   No Fences [10]...Garth Brooks

February 16, 1991
SINGLES
- HOT   Gonna Make You Sweat (Everybody Dance Now) [2]...C & C Music Factory Featuring Freedom Williams
- R&B   I'll Give All My Love To You [1]...Keith Sweat
- C&W   Brother Jukebox [2]...Mark Chesnutt
- A/C   *All The Man That I Need [1]...Whitney Houston

ALBUMS
- POP   To The Extreme [15]...Vanilla Ice
- R&B   The Future [3]...Guy
- C&W   No Fences [11]...Garth Brooks

February 23, 1991
SINGLES
- HOT   All The Man That I Need [1]...Whitney Houston
- R&B   Gonna Make You Sweat (Everybody Dance Now) [1]...C & C Music Factory Featuring Freedom Williams
- C&W   Walk On Faith [1]...Mike Reid
- A/C   All The Man That I Need [2]...Whitney Houston

ALBUMS
- POP   To The Extreme [16]...Vanilla Ice
- R&B   Do Me Again [1]...Freddie Jackson
- C&W   No Fences [12]...Garth Brooks

March 2, 1991
SINGLES
- HOT   All The Man That I Need [2]...Whitney Houston
- R&B   All The Man That I Need [1]...Whitney Houston
- C&W   Walk On Faith [2]...Mike Reid
- A/C   All The Man That I Need [3]...Whitney Houston

ALBUMS
- POP   Mariah Carey [1]...Mariah Carey
- R&B   Do Me Again [2]...Freddie Jackson
- C&W   No Fences [13]...Garth Brooks

March 9, 1991
SINGLES
- HOT   Someday [1]...Mariah Carey
- R&B   All The Man That I Need [2]...Whitney Houston
- C&W   I'd Love You All Over Again [1]...Alan Jackson
- A/C   All The Man That I Need [4]...Whitney Houston

ALBUMS
- POP   Mariah Carey [2]...Mariah Carey
- R&B   I'm Your Baby Tonight [7]...Whitney Houston
- C&W   No Fences [14]...Garth Brooks

March 16, 1991
SINGLES
- HOT   Someday [2]...Mariah Carey
- R&B   Written All Over Your Face [1]...Rude Boys
- C&W   I'd Love You All Over Again [2]...Alan Jackson
- A/C   *Coming Out Of The Dark [1]...Gloria Estefan

ALBUMS
- POP   Mariah Carey [3]...Mariah Carey
- R&B   I'm Your Baby Tonight [8]...Whitney Houston
- C&W   No Fences [15]...Garth Brooks

March 23, 1991
SINGLES
- HOT   One More Try [1]...Timmy -T-
- R&B   *I Like The Way (The Kissing Game) [1]...Hi-Five
- C&W   Loving Blind [1]...Clint Black
- A/C   Coming Out Of The Dark [2]...Gloria Estefan

ALBUMS
- POP   Mariah Carey [4]...Mariah Carey
- R&B   Business As Usual [1]...EPMD
- C&W   No Fences [16]...Garth Brooks

March 30, 1991
SINGLES
- HOT   Coming Out Of The Dark [1]...Gloria Estefan
- R&B   I Like The Way (The Kissing Game) [2]...Hi-Five
- C&W   Loving Blind [2]...Clint Black
- A/C   *You're In Love [1]...Wilson Phillips

ALBUMS
- POP   Mariah Carey [5]...Mariah Carey
- R&B   Business As Usual [2]...EPMD
- C&W   No Fences [17]...Garth Brooks

April 6, 1991

SINGLES
- HOT Coming Out Of The Dark [2]...Gloria Estefan
- R&B Do Me Again [1]...Freddie Jackson
- C&W Two Of A Kind, Workin' On A Full House [1]...Garth Brooks
- A/C You're In Love [2]...Wilson Phillips

ALBUMS
- POP Mariah Carey [6]...Mariah Carey
- R&B Ralph Tresvant [1]...Ralph Tresvant
- C&W No Fences [18]...Garth Brooks

April 13, 1991

SINGLES
- HOT I've Been Thinking About You [1]...Londonbeat
- R&B Wrap My Body Tight [1]...Johnny Gill
- C&W Down Home [1]...Alabama
- A/C You're In Love [3]...Wilson Phillips

ALBUMS
- POP Mariah Carey [7]...Mariah Carey
- R&B Ralph Tresvant [2]...Ralph Tresvant
- C&W No Fences [19]...Garth Brooks

April 20, 1991

SINGLES
- HOT You're In Love [1]...Wilson Phillips
- R&B Whatever You Want [1]...Tony! Toni! Tone!
- C&W Down Home [2]...Alabama
- A/C You're In Love [4]...Wilson Phillips

ALBUMS
- POP Mariah Carey [8]...Mariah Carey
- R&B Hi-Five [1]...Hi-Five
- C&W No Fences [20]...Garth Brooks

April 27, 1991

SINGLES
- HOT *Baby Baby [1]...Amy Grant
- R&B Whatever You Want [2]...Tony! Toni! Tone!
- C&W Down Home [3]...Alabama
- A/C Cry For Help [1]...Rick Astley

ALBUMS
- POP Mariah Carey [9]...Mariah Carey
- R&B New Jack City [1]...Soundtrack
- C&W No Fences [21]...Garth Brooks

May 4, 1991

SINGLES
- HOT Baby Baby [2]...Amy Grant
- R&B I'm Dreamin' [1]...Christopher Williams
- C&W Rockin' Years [1]...Dolly Parton with Ricky Van Shelton
- A/C Baby Baby [1]...Amy Grant

ALBUMS
- POP Mariah Carey [10]...Mariah Carey
- R&B New Jack City [2]...Soundtrack
- C&W No Fences [22]...Garth Brooks

May 11, 1991

SINGLES
- HOT Joyride [1]...Roxette
- R&B Call Me [1]...Phil Perry
- C&W If I Know Me [1]...George Strait
- A/C Baby Baby [2]...Amy Grant

ALBUMS
- POP Mariah Carey [11]...Mariah Carey
- R&B New Jack City [3]...Soundtrack
- C&W No Fences [23]...Garth Brooks

May 18, 1991

SINGLES
- HOT I Like The Way (The Kissing Game) [1]...Hi-Five
- R&B It Should've Been You [1]...Teddy Pendergrass
- C&W If I Know Me [2]...George Strait
- A/C Baby Baby [3]...Amy Grant

ALBUMS
- POP Out Of Time [1]...R.E.M.
- R&B New Jack City [4]...Soundtrack
- C&W Eagle When She Flies [1]...Dolly Parton

May 25, 1991

SINGLES
- HOT *I Don't Wanna Cry [1]...Mariah Carey
- R&B Kissing You [1]...Keith Washington
- C&W In A Different Light [1]...Doug Stone
- A/C Love Is A Wonderful Thing [1]...Michael Bolton

ALBUMS
- POP Time, Love & Tenderness [1]...Michael Bolton
- R&B New Jack City [5]...Soundtrack
- C&W No Fences [24]...Garth Brooks

June 1, 1991

SINGLES
- HOT I Don't Wanna Cry [2]...Mariah Carey
- R&B I Wanna Sex You Up [1]...Color Me Badd
- C&W Meet In The Middle [1]...Diamond Rio
- A/C Love Is A Wonderful Thing [2]...Michael Bolton

ALBUMS
- POP Out Of Time [2]...R.E.M.
- R&B New Jack City [6]...Soundtrack
- C&W No Fences [25]...Garth Brooks

June 8, 1991
SINGLES
- HOT More Than Words [1]...Extreme
- R&B I Wanna Sex You Up [2]...Color Me Badd
- C&W Meet In The Middle [2]...Diamond Rio
- A/C I Don't Wanna Cry [1]...Mariah Carey

ALBUMS
- POP Spellbound [1]...Paula Abdul
- R&B New Jack City [7]...Soundtrack
- C&W No Fences [26]...Garth Brooks

June 15, 1991
SINGLES
- HOT *Rush, Rush [1]...Paula Abdul
- R&B Power Of Love/Love Power [1]...Luther Vandross
- C&W If The Devil Danced (In Empty Pockets) [1]... Joe Diffie
- A/C Love Is A Wonderful Thing [3]...Michael Bolton

ALBUMS
- POP Spellbound [2]...Paula Abdul
- R&B New Jack City [8]...Soundtrack
- C&W No Fences [27]...Garth Brooks

June 22, 1991
SINGLES
- HOT Rush, Rush [2]...Paula Abdul
- R&B Power Of Love/Love Power [2]...Luther Vandross
- C&W The Thunder Rolls [1]...Garth Brooks
- A/C Love Is A Wonderful Thing [4]...Michael Bolton

ALBUMS
- POP EFIL4ZAGGIN [1]...N.W.A.
- R&B Power Of Love [1]...Luther Vandross
- C&W No Fences [28]...Garth Brooks

June 29, 1991
SINGLES
- HOT Rush, Rush [3]...Paula Abdul
- R&B How Can I Ease The Pain [1]...Lisa Fischer
- C&W The Thunder Rolls [2]...Garth Brooks
- A/C Rush, Rush [1]...Paula Abdul

ALBUMS
- POP Slave To The Grind [1]...Skid Row
- R&B Power Of Love [2]...Luther Vandross
- C&W No Fences [29]...Garth Brooks

July 6, 1991
SINGLES
- HOT Rush, Rush [4]...Paula Abdul
- R&B How Can I Ease The Pain [2]...Lisa Fischer
- C&W Don't Rock The Jukebox [1]...Alan Jackson
- A/C Rush, Rush [2]...Paula Abdul

ALBUMS
- POP For Unlawful Carnal Knowledge [1]...Van Halen
- R&B Make Time For Love [1]...Keith Washington
- C&W No Fences [30]...Garth Brooks

July 13, 1991
SINGLES
- HOT Rush, Rush [5]...Paula Abdul
- R&B Exclusivity [1]...Damian Dame
- C&W Don't Rock The Jukebox [2]...Alan Jackson
- A/C Rush, Rush [3]...Paula Abdul

ALBUMS
- POP For Unlawful Carnal Knowledge [2]...Van Halen
- R&B Make Time For Love [2]...Keith Washington
- C&W No Fences [31]...Garth Brooks

July 20, 1991
SINGLES
- HOT Unbelievable [1]...EMF
- R&B Exclusivity [2]...Damian Dame
- C&W Don't Rock The Jukebox [3]...Alan Jackson
- A/C Rush, Rush [4]...Paula Abdul

ALBUMS
- POP For Unlawful Carnal Knowledge [3]...Van Halen
- R&B Power Of Love [3]...Luther Vandross
- C&W No Fences [32]...Garth Brooks

July 27, 1991
SINGLES
- HOT *(Everything I Do) I Do It For You [1]...Bryan Adams
- R&B Baby I'm Ready [1]...Levert
- C&W I Am A Simple Man [1]...Ricky Van Shelton
- A/C Rush, Rush [5]...Paula Abdul

ALBUMS
- POP Unforgettable With Love [1]...Natalie Cole
- R&B Power Of Love [4]...Luther Vandross
- C&W No Fences [33]...Garth Brooks

August 3, 1991
SINGLES
- HOT (Everything I Do) I Do It For You [2]...Bryan Adams
- R&B Summertime [1]...D.J. Jazzy Jeff & The Fresh Prince
- C&W She's In Love With The Boy [1]...Trisha Yearwood
- A/C (Everything I Do) I Do It For You [1]...Bryan Adams

ALBUMS
- POP Unforgettable With Love [2]...Natalie Cole
- R&B Jungle Fever [1]...Stevie Wonder/Soundtrack
- C&W No Fences [34]...Garth Brooks

August 10, 1991
SINGLES
- HOT (Everything I Do) I Do It For You [3]...Bryan Adams
- R&B I Can't Wait Another Minute [1]...Hi-Five
- C&W She's In Love With The Boy [2]...Trisha Yearwood
- A/C (Everything I Do) I Do It For You [2]...Bryan Adams

ALBUMS
- POP Unforgettable With Love [3]...Natalie Cole
- R&B Jungle Fever [2]...Stevie Wonder/Soundtrack
- C&W No Fences [35]...Garth Brooks

August 17, 1991
SINGLES
- HOT (Everything I Do) I Do It For You [4]...Bryan Adams
- R&B Can You Stop The Rain [1]...Peabo Bryson
- C&W You Know Me Better Than That [1]...George Strait
- A/C (Everything I Do) I Do It For You [3]...Bryan Adams

ALBUMS
- POP Unforgettable With Love [4]...Natalie Cole
- R&B Power Of Love [5]...Luther Vandross
- C&W No Fences [36]...Garth Brooks

August 24, 1991
SINGLES
- HOT (Everything I Do) I Do It For You [5]...Bryan Adams
- R&B Can You Stop The Rain [2]...Peabo Bryson
- C&W You Know Me Better Than That [2]...George Strait
- A/C (Everything I Do) I Do It For You [4]...Bryan Adams

ALBUMS
- POP Unforgettable With Love [5]...Natalie Cole
- R&B Cooleyhighharmony [1]...Boyz II Men
- C&W No Fences [37]...Garth Brooks

August 31, 1991
SINGLES
- HOT (Everything I Do) I Do It For You [6]...Bryan Adams
- R&B Addictive Love [1]...BeBe & CeCe Winans
- C&W You Know Me Better Than That [3]...George Strait
- A/C (Everything I Do) I Do It For You [5]...Bryan Adams

ALBUMS
- POP Metallica [1]...Metallica
- R&B Cooleyhighharmony [2]...Boyz II Men
- C&W No Fences [38]...Garth Brooks

September 7, 1991
SINGLES
- HOT (Everything I Do) I Do It For You [7]...Bryan Adams
- R&B Addictive Love [2]...BeBe & CeCe Winans
- C&W Brand New Man [1]...Brooks & Dunn
- A/C (Everything I Do) I Do It For You [6]...Bryan Adams

ALBUMS
- POP Metallica [2]...Metallica
- R&B Boyz N The Hood [1]...Soundtrack
- C&W No Fences [39]...Garth Brooks

September 14, 1991
SINGLES
- HOT The Promise Of A New Day [1]...Paula Abdul
- R&B Let The Beat Hit 'Em [1]...Lisa Lisa & Cult Jam
- C&W Brand New Man [2]...Brooks & Dunn
- A/C (Everything I Do) I Do It For You [7]...Bryan Adams

ALBUMS
- POP Metallica [3]...Metallica
- R&B Boyz N The Hood [2]...Soundtrack
- C&W No Fences [40]...Garth Brooks

September 21, 1991
SINGLES
- HOT *I Adore Mi Amor [1]...Color Me Badd
- R&B Don't Wanna Change The World [1]...Phyllis Hyman
- C&W Leap Of Faith [1]...Lionel Cartwright
- A/C (Everything I Do) I Do It For You [8]...Bryan Adams

ALBUMS
- POP Metallica [4]...Metallica
- R&B Boyz N The Hood [3]...Soundtrack
- C&W No Fences [41]...Garth Brooks

September 28, 1991
SINGLES
- HOT I Adore Mi Amor [2]...Color Me Badd
- R&B I Adore Mi Amor [1]...Color Me Badd
- C&W Where Are You Now [1]...Clint Black
- A/C Time, Love And Tenderness [1]...Michael Bolton

ALBUMS
- POP Ropin' The Wind [1]...Garth Brooks
- R&B Boyz N The Hood [4]...Soundtrack
- C&W Ropin' The Wind [1]...Garth Brooks

October 5, 1991
SINGLES
- HOT Good Vibrations [1]...Marky Mark And The Funky Bunch Featuring Loleatta Holloway
- R&B Running Back To You [1]...Vanessa Williams
- C&W Where Are You Now [2]...Clint Black
- A/C Time, Love And Tenderness [2]...Michael Bolton

ALBUMS
- POP Use Your Illusion II [1]...Guns N' Roses
- R&B Can You Stop The Rain [1]...Peabo Bryson
- C&W Ropin' The Wind [2]...Garth Brooks

October 12, 1991
SINGLES
- HOT *Emotions [1]...Mariah Carey
- R&B Running Back To You [2]...Vanessa Williams
- C&W Keep It Between The Lines [1]...Ricky Van Shelton
- A/C Everybody Plays The Fool [1]...Aaron Neville

ALBUMS
- POP Use Your Illusion II [2]...Guns N' Roses
- R&B Can You Stop The Rain [2]...Peabo Bryson
- C&W Ropin' The Wind [3]...Garth Brooks

October 19, 1991
SINGLES
- HOT Emotions [2]...Mariah Carey
- R&B *Romantic [1]...Karyn White
- C&W Keep It Between The Lines [2]...Ricky Van Shelton
- A/C Too Many Walls [1]...Cathy Dennis

ALBUMS
- POP Ropin' The Wind [2]...Garth Brooks
- R&B Good Woman [1]...Gladys Knight
- C&W Ropin' The Wind [4]...Garth Brooks

October 26, 1991

SINGLES
- HOT   Emotions [3]...Mariah Carey
- R&B   It's So Hard To Say Goodbye To Yesterday [1]... Boyz II Men
- C&W   Anymore [1]...Travis Tritt
- A/C   Too Many Walls [2]...Cathy Dennis

ALBUMS
- POP   Ropin' The Wind [3]...Garth Brooks
- R&B   Different Lifestyles [1]...BeBe & CeCe Winans
- C&W   Ropin' The Wind [5]...Garth Brooks

November 2, 1991

SINGLES
- HOT   Romantic [1]...Karyn White
- R&B   Emotions [1]...Mariah Carey
- C&W   Anymore [2]...Travis Tritt
- A/C   When A Man Loves A Woman [1]...Michael Bolton

ALBUMS
- POP   Ropin' The Wind [4]...Garth Brooks
- R&B   Different Lifestyles [2]...BeBe & CeCe Winans
- C&W   Ropin' The Wind [6]...Garth Brooks

November 9, 1991

SINGLES
- HOT   Cream [1]...Prince And The N.P.G.
- R&B   Forever My Lady [1]...Jodeci
- C&W   Someday [1]...Alan Jackson
- A/C   When A Man Loves A Woman [2]...Michael Bolton

ALBUMS
- POP   Ropin' The Wind [5]...Garth Brooks
- R&B   As Raw As Ever [1]...Shabba Ranks
- C&W   Ropin' The Wind [7]...Garth Brooks

November 16, 1991

SINGLES
- HOT   Cream [2]...Prince And The N.P.G.
- R&B   Forever My Lady [2]...Jodeci
- C&W   Shameless [1]...Garth Brooks
- A/C   When A Man Loves A Woman [3]...Michael Bolton

ALBUMS
- POP   Ropin' The Wind [6]...Garth Brooks
- R&B   Forever My Lady [1]...Jodeci
- C&W   Ropin' The Wind [8]...Garth Brooks

November 23, 1991

SINGLES
- HOT   When A Man Loves A Woman [1]...Michael Bolton
- R&B   Tender Kisses [1]...Tracie Spencer
- C&W   Shameless [2]...Garth Brooks
- A/C   When A Man Loves A Woman [4]...Michael Bolton

ALBUMS
- POP   Ropin' The Wind [7]...Garth Brooks
- R&B   Apocalypse 91...The Enemy Strikes Black [1]... Public Enemy
- C&W   Ropin' The Wind [9]...Garth Brooks

November 30, 1991

SINGLES
- HOT   Set Adrift On Memory Bliss [1]...PM Dawn
- R&B   Are You Lonely For Me [1]...Rude Boys
- C&W   Forever Together [1]...Randy Travis
- A/C   That's What Love Is For [1]...Amy Grant

ALBUMS
- POP   Ropin' The Wind [8]...Garth Brooks
- R&B   Forever My Lady [1]...Jodeci
- C&W   Ropin' The Wind [10]...Garth Brooks

December 7, 1991

SINGLES
- HOT   Black Or White [1]...Michael Jackson
- R&B   I'll Take You There [1]...BeBe & CeCe Winans Featuring Mavis Staples
- C&W   For My Broken Heart [1]...Reba McEntire
- A/C   That's What Love Is For [2]...Amy Grant

ALBUMS
- POP   Achtung Baby [1]...U2
- R&B   Diamonds & Pearls [1]...Prince & The N.P.G.
- C&W   Ropin' The Wind [11]...Garth Brooks

December 14, 1991

SINGLES
- HOT   Black Or White [2]...Michael Jackson
- R&B   Private Line [1]...Gerald Levert
- C&W   For My Broken Heart [2]...Reba McEntire
- A/C   That's What Love Is For [3]...Amy Grant

ALBUMS
- POP   Dangerous [1]...Michael Jackson
- R&B   Death Certificate [1]...Ice Cube
- C&W   Ropin' The Wind [12]...Garth Brooks

December 21, 1991

SINGLES
- *HOT* **Black Or White** [3]...Michael Jackson
- *R&B* **I Love Your Smile** [1]...Shanice
- *C&W* **My Next Broken Heart** [1]...Brooks & Dunn
- *A/C* **Keep Coming Back** [1]...Richard Marx

ALBUMS
- *POP* **Dangerous** [2]...Michael Jackson
- *R&B* **Death Certificate** [2]...Ice Cube
- *C&W* **Ropin' The Wind** [13]...Garth Brooks

December 28, 1991

SINGLES
- *HOT* **Black Or White** [4]...Michael Jackson
- *R&B* **I Love Your Smile** [2]...Shanice
- *C&W* **My Next Broken Heart** [2]...Brooks & Dunn
- *A/C* **Keep Coming Back** [2]...Richard Marx

ALBUMS
- *POP* **Dangerous** [3]...Michael Jackson
- *R&B* **Death Certificate** [3]...Ice Cube
- *C&W* **Ropin' The Wind** [14]...Garth Brooks

SINGLES TITLE SECTION

Lists, alphabetically, all singles shown in the #1 Hits Section. The artist's name is listed next to each title. Below each title is a listing of the individual charts on which the record reached #1. The date the record first hit #1 on each chart is listed next to the chart. From 1950 through 1958, when *Billboard* published multiple charts, the charts are listed chronologically within each music category. The total weeks the record stayed at the #1 position on each chart is shown in parenthesis after the date. All B-sides shown in the #1 Hits Section are listed alphabetically in the back of this section.

CHART HEADINGS

- **POP** - Pop Singles (shown until the *Hot 100* begins on August 4, 1958)
- **HOT** - *Hot 100* singles
- **R&B** - R&B/Soul/Black Singles
- **C&W** - Country/Country & Western Singles
- **A/C** - Adult Contemporary/Easy Listening Singles

MULTIPLE CHART ABBREVIATIONS

- **BS** - *Best Sellers In Stores*
- **DJ** - *Most Played By Jockeys*
- **JB** - *Most Played In Juke Boxes*
- **HT** - *Hot 100*
- **TP** - *Top 100*

Cross references are shown throughout to aid in finding a title.

Please note the following when searching for titles:

Titles beginning with a contraction follow titles that begin with a similar non-contracted word. (Can't follows Can).

Titles such a "C.C. Rider" and "TSOP" will be found at the beginning of their respective letters; however, titles such as "D-I-V-O-R-C-E" and "L-O-V-E," which are spellings of words, are listed with their regular spellings.

A

ABC...*Jackson 5*
HOT - 4/25/70(2)
R&B - 4/4/70(4)

Abilene...*George Hamilton IV*
C&W - 9/14/63(4)

Above And Beyond...*Rodney Crowell*
C&W - 9/23/89(1)

Abracadabra...*Steve Miller Band*
HOT - 9/4/82(2)

Ace In The Hole...*George Strait*
C&W - 11/4/89(1)

Act Naturally...*Buck Owens*
C&W - 6/15/63(4)

Addicted...*Dan Seals*
C&W - 9/24/88(1)

Addicted To Love...*Robert Palmer*
HOT - 5/3/86(1)

Addicted To You...*Levert*
R&B - 10/1/88(2)

Addictive Love...*BeBe & CeCe Winans*
R&B - 8/31/91(2)

Admiral Halsey ..see: Uncle Albert

Adorable...*Drifters*
R&B - JB: 12/31/55(1)

Afraid Of Losing You Again ..see: (I'm So)

Africa...*Toto*
HOT - 2/5/83(1)

After All...*Cher & Peter Cetera*
A/C - 4/22/89(4)

After All The Good Is Gone...
Conway Twitty
C&W - 5/22/76(1)

After All This Time...*Rodney Crowell*
C&W - 5/27/89(1)

After The Fire Is Gone...
Conway Twitty & Loretta Lynn
C&W - 3/27/71(2)

After The Lovin'...
Engelbert Humperdinck
A/C - 12/4/76(2)

Afternoon Delight...
Starland Vocal Band
HOT - 7/10/76(2)

Against All Odds (Take A Look At Me Now)...*Phil Collins*
HOT - 4/21/84(3)

Ain't Misbehavin'...*Hank Williams, Jr.*
C&W - 5/17/86(1)

Ain't No Mountain High Enough...
Diana Ross
HOT - 9/19/70(3)
R&B - 10/3/70(1)

Ain't No Stoppin' Us Now...
McFadden & Whitehead
R&B - 6/2/79(1)

Ain't No Way To Treat A Lady...
Helen Reddy
A/C - 10/4/75(1)

Ain't Nobody...*Rufus & Chaka Khan*
R&B - 10/15/83(1)

Ain't Nothin' Goin' On But The Rent...*Gwen Guthrie*
R&B - 9/6/86(1)

Ain't Nothing Like The Real Thing...
Marvin Gaye & Tammi Terrell
R&B - 6/8/68(1)

Ain't Nuthin' In The World...
Miki Howard
R&B - 12/16/89(1)

Ain't She Somethin' Else...
Conway Twitty
C&W - 2/9/85(1)

Ain't That A Shame...*Pat Boone*
POP - JB: 9/17/55(2)

Ain't That A Shame...*Fats Domino*
R&B - BS: 6/11/55(11); DJ: 6/11/55(10);
        JB: 7/2/55(8)

Ain't That Peculiar...*Marvin Gaye*
R&B - 11/27/65(1)

Ain't Too Proud To Beg...*Temptations*
R&B - 6/25/66(8)

Alabam...*Cowboy Copas*
C&W - 8/22/60(12)

All Alone Am I...*Brenda Lee*
A/C - 11/10/62(5)

All Around The World...
Lisa Stansfield
R&B - 3/24/90(2)

All By Myself...*Fats Domino*
R&B - DJ: 10/29/55(3)

All For The Love Of Sunshine...
Hank Williams, Jr.
C&W - 9/5/70(2)

All I Do Is Think Of You...*Troop*
R&B - 6/30/90(1)

All I Ever Need Is You...
Kenny Rogers & Dottie West
C&W - 4/21/79(1)

All I Ever Need Is You...
Sonny & Cher
A/C - 11/27/71(5)

All I Have To Do Is Dream...
Everly Brothers
POP - BS: 5/12/58(4); TP: 5/19/58(3);
        DJ: 5/19/58(5)
R&B - BS: 5/19/58(5); DJ: 6/2/58(2)
C&W - BS: 6/2/58(3); DJ: 6/2/58(1)

All I Have To Offer You (Is Me)...
Charley Pride
C&W - 8/9/69(1)

All I Know...*Garfunkel*
A/C - 10/6/73(4)

All I Need...*Jack Wagner*
A/C - 1/12/85(2)

All My Ex's Live In Texas...
George Strait
C&W - 7/11/87(1)

All My Life...
Linda Ronstadt/Aaron Neville
A/C - 3/3/90(3)

All My Love (Bolero)...*Patti Page*
POP - DJ: 10/28/50(5)

All My Rowdy Friends (Have Settled Down)...*Hank Williams, Jr.*
C&W - 11/21/81(1)

All Night Long (All Night)...
Lionel Richie
HOT - 11/12/83(4)
R&B - 10/22/83(7)
A/C - 11/12/83(4)

All Of My Love...*Gap Band*
R&B - 12/23/89(2)

All Roads Lead To You...
Steve Wariner
C&W - 12/19/81(1)

All Shook Up...*Elvis Presley*
POP - BS: 4/13/57(8); TP: 4/20/57(8);
        DJ: 4/27/57(7); JB: 4/27/57(9)
R&B - BS: 4/29/57(4); DJ: 5/6/57(2);
        JB: 5/6/57(4)
C&W - JB: 5/13/57(1)

All The Gold In California...
Larry Gatlin & The Gatlin Brothers Band
C&W - 10/20/79(2)

All The Man That I Need...
Whitney Houston
HOT - 2/23/91(2)
R&B - 3/2/91(2)
A/C - 2/16/91(4)

All The Time...*Jack Greene*
C&W - 6/17/67(5)

All These Things...*Joe Stampley*
C&W - 7/4/76(1)

All This Love...*DeBarge*
A/C - 7/16/83(3)

All Those Years Ago...
George Harrison
A/C - 7/4/81(1)

All Time High...*Rita Coolidge*
A/C - 8/6/83(4)

All You Need Is Love...*Beatles*
HOT - 8/19/67(1)

Alley-Oop...*Hollywood Argyles*
HOT - 7/11/60(1)

Almost Paradise...Love Theme From Footloose...*Mike Reno & Ann Wilson*
A/C - 6/30/84(1)
(also see: Footloose)

Almost Persuaded...*David Houston*
C&W - 8/13/66(9)

Alone...*Heart*
HOT - 7/11/87(3)

Alone Again (Naturally)...
Gilbert O'Sullivan
HOT - 7/29/72(6)
A/C - 7/29/72(6)

Alone With You...*Faron Young*
C&W - DJ: 7/21/58(13)

Already It's Heaven...*David Houston*
C&W - 8/24/68(1)

Always...*Atlantic Starr*
HOT - 6/13/87(1)
R&B - 5/16/87(2)
A/C - 5/30/87(2)

Always Have Always Will...
Janie Frickie
C&W - 10/4/86(1)

Always Late (With Your Kisses)...
Lefty Frizzell
C&W - BS: 9/1/51(12); DJ: 9/15/51(6);
        JB: 9/29/51(6)

Always On My Mind...*Willie Nelson*
C&W - 5/8/82(2)

Always Wanting You...*Merle Haggard*
C&W - 4/12/75(2)
Am I Blue...*George Strait*
C&W - 11/7/87(1)
Am I Losing You...*Ronnie Milsap*
C&W - 5/9/81(1)
Am I That Easy To Forget...
Engelbert Humperdinck
A/C - 2/3/68(1)
Amanda...*Boston*
HOT - 11/8/86(2)
Amanda...*Waylon Jennings*
C&W - 6/30/79(3)
Amazing Love...*Charley Pride*
C&W - 12/15/73(1)
America...*Neil Diamond*
A/C - 6/13/81(3)
American Made...*Oak Ridge Boys*
C&W - 4/23/83(1)
American Pie...*Don McLean*
HOT - 1/15/72(4)
A/C - 1/15/72(3)
American Woman...*Guess Who*
HOT - 5/9/70(3)
Among My Souvenirs...*Marty Robbins*
C&W - 10/30/76(1)
And I Am Telling You I'm Not Going...*Jennifer Holliday*
R&B - 7/24/82(4)
And I Love You So...*Perry Como*
A/C - 5/26/73(1)
And The Beat Goes On...*Whispers*
R&B - 3/1/80(5)
Angel...*Aretha Franklin*
R&B - 8/4/73(2)
Angel...*Angela Winbush*
R&B - 11/14/87(2)
Angel Flying Too Close To The Ground...*Willie Nelson*
C&W - 3/21/81(1)
Angel In Disguise...
Earl Thomas Conley
C&W - 7/28/84(1)
Angel Of The Morning...*Juice Newton*
A/C - 4/11/81(3)
Angie...*Rolling Stones*
HOT - 10/20/73(1)
Angie Baby...*Helen Reddy*
HOT - 12/28/74(1)
A/C - 12/7/74(1)
Annie Had A Baby...*Midnighters*
R&B - BS: 9/25/54(2)
Annie's Song...*John Denver*
HOT - 7/27/74(2)
A/C - 7/6/74(3)
Another Brick In The Wall (Part II)...*Pink Floyd*
HOT - 3/22/80(4)
Another Day In Paradise...
Phil Collins
HOT - 12/23/89(4)
A/C - 12/2/89(5)
Another Lonely Song...*Tammy Wynette*
C&W - 2/23/74(2)
Another One Bites The Dust...*Queen*
HOT - 10/4/80(3)
Another Part Of Me...*Michael Jackson*
R&B - 9/17/88(1)

Another Saturday Night...*Sam Cooke*
R&B - 6/8/63(1)
Another Somebody Done Somebody Wrong Song ..see: (Hey Won't You Play)
Any Day Now...*Ronnie Milsap*
C&W - 7/3/82(1)
A/C - 6/19/82(5)
Any Love...*Luther Vandross*
R&B - 11/5/88(1)
Anymore...*Travis Tritt*
C&W - 10/26/91(2)
Anything For You...
Gloria Estefan & Miami Sound Machine
HOT - 5/14/88(2)
A/C - 4/23/88(3)
Anytime, Any Place, Anywhere...
Joe Morris
R&B - BS: 11/4/50(4); JB: 11/25/50(3)
April Love...*Pat Boone*
POP - DJ: 12/16/57(6); BS: 12/23/57(2); TP: 12/30/57(1)
Aqua Boogie...*Parliament*
R&B - 1/20/79(4)
Aquarius/Let The Sunshine In...
5th Dimension
HOT - 4/12/69(6)
A/C - 5/10/69(2)
Are You Ever Gonna Love Me...
Holly Dunn
C&W - 8/26/89(1)
Are You Happy Baby?...*Dottie West*
C&W - 2/28/81(1)
Are You Lonely For Me...*Rude Boys*
R&B - 11/30/91(1)
Are You Lonely For Me...
Freddie Scott
R&B - 2/11/67(4)
Are You Lonesome To-night?...
Elvis Presley
HOT - 11/28/60(6)
Are You On The Road To Lovin' Me Again...*Debby Boone*
C&W - 5/3/80(1)
Are You Sure Hank Done It This Way...*Waylon Jennings*
C&W - 11/15/75(1)
Are You Teasing Me...*Carl Smith*
C&W - DJ: 7/19/52(1)
Arthur's Theme (Best That You Can Do)...*Christopher Cross*
HOT - 10/17/81(3)
A/C - 9/26/81(4)
As Long As I'm Rockin' With You...
John Conlee
C&W - 5/26/84(1)
As Long As You Follow...
Fleetwood Mac
A/C - 1/28/89(1)
As Soon As I Hang Up The Phone...
Conway Twitty & Loretta Lynn
C&W - 8/17/74(1)
At Midnight (My Love Will Lift You Up)...*Rufus Featuring Chaka Khan*
R&B - 4/9/77(2)
At My Front Door...*El Dorados*
R&B - JB: 1/7/56(1)

At Seventeen...*Janis Ian*
A/C - 8/9/75(2)
At The Hop...*Danny & The Juniors*
POP - TP: 1/6/58(7); BS: 1/6/58(5); DJ: 1/27/58(3)
R&B - BS: 1/6/58(5)
At This Moment...
Billy Vera & The Beaters
HOT - 1/24/87(2)
A/C - 1/31/87(1)
Atomic Dog...*George Clinton*
R&B - 4/16/83(4)
Auf Wiederseh'n Sweetheart...
Vera Lynn
POP - BS: 7/12/52(9); DJ: 7/26/52(6); JB: 8/9/52(4)
Autumn Leaves...*Roger Williams*
POP - BS: 10/29/55(4)
Axel F...*Harold Faltermeyer*
A/C - 6/8/85(2)

B

B.B.D. (I Thought It Was Me)?...
Bell Biv DeVoe
R&B - 11/17/90(1)
B.J. The D.J....*Stonewall Jackson*
C&W - 2/15/64(1)
Babe...*Styx*
HOT - 12/8/79(2)
Baby Baby...*Amy Grant*
HOT - 4/27/91(2)
A/C - 5/4/91(3)
Baby, Baby (I Know You're A Lady)...
David Houston
C&W - 1/3/70(4)
Baby Blue...*George Strait*
C&W - 8/6/88(1)
Baby Bye Bye...*Gary Morris*
C&W - 3/2/85(1)
Baby Come Back...*Player*
HOT - 1/14/78(3)
Baby, Come To Me...
Patti Austin with James Ingram
HOT - 2/19/83(2)
A/C - 1/22/83(3)
Baby Come To Me...*Regina Belle*
R&B - 10/28/89(1)
Baby, Don't Do It...*"5" Royales*
R&B - BS: 2/21/53(3); JB: 2/28/53(3)
Baby Don't Forget My Number...
Milli Vanilli
HOT - 7/1/89(1)
Baby Don't Get Hooked On Me...
Mac Davis
HOT - 9/23/72(3)
A/C - 9/16/72(3)
Baby I Love You...*Aretha Franklin*
R&B - 8/26/67(2)
Baby, I Love Your Way/Freebird Medley (Free Baby)...*Will To Power*
HOT - 12/3/88(1)
Baby I'm-A Want You...*Bread*
A/C - 11/20/71(1)

280

Baby I'm For Real...*Originals*
R&B - 11/8/69(5)

Baby I'm Ready...*Levert*
R&B - 7/27/91(1)

Baby Love...*Supremes*
HOT - 10/31/64(4)
R&B - 10/31/64(4)

Baby Scratch My Back...*Slim Harpo*
R&B - 2/26/66(2)

Baby That's Backatcha...
Smokey Robinson
R&B - 5/24/75(1)

Baby, What About You...*Crystal Gayle*
C&W - 9/24/83(1)

Baby Workout...*Jackie Wilson*
R&B - 5/4/63(3)

Baby (You've Got What It Takes)...
Dinah Washington & Brook Benton
R&B - 2/8/60(10)

Baby's Got A New Baby...*S-K-O*
C&W - 3/14/87(1)

Baby's Got Her Blue Jeans On...
Mel McDaniel
C&W - 2/23/85(1)

Baby's Gotten Good At Goodbye...
George Strait
C&W - 4/1/89(1)

Back Home Again...*John Denver*
C&W - 11/30/74(1)
A/C - 10/26/74(2)

Back In Love Again ..see: (Every Time I Turn Around)

Back In My Arms Again...*Supremes*
HOT - 6/12/65(1)
R&B - 5/29/65(1)

Back In Stride...
Maze Featuring Frankie Beverly
R&B - 4/13/85(2)

Back In The High Life Again...
Steve Winwood
A/C - 8/1/87(3)

Back Stabbers...*O'Jays*
R&B - 9/9/72(1)

Back Street Affair...*Webb Pierce*
C&W - BS: 12/6/52(2); DJ: 12/13/52(4); JB: 1/17/53(2)

Back To Life (However Do You Want Me)...*Soul II Soul*
R&B - 10/7/89(1)

Backside Of Thirty...*John Conlee*
C&W - 5/5/79(1)

Bad...*Michael Jackson*
HOT - 10/24/87(2)
R&B - 10/17/87(3)

Bad, Bad Leroy Brown...*Jim Croce*
HOT - 7/21/73(2)

Bad, Bad Whiskey...*Amos Milburn*
R&B - BS: 1/6/51(1); JB: 1/13/51(3)

Bad Blood...*Neil Sedaka*
HOT - 10/11/75(3)

Bad Girls...*Donna Summer*
HOT - 7/14/79(5)
R&B - 7/21/79(1)

Bad Medicine...*Bon Jovi*
HOT - 11/19/88(2)

Ballad Of A Teenage Queen...
Johnny Cash
C&W - DJ: 2/3/58(10); BS: 2/17/58(8)

Ballad Of Davy Crockett...*Bill Hayes*
POP - BS: 3/26/55(5); DJ: 4/23/55(3); JB: 4/23/55(3)

Ballad Of Jed Clampett...
Flatt & Scruggs
C&W - 1/19/63(3)

Ballad Of The Green Berets...
SSgt Barry Sadler
HOT - 3/5/66(5)
A/C - 3/5/66(5)

Ballerina Girl...*Lionel Richie*
A/C - 2/7/87(4)

Band Of Gold...*Mel Carter*
A/C - 5/21/66(2)

Band On The Run...
Paul McCartney & Wings
HOT - 6/8/74(1)

Banda...*Herb Alpert*
A/C - 10/7/67(2)

Bar Room Buddies...
Merle Haggard & Clint Eastwood
C&W - 7/26/80(1)

Bargain Store...*Dolly Parton*
C&W - 3/29/75(1)

Batdance...*Prince*
HOT - 8/5/89(1)
R&B - 8/12/89(1)

Battle Of New Orleans...
Johnny Horton
HOT - 6/1/59(6)
C&W - 5/18/59(10)

Bayou Boys...*Eddy Raven*
C&W - 11/18/89(1)

Be My Love...*Mario Lanza*
POP - BS: 3/10/51(1)

Be Thankful For What You Got...
William DeVaughn
R&B - 6/1/74(1)

Beat It...*Michael Jackson*
HOT - 4/30/83(3)
R&B - 5/21/83(1)

Beauty Is Only Skin Deep...
Temptations
R&B - 9/24/66(5)

Because I Love You (The Postman Song)...*Stevie B*
HOT - 12/8/90(4)
A/C - 1/19/91(2)

Because Of You...*Tony Bennett*
POP - BS: 9/8/51(8); DJ: 9/22/51(8); JB: 9/29/51(10)

Because Of You...*Tab Smith*
R&B - BS: 12/8/51(1)

Bedtime Story...*Tammy Wynette*
C&W - 3/4/72(1)

Been To Canaan...*Carole King*
A/C - 1/13/73(1)

Before The Next Teardrop Falls...
Freddy Fender
HOT - 5/31/75(1)
C&W - 3/15/75(2)

Before You Go...*Buck Owens*
C&W - 6/26/65(6)

Begging To You...*Marty Robbins*
C&W - 2/8/64(3)

Beginnings...*Chicago*
A/C - 8/28/71(1)

Behind Closed Doors...*Charlie Rich*
C&W - 4/28/73(2)

Behind The Tear...*Sonny James*
C&W - 10/9/65(3)

Being With You...*Smokey Robinson*
R&B - 4/4/81(5)

Believe In Me...*Dan Fogelberg*
A/C - 6/23/84(1)

Ben...*Michael Jackson*
HOT - 10/14/72(1)

Beneath Still Waters...
Emmylou Harris
C&W - 5/10/80(1)

Bennie And The Jets...*Elton John*
HOT - 4/13/74(1)

Best Of My Love...*Eagles*
HOT - 3/1/75(1)
A/C - 2/1/75(1)

Best Of My Love...*Emotions*
HOT - 8/20/77(5)
R&B - 6/25/77(4)

(Best That You Can Do) ..see: Arthur's Theme

Best Thing That Ever Happened To Me...*Gladys Knight & The Pips*
R&B - 4/6/74(2)

Best Year Of My Life...*Eddie Rabbitt*
C&W - 1/12/85(1)

Bet Your Heart On Me...*Johnny Lee*
C&W - 12/5/81(1)

Bette Davis Eyes...*Kim Carnes*
HOT - 5/16/81(9)

Better Man...*Clint Black*
C&W - 6/10/89(1)

Big Bad John...*Jimmy Dean*
HOT - 11/6/61(5)
C&W - 11/20/61(2)
A/C - 10/23/61(10)

Big City...*Merle Haggard*
C&W - 4/10/82(1)

Big Girls Don't Cry...*4 Seasons*
HOT - 11/17/62(5)
R&B - 11/17/62(5)

Big Hunk O' Love...*Elvis Presley*
HOT - 8/10/59(2)

Big Wheels In The Moonlight...
Dan Seals
C&W - 2/18/89(1)

Billie Jean...*Michael Jackson*
HOT - 3/5/83(7)
R&B - 2/12/83(9)

Billy Bayou...*Jim Reeves*
C&W - 1/19/59(5)

Billy, Don't Be A Hero...
Bo Donaldson & The Heywoods
HOT - 6/15/74(2)

Bimbo...*Jim Reeves*
C&W - DJ: 1/9/54(3)

Bird Dog...*Everly Brothers*
POP - BS: 8/25/58(1)
C&W - BS: 9/8/58(6)

Birmingham Bounce...*Red Foley*
C&W - BS: 5/27/50(4); JB: 6/3/50(3)

Black & White...*Three Dog Night*
HOT - 9/16/72(1)
A/C - 10/7/72(1)

Black Cat...*Janet Jackson*
HOT - 10/27/90(1)

Black Night...*Charles Brown*
R&B - JB: 3/3/51(14); BS: 3/10/51(13)

Black Or White...*Michael Jackson*
HOT - 12/7/91(4)
still #1 as of the 1/4/92 chart
Black Sheep...*John Anderson*
C&W - 12/17/83(1)
Black Velvet...*Alannah Myles*
HOT - 3/24/90(2)
Black Water...*Doobie Brothers*
HOT - 3/15/75(1)
Blame It On The Rain...*Milli Vanilli*
HOT - 11/25/89(2)
Blanket On The Ground...
Billie Jo Spears
C&W - 4/26/75(1)
Blaze Of Glory...*Jon Bon Jovi*
HOT - 9/8/90(1)
Bless Your Heart...*Freddie Hart*
C&W - 8/12/72(2)
Blessed Are The Believers...
Anne Murray
C&W - 6/27/81(1)
Blinded By The Light...
Manfred Mann's Earth Band
HOT - 2/19/77(1)
Blood Red And Goin' Down...
Tanya Tucker
C&W - 9/29/73(1)
Blowin' In The Wind...
Peter, Paul & Mary
A/C - 8/3/63(5)
Blowin' In The Wind...*Stevie Wonder*
R&B - 8/27/66(1)
Blue Blue Day...*Don Gibson*
C&W - BS: 8/25/58(2)
Blue Christmas...*Ernest Tubb*
C&W - JB: 1/7/50(1)
Blue Eyes...*Elton John*
A/C - 9/11/82(2)
Blue Eyes Crying In The Rain...
Willie Nelson
C&W - 10/4/75(2)
Blue Light Boogie...*Louis Jordan*
R&B - BS: 9/9/50(7); JB: 9/30/50(4)
Blue Monday...*Fats Domino*
R&B - BS: 1/26/57(8); DJ: 1/26/57(7);
JB: 1/26/57(8)
Blue Moon...*Marcels*
HOT - 4/3/61(3)
R&B - 4/3/61(2)
Blue Moon With Heartache...
Rosanne Cash
C&W - 3/13/82(1)
Blue Shadows...*Lowell Fulsom*
R&B - BS: 10/28/50(1); JB: 10/28/50(4)
Blue Side Of Lonesome...*Jim Reeves*
C&W - 10/15/66(1)
Blue Skies...*Willie Nelson*
C&W - 9/2/78(1)
Blue Suede Shoes...*Carl Perkins*
C&W - JB: 4/7/56(3)
Blue Tango...*Leroy Anderson*
POP - BS: 5/17/52(5)
Blue Velvet...*Bobby Vinton*
HOT - 9/21/63(3)
A/C - 9/7/63(8)
Blueberry Hill...*Fats Domino*
R&B - DJ: 11/3/56(11); JB: 11/3/56(8);
BS: 11/24/56(8)

Bluer Than Blue...*Michael Johnson*
A/C - 6/17/78(3)
Blues, The...*Tony! Toni! Tone!*
R&B - 6/9/90(1)
Blues Stay Away From Me...
Delmore Brothers
C&W - JB: 1/14/50(1)
Bluest Eyes In Texas...
Restless Heart
C&W - 8/20/88(1)
Bo Diddley...*Bo Diddley*
R&B - JB: 6/25/55(2)
Bobbie Sue...*Oak Ridge Boys*
C&W - 4/3/82(1)
Boll Weevil Song...*Brook Benton*
A/C - 7/17/61(3)
Boogie Down...*Eddie Kendricks*
R&B - 2/9/74(3)
Boogie Fever...*Sylvers*
HOT - 5/15/76(1)
R&B - 6/5/76(1)
Boogie On Reggae Woman...
Stevie Wonder
R&B - 12/28/74(2)
Boogie Oogie Oogie...*Taste Of Honey*
HOT - 9/9/78(3)
R&B - 8/5/78(1)
Boogie Woogie Bugle Boy...
Bette Midler
A/C - 6/23/73(2)
Booted...*Roscoe Gordon*
R&B - BS: 3/15/52(1)
Bootzilla...*Bootsy's Rubber Band*
R&B - 3/25/78(1)
Bop...*Dan Seals*
C&W - 1/18/86(1)
Born Free...*Roger Williams*
A/C - 9/3/66(6)
Born To Be With You...*Sonny James*
C&W - 12/14/68(1)
Born To Boogie...*Hank Williams, Jr.*
C&W - 8/29/87(1)
Both To Each Other (Friends & Lovers)...*Eddie Rabbitt & Juice Newton*
C&W - 10/11/86(1)
Boy Named Sue...*Johnny Cash*
C&W - 8/23/69(5)
A/C - 8/30/69(2)
Brand New Key...*Melanie*
HOT - 12/25/71(3)
Brand New Man...*Brooks & Dunn*
C&W - 9/7/91(2)
Branded Man...*Merle Haggard*
C&W - 9/2/67(1)
Brandy (You're A Fine Girl)...
Looking Glass
HOT - 8/26/72(1)
Break Away...*Art Garfunkel*
A/C - 2/21/76(1)
Break It To Me Gently...
Aretha Franklin
R&B - 6/18/77(1)
Break It To Me Gently...*Juice Newton*
A/C - 10/9/82(2)
Breaking Up Is Hard To Do...
Neil Sedaka
HOT - 8/11/62(2)

Breaking Up Is Hard To Do...
Neil Sedaka
A/C - 2/7/76(1)
Breakout...*Swing Out Sister*
A/C - 11/7/87(2)
Bridge Over Troubled Water...
Aretha Franklin
R&B - 5/22/71(2)
Bridge Over Troubled Water...
Simon & Garfunkel
HOT - 2/28/70(6)
A/C - 2/28/70(6)
Bridge Washed Out...*Warner Mack*
C&W - 9/4/65(1)
Bright Lights, Big City...
Sonny James
C&W - 7/24/71(1)
Bring It On Home To Me...
Mickey Gilley
C&W - 8/21/76(1)
Broken Down In Tiny Pieces...
Billy "Crash" Craddock
C&W - 1/8/77(1)
Broken Hearted Me...*Anne Murray*
C&W - 12/1/79(1)
A/C - 10/13/79(5)
Broken Wings...*Mr. Mister*
HOT - 12/7/85(2)
Brother Jukebox...*Mark Chesnutt*
C&W - 2/9/91(2)
Brother Louie...*Stories*
HOT - 8/25/73(2)
Brown Sugar...*Rolling Stones*
HOT - 5/29/71(2)
Buckaroo...*Buck Owens*
C&W - 12/25/65(2)
Burn Rubber (Why You Wanna Hurt Me)...*Gap Band*
R&B - 2/14/81(2)
Burnin' Old Memories...*Kathy Mattea*
C&W - 11/11/89(1)
Bustin' Loose...
Chuck Brown & The Soul Searchers
R&B - 2/17/79(4)
But You Know I Love You...
Dolly Parton
C&W - 6/20/81(1)
Butterfly...*Charlie Gracie*
POP - JB: 4/13/57(2)
Butterfly...*Andy Williams*
POP - TP: 3/30/57(3); DJ: 3/30/57(2)
Bye Bye Love...*Everly Brothers*
C&W - BS: 7/15/57(7); DJ: 7/29/57(7)

C

C. C. Rider...*Chuck Willis*
R&B - DJ: 6/17/57(2)
Cajun Moon...*Ricky Skaggs*
C&W - 4/19/86(1)
Calcutta...*Lawrence Welk*
HOT - 2/13/61(2)
Call Me...*Blondie*
HOT - 4/19/80(6)

Call Me...*Aretha Franklin*
R&B - 3/21/70(2)
Call Me...*Phil Perry*
R&B - 5/11/91(1)
Call Me...*Skyy*
R&B - 2/6/82(2)
Call On Me...*Chicago*
A/C - 8/24/74(1)
Can I Change My Mind...*Tyrone Davis*
R&B - 2/1/69(3)
Can You Stand The Rain...*New Edition*
R&B - 2/4/89(2)
Can You Stop The Rain...*Peabo Bryson*
R&B - 8/17/91(2)
Can't Buy Me Love...*Beatles*
HOT - 4/4/64(5)
Can't Even Get The Blues...
Reba McEntire
C&W - 1/8/83(1)
Can't Fight This Feeling...
REO Speedwagon
HOT - 3/9/85(3)
**Can't Get Enough Of Your Love,
Babe**...*Barry White*
HOT - 9/21/74(1)
R&B - 9/7/74(3)
Can't Get Over You...
Maze Featuring Frankie Beverly
R&B - 9/23/89(1)
Can't Get Used To Losing You...
Andy Williams
A/C - 4/13/63(4)
Can't Help Falling In Love...
Elvis Presley
A/C - 1/13/62(6)
**Can't Keep A Good Man
Down**...*Alabama*
C&W - 11/9/85(1)
**(Can't Live Without Your) Love And
Affection**...*Nelson*
HOT - 9/29/90(1)
Can't Smile Without You...
Barry Manilow
A/C - 3/18/78(1)
Can't Stay Away From You...
Gloria Estefan & Miami Sound Machine
A/C - 2/13/88(1)
Can't Stop...*After 7*
R&B - 8/4/90(1)
**Can't Stop My Heart From Loving
You**...*O'Kanes*
C&W - 5/23/87(1)
Candy...*Cameo*
R&B - 1/31/87(2)
Candy Girl...*New Edition*
R&B - 5/14/83(1)
Candy Man...*Sammy Davis, Jr.*
HOT - 6/10/72(3)
A/C - 5/20/72(2)
Car Wash...*Rose Royce*
HOT - 1/29/77(1)
R&B - 12/25/76(2)
Caravan Of Love...
Isley, Jasper, Isley
R&B - 11/30/85(3)
Carefree Highway...*Gordon Lightfoot*
A/C - 10/19/74(1)

Careless Whisper...
Wham!/George Michael
HOT - 2/16/85(3)
A/C - 2/9/85(5)
Caribbean...*Mitchell Torok*
C&W - JB: 12/12/53(2)
**Caribbean Queen (No More Love On
The Run)**...*Billy Ocean*
HOT - 11/3/84(2)
R&B - 9/8/84(4)
Carolyn...*Merle Haggard*
C&W - 1/15/72(3)
Casanova...*Levert*
R&B - 8/22/87(2)
Casino Royale...*Herb Alpert*
A/C - 6/3/67(2)
Cast Your Fate To The Wind...
Sounds Orchestral
A/C - 5/1/65(3)
Cat's In The Cradle...*Harry Chapin*
HOT - 12/21/74(1)
Catch A Falling Star...*Perry Como*
POP - DJ: 3/24/58(1)
Cathy's Clown...*Everly Brothers*
HOT - 5/23/60(5)
R&B - 6/13/60(1)
Cathy's Clown...*Reba McEntire*
C&W - 7/29/89(1)
Cattle Call...*Eddy Arnold*
C&W - BS: 10/8/55(2)
Celebration...*Kool & The Gang*
HOT - 2/7/81(2)
R&B - 12/20/80(6)
Centerfold...*J. Geils Band*
HOT - 2/6/82(6)
Chain Of Fools...*Aretha Franklin*
R&B - 1/20/68(4)
Chains...*Patty Loveless*
C&W - 3/10/90(1)
Chair, The...*George Strait*
C&W - 12/21/85(1)
Chance Of Lovin' You...
Earl Thomas Conley
C&W - 12/8/84(1)
Chances Are...*Johnny Mathis*
POP - DJ: 10/21/57(1)
Change Of Heart...*Judds*
C&W - 1/14/89(1)
Chantilly Lace...*Jerry Lee Lewis*
C&W - 4/22/72(3)
Chapel Of Love...*Dixie Cups*
HOT - 6/6/64(3)
R&B - 6/6/64(3)
Chariots Of Fire - Titles...*Vangelis*
HOT - 5/8/82(1)
A/C - 4/3/82(5)
Charlie's Shoes...*Billy Walker*
C&W - 4/28/62(2)
Chattanooga Choo Choo...
Harpers Bizarre
A/C - 1/6/68(2)
Chattanoogie Shoe Shine Boy...
Red Foley
POP - JB: 2/11/50(8); BS: 2/18/50(4);
DJ: 2/25/50(2)
C&W - DJ: 1/21/50(13); BS: 2/4/50(12);
JB: 2/4/50(13)
Cherish...*Association*
HOT - 9/24/66(3)

Cherish...*David Cassidy*
A/C - 1/8/72(1)
Cherish...*Kool & The Gang*
R&B - 9/14/85(1)
A/C - 8/24/85(6)
Cherish...*Madonna*
A/C - 10/7/89(2)
Cherokee Maiden...*Merle Haggard*
C&W - 11/6/76(1)
**Cherry Pink And Apple Blossom
White**...*Perez "Prez" Prado*
POP - BS: 4/30/55(10); DJ: 5/21/55(6);
JB: 6/4/55(8)
Chica Boo...*Lloyd Glenn's Combo*
R&B - JB: 6/9/51(2)
Chipmunk Song...*Chipmunks*
HOT - 12/22/58(4)
Choice Of Colors...*Impressions*
R&B - 8/16/69(1)
Chokin' Kind...*Joe Simon*
R&B - 5/17/69(3)
Church On Cumberland Road...
Shenandoah
C&W - 4/22/89(2)
City Lights...*Mickey Gilley*
C&W - 2/1/75(1)
City Lights...*Ray Price*
C&W - 10/20/58(13)
City Of New Orleans...*Willie Nelson*
C&W - 11/3/84(1)
Clair...*Gilbert O'Sullivan*
A/C - 12/9/72(3)
Classical Gas...*Mason Williams*
A/C - 8/17/68(3)
Clock, The...*Johnny Ace*
R&B - BS: 7/18/53(5); JB: 8/1/53(4)
Close Enough To Perfect...*Alabama*
C&W - 10/30/82(1)
Close The Door...*Teddy Pendergrass*
R&B - 7/8/78(2)
Close To You...*Maxi Priest*
HOT - 10/6/90(1)
(also see: They Long To Be)
Closer I Get To You...
Roberta Flack & Donny Hathaway
R&B - 4/1/78(2)
Closer Than Close...*Jean Carne*
R&B - 8/2/86(2)
Closer Than Friends...*Surface*
R&B - 3/18/89(2)
Closer You Get...*Alabama*
C&W - 7/16/83(1)
Clouds, The...*Spacemen*
R&B - 12/7/59(3)
Clown, The...*Conway Twitty*
C&W - 4/17/82(1)
Coal Miner's Daughter...*Loretta Lynn*
C&W - 12/19/70(1)
Coca Cola Cowboy...*Mel Tillis*
C&W - 8/18/79(1)
Cold...*John Gary*
A/C - 12/23/67(2)
Cold Blooded...*Rick James*
R&B - 9/3/83(6)
Cold, Cold Heart...*Tony Bennett*
POP - BS: 11/3/51(6); JB: 12/8/51(3)
Cold, Cold Heart...*Hank Williams*
C&W - DJ: 5/12/51(1)

Cold Hearted...*Paula Abdul*
HOT - 9/2/89(1)
Cold Sweat...*James Brown*
R&B - 9/9/67(3)
Come Back To Me...*Janet Jackson*
A/C - 8/25/90(3)
Come From The Heart...*Kathy Mattea*
C&W - 7/1/89(1)
(Come Go With Me) ..see: If You're Ready
Come Live With Me...*Roy Clark*
C&W - 5/12/73(1)
Come Next Monday...*K.T. Oslin*
C&W - 11/24/90(2)
Come On Eileen...
Dexys Midnight Runners
HOT - 4/23/83(1)
Come On Over...*Olivia Newton-John*
A/C - 4/24/76(1)
Come On-a My House...
Rosemary Clooney
POP - BS: 7/28/51(6); DJ: 7/28/51(8); JB: 8/4/51(8)
Come See About Me...*Supremes*
HOT - 12/19/64(2)
Come Softly To Me...*Fleetwoods*
HOT - 4/13/59(4)
Come Together...*Beatles*
HOT - 11/29/69(1)
Come With Me...*Waylon Jennings*
C&W - 11/17/79(2)
Coming Out Of The Dark...
Gloria Estefan
HOT - 3/30/91(2)
A/C - 3/16/91(2)
Coming Up...*Paul McCartney*
HOT - 6/28/80(3)
Common Man...*John Conlee*
C&W - 5/21/83(1)
Control...*Janet Jackson*
R&B - 1/10/87(1)
Convoy...*C.W. McCall*
HOT - 1/10/76(1)
C&W - 12/20/75(6)
Cool It Now...*New Edition*
R&B - 11/24/84(1)
Could I Have This Dance...
Anne Murray
C&W - 11/15/80(1)
Could It Be I'm Falling In Love...
Spinners
R&B - 2/10/73(1)
Could've Been...*Tiffany*
HOT - 2/6/88(2)
A/C - 2/6/88(1)
Country Boy...*Ricky Skaggs*
C&W - 6/15/85(1)
Country Boy (You Got Your Feet In L.A.)...*Glen Campbell*
A/C - 12/27/75(1)
Country Bumpkin...*Cal Smith*
C&W - 5/18/74(1)
Country Girl...*Faron Young*
C&W - 11/9/59(4)
Country Girls...*John Schneider*
C&W - 4/6/85(1)
Country Is...*Tom T. Hall*
C&W - 11/16/74(1)

Coward Of The County...*Kenny Rogers*
C&W - 1/5/80(1)
(Cowboy And The Poet) ..see: Faster Horses
Cowboys And Clowns...*Ronnie Milsap*
C&W - 8/30/80(1)
Cowboys To Girls...*Intruders*
R&B - 5/11/68(1)
Cracklin' Rosie...*Neil Diamond*
HOT - 10/10/70(1)
Crazy...*Boys*
R&B - 9/22/90(1)
Crazy...*Kenny Rogers*
C&W - 3/30/85(1)
Crazy Arms...*Ray Price*
C&W - DJ: 6/23/56(20); BS: 7/28/56(11); JB: 7/28/56(1)
Crazy For You...*Madonna*
HOT - 5/11/85(1)
Crazy For Your Love...*Exile*
C&W - 3/16/85(1)
Crazy Little Thing Called Love...
Queen
HOT - 2/23/80(4)
Crazy Love...*Poco*
A/C - 3/10/79(7)
Cream...*Prince*
HOT - 11/9/91(2)
Crimson And Clover...
Tommy James & The Shondells
HOT - 2/1/69(2)
Crocodile Rock...*Elton John*
HOT - 2/3/73(3)
Cry...*Crystal Gayle*
C&W - 10/25/86(1)
Cry...*Johnnie Ray & The Four Lads*
POP - BS: 12/29/51(11); DJ: 1/5/52(10); JB: 1/26/52(9)
R&B - BS: 1/12/52(1); JB: 2/9/52(1)
Cry Baby...
Garnet Mimms & The Enchanters
R&B - 10/12/63(3)
Cry, Cry, Cry...*Highway 101*
C&W - 5/7/88(1)
Cry For Help...*Rick Astley*
A/C - 4/27/91(1)
Cry Myself To Sleep...*Judds*
C&W - 1/24/87(1)
Cry Of The Wild Goose...
Frankie Laine
POP - DJ: 3/11/50(2)
Crying In The Chapel...*Orioles*
R&B - BS: 8/22/53(4); JB: 8/29/53(5)
Crying In The Chapel...*Elvis Presley*
A/C - 5/22/65(7)
Crying My Heart Out Over You...
Ricky Skaggs
C&W - 4/24/82(1)
Crying Time...*Ray Charles*
A/C - 2/12/66(3)
Cupid's Boogie...
Little Esther/Johnny Otis Orchestra
R&B - JB: 7/8/50(1)
Cuts Both Ways...*Gloria Estefan*
A/C - 7/28/90(1)

D

Da'Butt...*E.U.*
R&B - 4/23/88(1)
Da Doo Ron Ron...*Shaun Cassidy*
HOT - 7/16/77(1)
Da Ya Think I'm Sexy?...*Rod Stewart*
HOT - 2/10/79(4)
Daddy Frank (The Guitar Man)...
Merle Haggard
C&W - 11/20/71(2)
Daddy Sang Bass...*Johnny Cash*
C&W - 1/4/69(6)
Daddy's Come Around...
Paul Overstreet
C&W - 2/2/91(1)
(Dallas Lovers' Song) ..see: Makin' Up For Lost Time
Dance, The...*Garth Brooks*
C&W - 7/14/90(3)
Dance Floor...*Zapp*
R&B - 8/21/82(2)
Dance With Me Henry (Wallflower)...
Georgia Gibbs
POP - JB: 5/14/55(3)
Dancin' Cowboys...*Bellamy Brothers*
C&W - 8/2/80(1)
Dancing Machine...*Jackson 5*
R&B - 5/11/74(1)
Dancing Queen...*Abba*
HOT - 4/9/77(1)
Dang Me...*Roger Miller*
C&W - 7/18/64(6)
Daniel...*Elton John*
A/C - 5/12/73(2)
Danny's Song...*Anne Murray*
A/C - 3/17/73(2)
Dark Lady...*Cher*
HOT - 3/23/74(1)
Darlene...*T. Graham Brown*
C&W - 11/5/88(1)
Darlin' Darlin' Baby (Sweet, Tender, Love)...*O'Jays*
R&B - 1/8/77(1)
Daughter Of Darkness...*Tom Jones*
A/C - 6/13/70(1)
Davy Crockett ..see: Ballad Of
Day Dreaming...*Aretha Franklin*
R&B - 4/22/72(1)
Daydream Believer...*Monkees*
HOT - 12/2/67(4)
Daydream Believer...*Anne Murray*
A/C - 3/1/80(1)
Daydreams About Night Things...
Ronnie Milsap
C&W - 9/20/75(2)
Daytime Friends...*Kenny Rogers*
C&W - 10/1/77(1)
Dazz...*Brick*
R&B - 11/27/76(4)
Dear John Letter...
Jean Shepard & Ferlin Huskey
C&W - BS: 8/29/53(6); JB: 10/10/53(4)

December, 1963 (Oh, What a Night)...
Four Seasons
HOT - 3/13/76(3)
Deep Purple...
Nino Tempo & April Stevens
HOT - 11/16/63(1)
Deeper Than The Holler...
Randy Travis
C&W - 1/28/89(1)
Deja Vu...*Dionne Warwick*
A/C - 1/19/80(1)
Delicado...*Percy Faith & his Orch.*
POP - BS: 7/5/52(1)
Delta Dawn...*Helen Reddy*
HOT - 9/15/73(1)
A/C - 8/4/73(2)
Desiree...*Neil Diamond*
A/C - 2/4/78(1)
Desperado Love...*Conway Twitty*
C&W - 9/6/86(1)
Devil In The Bottle...*T.G. Sheppard*
C&W - 2/15/75(1)
Devil Went Down To Georgia...
Charlie Daniels Band
C&W - 8/25/79(1)
Devil Woman...*Marty Robbins*
C&W - 9/1/62(8)
Dial My Heart...*Boys*
R&B - 12/10/88(1)
Diamonds...*Herb Alpert*
R&B - 6/20/87(2)
Diana...*Paul Anka*
POP - BS: 9/9/57(1)
R&B - BS: 9/23/57(2)
Didn't We Almost Have It All...
Whitney Houston
HOT - 9/26/87(2)
A/C - 9/19/87(3)
Died In Your Arms ..see: (I Just)
Different Worlds...*Maureen McGovern*
A/C - 9/8/79(2)
Diggin' Up Bones...*Randy Travis*
C&W - 11/8/86(1)
Dirty Diana...*Michael Jackson*
HOT - 7/2/88(1)
Disco Duck...*Rick Dees*
HOT - 10/16/76(1)
Disco Lady...*Johnnie Taylor*
HOT - 4/3/76(4)
R&B - 3/13/76(6)
Disco Nights (Rock-Freak)...*GQ*
R&B - 4/14/79(2)
Distant Drums...*Jim Reeves*
C&W - 5/21/66(4)
D-I-V-O-R-C-E...*Tammy Wynette*
C&W - 6/29/68(3)
Dixie On My Mind...
Hank Williams, Jr.
C&W - 8/1/81(1)
Dixie Road...*Lee Greenwood*
C&W - 7/20/85(1)
Dixieland Delight...*Alabama*
C&W - 4/16/83(1)
Dizzy...*Tommy Roe*
HOT - 3/15/69(4)
Do It Any Way You Wanna...
People's Choice
R&B - 9/27/75(1)

Do It ('Til You're Satisfied)...
B.T. Express
R&B - 10/19/74(1)
Do Me Again...*Freddie Jackson*
R&B - 4/6/91(1)
Do Me Baby...*Meli'sa Morgan*
R&B - 2/15/86(3)
Do That To Me One More Time...
Captain & Tennille
HOT - 2/16/80(1)
(Do The) Push And Pull...
Rufus Thomas
R&B - 2/6/71(2)
Do Wah Diddy Diddy...*Manfred Mann*
HOT - 10/17/64(2)
Do What You Do...*Jermaine Jackson*
A/C - 12/22/84(3)
Do Ya'...*K.T. Oslin*
C&W - 12/19/87(1)
Do You Get Enough Love...
Shirley Jones
R&B - 8/16/86(2)
(Do You Know Where You're Going To) ..see: Theme From Mahogany
Do You Know You Are My Sunshine...
Statler Brothers
C&W - 5/27/78(2)
Do You Love As Good As You Look...
Bellamy Brothers
C&W - 3/7/81(1)
Do You Love Me...*Contours*
R&B - 10/20/62(3)
(Do You Love Me) Just Say Yes...
Highway 101
C&W - 9/10/88(1)
Do You Love What You Feel...
Rufus & Chaka Khan
R&B - 12/15/79(3)
Do You Remember?...*Phil Collins*
A/C - 6/2/90(5)
Do You Wanna Go To Heaven...
T.G. Sheppard
C&W - 10/4/80(1)
Dock Of The Bay ..see: (Sittin' On)
Does Fort Worth Ever Cross Your Mind...*George Strait*
C&W - 1/5/85(1)
Doggie In The Window...*Patti Page*
POP - BS: 3/21/53(8); DJ: 3/28/53(7); JB: 3/28/53(7)
Doggin' Around...*Jackie Wilson*
R&B - 5/23/60(3)
Doing It To Death...
Fred Wesley & The J.B.'s
R&B - 7/7/73(2)
Dominique...*Singing Nun*
HOT - 12/7/63(4)
A/C - 12/7/63(4)
Don't...*Elvis Presley*
POP - BS: 2/10/58(5); TP: 3/10/58(1); DJ: 3/17/58(1)
Don't Ask Me Why...*Billy Joel*
A/C - 9/6/80(1)
Don't Be Cruel...*Bobby Brown*
R&B - 7/23/88(2)

Don't Be Cruel...*Elvis Presley*
POP - BS: 8/18/56(11); JB: 9/1/56(11); DJ: 9/8/56(8); TP: 9/15/56(7)
R&B - JB: 9/15/56(6); BS: 10/27/56(1)
C&W - JB: 9/15/56(10); BS: 9/29/56(5)
Don't Break The Heart That Loves You...*Connie Francis*
HOT - 3/31/62(1)
A/C - 3/24/62(4)
Don't Break The Heart That Loves You...*Margo Smith*
C&W - 2/18/78(2)
Don't Call Him A Cowboy...
Conway Twitty
C&W - 6/1/85(1)
Don't Cheat In Our Hometown...
Ricky Skaggs
C&W - 2/18/84(1)
Don't Close Your Eyes...
Keith Whitley
C&W - 8/13/88(1)
Don't Come Home A'Drinkin' (With Lovin' On Your Mind)...*Loretta Lynn*
C&W - 2/11/67(1)
Don't Disturb This Groove...*System*
R&B - 5/2/87(1)
Don't Expect Me To Be Your Friend...
Lobo
A/C - 2/3/73(2)
Don't Fight The Feelings Of Love...
Charley Pride
C&W - 6/30/73(1)
Don't Forbid Me...*Pat Boone*
POP - TP: 2/9/57(1); JB: 2/23/57(1)
Don't Give Up On Us...*David Soul*
HOT - 4/16/77(1)
A/C - 4/9/77(1)
Don't Go Breaking My Heart...
Elton John & Kiki Dee
HOT - 8/7/76(4)
A/C - 9/11/76(1)
Don't Go To Strangers...
T. Graham Brown
C&W - 5/2/87(1)
Don't It Make My Brown Eyes Blue...
Crystal Gayle
C&W - 8/27/77(4)
Don't Just Stand There ..see: (When You Feel Like You're In Love)
Don't Keep Me Hangin' On...
Sonny James
C&W - 8/8/70(4)
Don't Knock My Love...*Wilson Pickett*
R&B - 6/26/71(1)
Don't Know Much...
Linda Ronstadt/Aaron Neville
A/C - 10/28/89(5)
Don't Leave Me This Way...
Thelma Houston
HOT - 4/23/77(1)
R&B - 2/19/77(1)
Don't Let Me Cross Over...
Carl Butler & Pearl
C&W - 12/29/62(11)
Don't Let The Stars Get In Your Eyes...*Perry Como with The Ramblers*
POP - BS: 1/10/53(5); JB: 1/17/53(4); DJ: 1/24/53(3)

285

Don't Let The Stars Get In Your
  Eyes...Skeets McDonald
  C&W - JB: 12/27/52(3)
Don't Let The Stars Get In Your
  Eyes...Slim Willet
  C&W - DJ: 12/6/52(1)
Don't Make It Easy For Me...
  Earl Thomas Conley
  C&W - 4/7/84(1)
Don't Play That Song...
  Aretha Franklin
  R&B - 9/12/70(3)
Don't Pull Your Love/Then You Can
  Tell Me Goodbye...Glen Campbell
  A/C - 5/8/76(1)
Don't Rock The Jukebox...
  Alan Jackson
  C&W - 7/6/91(3)
Don't Say Goodnight (It's Time For
  Love)...Isley Brothers
  R&B - 4/19/80(4)
Don't Say No Tonight...Eugene Wilde
  R&B - 12/21/85(2)
Don't Sleep In The Subway...
  Petula Clark
  A/C - 7/15/67(3)
Don't Stop Believin'...
  Olivia Newton-John
  A/C - 9/18/76(1)
Don't Stop The Music...
  Yarbrough & Peoples
  R&B - 2/28/81(5)
Don't Stop 'Til You Get Enough...
  Michael Jackson
  HOT - 10/13/79(1)
  R&B - 9/8/79(5)
Don't Take It Away...Conway Twitty
  C&W - 5/12/79(1)
Don't Take It Personal...
  Jermaine Jackson
  R&B - 11/18/89(1)
Don't Take Your Guns To Town...
  Johnny Cash
  C&W - 2/23/59(6)
Don't The Girls All Get Prettier At
  Closing Time...Mickey Gilley
  C&W - 5/1/76(1)
Don't Underestimate My Love For
  You...Lee Greenwood
  C&W - 3/29/86(1)
Don't Wanna Change The World...
  Phyllis Hyman
  R&B - 9/21/91(1)
Don't Wanna Lose You...
  Gloria Estefan
  HOT - 9/16/89(1)
Don't Waste Your Time...
  Yarbrough & Peoples
  R&B - 5/26/84(1)
Don't We All Have The Right...
  Ricky Van Shelton
  C&W - 7/30/88(1)
Don't Worry...Marty Robbins
  C&W - 2/27/61(10)
Don't Worry Be Happy...
  Bobby McFerrin
  HOT - 9/24/88(2)

Don't Worry 'Bout Me Baby...
  Janie Fricke
  C&W - 7/10/82(1)
Don't You Ever Get Tired (Of Hurting
  Me)...Ronnie Milsap
  C&W - 3/11/89(1)
Don't You (Forget About Me)...
  Simple Minds
  HOT - 5/18/85(1)
Don't You Know...Della Reese
  R&B - 11/23/59(2)
Don't You Know How Much I Love
  You...Ronnie Milsap
  C&W - 10/8/83(1)
Don't You Know I Love You...Clovers
  R&B - BS: 9/1/51(2)
Don't You Want Me...Human League
  HOT - 7/3/82(3)
Door, The...George Jones
  C&W - 1/4/75(1)
Door Is Always Open...Dave & Sugar
  C&W - 7/10/76(1)
Door Is Still Open To My Heart...
  Dean Martin
  A/C - 11/14/64(1)
Double Crossing Blues...
  Little Esther/Johnny Otis Orchestra
  R&B - BS: 3/4/50(9); JB: 3/11/50(5)
Double Dutch Bus...Frankie Smith
  R&B - 7/18/81(4)
Down Home...Alabama
  C&W - 4/13/91(3)
Down Under...Men At Work
  HOT - 1/15/83(4)
Downtown...Petula Clark
  HOT - 1/23/65(2)
Downtown Train...Rod Stewart
  A/C - 1/20/90(1)
Dream Merchant...New Birth
  R&B - 8/16/75(1)
Dreamin'...Vanessa Williams
  R&B - 2/18/89(2)
Dreams...Fleetwood Mac
  HOT - 6/18/77(1)
Drifter...Sylvia
  C&W - 4/4/81(1)
Drinkin' My Baby (Off My Mind)...
  Eddie Rabbitt
  C&W - 4/17/76(1)
Drive...Cars
  A/C - 9/22/84(3)
Drivin' My Life Away...Eddie Rabbitt
  C&W - 8/23/80(1)
Drown In My Own Tears...Ray Charles
  R&B - DJ: 3/24/56(1); JB: 3/31/56(2)
Dueling Banjos...
  Eric Weissberg & Steve Mandell
  A/C - 2/17/73(2)
Duke Of Earl...Gene Chandler
  HOT - 2/17/62(3)
  R&B - 2/17/62(5)
Dukes Of Hazard ..see: Theme From

E

Early In The Morning...Gap Band
  R&B - 6/26/82(3)
Earth Angel...Penguins
  R&B - JB: 1/15/55(3); BS: 1/29/55(3);
  DJ: 2/19/55(1)
Easier Said Than Done...Essex
  HOT - 7/6/63(2)
  R&B - 7/20/63(2)
Easy...Commodores
  R&B - 7/16/77(1)
Easy Loving...Freddie Hart
  C&W - 9/11/71(3)
Easy On The Eyes...Eddy Arnold
  C&W - BS: 5/3/52(1)
Easy Question ..see: (Such An)
Ebony And Ivory...
  Paul McCartney & Stevie Wonder
  HOT - 5/15/82(7)
  A/C - 5/15/82(5)
Eddy's Song...Eddy Arnold
  C&W - BS: 1/31/53(3)
Eight Days A Week...Beatles
  HOT - 3/13/65(2)
(Eighteen Wheeler) ..see: Roll On
Eighteen Wheels And A Dozen
  Roses...Kathy Mattea
  C&W - 5/21/88(2)
El Paso...Marty Robbins
  HOT - 1/4/60(2)
  C&W - 12/21/59(7)
El Paso City...Marty Robbins
  C&W - 6/19/76(2)
Eleven Roses...Hank Williams, Jr.
  C&W - 7/1/72(2)
Elizabeth...Statler Brothers
  C&W - 3/17/84(1)
Elvira...Oak Ridge Boys
  C&W - 5/30/81(1)
Emotion...Helen Reddy
  A/C - 3/29/75(1)
Emotions...Mariah Carey
  HOT - 10/12/91(3)
  R&B - 11/2/91(1)
Empty Arms...Sonny James
  C&W - 4/10/71(4)
Encore...Cheryl Lynn
  R&B - 2/25/84(1)
End Of The World...Skeeter Davis
  A/C - 3/16/63(4)
Endless Love...
  Diana Ross & Lionel Richie
  HOT - 8/15/81(9)
  R&B - 8/22/81(7)
  A/C - 9/5/81(3)
Endlessly...Sonny James
  C&W - 11/28/70(3)
England Swings...Roger Miller
  A/C - 1/1/66(1)
(Enough Is Enough) ..see: No More
  Tears
Entertainer, The...Marvin Hamlisch
  A/C - 5/18/74(1)

Escapade...*Janet Jackson*
HOT - 3/3/90(3)
R&B - 3/10/90(1)

Escape (The Pina Colada Song)...
Rupert Holmes
HOT - 12/22/79(3)

Eternal Flame...*Bangles*
HOT - 4/1/89(1)
A/C - 4/8/89(2)

Eve Of Destruction...*Barry McGuire*
HOT - 9/25/65(1)

Even Now...*Barry Manilow*
A/C - 5/27/78(3)

Even The Nights Are Better...
Air Supply
A/C - 7/24/82(4)

Even Tho...*Webb Pierce*
C&W - DJ: 7/3/54(2)

(Evergreen) ..see: Love Theme From A Star Is Born

Everlasting Love...*Howard Jones*
A/C - 6/10/89(2)

Every Beat Of My Heart...*Pips*
R&B - 6/26/61(1)

Every Breath You Take...*Police*
HOT - 7/9/83(8)

Every Little Step...*Bobby Brown*
R&B - 4/15/89(1)

Every Rose Has Its Thorn...*Poison*
HOT - 12/24/88(3)

(Every Time I Turn Around) Back In Love Again...*L.T.D.*
R&B - 11/5/77(2)

Every Time Two Fools Collide...
Kenny Rogers & Dottie West
C&W - 4/22/78(2)

Every Time You Touch Me (I Get High)...*Charlie Rich*
A/C - 7/5/75(1)

Every Which Way But Loose...
Eddie Rabbitt
C&W - 2/10/79(3)

(Everybody Dance Now) ..see: Gonna Make You Sweat

Everybody Loves Somebody...
Dean Martin
HOT - 8/15/64(1)
A/C - 8/1/64(8)

Everybody Plays The Fool...
Aaron Neville
A/C - 10/12/91(1)

Everybody Wants To Rule The World...*Tears For Fears*
HOT - 6/8/85(2)

Everybody's Had The Blues...
Merle Haggard
C&W - 8/25/73(2)

Everybody's Somebody's Fool...
Connie Francis
HOT - 6/27/60(2)

Everyday...*Oak Ridge Boys*
C&W - 10/6/84(1)

Everyday People...
Sly & The Family Stone
HOT - 2/15/69(4)
R&B - 2/22/69(2)

(Everything I Do) I Do It For You...
Bryan Adams
HOT - 7/27/91(7)
A/C - 8/3/91(8)

Everything I Miss At Home...
Cherrelle
R&B - 12/17/88(1)

Everything Is Beautiful...
Ray Stevens
HOT - 5/30/70(2)
A/C - 5/23/70(3)

Everything She Wants...*Wham!*
HOT - 5/25/85(2)

Everything That Glitters (Is Not Gold)...*Dan Seals*
C&W - 7/5/86(1)

Everytime You Go Away...*Paul Young*
HOT - 7/27/85(1)
A/C - 8/10/85(2)

Everywhere...*Fleetwood Mac*
A/C - 1/16/88(3)

Exclusivity...*Damian Dame*
R&B - 7/13/91(2)

Express...*B.T. Express*
R&B - 3/8/75(1)

Eye Of The Tiger...*Survivor*
HOT - 7/24/82(6)

F

Face To Face...*Alabama*
C&W - 3/5/88(1)

Faith...*George Michael*
HOT - 12/12/87(4)

Fake...*Alexander O'Neal*
R&B - 7/25/87(2)

Faking Love...
T.G. Sheppard & Karen Brooks
C&W - 2/19/83(1)

Fallin' Again...*Alabama*
C&W - 7/9/88(1)

Fallin' In Love...
Hamilton, Joe Frank & Reynolds
HOT - 8/23/75(1)
A/C - 8/30/75(1)

Falling...*Melba Moore*
R&B - 2/14/87(1)

Fame...*David Bowie*
HOT - 9/20/75(2)

Family Affair...
Sly & The Family Stone
HOT - 12/4/71(3)
R&B - 12/4/71(5)

Famous Last Words Of A Fool...
George Strait
C&W - 4/9/88(1)

Fancy Free...*Oak Ridge Boys*
C&W - 11/7/81(1)

Fannie Mae...*Buster Brown*
R&B - 4/18/60(1)

Fantastic Voyage...*Lakeside*
R&B - 1/31/81(2)

Farther Up The Road...
Bobby "Blue" Bland
R&B - DJ: 9/2/57(2)

Faster Horses (The Cowboy And The Poet)...*Tom T. Hall*
C&W - 3/20/76(1)

Father Figure...*George Michael*
HOT - 2/27/88(2)

Feel Like Makin' Love...
Roberta Flack
HOT - 8/10/74(1)
R&B - 8/3/74(5)
A/C - 8/10/74(2)

Feelins'...
Conway Twitty & Loretta Lynn
C&W - 9/6/75(1)

Feels Good...*Tony! Toni! Tone!*
R&B - 9/1/90(2)

Feels So Good...*Chuck Mangione*
A/C - 5/13/78(1)

Feels So Right...*Alabama*
C&W - 7/18/81(2)

Fernando...*Abba*
A/C - 10/16/76(2)

Fever...*Little Willie John*
R&B - BS: 7/21/56(3); DJ: 7/21/56(5); JB: 9/1/56(1)

Ffun...*Con Funk Shun*
R&B - 1/7/78(2)

Fifteen Years Ago...*Conway Twitty*
C&W - 11/21/70(1)

Fifth Of Beethoven...*Walter Murphy*
HOT - 10/9/76(1)

50 Ways To Leave Your Lover...
Paul Simon
HOT - 2/7/76(3)
A/C - 2/28/76(2)

Fight The Power...*Isley Brothers*
R&B - 7/19/75(1)

Fightin' Side Of Me...*Merle Haggard*
C&W - 3/14/70(3)

Finally...*T.G. Sheppard*
C&W - 6/5/82(1)

Finally Got Myself Together (I'm A Changed Man)...*Impressions*
R&B - 6/22/74(2)

Finer Things...*Steve Winwood*
A/C - 4/25/87(3)

Fingertips...*Little Stevie Wonder*
HOT - 8/10/63(3)
R&B - 8/3/63(6)

Fire...*Ohio Players*
HOT - 2/8/75(1)
R&B - 1/25/75(2)

Fire & Smoke...*Earl Thomas Conley*
C&W - 7/11/81(1)

Fire I Can't Put Out...*George Strait*
C&W - 9/3/83(1)

Fire In The Night ..see: (There's A)

First Thing Ev'ry Morning (And The Last Thing Ev'ry Night)...*Jimmy Dean*
C&W - 8/7/65(2)

First Time...*Surface*
HOT - 1/26/91(2)
R&B - 1/19/91(1)
A/C - 2/2/91(2)
(also see: Remember)

First Time Ever I Saw Your Face...
Roberta Flack
HOT - 4/15/72(6)
A/C - 4/1/72(6)

Fishin' In The Dark...
Nitty Gritty Dirt Band
C&W - 10/17/87(1)

Fishnet... *Morris Day*
R&B - 3/12/88(2)

Fist City... *Loretta Lynn*
C&W - 4/20/68(1)

Five Long Years... *Eddie Boyd*
R&B - JB: 11/8/52(7); BS: 12/13/52(2)

Five Minutes... *Lorrie Morgan*
C&W - 4/14/90(1)

5-10-15 Hours... *Ruth Brown*
R&B - BS: 5/3/52(7); JB: 5/3/52(6)

Flame, The... *Cheap Trick*
HOT - 7/9/88(2)

Flamingo... *Earl Bostic*
R&B - BS: 12/29/51(4)

Flash Light... *Parliament*
R&B - 3/4/78(3)

Flashdance...What A Feeling...
Irene Cara
HOT - 5/28/83(6)

Flesh And Blood... *Johnny Cash*
C&W - 1/30/71(1)

Float On... *Floaters*
R&B - 8/13/77(6)

Fly Away... *John Denver*
A/C - 1/10/76(2)

Fly, Robin, Fly... *Silver Convention*
HOT - 11/29/75(3)
R&B - 11/15/75(1)

Folsom Prison Blues... *Johnny Cash*
C&W - 7/20/68(4)

Fool, Fool, Fool... *Clovers*
R&B - BS: 11/10/51(6); JB: 12/22/51(3)

Fool For You... *Ray Charles*
R&B - DJ: 8/6/55(1)

Fool For Your Love... *Mickey Gilley*
C&W - 6/25/83(1)

Fool Hearted Memory... *George Strait*
C&W - 8/28/82(1)

Fool (If You Think It's Over)...
Chris Rea
A/C - 9/9/78(3)

Fool On The Hill...
Sergio Mendes & Brasil '66
A/C - 9/7/68(6)

Foolish Beat... *Debbie Gibson*
HOT - 6/25/88(1)

Footloose... *Kenny Loggins*
HOT - 3/31/84(3)
(also see: Almost Paradise)

For All The Wrong Reasons...
Bellamy Brothers
C&W - 6/12/82(1)

For All We Know... *Carpenters*
A/C - 2/27/71(3)

For Loving You...
Bill Anderson & Jan Howard
C&W - 12/23/67(4)

For My Broken Heart... *Reba McEntire*
C&W - 12/7/91(2)

For The Good Times... *Ray Price*
C&W - 9/19/70(1)

For The Love Of Him... *Bobbi Martin*
A/C - 5/9/70(2)

For You... *Ricky Nelson*
A/C - 2/8/64(2)

Forever ..see: (I'll Be Loving You)

Forever And Ever, Amen...
Randy Travis
C&W - 6/13/87(3)

Forever My Lady... *Jodeci*
R&B - 11/9/91(2)

Forever Together... *Randy Travis*
C&W - 11/30/91(1)

Forever Your Girl... *Paula Abdul*
HOT - 5/20/89(2)

Forever's As Far As I'll Go...
Alabama
C&W - 1/26/91(1)

Forgiving You Was Easy...
Willie Nelson
C&W - 7/13/85(1)

Four Walls... *Jim Reeves*
C&W - DJ: 5/27/57(8)

Fourteen Carat Mind... *Gene Watson*
C&W - 1/9/82(1)

Forty Hour Week (For A Livin')...
Alabama
C&W - 8/3/85(1)

Frankenstein... *Edgar Winter Group*
HOT - 5/26/73(1)

Fraulein... *Bobby Helms*
C&W - DJ: 9/16/57(4); BS: 9/23/57(3)

Freebird ..see: Baby, I Love Your Way

Freeway Of Love... *Aretha Franklin*
R&B - 8/3/85(5)

Fresh... *Kool & The Gang*
R&B - 5/18/85(1)

Friends... *Razzy Bailey*
C&W - 6/6/81(1)

Friends And Lovers...
Gloria Loring & Carl Anderson
A/C - 9/6/86(2)
(also see: Both To Each Other)

Friends In Low Places... *Garth Brooks*
C&W - 10/6/90(4)

From A Distance... *Bette Midler*
A/C - 11/3/90(6)

From A Jack To A King...
Ricky Van Shelton
C&W - 3/18/89(1)

Fugitive, The... *Merle Haggard*
C&W - 3/4/67(1)

Full Of Fire... *Al Green*
R&B - 12/20/75(1)

Full Time Job... *Eddy Arnold*
C&W - DJ: 8/16/52(4)

Fun ..see: Ffun

Funkin' For Jamaica (N.Y.)...
Tom Browne
R&B - 10/4/80(4)

Funky Broadway... *Wilson Pickett*
R&B - 9/30/67(1)

Funky Worm... *Ohio Players*
R&B - 5/12/73(1)

Funkytown... *Lipps, Inc.*
HOT - 5/31/80(4)

Funny Face... *Donna Fargo*
C&W - 10/14/72(3)

G

Galveston... *Glen Campbell*
C&W - 4/19/69(3)
A/C - 3/29/69(6)

Gambler, The... *Kenny Rogers*
C&W - 12/16/78(3)

Game Of Love...
Wayne Fontana & The Mindbenders
HOT - 4/24/65(1)

(Games People Play) ..see: They Just Can't Stop It the

Games That Daddies Play...
Conway Twitty
C&W - 10/9/76(1)

Garden Party... *Rick Nelson*
A/C - 10/14/72(2)

Georgia On My Mind... *Ray Charles*
HOT - 11/14/60(1)

Georgia On My Mind... *Willie Nelson*
C&W - 6/10/78(1)

Get A Job... *Silhouettes*
POP - TP: 2/24/58(2)
R&B - DJ: 2/3/58(6); BS: 2/10/58(4)

Get Back...
Beatles with Billy Preston
HOT - 5/24/69(5)

Get Down, Get Down (Get On The Floor)... *Joe Simon*
R&B - 5/10/75(2)

Get Down Tonight...
K.C. & The Sunshine Band
HOT - 8/30/75(1)
R&B - 8/23/75(1)

Get It Right... *Aretha Franklin*
R&B - 8/20/83(2)

Get Off... *Foxy*
R&B - 8/26/78(2)

Get Off Of My Cloud... *Rolling Stones*
HOT - 11/6/65(2)

Get On The Good Foot... *James Brown*
R&B - 9/16/72(4)

Get Outta My Dreams, Get Into My Car... *Billy Ocean*
HOT - 4/9/88(2)
R&B - 4/16/88(1)

Get Ready... *Temptations*
R&B - 4/30/66(1)

Getaway... *Earth, Wind & Fire*
R&B - 8/7/76(2)

Ghostbusters... *Ray Parker Jr.*
HOT - 8/11/84(3)
R&B - 8/25/84(2)

Giddyup Go... *Red Sovine*
C&W - 1/8/66(6)

Girl From Ipanema...
Stan Getz/Astrud Gilberto
A/C - 7/18/64(2)

Girl I Got My Eyes On You... *Today*
R&B - 4/8/89(1)

Girl I'm Gonna Miss You...
Milli Vanilli
HOT - 9/23/89(2)

Girl Is Mine...
Michael Jackson/Paul McCartney
R&B - 1/15/83(3)
A/C - 12/25/82(4)

Girl On The Billboard...*Del Reeves*
C&W - 5/15/65(2)

Girlfriend...*Bobby Brown*
R&B - 12/27/86(2)

Girlfriend...*Pebbles*
R&B - 2/20/88(2)

Girls Night Out...*Judds*
C&W - 4/27/85(1)

Give It All You Got...*Chuck Mangione*
A/C - 2/23/80(3)

Give It To Me Baby...*Rick James*
R&B - 6/13/81(5)

Give It Up Or Turnit A Loose...
James Brown
R&B - 3/8/69(2)

Give Me Love - (Give Me Peace On Earth)...*George Harrison*
HOT - 6/30/73(1)

Give Me More, More, More (Of Your Kisses)...*Lefty Frizzell*
C&W - DJ: 2/2/52(3); JB: 2/9/52(3)

Give Me One More Chance...*Exile*
C&W - 11/17/84(1)

Give Me The Night...*George Benson*
R&B - 9/13/80(3)

Give Me Wings...*Michael Johnson*
C&W - 1/10/87(1)

Give The People What They Want...
O'Jays
R&B - 6/21/75(1)

Giving You The Benefit...*Pebbles*
R&B - 10/6/90(3)

Giving You The Best That I Got...
Anita Baker
R&B - 11/12/88(2)
A/C - 12/10/88(1)

Glory Of Love...*Peter Cetera*
HOT - 8/2/86(2)
A/C - 7/19/86(5)

Glory Of Love...*Five Keys*
R&B - BS: 9/22/51(4); JB: 10/20/51(2)

Glow-Worm...*Mills Brothers*
POP - JB: 12/6/52(3)

Go Away Little Girl...*Steve Lawrence*
HOT - 1/12/63(2)
A/C - 12/15/62(6)

Go Away Little Girl...*Donny Osmond*
HOT - 9/11/71(3)

Go Home...*Stevie Wonder*
A/C - 1/25/86(1)

Goin' Gone...*Kathy Mattea*
C&W - 1/30/88(1)

Goin' Home...*Fats Domino*
R&B - BS: 6/21/52(1)

Going, Going, Gone...*Lee Greenwood*
C&W - 3/10/84(1)

Going Where The Lonely Go...
Merle Haggard
C&W - 1/15/83(1)

Golden Ring...
George Jones & Tammy Wynette
C&W - 8/7/76(1)

Golden Rocket...*Hank Snow*
C&W - BS: 1/6/51(2); DJ: 1/27/51(1)

Golden Tears...*Dave & Sugar*
C&W - 3/3/79(3)

Gone...*Ferlin Husky*
C&W - BS: 4/6/57(10); DJ: 4/6/57(9); JB: 4/20/57(5)

Gone Too Far...*Eddie Rabbitt*
C&W - 5/17/80(1)

Gonna Fly Now (Theme From 'Rocky')...*Bill Conti*
HOT - 7/2/77(1)

Gonna Make You Sweat (Everybody Dance Now)...*C & C Music Factory Featuring Freedom Williams*
HOT - 2/9/91(2)
R&B - 2/23/91(1)

Gonna Take A Lot Of River...
Oak Ridge Boys
C&W - 10/29/88(1)

Good Hearted Woman...
Waylon & Willie
C&W - 2/21/76(3)

Good Lovin'...*Young Rascals*
HOT - 4/30/66(1)

Good Lovin' (Makes It Right)...
Tammy Wynette
C&W - 8/28/71(2)

Good Luck Charm...*Elvis Presley*
HOT - 4/21/62(2)

Good, The Bad And The Ugly...
Hugo Montenegro
A/C - 5/18/68(3)

Good Thing...*Fine Young Cannibals*
HOT - 7/8/89(1)

Good Times...*Chic*
HOT - 8/18/79(1)
R&B - 7/28/79(6)

Good Times...*Dan Seals*
C&W - 8/4/90(2)

Good Vibrations...*Beach Boys*
HOT - 12/10/66(1)

Good Vibrations...
Marky Mark & The Funky Bunch
HOT - 10/5/91(1)

Good Woman Blues...*Mel Tillis*
C&W - 11/27/76(2)

Goodnight Irene...
Gordon Jenkins & The Weavers
POP - BS: 8/19/50(13); JB: 8/26/50(12); DJ: 9/2/50(8)

Goodnight, Irene...
Ernest Tubb & Red Foley
C&W - BS: 8/26/50(2); JB: 8/26/50(3)

Got A Hold On Me...*Christine McVie*
A/C - 3/10/84(4)

Got My Heart Set On You...
John Conlee
C&W - 9/20/86(1)

Got My Mind Set On You...
George Harrison
HOT - 1/16/88(1)
A/C - 12/19/87(4)

Got The All Overs For You (All Over Me)...*Freddie Hart*
C&W - 12/9/72(3)

Got To Be Real...*Cheryl Lynn*
R&B - 1/6/79(1)

Got To Get You Into My Life...
Earth, Wind & Fire
R&B - 9/23/78(1)

Got To Get You Off My Mind...
Solomon Burke
R&B - 4/3/65(3)

Got To Give It Up...*Marvin Gaye*
HOT - 6/25/77(1)
R&B - 4/30/77(5)

Gotta Get You Home Tonight...
Eugene Wilde
R&B - 1/26/85(1)

Grand Tour...*George Jones*
C&W - 8/31/74(1)

Grandma Harp...*Merle Haggard*
C&W - 5/13/72(2)

Grandpa (Tell Me 'Bout The Good Old Days)...*Judds*
C&W - 5/10/86(1)

Grazing In The Grass...*Hugh Masekela*
HOT - 7/20/68(2)
R&B - 7/13/68(4)

Grease...*Frankie Valli*
HOT - 8/26/78(2)

Great Balls Of Fire...
Jerry Lee Lewis
C&W - BS: 1/6/58(2)

Great Pretender...*Platters*
POP - TP: 2/18/56(2); DJ: 2/18/56(2); JB: 2/25/56(1)
R&B - BS: 1/7/56(10); DJ: 1/7/56(11); JB: 1/28/56(9)

Greatest Love Of All...
Whitney Houston
HOT - 5/17/86(3)
A/C - 4/26/86(5)

Green Berets ..see: Ballad Of

Green Door...*Jim Lowe*
POP - TP: 11/3/56(3); JB: 11/17/56(3)

Green Onions...*Booker T. & The MG's*
R&B - 9/15/62(4)

Green Tambourine...*Lemon Pipers*
HOT - 2/3/68(1)

Groove Me...*King Floyd*
R&B - 1/2/71(4)

Groovin'...*Young Rascals*
HOT - 5/20/67(4)

Groovy Kind Of Love...*Phil Collins*
HOT - 10/22/88(2)
A/C - 10/8/88(3)

Guess Things Happen That Way...
Johnny Cash
C&W - DJ: 6/23/58(3); BS: 6/30/58(8)

Guitar Man...*Bread*
A/C - 9/9/72(1)
(also see: Daddy Frank)

Guitar Man...*Elvis Presley*
C&W - 3/14/81(1)

Guy Is A Guy...*Doris Day*
POP - JB: 5/24/52(1)

Gypsys, Tramps & Thieves...*Cher*
HOT - 11/6/71(2)

H

Half As Much...*Rosemary Clooney*
POP - JB: 7/26/52(3)
Half-Breed...*Cher*
HOT - 10/6/73(2)
Hands Off...*Jay McShann*
R&B - BS: 12/17/55(3); DJ: 12/17/55(2); JB: 1/14/56(2)
Handy Man...*James Taylor*
A/C - 9/3/77(1)
Hang On Sloopy...*McCoys*
HOT - 10/2/65(1)
Hang On To Your Heart...*Exile*
C&W - 11/16/85(1)
Hangin' On A String (Contemplating)...*Loose Ends*
R&B - 7/13/85(1)
Hangin' Tough...
New Kids On The Block
HOT - 9/9/89(1)
Hanky Panky...
Tommy James & The Shondells
HOT - 7/16/66(2)
Happening, The...*Supremes*
HOT - 5/13/67(1)
Happiest Girl In The Whole U.S.A....
Donna Fargo
C&W - 6/3/72(3)
Happy Birthday Darlin'...
Conway Twitty
C&W - 12/15/79(3)
Happy, Happy Birthday Baby...
Ronnie Milsap
C&W - 6/7/86(1)
Happy Heart...*Andy Williams*
A/C - 5/24/69(2)
Happy Organ...*Dave 'Baby' Cortez*
HOT - 5/11/59(1)
Happy People...*Temptations*
R&B - 2/8/75(1)
Happy Together...*Turtles*
HOT - 3/25/67(3)
Harbor Lights...*Sammy Kaye*
POP - BS: 11/18/50(2); JB: 11/18/50(4)
Hard Day's Night...*Beatles*
HOT - 8/1/64(2)
Hard Headed Woman...*Elvis Presley*
POP - BS: 7/21/58(2); DJ: 7/21/58(1)
Hard Luck Blues...*Roy Brown*
R&B - BS: 8/19/50(3)
Hard Rock Bottom Of Your Heart...
Randy Travis
C&W - 3/17/90(2)
Hard To Say I'm Sorry...*Chicago*
HOT - 9/11/82(2)
A/C - 8/21/82(3)
Harper Valley P.T.A....
Jeannie C. Riley
HOT - 9/21/68(1)
C&W - 9/28/68(3)
Have A Little Faith...*David Houston*
C&W - 5/11/68(1)
Have Mercy...*Judds*
C&W - 12/28/85(2)

Have Mercy Baby...*Dominoes*
R&B - JB: 6/14/52(10); BS: 6/28/52(7)
Have You Ever Loved Somebody...
Freddie Jackson
R&B - 2/21/87(2)
Have You Had Your Love Today...
O'Jays
R&B - 6/17/89(2)
Have You Looked Into Your Heart...
Jerry Vale
A/C - 2/6/65(1)
Have You Never Been Mellow...
Olivia Newton-John
HOT - 3/8/75(1)
A/C - 3/8/75(1)
Have You Seen Her...*Chi-Lites*
R&B - 11/20/71(2)
He Don't Love You (Like I Love You)...*Tony Orlando & Dawn*
HOT - 5/3/75(3)
A/C - 4/19/75(1)
He Got You...*Ronnie Milsap*
C&W - 10/23/82(1)
He Loves Me All The Way...
Tammy Wynette
C&W - 7/4/70(3)
He Stopped Loving Her Today...
George Jones
C&W - 7/5/80(1)
He Thinks I Still Care...*Anne Murray*
C&W - 7/6/74(2)
He Treats Your Daughter Mean ..see: (Mama)
He Will Break Your Heart...
Jerry Butler
R&B - 11/14/60(7)
He'll Have To Go...*Jim Reeves*
C&W - 2/8/60(14)
He's A Heartache (Looking For A Place To Happen)...*Janie Fricke*
C&W - 8/13/83(1)
He's A Rebel...*Crystals*
HOT - 11/3/62(2)
He's Back And I'm Blue...
Desert Rose Band
C&W - 6/25/88(1)
He's Got The Whole World (In His Hands)...*Laurie London*
POP - DJ: 4/14/58(4)
He's So Fine...*Chiffons*
HOT - 3/30/63(4)
R&B - 4/6/63(4)
He's The Greatest Dancer...
Sister Sledge
R&B - 3/31/79(1)
Head To Toe...*Lisa Lisa & Cult Jam*
HOT - 6/20/87(1)
R&B - 5/30/87(2)
Headache Tomorrow (Or A Heartache Tonight)...*Mickey Gilley*
C&W - 4/25/81(1)
Healing Hands...*Elton John*
A/C - 10/21/89(1)
Heart Healer...*Mel Tillis*
C&W - 3/5/77(1)
Heart Of Glass...*Blondie*
HOT - 4/28/79(1)

Heart Of Gold...*Neil Young*
HOT - 3/18/72(1)
Heartache Tonight...*Eagles*
HOT - 11/10/79(1)
Heartaches By The Number...
Guy Mitchell
HOT - 12/14/59(2)
Heartbeat In The Darkness...
Don Williams
C&W - 8/30/86(1)
Heartbreak Hotel...*Elvis Presley*
POP - BS: 4/21/56(8); TP: 5/5/56(7); JB: 5/5/56(8); DJ: 5/12/56(3)
C&W - BS: 3/17/56(17); DJ: 3/31/56(12); JB: 4/7/56(13)
Heartbreak Hotel...
Willie Nelson & Leon Russell
C&W - 9/1/79(1)
Heartbreak U.S.A....*Kitty Wells*
C&W - 7/10/61(4)
Heartbreaker...*Dolly Parton*
C&W - 9/30/78(3)
Heartbreaker...*Dionne Warwick*
A/C - 12/18/82(1)
Heartbroke...*Ricky Skaggs*
C&W - 11/13/82(1)
Heartlight...*Neil Diamond*
A/C - 10/23/82(4)
Hearts Aren't Made To Break (They're Made To Love)...*Lee Greenwood*
C&W - 7/12/86(1)
Hearts Of Stone...*Charms*
R&B - BS: 11/27/54(9); DJ: 1/22/55(2); JB: 1/29/55(3)
Hearts Of Stone...*Fontane Sisters*
POP - BS: 2/5/55(1); JB: 2/12/55(3)
Heat Wave...*Martha & The Vandellas*
R&B - 9/14/63(4)
Heaven...*Bryan Adams*
HOT - 6/22/85(2)
Heaven Is A Place On Earth...
Belinda Carlisle
HOT - 12/5/87(1)
Heaven Says Hello...*Sonny James*
C&W - 8/17/68(1)
Heaven's Just A Sin Away...*Kendalls*
C&W - 10/8/77(4)
Hell And High Water...
T. Graham Brown
C&W - 12/13/86(1)
Hello...*Lionel Richie*
HOT - 5/12/84(2)
R&B - 5/5/84(3)
A/C - 4/7/84(6)
Hello Darlin'...*Conway Twitty*
C&W - 6/6/70(4)
Hello, Dolly!...*Louis Armstrong*
HOT - 5/9/64(1)
A/C - 3/28/64(9)
Hello Goodbye...*Beatles*
HOT - 12/30/67(3)
Hello, I Love You...*Doors*
HOT - 8/3/68(2)
Hello Love...*Hank Snow*
C&W - 4/27/74(1)
Hello Stranger...*Yvonne Elliman*
A/C - 4/30/77(4)
Hello Stranger...*Barbara Lewis*
R&B - 7/6/63(2)

Hello Vietnam...*Johnny Wright*
C&W - 10/23/65(3)

Hello Walls...*Faron Young*
C&W - 5/8/61(9)

Help!...*Beatles*
HOT - 9/4/65(3)

Help Me...*Joni Mitchell*
A/C - 5/25/74(1)

Help Me Hold On...*Travis Tritt*
C&W - 5/12/90(1)

Help Me Make It Through The Night...
Sammi Smith
C&W - 2/13/71(3)

Help Me, Rhonda...*Beach Boys*
HOT - 5/29/65(2)

Help Me Somebody..."5" *Royales*
R&B - BS: 6/13/53(5); JB: 6/13/53(5)

Here And Now...*Luther Vandross*
R&B - 12/2/89(2)

Here Comes Honey Again...
Sonny James
C&W - 11/6/71(1)

Here I Am (Just When I Thought I Was Over You)...*Air Supply*
A/C - 11/7/81(3)

Here I Go Again...*Whitesnake*
HOT - 10/10/87(1)

Here In My Heart...*Al Martino*
POP - BS: 6/7/52(3); DJ: 6/28/52(3)

Here We Are...*Gloria Estefan*
A/C - 1/27/90(5)

Here You Come Again...*Dolly Parton*
C&W - 12/3/77(5)

Here's Some Love...*Tanya Tucker*
C&W - 10/2/76(1)

Hey! Baby...*Bruce Channel*
HOT - 3/10/62(3)

Hey, Good Lookin'...*Hank Williams*
C&W - DJ: 8/11/51(8)

Hey, Joe...*Carl Smith*
C&W - BS: 8/22/53(2); JB: 9/5/53(8); DJ: 9/12/53(4)

Hey Jude...*Beatles*
HOT - 9/28/68(9)

Hey Lover...*Freddie Jackson*
R&B - 12/3/88(1)

Hey Paula...*Paul & Paula*
HOT - 2/9/63(3)
R&B - 2/23/63(2)

Hey There...*Rosemary Clooney*
POP - BS: 9/25/54(6); DJ: 10/9/54(5); JB: 10/16/54(4)

Hey, Western Union Man...
Jerry Butler
R&B - 11/16/68(1)

(Hey Won't You Play) Another Somebody Done Somebody Wrong Song...*B.J. Thomas*
HOT - 4/26/75(1)
C&W - 5/17/75(1)
A/C - 3/22/75(1)

High Cotton...*Alabama*
C&W - 10/28/89(1)

Higher And Higher ..see: (Your Love Keeps Lifting Me)

Higher Ground...*Stevie Wonder*
R&B - 9/29/73(1)

Higher Love...*Steve Winwood*
HOT - 8/30/86(1)

Higher Plane...*Kool & The Gang*
R&B - 10/26/74(1)

Highway 40 Blues...*Ricky Skaggs*
C&W - 7/9/83(1)

Highwayman...
Waylon Jennings/Willie Nelson/ Johnny Cash/Kris Kristofferson
C&W - 8/17/85(1)

Hit The Road Jack...*Ray Charles*
HOT - 10/9/61(2)
R&B - 10/2/61(5)

Hold Me...*K.T. Oslin*
C&W - 1/7/89(1)

Hold Me, Thrill Me, Kiss Me...
Mel Carter
A/C - 8/28/65(1)

Hold On...*En Vogue*
R&B - 5/26/90(2)

Hold On...*Wilson Phillips*
HOT - 6/9/90(1)
A/C - 5/26/90(1)

Hold On! I'm A Comin'...*Sam & Dave*
R&B - 6/18/66(1)

Hold On To The Nights...*Richard Marx*
HOT - 7/23/88(1)

Holding Back The Years...*Simply Red*
HOT - 7/12/86(1)

Holding Her And Loving You...
Earl Thomas Conley
C&W - 11/26/83(1)

Holding On...*Steve Winwood*
A/C - 2/4/89(2)

Holding On (When Love Is Gone)...
L.T.D.
R&B - 9/9/78(2)

Hollywood Swinging...*Kool & The Gang*
R&B - 6/8/74(1)

Home...*Joe Diffie*
C&W - 11/10/90(1)

Home...*Stephanie Mills*
R&B - 11/25/89(1)

Honey...*Bobby Goldsboro*
HOT - 4/13/68(5)
R&B - 5/25/68(3)
A/C - 5/4/68(2)

Honey Hush...*Joe Turner*
R&B - JB: 12/5/53(8)

Honey Love...
Drifters featuring Clyde McPhatter
R&B - BS: 7/10/54(8); JB: 7/31/54(8)

Honey (Open That Door)...
Ricky Skaggs
C&W - 6/2/84(1)

Honeycomb...*Jimmie Rodgers*
POP - DJ: 9/23/57(4); BS: 9/30/57(2); TP: 10/7/57(2)
R&B - BS: 10/7/57(2); DJ: 10/14/57(1)

Honky Tonk...*Bill Doggett*
R&B - BS: 8/25/56(13); DJ: 9/29/56(5); JB: 10/20/56(1)

Honky Tonk Blues...*Charley Pride*
C&W - 4/12/80(1)

Honky Tonk Moon...*Randy Travis*
C&W - 10/8/88(1)

Honky Tonk Song...*Webb Pierce*
C&W - DJ: 5/20/57(1)

Honky Tonk Women...*Rolling Stones*
HOT - 8/23/69(4)

Honky Tonkin'...*Hank Williams, Jr.*
C&W - 8/7/82(1)

Honor Bound...*Earl Thomas Conley*
C&W - 4/13/85(1)

Hooked On A Feeling...*Blue Swede*
HOT - 4/6/74(1)

Hoop-Dee-Doo...
Perry Como/The Fontane Sisters
POP - DJ: 6/3/50(2)

Hope That We Can Be Together Soon...
Sharon Paige/Harold Melvin
R&B - 8/9/75(1)

Hope You're Feelin' Me (Like I'm Feelin' You)...*Charley Pride*
C&W - 10/18/75(1)

Horse With No Name...*America*
HOT - 3/25/72(3)

Hot Child In The City...*Nick Gilder*
HOT - 10/28/78(1)

Hot Diggity (Dog Ziggity Boom)...
Perry Como
POP - DJ: 5/5/56(1)

Hot Pants...*James Brown*
R&B - 8/7/71(1)

Hot Stuff...*Donna Summer*
HOT - 6/2/79(3)

Hotel California...*Eagles*
HOT - 5/7/77(1)

Hound Dog...*Elvis Presley*
POP - BS: 8/18/56(11); JB: 9/1/56(11)
R&B - JB: 9/15/56(6); BS: 10/27/56(1)
C&W - JB: 9/15/56(10); BS: 9/29/56(5)

Hound Dog...
Willie Mae "Big Mama" Thornton
R&B - BS: 4/18/53(6); JB: 4/25/53(7)

House Of The Rising Sun...*Animals*
HOT - 9/5/64(3)

Houston (Means I'm One Day Closer To You)...*Larry Gatlin & The Gatlin Brothers Band*
C&W - 12/24/83(2)

How Am I Supposed To Live Without You...*Michael Bolton*
HOT - 1/20/90(3)
A/C - 1/6/90(2)

How Am I Supposed To Live Without You...*Laura Branigan*
A/C - 9/3/83(3)

How Blue...*Reba McEntire*
C&W - 1/19/85(1)

How 'Bout Us...*Champaign*
A/C - 5/30/81(2)

How Can I Ease The Pain...
Lisa Fischer
R&B - 6/29/91(2)

How Can I Fall?...*Breathe*
A/C - 11/12/88(1)

How Can I Unlove You...*Lynn Anderson*
C&W - 10/16/71(3)

How Can You Mend A Broken Heart...
Bee Gees
HOT - 8/7/71(4)

How Deep Is Your Love...*Bee Gees*
HOT - 12/24/77(3)
A/C - 11/26/77(6)

How Do I Turn You On...*Ronnie Milsap*
C&W - 2/14/87(1)

How High The Moon...
Les Paul & Mary Ford
POP - BS: 4/21/51(9); DJ: 4/28/51(9); JB: 5/5/51(9)

How Long (Betcha' Got A Chick On The Side)...*Pointer Sisters*
R&B - 9/6/75(2)

How Long Will My Baby Be Gone...
Buck Owens & The Buckaroos
C&W - 4/6/68(1)

How Much More Can She Stand...
Conway Twitty
C&W - 5/8/71(1)

How Sweet It Is (To Be Loved By You)...*James Taylor*
A/C - 8/23/75(1)

How Will I Know...*Whitney Houston*
HOT - 2/15/86(2)
R&B - 3/8/86(1)
A/C - 2/15/86(1)

Human...*Human League*
HOT - 11/22/86(1)

Hungry Eyes...*Merle Haggard*
C&W - 5/10/69(1)

Hurt...*Juice Newton*
C&W - 2/8/86(1)

Hurting Each Other...*Carpenters*
A/C - 2/5/72(2)

Hurts Me To My Heart...*Faye Adams*
R&B - BS: 10/16/54(5); JB: 11/20/54(5)

Hustle, The...*Van McCoy*
HOT - 7/26/75(1)
R&B - 7/12/75(1)

I

I Adore Mi Amor...*Color Me Badd*
HOT - 9/21/91(2)
R&B - 9/28/91(1)

I Ain't Living Long Like This...
Waylon Jennings
C&W - 3/1/80(1)

I Ain't Never...*Mel Tillis*
C&W - 9/30/72(2)

I Almost Lost My Mind...*Pat Boone*
POP - JB: 7/28/56(4); TP: 8/4/56(2)

I Almost Lost My Mind...
Ivory Joe Hunter
R&B - BS: 2/18/50(2); JB: 2/25/50(5)

I Always Get Lucky With You...
George Jones
C&W - 7/30/83(1)

I Am A Simple Man...
Ricky Van Shelton
C&W - 7/27/91(1)

I Am Woman...*Helen Reddy*
HOT - 12/9/72(1)

I Believe In You...*Mel Tillis*
C&W - 7/8/78(1)

I Believe In You...*Don Williams*
C&W - 10/18/80(2)

I Believe In You (You Believe In Me)...*Johnnie Taylor*
R&B - 7/21/73(2)

I Belong To You...*Love Unlimited*
R&B - 2/15/75(1)

I Can Dream, Can't I?...
Andrews Sisters
POP - DJ: 1/7/50(5); BS: 1/14/50(4); JB: 1/21/50(3)

I Can Help...*Billy Swan*
HOT - 11/23/74(2)
C&W - 12/14/74(2)

I Can See Clearly Now...*Johnny Nash*
HOT - 11/4/72(4)
A/C - 11/4/72(4)

I Can Tell By The Way You Dance...
Vern Gosdin
C&W - 6/30/84(1)

I Can't Believe She Gives It All To Me...*Conway Twitty*
C&W - 1/22/77(1)

I Can't Believe That You've Stopped Loving Me...*Charley Pride*
C&W - 11/7/70(2)

I Can't Get Close Enough...*Exile*
C&W - 1/9/88(1)

I Can't Get Next To You...
Temptations
HOT - 10/18/69(2)
R&B - 10/4/69(5)

(I Can't Get No) Satisfaction...
Rolling Stones
HOT - 7/10/65(4)

I Can't Go For That (No Can Do)...
Daryl Hall & John Oates
HOT - 1/30/82(1)
R&B - 1/30/82(1)

I Can't Hear You No More...
Helen Reddy
A/C - 10/2/76(1)

I Can't Help Myself...*Four Tops*
HOT - 6/19/65(2)
R&B - 6/5/65(9)

I Can't Stop Loving You...
Ray Charles
HOT - 6/2/62(5)
R&B - 5/26/62(10)
A/C - 6/9/62(5)

I Can't Stop Loving You...
Conway Twitty
C&W - 9/23/72(1)

I Can't Wait Another Minute...
Hi-Five
R&B - 8/10/91(1)

I Can't Win For Losin' You...
Earl Thomas Conley
C&W - 2/28/87(1)

I Care...*Tom T. Hall*
C&W - 2/22/75(1)

I Cheated Me Right Out Of You...
Moe Bandy
C&W - 12/8/79(1)

I Could Get Used To You...*Exile*
C&W - 3/15/86(1)

I Could Never Love Another (After Loving You)...*Temptations*
R&B - 7/6/68(1)

I Couldn't Leave You If I Tried...
Rodney Crowell
C&W - 9/3/88(1)

I Couldn't Live Without Your Love...
Petula Clark
A/C - 8/27/66(1)

I Do It For You ..see: (Everything I Do)

I Don't Believe You've Met My Baby...*Louvin Brothers*
C&W - DJ: 3/17/56(2)

I Don't Care...*Webb Pierce*
C&W - BS: 7/16/55(12); JB: 7/30/55(12); DJ: 8/6/55(12)

I Don't Care...*Ricky Skaggs*
C&W - 7/31/82(1)

I Don't Care (Just as Long as You Love Me)...*Buck Owens*
C&W - 10/17/64(6)

I Don't Have The Heart...
James Ingram
HOT - 10/20/90(1)

I Don't Hurt Anymore...*Hank Snow*
C&W - BS: 6/19/54(20); DJ: 6/26/54(18); JB: 7/10/54(20)

I Don't Know...*Willie Mabon*
R&B - BS: 12/27/52(8); JB: 1/10/53(7)

I Don't Know A Thing About Love (The Moon Song)...*Conway Twitty*
C&W - 10/20/84(1)

I Don't Know Why You Don't Want Me...*Rosanne Cash*
C&W - 9/7/85(1)

I Don't Mind The Thorns (If You're The Rose)...*Lee Greenwood*
C&W - 12/7/85(1)

I Don't Need You...*Kenny Rogers*
C&W - 8/15/81(2)
A/C - 7/11/81(6)

I Don't See Me In Your Eyes Anymore...*Charlie Rich*
C&W - 6/15/74(1)

I Don't Wanna Cry...*Mariah Carey*
HOT - 5/25/91(2)
A/C - 6/8/91(1)

I Don't Wanna Go On With You Like That...*Elton John*
A/C - 8/20/88(1)

I Don't Wanna Play House...
Tammy Wynette
C&W - 10/14/67(3)

I Don't Want To Be A Memory...*Exile*
C&W - 7/14/84(1)

I Don't Want To Be Right ..see: (If Loving You Is Wrong)

I Don't Want To Have To Marry You...
Jim Ed Brown/Helen Cornelius
C&W - 9/11/76(2)

I Don't Want To Live Without You...
Foreigner
A/C - 5/14/88(1)

I Don't Want To Spoil The Party...
Rosanne Cash
C&W - 6/24/89(1)

I Fall To Pieces...*Patsy Cline*
C&W - 8/7/61(2)

I Feel A Song (In My Heart)...
Gladys Knight & The Pips
R&B - 11/30/74(2)

I Feel Fine...*Beatles*
HOT - 12/26/64(3)
I Feel For You...*Chaka Khan*
R&B - 11/3/84(3)
I Feel Good All Over...
Stephanie Mills
R&B - 7/4/87(3)
I Feel Like Loving You Again...
T.G. Sheppard
C&W - 1/31/81(1)
I Fell In Love Again Last Night...
Forester Sisters
C&W - 9/21/85(1)
I Forgot More Than You'll Ever Know...*Davis Sisters*
C&W - BS: 10/17/53(6); DJ: 10/17/53(8);
JB: 11/14/53(2)
I Forgot To Remember To Forget...
Elvis Presley
C&W - BS: 2/25/56(2); JB: 3/3/56(5)
I Get Around...*Beach Boys*
HOT - 7/4/64(2)
I Get The Fever...*Bill Anderson*
C&W - 11/19/66(1)
I Got Dreams...*Steve Wariner*
C&W - 10/7/89(1)
I Got Loaded...*Peppermint Harris*
R&B - JB: 11/10/51(2); BS: 12/22/51(1)
I Got Mexico...*Eddy Raven*
C&W - 6/16/84(1)
I Got My Mind Made Up (You Can Get It Girl)...*Instant Funk*
R&B - 3/17/79(3)
I Got The Feelin'...*James Brown*
R&B - 4/27/68(2)
I Got You Babe...*Sonny & Cher*
HOT - 8/14/65(3)
I Got You (I Feel Good)...
James Brown
R&B - 12/4/65(6)
I Gotcha...*Joe Tex*
R&B - 3/18/72(1)
I Guess I'm Crazy...*Jim Reeves*
C&W - 8/29/64(7)
I Guess It Never Hurts To Hurt Sometimes...*Oak Ridge Boys*
C&W - 5/5/84(1)
I Have Learned To Respect The Power Of Love...*Stephanie Mills*
R&B - 5/3/86(2)
I Hear A Symphony...*Supremes*
HOT - 11/20/65(2)
I Heard It Through The Grapevine...
Marvin Gaye
HOT - 12/14/68(7)
R&B - 12/14/68(7)
I Heard It Through The Grapevine...
Gladys Knight & The Pips
R&B - 12/2/67(6)
I Heard It Through The Grapevine...
Roger
R&B - 11/7/81(2)
I Honestly Love You...
Olivia Newton-John
HOT - 10/5/74(2)
A/C - 9/14/74(3)

I Just Called To Say I Love You...
Stevie Wonder
HOT - 10/13/84(3)
R&B - 10/13/84(3)
A/C - 10/13/84(3)
I Just Can't Get Her Out Of My Mind...*Johnny Rodriguez*
C&W - 4/5/75(1)
I Just Can't Help Believing...
B.J. Thomas
A/C - 8/22/70(1)
I Just Can't Stop Loving You...
Michael Jackson
HOT - 9/19/87(1)
R&B - 9/19/87(1)
A/C - 8/29/87(3)
(I Just) Died In Your Arms...
Cutting Crew
HOT - 5/2/87(2)
I Just Fall In Love Again...
Anne Murray
C&W - 3/24/79(3)
A/C - 2/10/79(4)
I Just Want To Be Your Everything...
Andy Gibb
HOT - 7/30/77(4)
I Just Want To Love You...
Eddie Rabbitt
C&W - 12/2/78(1)
I Just Wish You Were Someone I Love...*Larry Gatlin*
C&W - 2/11/78(1)
I Keep Coming Back...*Razzy Bailey*
C&W - 2/7/81(1)
I Knew You Were Waiting (For Me)...
Aretha Franklin & George Michael
HOT - 4/18/87(2)
I Know How He Feels...*Reba McEntire*
C&W - 12/3/88(1)
(I Know) I'm Losing You...
Temptations
R&B - 12/24/66(2)
I Know Where I'm Going...*Judds*
C&W - 7/18/87(1)
I Know (You Don't Love Me No More)...*Barbara George*
R&B - 1/20/62(4)
I Let The Stars Get In My Eyes...
Goldie Hill
C&W - JB: 2/7/53(3)
I Like The Way (The Kissing Game)...
Hi-Five
HOT - 5/18/91(1)
R&B - 3/23/91(2)
I Love...*Tom T. Hall*
C&W - 1/19/74(2)
I Love A Rainy Night...*Eddie Rabbitt*
HOT - 2/28/81(2)
C&W - 1/17/81(1)
A/C - 1/17/81(3)
I Love Music...*O'Jays*
R&B - 12/6/75(1)
I Love My Friend...*Charlie Rich*
C&W - 10/5/74(1)
A/C - 9/7/74(1)
I Love Rock 'N Roll...*Joan Jett*
HOT - 3/20/82(7)

I Love You A Thousand Ways...
Lefty Frizzell
C&W - DJ: 1/6/51(3)
I Love You Because...*Al Martino*
A/C - 5/25/63(2)
I Love You Because...*Leon Payne*
C&W - DJ: 1/14/50(2)
I Love You More Today...
Conway Twitty
C&W - 7/19/69(1)
I Love Your Smile...*Shanice*
R&B - 12/21/91(2)
still #1 as of the 1/4/92 chart
I Loved 'Em Every One...
T.G. Sheppard
C&W - 5/16/81(1)
I May Never Get To Heaven...
Conway Twitty
C&W - 9/8/79(1)
I Need Love...*L.L. Cool J*
R&B - 9/26/87(1)
I Need More Of You...
Bellamy Brothers
C&W - 4/20/85(1)
I Need To Be In Love...*Carpenters*
A/C - 7/10/76(1)
I Need You Now...*Eddie Fisher*
POP - BS: 11/13/54(3); DJ: 11/13/54(2);
JB: 12/4/54(2)
I Need You So...*Ivory Joe Hunter*
R&B - JB: 5/13/50(2)
I Never Loved A Man (The Way I Loved You)...*Aretha Franklin*
R&B - 3/25/67(7)
I Never Said I Love You...*Orsa Lia*
A/C - 4/28/79(1)
I Only Have Eyes For You...
Art Garfunkel
A/C - 10/11/75(1)
I Overlooked An Orchid...
Mickey Gilley
C&W - 11/2/74(1)
I Pity The Fool...*Bobby Bland*
R&B - 3/27/61(1)
I Really Don't Want To Know...
Eddy Arnold
C&W - JB: 5/15/54(1)
I Really Got The Feeling...
Dolly Parton
C&W - 1/20/79(1)
I Remember You...*Frank Ifield*
A/C - 10/20/62(1)
I Sang Dixie...*Dwight Yoakam*
C&W - 2/25/89(1)
I Saw Mommy Kissing Santa Claus...
Jimmy Boyd
POP - BS: 12/27/52(2)
I Second That Emotion...
Smokey Robinson & The Miracles
R&B - 1/13/68(1)
I See The Want To In Your Eyes...
Conway Twitty
C&W - 10/19/74(2)
I Shot The Sheriff...*Eric Clapton*
HOT - 9/14/74(1)
I Still Believe In You...
Desert Rose Band
C&W - 3/4/89(1)

I Still Haven't Found What I'm
Looking For...*U2*
   HOT - 8/8/87(2)
I Think I Love You...
Partridge Family
   HOT - 11/21/70(3)
I Think I'll Just Stay Here And
Drink...*Merle Haggard*
   C&W - 1/10/81(1)
I Think We're Alone Now...*Tiffany*
   HOT - 11/7/87(2)
I Told You So...*Randy Travis*
   C&W - 6/11/88(2)
I Walk Alone...*Marty Robbins*
   C&W - 11/9/68(2)
I Walk The Line...*Johnny Cash*
   C&W - JB: 7/21/56(6); DJ: 10/27/56(1)
I Wanna Be Loved...*Andrews Sisters*
   POP - DJ: 6/24/50(2)
I Wanna Be With You...
Isley Brothers
   R&B - 5/26/79(1)
I Wanna Be Your Lover...*Prince*
   R&B - 12/1/79(2)
I Wanna Dance With Somebody (Who
Loves Me)...*Whitney Houston*
   HOT - 6/27/87(2)
   A/C - 7/4/87(3)
I Wanna Dance With You...
Eddie Rabbitt
   C&W - 4/16/88(1)
I Wanna Live...*Glen Campbell*
   C&W - 5/18/68(3)
I Wanna Play House With You...
Eddy Arnold
   C&W - JB: 7/14/51(11); BS: 7/28/51(6)
I Wanna Sex You Up...*Color Me Badd*
   R&B - 6/1/91(2)
I Want Her...*Keith Sweat*
   R&B - 1/30/88(3)
I Want To Be Wanted...*Brenda Lee*
   HOT - 10/24/60(1)
I Want To Be With You Always...
Lefty Frizzell
   C&W - DJ: 5/26/51(11); BS: 6/9/51(6);
   JB: 6/9/51(5)
I Want To Be Your Man...*Roger*
   R&B - 12/19/87(1)
I Want To (Do Everything For You)...
Joe Tex
   R&B - 10/9/65(3)
I Want To Go With You...*Eddy Arnold*
   C&W - 4/9/66(6)
   A/C - 4/9/66(3)
I Want To Hold Your Hand...*Beatles*
   HOT - 2/1/64(7)
I Want To Know What Love Is...
Foreigner
   HOT - 2/2/85(2)
I Want To Walk You Home...
Fats Domino
   R&B - 9/21/59(1)
I Want You...*Marvin Gaye*
   R&B - 5/29/76(1)
I Want You Back...*Jackson 5*
   HOT - 1/31/70(1)
   R&B - 1/10/70(4)

I Want You, I Need You, I Love
You...*Elvis Presley*
   POP - BS: 7/28/56(1)
   C&W - BS: 7/14/56(2); JB: 8/11/56(1)
I Was Country When Country Wasn't
Cool...*Barbara Mandrell*
   C&W - 7/4/81(1)
I Was Made To Love Her...
Stevie Wonder
   R&B - 7/15/67(4)
I Went To Your Wedding...*Patti Page*
   POP - JB: 9/27/52(10); BS: 10/18/52(5);
   DJ: 11/15/52(1)
I Will Always Love You...
Dolly Parton
   C&W - 6/8/74(1)
   C&W - 10/16/82(1)
I Will Be There...*Dan Seals*
   C&W - 6/6/87(1)
I Will Follow Him...
Little Peggy March
   HOT - 4/27/63(3)
   R&B - 5/25/63(1)
I Will Survive...*Gloria Gaynor*
   HOT - 3/10/79(3)
I Wish...*Stevie Wonder*
   HOT - 1/22/77(1)
   R&B - 1/15/77(5)
I Wish It Would Rain...*Temptations*
   R&B - 2/17/68(3)
I Won't Come In While He's There...
Jim Reeves
   C&W - 3/25/67(1)
I Won't Hold You Back...*Toto*
   A/C - 4/30/83(1)
I Won't Last A Day Without You...
Carpenters
   A/C - 6/1/74(1)
I Won't Mention It Again...*Ray Price*
   C&W - 5/15/71(3)
I Won't Need You Anymore (Always
And Forever)...*Randy Travis*
   C&W - 11/21/87(1)
I Won't Take Less Than Your Love...
*Tanya Tucker with Paul Davis &
Paul Overstreet*
   C&W - 2/27/88(1)
I Wonder Do You Think Of Me...
Keith Whitley
   C&W - 9/9/89(1)
I Wonder If They Ever Think Of Me...
Merle Haggard
   C&W - 2/17/73(1)
I Wouldn't Change You If I Could...
Ricky Skaggs
   C&W - 3/19/83(1)
I Wouldn't Have Missed It For The
World...*Ronnie Milsap*
   C&W - 1/16/82(1)
I Wouldn't Want To Live If You
Didn't Love Me...*Don Williams*
   C&W - 9/21/74(1)
I Write The Songs...*Barry Manilow*
   HOT - 1/17/76(1)
   A/C - 12/13/75(2)
(I'd Be) A Legend In My Time...
Ronnie Milsap
   C&W - 1/25/75(1)

I'd Love To Lay You Down...
Conway Twitty
   C&W - 3/29/80(1)
I'd Love You All Over Again...
Alan Jackson
   C&W - 3/9/91(2)
I'd Love You To Want Me...*Lobo*
   A/C - 12/2/72(1)
I'd Rather Love You...*Charley Pride*
   C&W - 3/6/71(3)
I'd Really Love To See You
Tonight...*England Dan &
John Ford Coley*
   A/C - 8/21/76(1)
I'll Always Come Back...*K.T. Oslin*
   C&W - 4/23/88(1)
I'll Be Around...*Spinners*
   R&B - 10/14/72(5)
I'll Be Coming Back For More...
T.G. Sheppard
   C&W - 1/26/80(2)
I'll Be Doggone...*Marvin Gaye*
   R&B - 5/22/65(1)
I'll Be Good To You...
Brothers Johnson
   R&B - 6/12/76(1)
I'll Be Good To You...*Quincy Jones
Feat. Ray Charles & Chaka Khan*
   R&B - 1/20/90(2)
I'll Be Leaving Alone...
Charley Pride
   C&W - 7/9/77(1)
I'll Be Loving You (Forever)...
New Kids On The Block
   HOT - 6/17/89(1)
I'll Be Over You...*Toto*
   A/C - 10/25/86(2)
I'll Be There...*Jackson 5*
   HOT - 10/17/70(5)
   R&B - 10/10/70(6)
I'll Be There For You...*Bon Jovi*
   HOT - 5/13/89(1)
I'll Be True...*Faye Adams*
   R&B - BS: 2/6/54(1)
I'll Be True To You...*Oak Ridge Boys*
   C&W - 6/24/78(1)
I'll Be Your Everything...*Tommy Page*
   HOT - 4/14/90(1)
I'll Come Running Back To You...
Sam Cooke
   R&B - DJ: 1/27/58(1)
I'll Get Over You...*Crystal Gayle*
   C&W - 6/12/76(1)
I'll Give All My Love To You...
Keith Sweat
   R&B - 2/16/91(1)
I'll Go On Alone...*Marty Robbins*
   C&W - DJ: 1/24/53(2)
I'll Have To Say I Love You In A
Song...*Jim Croce*
   A/C - 4/27/74(1)
I'll Leave This World Loving You...
Ricky Van Shelton
   C&W - 11/19/88(2)
I'll Never Fall In Love Again...
Tom Jones
   A/C - 9/13/69(1)

I'll Never Fall In Love Again...
  Dionne Warwick
  A/C - 2/7/70(3)
I'll Never Find Another You...
  Sonny James
  C&W - 8/5/67(4)
I'll Never Get Out Of This World
  Alive...Hank Williams
  C&W - BS: 1/24/53(1)
I'll Never Stop Loving You...
  Gary Morris
  C&W - 11/23/85(1)
I'll Sail My Ship Alone...
  Moon Mullican
  C&W - JB: 6/17/50(4); BS: 7/22/50(1)
I'll Still Be Loving You...
  Restless Heart
  C&W - 3/21/87(1)
I'll Take You There...Staple Singers
  HOT - 6/3/72(1)
  R&B - 5/6/72(4)
I'll Take You There...BeBe & CeCe
  Winans Featuring Mavis Staples
  R&B - 12/7/91(1)
I'm A Believer...Monkees
  HOT - 12/31/66(7)
I'm A Ramblin' Man...Waylon Jennings
  C&W - 9/28/74(1)
(I'm A) Stand By My Woman Man...
  Ronnie Milsap
  C&W - 8/28/76(2)
I'm Coming Home...Johnny Mathis
  A/C - 9/29/73(1)
I'm Dreamin'...Christopher Williams
  R&B - 5/4/91(1)
I'm Easy...Keith Carradine
  A/C - 7/24/76(1)
I'm Every Woman...Chaka Khan
  R&B - 11/11/78(3)
I'm For Love...Hank Williams, Jr.
  C&W - 8/10/85(1)
I'm Gonna Get Married...Lloyd Price
  R&B - 9/7/59(3)
I'm Gonna Get You...Eddy Raven
  C&W - 5/14/88(1)
I'm Gonna Hire A Wino To Decorate
  Our Home...David Frizzell
  C&W - 8/14/82(1)
I'm Gonna Love You Just A Little
  More Baby...Barry White
  R&B - 5/26/73(2)
I'm Henry VIII, I Am...
  Herman's Hermits
  HOT - 8/7/65(1)
I'm In Love...Aretha Franklin
  R&B - 5/18/74(2)
  (also see: Look At Me)
I'm In Love...Evelyn King
  R&B - 8/15/81(1)
I'm In Love Again...Fats Domino
  DJ: 5/19/56(9); BS: 6/2/56(7);
  JB: 6/9/56(9)
I'm In The Mood...John Lee Hooker
  R&B - JB: 11/17/51(4)
I'm Just A Country Boy...
  Don Williams
  C&W - 11/5/77(1)

I'm Just Me...Charley Pride
  C&W - 7/31/71(4)
I'm Leaving It (All) Up To You...
  Donny & Marie Osmond
  A/C - 8/31/74(1)
I'm Leaving It Up To You...
  Dale & Grace
  HOT - 11/23/63(2)
  A/C - 11/23/63(2)
I'm Losing You ..see: (I Know)
I'm Mad...Willie Mabon & his Combo
  R&B - BS: 5/30/53(2)
I'm Moving On...Hank Snow
  C&W - BS: 8/19/50(21); DJ: 9/2/50(18);
  JB: 9/16/50(14)
I'm No Stranger To The Rain...
  Keith Whitley
  C&W - 4/8/89(2)
I'm Not Lisa...Jessi Colter
  C&W - 5/24/75(1)
I'm Only In It For The Love...
  John Conlee
  C&W - 9/10/83(1)
(I'm So) Afraid Of Losing You
  Again...Charley Pride
  C&W - 12/13/69(3)
I'm Sorry...John Denver
  HOT - 9/27/75(1)
  C&W - 11/8/75(1)
  A/C - 9/20/75(2)
I'm Sorry...Brenda Lee
  HOT - 7/18/60(3)
I'm Still Crazy...Vern Gosdin
  C&W - 9/2/89(1)
I'm Still In Love With You...
  Al Green
  R&B - 8/12/72(2)
I'm Telling You Now...
  Freddie & The Dreamers
  HOT - 4/10/65(2)
I'm Walkin'...Fats Domino
  R&B - BS: 3/23/57(6); JB: 3/23/57(5);
  DJ: 3/30/57(5)
I'm Walking Behind You...
  Eddie Fisher
  POP - JB: 7/4/53(7); DJ: 7/18/53(3);
  BS: 7/25/53(2)
I'm Your Baby Tonight...
  Whitney Houston
  HOT - 12/1/90(1)
  R&B - 12/1/90(2)
I'm Your Boogie Man...
  KC & The Sunshine Band
  HOT - 6/11/77(1)
I'm Yours...Elvis Presley
  A/C - 10/9/65(1)
I've Already Loved You In My Mind...
  Conway Twitty
  C&W - 9/24/77(1)
I've Always Been Crazy...
  Waylon Jennings
  C&W - 9/9/78(3)
I've Been Around Enough To Know...
  John Schneider
  C&W - 11/10/84(1)
I've Been Everywhere...Hank Snow
  C&W - 11/10/62(2)

I've Been Thinking About You...
  Londonbeat
  HOT - 4/13/91(1)
I've Been This Way Before...
  Neil Diamond
  A/C - 3/15/75(1)
I've Come To Expect It From You...
  George Strait
  C&W - 12/8/90(5)
I've Cried My Last Tear For You...
  Ricky Van Shelton
  C&W - 6/2/90(1)
I've Got A Tiger By The Tail...
  Buck Owens
  C&W - 2/20/65(5)
I've Got A Woman...Ray Charles
  R&B - JB: 5/7/55(1)
I've Got Love On My Mind...
  Natalie Cole
  R&B - 2/26/77(5)
I've Got To Use My Imagination...
  Gladys Knight & The Pips
  R&B - 1/19/74(1)
I've Gotta Be Me...Sammy Davis, Jr.
  A/C - 1/25/69(7)
(I've Had) The Time Of My Life...
  Bill Medley & Jennifer Warnes
  HOT - 11/28/87(1)
  A/C - 11/21/87(4)
Ice Ice Baby...Vanilla Ice
  HOT - 11/3/90(1)
If...Bread
  A/C - 4/24/71(3)
If...Perry Como
  POP - BS: 3/3/51(6); DJ: 3/3/51(8);
  JB: 3/31/51(5)
If Ever I See You Again...
  Roberta Flack
  A/C - 7/8/78(3)
If Ever You're In My Arms Again...
  Peabo Bryson
  A/C - 7/7/84(4)
If Hollywood Don't Need You...
  Don Williams
  C&W - 3/5/83(1)
If I Can't Have You...Yvonne Elliman
  HOT - 5/13/78(1)
If I Could Reach You...5th Dimension
  A/C - 10/28/72(1)
If I Could Turn Back Time...Cher
  A/C - 9/30/89(1)
If I Had You...Alabama
  C&W - 5/20/89(1)
If I Knew You Were Comin' I'd've
  Baked A Cake...Eileen Barton
  POP - DJ: 3/25/50(10); BS: 4/15/50(2);
  JB: 4/15/50(3)
If I Know Me...George Strait
  C&W - 5/11/91(2)
If I Said You Have A Beautiful Body
  Would You Hold It Against
  Me...Bellamy Brothers
  C&W - 5/19/79(3)
If I Were Your Woman...
  Gladys Knight & The Pips
  R&B - 1/23/71(1)

If It Ain't One Thing...It's Another...*Richard "Dimples" Fields*
R&B - 4/24/82(3)

If It Don't Come Easy...*Tanya Tucker*
C&W - 7/2/88(1)

(If Loving You Is Wrong) I Don't Want To Be Right...*Luther Ingram*
R&B - 7/8/72(4)

(If Loving You Is Wrong) I Don't Want To Be Right...*Barbara Mandrell*
C&W - 4/14/79(1)

If Not For You...*Olivia Newton-John*
A/C - 8/7/71(1)

If Only You Knew...*Patti LaBelle*
R&B - 1/28/84(4)

If The Devil Danced (In Empty Pockets)...*Joe Diffie*
C&W - 6/15/91(1)

If Tomorrow Never Comes...
Garth Brooks
C&W - 12/9/89(1)

If We Make It Through December...
Merle Haggard
C&W - 12/22/73(4)

If Wishes Came True...
Sweet Sensation
HOT - 9/1/90(1)

If You Ain't Lovin' (You Ain't Livin')...*George Strait*
C&W - 12/10/88(1)

If You Change Your Mind...
Rosanne Cash
C&W - 7/16/88(1)

If You Could Read My Mind...
Gordon Lightfoot
A/C - 2/20/71(1)

If You Don't Know Me By Now...
Harold Melvin & The Blue Notes
R&B - 11/18/72(2)

If You Don't Know Me By Now...
Simply Red
HOT - 7/15/89(1)
A/C - 6/24/89(6)

If You Ever Change Your Mind...
Crystal Gayle
C&W - 11/29/80(1)

If You Know What I Mean...
Neil Diamond
A/C - 7/17/76(2)

If You Leave Me Now...*Chicago*
HOT - 10/23/76(2)
A/C - 9/25/76(1)

If You Leave Me Tonight I'll Cry...
Jerry Wallace
C&W - 8/26/72(2)

If You Wanna Be Happy...*Jimmy Soul*
HOT - 5/18/63(2)
R&B - 6/1/63(1)

If You're Gonna Play In Texas...
Alabama
C&W - 10/27/84(1)

If You're Ready (Come Go With Me)...
Staple Singers
R&B - 12/8/73(3)

If You've Got The Money I've Got The Time...*Lefty Frizzell*
C&W - JB: 12/23/50(3)

If You've Got The Money I've Got The Time...*Willie Nelson*
C&W - 9/25/76(1)

Immigrant, The...*Neil Sedaka*
A/C - 5/10/75(1)

Impossible Dream...*Jack Jones*
A/C - 7/23/66(1)

In A Different Light...*Doug Stone*
C&W - 5/25/91(1)

In A Letter To You...*Eddy Raven*
C&W - 7/15/89(1)

In Love...*Ronnie Milsap*
C&W - 9/27/86(1)

In My Eyes...*John Conlee*
C&W - 1/21/84(1)

In The Arms Of Love...*Andy Williams*
A/C - 10/1/66(2)

In The Chapel in The Moonlight...
Dean Martin
A/C - 8/12/67(3)

In The Jailhouse Now...*Webb Pierce*
C&W - BS: 2/26/55(20); DJ: 3/5/55(15); JB: 3/5/55(21)

In The Midnight Hour...
Wilson Pickett
R&B - 8/7/65(1)

In The Misty Moonlight...*Dean Martin*
A/C - 1/20/68(2)

In The Rain...*Dramatics*
R&B - 3/25/72(4)

In The Year 2525 (Exordium & Terminus)...*Zager & Evans*
HOT - 7/12/69(6)
A/C - 8/16/69(2)

In Too Deep...*Genesis*
A/C - 6/13/87(3)

Incense And Peppermints...
Strawberry Alarm Clock
HOT - 11/25/67(1)

Indian Reservation...*Raiders*
HOT - 7/24/71(1)

Inner City Blues (Make Me Wanna Holler)...*Marvin Gaye*
R&B - 11/6/71(2)

Innocent Man...*Billy Joel*
A/C - 3/3/84(1)

Inseparable...*Natalie Cole*
R&B - 2/14/76(1)

Inside...*Ronnie Milsap*
C&W - 2/5/83(1)

Invisible Touch...*Genesis*
HOT - 7/19/86(1)

Is Anybody Goin' To San Antone...
Charley Pride
C&W - 4/18/70(2)

Is It Really Over?...*Jim Reeves*
C&W - 9/11/65(3)

Is It Still Over?...*Randy Travis*
C&W - 5/13/89(1)

Is It Wrong (For Loving You)...
Sonny James
C&W - 5/11/74(1)

Is That All There Is...*Peggy Lee*
A/C - 10/18/69(2)

Island Girl...*Elton John*
HOT - 11/1/75(3)

Islands In The Stream...
Kenny Rogers with Dolly Parton
HOT - 10/29/83(2)
C&W - 10/29/83(2)
A/C - 10/15/83(4)

It Ain't Cool To Be Crazy About You...*George Strait*
C&W - 12/6/86(1)

It Ain't Easy Bein' Easy...
Janie Fricke
C&W - 11/27/82(1)

It Ain't Nothin'...*Keith Whitley*
C&W - 1/13/90(1)

It Couldn't Have Been Any Better...
Johnny Duncan
C&W - 4/16/77(1)

It Might Be You...*Stephen Bishop*
A/C - 4/16/83(2)

It Must Be Him...*Vikki Carr*
A/C - 10/21/67(3)

It Must Be Love...*Don Williams*
C&W - 9/29/79(1)

It Must Have Been Love...*Roxette*
HOT - 6/16/90(2)

It Never Rains (In Southern California)...*Tony! Toni! Tone!*
R&B - 12/22/90(2)

It Only Hurts For A Little While...
Margo Smith
C&W - 7/1/78(1)

It Only Takes A Minute...*Tavares*
R&B - 9/20/75(1)

It Should've Been You...
Teddy Pendergrass
R&B - 5/18/91(1)

It Takes A Little Rain (To Make Love Grow)...*Oak Ridge Boys*
C&W - 5/30/87(1)

It Was A Very Good Year...
Frank Sinatra
A/C - 2/5/66(1)

It Was Almost Like A Song...
Ronnie Milsap
C&W - 7/16/77(3)

It Wasn't God Who Made Honky Tonk Angels...*Kitty Wells*
C&W - BS: 8/23/52(6); JB: 9/6/52(5)

It Would Take A Strong Strong Man...
Rick Astley
A/C - 10/1/88(1)

It'll Be Me...*Exile*
C&W - 11/1/86(1)

It's A Man's Man's Man's World...
James Brown
R&B - 6/4/66(2)

It's A Miracle...*Barry Manilow*
A/C - 4/26/75(1)

It's All In The Game...*Tommy Edwards*
POP - HT: 9/29/58(6); BS: 9/29/58(3)
R&B - BS: 9/29/58(3)

It's All In The Movies...
Merle Haggard
C&W - 11/29/75(1)

It's All Right...*Impressions*
R&B - 11/9/63(2)

It's All Wrong, But It's All Right...*Dolly Parton*
C&W - 5/6/78(2)

It's Been So Long...*Webb Pierce*
  C&W - BS: 7/11/53(6); DJ: 7/25/53(8);
  JB: 8/22/53(1)
It's Ecstasy When You Lay Down Next
  To Me...*Barry White*
  R&B - 10/1/77(5)
It's Four In The Morning...
  Faron Young
  C&W - 2/19/72(2)
It's Gonna Be Alright...*Ruby Turner*
  R&B - 2/17/90(1)
It's Gonna Take A Little Bit
  Longer...*Charley Pride*
  C&W - 7/22/72(3)
It's Gonna Take A Miracle...
  Deniece Williams
  R&B - 5/15/82(2)
It's Impossible...*Perry Como*
  A/C - 12/5/70(4)
It's In The Book...*Johnny Standley*
  POP - BS: 11/22/52(2)
It's Just A Matter Of Time...
  Brook Benton
  R&B - 3/9/59(9)
It's Just A Matter Of Time...
  Sonny James
  C&W - 2/14/70(4)
It's Just A Matter Of Time...
  Randy Travis
  C&W - 12/2/89(1)
It's Like We Never Said Goodbye...
  Crystal Gayle
  C&W - 4/19/80(1)
It's My Party...*Lesley Gore*
  HOT - 6/1/63(2)
  R&B - 6/15/63(3)
It's No Crime...*Babyface*
  R&B - 8/26/89(2)
It's Not Love (But It's Not Bad)...
  Merle Haggard
  C&W - 11/4/72(1)
It's Now Or Never...*Elvis Presley*
  HOT - 8/15/60(5)
It's Only Make Believe...
  Conway Twitty
  HOT - 11/10/58(2)
It's Sad To Belong...
  England Dan & John Ford Coley
  A/C - 6/25/77(5)
It's So Hard To Say Goodbye To
  Yesterday...*Boyz II Men*
  R&B - 10/26/91(1)
It's Still Rock And Roll To Me...
  Billy Joel
  HOT - 7/19/80(2)
It's Such A Pretty World Today...
  Andy Russell
  A/C - 8/5/67(1)
It's Such A Pretty World Today...
  Wynn Stewart
  C&W - 6/3/67(2)
It's Such A Small World...
  Rodney Crowell & Rosanne Cash
  C&W - 4/30/88(1)
It's The Little Things...*Sonny James*
  C&W - 11/18/67(5)

It's Time To Pay The Fiddler...
  Cal Smith
  C&W - 3/1/75(1)
It's Too Late...*Carole King*
  HOT - 6/19/71(5)
  A/C - 6/26/71(5)
It's You That I Need...*Enchantment*
  R&B - 2/25/78(1)
It's Your Thing...*Isley Brothers*
  R&B - 4/19/69(4)
Itsy Bitsy Teenie Weenie Yellow
  Polkadot Bikini...*Brian Hyland*
  HOT - 8/8/60(1)

J

Jack & Diane...*John Cougar*
  HOT - 10/2/82(4)
Jacob's Ladder...
  Huey Lewis & the News
  HOT - 3/14/87(1)
Jailhouse Rock...*Elvis Presley*
  POP - BS: 10/21/57(7); TP: 11/4/57(6);
  DJ: 11/25/57(2)
  R&B - BS: 10/21/57(5); DJ: 11/4/57(3)
  C&W - BS: 12/2/57(1)
Jam Tonight...*Freddie Jackson*
  R&B - 8/15/87(1)
Jambalaya (On The Bayou)...
  Hank Williams
  C&W - DJ: 9/6/52(14); BS: 10/4/52(14);
  JB: 10/11/52(12)
(Jammin') ..see: Master Blaster
Java...*Al Hirt*
  A/C - 2/22/64(4)
Jean...*Oliver*
  A/C - 9/20/69(4)
Jed Clampett ..see: Ballad Of
Jerk-Out...*Time*
  R&B - 8/25/90(1)
Jessie's Girl...*Rick Springfield*
  HOT - 8/1/81(2)
Jim Dandy...*Jim Dandy & The Gliders*
  R&B - DJ: 3/9/57(1)
Jimmy Mack...*Martha & The Vandellas*
  R&B - 5/13/67(1)
Jive Talkin'...*Bee Gees*
  HOT - 8/9/75(2)
Joanna...*Kool & The Gang*
  R&B - 1/14/84(2)
Jody's Got Your Girl And Gone...
  Johnnie Taylor
  R&B - 2/20/71(2)
Joe Knows How To Live...*Eddy Raven*
  C&W - 9/17/88(1)
Johnny Angel...*Shelley Fabares*
  HOT - 4/7/62(2)
Johnny B. Goode...
  Buck Owens & The Buckaroos
  C&W - 7/26/69(2)
Joker, The...*Steve Miller Band*
  HOT - 1/12/74(1)
Jolene...*Dolly Parton*
  C&W - 2/2/74(1)

Jose Cuervo...*Shelly West*
  C&W - 5/7/83(1)
Joshua...*Dolly Parton*
  C&W - 2/6/71(1)
Joy...*Teddy Pendergrass*
  R&B - 6/25/88(2)
Joy To The World...*Three Dog Night*
  HOT - 4/17/71(6)
Joyride...*Roxette*
  HOT - 5/11/91(1)
Judy In Disguise (With Glasses)...
  John Fred
  HOT - 1/20/68(2)
Juicy Fruit...*Mtume*
  R&B - 6/4/83(8)
Juke...*Little Walter*
  R&B - JB: 9/27/52(8); BS: 12/6/52(1)
Jukebox In My Mind...*Alabama*
  C&W - 9/8/90(4)
Jump...*Van Halen*
  HOT - 2/25/84(5)
Jump To It...*Aretha Franklin*
  R&B - 9/4/82(4)
Just A Dream...*Jimmy Clanton*
  R&B - BS: 8/25/58(1)
Just Another Love...*Tanya Tucker*
  C&W - 10/18/86(1)
Just Another Woman In Love...
  Anne Murray
  C&W - 7/21/84(1)
Just Because...*Anita Baker*
  R&B - 3/4/89(1)
Just Coolin'...*Levert*
  R&B - 3/11/89(1)
Just Get Up And Close The Door...
  Johnny Rodriguez
  C&W - 8/2/75(1)
Just Good Ol' Boys...
  Moe Bandy & Joe Stampley
  C&W - 9/22/79(1)
Just Got Paid...*Johnny Kemp*
  R&B - 5/28/88(2)
Just In Case...*Forester Sisters*
  C&W - 2/1/86(1)
(Just Like) Starting Over...
  John Lennon
  HOT - 12/27/80(5)
Just Married...*Marty Robbins*
  C&W - DJ: 5/26/58(1)
Just My Imagination...*Temptations*
  HOT - 4/3/71(2)
  R&B - 3/6/71(3)
Just Remember I Love You...*Firefall*
  A/C - 10/29/77(2)
Just Say Yes ..see: (Do You Love Me)
Just The Way You Are...*Billy Joel*
  A/C - 1/7/78(4)
Just To Be Close To You...*Commodores*
  R&B - 10/9/76(2)
Just To Satisfy You...
  Waylon Jennings & Willie Nelson
  C&W - 5/22/82(2)
Just To See Her...*Smokey Robinson*
  A/C - 5/16/87(1)
Just When I Needed You Most...
  Randy Vanwarmer
  A/C - 5/19/79(2)

297

Justify My Love...*Madonna*
HOT - 1/5/91(2)

K

Kansas City...*Wilbert Harrison*
HOT - 5/18/59(2)
R&B - 5/11/59(7)
Karma Chameleon...*Culture Club*
HOT - 2/4/84(3)
Kaw-Liga...*Hank Williams*
C&W - BS: 2/21/53(13); JB: 2/28/53(8); DJ: 3/7/53(8)
Keep Coming Back...*Richard Marx*
A/C - 12/21/91(2)
still #1 as of the 1/4/92 chart
Keep It Between The Lines...
Ricky Van Shelton
C&W - 10/12/91(2)
Keep It Comin' Love...
KC & The Sunshine Band
R&B - 9/24/77(1)
Keep Me In Mind...*Lynn Anderson*
C&W - 3/31/73(1)
Keep On Loving You...*REO Speedwagon*
HOT - 3/21/81(1)
Keep On Movin'...*Soul II Soul*
R&B - 7/8/89(2)
Keep On Singing...*Helen Reddy*
A/C - 4/13/74(2)
Keep On Truckin'...
Eddie Kendricks
HOT - 11/10/73(2)
R&B - 10/6/73(2)
Kentucky Gambler...*Merle Haggard*
C&W - 1/18/75(1)
Kentucky Waltz...*Eddy Arnold*
C&W - BS: 5/19/51(3); JB: 5/19/51(3)
Key Largo...*Bertie Higgins*
A/C - 3/20/82(2)
Kiddio...*Brook Benton*
R&B - 8/29/60(9)
Kids Of The Baby Boom...
Bellamy Brothers
C&W - 4/18/87(1)
Kids Say The Darndest Things...
Tammy Wynette
C&W - 6/16/73(1)
Killin' Time...*Clint Black*
C&W - 10/14/89(1)
Killing Me Softly With His Song...
Roberta Flack
HOT - 2/24/73(5)
Kind Of A Drag...*Buckinghams*
HOT - 2/18/67(2)
King Of The Road...*Roger Miller*
C&W - 3/27/65(5)
A/C - 2/13/65(10)
Kiss...*Prince*
HOT - 4/19/86(2)
R&B - 4/5/86(4)
Kiss An Angel Good Mornin'...
Charley Pride
C&W - 12/4/71(5)

Kiss And Say Goodbye...*Manhattans*
HOT - 7/24/76(2)
R&B - 5/22/76(1)
Kiss Him Goodbye...*Steam*
HOT - 12/6/69(2)
Kiss Of Fire...*Georgia Gibbs*
POP - DJ: 5/17/52(7); JB: 6/14/52(6)
Kiss On My List...
Daryl Hall & John Oates
HOT - 4/11/81(3)
Kiss You All Over...*Exile*
HOT - 9/30/78(4)
Kissing A Fool...*George Michael*
A/C - 11/26/88(1)
(Kissing Game) ..see: I Like The Way
Kissing You...*Keith Washington*
R&B - 5/25/91(1)
Knee Deep ..see: (not just)
Knock On Wood...*Eddie Floyd*
R&B - 11/19/66(1)
Knock On Wood...*Amii Stewart*
HOT - 4/21/79(1)
Knock Three Times...*Dawn*
HOT - 1/23/71(3)
Kokomo...*Beach Boys*
HOT - 11/5/88(1)
Kung Fu Fighting...*Carl Douglas*
HOT - 12/7/74(2)
R&B - 1/11/75(1)
Kyrie...*Mr. Mister*
HOT - 3/1/86(2)

L

La Bamba...*Los Lobos*
HOT - 8/29/87(3)
La Isla Bonita...*Madonna*
A/C - 5/23/87(1)
Ladies Night...*Kool & The Gang*
R&B - 11/3/79(3)
Lady...*Jack Jones*
A/C - 3/4/67(4)
Lady...*Kenny Rogers*
HOT - 11/15/80(6)
C&W - 11/22/80(1)
A/C - 11/15/80(4)
Lady Down On Love...*Alabama*
C&W - 10/22/83(1)
Lady Lay Down...*John Conlee*
C&W - 1/13/79(1)
Lady Marmalade...*LaBelle*
HOT - 3/29/75(1)
R&B - 2/22/75(1)
Land Of 1,000 Dances...
Wilson Pickett
R&B - 9/17/66(1)
Last Cheater's Waltz...*T.G. Sheppard*
C&W - 10/6/79(2)
Last Farewell...*Roger Whittaker*
A/C - 4/12/75(1)
Last One To Know...*Reba McEntire*
C&W - 12/12/87(1)
Last Song...*Edward Bear*
A/C - 3/3/73(2)

Last Time I Saw Him...*Diana Ross*
A/C - 2/16/74(3)
Last Train To Clarksville...*Monkees*
HOT - 11/5/66(1)
Laughter In The Rain...*Neil Sedaka*
HOT - 2/1/75(1)
A/C - 11/23/74(2)
Laura (What's He Got That I Ain't Got)...*Leon Ashley*
C&W - 9/30/67(1)
Lawdy Miss Clawdy...*Lloyd Price*
R&B - JB: 7/12/52(1); BS: 8/2/52(7)
Le Freak...*Chic*
HOT - 12/9/78(6)
R&B - 12/2/78(5)
Lead Me On...*Maxine Nightingale*
A/C - 7/7/79(7)
Lead Me On...
Conway Twitty & Loretta Lynn
C&W - 11/13/71(1)
Leader Of The Band...*Dan Fogelberg*
A/C - 2/6/82(2)
Leader Of The Pack...*Shangri-Las*
HOT - 11/28/64(1)
R&B - 11/28/64(1)
Lean On Me...*Club Nouveau*
HOT - 3/21/87(2)
Lean On Me...*Bill Withers*
HOT - 7/8/72(3)
R&B - 6/24/72(1)
Leap Of Faith...*Lionel Cartwright*
C&W - 9/21/91(1)
Learnin' The Blues...*Frank Sinatra*
POP - DJ: 7/9/55(2)
Leave A Tender Moment Alone...
Billy Joel
A/C - 9/8/84(2)
Leave Me Alone (Ruby Red Dress)...
Helen Reddy
A/C - 12/1/73(4)
Leave Me Lonely...*Gary Morris*
C&W - 2/7/87(1)
Leaving Louisiana In The Broad Daylight...*Oak Ridge Boys*
C&W - 2/9/80(1)
Leaving Me...*Independents*
R&B - 5/19/73(1)
Leaving On A Jet Plane...
Peter, Paul & Mary
HOT - 12/20/69(1)
A/C - 11/22/69(3)
Legend In My Time ..see: (I'd Be)
Legend Of Bonnie And Clyde...
Merle Haggard
C&W - 4/27/68(2)
Lesson...*Vikki Carr*
A/C - 2/10/68(1)
Lesson In Leavin'...*Dottie West*
C&W - 4/26/80(1)
Let 'Em In...*Wings*
A/C - 8/7/76(1)
Let It Be...*Beatles*
HOT - 4/11/70(2)
A/C - 4/11/70(4)
Let It Shine...*Olivia Newton-John*
A/C - 1/17/76(2)
Let It Whip...*Dazz Band*
R&B - 5/29/82(5)

Let Me Be The One...*Hank Locklin*
C&W - DJ: 12/19/53(3); JB: 1/2/54(2)
(Let Me Be Your) Teddy Bear...
Elvis Presley
POP - BS: 7/8/57(7); TP: 7/15/57(7);
DJ: 7/29/57(3)
R&B - BS: 9/2/57(1)
C&W - BS: 8/5/57(1)
Let Me Go, Lover...*Hank Snow*
C&W - DJ: 1/29/55(2)
Let Me Go, Lover!...*Joan Weber*
POP - DJ: 1/1/55(4); JB: 1/15/55(4);
BS: 1/22/55(2)
Let Me Love You Tonight...
Pure Prairie League
A/C - 6/28/80(3)
Let Me Tell You About Love...*Judds*
C&W - 9/30/89(1)
Let My Love Be Your Pillow...
Ronnie Milsap
C&W - 1/29/77(1)
Let Old Mother Nature Have Her Way...*Carl Smith*
C&W - DJ: 12/22/51(3); JB: 2/16/52(8);
BS: 3/8/52(6)
Let The Beat Hit 'Em...
Lisa Lisa & Cult Jam
R&B - 9/14/91(1)
Let The Good Times Roll...
Shirley & Lee
R&B - DJ: 9/1/56(3); JB: 9/8/56(3)
Let The Sunshine In ..see: Aquarius
Let Your Hair Down...*Temptations*
R&B - 2/2/74(1)
Let Your Love Flow...
Bellamy Brothers
HOT - 5/1/76(1)
Let's Chase Each Other Around The Room...*Merle Haggard*
C&W - 9/22/84(1)
Let's Dance...*David Bowie*
HOT - 5/21/83(1)
Let's Do It Again...*Staple Singers*
HOT - 12/27/75(1)
R&B - 11/22/75(2)
Let's Fall To Pieces Together...
George Strait
C&W - 9/1/84(1)
Let's Get It On...*Marvin Gaye*
HOT - 9/8/73(2)
R&B - 8/18/73(6)
Let's Get Serious...*Jermaine Jackson*
R&B - 5/17/80(6)
Let's Go Crazy...*Prince*
HOT - 9/29/84(2)
R&B - 10/6/84(1)
Let's Go Get Stoned...*Ray Charles*
R&B - 7/23/66(1)
Let's Go, Let's Go, Let's Go...
Hank Ballard
R&B - 11/7/60(3)
Let's Groove...*Earth, Wind & Fire*
R&B - 11/28/81(2)
Let's Hear It For The Boy...
Deniece Williams
HOT - 5/26/84(2)
R&B - 6/2/84(3)

Let's Stay Together...*Al Green*
HOT - 2/12/72(1)
R&B - 1/8/72(9)
Let's Stop Talkin' About It...
Janie Fricke
C&W - 3/31/84(1)
Let's Straighten It Out...*Latimore*
R&B - 11/2/74(2)
Let's Take The Long Way Around The World...*Ronnie Milsap*
C&W - 10/28/78(1)
Let's Wait Awhile...*Janet Jackson*
R&B - 3/14/87(1)
Letter, The...*Box Tops*
HOT - 9/23/67(4)
Lies...*En Vogue*
R&B - 9/15/90(1)
Life Turned Her That Way...
Ricky Van Shelton
C&W - 3/19/88(1)
Life's Highway...*Steve Wariner*
C&W - 6/14/86(1)
Light My Fire...*Doors*
HOT - 7/29/67(3)
Lightnin' Strikes...*Lou Christie*
HOT - 2/19/66(1)
Like A Prayer...*Madonna*
HOT - 4/22/89(3)
Like A Sad Song...*John Denver*
A/C - 10/9/76(1)
Like A Virgin...*Madonna*
HOT - 12/22/84(6)
Linda On My Mind...*Conway Twitty*
C&W - 3/8/75(1)
Lion Sleeps Tonight...*Tokens*
HOT - 12/18/61(3)
Lisbon Antigua...*Nelson Riddle*
POP - BS: 2/25/56(4); DJ: 3/3/56(2)
Listen To What The Man Said...*Wings*
HOT - 7/19/75(1)
Listen To Your Heart...*Roxette*
HOT - 11/4/89(1)
Little Bit More...
Melba Moore with Freddie Jackson
R&B - 11/8/86(1)
Little Bitty Tear...*Burl Ives*
A/C - 2/24/62(1)
Little Good News...*Anne Murray*
C&W - 12/3/83(1)
Little Jeannie...*Elton John*
A/C - 6/14/80(2)
Little Lies...*Fleetwood Mac*
A/C - 10/10/87(4)
Little Rock...*Reba McEntire*
C&W - 9/13/86(1)
Little Star...*Elegants*
POP - HT: 8/25/58(1)
R&B - BS: 9/1/58(4); DJ: 9/8/58(4)
Little Things...*Oak Ridge Boys*
C&W - 6/22/85(1)
Little Things Mean A Lot...
Kitty Kallen
POP - BS: 6/5/54(9); DJ: 6/12/54(8);
JB: 6/26/54(7)
Little Walter...*Tony! Toni! Tone!*
R&B - 6/11/88(1)

Live Fast, Love Hard, Die Young...
Faron Young
C&W - DJ: 6/18/55(3)
Live To Tell...*Madonna*
HOT - 6/7/86(1)
A/C - 5/31/86(3)
Livin' For The Weekend...*O'Jays*
R&B - 4/24/76(2)
Livin' For You...*Al Green*
R&B - 1/26/74(1)
Livin' On A Prayer...*Bon Jovi*
HOT - 2/14/87(4)
Living For The City...*Stevie Wonder*
R&B - 12/29/73(2)
Living In The Promiseland...
Willie Nelson
C&W - 6/28/86(1)
Living Proof...*Ricky Van Shelton*
C&W - 10/21/89(1)
Living Years...*Mike & The Mechanics*
HOT - 3/25/89(1)
A/C - 2/25/89(4)
Lizzie And The Rainman...
Tanya Tucker
C&W - 7/5/75(1)
Loco-Motion, The...*Grand Funk*
HOT - 5/4/74(2)
Loco-Motion, The...*Little Eva*
HOT - 8/25/62(1)
R&B - 8/25/62(3)
Lonely Again...*Eddy Arnold*
C&W - 4/15/67(2)
Lonely Boy...*Paul Anka*
HOT - 7/13/59(4)
Lonely Night (Angel Face)...
Captain & Tennille
A/C - 3/13/76(1)
Lonely Nights...*Mickey Gilley*
C&W - 2/6/82(1)
Lonely People...*America*
A/C - 2/15/75(1)
Lonely Teardrops...*Jackie Wilson*
R&B - 12/15/58(7)
Lonesome 7-7203...*Hawkshaw Hawkins*
C&W - 5/4/63(4)
Long And Winding Road...*Beatles*
HOT - 6/13/70(2)
Long Gone Lonesome Blues...
Hank Williams
C&W - DJ: 4/22/50(8); BS: 4/29/50(5);
JB: 5/6/50(4)
Long Hard Road (The Sharecropper's Dream)...*Nitty Gritty Dirt Band*
C&W - 8/25/84(1)
Long Line Of Love...
Michael Martin Murphey
C&W - 8/15/87(1)
Long Lonely Nights...*Clyde McPhatter*
R&B - DJ: 9/16/57(1)
Long Tall Sally...*Little Richard*
R&B - DJ: 4/14/56(5); JB: 4/14/56(8);
BS: 4/21/56(6)
Longer...*Dan Fogelberg*
A/C - 2/9/80(1)
Longest Time...*Billy Joel*
A/C - 5/19/84(2)
Longfellow Serenade...*Neil Diamond*
A/C - 11/16/74(1)

Look, The...*Roxette*
HOT - 4/8/89(1)
Look At Me (I'm In Love)...*Moments*
R&B - 6/28/75(1)
Look Away...*Chicago*
HOT - 12/10/88(2)
A/C - 12/3/88(1)
Lookin' For A Love...*Bobby Womack*
R&B - 3/16/74(3)
Lookin' For Love...*Johnny Lee*
C&W - 9/6/80(3)
Looking For A New Love...*Jody Watley*
R&B - 3/21/87(3)
Looking For Space...*John Denver*
A/C - 4/17/76(1)
Looks Like We Made It...
Barry Manilow
HOT - 7/23/77(1)
A/C - 6/4/77(3)
Loose Talk...*Carl Smith*
C&W - BS: 1/8/55(7); DJ: 1/8/55(6);
JB: 1/22/55(4)
Loosey's Rap...
Rick James/Roxanne Shante
R&B - 8/20/88(1)
Lord, I Hope This Day Is Good...
Don Williams
C&W - 2/27/82(1)
Lord Knows I'm Drinking...*Cal Smith*
C&W - 3/3/73(1)
Lord, Mr. Ford...*Jerry Reed*
C&W - 8/4/73(1)
(Lost Her Love) On Our Last Date...*Conway Twitty*
C&W - 5/27/72(1)
(Lost His Love) On Our Last Date...
Emmylou Harris
C&W - 1/22/83(1)
Lost In Emotion...
Lisa Lisa & Cult Jam
HOT - 10/17/87(1)
R&B - 10/3/87(1)
Lost In Love...*Air Supply*
A/C - 3/22/80(6)
Lost In The Fifties Tonight...
Ronnie Milsap
C&W - 9/28/85(2)
Lost In Your Eyes...*Debbie Gibson*
HOT - 3/4/89(3)
Lotta Love...*Nicolette Larson*
A/C - 2/3/79(1)
Louisiana Woman, Mississippi Man...
Conway Twitty & Loretta Lynn
C&W - 8/18/73(1)
Love And Affection ..see: (Can't Live Without Your)
Love Ballad...*L.T.D.*
R&B - 11/6/76(2)
Love Bites...*Def Leppard*
HOT - 10/8/88(1)
Love Child...*Supremes*
HOT - 11/30/68(2)
Love Come Down...*Evelyn King*
R&B - 10/2/82(5)
Love Don't Care (Whose Heart It Breaks)...*Earl Thomas Conley*
C&W - 7/27/85(1)

Love Hangover...*Diana Ross*
HOT - 5/29/76(2)
R&B - 5/15/76(1)
Love I Lost...
Harold Melvin & The Blue Notes
R&B - 11/24/73(2)
Love In The First Degree...*Alabama*
C&W - 12/26/81(2)
Love Is A House...*Force M.D.'s*
R&B - 9/5/87(2)
Love Is A Hurtin' Thing...*Lou Rawls*
R&B - 11/12/66(1)
Love Is A Many-Splendored Thing...
Four Aces
POP - BS: 10/8/55(2); DJ: 10/15/55(6);
TP: 11/12/55(3); JB: 11/12/55(3)
Love Is A Wonderful Thing...
Michael Bolton
A/C - 5/25/91(4)
Love Is Alive...*Judds*
C&W - 8/31/85(1)
Love Is Blue...*Paul Mauriat*
HOT - 2/10/68(5)
A/C - 2/17/68(11)
Love Is Forever...*Billy Ocean*
A/C - 12/20/86(3)
Love Is Here And Now You're Gone...
Supremes
HOT - 3/11/67(1)
R&B - 3/11/67(2)
Love Is In The Air...*John Paul Young*
A/C - 10/7/78(2)
Love Is Like A Butterfly...
Dolly Parton
C&W - 11/9/74(1)
Love Is On A Roll...*Don Williams*
C&W - 7/2/83(1)
Love Is Strange...*Mickey & Sylvia*
R&B - DJ: 3/16/57(2)
Love Is The Answer...
England Dan & John Ford Coley
A/C - 5/5/79(2)
Love Is The Foundation...
Loretta Lynn
C&W - 7/14/73(2)
(Love Is) Thicker Than Water...
Andy Gibb
HOT - 3/4/78(2)
Love Letters In The Sand...*Pat Boone*
POP - BS: 6/3/57(5); TP: 6/10/57(5);
DJ: 6/10/57(7)
L-O-V-E (Love)...*Al Green*
R&B - 4/12/75(2)
Love, Love, Love...*Webb Pierce*
C&W - BS: 10/22/55(8); DJ: 10/29/55(13);
JB: 11/5/55(9)
Love Machine...*Miracles*
HOT - 3/6/76(1)
Love Makes Things Happen...*Pebbles*
R&B - 1/26/91(2)
Love Me Do...*Beatles*
HOT - 5/30/64(1)
Love Me Down...*Freddie Jackson*
R&B - 1/5/91(2)
Love Me Over Again...*Don Williams*
C&W - 2/16/80(1)
Love Me Tender...*Elvis Presley*
POP - BS: 11/3/56(5); DJ: 11/3/56(5);
TP: 11/17/56(4); JB: 12/8/56(1)

Love Me Tonight ..see: (Turn Out The Light And)
Love Me With All Your Heart (Cuando Calienta El Sol)...
Ray Charles Singers
A/C - 5/30/64(4)
Love On A Two-Way Street...*Moments*
R&B - 5/16/70(5)
Love On Arrival...*Dan Seals*
C&W - 4/21/90(3)
Love Or Something Like It...
Kenny Rogers
C&W - 8/5/78(1)
Love Out Loud...*Earl Thomas Conley*
C&W - 6/17/89(1)
Love Overboard...
Gladys Knight & The Pips
R&B - 1/23/88(1)
Love Power...
Dionne Warwick & Jeffrey Osborne
A/C - 8/22/87(1)
(also see: Power Of Love)
Love Put A Song In My Heart...
Johnny Rodriguez
C&W - 12/13/75(1)
Love Rollercoaster...*Ohio Players*
HOT - 1/31/76(1)
R&B - 12/27/75(1)
Love Saw It...*Karyn White*
R&B - 4/22/89(2)
Love Song...*Anne Murray*
A/C - 2/9/74(1)
Love Song...*Oak Ridge Boys*
C&W - 8/20/83(1)
Love Story ..see: (Where Do I Begin)
Love Takes Time...*Mariah Carey*
HOT - 11/10/90(3)
R&B - 11/10/90(3)
A/C - 10/27/90(1)
Love Theme From A Star Is Born (Evergreen)...*Barbra Streisand*
HOT - 3/5/77(3)
A/C - 1/15/77(6)
Love Theme From Romeo & Juliet...
Henry Mancini
HOT - 6/28/69(2)
A/C - 6/7/69(8)
Love Train...*O'Jays*
HOT - 3/24/73(1)
R&B - 2/17/73(4)
Love Will Conquer All...
Lionel Richie
A/C - 11/22/86(2)
Love Will Find Its Way To You...
Reba McEntire
C&W - 4/2/88(1)
Love Will Keep Us Together...
Captain & Tennille
HOT - 6/21/75(4)
A/C - 6/7/75(1)
Love Will Lead You Back...
Taylor Dayne
HOT - 4/7/90(1)
A/C - 3/24/90(4)
Love Will Never Do (Without You)...
Janet Jackson
HOT - 1/19/91(1)

Love Will Turn You Around...
Kenny Rogers
C&W - 9/4/82(1)
A/C - 9/25/82(2)

Love Without End, Amen...
George Strait
C&W - 6/9/90(5)

Love Won't Let Me Wait...
Major Harris
R&B - 6/7/75(1)

Love You Down...*Ready For The World*
R&B - 12/13/86(2)

Love You Inside Out...*Bee Gees*
HOT - 6/9/79(1)

Love You Save...*Jackson 5*
HOT - 6/27/70(2)
R&B - 6/20/70(6)

Love Zone...*Billy Ocean*
R&B - 8/30/86(1)

Love's Gonna Live Here...*Buck Owens*
C&W - 10/19/63(16)

Love's Theme...
Love Unlimited Orchestra
HOT - 2/9/74(1)
A/C - 1/26/74(2)

Lovelite...*O'Bryan*
R&B - 6/23/84(1)

Lover's Question...*Clyde McPhatter*
R&B - 12/8/58(1)

Loves Me Like A Rock...*Paul Simon*
A/C - 9/8/73(2)

Lovin' Only Me...*Ricky Skaggs*
C&W - 7/8/89(1)

Lovin' You...*O'Jays*
R&B - 11/7/87(1)

Lovin' You...*Minnie Riperton*
HOT - 4/5/75(1)

Loving Blind...*Clint Black*
C&W - 3/23/91(2)

Loving Up A Storm...*Razzy Bailey*
C&W - 10/11/80(1)

Low Rider...*War*
R&B - 11/8/75(1)

Lucille...*Little Richard*
R&B - JB: 4/27/57(2)

Lucille...*Kenny Rogers*
C&W - 4/2/77(2)

Lucille (You Won't Do Your Daddy's Will)...*Waylon Jennings*
C&W - 6/4/83(1)

Luckenbach, Texas...*Waylon Jennings*
C&W - 5/21/77(6)

Lucky Charm...*Boys*
R&B - 4/1/89(1)

Lucy In The Sky With Diamonds...
Elton John
HOT - 1/4/75(2)

Lynda...*Steve Wariner*
C&W - 11/28/87(1)

M

MacArthur Park...*Donna Summer*
HOT - 11/11/78(3)

Mack The Knife...*Bobby Darin*
HOT - 10/5/59(9)

Made In Japan...*Buck Owens*
C&W - 7/15/72(1)

Maggie May...*Rod Stewart*
HOT - 10/2/71(5)

Magic...*Olivia Newton-John*
HOT - 8/2/80(4)
A/C - 7/19/80(5)

Make It Funky...*James Brown*
R&B - 10/2/71(2)

Make It Like It Was...*Regina Belle*
R&B - 2/3/90(1)

Make It Real...*Jets*
A/C - 6/25/88(3)

Make It With You...*Bread*
HOT - 8/22/70(1)

Make Love Stay...*Dan Fogelberg*
A/C - 4/9/83(1)

Make Love To Me!...*Jo Stafford*
POP - BS: 3/13/54(3); JB: 3/13/54(7); DJ: 4/3/54(3)

Make Me Lose Control...*Eric Carmen*
A/C - 7/16/88(3)

Make Me Yours...*Bettye Swann*
R&B - 7/22/67(2)

Make My Life With You...
Oak Ridge Boys
C&W - 2/16/85(1)

Make No Mistake, She's Mine...
Ronnie Milsap & Kenny Rogers
C&W - 9/12/87(1)

Make The World Go Away...
Eddy Arnold
C&W - 12/4/65(3)
A/C - 12/4/65(4)

Make You Sweat...*Keith Sweat*
R&B - 7/28/90(1)

Makin' Up For Lost Time (The Dallas Lovers' Song)...*Crystal Gayle & Gary Morris*
C&W - 2/15/86(1)

Mama Can't Buy You Love...*Elton John*
A/C - 8/25/79(1)

(Mama) He Treats Your Daughter Mean...*Ruth Brown*
R&B - BS: 3/7/53(5); JB: 3/21/53(5)

Mama He's Crazy...*Judds*
C&W - 8/4/84(1)

Mama Sang A Song...*Bill Anderson*
C&W - 10/27/62(7)

Mama Told Me (Not To Come)...
Three Dog Night
HOT - 7/11/70(2)

Mama Tried...*Merle Haggard*
C&W - 8/31/68(4)

Mama's Never Seen Those Eyes...
Forester Sisters
C&W - 6/21/86(1)

Mambo Baby...*Ruth Brown*
R&B - BS: 11/20/54(1); JB: 1/8/55(7)

Mammas Don't Let Your Babies Grow Up To Be Cowboys...*Waylon & Willie*
C&W - 3/4/78(4)

(Man In Motion) ..see: St. Elmo's Fire

Man In The Mirror...*Michael Jackson*
HOT - 3/26/88(2)
R&B - 3/26/88(1)

Mandolin Rain...
Bruce Hornsby & The Range
A/C - 3/21/87(3)

Mandy...*Barry Manilow*
HOT - 1/18/75(1)
A/C - 12/28/74(2)

Maneater...*Daryl Hall & John Oates*
HOT - 12/18/82(4)

Maniac...*Michael Sembello*
HOT - 9/10/83(2)

Margaritaville...*Jimmy Buffett*
A/C - 5/28/77(1)

Marie Laveau...*Bobby Bare*
C&W - 7/20/74(1)

Mary In The Morning...*Al Martino*
A/C - 7/1/67(2)

Mary Jo...*Four Blazes*
R&B - JB: 8/23/52(3)

Mashed Potato Time...*Dee Dee Sharp*
R&B - 4/28/62(4)

Master Blaster (Jammin')...
Stevie Wonder
R&B - 11/1/80(7)

Masterpiece...*Temptations*
R&B - 4/14/73(2)

May The Bird Of Paradise Fly Up Your Nose...*"Little" Jimmy Dickens*
C&W - 11/20/65(2)

Maybe Your Baby's Got The Blues...
Judds
C&W - 11/14/87(1)

Maybellene...*Chuck Berry*
R&B - DJ: 8/20/55(9); BS: 8/27/55(9); JB: 9/3/55(11)

Me And Bobby McGee...*Janis Joplin*
HOT - 3/20/71(2)

Me And Mrs. Jones...*Billy Paul*
HOT - 12/16/72(3)
R&B - 12/9/72(4)

Me And You And A Dog Named Boo...
Lobo
A/C - 5/15/71(2)

Me Myself And I...*De La Soul*
R&B - 6/10/89(1)

Meet In The Middle...*Diamond Rio*
C&W - 6/1/91(2)

Meet Me In Montana...
Marie Osmond with Dan Seals
C&W - 10/12/85(1)

Memories Are Made Of This...
Dean Martin
POP - DJ: 1/7/56(6); TP: 1/14/56(5); BS: 1/14/56(5); JB: 1/28/56(4)

Mercedes Boy...*Pebbles*
R&B - 5/21/88(1)

Mercy Mercy Me (The Ecology)...
Marvin Gaye
R&B - 8/14/71(2)

Message In Our Music...*O'Jays*
R&B - 10/30/76(1)

Mexican Joe...*Jim Reeves*
C&W - BS: 5/9/53(6); DJ: 6/6/53(7); JB: 6/6/53(9)

Mexico...*Bob Moore*
A/C - 10/9/61(1)

Miami Vice Theme...*Jan Hammer*
HOT - 11/9/85(1)

Michael...*Highwaymen*
HOT - 9/4/61(2)
A/C - 9/4/61(5)

Mickey...*Toni Basil*
HOT - 12/11/82(1)

Midnight...*Red Foley*
C&W - BS: 1/10/53(1)

Midnight Blue...*Melissa Manchester*
A/C - 6/21/75(2)

Midnight Hauler...*Razzy Bailey*
C&W - 10/3/81(1)

Midnight In Moscow...*Kenny Ball*
A/C - 3/3/62(3)

Midnight Train To Georgia...
Gladys Knight & The Pips
HOT - 10/27/73(2)
R&B - 10/20/73(4)

Mighty Love...*Spinners*
R&B - 3/2/74(2)

Mind Your Own Business...
Hank Williams, Jr.
C&W - 12/27/86(1)

Misery Loves Company...
Porter Wagoner
C&W - 3/10/62(2)

Miss You...*Rolling Stones*
HOT - 8/5/78(1)

Miss You Like Crazy...*Natalie Cole*
R&B - 6/3/89(1)
A/C - 6/3/89(1)

Miss You Much...*Janet Jackson*
HOT - 10/7/89(4)
R&B - 10/14/89(2)

Missing You...*Diana Ross*
R&B - 2/23/85(3)

Missing You...*John Waite*
HOT - 9/22/84(1)

M-I-S-S-I-S-S-I-P-P-I...*Red Foley*
C&W - JB: 7/15/50(1)

Missunderstanding...*Al B. Sure!*
R&B - 11/24/90(1)

Mister ..see: Mr.

Mistrustin' Blues...*Little Esther
with Mel Walker/The Johnny Otis Orch.*
R&B - JB: 4/15/50(4); BS: 5/6/50(4)

Moanin' The Blues...*Hank Williams*
C&W - DJ: 12/30/50(1)

Modern Day Romance...
Nitty Gritty Dirt Band
C&W - 9/14/85(1)

Mona Lisa...*Nat "King" Cole*
POP - DJ: 7/8/50(8); BS: 7/15/50(5);
JB: 7/22/50(5)
R&B - JB: 9/2/50(4)

Monday, Monday...
Mama's & The Papa's
HOT - 5/7/66(3)

Money For Nothing...*Dire Straits*
HOT - 9/21/85(3)

Money Honey...
Clyde McPhatter & The Drifters
R&B - BS: 11/21/53(11); JB: 11/21/53(1)

Monkey...*George Michael*
HOT - 8/27/88(2)

Monster Mash...*Bobby "Boris" Pickett*
HOT - 10/20/62(2)

Mony Mony "Live"...*Billy Idol*
HOT - 11/21/87(1)

Moody Blue...*Elvis Presley*
C&W - 2/19/77(1)

Moody River...*Pat Boone*
HOT - 6/19/61(2)

Moon Is Still Over Her Shoulder...
Michael Johnson
C&W - 5/9/87(1)

(Moon Song) ..see: I Don't Know A Thing About Love

Moonglow and Theme From "Picnic"...
Morris Stoloff
POP - DJ: 6/2/56(3)

Moonlighting...*Al Jarreau*
A/C - 7/25/87(1)

More And More...*Webb Pierce*
C&W - BS: 11/6/54(9); DJ: 11/6/54(8);
JB: 12/4/54(10)

More Than I Can Say...*Leo Sayer*
A/C - 12/27/80(3)

More Than The Eye Can See...
Al Martino
A/C - 11/11/67(2)

More Than Words...*Extreme*
HOT - 6/8/91(1)

More To Me...*Charley Pride*
C&W - 11/12/77(1)

Mornin' Ride...*Lee Greenwood*
C&W - 3/7/87(1)

Morning After...*Maureen McGovern*
HOT - 8/4/73(2)

Morning Dance...*Spyro Gyra*
A/C - 7/28/79(1)

Morning Desire...*Kenny Rogers*
C&W - 1/11/86(1)

Morning Has Broken...*Cat Stevens*
A/C - 5/13/72(1)

Morning Side Of The Mountain...
Donny & Marie Osmond
A/C - 1/25/75(1)

Morning Train (Nine To Five)...
Sheena Easton
HOT - 5/2/81(2)
A/C - 5/2/81(2)

Most Beautiful Girl...*Charlie Rich*
HOT - 12/15/73(2)
C&W - 11/24/73(3)
A/C - 11/10/73(3)

Mother-In-Law...*Ernie K-Doe*
HOT - 5/22/61(1)
R&B - 4/24/61(5)

Mother Popcorn (You Got To Have A Mother For Me)...*James Brown*
R&B - 8/2/69(2)

Mountain Music...*Alabama*
C&W - 5/1/82(1)

Mountain Of Love...*Charley Pride*
C&W - 3/20/82(1)

Movin'...*Brass Construction*
R&B - 5/8/76(1)

Movin' On...*Merle Haggard*
C&W - 7/12/75(1)

Mr. Big Stuff...*Jean Knight*
R&B - 7/3/71(5)

Mr. Blue...*Fleetwoods*
HOT - 11/16/59(1)

Mr. Custer...*Larry Verne*
HOT - 10/10/60(1)

Mr. Lee...*Bobbettes*
R&B - DJ: 9/30/57(4)

Mr. Lonely...*Bobby Vinton*
HOT - 12/12/64(1)

Mr. Sandman...*Chordettes*
POP - DJ: 11/27/54(7); BS: 12/4/54(7);
JB: 12/18/54(4)

Mr. Tambourine Man...*Byrds*
HOT - 6/26/65(1)

Mr. Telephone Man...*New Edition*
R&B - 2/2/85(3)

Mrs. Brown You've Got A Lovely Daughter...*Herman's Hermits*
HOT - 5/1/65(3)

Mrs. Robinson...*Simon & Garfunkel*
HOT - 6/1/68(3)

Music! Music! Music!...*Teresa Brewer*
POP - BS: 3/18/50(4); JB: 4/8/50(1)

Muskrat Love...*Captain & Tennille*
A/C - 10/30/76(4)

My Angel Baby...*Toby Beau*
A/C - 8/12/78(1)

My Babe...*Little Walter*
R&B - BS: 4/23/55(4); JB: 4/30/55(5);
DJ: 5/14/55(2)

My Baby Thinks He's A Train...
Rosanne Cash
C&W - 11/14/81(1)

My Boy...*Elvis Presley*
A/C - 4/5/75(1)

My Boyfriend's Back...*Angels*
HOT - 8/31/63(3)

My Cup Runneth Over...*Ed Ames*
A/C - 2/4/67(4)

My Ding-A-Ling...*Chuck Berry*
HOT - 10/21/72(2)

My Elusive Dreams...
David Houston & Tammy Wynette
C&W - 9/16/67(2)

My Eyes Adored You...*Frankie Valli*
HOT - 3/22/75(1)

My Eyes Can Only See As Far As You...*Charley Pride*
C&W - 5/8/76(1)

My Fantasy...
Teddy Riley Featuring Guy
R&B - 9/9/89(1)

My Favorite Memory...*Merle Haggard*
C&W - 11/28/81(1)

My First Love...*Atlantic Starr*
R&B - 5/27/89(1)

My Girl...*Temptations*
HOT - 3/6/65(1)
R&B - 1/30/65(6)

My Guy...*Mary Wells*
HOT - 5/16/64(2)
R&B - 5/16/64(2)

My Hang-Up Is You...*Freddie Hart*
C&W - 3/11/72(6)

My Heart...*Ronnie Milsap*
C&W - 5/31/80(3)

My Heart Belongs To Me...
Barbra Streisand
A/C - 7/30/77(4)

My Heart Has A Mind Of Its Own...
Connie Francis
HOT - 9/26/60(2)

N

My Heart Skips A Beat...*Buck Owens*
C&W - 5/16/64(7)

My Heroes Have Always Been Cowboys...*Willie Nelson*
C&W - 3/8/80(2)

My Hometown...*Bruce Springsteen*
A/C - 2/1/86(1)

My Life (Throw It Away If I Want To)...*Bill Anderson*
C&W - 5/17/69(2)

My Little Town...*Simon & Garfunkel*
A/C - 11/22/75(2)

My Love...*Petula Clark*
HOT - 2/5/66(2)

My Love...*Sonny James*
C&W - 5/16/70(3)

My Love...*Paul McCartney & Wings*
HOT - 6/2/73(4)
A/C - 6/2/73(3)

My Love...*Lionel Richie*
A/C - 5/21/83(4)

My Man...*Tammy Wynette*
C&W - 11/11/72(1)

My Maria...*B.W. Stevenson*
A/C - 9/22/73(1)

My Melody Of Love...*Bobby Vinton*
A/C - 11/9/74(1)

My, My, My...*Johnny Gill*
R&B - 7/14/90(2)

My Next Broken Heart...*Brooks & Dunn*
C&W - 12/21/91(2)

My Only Love...*Statler Brothers*
C&W - 3/9/85(1)

My Prayer...*Platters*
POP - BS: 8/4/56(2); TP: 8/18/56(5);
DJ: 8/18/56(3); JB: 8/25/56(1)
R&B - JB: 8/18/56(2); DJ: 8/25/56(2)

My Prerogative...*Bobby Brown*
HOT - 1/14/89(1)
R&B - 10/15/88(2)

My Sharona...*Knack*
HOT - 8/25/79(6)

My Shoes Keep Walking Back To You...*Ray Price*
C&W - DJ: 9/16/57(4)

My Song...
Johnny Ace with The Beale Streeters
R&B - BS: 9/27/52(9)

My Special Angel...*Bobby Helms*
C&W - BS: 12/9/57(4); DJ: 12/30/57(1)

My Special Angel...*Vogues*
A/C - 10/19/68(2)

My Sweet Lord...*George Harrison*
HOT - 12/26/70(4)

My Thang...*James Brown*
R&B - 7/20/74(2)

My True Story...*Jive Five*
R&B - 9/11/61(3)

My Woman My Woman, My Wife...
Marty Robbins
C&W - 5/2/70(1)

Nasty...*Janet Jackson*
R&B - 6/14/86(2)

Natural High...*Merle Haggard*
C&W - 6/8/85(1)

Navy Blue...*Diane Renay*
A/C - 3/21/64(1)

Near You...
George Jones & Tammy Wynette
C&W - 2/5/77(2)

Need You...*Sonny James*
C&W - 4/29/67(2)

Need You Tonight...*INXS*
HOT - 1/30/88(1)

Neither One Of Us (Wants To Be The First To Say Goodbye)...
Gladys Knight & The Pips
R&B - 3/17/73(4)

Nel Blu Dipinto Di Blu (Volare)...
Domenico Modugno
POP - HT: 8/18/58(5); BS: 8/18/58(5)

Never Be The Same...
Christopher Cross
A/C - 12/13/80(2)

Never Be You...*Rosanne Cash*
C&W - 1/25/86(1)

Never Been So Loved (In All My Life)...*Charley Pride*
C&W - 10/24/81(2)

Never Can Say Goodbye...*Jackson 5*
R&B - 5/1/71(3)

Never Gonna Fall In Love Again...
Eric Carmen
A/C - 6/19/76(1)

Never Gonna Give You Up...
Rick Astley
HOT - 3/12/88(2)
A/C - 3/12/88(3)

Never Gonna Let You Go...
Sergio Mendes
A/C - 6/18/83(4)

Never My Love...*5th Dimension*
A/C - 10/23/71(1)

Never Too Much...*Luther Vandross*
R&B - 10/24/81(2)

New Fool At An Old Game...
Reba McEntire
C&W - 3/25/89(1)

New Kid In Town...*Eagles*
HOT - 2/26/77(1)

New Looks From An Old Lover...
B.J. Thomas
C&W - 10/1/83(1)

Next In Line...*Conway Twitty*
C&W - 11/2/68(1)

Next Time I Fall...
Peter Cetera W/Amy Grant
HOT - 12/6/86(1)
A/C - 11/8/86(2)

Next To You, Next To Me...*Shenandoah*
C&W - 8/18/90(3)

Nice 'N' Slow...*Freddie Jackson*
R&B - 8/27/88(3)

Night ..also see: **Nite**

Night Chicago Died...*Paper Lace*
HOT - 8/17/74(1)

Night Fever...*Bee Gees*
HOT - 3/18/78(8)

Night Games...*Charley Pride*
C&W - 9/17/83(1)

Night The Lights Went Out In Georgia...*Vicki Lawrence*
HOT - 4/7/73(2)

Night They Drove Old Dixie Down...
Joan Baez
A/C - 9/4/71(5)

Night Train...*Jimmy Forrest*
R&B - JB: 3/15/52(7); BS: 3/22/52(6)

Nightingale...*Carole King*
A/C - 2/22/75(1)

Nightshift...*Commodores*
R&B - 3/16/85(4)

9 To 5...*Dolly Parton*
HOT - 2/21/81(2)
C&W - 1/24/81(1)
A/C - 2/28/81(2)
(also see: Morning Train)

96 Tears...
? (Question Mark) & The Mysterians
HOT - 10/29/66(1)

99 Miles From L.A....*Albert Hammond*
A/C - 5/24/75(1)

Nite And Day...*Al B. Sure!*
R&B - 4/30/88(3)

No Charge...*Melba Montgomery*
C&W - 5/25/74(1)

No Gettin' Over Me ..see: (There's)

No Help Wanted...*Carlisles*
C&W - DJ: 1/31/53(4); JB: 5/9/53(4)

No Matter How High...*Oak Ridge Boys*
C&W - 3/3/90(1)

No More Tears (Enough Is Enough)...
Barbra Streisand/Donna Summer
HOT - 11/24/79(2)

No Night So Long...*Dionne Warwick*
A/C - 9/20/80(3)

No One Is To Blame...*Howard Jones*
A/C - 6/28/86(1)

No Other Love...*Perry Como*
POP - DJ: 8/15/53(4)

Nobody...*Sylvia*
C&W - 8/21/82(1)

Nobody Does It Better...*Carly Simon*
A/C - 9/10/77(7)

Nobody Falls Like A Fool...
Earl Thomas Conley
C&W - 12/14/85(1)

Nobody In His Right Mind Would've Left Her...*George Strait*
C&W - 8/2/86(1)

Nobody Likes Sad Songs...
Ronnie Milsap
C&W - 6/23/79(1)

Nobody Loves Me Like You Do...
Anne Murray with Dave Loggins
C&W - 12/15/84(1)

Nobody's Home...*Clint Black*
C&W - 1/20/90(3)

North To Alaska...*Johnny Horton*
C&W - 1/9/61(5)

(not just) Knee Deep...*Funkadelic*
R&B - 10/13/79(3)

303

Nothing Compares 2 U...
Sinead O'Connor
HOT - 4/21/90(4)
Nothing From Nothing...*Billy Preston*
HOT - 10/19/74(1)
Nothing I Can Do About It Now...
Willie Nelson
C&W - 9/16/89(1)
Nothing's Gonna Stop Us Now...
Starship
HOT - 4/4/87(2)
A/C - 4/11/87(2)
Now And Forever (You And Me)...
Anne Murray
C&W - 4/26/86(1)

O

Oasis...*Roberta Flack*
R&B - 1/7/89(1)
Ocean Front Property...*George Strait*
C&W - 4/4/87(1)
Ode To Billie Joe...*Bobbie Gentry*
HOT - 8/26/67(4)
Off On Your Own (Girl)...*Al B. Sure!*
R&B - 8/6/88(2)
Oh, Baby Mine (I Get So Lonely)...
Johnnie & Jack
C&W - DJ: 6/12/54(2)
Oh Girl...*Chi-Lites*
HOT - 5/27/72(1)
R&B - 6/3/72(2)
Oh Girl...*Paul Young*
A/C - 9/22/90(3)
Oh Lonesome Me...*Don Gibson*
C&W - BS: 4/14/58(8); DJ: 4/14/58(8)
Oh! My Pa-Pa...*Eddie Fisher*
POP - BS: 1/2/54(8); DJ: 1/16/54(7);
JB: 1/30/54(6)
Oh, Pretty Woman...*Roy Orbison*
HOT - 9/26/64(3)
Oh Sheila...*Ready For The World*
HOT - 10/12/85(1)
R&B - 9/21/85(2)
Oh What A Dream...
Ruth Brown & Her Rhythmakers
R&B - BS: 9/4/54(4); JB: 9/25/54(8)
Oh, What A Night...*Dells*
R&B - 9/27/69(1)
(also see: December, 1963)
Okie From Muskogee...*Merle Haggard*
C&W - 11/15/69(4)
**(Old Dogs-Children And)
Watermelon Wine...***Tom T. Hall*
C&W - 1/27/73(1)
Old Fashioned Love Song...
Three Dog Night
A/C - 1/1/72(1)
Old Flame...*Alabama*
C&W - 4/18/81(1)
**Old Flames Can't Hold A Candle To
You...***Dolly Parton*
C&W - 9/27/80(1)

Old Man From The Mountain...
Merle Haggard
C&W - 8/24/74(1)
Old Songs...*Barry Manilow*
A/C - 11/28/81(3)
Older Women...*Ronnie McDowell*
C&W - 9/12/81(1)
On My Knees...
Charlie Rich with Janie Fricke
C&W - 12/9/78(1)
On My Own...
Patti LaBelle & Michael McDonald
HOT - 6/14/86(3)
R&B - 5/17/86(4)
**On Our Last Date ..see: (Lost Her [His]
Love)**
On Our Own...*Bobby Brown*
R&B - 8/5/89(1)
On Second Thought...*Eddie Rabbitt*
C&W - 2/17/90(2)
On The Other Hand...*Randy Travis*
C&W - 7/26/86(1)
On The Road Again...*Willie Nelson*
C&W - 11/8/80(1)
Once A Day...*Connie Smith*
C&W - 11/28/64(8)
Once In A Blue Moon...
Earl Thomas Conley
C&W - 5/3/86(1)
One...*Bee Gees*
A/C - 9/16/89(2)
One Bad Apple...*Osmonds*
HOT - 2/13/71(5)
One By One...*Kitty Wells & Red Foley*
C&W - JB: 7/31/54(1)
One Day At A Time...*Cristy Lane*
C&W - 6/21/80(1)
One Friend...*Dan Seals*
C&W - 1/16/88(1)
One Good Woman...*Peter Cetera*
A/C - 9/3/88(4)
100% Chance Of Rain...*Gary Morris*
C&W - 4/5/86(1)
One In A Million...*Johnny Lee*
C&W - 12/27/80(2)
One In A Million You...*Larry Graham*
R&B - 8/2/80(2)
One Less Bell To Answer...
5th Dimension
A/C - 1/2/71(1)
One Mint Julep...*Ray Charles*
R&B - 4/17/61(1)
One Moment In Time...
Whitney Houston
A/C - 10/29/88(2)
One More Night...*Phil Collins*
HOT - 3/30/85(2)
A/C - 3/30/85(3)
One More Try...*George Michael*
HOT - 5/28/88(3)
R&B - 6/18/88(1)
A/C - 5/28/88(3)
One More Try...*Timmy -T-*
HOT - 3/23/91(1)
One Nation Under A Groove...
Funkadelic
R&B - 9/30/78(6)

One Of A Kind (Love Affair)...
Spinners
R&B - 6/9/73(4)
One Of A Kind Pair Of Fools...
Barbara Mandrell
C&W - 11/19/83(1)
One Of These Nights...*Eagles*
HOT - 8/2/75(1)
One Piece At A Time...*Johnny Cash*
C&W - 5/29/76(2)
One Promise Too Late...*Reba McEntire*
C&W - 8/8/87(1)
One That You Love...*Air Supply*
HOT - 7/25/81(1)
1-2-3...
Gloria Estefan & Miami Sound Machine
A/C - 8/27/88(1)
One's On The Way...*Loretta Lynn*
C&W - 2/5/72(2)
Only Love Can Break A Heart...
Gene Pitney
A/C - 10/27/62(2)
Only Love Is Real...*Carole King*
A/C - 3/27/76(1)
Only One Love In My Life...
Ronnie Milsap
C&W - 7/15/78(3)
Only One You...*T.G. Sheppard*
C&W - 2/20/82(1)
Only The Lonely...*Sonny James*
C&W - 3/8/69(3)
Only The Strong Survive...
Jerry Butler
R&B - 4/5/69(2)
Only Yesterday...*Carpenters*
A/C - 5/3/75(1)
Only You...*Platters*
R&B - DJ: 10/22/55(5); BS: 10/29/55(7);
JB: 11/19/55(6)
Only You...*Ringo Starr*
A/C - 1/11/75(1)
Only You (Can Break My Heart)...
Buck Owens
C&W - 10/2/65(1)
Ooo La La La...*Teena Marie*
R&B - 4/9/88(1)
Open Up Your Heart...*Buck Owens*
C&W - 10/22/66(4)
Open Your Heart...*Madonna*
HOT - 2/7/87(1)
Operator...*Midnight Star*
R&B - 12/22/84(5)
Opposites Attract...*Paula Abdul*
HOT - 2/10/90(3)
Our Day Will Come...
Ruby & The Romantics
HOT - 3/23/63(1)
R&B - 3/23/63(2)
Our Love...*Natalie Cole*
R&B - 1/21/78(2)
Our Love Is On The Faultline...
Crystal Gayle
C&W - 6/11/83(1)
**Out Of My Head And Back In My
Bed...***Loretta Lynn*
C&W - 1/28/78(2)
Out Of Touch...*Daryl Hall John Oates*
HOT - 12/8/84(2)

Outa-Space...*Billy Preston*
R&B - 7/1/72(1)
Outstanding...*Gap Band*
R&B - 2/5/83(1)
Over And Over...*Dave Clark Five*
HOT - 12/25/65(1)
Overjoyed...*Stevie Wonder*
A/C - 4/12/86(2)
Owner Of A Lonely Heart...*Yes*
HOT - 1/21/84(2)

P

Paint It, Black...*Rolling Stones*
HOT - 6/11/66(2)
Paloma Blanca...
George Baker Selection
A/C - 2/14/76(1)
Papa Don't Preach...*Madonna*
HOT - 8/16/86(2)
Papa Don't Take No Mess...
James Brown
R&B - 10/12/74(1)
Papa Was A Rollin' Stone...
Temptations
HOT - 12/2/72(1)
Papa's Got A Brand New Bag...
James Brown
R&B - 8/14/65(8)
Paper Roses...*Marie Osmond*
C&W - 11/10/73(2)
A/C - 11/3/73(1)
Paperback Writer...*Beatles*
HOT - 6/25/66(2)
Paradise...*Sade*
R&B - 7/9/88(1)
Paradise Tonight...
Charly McClain & Mickey Gilley
C&W - 10/15/83(1)
Part Time Love...
Little Johnny Taylor
R&B - 10/19/63(1)
Part-Time Lover...*Stevie Wonder*
HOT - 11/2/85(1)
R&B - 10/19/85(6)
A/C - 10/26/85(3)
Party Doll...*Buddy Knox*
POP - BS: 3/30/57(1)
Party Time...*T.G. Sheppard*
C&W - 10/10/81(1)
Patricia...*Perez Prado*
POP - TP: 7/28/58(1); DJ: 7/28/58(1)
R&B - BS: 8/11/58(2); DJ: 8/25/58(1)
Payback, The...*James Brown*
R&B - 4/27/74(2)
Peace Train...*Cat Stevens*
A/C - 10/30/71(3)
Penny Lane...*Beatles*
HOT - 3/18/67(1)
Penny Lover...*Lionel Richie*
A/C - 11/17/84(4)
People...*Barbra Streisand*
A/C - 6/27/64(3)

People Got To Be Free...*Rascals*
HOT - 8/17/68(5)
Peppermint Twist...
Joey Dee & the Starliters
HOT - 1/27/62(3)
Personality...*Lloyd Price*
R&B - 6/29/59(4)
Philadelphia Freedom...
Elton John Band
HOT - 4/12/75(2)
Photograph...*Ringo Starr*
HOT - 11/24/73(1)
Physical...*Olivia Newton-John*
HOT - 11/21/81(10)
Pick Up The Pieces...*AWB*
HOT - 2/22/75(1)
Pillow Talk...*Sylvia*
R&B - 4/28/73(2)
(Pina Colada Song) ..see: Escape
Pink Champagne...*Joe Liggins*
R&B - JB: 5/27/50(13); BS: 6/3/50(11)
Place To Fall Apart...
Merle Haggard with Janie Fricke
C&W - 2/2/85(1)
Play, Guitar Play...*Conway Twitty*
C&W - 5/7/77(1)
Play That Funky Music...*Wild Cherry*
HOT - 9/18/76(3)
R&B - 9/4/76(2)
Please Come To Boston...*Dave Loggins*
A/C - 8/3/74(1)
Please Don't Go...
K.C. & The Sunshine Band
HOT - 1/5/80(1)
Please Don't Stop Loving Me...
Porter Wagoner & Dolly Parton
C&W - 10/12/74(1)
Please Don't Tell Me How The Story
Ends...*Ronnie Milsap*
C&W - 9/7/74(2)
Please Help Me, I'm Falling...
Hank Locklin
C&W - 5/16/60(14)
Please Love Me...*B.B. King*
R&B - JB: 7/4/53(3)
Please Mr. Please...
Olivia Newton-John
A/C - 7/12/75(3)
Please Mr. Postman...*Carpenters*
HOT - 1/25/75(1)
A/C - 1/18/75(1)
Please Mr. Postman...*Marvelettes*
HOT - 12/11/61(1)
R&B - 11/13/61(7)
Please Send Me Someone To Love...
Percy Mayfield
R&B - BS: 11/25/50(2); JB: 12/16/50(1)
Pleasure Principle...*Janet Jackson*
R&B - 8/8/87(1)
Pledging My Love...*Johnny Ace*
R&B - DJ: 2/12/55(10); BS: 2/19/55(9);
JB: 3/5/55(9)
Poetry Man...*Phoebe Snow*
A/C - 3/1/75(1)
Poison...*Bell Biv DeVoe*
R&B - 5/5/90(2)
Poison Ivy...*Coasters*
R&B - 10/5/59(4)

Poncho And Lefty...
Willie Nelson & Merle Haggard
C&W - 7/23/83(1)
Pony Time...*Chubby Checker*
HOT - 2/27/61(3)
R&B - 3/13/61(2)
Pool Shark...*Dave Dudley*
C&W - 5/9/70(1)
Poor Little Fool...*Ricky Nelson*
POP - HT: 8/4/58(2); BS: 8/4/58(2)
Poor Me...*Fats Domino*
R&B - DJ: 12/31/55(1)
Poor People Of Paris...*Les Baxter*
POP - DJ: 3/17/56(6); TP: 3/24/56(6);
BS: 3/24/56(4); JB: 4/14/56(3)
Poor Side Of Town...*Johnny Rivers*
HOT - 11/12/66(1)
Pop Muzik...*M*
HOT - 11/3/79(1)
(Pop, Pop, Pop, Pop) Goes My Mind...
Levert
R&B - 9/13/86(1)
Power Of Love...
Huey Lewis & The News
HOT - 8/24/85(2)
Power Of Love...*Joe Simon*
R&B - 8/26/72(2)
Power Of Love/Love Power...
Luther Vandross
R&B - 6/15/91(2)
Praying For Time...*George Michael*
HOT - 10/13/90(1)
Pride, The...*Isley Brothers*
R&B - 4/23/77(1)
Private Eyes...
Daryl Hall & John Oates
HOT - 11/7/81(2)
Private Line...*Gerald Levert*
R&B - 12/14/91(1)
Promise Of A New Day...*Paula Abdul*
HOT - 9/14/91(1)
Proud One...*Osmonds*
A/C - 9/13/75(1)
Puff The Magic Dragon...
Peter, Paul & Mary
A/C - 5/11/63(2)
Pure Love...*Ronnie Milsap*
C&W - 6/1/74(1)
Purple People Eater...*Sheb Wooley*
POP - TP: 6/9/58(6); BS: 6/9/58(6);
DJ: 6/23/58(4)
Push And Pull ..see: (Do The)
Put Your Dreams Away...*Mickey Gilley*
C&W - 10/2/82(1)

Q

Quarter To Three...*U.S. Bonds*
HOT - 6/26/61(2)

305

R

Race Is On...*Jack Jones*
A/C - 4/24/65(1)

Radio Heart...*Charly McClain*
C&W - 5/25/85(1)

Rag Doll...*4 Seasons*
HOT - 7/18/64(2)

Rag Mop...*Ames Brothers*
POP - BS: 2/11/50(1); DJ: 2/11/50(2)

Rags To Riches...*Tony Bennett*
POP - BS: 11/21/53(6); DJ: 11/28/53(7); JB: 12/5/53(8)

Rain, The...*Oran "Juice" Jones*
R&B - 9/20/86(2)

Raindrops Keep Fallin' On My Head...
B.J. Thomas
HOT - 1/3/70(4)
A/C - 12/13/69(7)

Rainy Day People...*Gordon Lightfoot*
A/C - 5/17/75(1)

Rainy Days And Mondays...*Carpenters*
A/C - 5/29/71(4)

Rainy Night In Georgia...
Brook Benton
R&B - 3/14/70(1)

Ramblin' Rose...*Nat "King" Cole*
A/C - 9/15/62(5)

Rapture...*Blondie*
HOT - 3/28/81(2)

Rated "X"...*Loretta Lynn*
C&W - 2/24/73(1)

Raunchy...*Ernie Freeman*
R&B - DJ: 1/6/58(2)

Raunchy...*Bill Justis*
R&B - DJ: 1/20/58(1)

Reach Out I'll Be There...*Four Tops*
HOT - 10/15/66(2)
R&B - 10/29/66(2)

Read 'Em And Weep...*Barry Manilow*
A/C - 12/24/83(6)

Ready For The Times To Get Better...
Crystal Gayle
C&W - 4/1/78(1)

Ready or Not...*After 7*
R&B - 4/21/90(2)

Real Love...
Kenny Rogers & Dolly Parton
C&W - 8/24/85(1)

Real Love...*Skyy*
R&B - 2/10/90(1)

Real Love...*Jody Watley*
R&B - 5/6/89(1)

Red Neckin' Love Makin' Night...
Conway Twitty
C&W - 1/23/82(1)

Red Red Wine...*UB40*
HOT - 10/15/88(1)

Redneck Girl...*Bellamy Brothers*
C&W - 12/11/82(1)

Reflex, The...*Duran Duran*
HOT - 6/23/84(2)

Release Me...*Esther Phillips*
R&B - 12/8/62(3)

Release Me...*Wilson Phillips*
HOT - 9/15/90(2)
A/C - 9/15/90(1)

Remember (The First Time)...
Eric Gable
R&B - 9/16/89(1)

Rescue Me...*Fontella Bass*
R&B - 10/30/65(4)

Respect...*Aretha Franklin*
HOT - 6/3/67(2)
R&B - 5/20/67(8)

Rest Your Love On Me...*Conway Twitty*
C&W - 5/2/81(1)

Reunited...*Peaches & Herb*
HOT - 5/5/79(4)
R&B - 4/28/79(4)

Rhinestone Cowboy...*Glen Campbell*
HOT - 9/6/75(2)
C&W - 8/25/75(3)
A/C - 8/2/75(1)

Rhumba Boogie...*Hank Snow*
C&W - BS: 3/31/51(8); JB: 4/21/51(5); DJ: 4/28/51(2)

Rhythm Nation...*Janet Jackson*
R&B - 1/13/90(1)

Rhythm Of The Night...*DeBarge*
R&B - 4/27/85(4)
A/C - 5/4/85(1)

Rhythm Of The Rain...*Cascades*
A/C - 3/2/63(2)

Ribbon Of Darkness...*Marty Robbins*
C&W - 6/19/65(1)

Rich Girl...*Daryl Hall & John Oates*
HOT - 3/26/77(2)

Ridin' My Thumb To Mexico...
Johnny Rodriguez
C&W - 10/13/73(2)

Right Down The Line...*Gerry Rafferty*
A/C - 9/30/78(4)

Right From The Start...
Earl Thomas Conley
C&W - 10/31/87(1)

Right Here Waiting...*Richard Marx*
HOT - 8/12/89(3)
A/C - 8/5/89(6)

Right Or Wrong...*George Strait*
C&W - 4/28/84(1)

Right Time Of The Night...
Jennifer Warnes
A/C - 4/16/77(1)

Ring My Bell...*Anita Ward*
HOT - 6/30/79(2)
R&B - 6/16/79(5)

Ring Of Fire...*Johnny Cash*
C&W - 7/27/63(7)

Ringo...*Lorne Greene*
HOT - 12/5/64(1)
A/C - 11/21/64(6)

Rip It Up...*Little Richard*
R&B - BS: 8/4/56(2); JB: 8/4/56(1)

Rise...*Herb Alpert*
HOT - 10/20/79(2)
R&B - 9/22/79(1)

Rock And Roll Lullaby...*B.J. Thomas*
A/C - 3/25/72(1)

Rock And Roll Waltz...*Kay Starr*
POP - BS: 2/18/56(1); TP: 2/25/56(4); JB: 3/3/56(6); DJ: 3/10/56(1)

Rock Around The Clock...*Bill Haley*
POP - BS: 7/9/55(8); DJ: 7/16/55(6); JB: 7/30/55(7)

Rock Me Amadeus...*Falco*
HOT - 3/29/86(3)

Rock Me Gently...*Andy Kim*
HOT - 9/28/74(1)

Rock Me Tonight (For Old Times Sake)...*Freddie Jackson*
R&B - 6/1/85(6)

Rock On...*Michael Damian*
HOT - 6/3/89(1)

Rock Steady...*Whispers*
R&B - 8/13/87(1)

Rock The Boat...*Hues Corporation*
HOT - 7/6/74(1)

Rock With You...*Michael Jackson*
HOT - 1/19/80(4)
R&B - 1/5/80(6)

Rock Your Baby...*George McCrae*
HOT - 7/13/74(2)
R&B - 7/6/74(2)

Rocket "88"...*Jackie Brenston*
R&B - BS: 6/9/51(3); JB: 6/23/51(5)

Rockin' Chair...*Gwen McCrae*
R&B - 6/14/75(1)

Rockin' Good Way (To Mess Around And Fall In Love)...
Dinah Washington & Brook Benton
R&B - 6/20/60(4)

Rockin' Me...*Steve Miller*
HOT - 11/6/76(1)

Rock-in Robin...*Bobby Day*
R&B - DJ: 10/6/58(3)

Rockin' With The Rhythm Of The Rain...*Judds*
C&W - 8/9/86(1)

Rockin' Years...
Dolly Parton with Ricky Van Shelton
C&W - 5/4/91(1)

Rocky...*Dickey Lee*
C&W - 11/22/75(1)

Roll On Big Mama...*Joe Stampley*
C&W - 5/3/75(1)

Roll On (Eighteen Wheeler)...*Alabama*
C&W - 3/24/84(1)

Roll With It...*Steve Winwood*
HOT - 7/30/88(4)
A/C - 8/6/88(2)

Rollin' With The Flow...*Charlie Rich*
C&W - 8/6/77(2)

Romantic...*Karyn White*
HOT - 11/2/91(1)
R&B - 10/19/91(1)

Romeo & Juliet ..see: Love Theme From

Room Full Of Roses...*Mickey Gilley*
C&W - 6/29/74(1)

Roots Of My Raising...*Merle Haggard*
C&W - 3/13/76(1)

Rose, The...*Bette Midler*
A/C - 5/10/80(5)

Rose, The...*Conway Twitty*
C&W - 3/12/83(1)

Rose Garden...*Lynn Anderson*
C&W - 12/26/70(5)

Rose In Paradise...*Waylon Jennings*
C&W - 4/25/87(1)

Roses Are Red...
Mac Band/McCampbell Brothers
R&B - 7/16/88(1)

Roses Are Red (My Love)...
Bobby Vinton
HOT - 7/14/62(4)
A/C - 7/28/62(4)

Round And Round...*Perry Como*
POP - BS: 4/6/57(1); DJ: 4/13/57(2);
TP: 4/20/57(1)

Rub-A-Dub-Dub...*Hank Thompson*
C&W - JB: 8/1/53(3)

Rub It In...*Billy "Crash" Craddock*
C&W - 8/3/74(2)

Rub You The Right Way...*Johnny Gill*
R&B - 5/19/90(1)

Rubberband Man...*Spinners*
R&B - 10/23/76(1)

Ruby Ann...*Marty Robbins*
C&W - 1/5/63(1)

Ruby, Baby...*Billy "Crash" Craddock*
C&W - 1/11/75(1)

Ruby Tuesday...*Rolling Stones*
HOT - 3/4/67(1)

Rudolph, The Red-Nosed Reindeer...
Gene Autry
POP - BS: 1/7/50(1)
C&W - DJ: 1/7/50(1)

Rumors...*Timex Social Club*
R&B - 7/19/86(2)

Run Away Child, Running Wild...
Temptations
R&B - 3/22/69(2)

Run, Woman, Run...*Tammy Wynette*
C&W - 10/24/70(2)

Runaround Sue...*Dion*
HOT - 10/23/61(2)

Runaway...*Del Shannon*
HOT - 4/24/61(4)

Runaway Train...*Rosanne Cash*
C&W - 11/12/88(1)

Running Back To You...
Vanessa Williams
R&B - 10/5/91(2)

Running Bear...*Sonny James*
C&W - 6/14/69(3)

Running Bear...*Johnny Preston*
HOT - 1/18/60(3)

Running Scared...*Roy Orbison*
HOT - 6/5/61(1)

Rush On Me ..see: (You're Puttin')

Rush, Rush...*Paula Abdul*
HOT - 6/15/91(5)
A/C - 6/29/91(5)

S

Sad Eyes...*Robert John*
HOT - 10/6/79(1)

Sad Movies (Make Me Cry)...
Sue Thompson
A/C - 10/16/61(1)

Saginaw, Michigan...*Lefty Frizzell*
C&W - 3/7/64(4)

Sailing...*Christopher Cross*
HOT - 8/30/80(1)

Sam...*Olivia Newton-John*
A/C - 3/12/77(2)

Sam's Place...*Buck Owens*
C&W - 5/13/67(3)

Same Old Me...*Ray Price*
C&W - 12/7/59(2)

San Antonio Stroll...*Tanya Tucker*
C&W - 10/25/75(1)

Sara...*Starship*
HOT - 3/15/86(1)
A/C - 2/22/86(3)

Satin Sheets...*Jeanne Pruett*
C&W - 5/26/73(3)

Satisfaction ..see: (I Can't Get No)

Satisfied...*Richard Marx*
HOT - 6/24/89(1)

Satisfied Mind...*Porter Wagoner*
C&W - DJ: 7/9/55(4)

Saturday Night...*Bay City Rollers*
HOT - 1/3/76(1)

Save The Last Dance For Me...
Drifters
HOT - 10/17/60(3)
R&B - 10/31/60(1)

Save The Overtime (For Me)...
Gladys Knight & The Pips
R&B - 5/28/83(1)

Save Your Heart For Me...
Gary Lewis & The Playboys
A/C - 8/7/65(3)

Save Your Kisses For Me...
Brotherhood Of Man
A/C - 6/12/76(1)

Save Your Love (For #1)...
Rene & Angela
R&B - 7/20/85(2)

Saving All My Love For You...
Whitney Houston
HOT - 10/26/85(1)
R&B - 9/7/85(1)
A/C - 10/5/85(3)

Say, Has Anybody Seen My Sweet Gypsy Rose...
Dawn featuring Tony Orlando
A/C - 8/18/73(3)

Say It Again...*Don Williams*
C&W - 8/14/76(1)

Say It Loud - I'm Black And I'm Proud...*James Brown*
R&B - 10/5/68(6)

Say Say Say...
Paul McCartney & Michael Jackson
HOT - 12/10/83(6)

Say You, Say Me...*Lionel Richie*
HOT - 12/21/85(4)
R&B - 1/11/86(2)
A/C - 12/7/85(5)

Say You'll Stay Until Tomorrow...
Tom Jones
C&W - 2/26/77(1)

School Day...*Chuck Berry*
R&B - DJ: 4/29/57(5); JB: 5/20/57(1);
BS: 5/27/57(1)

Sea Of Love...*Honeydrippers*
A/C - 12/15/84(1)

Sea Of Love...*Phil Phillips*
R&B - 10/12/59(1)

Search Is Over...*Survivor*
A/C - 6/22/85(4)

Searchin'...*Coasters*
R&B - BS: 6/3/57(13); JB: 6/10/57(2);
DJ: 6/24/57(7)

Seasons Change...*Expose*
HOT - 2/20/88(1)
A/C - 2/20/88(1)

Seasons In The Sun...*Terry Jacks*
HOT - 3/2/74(3)
A/C - 3/9/74(1)

Second Chance...*Thirty Eight Special*
A/C - 5/20/89(2)

Second Time Around...*Shalamar*
R&B - 2/16/80(1)

Secret Garden (Sweet Seduction Suite)...*Quincy Jones/Al B. Sure!/ James Ingram/El DeBarge/Barry White*
R&B - 3/17/90(1)

Secret Love...*Doris Day*
POP - BS: 2/27/54(1); DJ: 3/6/54(4)

Secret Love...*Freddy Fender*
C&W - 12/6/75(1)

Secret Lovers...*Atlantic Starr*
A/C - 4/5/86(1)

Send For Me...*Nat "King" Cole*
R&B - DJ: 8/19/57(2)

Send One Your Love...*Stevie Wonder*
A/C - 12/22/79(4)

Sensitivity...*Ralph Tresvant*
R&B - 12/15/90(1)

Sentimental Me...*Ames Brothers*
POP - DJ: 6/10/50(1)

Separate Lives...
Phil Collins & Marilyn Martin
HOT - 11/30/85(1)
A/C - 11/16/85(3)

September...*Earth, Wind & Fire*
R&B - 1/13/79(1)

Serpentine Fire...*Earth, Wind & Fire*
R&B - 11/19/77(7)

Set Adrift On Memory Bliss...
PM Dawn
HOT - 11/30/91(1)

Set 'Em Up Joe...*Vern Gosdin*
C&W - 7/23/88(1)

Seven Spanish Angels...
Ray Charles with Willie Nelson
C&W - 3/23/85(1)

Seven Year Ache...*Rosanne Cash*
C&W - 5/23/81(1)

Sexual Healing...*Marvin Gaye*
R&B - 11/6/82(10)

Sh-Boom...*Crew-Cuts*
POP - BS: 8/7/54(7); DJ: 8/7/54(9);
JB: 8/21/54(8)

Shadow Dancing...*Andy Gibb*
HOT - 6/17/78(7)

Shadows In The Moonlight...
Anne Murray
C&W - 7/21/79(1)
A/C - 6/16/79(3)

Shaft ..see: Theme From

Shake A Hand...*Faye Adams*
R&B - BS: 9/19/53(9); JB: 9/19/53(10)

Shake, Rattle, And Roll...*Joe Turner*
R&B - JB: 6/12/54(3)

(Shake, Shake, Shake) Shake Your Booty...*KC & The Sunshine Band*
HOT - 9/11/76(1)
R&B - 8/28/76(4)

Shake You Down...*Gregory Abbott*
HOT - 1/17/87(1)
R&B - 10/25/86(2)

Shakedown...*Bob Seger*
HOT - 8/1/87(1)

Shakey Ground...*Temptations*
R&B - 4/26/75(1)

Shame On The Moon...
Bob Seger & The Silver Bullet Band
A/C - 2/12/83(2)

Shame, Shame, Shame...
Shirley & Company
R&B - 3/1/75(1)

Shameless...*Garth Brooks*
C&W - 11/16/91(1)

Shanghai Breezes...*John Denver*
A/C - 5/8/82(1)

Share Your Love With Me...
Aretha Franklin
R&B - 8/23/69(5)

Share Your Love With Me...
Kenny Rogers
A/C - 10/24/81(2)

(Sharecropper's Dream) ..see: Long Hard Road

Shattered Dreams...*Johnny Hates Jazz*
A/C - 5/21/88(1)

She Ain't Worth It...
Glenn Medeiros & Bobby Brown
HOT - 7/21/90(2)

She And I...*Alabama*
C&W - 4/12/86(1)

She Believes In Me...*Kenny Rogers*
C&W - 6/9/79(2)
A/C - 5/26/79(2)

She Called Me Baby...*Charlie Rich*
C&W - 12/7/74(1)

She Can Put Her Shoes Under My Bed...*Johnny Duncan*
C&W - 5/20/78(1)

She Drives Me Crazy...
Fine Young Cannibals
HOT - 4/15/89(1)

She Got The Goldmine (I Got The Shaft)...*Jerry Reed*
C&W - 9/11/82(2)

She Keeps The Home Fires Burning...
Ronnie Milsap
C&W - 6/29/85(1)

She Left Love All Over Me...
Razzy Bailey
C&W - 3/27/82(1)

She Loves You...*Beatles*
HOT - 3/21/64(2)

She Needs Someone To Hold Her (When She Cries)...*Conway Twitty*
C&W - 2/3/73(2)

She Thinks I Still Care...
George Jones
C&W - 5/19/62(6)

She Works Hard For The Money...
Donna Summer
R&B - 7/30/83(3)

She's A Miracle...*Exile*
C&W - 7/6/85(1)

She's Actin' Single (I'm Drinkin' Doubles)...*Gary Stewart*
C&W - 5/10/75(1)

She's Crazy For Leavin'...
Rodney Crowell
C&W - 1/21/89(1)

She's Gone...*Tavares*
R&B - 12/21/74(1)

She's Got To Be A Saint...*Ray Price*
C&W - 12/30/72(3)

She's Got You...*Patsy Cline*
C&W - 3/31/62(5)

She's Got You...*Loretta Lynn*
C&W - 4/23/77(1)

She's In Love With The Boy...
Trisha Yearwood
C&W - 8/3/91(1)

She's Just An Old Love Turned Memory...*Charley Pride*
C&W - 3/12/77(1)

She's Like The Wind...
Patrick Swayze featuring Wendy Fraser
A/C - 2/27/88(2)

She's On The Left...*Jeffrey Osborne*
R&B - 9/24/88(1)

She's Pulling Me Back Again...
Mickey Gilley
C&W - 4/30/77(1)

She's Strange...*Cameo*
R&B - 4/7/84(4)

She's Too Good To Be True...*Exile*
C&W - 9/5/87(1)

She's Too Good To Be True...
Charley Pride
C&W - 11/18/72(3)

Sheila...*Tommy Roe*
HOT - 9/1/62(2)

Sherry...*4 Seasons*
HOT - 9/15/62(5)
R&B - 10/6/62(1)

Shine, Shine, Shine...*Eddy Raven*
C&W - 10/24/87(1)

Shining Star...*Earth, Wind & Fire*
HOT - 5/24/75(1)
R&B - 3/22/75(2)

Shoeshine Boy...*Eddie Kendricks*
R&B - 4/5/75(1)

Shoo-Be-Doo-Be-Doo-Da-Day...
Stevie Wonder
R&B - 6/1/68(1)

Shop Around...*Captain & Tennille*
A/C - 6/5/76(1)

Shop Around...*Miracles*
R&B - 1/16/61(8)

Short Fat Fannie...*Larry Williams*
R&B - DJ: 7/29/57(1)

Shot Gun Boogie...
Tennessee Ernie Ford
C&W - JB: 1/13/51(14); BS: 2/3/51(3); DJ: 2/24/51(1)

Shotgun...*Jr. Walker & The All Stars*
R&B - 3/13/65(4)

Shoulder To Cry On...*Charley Pride*
C&W - 4/14/73(1)

Shout...*Tears For Fears*
HOT - 8/3/85(3)

Show & Tell...*Peabo Bryson*
R&B - 7/1/89(1)

Show And Tell...*Al Wilson*
HOT - 1/19/74(1)

Show Her...*Ronnie Milsap*
C&W - 2/4/84(1)

Shower Me With Your Love...*Surface*
R&B - 7/29/89(1)

Shower The People...*James Taylor*
A/C - 8/28/76(1)

Sideshow...*Blue Magic*
R&B - 6/15/74(1)

Sign 'O' The Times...*Prince*
R&B - 4/11/87(3)

Signed, Sealed, Delivered I'm Yours...*Stevie Wonder*
R&B - 8/1/70(6)

Silly Love Songs...*Wings*
HOT - 5/22/76(5)
A/C - 5/29/76(1)

Sin...*Eddy Howard*
POP - DJ: 11/17/51(8); BS: 12/15/51(2); JB: 12/29/51(1)

Since I Met You Baby...
Ivory Joe Hunter
R&B - JB: 1/5/57(3); DJ: 1/12/57(1)

Since I Met You, Baby...*Sonny James*
C&W - 10/4/69(3)

Since You've Been Gone ..see: (Sweet Sweet Baby)

Sincerely...*McGuire Sisters*
POP - BS: 2/12/55(6); DJ: 2/12/55(10); JB: 3/5/55(7)

Sincerely...*Moonglows*
R&B - JB: 1/22/55(2); DJ: 2/5/55(1)

Sing...*Carpenters*
A/C - 3/31/73(2)

Sing A Song...*Earth, Wind & Fire*
R&B - 1/10/76(2)

Sing Me Back Home...*Merle Haggard*
C&W - 1/20/68(2)

Singing My Song...*Tammy Wynette*
C&W - 5/31/69(2)

Singing The Blues...*Guy Mitchell*
POP - TP: 12/8/56(9); BS: 12/8/56(9); DJ: 12/8/56(9); JB: 12/15/56(10)

Singing The Blues...*Marty Robbins*
C&W - DJ: 11/10/56(11); BS: 11/17/56(13); JB: 11/24/56(13)

Sir Duke...*Stevie Wonder*
HOT - 5/21/77(3)
R&B - 5/28/77(1)

Sister Golden Hair...*America*
HOT - 6/14/75(1)

(Sittin' On) The Dock Of The Bay...
Otis Redding
HOT - 3/16/68(4)
R&B - 3/16/68(3)

634-5789...*Wilson Pickett*
R&B - 3/12/66(7)

Sixteen Tons...*Tennessee Ernie Ford*
POP - BS: 11/26/55(7); DJ: 11/26/55(6); TP: 12/3/55(6); JB: 12/3/55(8)
C&W - BS: 12/17/55(10); JB: 12/31/55(7); DJ: 1/7/56(3)

Sixty-Minute Man...*Dominoes*
R&B - BS: 6/30/51(14); JB: 7/28/51(12)

Skeletons...*Stevie Wonder*
R&B - 11/28/87(2)

Skip A Rope...*Henson Cargill*
  C&W - 2/3/68(5)
Sledgehammer...*Peter Gabriel*
  HOT - 7/26/86(1)
Sleep Walk...*Santo & Johnny*
  HOT - 9/21/59(2)
Sleeping Single In A Double Bed...
  Barbara Mandrell
  C&W - 11/4/78(3)
Slide...*Slave*
  R&B - 7/30/77(1)
Slippery When Wet...*Commodores*
  R&B - 7/5/75(1)
Slow Burn...*T.G. Sheppard*
  C&W - 1/14/84(1)
Slow Down...*Loose Ends*
  R&B - 3/7/87(1)
Slow Hand...*Conway Twitty*
  C&W - 6/19/82(2)
Slow Poke...
  Pee Wee King & his Golden West Cowboys
  POP - JB: 1/5/52(3)
  C&W - JB: 11/3/51(15); DJ: 11/10/51(9);
    BS: 12/1/51(14)
Slowly...*Webb Pierce*
  C&W - BS: 2/20/54(17); DJ: 2/27/54(15);
    JB: 3/6/54(17)
Small Town Girl...*Steve Wariner*
  C&W - 3/28/87(1)
Smoke Gets In Your Eyes...*Platters*
  HOT - 1/19/59(3)
Smokie...*Bill Black's Combo*
  R&B - 1/11/60(4)
Smoky Mountain Rain...*Ronnie Milsap*
  C&W - 12/6/80(1)
  A/C - 2/21/81(1)
Smooth Operator...*Sade*
  A/C - 5/11/85(2)
Snap Your Fingers...*Ronnie Milsap*
  C&W - 8/1/87(1)
Snowbird...*Anne Murray*
  A/C - 8/29/70(6)
So Emotional...*Whitney Houston*
  HOT - 1/9/88(1)
So Many Ways...*Brook Benton*
  R&B - 11/16/59(3)
So Much In Love...*Tymes*
  HOT - 8/3/63(1)
So You Like What You See...*Samuelle*
  R&B - 10/27/90(2)
Soldier Boy...*Shirelles*
  HOT - 5/5/62(3)
Solid...*Ashford & Simpson*
  R&B - 12/1/84(3)
Solitaire...*Carpenters*
  A/C - 9/6/75(1)
Some Broken Hearts Never Mend...
  Don Williams
  C&W - 5/14/77(1)
Some Fools Never Learn...
  Steve Wariner
  C&W - 11/2/85(1)
Somebody Lied...*Ricky Van Shelton*
  C&W - 12/5/87(1)
Somebody Like Me...*Eddy Arnold*
  C&W - 11/26/66(4)
Somebody Should Leave...
  Reba McEntire
  C&W - 5/11/85(1)

Somebody Somewhere...*Loretta Lynn*
  C&W - 11/13/76(2)
Somebody's Gonna Love You...
  Lee Greenwood
  C&W - 11/12/83(1)
Somebody's Needin' Somebody...
  Conway Twitty
  C&W - 7/7/84(1)
Somebody's Watching Me...*Rockwell*
  R&B - 3/3/84(5)
Someday...*Mariah Carey*
  HOT - 3/9/91(2)
Someday...*Alan Jackson*
  C&W - 11/9/91(1)
Someday We'll Be Together...*Supremes*
  HOT - 12/27/69(1)
  R&B - 12/13/69(4)
Someday When Things Are Good...
  Merle Haggard
  C&W - 6/9/84(1)
Someone Could Lose A Heart Tonight...*Eddie Rabbitt*
  C&W - 2/13/82(1)
Someone Loves You Honey...
  Charley Pride
  C&W - 4/8/78(2)
Somethin' Stupid...
  Nancy & Frank Sinatra
  HOT - 4/15/67(4)
  A/C - 4/1/67(9)
Something Better To Do...
  Olivia Newton-John
  A/C - 10/18/75(3)
Something He Can Feel...
  Aretha Franklin
  R&B - 6/26/76(4)
Something In The Way (You Make Me Feel)...*Stephanie Mills*
  R&B - 8/19/89(1)
Sometimes...
  Bill Anderson & Mary Lou Turner
  C&W - 2/7/76(1)
Somewhere Between Right And Wrong...*Earl Thomas Conley*
  C&W - 12/18/82(1)
Somewhere Down The Road...
  Barry Manilow
  A/C - 2/20/82(2)
Somewhere My Love...
  Ray Conniff & The Singers
  A/C - 7/30/66(4)
Somewhere Tonight...*Highway 101*
  C&W - 12/26/87(2)
Song From Moulin Rouge (Where Is Your Heart)...*Percy Faith/Felicia Sanders*
  POP - BS: 5/16/53(10); DJ: 5/16/53(9);
    JB: 5/23/53(6)
Song Of Joy...*Miguel Rios*
  A/C - 6/27/70(2)
Song Of The South...*Alabama*
  C&W - 2/11/89(1)
Song Sung Blue...*Neil Diamond*
  HOT - 7/1/72(1)
  A/C - 6/3/72(7)
Songbird...*Barbra Streisand*
  A/C - 7/29/78(2)

Sophisticated Lady (She's A Different Lady)...*Natalie Cole*
  R&B - 6/19/76(1)
Sorry Seems To Be The Hardest Word...*Elton John*
  A/C - 12/18/76(1)
Soul Man...*Sam & Dave*
  R&B - 10/14/67(7)
Soul Song...*Joe Stampley*
  C&W - 1/20/73(1)
Soul Twist...*King Curtis*
  R&B - 4/14/62(2)
Sound Of Goodbye...*Crystal Gayle*
  C&W - 1/28/84(1)
(Sound Of Philadelphia) ..see: TSOP
Sounds Of Silence...
  Simon & Garfunkel
  HOT - 1/1/66(2)
Southern Nights...*Glen Campbell*
  HOT - 4/30/77(1)
  C&W - 3/19/77(2)
  A/C - 2/26/77(4)
Southern Rains...*Mel Tillis*
  C&W - 2/21/81(1)
Southern Star...*Alabama*
  C&W - 2/10/90(1)
Space Race...*Billy Preston*
  R&B - 11/17/73(1)
Spanish Eyes...*Al Martino*
  A/C - 1/8/66(4)
Spanish Harlem...*Aretha Franklin*
  R&B - 8/28/71(1)
Special Lady...*Ray, Goodman & Brown*
  R&B - 2/23/80(1)
Spinning Wheel...
  Blood, Sweat & Tears
  A/C - 8/2/69(2)
Spirit Of The Boogie...
  Kool & The Gang
  R&B - 5/31/75(1)
Splish Splash...*Bobby Darin*
  R&B - DJ: 8/4/58(2)
Spread My Wings...*Troop*
  R&B - 4/7/90(2)
St. Elmo's Fire (Man In Motion)...
  John Parr
  HOT - 9/7/85(2)
St. George And The Dragonet...
  Stan Freberg
  POP - BS: 10/10/53(4); DJ: 10/24/53(1)
Stagger Lee...*Lloyd Price*
  HOT - 2/9/59(4)
  R&B - 2/9/59(4)
Stand By Me...*Mickey Gilley*
  C&W - 8/9/80(1)
Stand By Me...*Ben E. King*
  R&B - 5/29/61(4)
Stand By My Woman Man ..see: (I'm A)
Stand By Your Man...*Tammy Wynette*
  C&W - 11/23/68(3)
Star Is Born ..see: Love Theme From
Star Wars Theme...*Meco*
  HOT - 10/1/77(2)
Stars on 45...*Stars on 45*
  HOT - 6/20/81(1)
Start Of A Romance...*Skyy*
  R&B - 5/13/89(2)

309

Staring Over ..see: (Just Like)
Starting Over Again...*Dolly Parton*
  C&W - 5/24/80(1)
Statue Of A Fool...*Jack Greene*
  C&W - 7/5/69(2)
Stay...*Maurice Williams*
  HOT - 11/21/60(1)
Stay In My Corner...*Dells*
  R&B - 8/10/68(3)
Stay Young...*Don Williams*
  C&W - 2/25/84(1)
Stayin' Alive...*Bee Gees*
  HOT - 2/4/78(4)
Step By Step...*New Kids On The Block*
  HOT - 6/30/90(3)
Step By Step...*Eddie Rabbitt*
  C&W - 10/17/81(1)
Step That Step...*Sawyer Brown*
  C&W - 5/18/85(1)
Stick-Up...*Honey Cone*
  R&B - 9/18/71(2)
Still...*Bill Anderson*
  C&W - 4/13/63(7)
Still...*Commodores*
  HOT - 11/17/79(1)
  R&B - 11/24/79(1)
Still Doin' Time...*George Jones*
  C&W - 12/12/81(1)
Still Losing You...*Ronnie Milsap*
  C&W - 8/18/84(1)
Stomp!...*Brothers Johnson*
  R&B - 4/5/80(2)
Stoned Love...*Supremes*
  R&B - 12/26/70(1)
Stop And Smell The Roses...*Mac Davis*
  A/C - 10/12/74(1)
Stop! And Think It Over...*Perry Como*
  A/C - 6/24/67(1)
Stop! In The Name Of Love...*Supremes*
  HOT - 3/27/65(2)
Stop To Love...*Luther Vandross*
  R&B - 1/17/87(1)
Story Of My Life...*Marty Robbins*
  C&W - DJ: 1/6/58(4); BS: 1/20/58(4)
Straight To The Heart...
  Crystal Gayle
  C&W - 2/21/87(1)
Straight Up...*Paula Abdul*
  HOT - 2/11/89(3)
Stranger On The Shore...
  Mr. Acker Bilk
  HOT - 5/26/62(1)
  A/C - 4/21/62(7)
Strangers In The Night...
  Frank Sinatra
  HOT - 7/2/66(1)
  A/C - 6/4/66(7)
Strawberry Letter 23...
  Brothers Johnson
  R&B - 8/6/77(1)
Streak, The...*Ray Stevens*
  HOT - 5/18/74(3)
Streets Of Bakersfield...
  Dwight Yoakam & Buck Owens
  C&W - 10/15/88(1)
Stripper, The...*David Rose*
  HOT - 7/7/62(1)
  A/C - 7/7/62(2)

Strong Enough To Bend...*Tanya Tucker*
  C&W - 10/22/88(1)
Strong Heart...*T.G. Sheppard*
  C&W - 8/23/86(1)
Stuck On You...*Elvis Presley*
  HOT - 4/25/60(4)
Stuck On You...*Lionel Richie*
  A/C - 8/4/84(5)
Stuck With You...
  Huey Lewis & the News
  HOT - 9/20/86(3)
  A/C - 9/20/86(3)
Stuff Like That...*Quincy Jones*
  R&B - 7/1/78(1)
(Such An) Easy Question...
  Elvis Presley
  A/C - 7/24/65(2)
Suddenly...*Billy Ocean*
  A/C - 5/25/85(2)
Sugar Daddy...*Bellamy Brothers*
  C&W - 4/5/80(1)
Sugar Shack...*Jimmy Gilmer/Fireballs*
  HOT - 10/12/63(5)
  R&B - 11/23/63(1)
Sugar, Sugar...*Archies*
  HOT - 9/20/69(4)
Sugar Town...*Nancy Sinatra*
  A/C - 1/21/67(2)
Sugartime...*McGuire Sisters*
  POP - DJ: 2/17/58(4)
Sukiyaki...*Kyu Sakamoto*
  HOT - 6/15/63(3)
  A/C - 6/8/63(5)
Sukiyaki...*Taste Of Honey*
  R&B - 5/9/81(1)
  A/C - 5/16/81(2)
Summer...*War*
  A/C - 9/4/76(1)
Summer In The City...*Lovin' Spoonful*
  HOT - 8/13/66(3)
Summer Place ..see: Theme From
Summer Wind...*Frank Sinatra*
  A/C - 10/15/66(1)
Summertime...
  D.J. Jazzy Jeff & The Fresh Prince
  R&B - 8/3/91(1)
Sunday In The South...*Shenandoah*
  C&W - 8/19/89(1)
Sunday Morning Coming Down...
  Johnny Cash
  C&W - 10/10/70(2)
Sundown...*Gordon Lightfoot*
  HOT - 6/29/74(1)
  A/C - 6/8/74(2)
Sunflower...*Glen Campbell*
  A/C - 8/27/77(1)
Sunshine On My Shoulders...
  John Denver
  HOT - 3/30/74(1)
  A/C - 3/16/74(2)
Sunshine Superman...*Donovan*
  HOT - 9/3/66(1)
Super Bad...*James Brown*
  R&B - 11/21/70(2)
Super Kind Of Woman...*Freddie Hart*
  C&W - 4/7/73(2)
Superman...*Donna Fargo*
  C&W - 4/21/73(1)

Supernatural Thing...*Ben E. King*
  R&B - 3/15/75(1)
Superstar...*Carpenters*
  A/C - 10/9/71(2)
Superstition...*Stevie Wonder*
  HOT - 1/27/73(1)
  R&B - 1/6/73(3)
Superwoman...*Karyn White*
  R&B - 1/14/89(3)
Surf City...*Jan & Dean*
  HOT - 7/20/63(2)
Surrender...*Elvis Presley*
  HOT - 3/20/61(2)
Suspicions...*Eddie Rabbitt*
  C&W - 8/11/79(1)
Suspicious Minds...*Elvis Presley*
  HOT - 11/1/69(1)
Sussudio...*Phil Collins*
  HOT - 7/6/85(1)
S.W.A.T. ..see: Theme From
Sweet Child O' Mine...*Guns N' Roses*
  HOT - 9/10/88(2)
Sweet Desire...*Kendalls*
  C&W - 11/25/78(1)
Sweet Dreams...*Emmylou Harris*
  C&W - 12/25/76(2)
Sweet Dreams (Are Made of This)...
  Eurythmics
  HOT - 9/3/83(1)
Sweet Little Sixteen...*Chuck Berry*
  R&B - BS: 3/10/58(3); DJ: 3/17/58(3)
Sweet Sticky Thing...*Ohio Players*
  R&B - 11/1/75(1)
Sweet Surrender...*Bread*
  A/C - 12/30/72(2)
Sweet Surrender...*John Denver*
  A/C - 2/8/75(1)
(Sweet Sweet Baby) Since You've
  Been Gone...*Aretha Franklin*
  R&B - 4/6/68(3)
Sweet Thing...
  Rufus Featuring Chaka Khan
  R&B - 2/21/76(2)
Sweet Woman Like You...*Joe Tex*
  R&B - 1/8/66(1)
Sweetest Taboo...*Sade*
  A/C - 2/8/86(1)
Sweetest Thing (I've Ever Known)...
  Juice Newton
  C&W - 1/30/82(1)
  A/C - 1/30/82(1)
Swingin'...*John Anderson*
  C&W - 3/26/83(1)
System Of Survival...
  Earth, Wind & Fire
  R&B - 12/12/87(1)

T

"T" 99 Blues...*Jimmy Nelson*
  R&B - JB: 11/3/51(1)

TSOP (The Sound Of Philadelphia)...
MFSB featuring The Three Degrees
HOT - 4/20/74(2)
R&B - 4/20/74(1)
A/C - 5/4/74(2)

Take Good Care Of Her...*Sonny James*
C&W - 6/18/66(2)

Take Good Care Of My Baby...
Bobby Vee
HOT - 9/18/61(3)

Take Me Down...*Alabama*
C&W - 7/24/82(1)

Take Me In Your Arms And Hold Me...
Eddy Arnold
C&W - JB: 1/28/50(1)

Take Me To The Next Phase...
Isley Brothers
R&B - 5/13/78(2)

Take Me To Your World...
Tammy Wynette
C&W - 3/9/68(2)

Take My Breath Away...*Berlin*
HOT - 9/13/86(1)

Take My Heart (You Can Have It If You Want It)...*Kool & The Gang*
R&B - 11/21/81(1)

Take On Me...*a-ha*
HOT - 10/19/85(1)

Take These Chains From My Heart...
Hank Williams
C&W - BS: 6/6/53(4)

Take This Job And Shove It...
Johnny Paycheck
C&W - 1/7/78(2)

Take Your Time (Do It Right)...
S.O.S. Band
R&B - 6/28/80(5)

Talk Back Trembling Lips...
Ernest Ashworth
C&W - 10/12/63(1)

Talk To Me...*Mickey Gilley*
C&W - 1/29/83(1)

Talking In Your Sleep...
Crystal Gayle
C&W - 8/19/78(2)

Talking Loud And Saying Nothing...
James Brown
R&B - 3/11/72(1)

Tall Dark Stranger...*Buck Owens*
C&W - 9/27/69(1)

Tammy...*Debbie Reynolds*
POP - DJ: 8/19/57(5); BS: 8/26/57(3); TP: 9/2/57(5)

Taste Of Honey...*Herb Alpert*
A/C - 10/30/65(5)

Tasty Love...*Freddie Jackson*
R&B - 11/15/86(4)

Tear Time...*Dave & Sugar*
C&W - 10/21/78(1)

Teardrops From My Eyes...*Ruth Brown*
R&B - BS: 12/9/50(11); JB: 12/23/50(7)

Tears Of A Clown...*Miracles*
HOT - 12/12/70(2)
R&B - 12/5/70(3)

Teddy Bear...*Red Sovine*
C&W - 7/17/76(3)
(also see: Let Me Be Your)

Teddy Bear Song...*Barbara Fairchild*
C&W - 3/17/73(2)

Teen Angel...*Mark Dinning*
HOT - 2/8/60(2)

Teenage Queen ..see: Ballad Of

Tell Her About It...*Billy Joel*
HOT - 9/24/83(1)
A/C - 9/24/83(2)

Tell It Like It Is...*Aaron Neville*
R&B - 1/7/67(5)

Tell Me A Lie...*Janie Fricke*
C&W - 12/10/83(1)

(Tell Me 'Bout The Good Old Days) ..see: Grandpa

Telstar...*Tornadoes*
HOT - 12/22/62(3)

Tender Kisses...*Tracie Spencer*
R&B - 11/23/91(1)

Tender Lie...*Restless Heart*
C&W - 12/17/88(1)

Tender Lover...*Babyface*
R&B - 1/6/90(1)

Tender Years...*George Jones*
C&W - 8/21/61(7)

Tennessee Bird Walk...
Jack Blanchard & Misty Morgan
C&W - 4/4/70(2)

Tennessee Flat Top Box...
Rosanne Cash
C&W - 2/13/88(1)

Tennessee Homesick Blues...
Dolly Parton
C&W - 9/8/84(1)

Tennessee River...*Alabama*
C&W - 8/16/80(1)

Tennessee Waltz...*Patti Page*
POP - JB: 12/16/50(13); BS: 12/30/50(9); DJ: 1/6/51(8)

Tequila...*Champs*
POP - TP: 3/17/58(5); BS: 3/17/58(5); DJ: 3/31/58(2)
R&B - BS: 3/31/58(4); DJ: 4/7/58(4)

Texas Women...*Hank Williams, Jr.*
C&W - 3/28/81(1)

Thank God For The Radio...*Kendalls*
C&W - 4/14/84(1)

Thank God I'm A Country Boy...
John Denver
HOT - 6/7/75(1)
C&W - 5/31/75(1)

Thank You (Falettinme Be Mice Elf Agin)...*Sly & The Family Stone*
HOT - 2/14/70(2)
R&B - 2/7/70(5)

Thank You Pretty Baby...*Brook Benton*
R&B - 8/10/59(4)

Thanks For My Child...
Cheryl Pepsii Riley
R&B - 11/26/88(1)

That Do Make It Nice...*Eddy Arnold*
C&W - JB: 10/22/55(2)

That Girl...*Stevie Wonder*
R&B - 2/20/82(9)

That Heart Belongs To Me...
Webb Pierce
C&W - DJ: 7/12/52(3)

That Rock Won't Roll...
Restless Heart
C&W - 11/15/86(1)

That Was A Close One...
Earl Thomas Conley
C&W - 7/4/87(1)

That Was Yesterday...*Donna Fargo*
C&W - 7/2/77(1)

That'll Be The Day...*Crickets*
POP - BS: 9/23/57(1)

That's All That Matters...
Mickey Gilley
C&W - 12/20/80(1)

That's Life...*Frank Sinatra*
A/C - 12/31/66(3)

That's My Pa...*Sheb Wooley*
C&W - 3/17/62(1)

That's The Thing About Love...
Don Williams
C&W - 8/11/84(1)

That's The Way (I Like It)...
KC & The Sunshine Band
HOT - 11/22/75(2)
R&B - 11/29/75(1)

That's The Way Love Goes...
Merle Haggard
C&W - 2/11/84(1)

That's The Way Love Goes...
Johnny Rodriguez
C&W - 2/16/74(1)

That's The Way Love Is...*Bobby Bland*
R&B - 3/9/63(2)

That's What Friends Are For...
Dionne & Friends
HOT - 1/18/86(4)
R&B - 1/25/86(3)
A/C - 1/11/86(2)

That's What Love Is For...*Amy Grant*
A/C - 11/30/91(3)

That's Why I Love You Like I Do...
Sonny James
C&W - 6/24/72(1)

Theme From A Summer Place...
Percy Faith
HOT - 2/22/60(9)

Theme From Mahogany (Do You Know Where You're Going To)...*Diana Ross*
HOT - 1/24/76(1)
A/C - 12/6/75(1)

Theme From Shaft...*Isaac Hayes*
HOT - 11/20/71(2)

Theme From S.W.A.T. ...
Rhythm Heritage
HOT - 2/28/76(1)

Theme From The Dukes Of Hazzard...
Waylon Jennings
C&W - 11/1/80(1)

Theme From Which Way Is Up...
Stargard
R&B - 2/4/78(2)

Then Came You...
Dionne Warwicke & Spinners
HOT - 10/26/74(1)

Then Who Am I...*Charley Pride*
C&W - 2/8/75(1)

311

Then You Can Tell Me Goodbye...
Eddy Arnold
C&W - 10/19/68(2)
(also see: Don't Pull Your Love)

There Goes My Baby...*Drifters*
R&B - 7/27/59(1)

There Goes My Everything...
Jack Greene
C&W - 12/24/66(7)

There! I've Said It Again...
Bobby Vinton
HOT - 1/4/64(4)
A/C - 1/4/64(5)

There Must Be More To Love Than This...*Jerry Lee Lewis*
C&W - 9/26/70(2)

There Stands The Glass...*Webb Pierce*
C&W - BS: 11/21/53(12); DJ: 12/5/53(6); JB: 12/5/53(9)

There Won't Be Anymore...
Charlie Rich
C&W - 3/9/74(2)

There You Go...*Johnny Cash*
C&W - JB: 3/2/57(5)

There'll Be Sad Songs (To Make You Cry)...*Billy Ocean*
HOT - 7/5/86(1)
R&B - 6/28/86(2)
A/C - 6/21/86(1)

(There's A) Fire In The Night...
Alabama
C&W - 1/26/85(1)

There's A Honky Tonk Angel (Who'll Take Me Back In)...*Conway Twitty*
C&W - 3/23/74(1)

There's A Kind Of Hush (All Over The World)...*Carpenters*
A/C - 4/3/76(2)

There's Been A Change In Me...
Eddy Arnold
C&W - DJ: 2/10/51(11); BS: 2/17/51(4)

(There's) No Gettin' Over Me...
Ronnie Milsap
C&W - 8/29/81(2)

There's No Stopping Your Heart...
Marie Osmond
C&W - 2/22/86(1)

There's No Way...*Alabama*
C&W - 5/4/85(1)

There's Nothing Better Than Love...
Luther Vandross with Gregory Hines
R&B - 5/9/87(1)

There's Something On Your Mind...
Bobby Marchan
R&B - 7/11/60(1)

These Boots Are Made For Walkin'...
Nancy Sinatra
HOT - 2/26/66(1)

These Dreams...*Heart*
HOT - 3/22/86(1)
A/C - 3/15/86(3)

They Just Can't Stop It the (Games People Play)...*Spinners*
R&B - 10/18/75(1)

(They Long To Be) Close To You...
Carpenters
HOT - 7/25/70(4)
A/C - 7/11/70(6)

Thicker Than Water ..see: (Love Is)

Thieves In The Temple...*Prince*
R&B - 9/29/90(1)

Thin Line Between Love & Hate...
Persuaders
R&B - 10/16/71(2)

Thing, The...*Phil Harris*
POP - BS: 12/2/50(4); DJ: 12/2/50(5); JB: 12/23/50(2)

Things Aren't Funny Anymore...
Merle Haggard
C&W - 5/4/74(1)

Things That I Used To Do...
Guitar Slim
R&B - JB: 1/30/54(14); BS: 2/13/54(6)

Think...*Aretha Franklin*
R&B - 6/15/68(3)

Think About Love...*Dolly Parton*
C&W - 3/8/86(1)

Think Of Laura...*Christopher Cross*
A/C - 2/4/84(4)

Think Of Me...*Buck Owens*
C&W - 7/2/66(6)

Thinkin' Of A Rendezvous...
Johnny Duncan
C&W - 12/11/76(2)

Third Man Theme...*Anton Karas*
POP - BS: 4/29/50(11)

3rd Man Theme...*Guy Lombardo*
POP - JB: 5/6/50(11)

This Bitter Earth...*Dinah Washington*
R&B - 7/25/60(1)

This Crazy Love...*Oak Ridge Boys*
C&W - 9/19/87(1)

This Diamond Ring...
Gary Lewis & The Playboys
HOT - 2/20/65(2)

This Guy's In Love With You...
Herb Alpert
HOT - 6/22/68(4)
A/C - 6/8/68(10)

This Is It...*Jim Reeves*
C&W - 5/1/65(3)

This Is The Time...*Billy Joel*
A/C - 1/10/87(3)

This Moment In Time...
Engelbert Humperdinck
A/C - 1/20/79(2)

This Old Heart Of Mine...
Rod Stewart with Ronald Isley
A/C - 4/21/90(5)

This Ole House...*Rosemary Clooney*
POP - BS: 11/6/54(1); JB: 11/13/54(3)

This One's For You...*Barry Manilow*
A/C - 11/13/76(1)

This Time...*Waylon Jennings*
C&W - 6/22/74(1)

This Time I've Hurt Her More Than She Loves Me...*Conway Twitty*
C&W - 1/31/76(1)

This Will Be...*Natalie Cole*
R&B - 10/4/75(2)

Those Were The Days...*Mary Hopkin*
A/C - 11/2/68(6)

Three Bells...*Browns*
HOT - 8/24/59(4)
C&W - 8/31/59(10)

Three Coins In The Fountain...
Four Aces Featuring Al Alberts
POP - JB: 7/24/54(1)

Three O'Clock Blues...*B.B. King*
R&B - JB: 2/2/52(5); BS: 2/9/52(5)

Three Time Loser...*Dan Seals*
C&W - 9/26/87(1)

Three Times A Lady...*Commodores*
HOT - 8/12/78(2)
R&B - 8/12/78(2)
A/C - 8/19/78(3)

Three Times In Love...*Tommy James*
A/C - 3/29/80(1)

Through The Years...*Kenny Rogers*
A/C - 3/6/82(2)

Throwing It All Away...*Genesis*
A/C - 10/11/86(2)

Thunder Rolls...*Garth Brooks*
C&W - 6/22/91(2)

Ticket To Ride...*Beatles*
HOT - 5/22/65(1)

Tide Is High...*Blondie*
HOT - 1/31/81(1)

Tie A Yellow Ribbon Round The Ole Oak Tree...*Dawn*
HOT - 4/21/73(4)
A/C - 4/7/73(2)

Tie Me Kangaroo Down, Sport...
Rolf Harris
A/C - 7/13/63(3)

Tight Fittin' Jeans...*Conway Twitty*
C&W - 9/26/81(1)

Tighten Up...*Archie Bell*
HOT - 5/18/68(1)
R&B - 5/18/68(2)

'Til I Can Make It On My Own...
Tammy Wynette
C&W - 4/10/76(1)

'Til I Gain Control Again...
Crystal Gayle
C&W - 2/12/83(1)

'Til I Get It Right...*Tammy Wynette*
C&W - 3/10/73(1)

Til The Rivers All Run Dry...
Don Williams
C&W - 3/27/76(1)

Till I Waltz Again With You...
Teresa Brewer
POP - BS: 2/14/53(5); DJ: 2/14/53(6); JB: 2/14/53(7)

'Till You're Gone...*Barbara Mandrell*
C&W - 7/17/82(1)

Timber, I'm Falling In Love...
Patty Loveless
C&W - 8/12/89(1)

Time After Time...*Cyndi Lauper*
HOT - 6/9/84(2)
A/C - 6/2/84(3)

Time In A Bottle...*Jim Croce*
HOT - 12/29/73(2)
A/C - 12/29/73(2)

Time, Love And Tenderness...
Michael Bolton
A/C - 9/28/91(2)

Time Of My Life ..see: (I've Had)

Time Passages...*Al Stewart*
A/C - 11/11/78(10)

Time, Time...*Ed Ames*
A/C - 6/17/67(1)
Time Will Reveal...*DeBarge*
R&B - 12/10/83(5)
Times Of Your Life...*Paul Anka*
A/C - 1/3/76(1)
Tin Man...*America*
A/C - 10/5/74(1)
Ting-A-Ling...*Clovers*
R&B - BS: 9/6/52(1); JB: 9/20/52(1)
To All The Girls I've Loved Before...*Julio Iglesias & Willie Nelson*
C&W - 5/12/84(2)
To Each His Own...
Faith Hope & Charity
R&B - 10/25/75(1)
To Know Him Is To Love Him...
Teddy Bears
HOT - 12/1/58(3)
To Know Him Is To Love Him...
Dolly Parton, Linda Ronstadt, Emmylou Harris
C&W - 5/16/87(1)
To Make Love Sweeter For You...
Jerry Lee Lewis
C&W - 3/1/69(1)
To See My Angel Cry...*Conway Twitty*
C&W - 11/8/69(1)
To Sir With Love...*Lulu*
HOT - 10/21/67(5)
Today's The Day...*America*
A/C - 6/26/76(2)
Together...*Connie Francis*
A/C - 8/7/61(1)
Together Again...*Ray Charles*
A/C - 4/30/66(3)
Together Again...*Emmylou Harris*
C&W - 4/24/76(1)
Together Again...*Buck Owens*
C&W - 6/6/64(2)
Together Forever...*Rick Astley*
HOT - 6/18/88(1)
Tom Dooley...*Kingston Trio*
HOT - 11/17/58(1)
Tomb Of The Unknown Love...
Kenny Rogers
C&W - 5/24/86(1)
Tomorrow (A Better You, A Better Me)...*Quincy Jones Featuring Tevin Campbell*
R&B - 6/16/90(1)
Tonight Carmen...*Marty Robbins*
C&W - 7/29/67(1)
Tonight's The Night (Gonna Be Alright)...*Rod Stewart*
HOT - 11/13/76(8)
Too Busy Thinking About My Baby...
Marvin Gaye
R&B - 6/7/69(6)
Too Gone Too Long...*Randy Travis*
C&W - 3/12/88(1)
Too Hot Ta Trot...*Commodores*
R&B - 2/18/78(1)
Too Late For Goodbyes...
Julian Lennon
A/C - 3/16/85(2)
Too Many Lovers...*Crystal Gayle*
C&W - 8/8/81(1)

Too Many Walls...*Cathy Dennis*
A/C - 10/19/91(2)
Too Much...*Elvis Presley*
POP - BS: 2/9/57(3); JB: 3/9/57(1)
Too Much Heaven...*Bee Gees*
HOT - 1/6/79(2)
Too Much Is Not Enough...
Bellamy Brothers/The Forester Sisters
C&W - 12/20/86(1)
Too Much On My Heart...
Statler Brothers
C&W - 11/30/85(1)
Too Much, Too Little, Too Late...
Johnny Mathis/Deniece Williams
HOT - 6/3/78(1)
R&B - 4/15/78(4)
A/C - 5/20/78(1)
Too Young...*Nat "King" Cole*
POP - BS: 6/23/51(5); DJ: 6/30/51(4); JB: 7/7/51(4)
Top Of The World...*Carpenters*
HOT - 12/1/73(2)
Topsy II...*Cozy Cole*
R&B - 10/27/58(6)
Torn Between Two Lovers...
Mary MacGregor
HOT - 2/5/77(2)
A/C - 12/25/76(2)
Tossin' And Turnin'...*Bobby Lewis*
HOT - 7/10/61(7)
R&B - 7/3/61(10)
Total Eclipse Of The Heart...
Bonnie Tyler
HOT - 10/1/83(4)
Touch A Hand, Make A Friend...
Oak Ridge Boys
C&W - 10/26/85(1)
Touch Me In The Morning...*Diana Ross*
HOT - 8/18/73(1)
A/C - 7/28/73(1)
Touch Me When We're Dancing...
Alabama
C&W - 11/29/86(1)
Touch Me When We're Dancing...
Carpenters
A/C - 8/22/81(2)
Touch The Hand...*Conway Twitty*
C&W - 7/19/75(2)
Toy Soldiers...*Martika*
HOT - 7/22/89(2)
Tragedy...*Bee Gees*
HOT - 3/24/79(2)
Trapped By A Thing Called Love...
Denise LaSalle
R&B - 10/30/71(1)
Travelin' Man...*Ricky Nelson*
HOT - 5/29/61(2)
Treasure Of Love...*Clyde McPhatter*
R&B - JB: 7/28/56(1)
Trip To Heaven...*Freddie Hart*
C&W - 8/11/73(1)
Trouble In Paradise...*Loretta Lynn*
C&W - 11/23/74(1)
True...*Spandau Ballet*
A/C - 10/8/83(1)
True Colors...*Cyndi Lauper*
HOT - 10/25/86(2)

True Love Ways...*Mickey Gilley*
C&W - 7/19/80(1)
Truly...*Lionel Richie*
HOT - 11/27/82(2)
A/C - 11/20/82(4)
Try A Little Kindness...
Glen Campbell
A/C - 11/15/69(1)
Try Me...*James Brown*
R&B - 2/2/59(1)
Tryin' To Beat The Morning Home...
T.G. Sheppard
C&W - 6/28/75(1)
Tryin' To Get The Feeling Again...
Barry Manilow
A/C - 5/1/76(1)
Tryin' To Love Two...*William Bell*
R&B - 4/2/77(1)
Trying To Love Two Women...
Oak Ridge Boys
C&W - 6/28/80(1)
Tulsa Time...*Don Williams*
C&W - 1/6/79(1)
Tumblin' Down...
Ziggy Marley & The Melody Makers
R&B - 12/24/88(2)
Turn Back The Hands Of Time...
Tyrone Davis
R&B - 5/2/70(2)
Turn It Loose...*Judds*
C&W - 3/26/88(1)
(Turn Out The Light And) Love Me Tonight...*Don Williams*
C&W - 11/1/75(1)
Turn The World Around...*Eddy Arnold*
C&W - 10/7/67(1)
Turn! Turn! Turn!...*Byrds*
HOT - 12/4/65(3)
Turn Your Love Around...
George Benson
R&B - 1/23/82(1)
Turned Away...*Chuckii Booker*
R&B - 7/22/89(1)
Turning Away...*Crystal Gayle*
C&W - 9/29/84(1)
Turning Point...*Tyrone Davis*
R&B - 2/7/76(1)
Twilight Time...*Platters*
POP - TP: 4/21/58(1); BS: 4/21/58(1); DJ: 5/12/58(1)
R&B - BS: 4/28/58(3)
Twinkle, Twinkle Lucky Star...
Merle Haggard
C&W - 2/20/88(1)
Twist, The...*Chubby Checker*
HOT - 9/19/60(1)
HOT - 1/13/62(2)
Twistin' The Nite Away...*Sam Cooke*
R&B - 3/24/62(3)
Two Dozen Roses...*Shenandoah*
C&W - 12/16/89(1)
Two Hearts...*Phil Collins*
HOT - 1/21/89(2)
A/C - 12/24/88(5)
Two Lovers...*Mary Wells*
R&B - 1/19/63(4)

313

Two More Bottles Of Wine...
  Emmylou Harris
  C&W - 6/17/78(1)
Two Of A Kind, Workin' On A Full House...*Garth Brooks*
  C&W - 4/6/91(1)

U

U ..see: You
Unanswered Prayers...*Garth Brooks*
  C&W - 1/12/91(2)
Unbelievable...*EMF*
  HOT - 7/20/91(1)
Unchain My Heart...*Ray Charles*
  R&B - 1/6/62(2)
Unchained Melody...*Les Baxter*
  POP - DJ: 5/14/55(2)
Unchained Melody...*Roy Hamilton*
  R&B - BS: 5/21/55(3)
Unchained Melody...*Al Hibbler*
  R&B - JB: 6/18/55(1)
Unchained Melody...
  Righteous Brothers
  A/C - 10/13/90(2)
Uncle Albert/Admiral Halsey...
  Paul & Linda McCartney
  HOT - 9/4/71(1)
Uncle Pen...*Ricky Skaggs*
  C&W - 10/13/84(1)
Undercover Angel...*Alan O'Day*
  HOT - 7/9/77(1)
Understand Your Man...*Johnny Cash*
  C&W - 4/4/64(6)
Until I Met You...*Judy Rodman*
  C&W - 7/19/86(1)
Until My Dreams Come True...
  Jack Greene
  C&W - 2/15/69(2)
Until You Come Back To Me (That's What I'm Gonna Do)...*Aretha Franklin*
  R&B - 1/12/74(1)
Up Where We Belong...
  Joe Cocker & Jennifer Warnes
  HOT - 11/6/82(3)
Upside Down...*Diana Ross*
  HOT - 9/6/80(4)
  R&B - 8/16/80(4)
Uptight (Everything's Alright)...
  Stevie Wonder
  R&B - 1/22/66(5)
Use Ta Be My Girl...*O'Jays*
  R&B - 5/27/78(5)

V

Valley Road...
  Bruce Hornsby & The Range
  A/C - 6/18/88(1)

Vaya Con Dios...*Les Paul & Mary Ford*
  POP - BS: 8/8/53(11); DJ: 8/8/53(3);
         JB: 8/22/53(9)
Venus...*Frankie Avalon*
  HOT - 3/9/59(5)
  A/C - 3/20/76(1)
Venus...*Bananarama*
  HOT - 9/6/86(1)
Venus...*Shocking Blue*
  HOT - 2/7/70(1)
Very Special Love Song...
  Charlie Rich
  C&W - 4/6/74(3)
  A/C - 3/30/74(2)
View To A Kill...*Duran Duran*
  HOT - 7/13/85(2)
Vision Of Love...*Mariah Carey*
  HOT - 8/4/90(4)
  R&B - 8/11/90(2)
  A/C - 8/4/90(3)
Vogue...*Madonna*
  HOT - 5/19/90(3)
(Volare) ..see: Nel Blu Dipinto Di Blu

W

Waitin' In Your Welfare Line...
  Buck Owens
  C&W - 2/19/66(7)
Waiting For A Star To Fall...
  Boy Meets Girl
  A/C - 12/17/88(1)
Wake Me Up Before You Go-Go...*Wham!*
  HOT - 11/17/84(3)
Wake Up Everybody...
  Harold Melvin & The Blue Notes
  R&B - 1/17/76(2)
Wake Up, Irene...*Hank Thompson*
  C&W - JB: 2/20/54(2)
Wake Up Little Susie...
  Everly Brothers
  POP - BS: 10/14/57(1); TP: 10/21/57(2);
         DJ: 10/28/57(4)
  R&B - DJ: 10/28/57(1)
  C&W - BS: 10/14/57(7); DJ: 10/28/57(8)
Walk Away From Love...*David Ruffin*
  R&B - 1/3/76(1)
Walk In The Black Forest...
  Horst Jankowski
  A/C - 7/10/65(2)
Walk Like A Man...*4 Seasons*
  HOT - 3/2/63(3)
Walk Like An Egyptian...*Bangles*
  HOT - 12/20/86(4)
Walk On By...*Leroy Van Dyke*
  C&W - 9/25/61(19)
Walk On Faith...*Mike Reid*
  C&W - 2/23/91(1)
Walk Right In...*Rooftop Singers*
  HOT - 1/26/63(2)
  A/C - 1/26/63(5)

Walk Through This World With Me...
  George Jones
  C&W - 4/1/67(2)
Walkin' Away...*Clint Black*
  C&W - 5/19/90(2)
Wallflower, The...*Etta James*
  R&B - DJ: 4/9/55(4)
  (also see: Dance With Me Henry)
Wanderer, The...*Eddie Rabbitt*
  C&W - 8/27/88(1)
Want Ads...*Honey Cone*
  HOT - 6/12/71(1)
  R&B - 5/29/71(3)
Wanted...*Perry Como*
  POP - BS: 4/10/54(8); DJ: 4/24/54(7);
         JB: 5/1/54(8)
War...*Edwin Starr*
  HOT - 8/29/70(3)
War Is Hell (On The Homefront Too)...*T.G. Sheppard*
  C&W - 11/20/82(1)
Washington Square...*Village Stompers*
  A/C - 11/2/63(3)
Wasted Days And Wasted Nights...
  Freddy Fender
  C&W - 8/9/75(2)
Watching Scotty Grow...
  Bobby Goldsboro
  A/C - 1/9/71(6)
Waterloo...*Stonewall Jackson*
  C&W - 7/27/59(5)
Watermelon Wine ..see: (Old Dogs-Children And)
Way Down...*Elvis Presley*
  C&W - 8/20/77(1)
Way He Makes Me Feel...
  Barbra Streisand
  A/C - 12/10/83(2)
Way I Want To Touch You...
  Captain & Tennille
  A/C - 11/8/75(2)
Way It Is...
  Bruce Hornsby & The Range
  HOT - 12/13/86(1)
  A/C - 12/6/86(2)
Way We Make A Broken Heart...
  Rosanne Cash
  C&W - 10/10/87(1)
Way We Were...*Barbra Streisand*
  HOT - 2/2/74(3)
  A/C - 1/12/74(2)
Way You Love Me...*Karyn White*
  R&B - 10/29/88(1)
Way You Make Me Feel...
  Michael Jackson
  HOT - 1/23/88(1)
  R&B - 12/26/87(4)
Ways To Love A Man...*Tammy Wynette*
  C&W - 10/25/69(2)
Wayward Wind...*Gogi Grant*
  POP - TP: 6/16/56(7); BS: 6/16/56(6);
         DJ: 6/23/56(8); JB: 6/30/56(4)
We Are Family...*Sister Sledge*
  R&B - 6/9/79(1)
We Are The World...*USA for Africa*
  HOT - 4/13/85(4)
  R&B - 5/4/85(2)
  A/C - 4/20/85(2)

We Believe In Happy Endings...
Earl Thomas Conley with Emmylou Harris
C&W - 10/1/88(1)

We Built This City...*Starship*
HOT - 11/16/85(2)

We Can Work It Out...*Beatles*
HOT - 1/8/66(3)

We Didn't Start The Fire...
Billy Joel
HOT - 12/9/89(2)

We'll Never Have To Say Goodbye Again...*England Dan & John Ford Coley*
A/C - 3/25/78(6)

We'll Sing In The Sunshine...
Gale Garnett
A/C - 9/26/64(7)

We're A Winner...*Impressions*
R&B - 3/9/68(1)

We're All Alone...*Rita Coolidge*
A/C - 11/12/77(1)

We're An American Band...*Grand Funk*
HOT - 9/29/73(1)

(We're Gonna) ..also see: Rock Around The Clock

We're Gonna Hold On...
George Jones & Tammy Wynette
C&W - 10/27/73(2)

We're Gonna Make It...*Little Milton*
R&B - 5/1/65(3)

We've Got Tonight...
Kenny Rogers & Sheena Easton
C&W - 4/9/83(1)

We've Only Just Begun...*Carpenters*
A/C - 10/10/70(7)

Wear My Ring Around Your Neck...
Elvis Presley
R&B - DJ: 5/5/58(3)

Wedding, The...*Julie Rogers*
A/C - 1/2/65(3)

Wedding Bell Blues...*5th Dimension*
HOT - 11/8/69(3)
A/C - 11/1/69(2)

Week In A Country Jail...*Tom T. Hall*
C&W - 1/31/70(2)

Weekend, The...*Steve Wariner*
C&W - 7/25/87(1)

Weekend In New England...
Barry Manilow
A/C - 1/8/77(1)

Weepin' And Cryin'...
Griffin Brothers
R&B - JB: 1/12/52(3)

Welcome Back...*John Sebastian*
HOT - 5/8/76(1)
A/C - 5/15/76(2)

West End Girls...*Pet Shop Boys*
HOT - 5/10/86(1)

What A Difference You've Made In My Life...*Ronnie Milsap*
C&W - 1/21/78(1)

What A Fool Believes...
Doobie Brothers
HOT - 4/14/79(1)

What A Man, My Man Is...
Lynn Anderson
C&W - 12/28/74(1)

(What A) Wonderful World...
Art Garfunkel with James Taylor & Paul Simon
A/C - 2/11/78(5)

What About Me?...*Kenny Rogers with Kim Carnes & James Ingram*
A/C - 11/3/84(2)

What Am I Gonna Do About You...
Reba McEntire
C&W - 1/17/87(1)

What Am I Gonna Do With You...
Barry White
R&B - 5/3/75(1)

What Am I Living For...*Chuck Willis*
R&B - DJ: 6/23/58(1)

What Are We Doin' In Love...
Kenny Rogers & Dottie West
C&W - 6/13/81(1)

What Cha' Gonna Do For Me...
Chaka Khan
R&B - 5/30/81(2)

What Does It Take (To Win Your Love)...*Jr. Walker & The All Stars*
R&B - 7/19/69(2)

What Goes On When The Sun Goes Down...*Ronnie Milsap*
C&W - 5/15/76(1)

What Have You Done For Me Lately...
Janet Jackson
R&B - 3/22/86(2)

What I'd Say...*Earl Thomas Conley*
C&W - 2/4/89(1)

What Kind Of Fool...
Barbra Streisand & Barry Gibb
A/C - 3/14/81(4)

What She Is (Is A Woman In Love)...
Earl Thomas Conley
C&W - 6/4/88(1)

What'd I Say...*Ray Charles*
R&B - 8/3/59(1)

What's A Memory Like You (Doing In A Love Like This)...*John Schneider*
C&W - 3/22/86(1)

What's Forever For...
Michael Martin Murphey
C&W - 9/25/82(1)

What's Going On...*Marvin Gaye*
R&B - 3/27/71(5)

What's Going On In Your World...
George Strait
C&W - 7/22/89(1)

What's He Doing In My World...
Eddy Arnold
C&W - 6/5/65(2)

(What's He Got That I Ain't Got) ..see: Laura

What's Love Got To Do With It...
Tina Turner
HOT - 9/1/84(3)

What's Your Mama's Name...
Tanya Tucker
C&W - 5/19/73(1)

Whatever Gets You Thru The Night...
John Lennon
HOT - 11/16/74(1)

Whatever Happened To Old Fashioned Love...*B.J. Thomas*
C&W - 5/14/83(1)

Whatever You Want...
Tony! Toni! Toné!
R&B - 4/20/91(2)

Wheel Of Fortune...*Kay Starr*
POP - BS: 3/15/52(9); DJ: 3/15/52(9); JB: 3/29/52(10)

Wheel Of Hurt...*Margaret Whiting*
A/C - 11/5/66(4)

Wheels...*Restless Heart*
C&W - 2/6/88(1)

When...*Kalin Twins*
R&B - DJ: 9/1/58(1)

When A Man Loves A Woman...
Michael Bolton
HOT - 11/23/91(1)
A/C - 11/2/91(4)

When A Man Loves A Woman...
Percy Sledge
HOT - 5/28/66(2)
R&B - 5/7/66(4)

When Doves Cry...*Prince*
HOT - 7/7/84(5)
R&B - 6/30/84(8)

When I Fall In Love...*Lettermen*
A/C - 1/6/62(1)

When I Need You...*Leo Sayer*
HOT - 5/14/77(1)
A/C - 4/23/77(1)

When I See You Smile...*Bad English*
HOT - 11/11/89(2)

When I Think Of You...*Janet Jackson*
HOT - 10/11/86(2)

When I Wanted You...*Barry Manilow*
A/C - 2/16/80(1)

When I'm Away From You...
Bellamy Brothers
C&W - 4/2/83(1)

When I'm Back On My Feet Again...
Michael Bolton
A/C - 7/7/90(3)

When I'm With You...*Sheriff*
HOT - 2/4/89(1)
A/C - 2/18/89(1)

When It's Springtime In Alaska...
Johnny Horton
C&W - 4/6/59(1)

When She Was My Girl...*Four Tops*
R&B - 10/10/81(2)

When The Snow Is On The Roses...
Ed Ames
A/C - 11/25/67(4)

When The Snow Is On The Roses...
Sonny James
C&W - 9/16/72(1)

When There's No You...
Engelbert Humperdinck
A/C - 4/3/71(1)

When We Make Love...*Alabama*
C&W - 6/23/84(1)

When Will I Be Loved...
Linda Ronstadt
C&W - 6/14/75(1)

When Will I See You Again...
Three Degrees
A/C - 12/14/74(1)

315

**(When You Feel Like You're In Love)
Don't Just Stand There**...*Carl Smith*
 C&W - DJ: 3/29/52(8); BS: 4/12/52(5);
   JB: 4/12/52(3)
When You Say Nothing At All...
 Keith Whitley
 C&W - 12/24/88(2)
When You're Hot, You're Hot...
 Jerry Reed
 C&W - 6/19/71(5)
Where Are You Now...*Clint Black*
 C&W - 9/28/91(2)
Where Did I Go Wrong...*Steve Wariner*
 C&W - 6/3/89(1)
Where Did Our Love Go...*Supremes*
 HOT - 8/22/64(2)
 R&B - 8/22/64(2)
Where Do Broken Hearts Go...
 Whitney Houston
 HOT - 4/23/88(2)
 A/C - 4/2/88(3)
(Where Do I Begin) Love Story...
 Andy Williams
 A/C - 3/20/71(4)
Where Do I Put Her Memory...
 Charley Pride
 C&W - 4/28/79(1)
Where Do The Nights Go...
 Ronnie Milsap
 C&W - 1/23/88(1)
Where Do We Go From Here...
 Stacy Lattisaw with Johnny Gill
 R&B - 2/24/90(1)
Where Does The Good Times Go...
 Buck Owens
 C&W - 2/18/67(4)
Where Is The Love...
 Roberta Flack & Donny Hathaway
 R&B - 8/5/72(1)
 A/C - 7/22/72(1)
(Where Is Your Heart) ..see: Song From Moulin Rouge
Where Were You When I Was Falling In Love...*Lobo*
 A/C - 9/29/79(2)
Which Way Is Up ..see: Theme From
White Knight...*Cledus Maggard*
 C&W - 2/14/76(1)
White Lightning...*George Jones*
 C&W - 4/13/59(5)
White Silver Sands...
 Bill Black's Combo
 R&B - 4/25/60(4)
White Sport Coat (And A Pink Carnation)...*Marty Robbins*
 C&W - JB: 5/20/57(5); DJ: 6/3/57(1);
   BS: 6/10/57(2)
Who Can It Be Now?...*Men At Work*
 HOT - 10/30/82(1)
Who'd She Coo?...*Ohio Players*
 R&B - 8/21/76(1)
Who's Cheatin' Who...*Charly McClain*
 C&W - 2/14/81(1)
Who's Gonna Mow Your Grass...
 Buck Owens
 C&W - 3/29/69(2)
Who's Holding Donna Now...*DeBarge*
 A/C - 7/20/85(3)

Who's Johnny...*El DeBarge*
 R&B - 7/12/86(1)
Who's Lonely Now...*Highway 101*
 C&W - 1/6/90(1)
Who's Making Love...*Johnnie Taylor*
 R&B - 11/23/68(3)
Who's That Girl...*Madonna*
 HOT - 8/22/87(1)
Whodunit...*Tavares*
 R&B - 5/21/77(1)
Whoever's In New England...
 Reba McEntire
 C&W - 5/31/86(1)
Whole Lot Of Shakin' Going On...
 Jerry Lee Lewis
 R&B - BS: 9/9/57(2); DJ: 9/9/57(1)
 C&W - BS: 9/9/57(2)
Why...*Frankie Avalon*
 HOT - 12/28/59(1)
Why Baby Why...*Charley Pride*
 C&W - 2/26/83(1)
Why Baby Why...
 Red Sovine & Webb Pierce
 C&W - DJ: 2/11/56(4); JB: 2/25/56(1);
   BS: 3/10/56(1)
Why Can't We Live Together...
 Timmy Thomas
 R&B - 1/27/73(2)
Why Do Fools Fall In Love...
 Teenagers featuring Frankie Lymon
 R&B - BS: 3/17/56(5); DJ: 3/31/56(2)
Why Does It Have To Be (Wrong or Right)...*Restless Heart*
 C&W - 8/22/87(1)
Why Don't You Believe Me...
 Joni James
 POP - BS: 11/29/52(4); DJ: 12/13/52(6);
   JB: 12/27/52(3)
Why Don't You Love Me...
 Hank Williams
 C&W - BS: 6/17/50(6); DJ: 6/24/50(10);
   JB: 7/22/50(5)
Why Don't You Spend The Night...
 Ronnie Milsap
 C&W - 3/22/80(1)
Why Have You Left The One You Left Me For...*Crystal Gayle*
 C&W - 1/27/79(2)
Why Lady Why...*Alabama*
 C&W - 12/13/80(1)
Why Me...*Kris Kristofferson*
 C&W - 7/7/73(1)
Why Not Me...*Judds*
 C&W - 12/22/84(2)
Why Not Me...*Fred Knoblock*
 A/C - 8/23/80(2)
Why'd You Come In Here Lookin' Like That...*Dolly Parton*
 C&W - 8/5/89(1)
Wichita Lineman...*Glen Campbell*
 C&W - 12/21/68(2)
 A/C - 12/14/68(6)
Wild And Blue...*John Anderson*
 C&W - 12/25/82(2)
Wild Side Of Life...*Hank Thompson*
 C&W - BS: 5/10/52(15); DJ: 5/17/52(8);
   JB: 5/24/52(15)

Wild Thing...*Troggs*
 HOT - 7/30/66(2)
Wild, Wild West...*Escape Club*
 HOT - 11/12/88(1)
Wildfire...*Michael Murphey*
 A/C - 6/14/75(1)
Will It Go Round In Circles...
 Billy Preston
 HOT - 7/7/73(2)
Will You Love Me Tomorrow...
 Shirelles
 HOT - 1/30/61(2)
Willow Weep For Me...*Chad & Jeremy*
 A/C - 1/23/65(1)
Winchester Cathedral...
 New Vaudeville Band
 HOT - 12/3/66(3)
 A/C - 12/3/66(4)
Wind Beneath My Wings...*Bette Midler*
 HOT - 6/10/89(1)
Window Up Above...*Mickey Gilley*
 C&W - 6/7/75(1)
Windy...*Association*
 HOT - 7/1/67(4)
Wings Of A Dove...*Ferlin Husky*
 C&W - 11/14/60(10)
Winner Takes It All...*Abba*
 A/C - 2/7/81(2)
Wish You Were Here...*Eddie Fisher*
 POP - DJ: 9/6/52(1)
Wishing Well...*Terence Trent D'Arby*
 HOT - 5/7/88(1)
 R&B - 4/2/88(1)
Wishing You Were Here...*Chicago*
 A/C - 12/21/74(1)
Witch Doctor...*David Seville*
 POP - TP: 4/28/58(3); BS: 4/28/58(2)
 R&B - DJ: 5/26/58(1)
With A Little Luck...*Wings*
 HOT - 5/20/78(2)
With One Exception...*David Houston*
 C&W - 7/22/67(1)
With Or Without You...*U2*
 HOT - 5/16/87(3)
Without Love (There Is Nothing)...
 Tom Jones
 A/C - 1/31/70(1)
Without You...*Nilsson*
 HOT - 2/19/72(4)
 A/C - 2/19/72(5)
Woke Up In Love...*Exile*
 C&W - 3/3/84(1)
Wolverton Mountain...*Claude King*
 C&W - 6/30/62(9)
Woman, A Lover, A Friend...
 Jackie Wilson
 R&B - 8/1/60(4)
Woman In Love...*Ronnie Milsap*
 C&W - 12/23/89(2)
Woman In Love...*Barbra Streisand*
 HOT - 10/25/80(3)
 A/C - 10/11/80(5)
Woman Needs Love (Just Like You Do)...*Ray Parker Jr. & Raydio*
 R&B - 5/16/81(2)
Woman Of The World (Leave My World Alone)...*Loretta Lynn*
 C&W - 4/12/69(1)

Woman (Sensuous Woman)...
Don Gibson
C&W - 9/2/72(1)

Woman To Woman...*Shirley Brown*
R&B - 11/16/74(2)

Woman's Gotta Have It...*Bobby Womack*
R&B - 6/17/72(1)

Wonder Could I Live There Anymore...*Charley Pride*
C&W - 7/25/70(2)

Wonder Of You...*Elvis Presley*
A/C - 6/20/70(1)

Wonderful Baby...*Don McLean*
A/C - 5/31/75(1)

Wonderful World ..see: (What A)

Wondering...*Webb Pierce*
C&W - DJ: 3/1/52(4)

Wonderland By Night...*Bert Kaempfert*
HOT - 1/9/61(3)

Wooden Heart...*Joe Dowell*
HOT - 8/28/61(1)
A/C - 8/14/61(3)

Word Up...*Cameo*
R&B - 10/4/86(3)

Words Get In The Way...
Miami Sound Machine
A/C - 8/23/86(2)

Work With Me Annie...*Midnighters*
R&B - BS: 5/22/54(7); JB: 7/3/54(4)

Workin' Man Blues...*Merle Haggard*
C&W - 8/16/69(1)

World Of Make Believe...
Bill Anderson
C&W - 2/9/74(1)

World Of Our Own...*Sonny James*
C&W - 3/16/68(3)

World We Knew (Over And Over)...
Frank Sinatra
A/C - 9/2/67(5)

World Without Love...*Peter & Gordon*
HOT - 6/27/64(1)

Would You Lay With Me (In A Field Of Stone)...*Tanya Tucker*
C&W - 3/30/74(1)

Would You Take Another Chance On Me...*Jerry Lee Lewis*
C&W - 1/8/72(1)

Wrap My Body Tight...*Johnny Gill*
R&B - 4/13/91(1)

Written All Over Your Face...
Rude Boys
R&B - 3/16/91(1)

Wurlitzer Prize (I Don't Want To Get Over You)...*Waylon Jennings*
C&W - 11/19/77(2)

Y

Ya Ya...*Lee Dorsey*
R&B - 11/6/61(1)

Yakety Yak...*Coasters*
POP - TP: 7/21/58(1)
R&B - BS: 6/23/58(7); DJ: 6/30/58(6)

Year That Clayton Delaney Died...
Tom T. Hall
C&W - 9/18/71(2)

Years...*Barbara Mandrell*
C&W - 2/23/80(1)

Yellow Rose...
Johnny Lee with Lane Brody
C&W - 4/21/84(1)

Yellow Rose Of Texas...*Mitch Miller*
POP - BS: 9/3/55(6); DJ: 9/3/55(6); JB: 10/1/55(6)

Yellow Roses...*Dolly Parton*
C&W - 11/25/89(1)

Yes, I'm Ready...
Teri DeSario with K.C.
A/C - 1/26/80(2)

Yes, Mr. Peters...
Roy Drusky & Priscilla Mitchell
C&W - 8/21/65(2)

Yesterday...*Beatles*
HOT - 10/9/65(4)

Yesterday Once More...*Carpenters*
A/C - 7/7/73(3)

Yesterday's Songs...*Neil Diamond*
A/C - 12/19/81(6)

Yesterday's Wine...
George Jones/Merle Haggard
C&W - 10/9/82(1)

You Again...*Forester Sisters*
C&W - 10/3/87(1)

You Ain't Seen Nothing Yet...
Bachman-Turner Overdrive
HOT - 11/9/74(1)

You Always Come Back (To Hurting Me)...*Johnny Rodriguez*
C&W - 6/9/73(1)

You And I...*Rick James*
R&B - 7/22/78(2)

You And I...
Eddie Rabbitt with Crystal Gayle
C&W - 12/4/82(1)

You And Me...*Tammy Wynette*
C&W - 10/16/76(2)
(also see: Now And Forever)

You And Me Against The World...
Helen Reddy
A/C - 7/27/74(1)

You Are...*Lionel Richie*
A/C - 2/26/83(6)

You Are My Everything...*Surface*
R&B - 11/4/89(2)

You Are My Lady...*Freddie Jackson*
R&B - 10/5/85(2)

You Are My Sunshine...*Ray Charles*
R&B - 12/15/62(3)

You Are My Treasure...*Jack Greene*
C&W - 4/13/68(1)

You Are The Sunshine Of My Life...
Stevie Wonder
HOT - 5/19/73(1)
A/C - 4/28/73(2)

You Beat Me To The Punch...
Mary Wells
R&B - 9/22/62(1)

You Belong To Me...*Jo Stafford*
POP - BS: 9/13/52(5); DJ: 9/13/52(12); JB: 9/13/52(2)

You Better Know It...*Jackie Wilson*
R&B - 10/19/59(1)

You Can Dream Of Me...*Steve Wariner*
C&W - 3/1/86(1)

You Can't Be A Beacon (If Your Light Don't Shine)...*Donna Fargo*
C&W - 7/27/74(1)

You Can't Deny It...*Lisa Stansfield*
R&B - 7/7/90(1)

You Can't Hurry Love...*Supremes*
HOT - 9/10/66(2)
R&B - 9/3/66(2)

You Can't Run From Love...
Eddie Rabbitt
C&W - 6/18/83(1)

U Can't Touch This...*M.C. Hammer*
R&B - 6/23/90(1)

You Could've Heard A Heart Break...
Johnny Lee
C&W - 11/24/84(1)

You Decorated My Life...*Kenny Rogers*
C&W - 11/3/79(2)

You Don't Bring Me Flowers...
Barbra Streisand & Neil Diamond
HOT - 12/2/78(1)

You Don't Have To Be A Star...
Marilyn McCoo & Billy Davis, Jr.
HOT - 1/8/77(1)
R&B - 11/20/76(1)

You Don't Have To Say You Love Me...
Elvis Presley
A/C - 11/28/70(1)

You Don't Have To Worry...*En Vogue*
R&B - 2/9/91(1)

You Don't Know Me...*Ray Charles*
A/C - 8/25/62(3)

You Don't Know Me...*Mickey Gilley*
C&W - 9/19/81(1)

You Don't Love Me Anymore...
Eddie Rabbitt
C&W - 8/12/78(1)

You Gave Me A Mountain...
Frankie Laine
A/C - 3/15/69(2)

You Give Good Love...*Whitney Houston*
R&B - 5/25/85(1)

You Give Love A Bad Name...*Bon Jovi*
HOT - 11/29/86(1)

You Got It...*Roy Orbison*
A/C - 3/25/89(2)

You Got It All...*Jets*
A/C - 3/7/87(2)

You Got The Love...
Rufus Featuring Chaka Khan
R&B - 12/14/74(1)

You Gotta Love Someone...*Elton John*
A/C - 12/15/90(5)

You Haven't Done Nothin...
Stevie Wonder
HOT - 11/2/74(1)
R&B - 9/28/74(2)

You Keep Me Hangin' On...*Supremes*
HOT - 11/19/66(2)
R&B - 11/26/66(4)

You Keep Me Hangin' On...*Kim Wilde*
HOT - 6/6/87(1)

You Know I Love You...*B.B. King*
R&B - BS: 11/8/52(2)

317

You Know Me Better Than That...
George Strait
C&W - 8/17/91(3)

You Lie...*Reba McEntire*
C&W - 11/3/90(1)

You Light Up My Life...*Debby Boone*
HOT - 10/15/77(10)
A/C - 11/19/77(1)

You Look So Good In Love...
George Strait
C&W - 1/7/84(1)

You Make Me Feel Like Dancing...
Leo Sayer
HOT - 1/15/77(1)

You Make Me Want To Make You Mine...*Juice Newton*
C&W - 10/19/85(1)

You Mean The World To Me...
David Houston
C&W - 11/4/67(2)

You Needed Me...*Anne Murray*
HOT - 11/4/78(1)

You Never Miss A Real Good Thing (Till He Says Goodbye)...*Crystal Gayle*
C&W - 1/15/77(1)

You Ought To Be With Me...*Al Green*
R&B - 12/2/72(1)

You Really Had Me Going...*Holly Dunn*
C&W - 11/17/90(1)

You Send Me...*Sam Cooke*
POP - BS: 12/2/57(2); TP: 12/9/57(3); DJ: 12/9/57(1)
R&B - BS: 11/25/57(6); DJ: 11/25/57(6)

You Should Be Dancing...*Bee Gees*
HOT - 9/4/76(1)

You Still Move Me...*Dan Seals*
C&W - 1/31/87(1)

You Take Me For Granted...
Merle Haggard
C&W - 5/28/83(1)

You Upset Me Baby...*B.B. King*
R&B - JB: 12/25/54(2)

You Were Always There...*Donna Fargo*
C&W - 7/28/73(1)

You Were On My Mind...*We Five*
A/C - 9/4/65(5)

You Will Know...*Stevie Wonder*
R&B - 3/5/88(1)

You Win Again...*Charley Pride*
C&W - 7/12/80(1)

You Won't See Me...*Anne Murray*
A/C - 6/22/74(2)

You You You...*Ames Brothers*
POP - DJ: 9/26/53(8); JB: 10/24/53(6)

You'll Lose A Good Thing...
Freddy Fender
C&W - 4/3/76(1)

You'll Lose A Good Thing...
Barbara Lynn
R&B - 8/4/62(3)

You'll Never Find Another Love Like Mine...*Lou Rawls*
R&B - 7/24/76(2)
A/C - 7/31/76(1)

You'll Never Walk Alone...
Roy Hamilton
R&B - BS: 3/27/54(8); JB: 5/8/54(5)

You're All I Need To Get By...
Marvin Gaye & Tammi Terrell
R&B - 8/31/68(5)

You're Gettin' To Me Again...
Jim Glaser
C&W - 9/15/84(1)

You're Gonna Ruin My Bad Reputation...*Ronnie McDowell*
C&W - 8/27/83(1)

(You're) Having My Baby...*Paul Anka*
HOT - 8/24/74(3)

You're In Love...*Wilson Phillips*
HOT - 4/20/91(1)
A/C - 3/30/91(4)

You're My Best Friend...*Don Williams*
C&W - 6/21/75(1)

You're My Jamaica...*Charley Pride*
C&W - 9/15/79(1)

You're My Man...*Lynn Anderson*
C&W - 6/5/71(2)

(You're My) Soul And Inspiration...
Righteous Brothers
HOT - 4/9/66(3)

You're No Good...*Linda Ronstadt*
HOT - 2/15/75(1)

You're Nobody Till Somebody Loves You...*Dean Martin*
A/C - 1/30/65(1)

You're Only Lonely...*J.D. Souther*
A/C - 11/17/79(5)

(You're Puttin') A Rush On Me...
Stephanie Mills
R&B - 10/10/87(1)

You're Sixteen...*Ringo Starr*
HOT - 1/26/74(1)

You're So Good When You're Bad...
Charley Pride
C&W - 11/6/82(1)

You're So Vain...*Carly Simon*
HOT - 1/6/73(3)
A/C - 1/20/73(2)

You're Still New To Me...
Marie Osmond with Paul Davis
C&W - 11/22/86(1)

You're The Best Break This Old Heart Ever Had...*Ed Bruce*
C&W - 3/6/82(1)

You're The Best Thing That Ever Happened To Me...*Ray Price*
C&W - 10/6/73(1)

You're The First, The Last, My Everything...*Barry White*
R&B - 1/18/75(1)

You're The First Time I've Thought About Leaving...*Reba McEntire*
C&W - 4/30/83(1)

You're The Inspiration...*Chicago*
A/C - 1/26/85(2)

You're The Last Thing I Needed Tonight...*John Schneider*
C&W - 8/16/86(1)

You're The One That I Want...
John Travolta & Olivia Newton-John
HOT - 6/10/78(1)

You're The Only One...*Dolly Parton*
C&W - 7/28/79(2)

You're The Only World I Know...
Sonny James
C&W - 1/23/65(4)

You're The Reason God Made Oklahoma...*David Frizzell & Shelly West*
C&W - 4/11/81(1)

You've Got A Friend...*James Taylor*
HOT - 7/31/71(1)
A/C - 7/31/71(1)

"You've Got" The Touch...*Alabama*
C&W - 4/11/87(1)

You've Lost That Lovin' Feelin'...
Righteous Brothers
HOT - 2/6/65(2)

You've Never Been This Far Before...
Conway Twitty
C&W - 9/8/73(3)

You've Really Got A Hold On Me...
Miracles
R&B - 2/16/63(1)

Young Blood...*Coasters*
R&B - BS: 6/3/57(1)

Young Hearts Run Free...*Candi Staton*
R&B - 6/5/76(1)

Young Love...*Tab Hunter*
POP - TP: 2/16/57(6); DJ: 2/16/57(6); BS: 3/2/57(4); JB: 3/2/57(5)

Young Love...*Sonny James*
POP - DJ: 2/9/57(1)
C&W - DJ: 2/2/57(9); BS: 2/16/57(7); JB: 2/23/57(3)

Young Love...*Judds*
C&W - 5/6/89(1)

Your Cheatin' Heart...*Hank Williams*
C&W - JB: 4/11/53(2); DJ: 5/2/53(6)

Your Heart's Not In It...*Janie Fricke*
C&W - 12/1/84(1)

Your Love...*Graham Central Station*
R&B - 8/30/75(1)

(Your Love Keeps Lifting Me) Higher And Higher...*Jackie Wilson*
R&B - 10/7/67(1)

Your Love's On The Line...
Earl Thomas Conley
C&W - 8/6/83(1)

Your Smile...*Rene & Angela*
R&B - 3/15/86(1)

Your Tender Loving Care...*Buck Owens*
C&W - 9/9/67(1)

Your Wildest Dreams...*Moody Blues*
A/C - 7/5/86(2)

B-sides

The following is an alphabetical listing of all B-sides which are listed with their A-side in the main section of this book.

Anyway You Want Me (That's How I Will Be)...*Elvis Presley*
POP - BS: 11/10/56; JB: 12/8/56

Baby I'm Burnin'...*Dolly Parton*
C&W - 1/20/79
Bernardine...*Pat Boone*
POP - BS: 6/3/57
Big River...*Johnny Cash*
C&W - BS: 3/3/58
Brand New Me...*Aretha Franklin*
R&B - 6/19/71

Claudette...*Everly Brothers*
POP - BS: 5/12/58
C&W - BS: 6/2/58
Come In Stranger...*Johnny Cash*
C&W - BS: 6/30/58

Devoted To You...*Everly Brothers*
POP - BS: 8/25/58
C&W - BS: 9/8/58
Don't Ask Me Why...*Elvis Presley*
POP - BS: 7/21/58

Everybody Is A Star...
Sly & The Family Stone
HOT - 2/14/70

For You Blue...*Beatles*
HOT - 6/13/70

Get Rhythm...*Johnny Cash*
C&W - JB: 7/21/56

He Ain't Heavy...He's My Brother...
Olivia Newton-John
A/C - 1/17/76
Heaven On Earth...*Platters*
POP - BS: 8/4/56

I Beg Of You...*Elvis Presley*
POP - BS: 2/10/58
I Can't Stop Lovin' You...*Don Gibson*
C&W - BS: 4/14/58
I Feel The Earth Move...*Carole King*
HOT - 6/19/71
I Was The One...*Elvis Presley*
POP - BS: 4/21/56; JB: 5/5/56
C&W - BS: 3/17/56; JB: 4/28/56

I'm A Man...*Bo Diddley*
R&B - JB: 6/25/55
I'm Gonna Fall Out Of Love With You...*Webb Pierce*
C&W - JB: 4/9/55
If You Were Me...*Webb Pierce*
C&W - BS: 10/22/55; JB: 11/5/55
Isn't It A Pity...*George Harrison*
HOT - 12/26/70

Just Call Me Lonesome...*Eddy Arnold*
C&W - JB: 10/22/55

Kentuckian Song...*Eddy Arnold*
C&W - BS: 10/8/55

Loving You...*Elvis Presley*
POP - BS: 7/8/57
R&B - BS: 9/2/57
C&W - BS: 8/5/57

My Baby Left Me...*Elvis Presley*
POP - BS: 7/28/56
C&W - BS: 7/14/56; JB: 8/11/56
My Blue Heaven...*Fats Domino*
R&B - BS: 6/2/56; JB: 6/9/56
Mystery Train...*Elvis Presley*
C&W - BS: 3/3/56; JB: 3/10/56

No Sugar Tonight...*Guess Who*
HOT - 5/9/70

Playing For Keeps...*Elvis Presley*
POP - BS: 2/9/57; JB: 3/9/57

Ready Teddy...*Little Richard*
R&B - JB: 8/4/56; BS: 8/11/56
Reason To Believe...*Rod Stewart*
HOT - 10/2/71

Scratch My Back (And Whisper in My Ear)...*Razzy Bailey*
C&W - 10/3/81
Send Me Some Lovin'...*Little Richard*
R&B - JB: 4/27/57
Slippin' And Slidin' (Peepin' And Hidin')...*Little Richard*
R&B - BS: 4/21/56; JB: 4/21/56

Sneaky Snake...*Tom T. Hall*
C&W - 2/22/75
Something...*Beatles*
HOT - 11/29/69
Stairway To Heaven...*O'Jays*
R&B - 4/24/76
Steamboat...*Drifters*
R&B - JB: 12/31/55
Summertime...*Sam Cooke*
POP - BS: 12/2/57

Think About It Darlin'...
Jerry Lee Lewis
C&W - 4/22/72
Train Of Love...*Johnny Cash*
C&W - JB: 3/2/57
Treat Me Nice...*Elvis Presley*
POP - BS: 10/21/57
R&B - BS: 11/11/57
C&W - BS: 12/2/57

What's The Reason I'm Not Pleasing You...*Fats Domino*
R&B - BS: 1/26/57; JB: 1/26/57
When The Swallows Come Back To Capistrano...*Pat Boone*
POP - BS: 12/23/57

You Done Me Wrong...*Ray Price*
C&W - BS: 7/28/56; JB: 7/28/56
You're The Reason I'm In Love...
Sonny James
C&W - BS: 3/16/57
Your Good For Nothing Heart...
Webb Pierce
C&W - BS: 7/16/55; JB: 8/6/55

ROYAL COURT OF #1s

This section lists the all-time biggest #1 hits and the all-time #1 hits of each major chart category as follows:

>Kings of the Singles
>
>Royal Court of Pop Singles
>Royal Court of R&B Singles
>Royal Court of Country Singles
>Royal Court of Adult Contemporary Singles
>
>Kings of the Albums
>
>Royal Court of Pop Albums
>Royal Court of R&B Albums
>Royal Court of Country Albums

The above listings are based on the most weeks at the #1 position. In the case of a tie, records are listed in chronological order.

Also included are:

>Triple Crown Winners
>Songs Reaching #1 on the Most Charts

KINGS OF THE SINGLES

Of all the singles listed in this book, the following records attained the most **weeks** at the #1 position.

I'm Moving On...Hank Snow
21 weeks at #1 on the Country charts in 1950

In The Jailhouse Now...Webb Pierce
21 weeks at #1 on the Country charts in 1955

ROYAL COURT OF *POP* SINGLES

ALL-TIME #1 HITS

The Tennessee Waltz...Patti Page
13 weeks at #1 in 1950

Goodnight, Irene...Gordon Jenkins and
The Weavers
13 weeks at #1 in 1950

ALL-TIME #1 HITS BY CHART CATEGORY

Best Sellers: Goodnight, Irene...Gordon Jenkins
and The Weavers
13 weeks at #1 in 1950

Disc Jockey: You Belong To Me...Jo Stafford
12 weeks at #1 in 1952

Juke Box: The Tennessee Waltz...Patti Page
13 weeks at #1 in 1950

Top 100: Singing The Blues...Guy Mitchell
9 weeks at #1 in 1956

Hot 100: You Light Up My Life...
Debby Boone
10 weeks at #1 in 1977
Physical...Olivia Newton-John
10 weeks at #1 in 1981

ALL-TIME #1 HITS BY DECADE

50s: The Tennessee Waltz...Patti Page
13 weeks at #1 in 1950
Goodnight, Irene...Gordon Jenkins
and The Weavers
13 weeks at #1 in 1950

60s: The Theme From "A Summer Place"...
Percy Faith
9 weeks at #1 in 1960
Hey Jude...The Beatles
9 weeks at #1 in 1968

70s: You Light Up My Life...Debby Boone
10 weeks at #1 in 1977

80s: Physical...Olivia Newton-John
10 weeks at #1 in 1981

ROYAL COURT OF R&B SINGLES

ALL-TIME #1 HITS

Sixty Minute Man...The Dominoes
14 weeks at #1 in 1951

Black Night...Charles Brown
14 weeks at #1 in 1951

Things That I Used To Do...Guitar Slim
14 weeks at #1 in 1954

ALL-TIME #1 HITS BY CHART CATEGORY

Best Sellers: Sixty Minute Man...The Dominoes
14 weeks at #1 in 1951
Disc Jockey: Blueberry Hill...Fats Domino
11 weeks at #1 in 1956
The Great Pretender...The Platters
11 weeks at #1 in 1956
Juke Box: Black Night...Charles Brown
14 weeks at #1 in 1951
Things That I Used To Do...
Guitar Slim
14 weeks at #1 in 1954
Hot R&B: Baby (You've Got What It Takes)
Dinah Washington &
Brook Benton
10 weeks at #1 in 1960
Tossin' And Turnin'...Bobby Lewis
10 weeks at #1 in 1961
I Can't Stop Loving You...
Ray Charles
10 weeks at #1 in 1962
Sexual Healing...Marvin Gaye
10 weeks at #1 in 1982

ALL-TIME #1 HITS BY DECADE

50s: Sixty Minute Man...The Dominoes
14 weeks at #1 in 1951
Black Night...Charles Brown
14 weeks at #1 in 1951
Things That I Used To Do...Guitar Slim
14 weeks at #1 in 1954
60s: Baby (You've Got What It Takes)...
Dinah Washington & Brook Benton
10 weeks at #1 in 1960
Tossin' And Turnin'...Bobby Lewis
10 weeks at #1 in 1961
I Can't Stop Loving You...Ray Charles
10 weeks at #1 in 1962
70s: Let's Stay Together...Al Green
9 weeks at #1 in 1972
80s: Sexual Healing...Marvin Gaye
10 weeks at #1 in 1982

ROYAL COURT OF *COUNTRY* SINGLES

ALL-TIME #1 HITS

I'm Moving On...Hank Snow
21 weeks at #1 in 1950

In The Jailhouse Now...Webb Pierce
21 weeks at #1 in 1955

ALL-TIME #1 HITS BY CHART CATEGORY

Best Sellers: I'm Moving On...Hank Snow
21 weeks at #1 in 1950

Disc Jockey: Crazy Arms...Ray Price
20 weeks at #1 in 1956

Juke Box: In The Jailhouse Now...
Webb Pierce
21 weeks at #1 in 1955

Hot Country: Walk On By...Leroy Van Dyke
19 weeks at #1 in 1961

ALL-TIME #1 HITS BY DECADE

50s: I'm Moving On...Hank Snow
21 weeks at #1 in 1950
In The Jailhouse Now...Webb Pierce
21 weeks at #1 in 1955

60s: Walk On By...Leroy Van Dyke
19 weeks at #1 in 1961

70s: My Hang-Up Is You...Freddie Hart
6 weeks at #1 in 1972
Convoy...C. W. McCall
6 weeks at #1 in 1975
Luckenbach, Texas (Back to the Basics of Love)...Waylon Jennings
6 weeks at #1 in 1977

80s: My Heart...Ronnie Milsap
3 weeks at #1 in 1980
Lookin' For Love...Johnny Lee
3 weeks at #1 in 1980
Coward Of The County...Kenny Rogers
3 weeks at #1 in 1980
Forever And Ever, Amen...Randy Travis
3 weeks at #1 in 1987

ROYAL COURT OF
ADULT CONTEMPORARY SINGLES

ALL-TIME #1 HIT

Love Is Blue...Paul Mauriat
11 weeks at #1 in 1968

ALL-TIME #1 HITS BY DECADE

60s: Love Is Blue...Paul Mauriat
11 weeks at #1 in 1968

70s: Time Passages...Al Stewart
10 weeks at #1 in 1978

80s: Lost In Love...Air Supply
6 weeks at #1 in 1980

I Don't Need You...Kenny Rogers
6 weeks at #1 in 1981

Yesterday's Songs...Neil Diamond
6 weeks at #1 in 1981

You Are...Lionel Richie
6 weeks at #1 in 1983

Read 'Em And Weep...Barry Manilow
6 weeks at #1 in 1983

Hello...Lionel Richie
6 weeks at #1 in 1984

Cherish...Kool & The Gang
6 weeks at #1 in 1985

Right Here Waiting...Richard Marx
6 weeks at #1 in 1989

If You Don't Know Me By Now...
Simply Red
6 weeks at #1 in 1989

KINGS OF THE ALBUMS

Of all the albums listed in this book, the following records attained the most weeks at the #1 position.

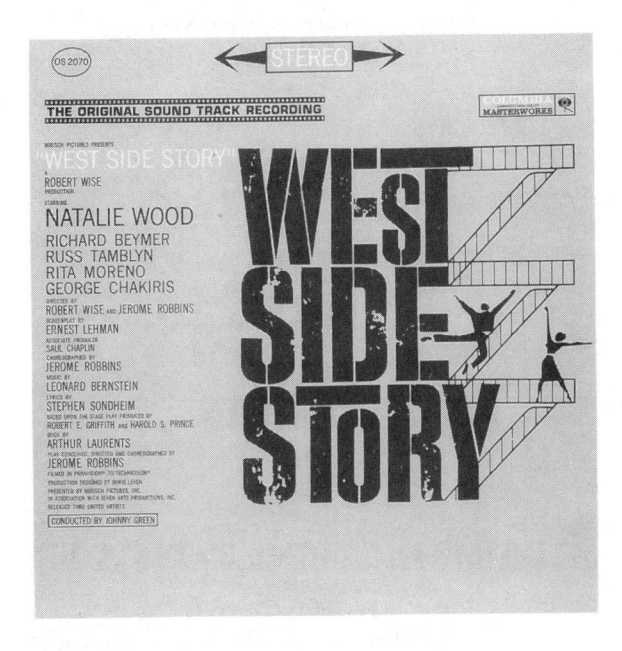

West Side Story...Soundtrack
54 weeks at #1 on the Pop charts in 1962

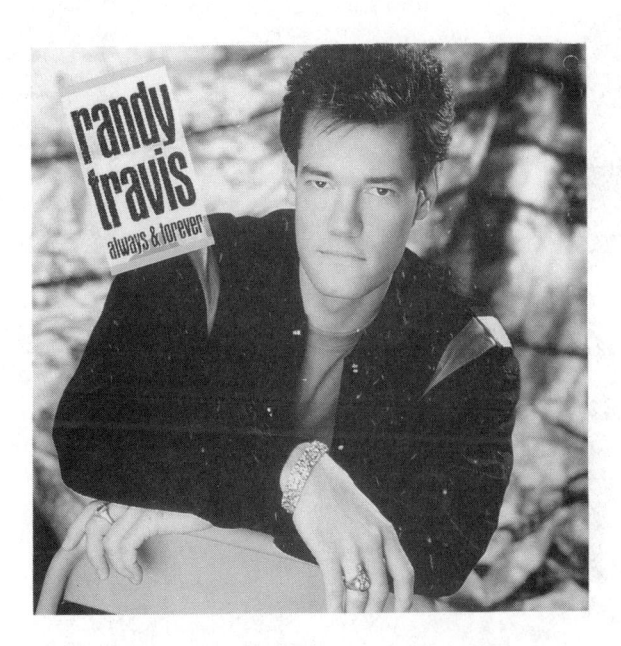

Always & Forever...Randy Travis
43 weeks at #1 on the Country charts in 1987

ROYAL COURT OF *POP* ALBUMS

ALL-TIME #1 ALBUM

West Side Story...Soundtrack
54 weeks at #1 in 1962

ALL-TIME #1 ALBUMS BY DECADE

50s: Calypso...Harry Belafonte
31 weeks at #1 in 1956
South Pacific...Soundtrack
31 weeks at #1 in 1958

60s: West Side Story...Soundtrack
54 weeks at #1 in 1962

70s: Rumours...Fleetwood Mac
31 weeks at #1 in 1977

80s: Thriller...Michael Jackson
37 weeks at #1 in 1983

ROYAL COURT OF R&B ALBUMS

ALL-TIME #1 ALBUM

Thriller...Michael Jackson
37 weeks at #1 in 1983

ALL-TIME #1 ALBUMS BY DECADE

60s: The Temptations Sing Smokey...
The Temptations
18 weeks at #1 in 1965

70s: Songs In The Key Of Life...Stevie Wonder
20 weeks at #1 in 1976

80s: Thriller...Michael Jackson
37 weeks at #1 in 1983

ROYAL COURT OF *COUNTRY* ALBUMS

ALL-TIME #1 ALBUM

Always & Forever...Randy Travis
43 weeks at #1 in 1987

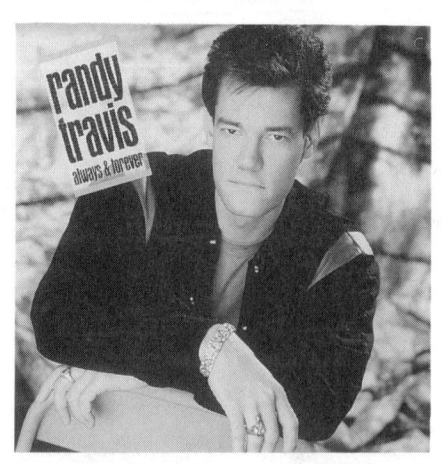

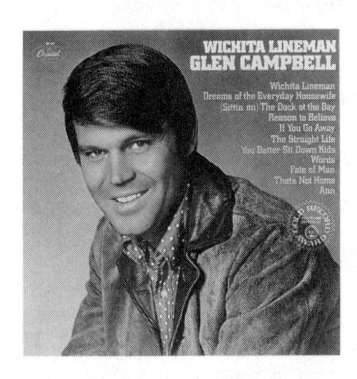

ALL-TIME #1 ALBUMS BY DECADE

60s: Wichita Lineman...Glen Campbell
20 weeks at #1 in 1968
Johnny Cash At San Quentin...Johnny Cash
20 weeks at #1 in 1969
70s: Kenny...Kenny Rogers
25 weeks at #1 in 1979
80s: Always & Forever...Randy Travis
43 weeks at #1 in 1987

TRIPLE CROWN WINNERS

To qualify as a triple crown winner a record must hit #1 on three major singles chart categories (ex.: Pop/R&B/C&W). Hitting #1 on multiple charts within a specific category such as Pop does not qualify a record for the triple crown. The date the record became a simultaneous #1 hit is shown next to the title.

POP, R&B and COUNTRY CHART

DATE

9/15/56	Don't Be Cruel/Hound Dog	Elvis Presley
5/13/57	All Shook Up	Elvis Presley
9/02/57*	(Let Me Be Your) Teddy Bear	Elvis Presley
10/28/57	Wake Up Little Susie	The Everly Brothers
12/02/57*	Jailhouse Rock	Elvis Presley
6/02/58	All I Have To Do Is Dream	The Everly Brothers

POP, R&B and ADULT CONTEMPORARY CHART

6/09/62	I Can't Stop Loving You	Ray Charles
5/04/74*	TSOP (The Sound Of Philadelphia)	MFSB featuring The Three Degrees
8/10/74	Feel Like Makin' Love	Roberta Flack
6/03/78*	Too Much, Too Little, Too Late	Johnny Mathis/Deniece Williams
8/19/78	Three Times A Lady	Commodores
9/05/81	Endless Love	Diana Ross & Lionel Richie
11/12/83	All Night Long (All Night)	Lionel Richie
5/12/84	Hello	Lionel Richie
10/13/84	I Just Called To Say I Love You	Stevie Wonder
5/04/85*	We Are The World	USA for Africa
10/26/85*	Saving All My Love For You	Whitney Houston
11/02/85	Part-Time Lover	Stevie Wonder
1/11/86*	Say You, Say Me	Lionel Richie
1/25/86*	That's What Friends Are For	Dionne & Friends
3/08/86*	How Will I Know	Whitney Houston
7/05/86*	There'll Be Sad Songs (To Make You Cry)	Billy Ocean
6/13/87*	Always	Atlantic Starr
9/19/87*	I Just Can't Stop Loving You	Michael Jackson
6/18/88*	One More Try	George Michael
8/11/90	Vision Of Love	Mariah Carey
11/10/90*	Love Takes Time	Mariah Carey
2/02/91*	The First Time	Surface
3/02/91	All The Man That I Need	Whitney Houston

POP, COUNTRY and ADULT CONTEMPORARY CHART

11/20/61	Big Bad John	Jimmy Dean
5/25/68*	Honey	Bobby Goldsboro
12/15/73*	The Most Beautiful Girl	Charlie Rich
5/17/75*	(Hey Won't You Play) Another Somebody Done Somebody Wrong Song	B.J. Thomas
9/06/75*	Rhinestone Cowboy	Glen Campbell
11/08/75*	I'm Sorry	John Denver
4/30/77*	Southern Nights	Glen Campbell
11/22/80	Lady	Kenny Rogers
2/28/81*	I Love A Rainy Night	Eddie Rabbitt
2/28/81*	9 To 5	Dolly Parton
10/29/83	Islands In The Stream	Kenny Rogers with Dolly Parton

*: triple crown achieved as of this date but not on all charts simultaneously

SONGS REACHING #1 ON THE MOST CHARTS

During the years 1950-1958, *Billboard* published multiple singles charts for each major type of music (POP, R&B, C&W). These charts included *Best Sellers In Stores*, *Most Played By Jockeys*, and *Most Played In Juke Boxes*, as well as the *Top 100* and *Hot 100* charts for pop music. (See *Researching The Charts* for a complete explanation of these multiple charts.) Below is a listing of songs which hit #1 on the most charts (ex.: "All Shook Up" reached #1 on four Pop charts (*Top 100*, *Best Sellers*, *Disc Jockey* and *Juke Box*), three R&B charts (*Best Sellers*, *Disc Jockey* and *Juke Box*) and one Country chart (*Juke Box*), for a total of eight charts).

Total Charts	Date First Hit #1	Title	Artist
8	8/18/56	Don't Be Cruel	Elvis Presley
8	4/13/57	All Shook Up	Elvis Presley
7	11/26/55	Sixteen Tons	Tennessee Ernie Ford
7	3/17/56	Heartbreak Hotel	Elvis Presley
7	5/12/58	All I Have To Do Is Dream	The Everly Brothers
6	1/21/50	Chattanoogie Shoe Shine Boy	Red Foley
6	1/07/56	The Great Pretender	The Platters
6	8/04/56	My Prayer	The Platters
6	8/18/56	Hound Dog	Elvis Presley
6	10/14/57	Wake Up Little Susie	The Everly Brothers
6	10/21/57	Jailhouse Rock	Elvis Presley
5	12/29/51	Cry	Johnnie Ray & The Four Lads
5	7/08/57	(Let Me Be Your) Teddy Bear	Elvis Presley
5	9/23/57	Honeycomb	Jimmie Rodgers
5	11/25/57	You Send Me	Sam Cooke
5	3/17/58	Tequila	The Champs

Total Charts: Total number of charts on which the record hit the #1 position

Date First Hit #1: Earliest date record hit #1 on any of the charts

JUST FOR

Only Joel Whitburn's Record Research Books List Every

When the talk turns to music, more people turn to Joel Whitburn's Record Research Collection than to any other reference source.

That's because these are the **only** books that get right to the bottom of *Billboard*'s major charts, with **complete, fully accurate chart data on every record ever charted**. So they're quoted with confidence by DJ's, music show hosts, program directors, collectors and other music enthusiasts worldwide.

Each book lists every record's significant chart data, such as peak position, debut date, peak date, weeks charted, label, record number and much more, all conveniently arranged for fast, easy reference. Most books also feature artist biographies, record notes, RIAA Platinum/Gold Record certifications, top artist and record achievements, all-time artist and record rankings, a chronological listing of all #1 hits, and additional in-depth chart information.

And now, the new large-format **Billboard Hot 100 Charts** book series takes chart research one step further, by actually reproducing weekly "Hot 100" charts by decade.

Joel Whitburn's Record Research Collection. #1 on **everyone's** hit list.

TOP POP SINGLES 1955-1990
Nearly 20,000 Pop singles - every "Hot 100" hit - arranged by artist. $70.00 Hardcover/$60.00 Softcover.

POP SINGLES ANNUAL 1955-1990
A year-by-year ranking, based on chart performance, of the nearly 20,000 Pop hits. $70.00 Hardcover/$60.00 Softcover.

THE BILLBOARD HOT 100 CHARTS:
THE SIXTIES 1960-1969
THE SEVENTIES 1970-1979
THE EIGHTIES 1980-1989
Three complete collections of the actual weekly "Hot 100" charts from each decade, reproduced in black-and-white at 70% of original size. Deluxe Hardcover. $90.00 each.

TOP POP ALBUMS 1955-1985
The 14,000 LPs that ever appeared on *Billboard*'s Pop albums charts, arranged by artist. Softcover. $50.00.

POP MEMORIES 1890-1954
The only documented chart history of early American popular music, arranged by artist. $50.00. Softcover.

TOP COUNTRY SINGLES 1944-1988
An artist-by-artist listing of every "Country" single ever charted. $60.00 Hardcover/$50.00 Softcover.

THE RECORD

Record To Ever Appear On Every Major Billboard Chart.

TOP R&B SINGLES 1942-1988
Every "Soul," "Black," "Urban Contemporary" and "Rhythm & Blues" charted single, listed by artist. $60.00 Hardcover/$50.00 Softcover.

BILLBOARD'S TOP 10 CHARTS 1958-1988
1,550 actual, weekly Top 10 Pop singles charts in the original "Hot 100" chart format. $50.00. Softcover.

BILLBOARD #1 HITS 1950-1991
A week-by-week listing of every #1 single and album from Billboard's Pop, R&B, Country and Adult Contemporary charts. Softcover. $35.00.

BILLBOARD'S TOP 3000+ 1955-1990
Every single that ever appeared in the Top 10 of *Billboard*'s Pop charts, ranked by all-time popularity. Softcover. $25.00.

DAILY #1 HITS 1940-1989
A day-by-day listing of the #1 Pop records of the past 50 years. Spiral-bound softcover. $25.00.

MUSIC YEARBOOKS 1983/1984/1985/1986
The complete story of each year in music, covering *Billboard*'s biggest singles and albums charts. Softcover. $35.00 each.

MUSIC & VIDEO YEARBOOKS
1987/1988/1989/1990/1991
Comprehensive, yearly updates on *Billboard*'s major singles, albums and videocassettes charts. Softcover. $35.00 each.

For complete book descriptions and ordering information, call, write or fax today.

Record Research
The World's Leading Authority
On Recorded Entertainment

RECORD RESEARCH INC.
P.O. Box 200
Menomonee Falls, WI 53052-0200
Phone: 414-251-5408
Fax: 414-251-9452

The RECORD RESEARCH Collection

Book Title	Quantity	Price	Total
1. Billboard Hot 100 Charts — The Sixties (Hardcover)	_____	$90.00	_____
2. Billboard Hot 100 Charts — The Seventies (Hardcover)	_____	$90.00	_____
3. Billboard Hot 100 Charts — The Eighties (Hardcover)	_____	$90.00	_____
4. Top Pop Singles 1955-1990 (Hardcover)	_____	$70.00	_____
5. Top Pop Singles 1955-1990 (Softcover)	_____	$60.00	_____
6. Pop Singles Annual 1955-1990 (Hardcover)	_____	$70.00	_____
7. Pop Singles Annual 1955-1990 (Softcover)	_____	$60.00	_____
8. Top Country Singles 1944-1988 (Hardcover)	_____	$60.00	_____
9. Top Country Singles 1944-1988 (Softcover)	_____	$50.00	_____
10. Top R&B Singles 1942-1988 (Hardcover)	_____	$60.00	_____
11. Top R&B Singles 1942-1988 (Softcover)	_____	$50.00	_____
12. Pop Memories 1890-1954	_____	$50.00	_____
13. Top 10 Charts 1958-1988	_____	$50.00	_____
14. Top Pop Albums 1955-1985	_____	$50.00	_____
15. Billboard #1's 1950-1991	_____	$35.00	_____
16. Top 3000+ 1955-1990	_____	$25.00	_____
17. Daily #1 Hits 1940-1989	_____	$25.00	_____
18. Music & Video Yearbook 1990	_____	$35.00	_____
19. Music & Video Yearbook 1989	_____	$35.00	_____
20. Music & Video Yearbook 1988	_____	$35.00	_____
21. Music & Video Yearbook 1987	_____	$35.00	_____

(1983-1986 Music Yearbooks are available at $35.00 each.)

All books are softcover except items 1, 2, 3, 4, 6, 8, & 10.

Shipping & Handling (see below) .... _____

Total Payment $_____

Shipping & Handling

All U.S. orders add $5.00 for the first book ordered and $2.00 for each additional book.

All Canadian and foreign orders add $6.00 for the first book ordered and $3.00 for each additional book. Canadian and foreign orders are shipped via surface mail and must be paid in U.S. dollars. Call or write for air mail shipping rates.

For more information on the complete line of *Record Research* books, please write for a free catalog.

Payment Method   ☐ Check   ☐ Money Order
                     ☐ MasterCard   ☐ VISA

MasterCard or VISA # __ __ __ __   __ __ __ __   __ __ __ __   __ __ __ __

Expiration Date _____ / _____
                  Mo.   Yr.

Signature _____

To Charge Your Order By Phone, Call 414-251-5408 or
Fax 414-251-9452 (office hours: 8AM-5PM CST)

Name _____
Address _____
City _____
State _____ ZIP _____

Record Research Inc.
P.O. Box 200
Menomonee Falls, WI 53052-0200

Record Research
The World's Leading Authority On Recorded Entertainment